MODERN
Real Estate
Practice IN
NORTH CAROLINA

FIFTH EDITION

Fillmore W. Galaty

Wellington J. Allaway

Robert C. Kyle

Gary W. Taylor, DREI,
Consulting Editor

DISCARD

Dearborn™
Real Estate Education

This publication is designed to provide accurate and authoritative information in regard to the subject matter covered. It is sold with the understanding that the publisher is not engaged in rendering legal, accounting or other professional service. If legal advice or other expert assistance is required, the services of a competent professional person should be sought.

Senior Vice President and General Manager: Roy Lipner
Publisher and Director of Distance Learning: Evan Butterfield
Development Editor: Michael J. Scafuri
Editorial Production Manager: Bryan Samolinski
Senior Typesetter: Janet Schroeder
Creative Director: Lucy Jenkins

Published by Dearborn™ Real Estate Education
a division of Dearborn Financial Publishing, Inc.®
30 South Wacker Drive
Chicago, IL 60606-7481
(312) 836-4400
http://www.dearbornRE.com

Printed in the United States of America.

03 04 05 10 9 8 7 6 5 4 3   2 1

Library of Congress Cataloging-in-Publication Data

Galaty, Fillmore W.
    Modern real estate practice in North Carolina / Fillmore W. Galaty, Wellington J. Allaway, Robert C. Kyle; Gary W. Taylor, consulting editor—5th ed.
        p. cm.
    Includes bibliographical references and index.
    ISBN 0-7931-6458-3
    1. Vendors and purchasers—North Carolina.   2. Real estate business—Law and legislation—North Carolina.   3. Real property—North Carolina.   I. Allaway, Wellington J.   II. Kyle, Robert C.   III. Taylor, Gary W.   IV. Title.
    KFN7526.G35   2000
    346.75604'37—dc21   00-028003

Contents

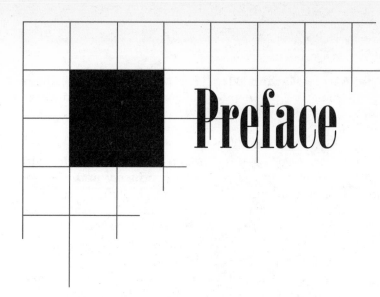

Preface

Since its first printing in 1994, *Modern Real Estate Practice in North Carolina* has provided thousands of readers with valuable real estate information, presented in a logical and accessible manner. Specifically tailored to North Carolina law and practice, *Modern Real Estate Practice in North Carolina* sets the standard for real estate textbooks, whether it is used to prepare for the licensing examination, for a college or university program or simply for personal knowledge.

FEATURES

Real estate students and instructors alike will appreciate the following features:

- **NEW!** Math rationales have been added for the chapter quizzes and sample state exam to aid in reviewing and studying math concepts and applications.
- Each chapter opens with **learning objectives** that tell you what concepts and information you should be able to identify, describe, explain and distinguish when you've finished.
- **Key terms** are provided at the beginning of each chapter. This feature not only lets you know what terms you should be alert for as you read but helps your study and review process as well.
- **Margin notes** help direct readers' attention to important vocabulary terms, concepts and study tips. The margin notes help readers move more easily through the text, locate issues for review, and serve as memory prompts for more efficient and effective studying.
- **For Example** scenarios help illustrate how issues of fair housing, agency, and brokerage affect real estate professionals and real estate transactions.
- **Chapter review** and **sample exam questions** contain many fact-pattern problems that encourage students to understand and apply information rather than just memorize. Additionally, Chapter 14, "Closing the Real Estate Transaction," contains a story problem that requires that students fill out a blank HUD-1 settlement statement. The Answer Key contains the filled-out version, which shows students how to calculate debits and credits to the buyer and seller.

- **Chapter 20, "Real Estate Mathematics,"** will help students establish the basic math principles that real estate professionals use when working with clients or customers.

One thing, however, has stayed the same. As in the first four editions, the goal of *Modern Real Estate Practice in North Carolina,* 5th Edition is to help students understand the dynamics of the real estate industry and prepare for their licensing exam. In this edition, we've met that challenge, providing you with the critical information you need to pass the real estate examination, buy or sell property, or establish a real estate career.

A FINAL NOTE

We love to hear from our readers. Please take a few moments to let us know what you thought of this textbook. Did it help you? Has your understanding of real estate increased? How did you do on your course or license exam? Please indicate that you used the fifth edition of *Modern Real Estate Practice in North Carolina* and send your comments to Dearborn™ Real Estate Education, Attention: Editorial Department, 30 South Wacker Drive, Chicago, IL 60606-7481, or contact us through our web site, http://www.dearbornRE.com.

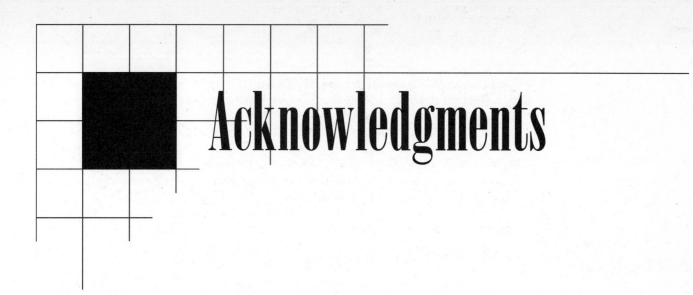

Acknowledgments

CONSULTING EDITOR

The authors would particularly like to thank Gary W. Taylor of Matthews, North Carolina, who served as consulting editor for this fifth edition of *Modern Real Estate Practice in North Carolina.* As a real estate instructor and former Director of Education at the Mingle Institute of Real Estate, Mr. Taylor has helped countless students begin successful careers in real estate. Mr. Taylor holds the highly respected DREI (distinguished real estate instructor) designation and has served as president of the North Carolina Real Estate Educators' Association.

REVIEWERS

For their input in the development of this fifth edition, the authors wish to thank the following individuals:

Deborah Carpenter, Fonville Morisey Center for Real Estate Studies
Cindy Chandler, DREI, The Chandler Group
Vicki Ferneyhough, DREI, Fonville Morisey Center for Real Estate Studies
Bill Gallagher, DREI, GRI, ITI, Bill Gallagher School of Real Estate
Mike Hughes, Wake Technical Community College
C. Douglas Long, Guilford Technical Community College
Saundra R. Martin, Central Piedmont Community College
Timothy Jay Niewald, Sandhills Community College
Sharon L. Pelt, Vice President of Career Development, Fonville Morisey Realty, Inc.
Kim Stotesbury, DREI, GRI, ITI, Rowan Cabarrus Community College

The authors also thank the following members of the North Carolina Editorial Review Board for their gracious participation in the initial development of this textbook:

George Bell, George Bell Productions, Ltd.
Ann Bowman, Landmark Real Estate, Inc.
Thomas J. Daniel, Fayette Real Estate Institute
Thomas A. Fallon, Spectrum Real Estate Training Center

ACKNOWLEDGMENTS

Glen Hamilton, Craven Community College
Lois G. Hobbs, DREI, Monk Real Estate Training Center
Howard Logue, Adcock and Associates Real Estate
C. Douglas Long, Guilford Technical Community College
Saundra R. Martin, Central Piedmont Community College
Sharon Montague, Asheville Real Estate Academy
Susan Wall, DREI, The Prudential Carolinas Realty
Roger Weeks, Central Piedmont Community College
Robert Whitaker, Jr., Whitaker & Associates
Robert L. Wroe, Jr., Broker and Instructor

1 Basic Real Estate Concepts

When you've finished reading this chapter, you should be able to

- **describe** the physical and economic characteristics of real property; the concept of land use and development, including highest and best use; and the advantages and disadvantages of real estate investments.

- **identify** the various careers, areas of real estate specializations and the professional organizations that support them.

- **explain** the operation of supply and demand in the real estate market.

- **define** these *key terms:*

broker	highest and best use	real property
business cycles	land	salesperson
chattels	market	situs
demand	personal property	supply
heterogeneity	real estate	

INTRODUCTION

It is important that real estate students understand the basic characteristics of real estate, how real estate is used and the real estate market. This chapter presents those fundamental concepts and lays the foundation for the exciting and challenging study of real estate practice.

GENERAL CHARACTERISTICS OF REAL ESTATE

There are two major classifications of property; real property and personal property. (Personal property is sometimes referred to as *personalty.*) The distinction between these two types of property is an important one. **Real property** is defined as the land, everything that is permanently attached to

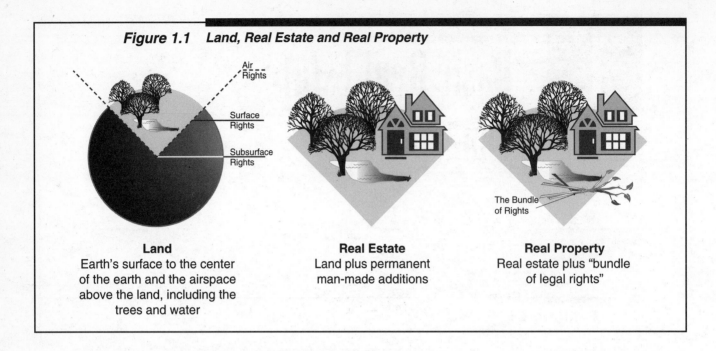

Figure 1.1   Land, Real Estate and Real Property

Air Rights

Surface Rights

Subsurface Rights

Land
Earth's surface to the center of the earth and the airspace above the land, including the trees and water

Real Estate
Land plus permanent man-made additions

The Bundle of Rights

Real Property
Real estate plus "bundle of legal rights"

the land and everything that is appurtenant to (or goes with) the land. **Personal property** is considered to be all property that does not fit the definition of real property. The primary characteristic of personal property is movability. Items of personal property, also referred to as **chattels,** include such tangibles as chairs, tables, clothing, money, bonds and bank accounts. In other words, a chattel is *an item of movable personal property.*

Land, Real Estate and Real Property

The words *land, real estate* and *real property* are often used interchangeably. However, for a full understanding of the nature of real estate and the laws that affect it, licensees need to be aware of subtle yet important differences in meaning.

Land. **Land** is defined as the earth's surface extending downward to the center of the earth and upward to infinity, including things permanently attached by nature, such as trees and water (see Figure 1.1).

The term *land* thus refers not only to the surface of the earth but also to the underlying soil and things that are naturally attached to the land, such as boulders and trees. Land also includes the minerals and substances below the earth's surface together with the airspace above the land up to infinity. The surface, subsurface and airspace can be owned separately as surface rights, subsurface rights and air rights and can be severed by separate conveyance. A specific tract of land is commonly referred to as a *parcel.*

Real estate. **Real estate** is defined as land at, above and below the earth's surface, including all things permanently attached to it, whether natural or artificial (see Figure 1.1). The term *real estate* is thus somewhat broader than the term *land* and includes not only the physical components of the land provided by nature but also all permanent improvements on and to the land. Land is also referred to as *improved* when streets, utilities, sewers and other improvements are brought to the land, thus making the land suitable for building.

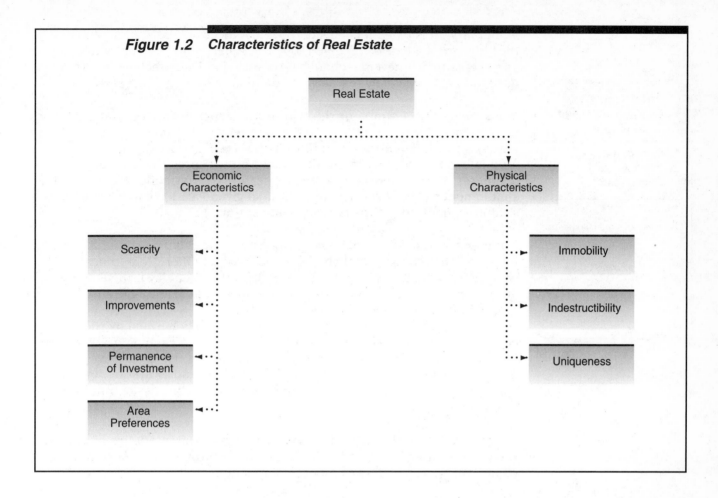

Figure 1.2   Characteristics of Real Estate

Real property.   Real property is defined as the interests, benefits and rights inherent in the ownership of real estate (see Figure 1.1).

The broader term *real property* includes the physical surface of the land, what lies below it, what lies above it and what is permanently attached to it, as well as all the rights of ownership (including the right to possess, sell, lease and enjoy the land).

In Practice   When people talk about buying or selling houses, office buildings, land and the like, they usually call all of these things real estate. For all practical purposes, the term is synonymous with real property, as defined here. Thus, in everyday usage, real estate includes the legal rights of ownership specified in the definition of real property. Sometimes the term realty is used instead.

Physical and Economic Characteristics of Real Property

There are seven characteristics that define the nature of real property and affect its use. These characteristics fall into two broad categories: physical characteristics and economic characteristics (see Figure 1.2).

Physical characteristics.   Land has three physical characteristics that set it apart from other commodities: immobility, indestructibility and uniqueness.

Immobility. It is true that some of the substances of land are removable and that topography can be changed, but the geographic location of any given parcel of land can never be changed. Because land is immobile, the rights to use land are more easily regulated than are other forms of property use.

Indestructibility. Land is durable and indestructible (or permanent). The permanence of land, coupled with the long-term nature of the improvements placed on it, has tended to stabilize investments in land. However, while land is indestructible, the improvements on it depreciate and can become obsolete, thereby reducing values—perhaps drastically. (Depreciation should not be confused with the fact that a given location can become undesirable economically, thus creating a ghost town.)

Uniqueness. No two parcels of land are ever exactly the same. Although they may share substantial similarity, all parcels differ geographically. The uniqueness of land is also referred to as its **heterogeneity** or *nonhomogeneity*. In fact, it is the uniqueness of each parcel of land that gives rise to the remedy of *specific performance* for the breach of a real estate contract. Under the doctrine of specific performance, the party harmed by the breach of a real estate contract can ask a judge to force the breaching party to carry out the terms of the contract rather than ordering the breaching party to pay monetary damages. Because each parcel of land is unique, monetary damages cannot compensate the damaged party for the loss of that particular parcel.

Economic characteristics. The basic economic characteristics of land are the factors that influence its value as an investment: scarcity, improvements, permanence of investment and area preferences.

Scarcity. Although land is not thought of as a rare commodity, its total supply is fixed. Even though a considerable amount of land in the United States is still not used or inhabited, the supply of land in a given location or of a particular quality may be limited, thus creating increased demand for that specific land. Because no more land can be produced, the increasing use of land has a positive impact on value.

Improvements. Any addition or change to land or a building that affects the property's value is referred to as an *improvement.* Improvements of a private nature, such as the house, fencing, etc., are referred to as *improvements **on** the land,* whereas improvements of a public nature, such as sidewalks, sewer systems, curbing, etc., are referred to as *improvements **to** the land.* Additions or alterations to the property that are merely repairs or replacements may not be considered to be improvements. Agents should be aware that the term *improved land* has two meanings. If buildings are constructed on the land, the buildings can be considered "improvements." If the land has been prepared for development, such as with grading, installation of utilities, etc., the land may be referred to as *improved land.*

Building an improvement on one parcel of land affects the value and utilization of neighboring tracts and can have a direct bearing on whole communities. For example, improving a parcel by constructing a shopping center or selecting it as the site for an atomic reactor can directly influence a large area. Such land improvements can influence not only other parcels and other communities favorably or unfavorably, they may affect the use, value and price of the land.

Permanence of investment. Once land is improved, the total capital and labor used to build the improvement represents a large fixed investment. Although even a well-built structure can be razed to make way for a newer building or another use of the land, improvements such as drainage, electricity, water and sewer systems remain because they generally cannot be dismantled or removed economically. The owner has no way to transfer the investment to another parcel of land. The return on such investments, therefore, tends to be long-term and relatively stable. This permanence generally makes improved real estate unsuitable for short-term, rapid-turnover investing.

Area preferences (location). Area preference, sometimes called *location*, refers to people's choices and tastes regarding a given area. Location is one of the most important economic characteristics of land. **Situs** is a related term regarding location that takes into consideration social factors in addition to economic factors.

GENERAL CONCEPTS OF LAND USE AND INVESTMENT

The various characteristics of a parcel of real estate affect its desirability for a specific use. For example, contour and elevation of the parcel, transportation and availability of natural resources such as water all affect the use that can be made of a property, and the way in which a property is used has a dramatic impact on the value of that property.

Highest and Best Use   The **highest and best use** is the use that will give the owners the greatest actual return on their investment. Extensive studies are often prepared to determine whether a property is being properly utilized. For example, a highest-and-best-use study may show that a parking lot in a busy downtown area or a farm surrounded by urbanized land is not the highest and best use of the property.

If a property can be put to its highest and best use, its value will increase. For example, if the highest and best use of a piece of property is as a high-rise office building rather than a parking lot, changing its use accordingly will increase its value and also will give the owners the highest return on their investment.

Although a property can have only one highest and best use at any given time, the highest and best use can change. Because of changes in socioeconomic conditions, a property's highest and best use may be a retail shopping center today but a large apartment complex five years from now.

Land-Use Controls   The potential uses of a property are limited by various land-use controls. Property owners cannot simply decide to tear down their single-family home and replace it with a convenience store. Chances are they would be violating a land-use law.

The control and regulation of land use are accomplished through both public and private land-use controls, discussed in Chapter 5.

Real Estate as an Investment

Real estate, no matter what its use, is virtually always considered an investment. Customers often expect a real estate broker or salesperson to act as an investment counselor. Though brokers and salespeople should possess a basic knowledge of real estate investment, they should always refer a potential real estate investor to a competent accountant, lawyer or investment specialist who can give expert advice regarding the investor's specific interest or objective.

However, real estate practitioners should possess a rudimentary knowledge of real estate investment so they can deal with customers on a basic level. Such knowledge begins with a brief examination of the traditional advantages and disadvantages of investing in real estate.

Advantages of real estate investment. Historically, well-located and fairly priced real estate investments have shown a good rate of return, often higher than the prevailing interest rate charged by mortgage lenders. Theoretically, this means that an investor can use the leverage of borrowed money to finance a real estate purchase and feel relatively sure that, if held long enough, the asset will yield more money than it costs to finance the purchase. It should be remembered that part of the return must make up for the value lost by a depreciating asset.

Most real estate values tend to keep pace with the rate of inflation. Such an inflation hedge provides the prudent real estate investor with relative assurance that if the purchasing power of the dollar decreases, the value of the investor's assets will increase to offset the inflationary effects. In addition, real estate entrepreneurs may enjoy various tax advantages, which are discussed in detail in Chapter 18.

Disadvantages of real estate investment. Unlike stocks and bonds, real estate is not a liquid asset. This means that an investor may not be able to sell real estate quickly without taking a loss. Contrast this with the investor in listed stocks, who needs only call a stockbroker to liquidate assets when funds are needed quickly. Even though a real estate investor may raise a limited amount of cash by refinancing the property, that property is usually listed with a real estate broker, and the investor may have to sell at a substantially lower price than full market value to facilitate a quick sale.

In addition, it is difficult to invest in real estate without some degree of expert advice. Investment decisions must be based on a careful study of all the facts in a given situation, reinforced by a broad and thorough knowledge of real estate and the manner in which it affects and is affected by the marketplace—the human element. Unsophisticated investors should seek legal and tax counsel before making any real estate investments.

Rarely can a real estate investor sit idly by and watch his or her money grow. Management decisions must be made. For example, should the investor manage the property personally or would it be preferable to hire a professional property manager? How much rent should be charged? How should repairs and tenant grievances be handled? Is sweat equity (physical improvements accomplished by the investor personally) required to make the asset profitable?

Finally, and most important, a high degree of risk often is involved in real estate investment. There is always the possibility that an investor's property will decrease in value during the period it is held or that it will fail to generate sufficient income to make it profitable. External influences beyond the investor's control may come into play in negative or positive ways, affecting the value of the investment.

THE SCOPE OF THE REAL ESTATE BUSINESS

Billions of dollars' worth of real estate is sold each year in the United States. Adding to this great volume of sales are rental collections by real estate management firms, appraisals of properties ranging from vacant land to modern office and apartment buildings and the lending of money through mortgage loans on real estate.

Millions of people depend on some aspect of the real estate business for their livelihood. As the technical aspects of real estate activities become more complex, real estate offices require an increasing number of people properly trained to handle such transactions. Many professionals and business organizations, such as lawyers, architects, surveyors, accountants and tax specialists, banks, trust companies, and abstract and title insurance companies also depend on the real estate specialist.

Real Estate: A Business of Many Specializations

Despite the size and complexity of the real estate business, many people think of it as comprising only brokers and salespeople. Actually, today's real estate industry employs millions of knowledgeable individuals who are well trained in specialty areas such as appraisal, property management, financing, development, counseling and education. Each of these areas is a business unto itself, but every real estate professional must have a basic knowledge of all of these specializations to be successful.

Real Estate Professions

Brokerage. The business of bringing together people interested in making a real estate transaction is called *brokerage*. Usually, the **broker** acts as an agent who negotiates the sale, purchase or rental of property on behalf of others for a fee or commission. In any transaction, there may be a **salesperson** working on behalf of the broker. The commission, generally a percentage of the amount of the transaction, is usually paid by the seller in a sales transaction or by the owner in a rental transaction (although it can be paid by any party). Brokerage is further discussed in Chapter 6.

North Carolina's license law (G.S. 93A-1 & 2.) stipulates that a person must be licensed as a real estate broker if he or she lists or offers to list; sells or offers to sell; buys or offers to buy; auctions or offers to auction; negotiates the purchase, sale or exchange of; leases or offers to lease; or rents or offers to rent any real estate for others for compensation or the promise of compensation. The license law also requires that a licensed salesperson who engages in any of these activities must be under the supervision of a real estate broker.

Appraisal. The process of estimating the value of a parcel of real estate is *appraisal*. Although brokers must have some understanding of valuation as part of their training, qualified appraisers are generally employed when property is financed or is sold by court order. The appraiser must have sound judgment, experience and a detailed knowledge of the methods of valuation and also be licensed as an appraiser. Appraisal is covered in Chapter 16.

Property management. Someone who operates a property for its owner is involved in *property management.* The property manager may be responsible for soliciting tenants, collecting rents, altering or constructing new space for tenants, ordering repairs and generally maintaining the property. The manager's basic responsibility is to protect the owner's investment and maximize the owner's return on the investment. Property management is discussed in Chapter 11.

Financing. The business of providing the funds necessary to complete real estate transactions is called *financing.* Most transactions are financed by means of a loan secured by a mortgage or deed of trust by which the property is pledged as security for the eventual payment of the loan. This and other methods of real estate financing are examined in Chapters 12 and 13.

Property development. This specialty includes the work of developers, or subdividers, who purchase raw land, divide it into lots, build roads and install sewer systems. Property development also includes the skills of architects and builders, who improve the building lots with houses and other buildings and who sell the improved real estate, either themselves or through brokerage firms. Property development is discussed in Chapter 5. House construction is discussed in Chapter 15.

Counseling. Providing competent independent advice and guidance on a variety of real estate problems is known as *counseling.* A counselor attempts to furnish the client with direction in choosing alternative courses of action. Increasing the client's knowledge is every counselor's function in rendering services.

Education. Education is the provision of information to both the real estate practitioner and the consumer. Colleges and universities, private schools and trade organizations conduct courses and seminars on all aspects of the business, from the principles of the prelicensing program to the technical aspects of tax and exchange law.

Other areas. Many other specialties and professionals are also part of the real estate business. Practitioners associated with mortgage banking firms and those who negotiate mortgages for banks and savings and loan associations are examples of professionals associated with these other areas of specialty. Members of corporate real estate departments as well as officials and employees of government agencies such as zoning boards and assessing offices are further examples.

Professional organizations. The real estate business has many trade organizations, the largest being the National Association of REALTORS® (NAR). Organized in 1908, NAR sponsors various affiliated organizations that offer professional designations to brokers, salespeople and others who complete required courses (see Table 1.1). NAR, along with the state and local boards, serves the interests of its members by keeping them informed of developments in their fields, publicizing the services of its members, improving standards and practices and recommending or taking positions on public legislation or regulations affecting the operations of members and member firms.

Table 1.1   National Association of REALTORS® Institutes and Professional Designations

Institute	Designation(s)
NAR • National Association of REALTORS®	Graduate REALTORS® Institute (GRI)
ASREC • American Society of Real Estate Counselors	Certified International Property Specialist (CIPS)
CIREI • Commercial-Investment Real Estate Institute	Counselor of Real Estate (CRE)
IREM • Institute of Real Estate Management	Certified Commercial Investment Member (CCIM)
RLI • REALTORS® Land Institute	Certified Property Manager® (CPM®)
RNMI • REALTORS® National Marketing Institute	Accredited Management Organization® (AMO®)
SIOR • Society of Industrial and Office REALTORS®	Accredited Resident Manager® (ARM®)
WCR • Women's Council of REALTORS®	Accredited Land Consultant (ALC)
	Certified Real Estate Brokerage Manager (CRB)
	Certified Residential Specialist (CRS)
	Professional Real Estate Executive (PRE)
	Leadership Training Graduate (LTG)

The majority of local real estate associations throughout the United States and Canada are affiliated with NAR. Members of the North Carolina Association of REALTORS® and affiliated local boards subscribe to the association's strict Code of Ethics and are entitled to be known as REALTORS® or REALTOR-ASSOCIATES®. The term REALTORS® is a registered trademark. In North Carolina there are approximately 75,000 licensed brokers and salespeople, of whom approximately 23,000 are REALTORS®. All REALTORS® are licensees, but not all licensees are REALTORS®.

Among the many other professional associations is the National Association of Real Estate Brokers (NAREB), whose members also subscribe to a code of ethics. Members of NAREB are known as *Realtists*.

Uses of Real Property

Just as there are many areas of specialization within the real estate industry, there are many different types of property in which to specialize. According to its use, real estate can generally be classified into one of five categories:

1. Residential—all property used for housing, from acreage to small city lots, both single-family and multifamily, in urban, suburban and rural areas
2. Commercial—business property, including offices, shopping centers, stores, theaters, hotels and parking facilities

---

Five Categories of Real Property

1. Residential
2. Commercial
3. Industrial
4. Agricultural
5. Special-purpose

---

3. Industrial—warehouses, factories, land in industrial districts and power plants
4. Agricultural—farms, timberland, ranches and orchards
5. Special-purpose—churches, schools, cemeteries and government-held lands

The market for each of these types of properties can be further subdivided into the sales market, which involves the transfer of title, and the rental market, which involves the transfer of space on a rental basis.

In Practice   Although in theory a real estate person or firm can perform all the services listed above and handle all five classes of property, this is rarely done except in small towns. Most real estate firms tend to specialize to some degree, especially in urban areas. In some cases, a real estate licensee may perform only one service for one type of property. Residential property brokers and industrial property appraisers are two examples of such specialization.

THE REAL ESTATE MARKET

In literal terms, a **market** is a place where goods are bought and sold, where value for those goods is established and where it is advantageous for buyers and sellers to trade. The function of the market is to facilitate this exchange by providing a setting in which the supply and demand forces of the economy can establish market value. The real estate market is a free market and is local in nature.

Supply and Demand

When supply increases and demand remains stable, prices go down. When demand increases and supply remains stable, prices go up.

The economic forces of supply and demand continually interact in the market to establish and maintain price levels. Essentially, when **supply** increases, prices drop as more producers compete for buyers; when **demand** increases, prices rise as more buyers compete for the product.

Production slows or stops during a period of oversupply. When the market cannot meet the demand, production increases to take advantage of demand. Supply and demand are balanced at what is called the *point of equilibrium.*

For Example Here's how one broker describes market forces: "In my 17 years in real estate, I've seen supply and demand in action many times. When a car maker relocated its factory to my region a few years back, hundreds of people wanted to buy the few higher-bracket houses for sale at the time. Those sellers were able to ask ridiculously high prices for their properties, and two houses actually sold for more than the asking prices! On the other hand, when the naval base closed and 2,000 civilian jobs were transferred to other parts of the country, it seemed like every other house in town was for sale. We were practically giving houses away to the few people who were buying."

Supply and demand in the real estate market. Characteristics of the goods in the marketplace determine how quickly the forces of supply and demand will be able to achieve equilibrium. Such characteristics are the degree of standardization of the product, the mobility and financial stability of the product and the mobility of the parties (buyer and seller).

Real estate is not a standardized product; no two parcels can ever be exactly alike. Each parcel of real estate is unique because it has its own geographic location.

Because real estate is fixed in nature (immobile), it cannot be moved from area to area to satisfy the pressures of supply and demand. Property buyers are also generally limited in their mobility—retirees are a major exception in regard to residences. For these reasons, the real estate business has tended toward local markets, where offices can maintain detailed familiarity with market conditions and available units. The increasing mobility of the population, however, and the growing impact of new technologies in communication and data handling have resulted in the geographic expansion of real estate firms.

Where standardization and mobility are relatively great, the forces of supply and demand balance relatively quickly. But because of real estate's characteristics of uniqueness and immobility, the real estate market is generally relatively slow to adjust. To a certain extent, the product can be removed from the market (as when a home offered for resale is withdrawn), yet an oversupply of product usually results in a lowering of price levels. Because development and construction of real estate take a considerable period of time from conception to completion, increases in demand also may not be met immediately. Building and housing construction may occur in uneven spurts of activity owing to such factors.

Factors affecting supply. Factors that tend to affect supply in the real estate market include the labor force, construction costs, government controls and monetary or financial policies.

Labor force and construction costs. A shortage of labor in the skilled building trades, an increase in the cost of building materials, or a scarcity of materials tend to decrease the amount of housing built or increase its cost. The impact of the labor force on price levels depends on the extent to which higher costs can be passed on to the buyer or renter in the form of higher purchase prices or rents. Technological advances that result in lower-priced materials and more efficient means of construction may tend to counteract some price increases.

Government controls and financial policies. Government monetary policy can have a substantial impact on the real estate market. The Federal Reserve Board and government agencies such as the Federal Housing Administration (FHA) and Ginnie Mae (formerly the Government National Mortgage Association, GNMA), as well as Freddie Mac (formerly the Federal Home Loan Mortgage Corporation, FHLMC), can affect the amount of money available to lenders for mortgage loans (see Chapter 12). In addition, the government can influence the amount of money available for real estate investment through its fiscal and monetary policies. Such policies include the amount of money taken out of circulation, taxation and the amount of money the government puts into circulation through spending programs ranging from welfare to farm subsidies.

At the local level, real estate taxation is one of the primary sources of revenue for government. Policies on taxation of real estate can have either positive or negative effects. Tax incentives have been one way for communities to attract new businesses and industries to their areas. And, of course, along with these enterprises come increased employment and expanded residential real estate markets.

Local governments also can affect market operations and the development and construction of real estate by applying land-use controls. Building codes and zoning ordinances are used by communities to control the use of land. Real estate values and markets are thereby stabilized. Community amenities—for example, churches, schools and parks—and efficient government policies are influential factors affecting the real estate market. Local governments can negatively influence development by imposing excessive fees or overly restrictive zoning and business codes.

Factors affecting demand. Factors that tend to affect demand in the real estate market include population, demographics, and employment and wage levels.

Population. Because shelter (whether in the form of owned or rented property) is a basic human need, the general need for housing grows as the population grows. Even though the total population of the country may continue to increase, growth is not uniform. Some areas grow faster than others, and some do not grow at all. We even have modern-day ghost towns, where the exhaustion of natural resources or the termination of an industrial operation has resulted in a mass exodus of population.

Demographics. Not only population but the makeup of that population—demographics—affects demand. Family size and the ratio of adults to children, the number of people moving into retirement care facilities and retirement communities, the effect of doubling up (two or more families using one housing unit) and the changing number of single-parent households all contribute to the amount and type of housing needed. Also pertinent are the number of young people who would prefer to rent or own their own residences but for economic reasons have roommates or remain in their parents' homes.

Employment and wage levels. Home ownership and rental decisions are closely related to ability to pay. Employment opportunities and wage levels in a small community can be affected drastically by decisions made by major employers in the area. Individuals involved in the real estate market in such communities must keep well informed about the business plans of local employers.

To estimate how changes in wage levels will affect people's decisions concerning real estate, it is also important to look for trends in how individual income is likely to be used. General trends in the economy (availability of mortgage money, interest rates, rate of inflation and the like) will influence an individual's spending decisions.

Business cycles. The upward and downward fluctuations in business activity are called **business cycles.** Although business cycles often seem to recur within a certain number of years, they are actually caused primarily by forces such as population growth, taxes, interest rates, wars and oil embargoes. A business cycle can generally be characterized by four stages: expansion, recession, depression and revival. The movements of a cycle are usually gradual and indistinct.

The real estate cycle. The real estate market is slow in adjusting to variations in supply and demand. Because one factor of a real estate cycle is building activity, the time lag between the demand for units and the completion of those units causes real estate cycles to peak after the rest of the economy does and to take longer to recover from depressed periods than do other economic sectors. The local character of the real estate market creates many local conditions that may not correspond to the general movement of a real estate cycle.

Governmental anticyclical efforts. Ever since the Great Depression of the 1930s, the federal government has attempted to establish fiscal and monetary policies to prevent extreme fluctuations in the business cycle. By increasing government spending during times of recession and taking money out of circulation through taxation and control of lending institutions during times of inflation/expansion, the government attempts to promote steady, gradual economic growth.

SUMMARY

The special nature of land as an investment is apparent in both its physical and economic characteristics. Physically, land is immobile, indestructible and unique. Its economic characteristics are controlled by such factors as scarcity, improvements, permanence of investment and area preferences.

Although most people think of land as the surface of the earth, land is the earth's surface and also the mineral deposits under the earth and the air above it. The term *real estate* further expands this definition to include all natural and manmade improvements attached to the land. *Real property* is the term used to describe all the legal rights associated with ownership of real estate. Real property is immovable.

All property that does not fit the definition of real estate is classified as personal property, or chattels. Personal property can be moved. A chattel is an item of movable personal property.

The value of land is affected by its highest and best use and by the land-use controls that specify the possible uses of a piece of land.

Although selling is the most widely recognized activity of the real estate business, the industry also involves many other services, such as appraisal, property management, property development and subdivision, counseling and property financing. Most real estate firms specialize in only one or two of these areas. However, the highly complex and competitive nature of our society requires that a real estate professional be an expert in a number of fields.

Real property can be classified according to its general use as residential, commercial, industrial, agricultural or special-purpose. Although many brokers deal with more than one type of real property, they usually specialize to some degree.

A market is a place where goods and services can be bought and sold and price levels established. The ideal market allows for a continual balancing of the forces of supply and demand. Because of its unique characteristics, real estate is relatively slow to adjust to the forces of supply and demand.

The supply of and demand for real estate are affected by many factors. Those that bear on supply include labor availability and construction costs as well as government monetary controls and fiscal policy. Elements that influence demand include population and demographics, employment and wage levels, interest rates and taxes. If demand is high and supply is low, there is a "seller's market"; if demand is low and supply is high, there is a "buyer's market."

Fluctuations of business activity in this country are observed in cycles. Business cycles occur in four stages: expansion, recession, depression and revival. The real estate cycle involves similar stages, but it tends to peak after the rest of the economy does and it takes longer to recover than do other sectors of the business community.

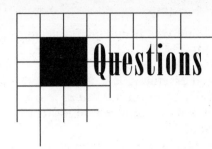

Questions

1. Which of the following BEST defines real estate?
   a. Land and the air above it
   b. Land and the buildings permanently affixed to it
   c. Land and all things permanently affixed to it
   d. Land and the mineral rights in the land

2. Which of the following is NOT a physical characteristic of land?
   a. Indestructibility   c. Immobility
   b. Scarcity   d. Uniqueness

3. The term *nonhomogeneity* refers to which of the following?
   a. Scarcity   c. Mobility
   b. Uniqueness   d. Indestructibility

4. Area preference, or situs, refers to
   I. location.
   11. a physical characteristic of the building on the land.
   a. I only
   b. II only
   c. Both I and II
   d. Neither I nor II

5. Which of the following physical and economic factors would a land developer take into consideration when determining the optimum use of a parcel of land?
   a. Transportation
   b. Available natural resources
   c. Contour and elevation
   d. All of the above

6. Which of the following is NOT an economic characteristic of real estate?
   I. Indestructibility
   II. Improvements
   III. Scarcity
   a. I only
   b. I and II only
   c. I and III only
   d. I, II and III

7. A theater or hotel is an example of
   I. industrial real estate.
   II. special-purpose real estate.
   a. I only
   b. II only
   c. Both I and II
   d. Neither I nor II

8. Factors that influence the demand for real estate include the
   a. number of real estate brokers in the area
   b. number of full-time real estate salespeople in the area.
   c. wage levels and employment opportunities in the area.
   d. price of new homes being built in the area.

9. The designation REALTOR® refers to
   a. any person whose business involves real estate.
   b. any licensed real estate broker.
   c. an active member of a state association or local board affiliated with the National Association of REALTORS®.
   d. an active member of the National Association of Real Estate Brokers.

10. Which of the following statements is true of business cycles?
    a. They involve periods of expansion, recession, depression and revival.
    b. They are dictated by the number of real estate professionals practicing real estate on a full-time basis.
    c. They have to do with the ethnic and religious characteristics of the area.
    d. They do not exist in the real estate and building industries.

11. All of the following factors tend to affect supply EXCEPT
    a. the labor force.
    b. construction costs.
    c. government controls.
    d. demographics.

12. Real estate can be a poor investment if
    a. inflation is high.
    b. the investor can hold on to the investment for a long period of time.
    c. the investor needs ready cash.
    d. land values are increasing.

13. In general, when the supply of a certain commodity increases, prices
    I. tend to rise.
    II. tend to drop.
    III. can no longer be established.
    a. I only
    b. II only
    c. I and III only
    d. Neither I, II nor III

14. In general terms, a market refers to which of the following?
    a. Place where sellers come to sell their goods
    b. Amount of goods available at a given price
    c. Quality of goods available to the public
    d. Forum where the cost of goods is established

15. The demand for real estate in a particular community is LEAST affected by
    a. population.
    b. wage levels.
    c. employment.
    d. international trade.

16. The real estate market is considered local in character for all EXCEPT which of the following reasons?
    a. Land is fixed or immobile.
    b. Most people are not mobile enough to take advantage of available real estate in distant areas.
    c. Local controls can have a significant impact on the market.
    d. Most people are mobile enough to take advantage of available real estate in distant areas.

17. Compared with typical markets, the real estate market
    a. is national in scope.
    b. is always stable and is not affected by supply or demand.
    c. does not affect any other industry but its own.
    d. is local in nature and is slow to respond to the forces of supply and demand.

18. Which of the following statements is true?
    a. All licensees are REALTORS®.
    b. All REALTORS® are licensees.
    c. Both a and b are true.
    d. Neither a nor b is true.

2 Property Ownership and Interests

LEARNING OBJECTIVES

When you've finished reading this chapter, you should be able to

- **explain** the concept of the "bundle of legal rights"; the characteristics of real estate; types of freehold estates; property taxation laws and procedures; and how real property is assessed and taxed.

- **describe** all types of fixtures and be able to identify items that may or may not be fixtures by applying all parts of the Total Circumstances Test.

- **describe** the different types of real property ownership.

- **define** these *key terms:*

ad valorem	fixture	remainder interest
agricultural fixtures	freehold estate	reversionary interest
air rights	future interests	riparian rights
appurtenant	joint tenancy	severalty
assessment	lien	severance
bundle of legal rights	life estate	special assessment
chattel fixture	littoral rights	subsurface rights
condition subsequent	mass appraisal	(mineral rights)
condominium	nonfreehold estate	surface rights
cooperative	(leasehold estate)	tenancy by the entirety
deed restriction	North Carolina	tenancy in common
easement	Condominium Act of	time-share
easement appurtenant	1986	Total Circumstances
easement in gross	party walls	Test
encroachment	planned unit	town house
encumbrance	development (PUD)	trade fixture
fee simple absolute	priority	Uniform Commercial
fee simple defeasible	proprietary lease	Code (UCC)
fee simple	pur autre vie	waste
determinable		

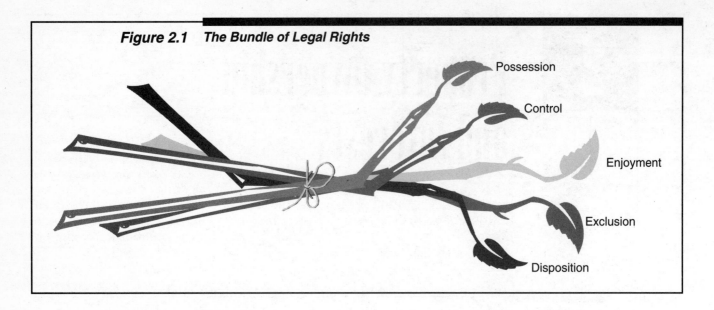

Figure 2.1   *The Bundle of Legal Rights*

Possession

Control

Enjoyment

Exclusion

Disposition

THE CONCEPT OF PROPERTY

The unique nature of real estate has given rise to a distinctive set of laws and rights. Even the simplest of real estate transactions brings into play a complex body of laws, and licensees must understand not only the effect of these laws but also how the laws define real property.

The Bundle of Legal Rights

Real property is often described as a **bundle of legal rights.** This is a "legal relationship" between the owner and the property. In other words, a purchaser of real estate is actually buying the rights of ownership held by the seller. The rights of ownership (see Figure 2.1) include the right to control the property within the framework of the law, the right of exclusion (to keep others from entering or using the property), the right of possession, the right of disposition (to sell, will or otherwise dispose of the property) and the right of enjoyment (to use the property in any legal manner).

The concept of the bundle of rights comes from old English law and a populace that, for the most part, could not read or write. Therefore, a seller transferred property by giving the purchaser a bundle of bound sticks from a tree on the property. This process was referred to as a *livery of seisin.* The purchaser who held the bundle also owned the tree from which the sticks came and the land to which the tree was attached. Because the rights of ownership can be separated and individually transferred, the sticks became symbolic of those rights.

Appurtenances

An *appurtenance* is defined as a right or privilege that goes along with the ownership of land. Some of these rights include subsurface rights (mineral rights), air rights and water rights. An appurtenance is generally transferred along with the property to the new owner.

Subsurface and air rights. **Surface rights** are simply the rights to use the surface of the earth. However, real property ownership also can include **subsurface rights (mineral rights),** which are the rights to the natural resources lying below the earth's surface. A transfer of surface rights may, however, be accomplished without the transfer of subsurface rights.

For example, a landowner could sell the rights to any oil and gas found in the land to an oil company. The landowner then could sell his or her remaining interest, reserving the rights to all coal found in the land. After the sale, three parties would have ownership interests in the real estate: the oil company would own all oil and gas, the seller would own all coal and the new landowner would own the rights to the rest of the real property.

The rights to use the air above the land also may be sold or leased independently of the land. Such **air rights** are an increasingly important part of real estate, particularly in large cities, where air rights over railroads have been purchased to construct huge office buildings such as the Pan-Am Building in New York City and the Merchandise Mart in Chicago. To construct such a building, the developer must purchase not only the air rights but also numerous small portions of the land's surface for the building's foundation supports, called *caissons*.

Until the development of airplanes, a property's air rights were considered to be unlimited. Today, however, the courts permit reasonable interference with these rights, such as those necessary for aircraft, as long as the owner's right to use and occupy the land is not unduly lessened. Governments and airport authorities often purchase air rights adjacent to an airport to provide approach patterns for air traffic.

With the continuing development of solar power, air rights—more specifically, sun rights—have been redefined by the courts. They consider tall buildings that block sunlight from smaller solar-powered buildings to be interfering with the smaller buildings' sun rights.

In summary, one parcel of real property may be owned by many people, each holding a separate right to a different part of the real estate. These rights may be severed by separate conveyance. Thus, there may exist at the same time

- an owner of the surface rights,
- an owner of the subsurface mineral rights,
- an owner of the subsurface gas and oil rights, and
- an owner of the air rights.

Water rights. One of the interests that may attach to the ownership of real estate is the right to use adjacent bodies of water. In North Carolina, the ownership of water and the land adjacent to it is determined by the doctrine of riparian rights.

Riparian rights are granted to owners of land located along the course of a river, stream or lake. Such an owner has the unrestricted right to use the water, provided such use does not harm owners upstream or downstream by interrupting or altering the flow of the water or by contaminating it. In addition, an owner of land that borders a nonnavigable waterway owns the land under the water to the exact center of the waterway. In North Carolina, land adjoining navigable rivers is owned only to the banks of the river (see Figure 2.2). Navigable waters are considered public highways on which the public has an easement or a right to travel.

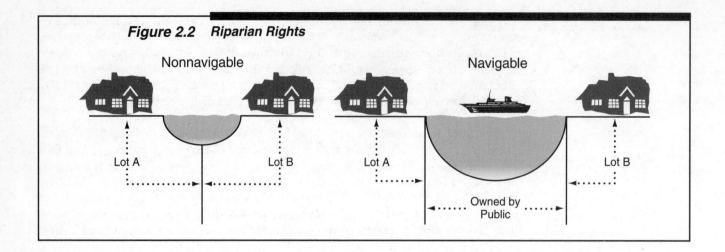

Figure 2.2   *Riparian Rights*

Littoral rights. Closely related to riparian rights are the *littoral rights* of owners whose land borders large, navigable lakes and oceans. Owners with littoral rights enjoy unrestricted use of navigable waters but own the land adjacent to the water only up to the mean high-water mark (see Figure 2.3). All land below this point is owned by the government. (The strip of land between high and low tide lines belongs to the state of North Carolina and is called the *foreshore.*)

Riparian and littoral rights are **appurtenant** (attached) to the land and cannot be retained when the property is sold. This means that the right to use the water belongs to whoever owns the bordering land and cannot be retained by a former owner after the land is sold.

The quantity of land can be affected by the natural action of the water. An owner is entitled to all land created by *accretion,* or an increase in land resulting from the deposit of soil by the water. If water recedes or disappears, new land is acquired by *reliction.*

Erosion, the gradual wearing away of land caused by flowing water or other natural forces, may cause an owner to lose land. When an act of nature such as a flood removes soil, this is known as *avulsion.*

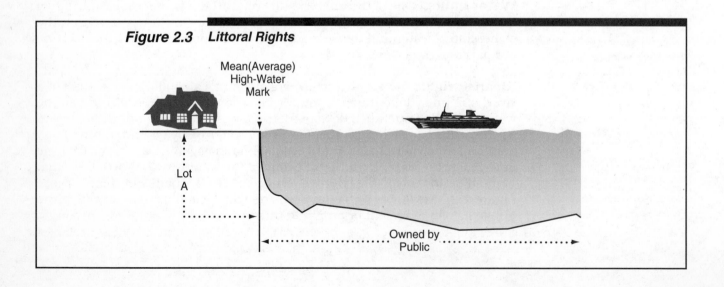

Figure 2.3   *Littoral Rights*

Figure 2.4   Real versus Personal Property

Real Estate	Personal Property	Fixture	Trade Fixture
Land and anything permanently attached to it	Movable items not attached to real estate; items severed from real estate	Item of personal property converted to real estate by attaching it to the real estate with the intention that it become permanently a part thereof	Item of personal property attached to real estate that is owned by a tenant and is used in a business; legally removable by tenant

---

Fixtures: Real Property versus Personal Property

As discussed in Chapter 1, real property is defined as the land, everything attached to the land and everything appurtenant to the land. Personal property is defined as everything that is not real property (see Figure 2.4). While the distinction between real and personal property is important to all real estate transactions, it is not always obvious. For instance, is a pile of lumber in the backyard of a house personal property or part of the real property? What about the drapes or an antique mirror attached to the wall of a home? If these items are considered personal property, they can be taken by the seller when he or she moves out of the house. On the other hand, if these items are considered real property, the buyer becomes their new owner and the seller cannot remove them. Real estate agents must be careful to see that both parties to a real estate transaction understand clearly which items are real property and which items are personal property to prevent confusion and disappointment at closing.

Mobile homes. A mobile home is generally considered to be personal property, even though its mobility may be limited to a single trip to a mobile-home park. A mobile home may, however, be considered real property if it is permanently affixed to land, as prescribed by state law.

Plants. Trees and crops generally fall into one of two classes. Trees, perennial bushes and grasses that do not require annual cultivation (*fructus naturales*—fruits of nature) are considered real property. Annual crops of wheat, corn, vegetables and fruit, known as *emblements* (*fructus industriales*—fruits of industry), are generally considered personal property. But as long as an annual crop is growing, it will be transferred as part of the real property if no special provision is made in the sales contract. A tenant may reenter land, if necessary, to harvest crops that result from the tenant's labor.

It is possible to change an item of real property to personal property by *severance*. For example, a growing tree is real estate until the owner cuts down the tree and thereby severs it from the earth. Similarly, an apple becomes personal property once it is picked from a tree, and a crop of wheat becomes personal property once it is harvested. Severance also may be the result of a

The term used in law for plants that do not require annual cultivation (such as trees and shrubbery) is *fructus naturales* (fruits of nature); emblements are known in law as *fructus industriales* (fruits of industry).

contract. For example, if the owner of an apple orchard sells the apple crop while it is still ripening on the trees, the crop has been severed (and thus turned into personal property) even though it is still physically attached to the trees.

It is also possible to change personal property into real property. If a land-owner buys cement, stones and sand and constructs a concrete walk on the land, the component parts of the concrete, which were originally personal property, are converted into real property. They have become a permanent improvement on the land. This process is called *annexation.*

Classification of fixtures. In considering the differences between real property and personal property, it is important to be able to distinguish between a fixture and personal property.

An item that was once personal property but has been so affixed to land or a building that the law construes it to be part of the real estate is a **fixture.** Examples of fixtures are heating plants, elevator equipment in highrise buildings, radiators, kitchen cabinets, light fixtures and plumbing fixtures. *If an item is a fixture it automatically transfers with the property unless excepted by either party to the contract.* As a matter of fact, almost any item that has been added as a permanent part of a building is considered a fixture.

Legal tests of a fixture. The **Total Circumstances Test** is a legal test applied by the courts to determine whether an item is a fixture (and there-fore part of the real property) or personal property. All four parts of the test must be applied, but intention is the major part of the test.

Legal Tests of a Fixture: 1. Intention 2. Relationship 3. Method of annexation 4. Adaptation to real estate	1. **Intention of the annexor:** Did the person who installed the item intend it to remain permanently or be removable? (The courts look at objective evidence of the party's intent, not his or her subjective intent. In other words, the courts look at the facts surrounding the situation and determine what a reasonable person would have intended by them.) 2. **Relationship of the parties:** Is the person making the attachment an owner or a tenant? It is presumed that an owner intends a permanent attachment (the item becomes a fixture), while a tenant intends a temporary attachment (the item remains personal property). The greater the legal relationship the annexor has to the real property, the greater the likelihood the item will be declared a fixture. 3. **Method of annexation:** How permanently was the item attached? Can it be removed without causing damage? 4. **Adaptation to real estate:** Is the item being used as real property or personal property?

These four tests are easy to remember by using the acronym IRMA:

      I,   Intention
      R,   Relationship of the parties
      M,   Method of annexation
      A,   Adaptation to the real estate

Although these tests seem simple, court decisions have not been consistent regarding what constitutes a fixture. Articles that appear to be permanently affixed have sometimes been held by the courts to be personal property, whereas items that do not appear to be permanently attached have been held to be fixtures.

In the sale of property, the one certain way to avoid confusion over the nature of an article is for the parties to enter into a written agreement that establishes which items are considered part of the real property. A real estate broker or salesperson should ensure that a sales contract includes a list of all articles that are being included in the sale, particularly if there is any doubt as to whether they are permanently attached fixtures. Articles that might cause confusion include freestanding appliances, invisible fencing and controls, lightbulbs, above-ground pools and swing sets.

In Practice   The NCAR Standard Form 2, "The Offer to Purchase and Sales Contract," dated 1999, in paragraph 2, lists items that are normally fixtures and provides for items that may be excepted by the seller or buyer. "**2. FIXTURES:** The following items, if any, are included in the purchase price free of liens: any built-in appliances, light fixtures, ceiling fans, attached floor coverings, blinds, shades, drapery rods and curtain rods, brackets and all related hardware, window and door screens, storm windows, combination doors, awnings, antennas, satellite dishes and receivers, burglar/fire/smoke alarms, pool and spa equipment, solar energy systems, attached fireplace screens, gas logs, fireplace inserts, electric garage door openers with controls, outdoor plants and trees, (except those in movable containers), basketball goals, storage sheds, mailboxes, wall and/or door mirrors, and any other items *attached or affixed to the Property, EXCEPT the following items:*_____.*"*

Trade fixtures. An article owned by a tenant and attached to a rented space or building for use in conducting a business is a **trade fixture,** or a **chattel fixture.** Examples of trade fixtures are bowling alleys, store shelves, bars and restaurant equipment. Do not confuse trade fixtures, items the tenant installs to further his or her trade or business, with "up-fits" installed by the landlord while preparing the property for the tenant's occupancy.

Trade fixtures differ from other types of fixtures in three ways:

1. Fixtures are part of the real property and belong to the owner of that property. Trade fixtures are usually owned and installed by a tenant for his or her use and are the tenant's personal property.
2. Fixtures are considered a permanent part of a building, but trade fixtures are removable. Trade fixtures may be attached to a building in the same manner as other fixtures. However, due to the relationship of the parties (landlord and tenant), the law gives a tenant the right to remove trade fixtures, provided the removal is completed before the term of the lease expires and the rented space is restored to approximately its original condition.

3. Because fixtures are legally construed to be real property, they are included in any sale or mortgage of the real property. Trade fixtures are not included in the sale or mortgage of real property except by special agreement.

Trade fixtures that are not removed at the end of the lease become the real property of the landlord. Acquiring the property in this way is known as *accession.*

For Example Paul's Pizza leases space in a small shopping center. Paul bolted a large iron oven to the floor of the unit. When Paul's Pizza goes out of business or relocates, Paul will be able to take his pizza oven with him if he can repair the bolt-holes in the floor; the oven is a trade fixture. On the other hand, if the pizza oven was brought into the restaurant in pieces, welded together, then set in concrete, Paul might not be able to remove it without causing structural damage. In that case, the oven might become a fixture.

Agricultural fixtures. There is a special class of fixtures in North Carolina: **agricultural fixtures.** While fixtures used in a farming operation would seem to fall into the category of trade fixtures, in North Carolina agricultural fixtures are considered real property rather than personal property. Thus, if a tenant farmer installed feeding troughs during the tenancy, they would be considered real property and could not be removed by the tenant at the end of the lease.

Effect of the Uniform Commercial Code (UCC). All brokers should be aware of the effect of the **Uniform Commercial Code (UCC)** on fixtures. According to the UCC, if a homeowner purchases an item on credit (a dishwasher, for example) and gives the creditor a security agreement, that item remains personal property and may be removed by the creditor in the event of default. When the item has been paid for in full, it becomes real property. Suppose the homeowner decides to sell her home before the dishwasher has been paid for. She could remove the dishwasher when she moves out of the house because it is still her personal property. On the other hand, she may leave the dishwasher behind and the buyer might assume that it is real property that was included in the purchase price. The buyer may be surprised to learn that he must pay the secured creditor the outstanding balance or risk having the appliance repossessed. All homebuyers should make sure there are no security agreements filed on property within the home. This is normally included in the title search the buyer's lawyer will perform. The filing of the security agreement in effect makes the fixture an item of personal property until it is paid for.

ESTATES IN REAL PROPERTY

The amount and kind of interest that a person has in real property is called an *estate in land.* An estate may be defined as the degree, quantity, nature and extent of interest one has in real property. Estates in land are divided into two major classifications: (1) nonfreehold estates or leasehold estates (those involving tenants) and (2) freehold estates (those involving ownership) (see Figure 2.5). (Nonfreehold estates are discussed in detail in Chapter 10.)

Figure 2.5   *Estates and Interests in North Carolina Real Estate*

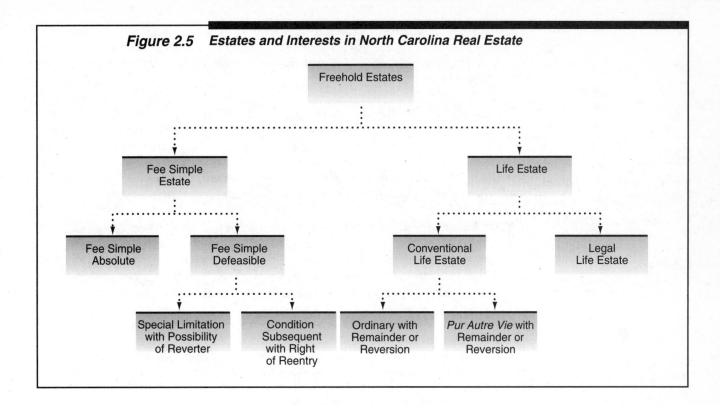

Freehold estates are estates of indeterminable length, such as those existing for a lifetime or forever. These include the

- fee simple estate (can pass by inheritance),
- defeasible fee estate (can pass by inheritance),
- ordinary conventional life estate with remainder or reversion (does not pass by inheritance) and
- pur autre vie estate with remainder or reversion (can pass by inheritance).

The first two of these estates continue for an indefinite period and are inheritable by the heirs of the owner. The third and fourth terminate on the death of the person on whose life they are based.

Nonfreehold, or **leasehold, estates** include any estate that is not a freehold estate. These are the

- estate for years,
- estate from year to year,
- estate at will and
- estate at sufferance.

Fee Simple Estate   A holder of an estate in fee simple is entitled to all rights in the property. An estate in fee simple is the highest type of interest in real estate recognized by law. It is complete ownership. This estate is of unlimited duration. When the owner dies, the estate passes to the owner's heirs or devisees (as provided in the owner's will). A fee simple estate is thus an estate of inheritance and is always legally transferable, but it is not always free of encumbrances.

Fee simple absolute. A fee simple ownership, on which there are no limitations (other than the governmental powers) is a **fee simple absolute**. In common usage, the terms *fee* and *fee simple* are used interchangeably with fee simple absolute.

Fee simple defeasible. A **fee simple defeasible** (or *defeasible fee estate*) is qualified and may be lost (or defeated) on the occurrence or nonoccurrence of a specified event. A fee simple may be qualified by a **condition subsequent** that dictates some action or activity that the new owner must not perform. The former owner retains a right of reentry so that if the condition is broken, the former owner can retake possession of the property.

> **For Example** A grant of land on the condition that there be no consumption of alcohol on the premises is a fee simple on condition subsequent. If alcohol is consumed on the property, the former owner has the right to reacquire full ownership. It will be necessary for the grantor (or the grantor's heirs or successors) to go to court to assert that right. There is no automatic right of reversion.

A **fee simple determinable** is similar to a fee simple subsequent, in that a special condition is connected to the estate. In a fee simple determinable estate, the ownership is held "so long as" or "during the period" the condition or limitation is maintained. The former owner, or his or her heirs or successors retains the right of reversion and so automatically reacquires full ownership if the special condition ceases to exist.

> **For Example** A grant of land from Aunt Fran to her church so long as the land is used only for religious purposes is a fee simple determinable (with a special limitation). If the church uses the land for a nonreligious purpose, title automatically reverts back to Aunt Fran (or her heirs or successors).

Do not confuse the two estates. The difference between them is in the language used to create the estate. A *fee simple estate qualified by a condition subsequent* is conveyed "provided that," or "on the condition that." The language used for a *fee simple determinable estate* is based on time. It is conveyed "as long as." Both of these defeasible estates are the same as far as possession and use are concerned.

Because they will take effect only at some time in the future (if at all), the right of entry and the possibility of reverter are called **future interests**.

Life Estate

A **life estate** is an estate in land that is limited in duration to the life of the owner or to the life or lives of some other designated person or persons (see Figure 2.6).

An ordinary life estate is limited to the lifetime of the owner of the life estate (the life tenant). An ordinary life estate ends with the death of the person to whom it was granted (see Figure 2.7).

> **For Example** Broderick wants his children ultimately to have ownership of a piece of property. But he wants his mother to be able to live on it for as long as she lives. So Broderick deeds the property to his mother for her life. When she dies, the ownership of the property will revert to his children.

Fee simple defeasible: "on the condition that"

Fee simple determinable: "so long as" "while" "during"

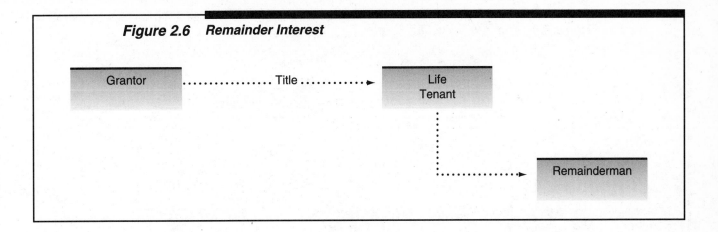

Figure 2.6 Remainder Interest

There is also an estate known as an estate for the life of another; the legal term being *life estate **pur autre vie*** (See Figure 2.8).

For Example Austin, a 67-year-old man, owns fee simple title to Blackacre Farms. He conveys a life estate in Blackacre Farms to his brother Carl for the life of Denise, Carl's daughter and Austin's niece. Carl has the right to enjoy the ownership of the property and is the life tenant, but Denise is the measuring life. Should Denise die, Carl's estate will terminate and revert to Austin, Austin's heirs or to a named remainderman. The measuring life has no present or future ownership interest in the property.

While a life estate is not considered an estate of inheritance, a life estate pur autre vie can be inherited by the life tenant's heirs, but only until the death of the person against whose life the estate is measured. For example, if Carl died before Denise, Carl's heirs would inherit Carl's life estate. However, their life estate would terminate on the death of Denise.

Remainder and reversion. A fee simple owner who creates a life estate must consider the future ownership of the property after the termination of the life estate. The future interest may take one of two forms:

1. **Remainder interest:** The grantor names someone other than himself or herself to receive title to the property when the life estate terminates. This occurred in our example with Broderick. He provided that his children would receive title when his mother's life estate terminated. The person(s) named (the children, in our example) is said

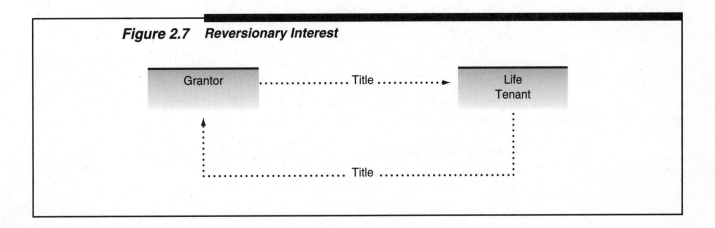

Figure 2.7 Reversionary Interest

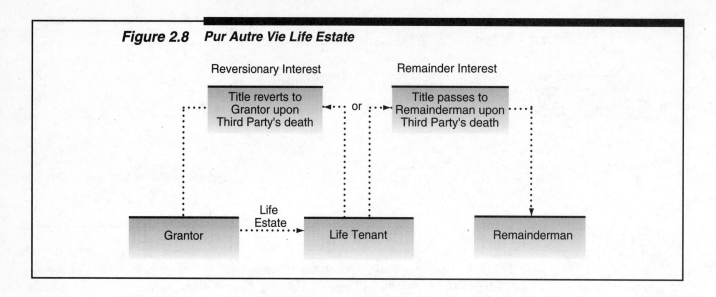

Figure 2.8   Pur Autre Vie Life Estate

to own a remainder interest and is called a *remainderman*. A remainder interest is a *nonpossessory estate*—a future interest. This interest can be sold.

2. **Reversionary interest:** If the grantor does not name a remainderman, then ownership returns to the grantor when the life estate terminates. If the grantor is deceased when the life estate terminates, the property goes to the grantor's heirs or devisees. This interest or estate is called a *reversion* and is also a future interest.

When the life estate terminates, the holder of the future interest (the remainder or reversion) will be the owner of a fee simple estate.

A life tenant's interest in real property is a true ownership interest. In general, the life tenant is not answerable to the holder of the future interest. A life tenant is entitled to all income and profits arising from the property during the life tenancy. A life tenant also may use some of the property's resources to maintain the property. For example, a life tenant may sell some of the timber growing on the property to pay for damages caused by a flood. This right is referred to as *estovers*. A life tenant also can sell or mortgage his or her life tenancy, although there may be few parties willing to purchase or lend money that is secured by such a limited interest.

A life tenant's rights are not absolute, however. A life tenant can enjoy the rights of the land but cannot encroach on those of the reversioner or remainderman. In other words, the life tenant cannot perform any act that would permanently injure the land or property. For example, a life tenant would not be allowed to destroy an orchard on the property just because he or she didn't want to bother with it. This kind of injury to real estate is known in legal terms as **waste**. Those with a future interest in the property could bring legal action for damages or seek an injunction against the life tenant.

Conventional life estate. A conventional life estate is created by grant from the owner of the fee simple estate. The owner retains a reversionary interest in the property or names a remainderman.

Legal life estate. A legal life estate is one created by statute in some states. A legal life estate becomes effective automatically by operation of law on the occurrence of certain events. Dower and curtesy are the forms of legal life estate currently used in some states. Dower is a wife's right to a life estate in her husband's property after his death; curtesy is a husband's right to a life estate in his wife's property after her death.

North Carolina has abolished dower and curtesy and has set up a system of intestate succession in their place. Intestate statutes provide for the distribution of the property of an intestate person, who is someone who dies without a valid will.

OWNERSHIP OF REAL PROPERTY

A fee simple estate in land may be held in (1) severalty, which means that title is held by one owner (sometimes referred to as *sole ownership*), or (2) co-ownership, cotenancy or concurrent ownership, where title is held by two or more persons at the same time.

The manner in which property is owned is important to the real estate broker for two reasons: (1) the form of ownership existing when a property is sold determines who must sign the various documents involved (listing contract, acceptance of offer to purchase or sales contract, and deed) and (2) the purchaser must determine in what form to take title. For example, a sole purchaser generally takes title in his or her name alone, and a tenancy in severalty is created. However, if there are two or more purchasers, they may take title in a tenancy in common, in joint tenancy or in tenancy by the entirety. When questions about these forms are raised by the parties to a transaction, the real estate broker should recommend that the parties seek legal and tax advice.

Ownership in Severalty When title to real estate is vested in (presently owned by) one person or a single entity, such as a partnership, corporation or limited liability company (LLC), that person or entity is said to own the property in **severalty.** This person or entity is also referred to as the *sole owner.*

Co-Ownership When title to one parcel of real estate is vested in two or more persons or organizations, those parties are said to be *co-owners,* or *concurrent owners,* of the property. There are several forms of co-ownership, each having unique legal characteristics. The three forms recognized in North Carolina are

1. tenancy in common,
2. joint tenancy and
3. tenancy by the entirety.

Forms of Co-Ownership in North Carolina

1. Tenancy in common
2. Joint tenancy
3. Tenancy by the entirety

Tenancy in common. A parcel of real estate may be owned by two or more people in what is known as a **tenancy in common.** There are two important characteristics of a tenancy in common. First, the ownership interest of a tenant in common is an undivided interest; there is a unity of possession among the co-owners. This means that although a tenant in common may hold, for example, a one-half or one-third interest in a property, it is impossible to distinguish physically which specific half or third of the property the tenant in common owns. The deed creating a tenancy in common may or

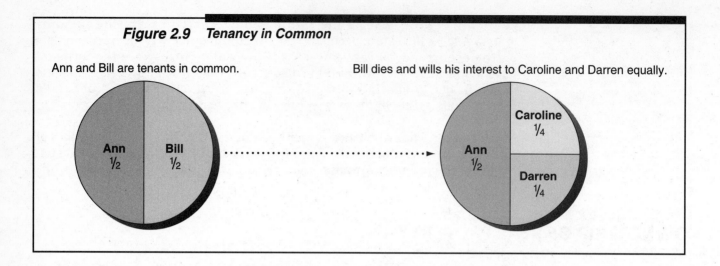

Figure 2.9   Tenancy in Common

Ann and Bill are tenants in common.

Ann
½

Bill
½

Bill dies and wills his interest to Caroline and Darren equally.

Ann
½

Caroline
¼

Darren
¼

may not state the fractional interest held by each co-owner; if no fractions are stated, the tenants are presumed to hold equal shares. For example, if five people hold title, each would own an undivided one-fifth interest.

The second important characteristic of a tenancy in common is that each owner holds his or her undivided interest in severalty and can sell, convey, mortgage or transfer that interest through the right of partition. On the death of a co-owner, that tenant's undivided interest passes to his or her heirs through a probate proceeding. The interest of a deceased tenant in common does not pass to another tenant in common unless the surviving co-owner is an heir or a purchaser (see Figure 2.9).

When two or more unmarried people acquire title to a parcel of real estate and the deed does not stipulate the type of tenancy created, by operation of law they acquire title as tenants in common.

Termination of co-ownership by partition suit. Each co-owner of real estate has an absolute right to force a "partition" of the land by voluntary action and agreement, which will divide their real estate according to their interests. When a division among co-owners cannot be agreed on voluntarily, the division can be ordered by a court in a suit for partition. The court may actually divide the land into pro rata parcels or, if this cannot be done, may order the property sold and the proceeds divided proportionately among the owners.

Joint tenancy. Most states recognize some form of **joint tenancy** in property owned by two or more people. With joint tenancy, the ownership shares are always equal. The feature that distinguishes a joint tenancy from a tenancy in common is the right of survivorship. The death of one of the joint tenants does not destroy the ownership unit; it only reduces by one the number of people who make up the unit. As each successive joint tenant dies, the surviving joint tenant(s) acquires the interest of the deceased joint tenant. The joint tenancy continues until there is only one owner, who then holds title in severalty. The last surviving joint tenant has the same rights to dispose of the property as any sole owner (see Figure 2.10).

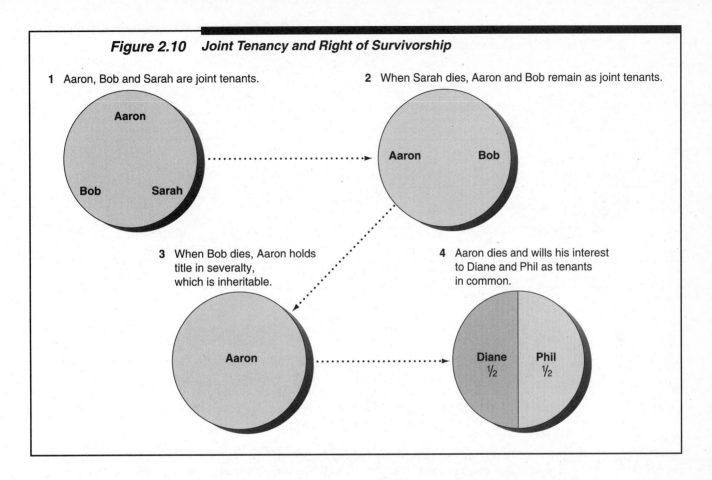

Figure 2.10 *Joint Tenancy and Right of Survivorship*

1 Aaron, Bob and Sarah are joint tenants.

2 When Sarah dies, Aaron and Bob remain as joint tenants.

3 When Bob dies, Aaron holds title in severalty, which is inheritable.

4 Aaron dies and wills his interest to Diane and Phil as tenants in common.

North Carolina does not favor the right of survivorship for a joint tenancy. The right of survivorship can be created if the deed is worded in exact compliance with North Carolina court decisions, making it clear that the right of survivorship is intended. Otherwise, North Carolina statutes provide that on the death of a joint tenant, the decedent's estate does not pass to the surviving joint tenant but instead goes to his or her heirs in the same manner as estates held by tenancy in common. In other words, unless the deed is worded exactly right, a joint tenancy can be created, but the right of survivorship does not apply. Note that where a right of survivorship is created, if one joint tenant owner conveys his or her interest to another person, that right of survivorship will be destroyed. The new owner becomes a tenant in common with the other owners because title is conveyed at a separate time.

A lawyer should always be consulted if the parties to a transaction insist on the right of survivorship. There are many technical requirements that must be met before a court will recognize a joint tenancy with a right to survivorship.

Tenancy by the entirety. **Tenancy by the entirety** is a special form of tenancy in which the owners are husband and wife. Each spouse has an equal, undivided interest in the property; each, in essence, owns the entire estate. On the death of one spouse, full title automatically passes to the surviving spouse. The transfer of the interest of the deceased spouse may be recorded by filing a certificate of death, an affidavit or a certificate of transfer, as provided by law.

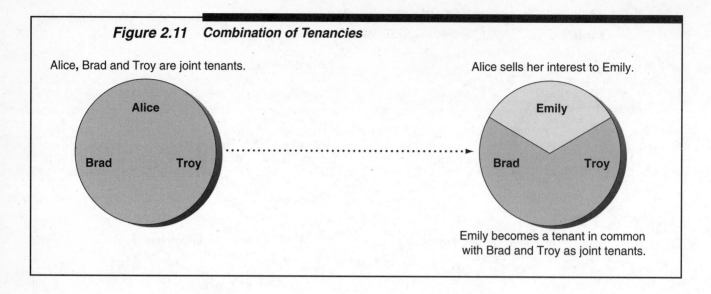

Figure 2.11   Combination of Tenancies

Alice, Brad and Troy are joint tenants.

Alice sells her interest to Emily.

Emily becomes a tenant in common with Brad and Troy as joint tenants.

The distinguishing characteristics of tenancy by the entirety are

- the owners must be husband and wife when title is received;
- the owners have rights of survivorship;
- during the owners' lives, title can be conveyed only by a deed signed by both parties (one party cannot convey a one-half interest); and
- there is generally no right to partition.

Any conveyance to a husband and wife by deed or will creates a tenancy by the entirety unless specifically stated otherwise. A tenancy by the entirety may be terminated by the death of either spouse, by divorce (leaving the parties as tenants in common) or by the mutual agreement of both spouses. Note that a husband and wife can choose another form of ownership for property that is owned during marriage—tenancy by the entirety is not the only available option. Furthermore, property that is jointly owned before marriage (or owned in severalty by one of the spouses) does not automatically become a tenancy by the entirety simply by virtue of the fact of marriage. If a couple owned property before marriage as tenants in common, they will continue to own the property as tenants in common unless the husband and wife choose to change the method of ownership.

Hybrid Forms of Ownership

Some forms of ownership are called *hybrid forms of ownership* because they contain elements of both ownership in severalty and concurrent ownership (see Figure 2.11).

Condominium ownership. The **condominium** form of ownership of apartment buildings was popular in Europe for many years before gaining wide acceptance in the United States. Condominium laws, often called *horizontal property acts*, have been enacted in every state, including North Carolina. Under these laws, the occupant/owner of each apartment holds a fee simple title to the apartment (which is often called *title to airspace*) and also a specified share of the indivisible parts of the building and land, known as the *common elements* (see Figure 2.12). The individual unit owners in a condominium own these common elements together as tenants in common. The individual unit owners pay their own separate property taxes and mortgage payments and typically belong to an owners' association that manages the condominium complex.

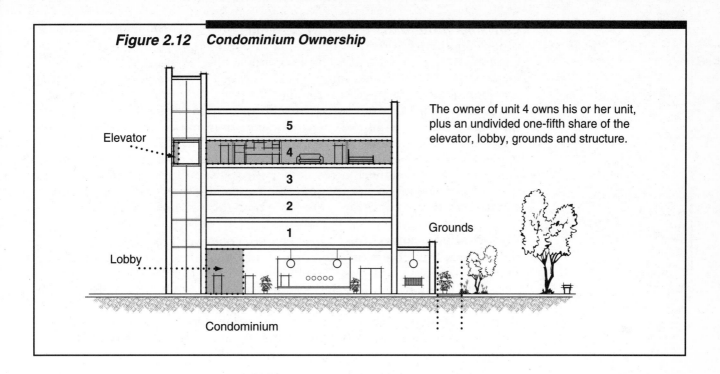

Figure 2.12   Condominium Ownership

The owner of unit 4 owns his or her unit, plus an undivided one-fifth share of the elevator, lobby, grounds and structure.

The condominium form of ownership is usually used for apartment buildings. These may range from freestanding highrise buildings to townhouse-like arrangements. The common elements include such items as the land, exterior structure, hallways, elevators, stairways and roof. In some instances, lawns and recreational facilities such as swimming pools, clubhouses, tennis courts and golf courses also may be considered common elements. In addition, the condominium form of ownership is used for other types of properties such as commercial properties, office buildings and multiuse buildings that contain offices and shops as well as residential units.

Creation of a condominium. North Carolina law (the **North Carolina Condominium Act of 1986**) specifies that a condominium is created and established when the developer of the property executes and records a declaration of its creation in the county where the property is located. The declaration must include any covenants, conditions or restrictions on the use of the property. The developer must file a plat map or plan of the condominium property, buildings and any other improvements. The developer also must prepare a set of bylaws. The bylaws usually provide for

- the creation of a unit owners' association giving a vote to each unit owner,
- the election of a board of managers from among the unit owners,
- the duties of the board of managers,
- the compensation of its members,
- their method of election and removal,
- whether a managing agent is to be engaged and
- the method of collecting the unit owners' association monthly dues from each member to cover the costs of management and maintenance of the common areas.

Consumer protection. The North Carolina law also requires disclosure and other consumer protection measures in connection with new residential condominium unit sales in the form of public offering statements and resale certificates. The developer must disclose all ownership and other appropriate documents to the purchaser before the purchase contract is signed. The purchaser then has a seven-day rescission period, which begins after the purchase contract is signed. At any time during that seven-day period, the purchaser can cancel the sale and receive a full refund of any earnest money deposit. On a resale unit (a sale of a condominium other than the original sale from the developer), a resale certificate detailing the monthly dues assessment and any other fees payable by a unit owner must be given to a purchaser prior to conveyance. There is no right to cancel on resales.

Cooperative ownership. Under the usual **cooperative** arrangement, title to land and building is held by a corporation (or land trust). The building management sets a price for each apartment in the building. Each purchaser of an apartment in the building receives stock in the corporation when he or she pays the agreed-on price for the apartment. The purchaser then becomes a shareholder of the corporation and, by virtue of that stock ownership, receives a **proprietary lease** to his or her apartment for the life of the corporation.

The cooperative building's real estate taxes are assessed against the corporation as owner. Generally, the mortgage is signed by the corporation, creating one lien on the entire parcel of real estate. Taxes, mortgage interest and principal, and operating and maintenance expenses are shared by the tenant/shareholders in the form of monthly assessments.

While the cooperative tenant/owners do not actually own an interest in real estate (they own stock, which is personal property), for all practical purposes they control the property through their stock ownership and their voice in the management of the corporation. The bylaws of the corporation generally provide that each prospective purchaser of an apartment lease must be approved by an administrative board.

Townhouse ownership. **Townhouse** projects are typically a group of two-story or three-story units that are horizontally attached to each other; that is, they share **party walls**. Each townhouse unit is individually owned; the homeowner association owns the common areas. Townhouse ownership is similar to condominium ownership with one fundamental difference: the owner of each townhouse unit also owns the land on which that unit is built. A developer may choose to build a townhouse project rather than a condominium project because of all the rules and regulations that govern condominiums.

Time-share ownership. A **time-share** is any right to occupy a unit of real property during five or more separated time periods (usually consisting of one or two weeks) over a period of at least five years. Time-sharing permits multiple purchasers to buy interests in real estate—usually a unit of a resort hotel, an apartment or a condominium—with each purchaser having a right to use the facility for a specific time period. For instance, a time-share owner may have the right to use an oceanfront apartment for the first three weeks of June every calendar year.

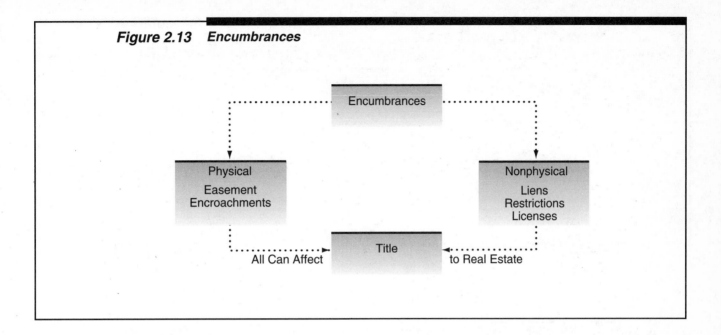

Figure 2.13 Encumbrances

North Carolina statutes regulate the development and sale of time-shares. For example, all time-share projects must be registered with the state, developers must give prospective purchasers public offering statements and purchasers have a five-day cancellation period during which they can cancel the purchase without penalty. [See Article 4, *Real Estate Licensing in North Carolina.*]

Planned unit development. A **planned unit development (PUD)** is really a method of real estate development, not ownership. The major feature of a PUD is flexible zoning. It differs from a normal subdivision in that buildings are clustered together (rather than complying with normal lot size and setback requirements), leaving more room for open spaces and recreational areas. Sometimes PUDs include a variety of land uses as well. For example, instead of being solely single-family residential, a PUD also may include some multifamily complexes as well as some retail or commercial uses. Typically, residential owners receive title to their individual units, while the homeowners' association typically has title to the other areas of the development.

ENCUMBRANCES ON REAL PROPERTY

A claim, charge or liability that attaches to and is binding on real estate is called an **encumbrance.** An encumbrance is anything that affects title to real estate (see Figure 2.13). It is a right or interest held by a party who is not the fee owner of the property. An encumbrance may affect the value or obstruct the use of the property, but it does not necessarily prevent a transfer of title.

Liens A charge against property that provides security for a debt or an obligation of the property owner is a **lien.** If the obligation is not repaid, the lienholder, or creditor, has the right to have it paid out of the debtor's property, usually from the proceeds of a court sale. Real estate taxes, mortgages and trust

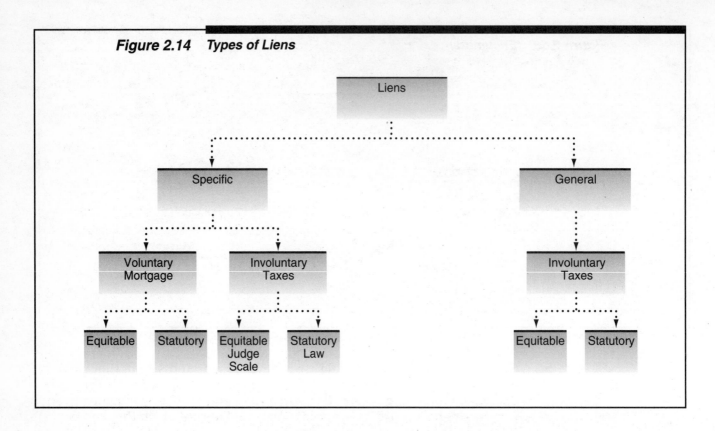

Figure 2.14* *Types of Liens

deeds, judgments and mechanics' liens may all represent liens against an owner's real estate. A lien does not constitute ownership; it is a type of encumbrance. Note, however, that whereas all liens are encumbrances, not all encumbrances are liens.

Liens fall into several categories, based on how they are created. A voluntary lien is contractual or consensual and is created by the debtor's action, as when someone takes out a mortgage loan to buy real estate. An involuntary lien is created by law and can be either statutory or equitable. Liens may be further classified as general or specific, as illustrated in Figure 2.14.

Specific liens. A specific lien is secured by a specific parcel of property and affects only that particular property.

Mortgage and deed of trust liens. In general, a mortgage or deed of trust lien is a voluntary lien on real estate given to a lender by a borrower as security for a real estate loan. It becomes a lien on real property when the lender records the mortgage or deed of trust in the office of the register of deeds in the county where the property is located. Mortgage and deed of trust liens are the most common form of lien or encumbrance. Mortgages and mortgage liens are discussed in detail in Chapter 12.

Real property tax and special assessment liens. If a property owner fails to pay the taxes levied by a city or county on his or her property, the unpaid tax becomes a specific, involuntary lien on that property. The lien attaches to the property on the date the property is listed (January 1 of each year) and takes priority over all other liens. Real property is taxed on an *ad valorem* basis, which means *according to value.*

In addition to the ad valorem real estate taxes, special assessment (improvement) taxes may be levied against real property. The purpose of these taxes is to pay for an improvement that has benefited the taxed property, such as street paving or the installation of a sewer system.

Both ad valorem and special assessment tax liens are valid for ten years. (Property taxes are discussed in more detail later in this chapter.)

Mechanics' liens. The purpose of the mechanic's lien is to give security to those who perform labor or furnish material in the improvement of real property. A mechanic's lien is a specific, involuntary lien and is available to contractors, subcontractors, architects, equipment lessors, surveyors, laborers and others. This type of lien is filed when the owner has not paid for the work or when the general contractor has been paid but has not paid the subcontractors or suppliers.

To be entitled to a mechanic's lien, the person who did the work must have had a contract (express or implied) with the owner or the owner's authorized representative. A person claiming a mechanic's lien must file the lien claim within 120 days after last furnishing the labor or materials; the lien takes effect from the date that person first furnished the labor or materials. The action to enforce a properly filed mechanic's lien must be brought within 180 days after a worker last furnished labor or materials.

General liens. General liens affect all the property of a debtor, both real and personal, rather than a specific parcel of real property.

Judgments. A judgment is a decree issued by a court. When the decree provides for the awarding of money and sets forth the amount of money owed by the debtor to the creditor, the judgment is referred to as a *money judgment.*

When a judgment is properly docketed in a county (entered and indexed in a judgment book), that judgment becomes a lien on all of the real estate and personal property owned by the judgment debtor in that county. Real estate of the judgment debtor in other counties is not affected unless the judgment is docketed in those counties as well. A judgment lien is good for ten years from the date of the judgment.

Personal property tax liens. A personal property tax is assessed on certain types of personal property. If unpaid, this tax becomes a general, involuntary lien against all the property owned by the taxpayer.

State tax liens. Both unpaid state inheritance taxes and unpaid state income taxes give rise to general, involuntary liens against all property owned by the individual taxpayer. Both types of liens last for ten years.

Federal tax liens. An Internal Revenue Service (IRS) tax lien results from a person's failure to pay any portion of federal IRS taxes, such as income and withholding taxes. A federal tax lien is a general; involuntary lien on all real and personal property held by the delinquent taxpayer. Its priority is based on the date of filing or recording; it does not supersede previously recorded liens.

Effects of liens on title. Although the fee simple estate held by a typical real estate owner can be reduced in value by the lien rights of others, the owner is still free to convey title to a willing purchaser. The purchaser will, however, buy the property subject to any liens because liens run with the land; that is, they will bind successive owners if steps are not taken to clear the liens.

Remember, liens attach to the property, not to the property owner. Thus, although a purchaser who buys real estate under a delinquent lien is not responsible for payment of the debt secured by the lien, he or she faces a possible loss of the property if the creditors take court action to enforce the payment of their liens.

Priority of liens. Real estate taxes and special assessments generally take **priority** over all other liens. Therefore, if the property is sold through a court-ordered sale to satisfy unpaid debts or obligations, outstanding real estate taxes, personal property taxes and special assessments will be paid from the proceeds first. The remainder of the proceeds will be used to pay other outstanding liens in the order of the date and time they were filed. The first lien to be filed is the first lien to be paid. (This is called a *pure race system* of determining lien priority.) One exception to this rule is the mechanic's lien: the priority of a mechanic's lien dates back to the date the labor began or materials were first provided rather than to the date the lien was filed.

Restrictions (Restrictive Covenants and/or Protective Covenants)

Deed restrictions are another type of encumbrance on real property. Deed restrictions (also referred to as *conditions, covenants* and *restrictions*) are private agreements placed in the public record that affect the use of land. They are usually imposed by an owner of real estate when property is sold and are included in the seller's deed to the buyer. Deed restrictions typically would be imposed by a developer or subdivider for the purpose of maintaining specific standards in a subdivision, and they would be listed in the original development plans for the subdivision filed in the public record. Deed restrictions are discussed further in Chapter 4.

Lis Pendens

A judgment or another decree affecting real estate is rendered at the conclusion of a lawsuit. Generally, there is a considerable time lag between the filing of a lawsuit and the rendering of a judgment. When any suit is filed that affects title to a specific parcel of real estate (such as a foreclosure suit), the person bringing the lawsuit may file a lis pendens (Latin for "litigation pending"). When a lis pendens is filed, anyone acquiring an interest in the property takes that interest subject to any judgment or decree the court may issue. It is not a lien but rather a notice that there is an action or lawsuit pending that may adversely affect the title. The lis pendens acts more like an encumbrance against the title.

For Example If a lender is filing a foreclosure suit against a property owner, it will file a lis pendens against the property. If the property owner should sell the property during the course of the legal action, the new purchaser would take title subject to the outcome of the foreclosure action.

Easements

A right to use the land of another for a particular purpose is called an **easement.** Easements are not a form of ownership; they merely grant the use of the property. There are two types of easements: appurtenant and in gross.

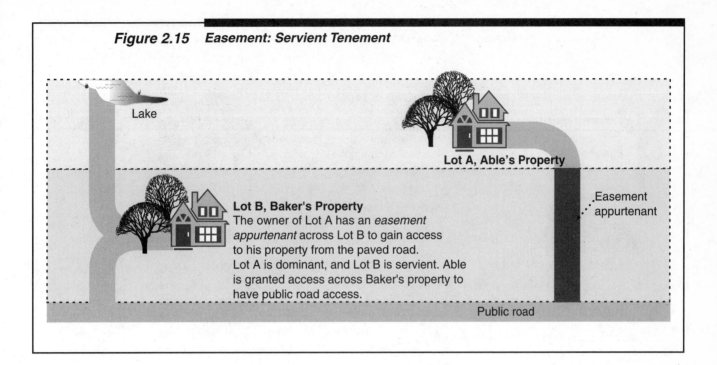

Figure 2.15 Easement: Servient Tenement

Lake

Lot A, Able's Property

Lot B, Baker's Property
The owner of Lot A has an *easement appurtenant* across Lot B to gain access to his property from the paved road. Lot A is dominant, and Lot B is servient. Able is granted access across Baker's property to have public road access.

Easement appurtenant

Public road

Easement appurtenant. An easement that is annexed to the ownership of one parcel of land and used for the benefit of another parcel of land is an **easement appurtenant.** For an easement appurtenant to exist, two adjacent tracts of land must be owned by different parties. The tract over which the easement runs is known as the *servient tenement;* the tract that benefits from the easement is known as the *dominant tenement* (see Figures 2.15 and 2.16).

For Example If Able and Baker own adjacent properties in a lake resort community and only Able's property borders the lake, Able may grant Baker an easement across Able's property so that Baker can have access to the lake. Able's property is the servient tenement; Baker's property is the dominant tenement. Baker's property benefits from the easement because it now has lake access, which didn't exist before the easement was granted.

An easement appurtenant is considered part of the dominant tenement, and if the dominant tenement is conveyed to another party, the easement passes with the title. In legal terms, the easement "runs with the land."

A *party wall* is an exterior wall of a building that straddles the boundary line between two owners' lots, with half of the wall on each lot. Each lot owner owns the half of the wall on his or her lot, and each has an easement appurtenant in the other half of the wall for support of his or her building. A written party-wall agreement should be used to create the easement rights. Expenses to build and maintain the wall are usually shared. A party driveway shared by adjoining owners and straddling the property boundary also should be created by written agreement, specifying responsibility for expenses.

Easement in gross. A mere personal interest in or right to use the land of another is an **easement in gross.** The right of use belongs to an individual

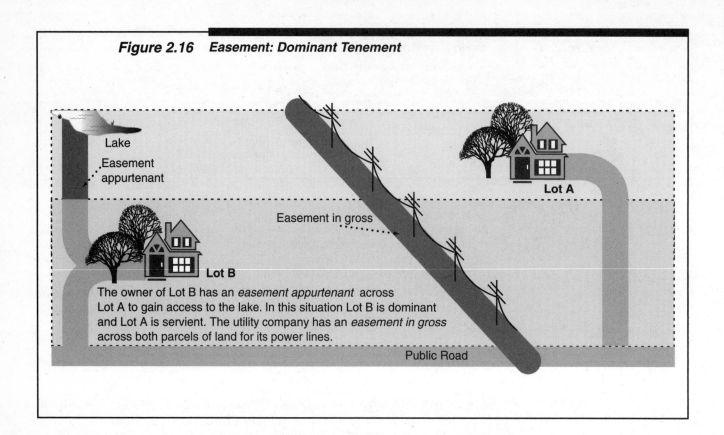

Figure 2.16   *Easement: Dominant Tenement*

Lake

Easement appurtenant

Lot A

Easement in gross

Lot B

The owner of Lot B has an *easement appurtenant* across Lot A to gain access to the lake. In this situation Lot B is dominant and Lot A is servient. The utility company has an *easement in gross* across both parcels of land for its power lines.

Public Road

(whether a person or a corporation) and is not appurtenant to any ownership estate in land. In other words, an easement in gross benefits a person or an entity, not a parcel of property. Examples of easements in gross are the easement rights a railroad has in its right-of-way or the right-of-way for a pipeline or high-tension power line. Commercial easements in gross may be assigned or conveyed and may be inherited. However, personal easements in gross usually are not assignable and terminate on the death of the easement owner.

Creating an easement. To create an easement, there must be two separate parties, one of whom is the owner of the land over which the easement runs. It is impossible for the owner of a parcel of property to have an easement over his or her own land. Thus, where a valid easement exists and the dominant tenement is subsequently acquired by the owner of the servient tenement, the easement is extinguished. The person who has the easement interest has a nonpossessory interest in the land. The owner of the land burdened by the easement has a possessory interest in the land (the owner can use and possess the land), but the owner cannot interfere with the easement holder's rights.

Easements may be created in a number of ways:

- *Express grant.* An easement is commonly created by a written agreement between the parties establishing the easement right. Easements are often created in a deed from the owner of the property over which an easement will run.

- *Express reservation.* An easement can be created by the grantor in a deed of conveyance by reserving an easement over the sold land.
- *Necessity.* An easement by necessity, or easement by implication of law, arises because all owners must have rights of ingress to and egress from their land— they cannot be landlocked. If a grantor has conveyed property that is completely surrounded by the grantor's property (thus landlocking the grantee), an easement by necessity will be created.
- *Prescription.* When a claimant has made use of another's land for a certain period of time, as defined by state law, an easement by prescription is acquired. This prescriptive period is 20 years in North Carolina. The claimant's use must have been continuous, exclusive and without the owner's approval. Additionally, the use must have been visible, open and notorious, so that the owner could have readily learned of it. A property owner can prevent an easement by prescription from being created by giving the user permission.
- *Condemnation.* An easement by condemnation is acquired for a public purpose, through the power of eminent domain. Eminent domain is the power of a government or quasi-government entity to take property for a public use, after paying the owner just compensation. Examples are taking land to put in a power line or widen a road. In both cases, the owner must be compensated for any loss in property value.

Terminating an easement. An easement may be terminated

- when the purpose for which the easement was created no longer exists;
- if the easement holder becomes the owner of the land where the easement is located (a situation called a *merger*);
- by release of the right of easement to the owner of the servient tenement;
- by abandonment of the easement (the intention of the parties is the determining factor);
- by nonuse of a prescriptive easement;
- by adverse possession by the owner of the servient tenement;
- by destruction of the servient tenement, as in the demolition of a party wall;
- by nonrecordation;
- by lawsuit (an action to quiet title) against someone claiming the easement; or
- by excessive use, as when a residential use is converted to commercial purposes.

Encroachments   An **encroachment** arises when a building (or some portion of it), a fence or a driveway illegally extends beyond the land of its owner and covers some land of an adjoining owner, a street or an alley. For instance, two landowners are neighbors. The garage of one landowner actually extends about one foot onto the neighbor's property. This is an encroachment.

Encroachments are usually disclosed by either a physical inspection of the property or a location survey. A location survey shows the location of all improvements located on a property and determines whether any improvements extend over the lot lines. If the building on a lot encroaches on neighboring land, the neighbor may be able either to recover damages or to secure removal of the portion of the building that encroaches. Encroachments of long standing (for the prescriptive period of 20 years in North Carolina) may give rise to easements by prescription. The primary reason for a property survey is to ensure no encroachments have occurred. The legal effect of an encroachment is to make both titles unmarketable.

In Practice   Because an undisclosed encroachment could render a title unmarketable, the existence of an encroachment should be noted in a listing agreement, and the sales contract governing the transaction should be made subject to the existence of the particular encroachment. Encroachments are not disclosed by the usual title evidence provided in a real estate sale unless a survey is submitted while the examination is being made. Mortgage lenders may resist loans on properties with serious encroachments.

PROPERTY TAXATION IN NORTH CAROLINA

The ownership of real estate is subject to certain government powers. One of these powers is the right of state and local governments to impose tax liens for the support of their governmental functions. This power to tax comes from the state constitution and is considered to be a constitutional power rather than a police power. Because the location of real estate is permanently fixed, the government can levy taxes with a high degree of certainty that the taxes will be collected. Furthermore, because the lien for taxes levied on real estate has priority over other previously recorded liens, the tax lien will be the first lien to be paid from the proceeds of a court-ordered sale of the real estate.

Real estate taxes fall into two categories: (1) general real estate, or ad valorem, taxes and (2) special assessment, or improvement, taxes. Both of these taxes are levied against specific parcels of property and automatically become liens on those properties.

General Tax (Ad Valorem Tax)   General real estate taxes are levied for the general support of the government agency authorized to impose the levy. These taxes are known as *ad valorem taxes* because the amount of the tax varies in accordance with the value of the property being taxed. In North Carolina, the *Machinery Act* governs ad valorem taxes.

Property subject to taxation. All real property in North Carolina is subject to taxation. Although counties and municipalities determine real estate property tax rates within their jurisdictions on a statewide basis, the Machinery Act regulates real property taxation standards, standards for assessment, standards for appraisal and requirements for tax-exempt status. Property generally considered exempt includes that owned by nonprofit religious, educational and charitable organizations; property owned by the elderly and handicapped; agricultural, horticultural and forest lands; and some properties with energy-efficient heating and cooling systems.

Taxation timetable. In January of each tax year, all taxable real property must be listed in the county in which it is located. All listed property is assessed at its fair market value. Real property is appraised based on a statutory schedule and then is reappraised every eight years, a process referred to as *octennial reappraisal*. Real property may be reassessed more frequently than every eight years. In addition, the county may choose to make horizontal adjustments in the fourth year after reappraisal. This means the values of certain types of property or of properties within certain areas may be uniformly adjusted up to current value by applying an "across the board" percentage increase or decrease.

Each county or municipality determines the appropriate tax rate every year as part of its budgeting process. The rate is calculated by dividing the total amount of revenue needed by the total assessed value of all the property in the county or city. The tax rate must be established by July 1 of each year. Tax rates are usually expressed as a certain dollar amount per $100 of value.

For Example If the tax rate were $.90 per $100 of value, a $90,000 home would get a tax bill for $810.

$$\$90,000 \div \$100 \times .90 = \$810$$

If the tax rate were only $.80 per $100 of value, the same $90,000 home would get a tax bill for $720.

$$\$90,000 \div \$100 \times .80 = \$720$$

Each year's taxes are legally due and payable on September 1. However, because interest does not begin accruing until early in January of the following year, most people pay their real property taxes in late December. It is worth noting that even though cities and counties operate under a fiscal year (beginning on July 1 and ending on June 30), taxes are prorated based on the calendar year (see Figure 2.17).

Property tax liens. As noted earlier, property taxes are liens that attach to real property as of the listing date. In other words, even though property taxes are not due until September 1 of any given year, the tax lien takes effect the previous January 1. Remember, this tax lien takes priority over all other liens.

Appraisal and Assessment

The *appraisal* of real property may be defined as a process or an opinion as to value of property and how that value is communicated (see Chapter 16). The **assessment** is an official valuation of property for the purpose of establishing assessed value for tax purposes. Even though similar in concept, the techniques used in appraisal and assessment are quite different. Tax assessors do not have the time to assess individual properties, as do appraisers for other reasons such as loan applications. In the assessment process one method routinely used is the **mass appraisal** technique that determines assessed value for all lands in a given area by applying an overall percentage increase or decrease. This method is often used in conjunction with a "horizontal adjustment." Real property may be subject to reassessment if substantial improvements are added to the property.

Special Assessments

Special assessments, the second category of real estate taxes, are special taxes levied on real estate for public improvements to that real estate. Property owners in the area of the improvements are required to pay for them

Figure 2.17   Taxation Timetable

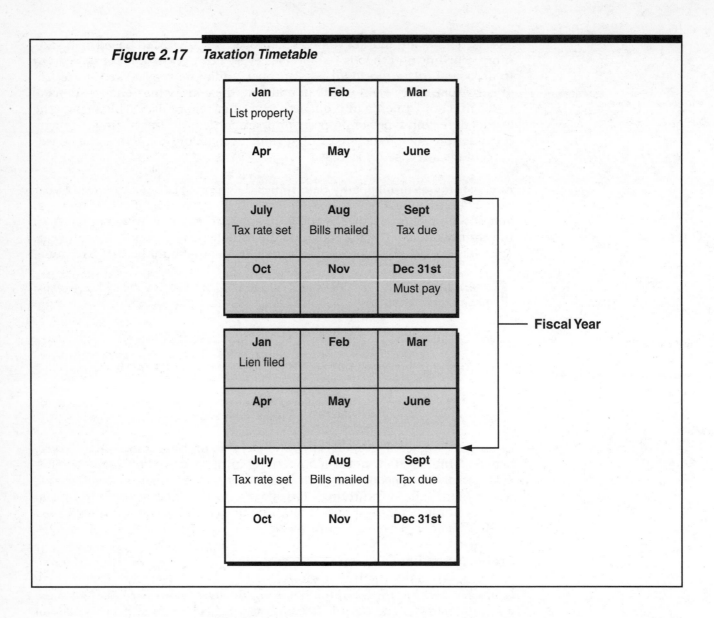

Jan	Feb	Mar
List property		

Apr	May	June

July	Aug	Sept
Tax rate set	Bills mailed	Tax due

Oct	Nov	Dec 31st
		Must pay

Jan	Feb	Mar
Lien filed		

Apr	May	June

July	Aug	Sept
Tax rate set	Bills mailed	Tax due

Oct	Nov	Dec 31st

— Fiscal Year

because their properties benefit directly from the improvements. Special assessments are authorized for the installation of paved streets, curbs, gutters, sidewalks, storm sewers, street lighting, beach erosion drainage projects and water control, to mention just a few. These improvements increase the value of the affected properties, so the owners are, in effect, merely reimbursing the taxing entity for that increase. Either a county or a city may levy the special assessment, and statutes regulate how the assessment is to be prorated and levied. The assessment could be based on the cost per front foot or on the total area of the land that benefits. Basic procedures by the county board of commissioners for levying special assessments are

- adoption of a preliminary resolution;
- provision of specific information, to include a public hearing;
- issue of proper notice to affected landowners;
- separation of a final resolution, to include costs and preparing assessment rolls; and
- final hearing, held after proper notice and information is given to the tax collector.

Like ad valorem taxes, special assessment liens enjoy priority over other types of liens. (However, they do not take precedence over ad valorem taxes.)

SUMMARY

Different rights to the same parcel of real estate may be owned and controlled by different parties, one owning surface rights, one owning air rights and one or more owning subsurface rights. These rights can be severed by separate instruments.

When articles of personal property are permanently affixed to land, they may become fixtures. As such, they are considered a part of the real estate and become subject to any existing mortgage on the property. Personal property attached to real estate by a tenant for the purpose of his or her business is classified as a trade, or chattel, fixture and remains personal property.

Four legal tests determine if an item is a fixture or not: intent, relationship of the annexing party to the property, method of annexation and adaptability (which may be referred to as the *Total Circumstances Test*).

An estate is the degree, quantity, nature and extent of interest a person holds in land. Freehold estates are estates of indeterminate length. Less-than-freehold estates are called *nonfreehold,* or *leasehold, estates,* and they concern tenants. A parcel of land may be a freehold and nonfreehold at the same time.

A freehold estate may be a fee simple estate or a life estate. A fee simple estate can be absolute or defeasible on the happening of some event. A conventional life estate is created by the owner of a fee estate; a legal life estate is created by law. Legal life estates include dower and curtesy, which North Carolina does not recognize.

Estates of inheritance include fee simple, fee simple determinable, fee simple subject to a condition subsequent and life estate pur autre vie. Estates not of inheritance include conventional life estates and marital life estates.

Encumbrances against real estate may be in the form of liens, deed restrictions, easements and encroachments. A fee simple estate is always transferable, but may not always be free of encumbrances.

An easement is the right acquired by one person to use another's real estate. There are two types of easements: easement appurtenant and easement in gross. An easement appurtenant involves two separately owned tracts. The tract benefited is known as the *dominant tenement;* the tract subject to the easement is called the *servient tenement.* An appurtenant easement is an encumbrance to the servient estate and a benefit to the dominant estate. An easement in gross is a personal right, such as that granted to utility companies to maintain poles, wires and pipelines. An easement in gross is a personal right; it is not transferable and ends with the death of the grantee.

An encroachment is an unauthorized use of another's real estate. The net effect of an encroachment is to make titles to both properties unmarketable.

Sole ownership, or ownership in severalty, indicates that title is held by one person or entity. Under the designation *co-ownership,* there are several ways in which title to real estate can be held concurrently by more than one person. Currently, co-ownership in North Carolina may be held by joint tenancy, tenancy in common or tenancy by the entirety.

Hybrid forms of ownership combine elements of ownership in severalty and concurrent ownership. Such forms of ownership include ownership of condominiums, cooperatives, time-shares and townhouses.

Liens are claims, or charges, of creditors or tax officials against the real and personal property of a debtor. A lien is a type of encumbrance. Liens are either general, covering all real and personal property of a debtor/owner, or specific, covering only the specific property described in the mortgage, tax bill or other document. The life of a general lien is ten years from the rendition of the judgment.

With the exception of real estate tax liens and mechanics' liens, the priority of liens is determined by the order in which they are placed in the public record of the county in which the debtor's property is located.

Real estate taxes are levied annually by local taxing authorities. Tax liens are generally given priority over other liens. Payments are required before stated dates, after which penalties accrue. Special assessments are levied to allocate the cost of improvements such as new sewers, sidewalks, curbs or paving to the real estate that benefits from them. Special assessment liens also are given priority over most other liens.

Questions

1. Real property is often referred to as a *bundle of legal rights.* Which of the following is NOT among these rights?
   a. Right of exclusion
   b. Right to use the property for illegal purposes
   c. Right of enjoyment
   d. Right to sell or otherwise convey the property

2. A fixture is considered to be
   I. real estate.
   II. personal property.
      a. I only
      b. II only
      c. Both I and II
      d. Neither I nor II

3. A construction firm builds an office center over a railroad right-of-way. This means that
   a. trains can no longer operate on the tracks under the building during business hours because the noise would disturb occupants of the office center.
   b. the construction firm has built the office center using the subsurface rights to the property.
   c. the construction firm has built the office center using the air rights over the railroad right-of-way.
   d. in building the office center the construction firm is in violation of North Carolina law.

4. A tenant firmly attaches appropriate appliances for his restaurant business on the leased premises. These appliances are
   I. trade fixtures.
   II. personal property.
   III. part of the real estate once they are installed.
      a. I only
      b. II only
      c. III only
      d. I and II only

5. Jerry and Ann Edwards are building a new enclosed front porch on their home. The lumber dealer with whom they are contracting has just unloaded a truckload of lumber that will be used to build the porch on their property. At this point, the lumber is considered a
   a. fixture that is real estate.
   b. chattel that is personal property.
   c. fixture that is personal property.
   d. chattel that is real estate.

6. When the Edwardses' new front porch, as described in question 5, is complete, the lumber that the dealer originally delivered will be considered a
   a. fixture that is real estate.
   b. chattel that is personal property.
   c. fixture that is personal property.
   d. chattel that is real estate.

7. Anne Ferneding is renting a single-family home under a one-year lease. Two months into the lease, she installs awnings over the building's front windows to keep the sun away from some delicate hanging plants. Which of the following statements is true?
   a. Anne must remove the awnings when she vacates or leave them for the landlord.
   b. Because of their nature, the awnings are considered real property.
   c. The awnings are considered fixtures.
   d. Because of the nature of the property, the awnings are considered trade fixtures.

8. Aaron Heffner purchases a parcel of land and sells the mineral rights to an exploration company. This means that, with regard to this property, Aaron now owns all EXCEPT which of the following rights?
   a. Air
   b. Surface
   c. Subsurface
   d. Air and subsurface

9. *Qualified fee* generally means that the estate will terminate on
   I. the death of the grantor.
   II. the death of the grantee.
   III. certain events or changes in use.
      a. I only
      b. II only
      c. III only
      d. I and III only

10. The term *dower* refers to which of the following?
   a. Conventional life estate in real property
   b. Ownership of a homestead
   c. Marital right
   d. Common law

11. Ed Roberts has the legal right to pass over the land owned by his neighbor. This is an
   a. estate in land.   c. emblement.
   b. easement.   d. encroachment.

12. Which of the following describes a life estate?
   a. Estate conveyed from Andrew to Betty for life
   b. Estate held by Andrew and Betty as co-owners with right of survivorship
   c. Estate with use conditions
   d. Fee simple estate

13. An estate in land that will automatically extinguish on the occurrence of a specified event is called a
   I. right of entry.
   II. fee simple determinable.
   III. reversionary interest.
      a. I only
      b. II only
      c. I and III only
      d. II and III only

14. A purchaser of real estate learns that her ownership rights will continue forever and that no other person can claim to be the owner or has any ownership control over the property. This person owns a
   a. fee simple interest.
   b. life estate.
   c. determinable fee estate.
   d. fee simple on condition subsequent.

15. Joan owned the fee simple title to a vacant lot adjacent to a hospital and was persuaded to make a gift of the lot. She wanted to have some control over its use, so her attorney prepared her deed to convey ownership of the lot to the hospital "so long as it is used for hospital purposes." After completion of the gift, the hospital owned a(n)
   a. fee simple absolute estate.
   b. easement.
   c. fee simple determinable.
   d. leasehold estate.

16. After Sacksteder had purchased his house and moved in, he discovered that his neighbor regularly uses Sacksteder's driveway to reach a garage located on the neighbor's property. Sacksteder's lawyer explained that ownership of the neighbor's real estate includes an easement over the driveway. Sacksteder's property is called
   a. the dominant tenement.
   b. a freehold.
   c. a leasehold.
   d. the servient tenement.

17. When a fee simple estate in a parcel of North Carolina real estate is conveyed by a deed to two or more owners other than husband and wife without designating the nature of their co-ownership, they are assumed to be
   a. tenants by the entirety.
   b. survivors.
   c. tenants in common.
   d. joint tenants.

18. A tenant in common owns an
   I. undivided interest.
   II. interest that must be equally divided.
      a. I only
      b. II only
      c. Both I and II
      d. Neither I nor II

19. A purchaser under the cooperative form of
   ownership receives
   I. a lease for the unit.
   II. stock in the cooperative corporation.
      a. I only
      b. II only
      c. Both I and II
      d. Neither I nor II

20. If property is held by two or more owners
   as tenants in common, the interest of a
   deceased co-owner will pass to the
      a. remaining owner or owners.
      b. heirs of the deceased.
      c. trust under which the property was
         owned.
      d. state by the law of escheat, regardless of
         whether the deceased has any heirs.

21. A condominium is created when
      a. the construction of the improvements is
         completed.
      b. the owner or developer files a
         declaration of condominium in the
         public record.
      c. the condominium owners' association is
         established.
      d. all of the unit owners file documents in
         the public records asserting their
         decision.

22. Ownership that allows possession for only
   a specific time each year is a
      a. cooperative.   c. condominium.
      b. time-share.   d. syndicate.

23. In North Carolina, real property must be
   reassessed every
      a. four years.   c. eight years.
      b. six years.   d. ten years.

24. Which of the following taxes is (are) used to
   distribute the cost of public services
   among real estate owners?
      a. Personal property tax
      b. Sales tax
      c. Real property tax
      d. All of the above

25. Which of the following liens usually would
   be given higher priority?
      a. Mortgage dated last year
      b. Current real estate tax
      c. Mechanic's lien for work started before
         the mortgage was made
      d. Judgment rendered yesterday

26. Green is the owner of a fee simple estate.
   The estate has a lien on it for real property
   taxes. The property
      a. is freely transferable, even though it has
         a lien on it.
      b. cannot be transferred until the lien is
         repaid.
      c. may be transferred to the lienholder
         only.
      d. automatically reverts to the previous
         owner because it is encumbered with a
         lien.

27. Estevez has a freehold estate in a single-
   family home. She rents the home to a
   young couple.
      a. Estevez no longer has a freehold estate,
         because a freehold estate and a
         leasehold (nonfreehold) estate cannot
         exist in the same property.
      b. Estevez must give up her freehold estate
         in order to rent the property to others.
      c. The tenants now own the freehold estate
         in the property.
      d. Estevez has a freehold estate in the
         property, and the tenants have a
         leasehold estate in the property.

28. David owns property that is bordered by a
   small stream. His property ends
      a. at the mean high-water mark of the
         stream.
      b. at the stream border.
      c. at the center of the stream.
      d. five feet before the stream border.

29. Martha owns property that borders a large, navigable lake. Her property ends
    a. at the mean high-water mark of the lake.
    b. at the lake border.
    c. at the center of the lake.
    d. five feet before the lake border.

30. The ad valorem property tax rates may be adjusted
    a. every year.　　　c. every four years.
    b. every two years.　d. every eight years.

31. What is the assessed value of a house located in the city limits if the city tax rate is $.80 per $100, the county tax rate is $.50 per $100 and the owner's annual taxes are $1,600?
    a. $20,000.33　　c. $123,076.92
    b. $32,000.92　　d. $52,000.00

32. What is the monthly tax liability on a property assessed at $133,000 if the published tax rate is $1.678 per $100 of assessed value?
    a. $2,231.74　　c. $1,950.00
    b. $185.98　　　d. $3,234.00

33. If you recently paid $2,000 in annual property taxes and the assessed value of your house is $184,000, what is the tax rate?
    a. $1.09/$100　　c. $1.33/$100
    b. $1/$100　　　 d. $119/$100

34. Which of the following are considered to be real property?
    I. Potted flowering plants
    II. Ornamental trees
    III. Crops
    a. I only
    b. II only
    c. III only
    d. I and II

35. Which of the following is (are) considered to be real property?
    I. Mailbox by the street
    II. Fireplace tools
    a. I only
    b. II only
    c. Both I and II
    d. Neither I nor II

36. A buyer and a seller/developer executed a purchase contract for a condominium on May 6, 2000, with the buyer putting down $5,000 in earnest money. The buyer changed her mind and notified the seller on May 11, 2000, that she was rescinding the contract. Which of the following is true?
    a. The buyer can legally cancel the contract and have the earnest money refunded.
    b. The buyer cannot cancel the contract because the three-day right of rescission has passed.
    c. The buyer can cancel only if she forfeits the earnest money.
    d. The buyer cannot cancel the contract because there is no right of rescission.

37. A dirt road that runs adjacent to your property is paved by ABC Paving Company under city contract. As property owner, you would pay for this in the form of
    a. ad valorem real property taxes.
    b. personal property taxes.
    c. an invoice from the contractor.
    d. a special assessment.

38. Which of the following statements is true?
    I. A life estate is a freehold estate.
    II. It is possible to have a freehold estate and a nonfreehold estate on the same property at the same time.
    a. I only
    b. II only
    c. Both I and II
    d. Neither I nor II

39. Tenants in common can do all of the following EXCEPT
    a. sell their interest.
    b. will their interest.
    c. exclude other tenant owners from the property.
    d. have their interest partitioned.

40. What forms of concurrent ownership can be jointly held only by husband and wife?
    I. Tenancy in common
    II. Tenancy by the entirety
    III. Estate for years
    a. I only
    b. II only
    c. II and III only
    d. I, II and III

41. What forms of concurrent ownership may be jointly held by husband and wife?
    I. Tenancy in common
    II. Tenancy by the entirety
       a. I only
       b. II only
       c. Both I and II
       d. Neither I nor II

42. Which of the following would NOT be considered in determining if an item is a fixture?
    a. Intent
    b. Adaptability
    c. Value
    d. Method of attachment

43. Concerning ownership as a joint tenancy, which of the following statements are true?
    I. A joint tenancy has the incident of the doctrine of survivorship.
    II. Joint tenants must hold the same land with unequal interests.
    III. Joint tenants must hold equal undivided interest in the property.
    IV. It is a form of concurrent ownership used widely in North Carolina.
       a. I and II only
       b. I and III only
       c. III and IV only
       d. II and IV only

44. Lis pendens is
    a. a recorded document that prevents transfer of title.
    b. a recorded notice that a legal action has been commenced against the property owner.
    c. both a and b.
    d. neither a nor b.

45. All of the following are characteristics of a fee simple title except that it is
    a. free from encumbrances.
    b. of indefinite duration.
    c. transferable with or without valuable consideration.
    d. transferable by will or intestate succession.

46. William, Frank, and Jane are joint tenants. Jane sells her interest to Lloyd, and then Frank dies. As a result,
    a. Frank's heirs, Lloyd and William are joint tenants.
    b. Frank's heirs and William are joint tenants.
    c, William, Lloyd and Frank's heirs are tenants in common
    d. William and Lloyd are tenants in common.

47. The state wants to condemn a strip of land through a farm for a highway. The state can do this because of its
    I. police power.
    II. power of eminent domain.
       a. I only
       b. II only
       c. Both I and II
       d. Neither I nor II

48. All of the following terms are related to easements EXCEPT
    a. by necessity.
    b. conditions, covenants and restrictions.
    c. appurtenant.
    d. servient tenant.

3 Property Description

LEARNING OBJECTIVES

When you've finished reading this chapter, you should be able to

- **explain** the importance of an accurate legal description and **list** those documents requiring legal descriptions.

- **discuss** the three acceptable methods of property description, **give** examples and **know** the characteristics of each.

- **learn** the various land measurements used in real estate practices.

- **define** these *key terms:*

legal description	monument	reference to a recorded
metes-and-bounds	plat map	plat (lot-and-block or
description	point of beginning	recorded plat system)
	(POB)	survey

DESCRIBING LAND

One of the essential elements of a valid deed is an accurate, acceptable, legal description of the land being conveyed. The real estate involved must be identifiable from the wording of the deed and with reference to only the documents named in the deed. The courts have usually held that a description of land is legally sufficient if a competent surveyor can locate the real estate in question.

A **legal description** is an exact way of describing real estate in a contract, a deed, a mortgage or another document that will be accepted by a court of law. While street addresses are not sufficient legal descriptions, the legal description in a deed or mortgage may be followed by the words *commonly known as* and the street address. The street address standing alone is referred to as an *informal description.*

An average parcel of land has been conveyed and transferred many times in the past. The description of the land in a deed, a mortgage or another instrument should be the same as that used in the previous instrument of conveyance. Discrepancies, errors and legal problems can be avoided or reduced if this practice is followed in drawing up subsequent conveyances.

In Practice   One of the most frequent causes of lawsuits against licensees is inaccurate monuments and lot lines. Buyers need to be confident that the property they are purchasing is in fact what they believe they are paying for. Relying on old surveys is not necessarily a good idea; the property should be resurveyed by a competent land surveyor, whether or not the lender requires it. Licensees should be very careful when stating the location of boundary lines. Licensees should encourage prospective buyers to hire a registered land surveyor if they plan to install fences or add to the buildings on their property. Recent flooding in North Carolina points out the need to be sure that buyers are informed about whether their property is in a flood plain.

METHODS OF DESCRIBING REAL ESTATE

There are four basic methods of describing real estate: (1) metes and bounds, (2) reference to recorded plat (lot and block), (3) reference to a publicly recorded document that contains a legal description and (4) the rectangular (government) survey, *which is not used in North Carolina.* A combination of methods also may be used. In North Carolina, land is described using the metes-and-bounds method of description, reference to a recorded plat method or reference to a publicly recorded document such as a deed.

Government Survey System   The original 13 colonies were never surveyed under this system, which was established by Congress in 1785 to describe properties in an expanding country. The system uses intersecting lines, called *meridians* and *range lines*, that impose grids over the land, forming townships. As North Carolina is one of the original colonies, it has never been surveyed under this system. ***This method of property description is not tested on the state examination.***

Metes and Bounds   A **metes-and-bounds description** is the earliest form of legal description used in the United States and is still the primary method of describing property in the original 13 colonies. It makes use of the boundaries and measurements of the land in question. This description shows the boundaries of the parcel and where they meet. Such a description starts at a definitely designated place called the **point of beginning (POB)** and proceeds around the boundaries of the tract (clockwise or counterclockwise) by reference to linear measurements and compass directions, referred to as *calls.* Each call shows the distance (metes) and direction (bounds). Each call begins with either North or South (the cardinal directions), then the number of degrees East or West, using a surveyor's compass. A metes-and-bounds description always ends at the POB so that the tract being described has *closure.*

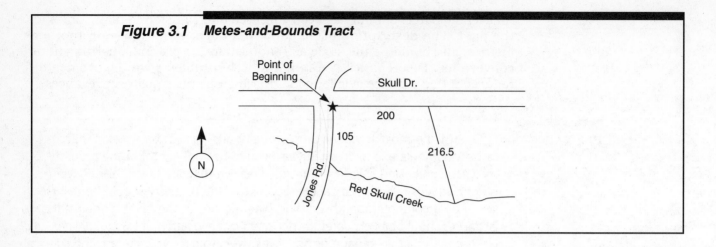

Figure 3.1   *Metes-and-Bounds Tract*

In a metes-and-bounds description, the actual distance between monuments takes precedence over any linear measurement set forth in the description if the two measurements differ. **Monuments** are fixed objects used to establish real estate boundaries. Natural objects such as stones, large trees, lakes and streams, as well as streets, highways and markers placed by surveyors, are commonly used as monuments. Measurements often include the words *more or less;* the location of the monuments is more important than the distance stated in the wording. Problems are created in some instances when a monument has shifted or disappeared over the years.

An example of a metes-and-bounds description of a parcel of land (pictured in Figure 3.1) follows:

> A tract of land located in _____ , _____ , described as follows: Beginning at the intersection of the east line of Jones Road and the south line of Skull Drive; thence north 90° east along the south line of Skull Drive 200 feet; thence south 15° east 216.5 feet, more or less, to the center thread of Red Skull Creek; thence north 4° west along the center line of said creek to its intersection with the east line of Jones Road; thence north 105 feet, more or less, along the east line of Jones Road to the place of beginning.

When used to describe property within a town or city, a metes-and-bounds description may begin as follows:

> Beginning at a point on the southerly side of Kent Street, 100 feet easterly from the corner formed by the intersection of the southerly side of Kent Street and the easterly side of Broadway; thence . . .

In this description, the POB is given by reference to the intersection. The description must close by returning to the POB.

Metes-and-bounds descriptions may be very complex and should be handled with extreme care. When they include compass directions of the various lines and concave or convex curved lines, they can be difficult to understand. In such cases, the advice and counsel of a surveyor should be sought.

Figure 3.2   Subdivision Plat Map

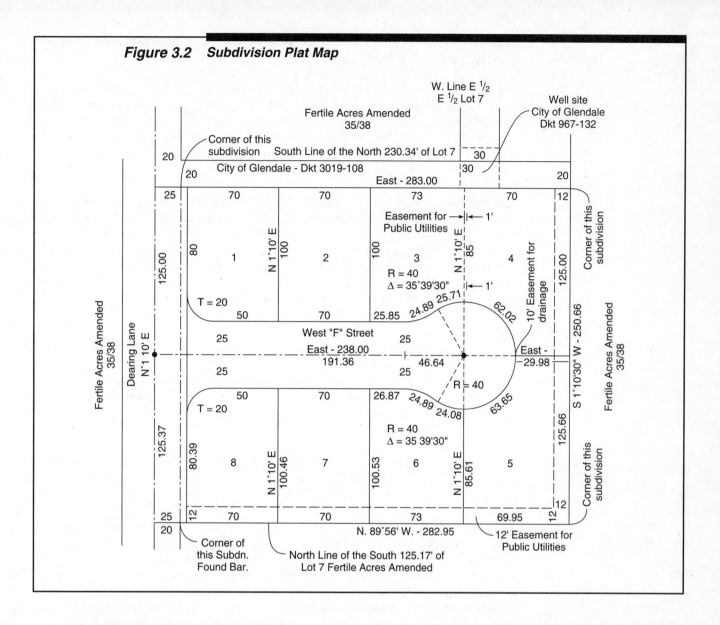

Reference to a Recorded Plat (Lot and Block)

The second method of land description used in North Carolina is by **reference to a recorded plat** (the **lot-and-block** or **recorded plat system**). It is a system that uses lot and block numbers—referred to as a *plat* or *subdivision*—placed in the registry of deeds of the county where the land is located. This is the most common and worry-free method of describing property in urban areas.

The first step in subdividing land is the preparation of a **plat map**—by a licensed surveyor or engineer—as illustrated in Figure 3.2.

On this plat map, the land is divided into numbered or lettered blocks and lots, and streets or access roads for public use are indicated. Lot sizes and street details must be indicated completely and must comply with all local ordinances and requirements. When properly signed and approved, the subdivision plat must be recorded in the county in which the land is located; it thereby becomes part of the legal description. In describing a lot from a recorded subdivision plat, the lot and block number, name or number of the subdivision plat and name of the county and state are used. The plat must be recorded in the public records to be a legally acceptable property description. For example:

> Being all of Lot Number Forty-one (41) as shown and designated on a certain map prepared by John Doe, C.E., dated May 16, 1980, entitled "Plan of Bradford Extension," which said map is duly recorded in Map Book 7 at Page 32, in the Office of the Register of Deeds of Craven County, to which map reference is hereby made for a further and better description. Less and except any existing road right of ways of record.

Sometimes, property is described by reference to a previous deed for the same property. The previous deed will contain a land description, which is then incorporated into the current deed by reference. For example, if a deed dated September 17, 1993, included the above description by reference to a recorded plat, a deed prepared four years later that conveyed the same property could incorporate that same description by referring to the previous deed. Deeds do not make reference to buildings on the property.

Informal References

The use of informal references in describing property can often lead to legal problems, but informal references may be sufficient if they enable a surveyor to precisely locate the parcel of real estate. A street address is a good example of an informal reference, and is often used in a listing contract and short-term rental agreements. Any contract to convey a real property interest and any type of deed should always contain a legally acceptable description.

Preparation and Use of a Survey

Legal descriptions should not be changed, altered or combined without adequate information from a competent authority such as a surveyor or title lawyer. Legal descriptions should always include the name of the county and state in which the land is located.

A licensed land surveyor is trained and authorized to locate a given parcel of land and to determine its legal description. The surveyor does this by preparing a **survey,** which sets forth the legal description of the property, and a survey sketch, which shows the location and dimensions of the parcel. When a survey also shows the location, size and shape of buildings located on the lot, it is referred to as a *physical survey,* a *mortgage location survey* or an *identification survey.* When a survey shows the "lay of the land" such as where there are hills and valleys, it is called a **topographic** or **topo survey**. Surveys are required in many real estate transactions, such as when conveying a portion of a given tract of land, conveying real estate as security for a mortgage loan, showing the location of new construction, locating roads and highways and determining the legal description of the land on which a particular building is located. When underwriting a real estate loan, the lender will require an up-to-date survey of the security property to make sure that there are no encroachments on the property because an encroachment would render the title to the property unmarketable. Encroachments could be across boundary lines, easements, or setbacks.

Reference to a Recorded Deed

The third method of land description used in North Carolina is by reference to a publicly recorded document, usually a deed. It is a system that references a deed to the identical property. This deed typically contains a legal description of the property that is to be conveyed.

| **In Practice** | When filling in the blanks of a sales contract, an agent should exercise great care to ensure that a proper and accurate legal description is used. Never list the legal description as "N/A" for not applicable. |

Because legal descriptions of newly subdivided land, once recorded, affect title to real estate, they should be prepared only by a registered surveyor or a lawyer. Real estate licensees who attempt to draft legal descriptions create potential risks for themselves and their clients and customers. [See G.S. 93A-6(a)(11), and Rule A.0111.] Furthermore, when entered on a document of conveyance, legal descriptions should be copied with care. For example, an incorrectly worded legal description in a sales contract may obligate the seller to convey or the buyer to purchase more or less land than either one intended. Title problems can arise for the buyer who seeks to convey the property at a future date.

MATH CONCEPTS

Land Acquisition Costs

To calculate the cost of purchasing land, use the same unit in which the cost is given. Costs quoted per square foot must be multiplied by the proper number of square feet; costs quoted per acre must be multiplied by the proper number of acres; and so on.

To calculate the cost of a parcel of land of three acres at $1.10 per square foot, convert the acreage to square feet before multiplying:

43,560 square feet per acre × 3 acres = 130,680 square feet
130,680 square feet × $1.10 per square foot = $143,748

To calculate the cost of a parcel of land of 17,500 square feet at $60,000 per acre, convert the cost per acre into the cost per square foot before multiplying by the number of square feet in the parcel:

$60,000 per acre ÷ 43,560 square feet per acre = $1.38 (rounded) per square foot
17,500 square feet × $1.38 per square foot = $24,150

SUMMARY

Documents affecting or conveying interests in real estate must contain accurate descriptions of the property involved. Four methods of legal description of land are used in the United States: (1) metes and bounds, (2) reference to recorded plat (lot and block), (3) reference to publicly recorded document (deed) and (4) rectangular (government) survey. The last method is not used in North Carolina. A legal description is a precise method of identifying a parcel of land. A property's description should always be the same as the one used in previous documents. The primary method of property descriptions in the original 13 colonies is the metes-and-bounds method.

In a metes-and-bounds description, the actual location of monuments takes precedence over the written linear measurement in a document. When property is described by metes and bounds, the description must always enclose a tract of land; that is, the boundary line must end at the point at which it started.

Land in every state can be subdivided into lots and blocks by means of a recorded plat of subdivision. An approved plat of survey that shows the division into blocks, giving the size, location and designation of lots and specifying the location and size of streets to be dedicated for public use, is filed for record in the recorder's office of the county in which the land is located. It is possible to resubdivide portions of a previously recorded subdivision.

The services of licensed surveyors are necessary in the conduct of the real estate business. A plat prepared by a surveyor is the usual method of certifying the legal description of a certain parcel of land. Mortgage location (or identification) surveys are customarily required in purchases of real estate when a mortgage or new construction is involved.

Questions

1. In a sales contract, which of the following is an acceptable description of property?
   a. Plat name
   b. Johnson property
   c. Legal description
   d. Lot number

2. A monument is used in which of the following types of legal descriptions?
   a. Lot and block
   b. Metes and bounds
   c. Rectangular survey
   d. Government survey

3. In describing real estate, the system that uses feet, degrees and natural markers as monuments is the
   a. rectangular survey.
   b. metes-and-bounds description.
   c. government survey.
   d. lot and block system.

Answer questions 4 through 7 according to the information given on the plat of Mountainside Manor in Figure 3.3.

4. Which of the following statements is true?
   a. Lot 9, Block A is larger than Lot 12 in the same block.
   b. The plat for the lots on the southerly side of Wolf Road between Goodrich Boulevard and Carney Street is found on Sheet 3.
   c. Lot 8, Block A has the longest road frontage.
   d. Lot 11, Block B has more frontage than Lot 2, Block A.

5. Which of the following lots has the most frontage on Jasmine Lane?
   a. Lot 10, Block B   c. Lot 1, Block A
   b. Lot 11, Block B   d. Lot 2, Block A

6. "Beginning at the intersection of the east line of Goodrich Boulevard and the south line of Jasmine Lane and running south along the east line of Goodrich Boulevard a distance of 230 feet; thence east parallel to the north line of Wolf Road a distance of 195 feet; thence northeasterly on a course N 22° E a distance of 135 feet; and thence northwesterly along the south line of Jasmine Lane to the point of beginning." Which lots are described here?
   a. Lots 13, 14 and 15, Block A
   b. Lots 9, 10 and 11, Block B
   c. Lots 1, 2, 3 and 15, Block A
   d. Lots 7, 8 and 9, Block A

7. On the plat, how many lots have easements?
   a. One   c. Three
   b. Two   d. Four

Figure 3.3 **Plat of Mountainside Manor Subdivision**

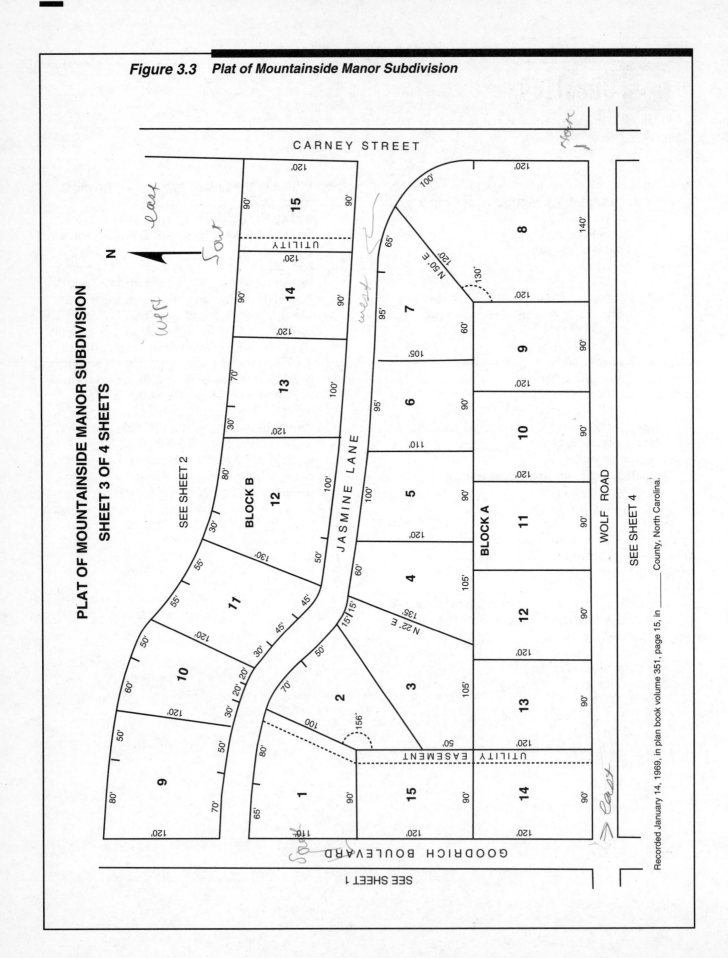

PLAT OF MOUNTAINSIDE MANOR SUBDIVISION
SHEET 3 OF 4 SHEETS

Recorded January 14, 1969, in plan book volume 351, page 15, in _____ County, North Carolina.

4 Transfer of Title to Real Property

LEARNING OBJECTIVES

When you've finished reading this chapter, you should be able to

- **identify** and understand the methods of transferring title, and **explain** the difference between voluntary and involuntary alienation of title.

- **identify** the essential and nonessential elements of a deed.

- **describe** the three major types of deeds used in North Carolina.

- **explain** the processes of title examination and recordation.

- **define** these *key terms:*

abstract of title	delivery and	marketable title
actual notice	acceptance	Marketable Title Act
adverse possession	excise tax	quitclaim deed
ALTA policy	general warranty deed	recording
certificate of title	grantee	revenue stamps
chain of title	granting clause	special warranty deed
Conner Act	grantor	title insurance
constructive notice	intestate	voluntary alienation
deed	involuntary alienation	will

METHODS OF TRANSFERRING TITLE

Title to real estate means the right to or ownership of the land. The word *title* also is used to refer to the documentary evidence of the right of ownership, such as a deed. The word *title* refers to a summation of all the things property owners have to prove and protect their ownership interest in property. The term *title* has two functions: it represents the bundle of legal rights the owner possesses in the real estate and it denotes the facts that, if proven, enable a person to recover or retain ownership or possession of a parcel of real estate.

Figure 4.1   Legal Terms for Parties in Real Estate Transactions

In reference to parties to a real estate instrument, such as a deed, the parties are referred to in legal terms such as *grantor* and *grantee.* The "OR" is the giver of the paper, and the "EE" is the receiver of the paper.

Type of Document	Giver	Receiver
Deed	Grantor (Seller)	Grantee (Buyer)
Offer	Offeror (Buyer)	Offeree (Seller)
Counteroffer	Offeror (Seller)	Offeree (Buyer)
Lease	Lessor (Landlord)	Lessee (Tenant)
Mortgage	Mortgagor (Buyer)	Mortgagee (Lender)
Option	Optionor (Seller)	Optionee (Buyer)

A parcel of real estate may be transferred voluntarily by sale or gift, or it may be taken involuntarily by operation of law. In addition, it may be transferred by will or descent after a person has died. Transfer of title is referred to as *alienation,* which means the act of transferring property to another.

Voluntary Alienation

Voluntary alienation (transfer) of title may be made by either gift or sale. Voluntary alienation is done with the wishes and consent of the property owner. To transfer title by voluntary alienation during his or her lifetime, an owner must use some form of deed.

A **deed** is a written instrument by which an owner of real estate intentionally conveys his or her right, title or interest in the parcel of real estate to another. A deed is evidence of title. The owner is referred to as the **grantor,** and the person who receives title is called the **grantee** (see Figure 4.1). A deed is executed (signed) only by the grantor(s). The grantee(s) does not sign the deed.

Requirements for a valid conveyance. A valid deed in North Carolina must contain certain essential elements, including the following:

- The deed must be in writing.
- The grantor must have the legal capacity to execute a deed.
- Both the grantor and the grantee must be identified.
- There must be adequate words of conveyance.
- There must be an accurate legal description of the property conveyed.
- The deed must be signed by the grantors.
- The deed must be delivered and voluntarily accepted.

A **grantor** conveys property to a grantee.

A **grantee** receives property from a grantor.

A **deed** is the instrument that conveys property from a grantor to a grantee.

In writing. All deeds must be in writing, in accordance with the requirements of the statute of frauds, which states "an oral deed cannot be enforced."

Grantor. A grantor must have a legal existence, be of lawful age and be legally competent in order to convey title to real estate. A minor (a person who has not reached majority) does not have legal capacity to transfer title, so any attempted conveyance by a minor is void. In North Carolina, a person is a minor until he or she reaches 18 years of age.

A grantor generally is held to have sufficient mental capacity to execute a deed if he or she is capable of understanding the action. A deed executed by a person while mentally impaired (for example, by intoxication) is only voidable—it is not void. A deed executed by a person who has been judged legally incompetent is considered to be void.

Identification of grantor and grantee. To be valid, a deed must name both the grantor and the grantee in such a way that they are readily identifiable. Furthermore, the grantee must be a real person, either a natural person or an artificial person, such as a corporation. A deed naming as the grantee a fictitious person, a company that does not exist or a society or club that is not properly incorporated is considered void. The grantee cannot be a dead person.

Words of conveyance. A deed of conveyance transfers a present interest in real estate, and it must contain words that state the grantor's intention to convey the property at this time. An expression of intent to convey at some future time is inadequate. Such words of conveyance are often called the **granting clause.** Depending on the type of deed and the obligations agreed to by the grantor, the wording is generally *convey and warrant; grant; grant, bargain and sell;* or *remise, release and quitclaim.*

Legal description. To be valid, a deed must contain an acceptable, accurate, legal description of the real estate conveyed. Land is considered to be described adequately if a competent surveyor could locate the property from the description used. The rules relative to describing real estate were discussed in the previous chapter.

Signature of grantor. To be valid, a deed must be signed by all the grantors (or their authorized agents) named in the deed. If the grantor is married, both the grantor and his or her spouse must sign the deed. The grantee need not sign the deed.

Delivery. Before a transfer of title by conveyance can take effect, there must be **delivery and acceptance;** that is, actual *delivery* of the deed by the grantor and either actual or implied *acceptance* by the grantee. Delivery may be made by the grantor to the grantee personally or to a third party who is authorized by the grantee to accept the deed (such as a lawyer). Title is said to *pass* when a deed is delivered and voluntarily accepted. The effective date of the transfer of title from the grantor to the grantee is the date of delivery of the deed itself.

Elements that are not required. Nonessential elements often appear in deeds, but are not required for validity. Nonessential elements include the following:

- Deeds do not have to be *witnessed.*
- Deeds do not have to be *dated* (although, for practical matters, it may be wise to do so).

- Deeds do not have to include a statement as to the amount of *consideration* (the amount of money that was paid for the property).
- Deeds do not have to be *acknowledged (notarized)*.
- Deeds do not have to be *recorded*.
- Effective in 1999, deeds do not have to be *sealed* in North Carolina to be valid. Standard deed forms may continue to have the word "seal" after the signature; however, it is no longer required to create a valid deed.

Note that acknowledgment is necessary before a deed can be recorded, and recording a deed is necessary to protect the grantee's rights in the property. Recording is discussed later in this chapter.

Types of Deeds

Three common forms of deeds (the general warranty deed, the special warranty deed and the quitclaim deed) and several types of special-purpose deeds are used in North Carolina.

General warranty deed. For a purchaser of real estate, a **general warranty deed** provides greater protection than any other deed. It is the best deed for the grantee, but it gives the grantor the greatest degree of liability. It is referred to as a *general warranty deed* or simply a *warranty deed* because the grantor is legally bound by certain basic covenants or warranties:

> **General Warranty Deed**
>
> Four covenants:
>
> 1. Covenant of seisin
> 2. Covenant against encumbrances
> 3. Covenant of quiet enjoyment
> 4. Covenant of warranty forever

- *Covenant of seisin and the right to convey:* The grantor warrants that he or she is the owner of the property and has the right to convey title to it. Delivery of seisin is the actual transfer of title.
- *Covenant against encumbrances:* The grantor warrants that the property is free from any liens or encumbrances except those of record. Encumbrances would generally include such items as mortgages, mechanics' liens, real estate tax liens and easements.
- *Covenant of quiet enjoyment:* The grantor guarantees that the grantee's title will be good against third parties who might bring court actions to establish superior title to the property. If the grantee's title is found to be inferior, the grantor is liable for damages.
- *Covenant of warranty forever:* The grantor guarantees that if at any time in the future the title fails, he or she will compensate the grantee for the loss sustained. However, it is in the best interest of the grantee to obtain title insurance because at the time of a later claim, the grantor may be dead or financially insolvent.

These covenants in a general warranty deed are not limited to matters that occurred during the time the grantor owned the property; they extend back to its origin. An example of a general warranty deed appears in Figure 4.2. Note that the first three covenants are most important.

> **Special Warranty Deed**
>
> *Two warranties:*
>
> 1. Warranty that grantor received title
> 2. Warranty that property was unencumbered by grantor

Special warranty deed (limited warranty deed). A conveyance that carries only one covenant is called a **special warranty deed** (also known as a *limited warranty deed*). The grantor warrants only that the property was not encumbered during the time he or she held title except as noted in the deed. Special warranty deeds generally contain the words *remise, release, alienate and convey* in the granting clause. Any additional warranties to be included must be specifically stated in the deed. An example of a special warranty deed appears in Figure 4.3.

Figure 4.2 *General Warranty Deed*

NORTH CAROLINA GENERAL WARRANTY DEED

Excise Tax: _____

Parcel Identifier No._____ Verified by _____ County on the ____ day of_____, 20__
By:_____

Mail/Box to: _____

This instrument was prepared by:_____

Brief description for the Index: _____

THIS DEED made this _____ day of _____, 20___, by and between

GRANTOR	GRANTEE

Enter in appropriate block for each party: name, address, and, if appropriate, character of entity, e.g. corporation or partnership.

The designation Grantor and Grantee as used herein shall include said parties, their heirs, successors, and assigns, and shall include singular, plural, masculine, feminine or neuter as required by context.

WITNESSETH, that the Grantor, for a valuable consideration paid by the Grantee, the receipt of which is hereby acknowledged, has and by these presents does grant, bargain, sell and convey unto the Grantee in fee simple, all that certain lot or parcel of land situated in the City of _____, _____ Township, _____ County, North Carolina and more particularly described as follows:

The property hereinabove described was acquired by Grantor by instrument recorded in Book _____ page _____.

A map showing the above described property is recorded in Plat Book_____ page _____.

NC Bar Association Form No. 3 © 1976, Revised © 1977, 2002   + James Williams & Co., Inc.
Printed by Agreement with the NC Bar Association - 1981   www.JamesWilliams.com

Figure 4.2   *General Warranty Deed (continued)*

TO HAVE AND TO HOLD the aforesaid lot or parcel of land and all privileges and appurtenances thereto belonging to the Grantee in fee simple.

And the Grantor covenants with the Grantee, that Grantor is seized of the premises in fee simple, has the right to convey the same in fee simple, that title is marketable and free and clear of all encumbrances, and that Grantor will warrant and defend the title against the lawful claims of all persons whomsoever, other than the following exceptions:

IN WITNESS WHEREOF, the Grantor has duly executed the foregoing as of the day and year first above written.

_____ (SEAL)
(Entity Name)

USE BLACK INK ONLY

By:_____ (SEAL)
    Title:_____

By:_____ (SEAL)
    Title:_____

By:_____ (SEAL)
    Title:_____

SEAL-STAMP   USE BLACK INK ONLY

State of North Carolina - County of _____

I, the undersigned Notary Public of the County and State aforesaid, certify that _____ personally appeared before me this day and acknowledged the due execution of the foregoing instrument for the purposes therein expressed. Witness my hand and Notarial stamp or seal this_____ day of _____, 20__.

My Commission Expires:_____   _____
                                                        Notary Public

---

SEAL-STAMP   USE BLACK INK ONLY

State of North Carolina - County of _____

I, the undersigned Notary Public of the County and State aforesaid, certify that _____ personally came before me this day and acknowledged that _he is the _____ of _____, a North Carolina or _____ corporation/limited liability company/general partnership/limited partnership (strike through the inapplicable), and that by authority duly given and as the act of each entity, _he signed the forgoing instrument in its name on its behalf as its act and deed. Witness my hand and Notarial stamp or seal this _____ day of _____, 20__.

My Commission Expires:_____   _____
                                                        Notary Public

---

SEAL-STAMP   USE BLACK INK ONLY

State of North Carolina - County of _____

I, the undersigned Notary Public of the County and State aforesaid, certify that _____
_____
_____

Witness my hand and Notarial stamp or seal this _____ day of _____, 20__.

My Commission Expires:_____   _____
                                                        Notary Public

---

The foregoing Certificate(s) of _____ is/are certified to be correct.
This instrument and this certificate are duly registered at the date and time and in the Book and Page shown on the first page hereof.

_____ Register of Deeds for _____ County

By:_____ Deputy/Assistant - Register of Deeds

NC Bar Association Form No. 3 © 1976, Revised © 1977, 2002   * James Williams & Co., Inc.
Printed by Agreement with the NC Bar Association - 1981   www.JamesWilliams.com

Figure 4.3 *Special Warranty Deed*

NORTH CAROLINA SPECIAL WARRANTY DEED

Excise Tax: _____

Parcel Identifier No._____ Verified by _____ County on the ____ day of_____, 20__
By: _____

Mail/Box to: _____

This instrument was prepared by:_____

Brief description for the Index: _____

THIS DEED made this _____ day of _____, 20___, by and between

GRANTOR	GRANTEE

Enter in appropriate block for each party: name, address, and, if appropriate, character of entity, e.g. corporation or partnership.

The designation Grantor and Grantee as used herein shall include said parties, their heirs, successors, and assigns, and shall include singular, plural, masculine, feminine or neuter as required by context.

WITNESSETH, that the Grantor, for a valuable consideration paid by the Grantee, the receipt of which is hereby acknowledged, has and by these presents does grant, bargain, sell and convey unto the Grantee in fee simple, all that certain lot or parcel of land situated in the City of _____, _____Township, _____ County, North Carolina and more particularly described as follows:

The property hereinabove described was acquired by Grantor by instrument recorded in Book _____ page _____.

A map showing the above described property is recorded in Plat Book_____ page _____.

NC Bar Association Form No. 6 © 1977, 2002   + James Williams & Co., Inc.
Printed by Agreement with the NC Bar Association - 1981   www.JamesWilliams.com

SOURCE: This form is used with the permission of the North Carolina Bar Association who has copyrighted this form and others.

Figure 4.3   Special Warranty Deed (continued)

TO HAVE AND TO HOLD the aforesaid lot or parcel of land and all privileges and appurtenances thereto belonging to the Grantee in fee simple.

And the Grantor covenants with the Grantee, that Grantor has nothing to impair such title as Grantor received, and Grantor will warrant and defend the title against the lawful claims of all persons claiming by, under or through Grantor, other than the following exceptions:

IN WITNESS WHEREOF, the Grantor has duly executed the foregoing as of the day and year first above written.

_____   _____(SEAL)
         (Entity Name)

By:_____   _____(SEAL)
     Title:_____

By:_____   _____(SEAL)
     Title:_____

By:_____   _____(SEAL)
     Title:_____

USE BLACK INK ONLY

SEAL-STAMP

State of North Carolina - County of _____

I, the undersigned Notary Public of the County and State aforesaid, certify that _____
_____ personally appeared before me this day and acknowledged the due execution of the foregoing instrument for the purposes therein expressed. Witness my hand and Notarial stamp or seal this _____ day of _____, 20__.

My Commission Expires:_____ _____

                       Notary Public

SEAL-STAMP

State of North Carolina - County of _____

I, the undersigned Notary Public of the County and State aforesaid, certify that _____
_____ personally came before me this day and acknowledged that _he is the _____ of _____,
a North Carolina or _____ corporation/limited liability company/general partnership/limited partnership (strike through the inapplicable), and that by authority duly given and as the act of each entity, _he signed the forgoing instrument in its name on its behalf as its act and deed. Witness my hand and Notarial stamp or seal this _____ day of _____, 20__.

My Commission Expires:_____

                       Notary Public

SEAL-STAMP

State of North Carolina - County of _____

I, the undersigned Notary Public of the County and State aforesaid, certify that _____
_____ personally appeared before me this day and acknowledged the due execution of the foregoing instrument for the purposes therein expressed. Witness my hand and Notarial stamp or seal this _____ day of _____, 20__.

My Commission Expires:_____

                       Notary Public

The foregoing Certificate(s) of _____ is/are certified to be correct. This instrument and this certificate are duly registered at the date and time and in the Book and Page shown on the first page hereof.

_____ Register of Deeds for _____ County

By:_____ Deputy/Assistant - Register of Deeds

NC Bar Association Form No. 6 © 1977, 2002   + James Williams & Co., Inc.
Printed by Agreement with the NC Bar Association - 1981   www.JamesWilliams.com

Quitclaim deed (non-warranty deed). A **quitclaim deed** (non-warranty deed) provides the grantee with the least protection of any deed. It carries no covenant or warranties and conveys only such interest, if any, that the grantor may have when the deed is delivered. By a quitclaim deed, the grantor only *remises, releases and quitclaims* his or her interest in the property to the grantee. The deed might convey an easement; it might reconvey equitable title back to a seller; it might convey nothing at all. An example of a quitclaim deed appears in Figure 4.4.

Quitclaim Deed

No express or implied covenants or warranties

- Used primarily to convey less than fee simple or to cure a title defect

---

If the grantor under a quitclaim deed has no interest in the property described, the grantee acquires nothing by virtue of the quitclaim deed; nor does he or she acquire any right of warranty against the grantor. A quitclaim deed can convey title as effectively as a warranty deed if the grantor has good title when the deed is delivered, but it provides none of the guarantees of a warranty deed.

A quitclaim deed is frequently used to cure a defect, called a *cloud on the title*, in the recorded history of a real estate title. For example, if the name of the grantee is misspelled on a warranty deed placed in the public record, a quitclaim deed with the correct spelling may be executed to the grantee to perfect the title. A quitclaim deed is also used when a grantor allegedly has inherited property but is not certain of the validity of the title of the decedent from whom the property was inherited. The use of a warranty deed in such an instance could carry with it obligations of warranty, while a quitclaim deed would convey only the grantor's interest.

In Practice   A licensed real estate agent in North Carolina is prohibited from drafting a deed for others and is also prohibited from filling in the blanks of a deed form for others. While a licensed real estate agent may prepare a deed to convey his or her own property, an attorney should be consulted for all deed preparations

---

Special-Purpose Deeds

Correction deed. A correction deed is used when there has been an error in a previous deed. For example, if the description of the property in the original deed was incorrect, a correction deed will be used to make the correction.

Deed of gift. When a grantor conveys property as a gift (that is, no consideration or only token consideration has been accepted for the property), a deed of gift is used. A deed of gift must be recorded within two years or it becomes void. Because no consideration is exchanged, there is no need to affix revenue stamps to the deed.

Deed of release. A deed of release is used to release a parcel of property from a mortgage or deed of trust lien when the real estate loan has been paid in full.

Deed in lieu of foreclosure. A deed in lieu of foreclosure is used when a mortgagor has defaulted on the mortgage loan and wants to avoid a foreclosure action. The debtor simply gives the lender a deed in lieu of foreclosure and thus is spared both the foreclosure procedure and the possibility of a

Figure 4.4   *Quitclaim Deed (Non-Warranty Deed)*

NORTH CAROLINA NON-WARRANTY DEED

Excise Tax: _____

Parcel Identifier No. _____ Verified by _____ County on the ____ day of _____, 20__

By: _____

Mail/Box to: _____

This instrument was prepared by: _____

Brief description for the Index: _____

THIS DEED made this _____ day of _____, 20___, by and between

GRANTOR	GRANTEE

Enter in appropriate block for each party: name, address, and, if appropriate, character of entity, e.g. corporation or partnership.

The designation Grantor and Grantee as used herein shall include said parties, their heirs, successors, and assigns, and shall include singular, plural, masculine, feminine or neuter as required by context.

WITNESSETH, that the Grantor, for a valuable consideration paid by the Grantee, the receipt of which is hereby acknowledged, has and by these presents does grant, bargain, sell and convey unto the Grantee in fee simple, all that certain lot or parcel of land situated in the City of _____, _____ Township, _____ County, North Carolina and more particularly described as follows:

The property hereinabove described was acquired by Grantor by instrument recorded in Book _____ page _____.

A map showing the above described property is recorded in Plat Book_____ page _____.

NC Bar Association Form No. 7 © 1977, 2002   + James Williams & Co., Inc.
Printed by Agreement with the NC Bar Association - 1981   www.JamesWilliams.com

Figure 4.4   Quitclaim Deed (Non-Warranty Deed) (continued)

TO HAVE AND TO HOLD the aforesaid lot or parcel of land and all privileges and appurtenances thereto belonging to the Grantee in fee simple.

The Grantor makes no warranty, express or implied, as to title to the property hereinabove described.

   IN WITNESS WHEREOF, the Grantor has caused this instrument to be duly executed and delivered.

_____   _____(SEAL)
               (Entity Name)

By:_____   _____(SEAL)
       Title:_____

By:_____   _____(SEAL)
       Title:_____

By:_____   _____(SEAL)
       Title:_____

USE BLACK INK ONLY

SEAL-STAMP   State of North Carolina - County of _____

USE BLACK INK ONLY

I, the undersigned Notary Public of the County and State aforesaid, certify that _____
_____ personally appeared before me this day and acknowledged the due execution of the foregoing instrument for the purposes therein expressed. Witness my hand and Notarial stamp or seal this _____ day of _____, 20__.

My Commission Expires:_____   _____
                                                                   Notary Public

---

SEAL-STAMP   State of North Carolina - County of _____

USE BLACK INK ONLY

I, the undersigned Notary Public of the County and State aforesaid, certify that _____
_____ personally came before me this day and acknowledged that _he is the _____ of _____, a North Carolina or _____ corporation/limited liability company/general partnership/limited partnership (strike through the inapplicable), and that by authority duly given and as the act of each entity, _he signed the forgoing instrument in its name on its behalf as its act and deed. Witness my hand and Notarial stamp or seal this _____ day of _____, 20__.

My Commission Expires:_____   _____
                                                                   Notary Public

---

SEAL-STAMP   State of North Carolina - County of _____

USE BLACK INK ONLY

I, the undersigned Notary Public of the County and State aforesaid, certify that _____
_____ personally appeared before me this day and acknowledged the due execution of the foregoing instrument for the purposes therein expressed. Witness my hand and Notarial stamp or seal this _____ day of _____, 20__.

My Commission Expires:_____   _____
                                                                   Notary Public

---

The foregoing Certificate(s) of _____ is/are certified to be correct.
This instrument and this certificate are duly registered at the date and time and in the Book and Page shown on the first page hereof.
_____ Register of Deeds for _____ County

By:_____   Deputy/Assistant - Register of Deeds

NC Bar Association Form No. 7 © 1977, 2002   + James Williams & Co., Inc.
Printed by Agreement with the NC Bar Association - 1981   www.JamesWilliams.com

deficiency judgment (see Chapter 12). Significant tax issues can arise when a deed in lieu of foreclosure is used; competent legal or tax advice always should be obtained.

Trustee's deed. A deed of conveyance executed by a trustee is a trustee's deed and is used when a trustee named in a will, trust agreement or trust deed conveys the real estate to anyone other than the trustor. The trustee's deed sets forth the fact that the trustee executes the instrument in accordance with the powers and authority granted to him or her by the trust instrument.

Deeds executed pursuant to court order. This classification covers deeds such as a sheriff's deed, a tax deed, a guardian's deed and an executor's deed. These deeds are used to convey title to property that is transferred by court order or by will.

One characteristic of special-purpose deeds is that the full consideration is usually stated in the deed. This is done because the deed is executed pursuant to a court order; because the court has authorized the sale of the property for a given amount of consideration, this amount should be exactly stated in the document.

Revenue Stamps (Excise Tax)

All sellers of real property in North Carolina must pay an **excise tax,** which is based on the purchase price of the property. The statute states, "There is levied an excise tax on each deed, instrument, or writing by which any interest in real property is conveyed to another person." The **revenue stamps** that must be affixed to each deed are proof that this excise tax has been paid. The amount of the tax is $1 for every $500 of consideration or fraction thereof and always is expressed as a whole dollar amount.

To calculate the amount of revenue stamps, round the sales price up to the nearest $500, divide by 500, and multiply by $1. For example, suppose the purchase price is $89,250. Round up the price to $89,500, and divide by 500. This gives you 179. Multiply 179 by $1 and you have determined that the seller will need to pay $179 for revenue stamps.

Here's another example. Suppose the purchase price is $94,750. Round up the price to $95,000, and divide by 500. This gives you 190. Multiply 190 by $1. The seller will need to pay $190 for revenue stamps.

The statute establishing the payment of the revenue stamp excise tax exempts certain types of conveyances, such as transfer by a government entity, transfer by will or intestate succession because of death, transfer by deed of gift when no consideration is paid, transfer by merger or consolidation and transfer by instruments securing a debt, such as a mortgage and/ or deed of trust.

Involuntary Alienation

Title to property also can be transferred by **involuntary alienation**—that is, without the owner's wishes or consent (see Figure 4.5). Such transfers are usually carried out by operation of law and range from government condemnation of land for public use to the sale of property to satisfy delinquent tax or mortgage liens.

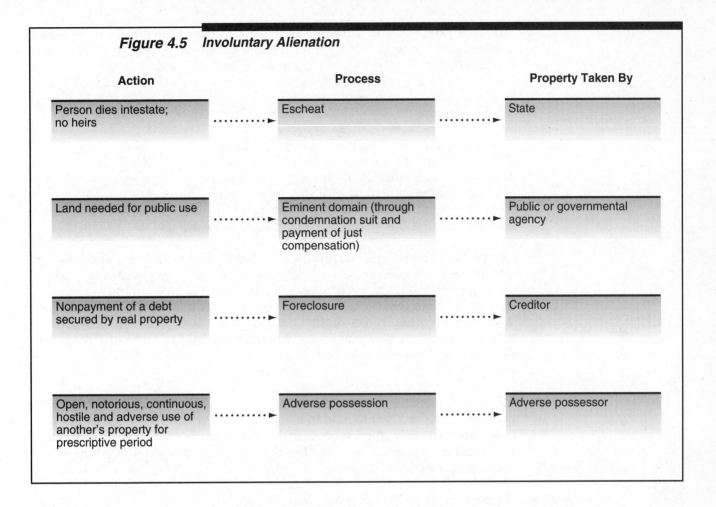

Figure 4.5 Involuntary Alienation

Action	Process	Property Taken By
Person dies intestate; no heirs	Escheat	State
Land needed for public use	Eminent domain (through condemnation suit and payment of just compensation)	Public or governmental agency
Nonpayment of a debt secured by real property	Foreclosure	Creditor
Open, notorious, continuous, hostile and adverse use of another's property for prescriptive period	Adverse possession	Adverse possessor

Escheat. When a person dies intestate (without a will) and leaves no heirs, the title to his or her real estate passes to the state by the state's power of escheat.

Eminent domain. Federal, state and local governments; school boards; some government agencies; and certain public and quasi-public corporations and utilities have the power of eminent domain. Under this power, private property may be taken for public use through a suit for condemnation. The exercise of eminent domain is subject to a court's determination of three necessary conditions: (1) that the use is for the benefit of the public; (2) that an equitable amount of compensation, as set by the court, will be paid to the owner; and (3) that the rights of the property owner will be protected by due process of law. North Carolina also recognizes a "quick take" method of condemnation. When authorized by law, title and possession of private property can immediately be transferred to the public authority.

Lien foreclosure. Land also may be transferred without an owner's consent to satisfy debts contracted by the owner that have become liens against the property. In such cases, the liens are foreclosed, the property is sold and the proceeds of the sale are applied to pay off the debts. Debts that could be foreclosed include mortgage loans, real estate taxes, mechanics' liens and general judgments against the property owner.

Adverse possession. **Adverse possession** is another means of involuntary transfer. For a person to make a claim of ownership under adverse possession they must have some reason to believe the land is theirs. An owner who does not use or inspect his or her land for a number of years may lose title to another person who makes a claim to the land, takes possession and, most importantly, uses the land. The possession of the claimant must be

- open and notorious (well known to others),
- continuous (uninterrupted for the required period),
- hostile (without the permission of the owner),
- exclusive (not shared with the owner) and
- adverse to the true owner's possession (the adverse possessor must believe that the land occupied is his or her own).

In North Carolina, the required period of continuous possession varies widely, depending on the circumstances. If the adverse possessor is trying to acquire privately owned property and has color of title (a faulty document that purports to give the adverse possessor title), the period of possession is 7 years. If there is no color of title, the period of possession is 20 years. If the adverse possessor is trying to acquire property that is owned by the state, the period of possession is 21 years with color of title and 30 years without color of title.

Even if the adverse possessor fulfills all the legal requirements for adverse possession, he or she must go to court to get clear title to the property. This is done with a quiet title action. It is difficult to prove title by adverse possession, and until a court decides that title has been acquired, the claimant's title is considered to be unmarketable.

Transfer of a Deceased Person's Property

By descent (intestate succession). Every state, including North Carolina, has a law known as a *statute of descent and distribution.* When a person dies **intestate** (without having left a will), the decedent's real estate and personal property pass to the decedent's heirs according to this statute. In effect, the state makes a will for anyone who did not do so. A court appoints a person to distribute the deceased's property according to the provisions of the statute. This person is called an *administrator* if a man or an *administratrix* if a woman. North Carolina's provisions for intestate succession are quite complicated, and a lawyer should be consulted when intestate questions arise.

Transfer of title by will. A **will** is an instrument made by a mentally competent owner to convey title to real and personal property on the owner's death. A will takes effect only after death; until that time, any property covered by the will can be conveyed by the owner and thus removed from the owner's estate. An ownership interest that contains survivorship rights cannot be affected by a will. In North Carolina, if a husband and wife own property as tenants by the entirety, the property cannot pass by will. Neither spouse can disinherit the other spouse by will.

The gift of real property by will is known as a *devise,* and a person who receives property by will is known as a *devisee.* Technically, an heir is one who takes property by the law of descent, but the term is commonly used to include devisees as well. A legacy or bequest is a gift of personal property; the person receiving personal property is known as a *beneficiary.*

TITLE ASSURANCE

Under the terms of a typical real estate sales contract, the seller is required to deliver **marketable title** to the buyer at the closing. To be marketable, a title must meet five criteria: (1) be free from any significant liens and encumbrances; (2) disclose no serious defects; (3) be free of doubtful questions of law or fact to prove its validity; (4) protect a purchaser from the hazard of litigation or any threat to quiet enjoyment of the property; and (5) convince a reasonably well-informed and prudent person, acting on business principles and willful knowledge of the facts and their legal significance, that he or she could in turn sell or mortgage the property at a fair market value.

Most people spend more money on the purchase of real estate than on any other single item. Therefore, it is understandable that buyers want to be sure they get what they pay for—marketable title to the property. So while a deed might contain several warranties of title, the buyer may insist on a title search to make sure he or she is getting marketable title.

Title Search

A title search is the examination of all public records that might affect a title. The title examiner tries to establish a **chain of title,** which shows the record of ownership of the property over a period of time, depending on the length of the title search. In the United States, chains of title in colonial states frequently date back to a grant from the king of England. In those states admitted to the Union after the formation of the United States, the deeds of conveyance in the chain of title generally stem from the patent issued by the U.S. government. A title search, or title examination, can be performed by a lawyer or a trained paralegal, but only attorneys may give an opinion. In North Carolina real estate agents are prohibited from giving an opinion on the condition of a title.

Through the chain of title, the ownership of the property can be traced backward from its present owner to its source. Ownership is traced by means of searching the *grantee and grantor indexes* that are kept in the register of deeds' offices. Under this system, all documents relating to a parcel of property are indexed under the names of the grantors and the grantees, not under the property itself.

If there is a period for which ownership is unaccounted, there is a gap in the chain. In such cases, it is usually necessary to establish ownership by a court action called a *suit to quiet title.* The court's judgment, following a proceeding in which all possible claimants are allowed to present evidence, then can be filed. A suit to quiet title may be required when, for instance, a grantor has acquired title under one name and conveyed title under a different name. Title acquired by adverse possession also can be established of record by a quiet title action.

When a title examination is conducted, the title examiner lists each instrument in chronological order along with information relative to taxes, judgments, special assessments and the like. The title examiner concludes with an opinion of title indicating which records were examined and when and stating the examiner's opinion of the quality of the title. The grantor and grantee index system is used in North Carolina to examine the title. Any defect of title will appear in the grantor index.

Title Insurance   A **title insurance** policy is a contract by which a title insurance company agrees, subject to the terms of its policy, to indemnify (that is, to compensate or reimburse) the insured (the owner, the mortgagee or another interest holder) against any losses sustained as a result of defects in a title that existed at the time the policy was issued, other than those exceptions listed in the policy. A title insurance policy may be used in addition to an **abstract of title** or a **certificate of title.**

Title companies issue various forms of title insurance policies, the most common of which are the owner's title insurance policy and the mortgagee's title insurance policy. As the names indicate, each type of policy is issued to insure specific interests. An owner's policy insures an owner's interest in property; a mortgagee's policy insures a lender's interest in property. The owner's coverage is usually the face amount of the purchase price. The lender's coverage is limited to the loan amount. It is of a "diminishing liability."

A standard coverage policy usually insures against defects that may be found in the public records plus many defects not found there. The extended coverage provided by an **ALTA** (American Land Title Association) **policy** includes all the protection of a standard policy plus additional protection to cover risks that may be discovered only through inspection of the property (including rights of persons in actual possession of the land, even if unrecorded) or revealed by examination of an accurate survey. The company does not insure against any defects in or liens against the title that are found by the title examination and listed in the standard policy.

The ALTA owner's title insurance policy protects the owner against title defects not found in the public records, such as

- falsification of the records;
- misrepresentation of the true owner(s) of the land;
- old unsettled estates;
- forged deeds, releases or wills;
- instruments executed under a fabricated or expired power of attorney;
- errors in copying and indexing;
- deeds delivered after the death of a grantor or grantee or without consent of the grantor;
- mistakes in recording legal documents;
- undisclosed or missing heirs;
- birth or adoption of children after the date of the will;
- deeds by persons of unsound mind;
- deeds by persons supposedly single but secretly married; and
- deeds by minors.

The consideration for the policy (the premium) is paid once at closing for the life of the policy. This one-time premium paid at closing keeps the policy in effect as long as the owner or heirs have an interest in the property. The maximum loss for which the company may be liable cannot exceed the face amount of the policy (unless the amount of coverage has been extended by use of an inflation rider). When a title company settles a claim covered by a policy, it can then "step into the shoes" of the insured party and seek compensation from anyone responsible for the settled claim.

Table 4.1 **Owner's Title Insurance Policy**

Standard Coverage	**Extended Coverage**	**Not Covered by Either Policy**
1. Defects found in public records	Standard coverage plus defects discoverable through:	1. Defects and liens listed in policy
2. Forged documents	1. Property inspection, including unrecorded rights of persons in possession	2. Defects known to buyer
3. Incompetent grantors		3. Changes in land use brought about by zoning ordinances
4. Incorrect marital statements	2. Examination of survey	
5. Improperly delivered deeds	3. Unrecorded liens not known by policyholder	

With the owner's title insurance policy, if the insured owner were to lose title because of a covered claim, the title company would pay the owner the value of the property up to the face amount of the policy (plus the amount covered in the policy's available inflation clause). The title company also assumes any costs incurred in the defense of the title. ALTA coverage is summarized in Table 4.1.

North Carolina is considered an approved attorney state. That means that title searches are performed by an attorney rather than by a title insurance company. When the title search is completed, the attorney submits a preliminary opinion on title to the title insurance company, which, in essence, serves as an application for title insurance. Based on the preliminary opinion on title, the title insurance company issues a title commitment. The title commitment includes a description of the title insurance policy; the name of the insured party; the legal description of the real estate; the estate or interest covered; a schedule of all exceptions, consisting of encumbrances and defects found in the public records; and conditions and stipulations under which the commitment is issued. The title commitment is used at closing as assurance of a clear title to the property in question.

After closing, the attorney issues a final opinion on title, which includes recording information for the deed and deed of trust and so forth. The final opinion on title goes to the title insurance company, which issues the title insurance policy based on this information. Under the title insurance policy, the title insurance company promises to defend the title as insured, as well as to pay any claims against the property if the title proves to be defective. The opinion issued by the attorney is just that, an *opinion* based on the search of public records. It is not a guarantee of good title.

In Practice   Before a lender will forward money on a loan secured by real estate, it normally orders a title search at the expense of the borrower to assure itself that there are no recorded liens superior in priority to its mortgage on the property.

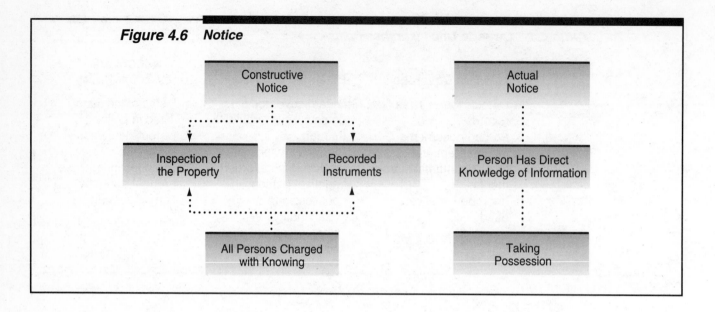

Figure 4.6   Notice

Constructive Notice → Inspection of the Property / Recorded Instruments → All Persons Charged with Knowing

Actual Notice → Person Has Direct Knowledge of Information → Taking Possession

Title Recordation

Both title insurance and title examinations depend on the fact that all conveyances of real property, as well as other interests in real property, must be recorded. All owners or parties interested in real estate need to record, or file, all documents affecting their interests in the real estate to give public notice to the world of those interests (see Figure 4.6). This public notice is called **constructive notice.** Physically taking possession of the property is **actual notice.**

Necessity for recording. Before buying a parcel of property, a potential purchaser wants to know that the seller can convey good title to the property as well as what liens and encumbrances affect that title. Through the process of **recording,** documents that affect property ownership are readily available as matters of public record. Thus, a person can inspect the documents that affect a property before making a decision about purchasing it.

For Example A purchaser offering cash for a property might want to be sure that the seller has paid in full, before the settlement takes place, all of the debts outstanding against the property. By inspecting the recorded documents the purchaser could determine what debts encumber the property.

To serve as public notice, all instruments in writing affecting any estate, right, title or interest in land must be recorded with the register of deeds in the county where the land is located. Everyone interested in the title to a parcel of property can thus receive notice of the various interests of all other parties. Because North Carolina is a pure race state (see below), recording gives legal priority to those interests that are recorded first.

Conner Act. The **Conner Act** is a state law that provides that many types of real estate documents are not valid as to third parties unless they are recorded. The documents covered include deeds, mortgages, installment land contracts, assignments, options, leases of more than three years, easements and restrictive covenants. Under the Conner Act, if a purchaser fails to record his or her deed but a subsequent purchaser does, the subsequent purchaser's title takes precedence over the first purchaser's title. This kind of recording statute is called a *pure race statute:* whoever records first prevails, even if that purchaser had personal knowledge of a previous interest that was unrecorded.

For Example Suppose Zackermann sells her property to Sands. Sands fails to record his deed. Two weeks later, Zackermann sells the same property (even though it is no longer hers) to Hanson. Hanson suspects that Zackermann no longer owns the property but accepts the deed and quickly records it. Because Hanson recorded his deed, he now has marketable title to the property, and Sands is out of luck.

Marketable Title Act. North Carolina's *Marketable Title Act* provides that if a chain of title can be traced back for 30 years without problem, it becomes marketable title. Any conflicting claims outside this chain of title may be extinguished. The practical effect of this act is to eliminate obsolete defects in the chain of title.

SUMMARY

Title to real estate is the right to and evidence of ownership of the land. It may be transferred by voluntary alienation, involuntary alienation, will or descent.

The voluntary transfer of an owner's title is made by a deed. Requirements of a valid deed include a grantor with the legal capacity to contract, a readily identifiable grantee, a granting clause, a legal description of the property, delivery and acceptance, a seal and the signature of the grantor. Deeds are subject to a state excise tax (revenue stamps) when they are recorded. Title to the property passes when the grantor delivers a deed to the grantee and it is accepted.

The obligations of a grantor are determined by the form of the deed—that is, whether it is a general warranty deed, special warranty deed or quitclaim deed. A general warranty deed provides the greatest protection of any deed because it binds the grantor to certain covenants or warranties. The general warranty deed gives the grantor the greatest degree of liability, while it gives the grantee the greatest degree of protection. It is the best deed for the grantee. A special warranty deed warrants only that the real estate is not encumbered, except as stated in the deed. A quitclaim deed carries with it no warranties whatsoever and conveys only the interest, if any, the grantor possesses in the property.

An owner's title may be transferred without his or her permission by a court action such as a foreclosure or judgment sale, a tax sale, condemnation under the right of eminent domain, adverse possession or escheat. These are forms of involuntary alienation. Eminent domain is the right of the government to take private property; condemnation is the process by which it is done.

The real estate of an owner who makes a valid will (who dies testate) passes to the devisees through the probating of the will. The title of an owner who dies without a will (intestate) passes according to the provisions of the law of descent of the state in which the real estate is located.

The purpose of the recording acts is to give legal, public and constructive notice to the world of parties' interests in real estate. The recording provisions have been adapted to a system and order in the transfer of real estate. Without them, it would be virtually impossible to transfer real estate from one party to another. The interests and rights of the various parties in a particular parcel of land must be recorded so that such rights will be legally effective against third parties who have no knowledge or notice of the rights. Recordation is not essential to make a document valid.

Title evidence shows whether a seller is conveying marketable title. Marketable title is generally one that is so free from significant defects that the purchaser can be insured against having to defend the title. Title insurance protects the policy owner from defects in the title, except those specially excluded from the insurance policy. The title insurance premium is a one-time cost, usually paid at closing by the buyer, and it remains in effect as long as the buyer or the buyer's heirs own the property.

Questions

1. In North Carolina, the statutory period for adverse possession (without color of title) is an uninterrupted period of how many years?
   a. 30
   b. 7
   c. 3
   d. 20

2. When property is sold for $75,000, the revenue stamp tax would be
   a. $150.
   b. $100.
   c. $135.
   d. $125.

3. Which of the following statements is true of a deed that is signed but not delivered?
   a. It passes title.
   b. It passes no legal title.
   c. It is void.
   d. It is illegal.

4. Title to real estate may be transferred during a person's lifetime by which of the following means?
   a. Escheat
   b. Descent
   c. Involuntary alienation
   d. Devise

5. A deed that an owner of real estate may use to voluntarily transfer a right, a title or an interest in real estate may be what type of deed?
   a. Sheriff's
   b. Warranty
   c. Foreclosure
   d. Trustee's

6. An owner of real estate who was adjudged legally incompetent made a will during his stay at a nursing home. He later died and was survived by a wife and three children. His real estate passed
   a. to his wife.
   b. to the heirs mentioned in his will.
   c. according to the state law of intestate succession.
   d. to the state.

7. Revenue stamps on real estate conveyances are usually paid
   a. by the grantee.
   b. to the state real estate commission.
   c. by the grantor.
   d. by the real estate agent.

8. Which of the following is NOT a means of title transfer by involuntary alienation?
   a. Eminent domain
   b. Escheat
   c. Foreclosure
   d. Deed

9. Deeds conveying North Carolina real estate require the signature of the
   I. grantor.
   II. grantee.
   a. I only
   b. II only
   c. Both I and II
   d. Neither I nor II

10. Which of the following best describes the covenant of quiet enjoyment?
    a. The grantor promises to obtain and deliver any instrument needed to make the title good.
    b. The grantor guarantees that if the title fails in the future, he or she will compensate the grantee.
    c. The grantor warrants that he or she is the owner of the property and has the right to convey title to it.
    d. The grantor ensures that the title will be good against the title claims of third parties.

11. A purchaser went to the registry of deeds to check the public records. She found that the seller was the grantee in the last recorded deed and that no mortgage was on record against the property. Therefore, the purchaser may assume which of the following?
    a. All taxes are paid, and no judgments are outstanding.
    b. The seller has good title.
    c. The seller did not mortgage the property.
    d. No one else is occupying the property.

12. Which of the following statements is true of the person who examines the chain of title for a parcel of real estate?
    a. He or she writes a brief history of the record of ownership of the property.
    b. He or she ensures the condition of the title.
    c. He or she inspects the property.
    d. He or she issues a guarantee as to the quality of the title.

13. Which of the following statements best explains why instruments affecting real estate are recorded in the public records of the county where the property is located?
    I. Recording gives constructive notice to the world of the rights and interests in a particular parcel of real estate.
    II. The instruments must be recorded to comply with the terms of the statute of frauds.
    III. Recording proves the execution of the instrument.
    a. I only
    b. II only
    c. III only
    d. II and III only

14. *Chain of title* refers to which of the following?
    a. Summary of all instruments and legal proceedings affecting a specific parcel of land
    b. Series of links measuring 7.92 inches each
    c. Instrument or document that protects the insured parties (subject to specific exceptions) against defects in the examination of the record and hidden risks such as forgeries, undisclosed heirs, errors in the public records and so forth
    d. Succession of conveyances from some starting point whereby the present owner derives title

15. A title insurance policy with standard coverage generally covers all of the following EXCEPT
    a. forged documents.
    b. incorrect marital statements.
    c. rights of parties in possession.
    d. incompetent grantors.

16. What is meant by *condemnation?*
    a. The right of the government to take private property
    b. The same as eminent domain
    c. The process by which eminent domain is exercised
    d. Adverse possession with just compensation

17. Which of the following is NOT a necessary condition of eminent domain?
    a. Use benefits the public
    b. Property is to be given to the owner of a quasi-public corporation
    c. Property owner is protected by due process of law
    d. Just compensation is paid to the property owner

18. Which of the following real estate documents is LEAST LIKELY to be recorded?
    a. Deed
    b. Month-to-month lease
    c. Option contract
    d. Land contract

19. When title passes to a third party on the death of the life tenant, what is the third party's interest in the property?
    a. Remainder   c. Pur autre vie
    b. Reversionary   d. Redemption

20. Which of the following documents always would be discovered in a search of the public records?
    a. Encroachments
    b. Rights of parties in possession
    c. Inaccurate surveys
    d. Mechanic's lien

21. In North Carolina, the statutory period of possession required to acquire title by adverse possession with color of title is how many years?
    a. 7   c. 21
    b. 12   d. 27

5 Land-Use Controls

LEARNING OBJECTIVES

When you've finished reading this chapter, you should be able to

- **identify** the types of public and private land use controls and how they may affect an owner's use of the property.

- **understand** the development of the master (comprehensive) plan and how it affects the development, control and use of property.

- **explain** the stages in developing a subdivision, including compliance with zoning, regulations, building codes and the approval process.

- **understand** land-use controls and real estate agents' disclosure responsibilities.

- **define** these *key terms:*

Americans with Disabilities Act (ADA)	developer	master plan
	direct public ownership	minimum standards
	enabling act	property report
buffer zone	Federal Emergency	protective covenant
building code	Management	restrictive covenant
building permit	Agency (FEMA)	subdivider
certificate of occupancy	gridiron pattern	subdivision
	Interstate Land Sales	variance
clustering	Full Disclosure Act	zoning board of
conditional-use permit	laches	adjustment
covenant	legal nonconforming	zoning ordinances
curvilinear system	use	

The regulation of land use is accomplished through public land-use controls, private land-use controls (deed restrictions) and public ownership of land—including parks, schools and expressways—by federal, state and local governments.

PUBLIC LAND-USE CONTROLS

The *police power* of the states is their inherent authority to create and adopt regulations necessary to protect the public health, safety and general welfare. The states, in turn, allow counties, cities and towns to make regulations in keeping with general laws. The largely urban population and the increasing demands placed on our limited natural resources have made it necessary for cities, towns and villages to increase limitations on the private use of real estate. There are now controls over noise, air and water pollution as well as population density.

Public land-use controls include

- planning,
- zoning,
- subdivision regulations,
- codes that regulate building construction and
- environmental protection legislation.

The Master Plan   The primary method by which local governments recognize development goals is through the formulation of a comprehensive **master plan,** also commonly referred to as a *general plan.* Cities and counties develop master plans to ensure that social and economic needs are balanced against environmental and aesthetic concerns.

The master plan is both a statement of policies and a presentation of how those policies can be realized. As created by the city, county or regional *planning commission,* a typical master plan provides for

- *land use,* including standards of population density and economic development;
- *public facilities,* including schools, civic centers and utilities;
- *circulation,* including public transportation and highways;
- *conservation* of natural resources; and
- *noise abatement.*

Both economic and physical surveys are essential in preparing a master plan. Countywide plans also must include the coordination of numerous civic plans and developments to ensure orderly city growth with stabilized property values. City plans are put into effect by the enactment and enforcement of zoning ordinances.

Zoning   The provisions of the master plan are implemented by zoning ordinances. **Zoning ordinances** are laws imposed by local government authorities (such as cities and counties) that regulate and control the use of land and structures within designated districts or zones. Zoning regulates and affects such things as use of the land, lot sizes, types of structures permitted, building heights, setbacks (the minimum distance away from streets or sidewalks that structures may be built) and density (the ratio of land area to structure area or population).

Zoning powers are conferred on municipal governments by North Carolina's **enabling act** through the general assembly. There are no nationwide or statewide zoning ordinances; zoning is local in nature. (State and federal governments may, however, regulate land use through special legislation, such as scenic easement and coastal management laws.)

Zoning ordinances generally divide land use into use classifications: residential, commercial, industrial and agricultural. Many communities now include *cluster zoning* and *multiple-use zoning;* the latter permits planned unit developments (PUDs).

To ensure adequate control, land-use areas are further divided into subclasses. Residential areas may be subdivided to provide for detached single-family dwellings, semidetached structures containing not more than four dwelling units, walkup apartments or highrise apartments. Some communities require the use of **buffer zones**—such as landscaped parks and playgrounds—to separate and screen residential areas from nonresidential areas.

Adoption of zoning ordinances. Today, almost all cities have enacted comprehensive zoning ordinances governing the use of land located within corporate limits. Many states have enacted legislation that provides that the use of land located within one to three miles of an incorporated area must receive the approval and consent of the incorporated area, even if the property is not contiguous to the village, town or city.

Zoning ordinances must not violate the rights of property owners (as provided under the due-process provisions of the Fourteenth Amendment to the U.S. Constitution) or the various provisions of the North Carolina State Constitution. If the means used to regulate the use of property are destructive, unreasonable, arbitrary or confiscatory, the legislation is usually considered void. Tests commonly applied in determining the validity of ordinances require that

- the power be exercised in a reasonable manner;
- the provisions be clear and specific;
- the ordinance be free from discrimination;
- the ordinance promote public health, safety and general welfare under the police power concept; and
- the ordinance apply to all property in a similar manner.

When land is taken for public use by the government's power of eminent domain, the owner must receive compensation. When *downzoning* occurs in an area—for instance, when land zoned for residential construction is rezoned for conservation or recreational purposes only—the state is ordinarily not responsible for compensating property owners for any resulting loss of value. However, if the courts find that a "taking" has occurred, the downzoning will be held to be an unconstitutional attempt to use the power of eminent domain without providing fair compensation to the property owner. (See Chapter 4 for a discussion of eminent domain.)

Zoning laws are generally enforced by requiring that building permits be obtained before property owners can build on their land. A permit will not be issued unless a proposed structure conforms to the permitted zoning, among other requirements.

Legal nonconforming use. It is not unusual to find real property improvements that were legally created before the enactment of the current zoning law. This is referred to as a **legal nonconforming use** of the property. Nonconforming use can apply to the way the land is used, the type of structure that is on the property, the way the structure is used or even the lot size itself. For instance, a small factory building may be the last one left in a neighborhood that was once industrial but has since been zoned for residential use. The property owner has a "matter of right" to continue this nonconforming preexisting use.

Nonconforming uses are generally not permitted to continue indefinitely. Zoning statutes may prohibit the reconstruction of a building that is destroyed by fire or otherwise dismantled if it doesn't conform to current zoning requirements.

Illegal nonconforming use. An illegal nonconforming use is one that violates the zoning laws at the time it is put into place. For example, operating a gas station in a single-family residential zone would be an illegal use. The zoning body (city or county) can go to court to stop an illegal use at any time. To create an illegal nonconforming use is a misdemeanor.

Zoning variations. Each time a plan is created or a zoning ordinance enacted, some owners are inconvenienced and want to change the use of their property. **Zoning boards of adjustment** have been established in most communities to hear complaints about the effects of zoning ordinances on specific parcels of property. Petitions may be presented to the board for variances or exceptions to the zoning law. Generally, such owners may appeal for either a conditional-use permit or a variance to allow a use that does not meet zoning requirements.

> *Conditional-use permits* allow nonconforming but related land uses.
>
> *Variances* permit prohibited land uses to avoid undue hardship.

A **conditional-use,** or *special-use*, **permit** is provided for in the zoning laws. It is granted to a property owner who wishes to use property in a special way that is in the public interest—such as a church in a residential district. A **variance** may be sought to provide a deviation from an ordinance.

For Example If an owner's lot is level next to a road but slopes steeply 30 feet away from the road, the zoning board may allow a variance so the owner can build closer to the road than the setback requirement allows. Otherwise, the lot could not be used.

As discussed in Chapter One under highest and best use, it is in the public interest to put land to use rather than have it lie fallow. But to get a variance, the property owner must prove that he or she will suffer a substantial hardship if the variance is not granted and that the hardship was not created by the owner.

A property owner can change the zoning classification of a parcel of real estate by obtaining an amendment to the official zoning map, which is part of the original zoning ordinance for the area. The proposed amendment must be brought before a public hearing on the matter and approved by the governing body of the community. When local officials fail to grant the desired relief from zoning regulations, the unhappy property owner can appeal to the courts, which may override the local officials and even the voters.

Overlay districts. An *overlay district* is a type of district or zone that is superimposed over another type of zone. The overlay zone can modify the use of the original zone. A common example is when an area that is zoned single-family residential is also designated as a flood zone. This means that additional restrictions and regulations are imposed on developments and improvements in that area.

Historic preservation zoning. The purpose of historic preservation zoning is to preserve historic buildings and sites that are irreplaceable. An owner whose property falls within a historic preservation zone may have difficulty changing or upgrading the exterior of a structure on the property.

Before making material changes to a property located in a designated historic district or to individual property designated as a historic property, the owner must obtain a *certificate of appropriateness.* This certificate confirms that the local historic district commission has approved of the changes to be made to the property.

Aesthetic zoning. In North Carolina, an area can be zoned strictly for aesthetic considerations. Thus, a property's value can be decreased for the public good of an aesthetically pleasing neighborhood.

Spot zoning. When a particular property or group of properties is rezoned to permit a use different from the neighboring properties' use, it is referred to as *spot zoning.* If the purpose of the spot zoning is to increase the value of a particular owner's property, it is illegal.

Agents Duty to Disclose Zoning

Agents' responsibilities concerning knowledge of land-use controls vary. Agents working with urban properties—both commercial and residential— usually have more responsibilities and require more knowledge than agents working in more rural areas. Residential agents may require more knowledge of subdivision regulations, street disclosure laws and protective covenants than commercial agents, who may require more knowledge about rezoning, variances and special-use permits.

Agents should be able to recognize situations such as mixed use and property alterations where a closer check of zoning may be necessary. An agent should never make improper assumptions about the zoning of a property on behalf of a client or customer. Proper disclosure of zoning and protective covenants should be routinely made before the buyer signs an offer to purchase. A listing agent should acquire copies of any deed restrictions and protective covenants at the time of taking the listing.

Subdivision Regulations

There is *no uniform planning and land development legislation that affects the entire country.* Laws governing subdividing and land planning are controlled by the state and by local governing bodies of the county, city, town or village where the land is located. Local regulations are by no means uniform throughout the country but reflect customs and local climate, health and hazardous conditions. Despite the local nature of land-use laws, rules and regulations developed by government agencies such as the Federal Housing Administration (FHA) have provided certain *minimum standards* that have served as usable guides. A large number of local governments have established higher standards for subdividers of land under their jurisdiction.

> ### Subdivision Regulations
>
> 1. Division of land into two or more lots
> 2. Cities and counties implement subdivision regulations
> 3. Planning boards have administrative responsibilities
> 4. Must be approved before selling lots
> 5. Comply with street disclosure laws
> 6. Protective covenants are enforceable

In North Carolina, state law defines the term **subdivision** as "all divisions of a tract or parcel of land into two or more lots, building sites or other divisions for the purpose of sale or building development (whether immediate or future) and includes all division of land involving the dedication of a new street or a change in existing streets." There are two exceptions to this definition of subdivision. The following two types of parcels are not considered subdivisions: (1) a division of land if each parcel has more than 10 acres with no street right-of-way dedication and (2) a division of land no larger than two acres into no more than three lots with no street right-of-way dedication involved, when the parcel is owned by a single entity.

Although the recording of a plat of subdivision of land prior to public sale for residential or commercial use is usually required, land planning precedes the actual subdividing process. The land development plan must comply with the overall *master plan* adopted by the county, city, town or village. The basic city plan and zoning requirements are not inflexible, but long, expensive (and frequently complicated) hearings are usually required before alterations can be authorized. Approval of the subdivision plat is, however, a necessary step before recording.

Most cities, villages and other areas that are incorporated under state laws have *planning commissions*. Depending on how the particular group is organized, such a committee or commission may have only an advisory status to the council or trustees of the community. In other instances, the commission may have authority to approve or disapprove plans.

Communities establish strict criteria before approving new subdivisions. Frequent requirements are *dedication* of land for streets, schools and parks; assurance by *bonding* that sewer and street costs will be paid or that such improvements will be completed before construction begins; and *compliance with zoning ordinances* governing use and lot size, along with fire and safety ordinances.

Because of the fear that they may pollute streams, rivers, lakes and underground water sources, septic systems are no longer authorized in many areas, and an environmentally approved sewage-disposal arrangement must be included in a land development plan. The shortage of water has caused great concern, and local authorities usually require that land planners submit information on how they intend to satisfy sewage-disposal and water-supply requirements. Development and septic tank installation may first require a *percolation test* of the soil's absorption and drainage capacities. Frequently, a planner will also have to submit an *environmental impact report*.

Subdivision process. The process of subdivision normally involves three distinct stages of development: (1) the initial planning stage, (2) the final planning stage and (3) the disposition, or start-up.

During the *initial planning stage*, the **subdivider** seeks out raw land in a suitable area. Once the land is located, the property is analyzed for its highest and best use, and preliminary subdivision plans are drawn up accordingly. Close contact is initiated between the subdivider and local planning and zoning officials. If the project requires zoning variances, negotiations for these begin. The subdivider also locates financial backers and initiates marketing strategies.

The *final planning* stage is basically a follow-up of the initial stage. Final plans are prepared, approval is sought from local officials, permanent financing is obtained, the land is purchased, final budgets are prepared and marketing programs are designed.

The *disposition,* or *start-up,* carries the subdividing process to a conclusion. Subdivision plans are recorded with local officials, and streets, sewers and utilities are installed. Buildings, open parks and recreational areas are constructed and landscaped if they are part of the subdivision plan. Marketing programs are then initiated, and title to the individual parcels of subdivided land is transferred as the lots are sold.

A developer of a subdivision must have streets approved, based on construction standards set by the North Carolina Department of Transportation, and must declare the streets to be for public or private use. Regardless of the age of the subdivision, real estate licensees should determine if the streets are public or private before making any statements to that effect. Agents must also disclose to buyers whether subdivision streets will be public or private prior to selling or conveying the lot, pursuant to North Carolina disclosure laws (G.S. 136-102.6).

Real estate licensees should be well aware of the needed verification of approved subdivisions, especially in regards to selling recently subdivided lots. Before selling or listing lots in newly subdivided land, an agent should check with the Register of Deeds Office in the county where the lot is located to ensure the plat has been properly recorded. Approval must be granted by the proper county agency (usually a planning board) before recordation can take place. An agent who sells a lot before approval of the subdivision is granted may be subject to a civil lawsuit or may be criminally prosecuted as well as face disciplinary action by the North Carolina Real Estate Commission.

Plat of subdivision. The subdivider's completed plat of subdivision, a map of the development indicating the location and boundaries of individual properties, must contain all necessary approvals of public officials and must be recorded in the county where the land is located.

The plat will be the basis for future conveyance, so the subdivided land should be measured carefully, with all lot sizes and streets noted by the surveyor and entered accurately on the document. Survey monuments should be established, and measurements should be made from these monuments, with the location of all lots carefully marked. Salespersons engaged to sell subdivided land should be certain that the subdivision has been approved by the appropriate government body. In cities or counties that have subdivision ordinances, criminal penalties may be levied against a seller or a seller's agent who attempts to sell land subject to those ordinances without proper government approval.

Covenants and restrictions. Deed restrictions, discussed in more detail later in this chapter, are usually originated and recorded by a subdivider as a means of *controlling and maintaining the desirable quality and character of the subdivision.* These restrictions can be included in the subdivision plat or they may be set forth in a separate recorded instrument, commonly referred to as a *declaration of restrictions.*

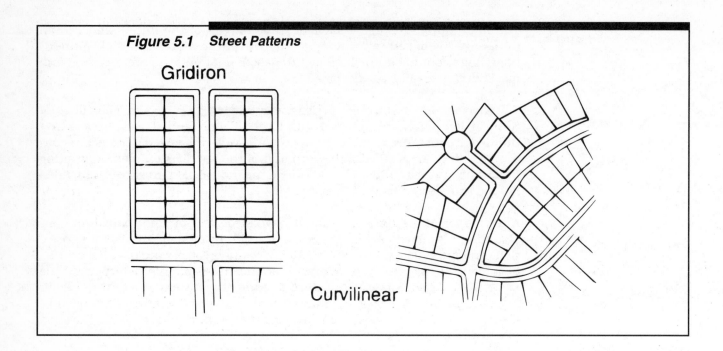

Figure 5.1   Street Patterns

Gridiron

Curvilinear

Deed restrictions may include the size of structures that can be built; the cost—often the minimum cost—of structures that can be built; the number of structures that can be built; or even architectural styles, fence heights or outbuildings that can be built on the land.

FHA standards. FHA **minimum standards** have been established for residential-area subdivisions that are to be submitted for approval for FHA loan insurance. The primary minimum standards established by the FHA are the following:

- Streets must comply with approved widths and must be paved.
- The area must be free from hazards such as airplane landing fields, heavy through traffic and excessive noise or air pollution.
- Each lot must have access to all utilities.
- Provisions for shopping, schools, churches, recreation and transportation must be available.
- Lots must comply with minimum, and in some cases maximum, size requirements.
- Plans for construction must be approved and must meet minimum standards.
- Uniform building setbacks and lot lines usually are required.
- Minimum landscaping usually is required.

FHA standards also apply to building construction. Since 1986, in recognition of the more stringent local codes in effect, the FHA has allowed local building codes (where preapproved by HUD—the Department of Housing and Urban Development) to serve as the standards. Exceptions generally include site condition standards, thermal (insulation) standards and certain other material standards.

Street patterns. By varying street patterns and clustering housing units, a subdivider can increase the amount of open and recreational space in a development. Two of these patterns are illustrated in Figure 5.1.

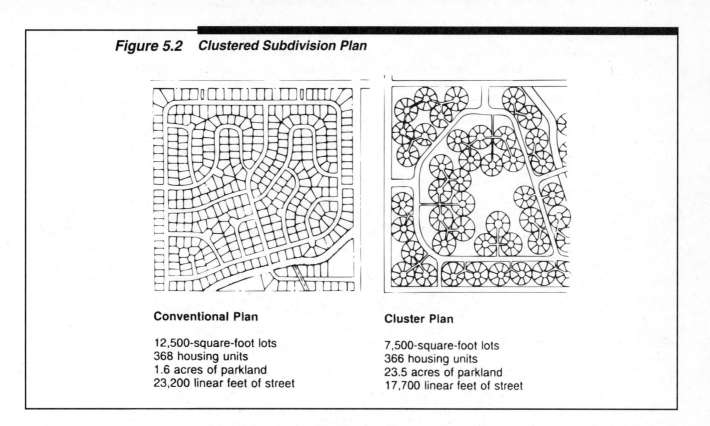

Figure 5.2   *Clustered Subdivision Plan*

Conventional Plan

12,500-square-foot lots
368 housing units
1.6 acres of parkland
23,200 linear feet of street

Cluster Plan

7,500-square-foot lots
366 housing units
23.5 acres of parkland
17,700 linear feet of street

The **gridiron pattern** evolved out of the rectangular survey system. Featuring large lots, wide streets and limited-use service alleys, the system works reasonably well, up to a point. An overabundance of grid-patterned streets often results in monotonous neighborhoods, with all lots facing busy streets. Sidewalks are usually located adjacent to the streets, and the system provides for little or no open, park or recreational space.

The **curvilinear system** integrates major arteries of travel with smaller secondary and cul-de-sac streets carrying minor traffic. Small open parks are often provided at intersections.

Clustering for open space.   By slightly reducing lot sizes and **clustering** lots around varying street patterns, a **developer** can house as many people in the same area as could be housed using traditional subdividing plans, but with substantially increased tracts of open space.

For example, compare the two illustrations in Figure 5.2. The first is a plan for a conventionally designed subdivision containing 368 housing units. It uses 23,200 linear feet of street and leaves only 1.6 acres open for park areas. Contrast this with the second subdivision pictured. Both subdivisions are equal in size and terrain. But when lots are minimally reduced in size and clustered around limited-access cul-de-sac streets, the number of housing units remains nearly the same (366), with less street area (17,700 linear feet) and drastically increased open space (23.5 acres). In addition, with modern building designs this clustered plan could be modified to accommodate 550 patio homes or 1,100 townhouses.

Interstate Land Sales Full Disclosure Act

To protect consumers from "overenthusiastic sales promotions" in interstate land sales, Congress passed the **Interstate Land Sales Full Disclosure Act.** The law requires those engaged in the interstate sale or leasing of subdivision lots to file a *statement of record* and *register* the details of the land with HUD. The act exempts the sale of lots in a subdivision containing fewer than 25 lots. Interstate sales or leasing activities include out-of-state mailers, newspaper ads, television advertising directed to out-of-state buyers and out-of-state telephone solicitation. Licensees involved in interstate selling of lots across state lines that come under this act should seek legal advice to ensure full compliance.

If a development contains 25 or more lots, the developer must furnish prospective buyers with a **property report** containing all essential information about the property, such as

- distance over paved roads to nearby communities,
- number of homes currently occupied,
- soil conditions affecting foundations and septic systems,
- type of title a buyer receives and
- existence of liens.

The property report must be given to a prospective purchaser at least *three business days* before a sales contract is signed.

A purchaser of a lot covered by the act has a week to change his or her mind about the sale. The purchaser can revoke the sales contract—at his or her option—until midnight of the seventh day following the signing of the contract. If a buyer signs a contract to purchase a lot covered by the act and fails to receive a property report, the purchaser has two years in which to revoke the contract.

If the seller misrepresents the property in any sales promotion, anyone induced to purchase a lot by the promotion can sue the seller for civil damages. Failure to comply with the law also may subject a seller to criminal penalties of fines and imprisonment.

Building Codes

North Carolina has enacted a series of statewide **building codes** containing requirements as to construction standards, and the primary purpose is safety. Most cities, towns and counties have enacted ordinances that enforce these *minimum construction standards* that must be met when repairing or erecting buildings. This enforcement is through the local building inspectors certified by the North Carolina Department of Insurance. These building codes set the requirements for kinds of materials, sanitary equipment, electrical wiring, fire prevention standards and the like.

Most communities require the issuance of a **building permit** by the city clerk or another official before a person can build a structure or alter or repair an existing building on property within the municipality. The permit requirement allows officials to verify compliance with building codes and zoning ordinances as they examine the plans and inspect the work. Once the completed structure has been inspected and found satisfactory, the city inspector issues a **certificate of occupancy**.

If the construction violates a deed restriction (discussed later in this chapter), the issuance of a building permit will not cure this violation. A building permit is merely evidence of the applicant's compliance with municipal regulations.

Flood Hazard Regulations and Insurance

The Federal Emergency Management Agency (FEMA) has designated many areas bordering on rivers and streams as *flood hazard areas,* which are subject to federal regulations concerning improvements and construction in those areas. FEMA produces maps that designate these flood hazard areas, and flood insurance is required under the National Flood Insurance Program if a federally related mortgage loan is to be used for properties within those areas. The lender will insist on appropriate flood insurance, which the buyer can purchase from most regular insurance companies that sell homeowners' policies. The basic standard homeowners' policies do not cover flood damage. Land located in these flood hazard areas is subject to restrictions in terms of location, types of improvements and elevations of the improvements. Real estate licensees should inform any potential buyers of possible flood areas and have them acquire a copy of the latest property survey.

Highway Access Restrictions

Access to a public road or street is important to any buyer, and the agent should make sure that public road access is available. If any government entity takes away road access, the owner must be compensated under eminent domain. If there is any planned construction of new highways, freeways, loop roads, etc., real estate licensees are expected to be aware of this and make full disclosure to any potential customer or client. Changes in road access have a great impact on value and usability of the property. Failure of a real estate licensee to properly disclose material facts about road access could lead to disciplinary action by the Real Estate Commission [see G.S. 93A-6(a)(1)].

In Practice

The subject of city planning, zoning and restriction of the use of real estate is extremely technical, and interpretation of the law is not altogether clear. Real estate agents should never offer advice on whether a particular use will be allowed or whether a variance or special-use permit will be granted. Questions concerning any of these subjects in relation to real estate transactions should be referred to legal counsel.

Environmental Protection Legislation

Federal and state legislators have passed a number of environmental protection laws in an attempt to respond to the growing public concern over the improvement and preservation of America's natural resources. (See Chapter 19 for further discussion on environmental issues.)

The various states have responded to the environmental issue by passing a variety of local environmental protection laws regarding all forms of pollution—air, water, noise and solid-waste disposal. Many states have enacted laws that prevent builders or private individuals from considering septic tanks or other waste disposal systems in certain areas, particularly where streams, lakes and rivers are affected. In addition to the state and federal governments, cities and counties also frequently pass environmental legislation (see Figure 5.3).

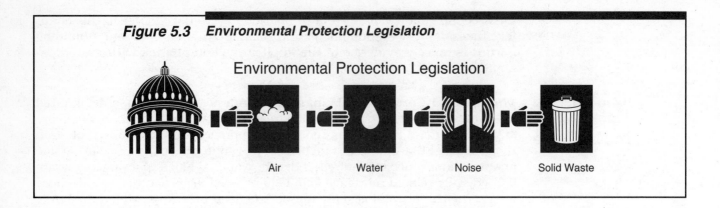

Figure 5.3   *Environmental Protection Legislation*

Environmental Protection Legislation

Air   Water   Noise   Solid Waste

Americans with Disabilities Act (ADA)

The federal government has recently mandated that newer buildings and older public buildings that undergo remodeling must meet the standards of the **Americans with Disabilities Act (ADA).** The purpose of this legislation is to facilitate accessibility and mobility by ramp construction, safety rails, wider doors and other accommodations. (See Chapter 7 for further discussion on ADA.)

PRIVATELY IMPOSED LAND-USE CONTROLS

Private land-use controls are put in place by individual property owners, usually when they transfer property. When property is conveyed, a property owner can include restrictions in the deed that limit the new owner's use of the property. For example, the property may be conveyed on the condition that it be used only as a bird sanctuary.The most common examples of private land-use controls are the restrictions imposed by subdivision developers. All those who purchase lots in a subdivision promise to abide by the developer's restrictions, which usually include provisions requiring regular property maintenance and restrictions on parking, the height of fences and so on.

There is a distinction between restrictions on the grantee's right to *sell* and restrictions on the grantee's right to *use.* In general, provisions in a deed conveying a fee simple estate with restrictions on the grantee's right to sell, mortgage or convey it are void. Such restrictions attempt to limit the basic principle of the *free alienation (transfer) of property;* the courts consider them against public policy and therefore unenforceable.

A subdivider may establish restrictions on the right to use land through a **covenant** in a deed or by reference to a separate recorded declaration, called a *declaration of restrictive covenants.* When a lot in that subdivision is conveyed by an owner's deed, the deed refers to the plat or declaration of restrictions and incorporates these restrictions as limitations on the title conveyed by the deed. In this manner, the restrictive covenants are included in the deed by reference and become binding on all grantees. Such covenants or restrictions usually relate to type of building; use to which the land may be put; type of construction, height, setbacks and square footage; and cost. Private use restrictions are used primarily to protect property from traffic odors, noise, etc., and need not pass the test of promoting the public welfare, the test that public use restrictions must pass.

In Practice
The term **restrictive covenant** is being replaced by the term **protective covenant.** Both have essentially the same meaning, which is defined by the North Carolina Real Estate Commission as follows: "Protective covenants are enforceable conditions that restrict the manner in which an owner may use his/her property" (1997-1998 Update Course). The term *protective covenant* is a more modern term and better implies the intended use, which is to protect owners from uses that may have an adverse affect on value or enjoyment.

Use restrictions usually are considered valid if they are reasonable and are for the benefit of all property owners in the subdivision. If, however, such restrictions are too broad in their terms, they prevent the free transfer of property. If they are "repugnant" to the estate granted, they are probably not enforceable. If any restrictive covenant or condition is considered ineffective by a court, the property is freed from the invalid covenant or condition. Note that deed restrictions can be more restrictive on an owner's use than zoning ordinances. The more restrictive of the two takes precedence.

Subdivision restrictions give each lot owner the right to apply to the court for an injunction or legal action to prevent a neighboring lot owner from violating the recorded restrictions. If granted, the court injunction directs the violator to stop or remove the violation on penalty of being in contempt of court. The court retains the power to punish the violator for failure to obey the court order. If adjoining lot owners stand idly by while a violation is being committed, they can *lose the right* to the court's injunction by their inaction; the court might claim their right was lost through **laches**—that is, loss of a right through undue delay or failure to assert it.

GOVERNMENT OWNERSHIP

Over the years, the government's general policy has been to encourage private ownership of land. A certain amount of land is owned by the government for such uses as municipal buildings, state legislative houses, schools and military stations. Such **direct public ownership** is a means of land control.

Publicly owned streets and highways serve a necessary function for the entire population. Public land is often used for recreational purposes as well. National and state parks and forest preserves create areas for public use and recreation and at the same time help to conserve our natural resources. At present, the federal government owns approximately 775 million acres of land, nearly one-third of the total area of the United States. At times, the federal government has held title to as much as 80 percent of the nation's total land area.

SUMMARY

The control of land use is exercised in three ways: through public controls, private (or nongovernment) controls and government ownership of land.

Public controls are ordinances based on the states' police powers to protect the public health, safety and welfare. Through power conferred by state enabling acts, local governments enact comprehensive master plans, and any zoning must be in accordance with the master plan.

Zoning ordinances carrying out the provisions of the master plan segregate residential areas from business and industrial zones and control not only land use but also height and bulk of buildings and density of populations. Zoning enforcement problems involve boards of adjustment, conditional-use permits, variances and exceptions, and nonconforming uses. Zoning ordinances are local in nature; there are no statewide zoning ordinances.

A subdivider buys undeveloped acreage, divides it into smaller parcels and develops or sells it. A builder builds homes on the lots and sells them through the builder's own sales organization or through local real estate brokerage firms. A developer may be a subdivider or a builder who also subdivides. Land development must comply with the master plans adopted by counties, cities, towns or villages. This may entail approval of land-use plans by local planning committees or commissioners.

The process of subdivision includes dividing the tract of land into lots and blocks and providing for utility easements, as well as laying out street patterns and widths. Generally, a subdivider must record a completed plat of subdivision, with all necessary approvals of public officials, in the county where the land is located. Subdividers usually place restrictions on the use of all lots in a subdivision as a general plan for the benefit of all lot owners.

Subdivided-land sales are regulated on the federal level by the Interstate Land Sales Full Disclosure Act. This law requires that developers engaged in interstate land sales in a subdivision containing 25 or more lots register the details of the land with HUD. At least three business days before any sales contract is signed, such developers also must provide prospective purchasers with a property report containing all essential information about the property in any development that exceeds 25 lots. Subdivided-land sales are also regulated by individual state statutes.

Building codes specify standards for construction, plumbing, sewers, electrical wiring and equipment.

In addition to land-use control on the local level, state governments and the federal government have passed laws regarding flood hazard insurance and highway access restrictions. They also have occasionally intervened when necessary to preserve natural resources through environmental legislation.

Private controls are exercised by owners, generally subdividers, who control use of subdivision lots by deed restrictions designed to apply to all lot owners. The usual recorded restrictions may be enforced by adjoining-lot owners obtaining a court injunction to stop a violator. Private restrictions need not promote the public welfare and safety, as must public restrictions.

Public ownership provides land for such public purposes as parks, highways, schools and municipal buildings.

Questions

1. A provision in a subdivision declaration used as a means of forcing the grantee to live up to the terms under which he or she holds title to the land is a
   a. restrictive covenant.
   b. reverter.
   c. loss through laches.
   d. conditional-use clause.

2. Tests commonly applied in determining the validity of zoning ordinances require all of the following EXCEPT that the
   a. power be exercised in a reasonable manner.
   b. ordinance be free from discrimination.
   c. ordinance apply to all property in a similar manner.
   d. ordinance causes a loss of property value for the good of the community.

3. Public land-use controls include all of the following EXCEPT
   a. subdivision regulations.
   b. deed restrictions.
   c. environmental protection laws.
   d. master plan specifications.

4. Zoning powers are conferred on municipal governments by
   I. state enabling acts.
   II. eminent domain.
      a. I only
      b. II only
      c. Both I and II
      d. Neither I nor II

5. Zoning laws are generally enforced by
   a. zoning boards of adjustment.
   b. ordinances stipulating that building permits will not be issued unless the proposed structure conforms to zoning ordinances.
   c. deed restrictions.
   d. the North Carolina Secretary of State.

6. Zoning boards of adjustment are established to hear complaints about
   a. restrictive covenants.
   b. the effects of a zoning ordinance.
   c. building codes.
   d. the effects of public ownership.

7. The police power allows regulation of all of the following EXCEPT
   a. number of buildings.
   b. size of buildings.
   c. building ownership.
   d. building occupancy.

8. The purpose of a building permit is to
   I. override a deed restriction.
   II. maintain municipal control over the volume of building.
   III. provide evidence of compliance with municipal regulations.
      a. I only
      b. II only
      c. III only
      d. I, II and III

9. Dinwiddie owns a vacant lot in a residential neighborhood. His friends in the city government manage to change the zoning on his lot to commercial, so he can increase his profits on the property. This type of zoning is called
   a. spot zoning.
   b. a nonconforming use.
   c. an illegal use.
   d. a variance.

10. The grantor of a deed may place effective restrictions on the
   I. right to sell the land.
   II. use of the land.
      a. I only
      b. II only
      c. Both I and II
      d. Neither I nor II

11. A new zoning code is enacted. A building that is permitted to continue in its former use even though that use does not conform to a new zoning ordinance is an example of a(n)
    a. legal nonconforming use.
    b. variance.
    c. special use.
    d. inverse condemnation.

12. To determine whether a location can be put to future use as a retail store, one would examine the
    a. building code.
    b. list of permitted nonconforming uses.
    c. housing code.
    d. zoning code.

13. Which of the following probably would NOT be included in a list of deed restrictions?
    a. Types of buildings that may be constructed
    b. Allowable ethnic origins of purchasers
    c. Activities that are not to be conducted at the site
    d. Minimum size of buildings to be constructed

14. A restriction in a seller's deed may be enforced by which of the following?
    a. Court injunction
    b. Zoning board of adjustment
    c. City building commission
    d. State legislature

15. Julie & Janelle Enterprises just purchased a vacant lot, and the owners want to build a dress shop to expand their business. The plans drawn up by the architect extend the building two feet beyond the setback requirements for that location. To construct the building legally, the owners must obtain a
    a. nonconforming-use permit.
    b. license.
    c. variance.
    d. permit issued by the state.

16. To control and maintain the quality and character of a subdivision, a developer will establish which of the following?
    I. Easements
    II. Deed restrictions
    III. Building codes
    a. I only
    b. II only
    c. III only
    d. I and III only

17. A neighborhood in Central City consists of very old buildings. The neighborhood is subject to a special zoning that makes it very difficult for property owners to tear down a building and replace it with a modern one. This type of zoning is called
    a. historic preservation zoning.
    b. spot zoning.
    c. zoning amendments.
    d. a taking.

18. A map illustrating the sizes and locations of streets and lots in a subdivision is called a
    a. gridiron pattern.
    b. survey.
    c. plat of subdivision.
    d. property report.

19. In complying with the Interstate Land Sales Full Disclosure Act, which of the following information need *not* be included in a property report given to a land buyer?
    a. Soil conditions affecting foundations
    b. Financial condition of the seller
    c. Number of homes currently occupied, categorized by race of occupants
    d. Existence of liens

20. When there is a violation of a restrictive covenant, the best remedy of other property owners is to
    a. go to the zoning commission.
    b. go to the city council.
    c. go to the developer.
    d. hire an attorney and go to court.

21. If present zoning ordinances cause an undue hardship for the property owner, they may be able to have it changed by city officials under which of the following?
    a. Nonconforming use
    b. Variance
    c. Spot zoning
    d. Special-use permit

22. Mr. Jones owns a gas station at the edge of town, and pursuant to a comprehensive plan, the city zones the land as residential. Which of the following statements is true?
    I. The gas station can continue to operate under a variance.
    II. The gas station may continue to operate forever as a nonconforming use.
    a. I only
    b. II only
    c. Both I and II
    d. Neither I nor II

23. Generally, zoning laws are enforced by
    I. zoning boards of adjustment.
    II. ordinances stipulating that building permits will not be issued unless the proposed structures conform to the zoning ordinances.
    III. deed restrictions.
    a. I only
    b. II only
    c. III only
    d. I, II and III

6 Real Estate Brokerage and the Law of Agency

LEARNING OBJECTIVES

When you've finished reading this chapter, you should be able to

- **identify** all types of agency relationships and characteristics of each (single, subagency, dual agency and designated agency) and **explain** how fiduciary relationships are established and terminated.

- **differentiate** between client-level and customer-level responsibilities of the agent.

- **explain** agency disclosure requirements in North Carolina; how, when and to whom proper disclosures must be made in agency agreements.

- **describe** an agent's responsibility to a principal (client) and to a customer (third party) and **explain** the duties and liabilities of principals to their agents.

- **define** these *key terms:*

agent	fiduciary	puffing
allocating markets or customers	fraud	ratification
antitrust laws	general agent	ready, willing and able buyer
brokerage	group boycotting	special agent
buyer brokerage	implied agreement	stigmatized property
caveat emptor	independent contractor	subagent
COALD	material fact	tort
commission	negligent misrepresentation	universal agent
designated agency	negligent omission	willful misrepresentation
dual agency	price-fixing	willful omission
employee	principal	
express agreement		

INTRODUCTION TO BROKERAGE AND AGENCY

The nature of real estate brokerage services, particularly those provided in residential sales transactions, has changed significantly in recent years. Through the 1950s, real estate brokerage firms were primarily one-office, minimally staffed, family-run operations. The broker listed the owner's property for sale and found a buyer without assistance from other companies. Then the sale was negotiated and closed. It was relatively clear that the broker represented the seller's interests.

In the 1960s, however, the ways buyers and sellers were brought together in a transaction began to change. Brokers started to share information about properties they had listed, which resulted in two brokers cooperating with one another to sell a property. Brokers formalized this exchange of information by creating multiple-listing services (MLSs). By increasing exposure to potential buyers, the MLS expedited sales and thus became a widely used industry service.

Unfortunately, confusion quickly arose over whom the broker represented in these cooperative transactions. With two different brokers involved in a sale, the natural assumption was that there was a clear division of responsibility. The broker who had the property listed for sale represented the seller; the broker who found the buyer represented the buyer. However, this was not the case. In these shared transactions, both brokers represented the seller. Generally, the MLSs provided for a *unilateral subagency,* which was created when a seller listed his or her property with a listing broker or firm. The listing broker then submitted the listing to the MLS so the listing could be shared with other MLS members. These MLS members immediately became subagents of the seller; the seller became their client. This common "traditional view" of agency began to erode when buyers became concerned about having their own representation.

Such misunderstandings ultimately led buyers to question exactly how their interests were being protected. This helped spur a growing trend in which consumers began to demand that their rights be protected so that they could make informed decisions. In many states, lawmakers have departed from the common-law doctrine of **caveat emptor**—let the buyer beware— toward greater consumer protection. Buyers seek not only accurate, factual information but also advice, particularly as real estate transactions have become much more complex. They view the real estate licensee as the expert on whom they can rely to guide them. Today, buyers seek representation. However, North Carolina is still considered to be a "caveat emptor" state.

THE LAW OF AGENCY

The basic framework of the law that governs the legal responsibilities of the broker to the people he or she represents—known as the *law of agency*—has not changed. But its *application* has. Brokers are reevaluating their services. They are determining whether they will represent the seller, the buyer or both (if permitted by state law) in the sale or rental of property. They also must decide how they will cooperate with other brokers on a transaction. In short, the brokerage business is undergoing many changes as brokers focus on ways to enhance their services to buyers and sellers.

Figure 6.1   *Definitions in Agency Law*

The North Carolina Real Estate Commission strongly encourages the broker-in-charge (BIC) of a real estate firm to have a written office policy as to the type of agency the firm will practice. It is the firm that is technically the agent. The company policy should cover whether the firm will practice seller single agency only, buyer single agency only, or dual and designated agency. Which party the firm will represent is a decision that is largely based on economics. For instance, a single-agency practice could lead to a loss of income. Whichever form of representation the firm adopts, the written policy should clearly state how that type of agency representation will be exercised. The written policy also should explain how the firm will enter into cooperative relationships among other firms, how it will arrange commission splits, and how it implements disclosure requirements.

GENERAL AGENCY DEFINITIONS

Real estate brokers and salespeople are commonly referred to as **agents.** Legally, however, the term refers to a strictly defined legal relationship. In the real estate industry, it is the relationship a party has with buyers and sellers. In the *law of agency,* the body of law that governs these relationships, the following terms have specific definitions (see Figure 6.1):

> An agent is a person authorized to act on behalf of another.

- *Agent*—the individual who is authorized and consents to represent the interests of another person. In the real estate industry, principals are hiring an entire company to represent them. Even though "the firm" is the agent, the broker-in charge would be personally accountable for agency law compliance.
- *Subagent*—one who is employed by a person already acting as an agent (such as a salesperson licensed under a broker who is employed under the terms of a listing agreement). Simply stated, a subagent is "an agent of an agent."
- *Principal*—the individual who hires and delegates to the agent through a brokerage contract the responsibility of representing his or her interests. In the real estate business, the **principal** is the buyer, seller, landlord or tenant.
- *Agency*—the fiduciary relationship between the principal and the agent.

- *Subagency*—the fiduciary relationship between the subagent and the agent.
- *Fiduciary*—a relationship in which the agent is placed in the position of trust and confidence to the principal.
- *Client*—the principal.
- *Customer*—the third party for whom some level of service is provided.

The principal-agent relationship evolved from the master-servant relationship under English common law. The servant owed absolute loyalty to the master. This loyalty superseded the servant's personal interest as well as any loyalty the servant might owe to others. The agent owes the principal similar loyalty. As masters used the services of servants to accomplish what they could not or did not want to do for themselves, the principal uses the services of the agent. The agent is regarded as an expert on whom the principal can rely for specialized professional advice.

> An agent works *for* the client and **with** the customer.

There is a distinction between the level of services that agents provide to *clients* and the level they provide to customers. The *client* is the principal to whom the agent gives advice and counsel. The agent is entrusted with certain *confidential information* and has *fiduciary responsibilities* (discussed in greater detail later in this chapter) to the principal. In contrast, the *customer* is entitled to factual information and fair and honest dealings as a consumer but does not receive advice and counsel or confidential information about the principal. The agent works *for* the principal and *with* the customer. Essentially, the agent is an advocate for the principal.

The relationship between the principal and agent must be consensual: the principal *delegates* authority; the agent *consents* to act. The parties must mutually agree to form the relationship. An agent may be authorized by the principal to use the assistance of others, called **subagents** of the principal.

BROKERAGE DEFINED

Before discussing the intricacies of agency, it is important to look more closely at the parties who provide the client and customer services in a real estate agency relationship (see Figure 6.2).

Brokerage is the business of bringing buyers and sellers together in the marketplace. Buyers and sellers in many fields of business employ the services of brokers to facilitate complex business transactions. In the real estate business, a *broker* is defined as a person who is licensed to buy, sell, exchange, manage or lease real property for others and to charge a fee for his or her services. The real estate salesperson works on behalf of, and is licensed to represent, the broker (see G.S. 93A-1, G.S. 93A-2).

The principal who employs the broker may be a seller, a prospective buyer, an owner (landlord) who wishes to lease out property or a person (tenant) seeking property to rent. The real estate broker acts as the agent of the principal, and the salesperson acts as the subagent of the principal. The principal usually compensates the broker with a **commission,** contingent on the broker's successfully performing the service for which he or she was employed. That service generally involves negotiating a transaction with a prospective purchaser, seller, landlord or tenant who is ready, willing and able to complete the contract. However, the source of compensation does not necessarily dictate the agency relationship.

In a typical real estate listing contract, the seller will authorize the broker to use salespeople employed by the broker as well as other *cooperating brokers* (members of the MLS). Cooperating brokers may act as subagents of the principal and may in turn employ their own salespeople. The relationship of a salesperson to an employing broker is also an agency relationship. The salesperson is thus the agent of the broker in addition to being the subagent of the principal.

REALTOR® Board/Association MLSs may not require that members make blanket offers of subagency to other members. Instead, MLS members must offer cooperation with compensation to other members. Thus, other members of the MLS may find a buyer for listed property while working as a subagent of the listing agent or as an agent of the buyer. The cooperating agent then will receive a portion of the commission when the sale closes. While all offers of cooperation must be accompanied by an offer of compensation, the listing broker may offer differing amounts to subagents and to buyer agents.

Classification of Agency Relationships

An agent may be classified as a universal agent, a general agent or a special agent, based on the nature of his or her authority.

A **universal agent** is a person who is empowered to do anything the principal could do personally. There are virtually no limits to the universal agent's authority to act on behalf of the principal. This type of agency is seldom practiced in a typical real estate transaction.

A **general agent** may represent the principal in a broad range of matters *related to a particular business or activity.* The general agent may, for example, bind the principal to any contracts within the scope of the agent's authority. This type of agency can be created by a *general power of attorney,* which makes the agent an *attorney-in-fact.* A real estate broker typically does not have this scope of authority as an agent in a real estate sales transaction. A property manager may be considered to be a general agent.

A **special agent** is authorized to represent the principal in only one specific act or business transaction, and under detailed instructions. A real estate broker is usually a special agent. If hired by a seller, the broker's duty is limited to finding a **"ready, willing and able" buyer** for the property. A special agent for a buyer has the limited responsibility of finding a property that fits the buyer's criteria. As a special agent, the broker may not bind the principal to any contract. A *special power of attorney* is another means of authorizing an agent to carry out only a specified act or acts. It is important to remember that a special agency gives *limited authority.*

For Example You are very busy with an important project, so you give your colleague $5 and ask him to buy your lunch. Your colleague is your general agent; you have limited his scope of authority to a particular business (buying your lunch), and established the amount that may be spent (up to $5). Still, he has broad discretion in selecting what you will eat and where he will buy it. However, if you had told your colleague, "Please buy me a Number 3 salad at Lettuce Eat Lettuce," you would have further limited his authority to a very specific task. Your colleague, therefore, would have been your special agent.

Creation of Agency

Agents are employed for their expertise. However, providing services does not in itself create an agency relationship. No agency exists without mutual consent between the principal and the agent. The agent consents to undertake certain duties on behalf of the principal, subject to the principal's control. The principal authorizes the agent to perform these acts when dealing with others.

Common law agency relationships can be created in the following ways:

- With a written listing contract whereby a seller employs an agent to produce a buyer for the property: the seller is the principal, the broker is the seller's agent
- With a buyer agency contract whereby a prospective buyer hires a broker to locate properties for the buyer with buyer representation: the buyer is the principal, the broker is the buyer's agent
- With a dual-agency contract whereby the broker legally represents both parties; both seller and buyer are principals, broker is agent to both, but written informed consent from both parties is required
- With a property management contract whereby the owner of rental properties engages the services of a broker to rent and manage the property; the owner is the principal and the broker is the property manager/agent
- With an in-house brokerage employment contract whereby a licensee signs an employment agreement with a broker that defines the legal and agency relationship between them
- By the conduct of the parties (implied agency)

(These agency agreements and examples of each are fully discussed in Chapter 8.)

Scope of Authority

Under general agency law principles, an agency relationship can be created by either an oral or a written agency agreement between the principal and the agent. It also can be implied from words or conduct. To ensure that all parties have a clear understanding of the agency relationship, it is in everyone's best interest to create an agency relationship through an expression of agreement rather than through implication. Principal and agent may make an **express agreement** (written or oral).

An agency also can be created by **implied agreement** when principal and agent, without formally agreeing to the agency, act as if one exists. However, an implied contract will not be established simply on trade custom and practice. There must be sufficient evidence to show that the principal authorized the agent to perform acts under circumstances in which a reasonable principal would be expected to compensate the agent for the services. The fact that a seller simply allows a broker to show the property is not sufficient to create an implied agency agreement, nor are implied agency agreements permitted under North Carolina real esate license law.

When someone claims to be an agent but there is no agreement, the "principal" can establish an agency by **ratification** (apparent authority)—in other words, by performing any act that accepts (ratifies) the conduct of the agent as that of an agent.

If someone has stated incorrectly that another person is his or her agent and a third person has relied on that representation, an agency relationship may have been created by estoppel. In such event, in dealing with the "agent" the "principal" cannot later deny the existence of an agency.

Compensation. Because the source of compensation does not determine agency, the agent does not necessarily represent the person who pays the commission. In fact, agency can exist even if there is no fee involved (a gratuitous agency). Buyers and sellers can make any agreement they choose about compensating the broker, regardless of which one is the agent's principal. For example, the seller could agree to pay a commission to the broker who is the buyer's agent. The listing agreement should state how the agent is being compensated.

Termination of Agency

When an agent completes his or her assignment, the agency relationship ends, as does all responsibility to that former principal. An agency agreement may be terminated at any time for any of the following reasons:

- Completion or fulfillment of the purpose for which the agency was created
- Expiration of the terms of the agency
- Mutual agreement to terminate the agency
- Breach by one of the parties, such as abandonment by the agent or revocation by the principal (The breaching party might be liable for damages.)
- By operation of law, as in a bankruptcy of the principal (because title to the property would be transferred to a court-appointed receiver)
- Destruction or condemnation of the property
- Death or incapacity of either party (Notice of death is not necessary. Note that if a property is listed with a brokerage firm and the listing agent dies, the listing would not be terminated.)

AGENCY RELATIONSHIPS

A variety of agency relationships may be created. The distinctions between them are not always clear. When consumers feel their individual interests have not been adequately protected, licensees may face legal and ethical problems. The broker must decide the agency policy and procedures for the firm, determine who will be represented, disclose the agency alternatives to each party, then act according to the agency relationship defined.

In North Carolina every agreement for brokerage services in real estate transactions shall be in writing [See Rule A.0104(a)]. Real estate agency relationships typically are created with a *property management agreement,* or buyer *or tenant* agency agreement. Listing agreements will be discussed in detail in Chapter 8.

Single Agency

In a single-agency situation, the broker exclusively represents either the buyer or the seller in a transaction. The agent represents one client; any third party is a customer. In the past, particularly in residential sales, brokers almost always represented the seller. The broker served the seller as the client, and other agents in the firm were subagents of the seller. In this case, prospective buyers do not have a client-based relationship with anyone. Rather, they are the customers (the third parties), to whom licensees are responsible only within the scope of their legal and ethical responsibilities to consumers. Consequently, buyers must take responsibility for pro-

A *single-agent* represents either the buyer or the seller in a transaction.

tecting their own interests in a transaction—in essence, they are represented by no one other than themselves. Brokers may choose to exclusively represent buyers as their clients. In this case, the sellers are the customers. Because of the growing awareness that buyers also deserve the degree of representation available in a client-based relationship, more buyers are seeking brokers to represent them.

A single-agency broker may represent both sellers and buyers. However, in single agency, the broker does not represent both parties in the same transaction. This limitation avoids conflicting fiduciary duties and results in client-based service and loyalty to only one client. Single agency precludes selling one's own listings if the agent is acting as a buyer's agent

Buyer as Principal

When a buyer contracts with a broker to locate property and represent his or her interests in the transaction, the buyer is the *principal*—the broker's client. The broker as *agent* is strictly accountable to the buyer. The seller is the customer.

In the past, it was simple: brokers always represented sellers, and buyers were expected to look out for themselves. With the widespread use of MLSs and subagency, a buyer often had the mistaken impression that the subagent was the buyer's agent, although the reality was that both agent and subagent represented the seller's interest. Today, however, many residential brokers and salespersons are discovering opportunities of buyer representation. Some brokers and salespersons have become specialists in the emerging field of **buyer brokerage,** representing buyers exclusively. Real estate commissions (including the North Carolina Real Estate Commission) across the country have developed rules and procedures to regulate such buyers' brokers, and local real estate associations have developed agency representation forms and other materials for them to use. The agency disclosure forms are discussed in Chapter 8. Professional organizations offer assistance, certification, training and networking opportunities for buyers' agents.

A buyer or tenant agency relationship is established in the same way as any other agency agreement: by *express* contract or agreement, *which may be oral initially, but which must be reduced to writing no later than the time an offer is extended by any party to the transaction. If the agent seeks to restrict the buyer's right to work with other agents or independently or to bind the client to the agent for any specified period, then the buyer agency agreement must be in writing from the formation of the restricted relationship.* The buyer's agent may receive a flat fee or a share of the commission or both, depending on the terms of the agency agreement.

A *subagent* is the agent of an agent. The person designated by an agent to assist in performing client based functions on behalf of the principal.

Subagency. A subagency is created when one broker, usually the seller's agent, appoints other brokers (with the authority of the seller) to assist in performing client-based functions on the principal's behalf. These cooperating brokers have the same fiduciary obligations to the seller as the listing broker, assisting in producing a ready, willing and able buyer for the property. The listing broker and the seller now become liable for the conduct of all of the cooperating brokers and their salespeople in protecting the fiduciary responsibility to the seller (see Figure 6.2). It is also important to note that when a real estate broker/firm becomes an agent under an agency agreement with a principal, all individual real estate agents affiliated with the broker/firm automatically become subagents of the principal, unless there is a specific agreement to the contrary.

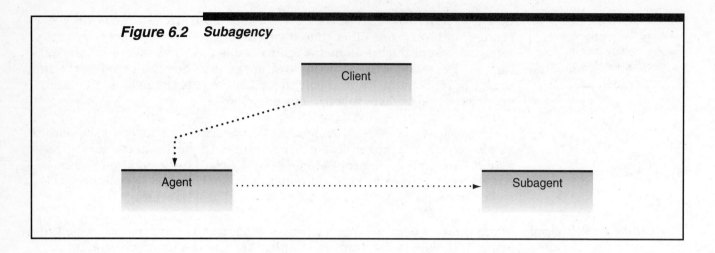

Figure 6.2   Subagency

For Example If you give your colleague $5 and ask him to buy your lunch, your colleague is your agent. If your colleague is busy, he may hand your money to a friend, along with your instructions. The friend is a subagent—an agent of your agent. Your colleague's friend is still responsible for buying your lunch in accordance with your instructions. The subagent, like the agent, is ultimately responsible to you, the principal.

Dual and Designated Agency

The appropriate paragraphs of Rule A.0104 are quoted below.

(i) A firm which represents more than one party in the same real estate transaction is a dual agent and, through the brokers and salespersons associated with the firm, shall disclose its dual agency to the parties.

(j) When a firm represents both the buyer and seller in the same real estate transaction, the firm may, with the prior express approval of its buyer and seller clients, designate one or more individual agents associated with the firm to represent only the interest of the seller and one or more other individual brokers and salespersons associated with the firm to represent only the interests of the buyer in the transaction. The authority for designated agency must be reduced to writing not later than the time that the parties are required to reduce their dual agency agreement to writing in accordance with subsection (d) of this rule. An individual broker or salesperson shall not be so designated and shall not undertake to represent only the interest of one party if the broker or salesperson has actually received confidential information concerning the other party in connection with the transaction. A broker-in-charge shall not act as a designated agent for a party in a real estate sales transaction when a salesperson under his supervision will act as a designated agent for another party with a competing interest.

(k) When a firm acting as a dual agent designates an individual broker or salesperson to represent the seller, the broker or salesperson so designated shall represent only the interest of the seller and shall not, without the seller's permission, disclose to the buyer or a broker or salesperson designated to represent the buyer:

(1) that the seller may agree to a price, terms, or any conditions of sale other than those established by the seller;

(2) the seller's motivation for engaging in the transaction unless disclosure is otherwise required by statute or rule; and

(3) any information about the seller which the seller has identified as confidential unless disclosure of the information is otherwise required by statute or rule.

(l)   When a firm acting as a dual agent designates an individual broker or salesperson to represent the buyer, the broker or the salesperson so designated shall represent only the interest of the buyer and shall not, without the buyer's permission, disclose to the seller or a broker or salesperson designated to represent the seller:

(1) that the buyer may agree to a price, terms, or any conditions of sale other than those offered by the buyer;

(2) the buyer's motivation for engaging in the transaction unless disclosure is otherwise required by statute or rule; and

(3) any information about the buyer which the buyer has identified as confidential unless disclosure of the information is otherwise required by statute or rule.

(m) A broker or salesperson designated to represent a buyer or seller in accordance with Section (j) of this Rule shall disclose the identity of all of the brokers and salespersons so designated to both the buyer and the seller. The disclosure shall take place no later than the presentation of the first offer to purchase or sell.

(n) When an individual broker or salesperson represents both the buyer and seller in the same real estate sales transaction pursuant to a written agreement authorizing dual agency, the parties may provide in the written agreement that the broker or salesperson shall not disclose the following information about one party to the other without written permission from the party about whom the information pertains:

(1) that a party may agree to a price, terms, or any conditions of sale other than those offered;

(2) the motivation of a party for engaging in the transaction, unless disclosure is otherwise required by statute or rule; and

(3) any information about a party which that party has identified as confidential, unless disclosure is otherwise required by statute or rule.

Dual Agency   In a **dual-agency** situation, the broker represents two principals in the same transaction. Dual agency requires that the agent be equally loyal to two separate principals at the same time. The challenge is to fulfill the fiduciary obligations to one principal without compromising the other. Under the strict terms of the law of agency, dual agency seems to be a logical impossibility. How can one person "serve two masters," especially when their interests are not only separate but may also be opposite? Because agency originates with the broker, dual agency arises when the broker is the

A *dual agent* represents two principals in the same transaction.

agent of both parties in the same transaction. The salespeople, as agents of the broker, have fiduciary responsibilities to the same principals as well. A real estate broker or salesperson representing one party in a transaction shall not undertake to represent another party in the same transaction without the express approval of both parties.

Considerable debate exists in the real estate industry as to how brokers can represent both buyers and sellers in the same transaction. Recently, several states have passed laws in an attempt to avoid dual agency, particularly when the buyer-principal wants to purchase a property listed by the same broker-agent (known as an *in-house sale*). Under these laws, the broker can designate certain licensees within the firm who are the legal representatives of a principal. The broker will not be considered a dual agent as long as the designated legal representative for each principal in the transaction is not the same salesperson. In effect, these laws create a *split agency*, which is quite a departure from the common doctrines of the law of agency. It is expected that there will be a number of other legislative developments as states wrestle with the issue of dual agency.

For Example Mark, a real estate broker, is the agent for the owner of Roomy Manor, a large mansion. Jennifer, a prospective buyer, comes into Mark's office and asks him to represent her in her search for a modest home. After several weeks of activity, including two offers unsuccessfully negotiated by Mark, Jennifer spots the For Sale sign in front of Roomy Manor. She tells Mark that she wants to make an offer and asks for his advice on a likely price range. Mark is now in the difficult position of being a dual agent; Mark represents the seller (who naturally is interested in receiving the highest possible price) and the buyer (who is interested in making a successful low offer).

Undisclosed dual agency. A broker may not intend to create a dual agency. However, by a salesperson's words and actions, it can occur *unintentionally* or *inadvertently*. Sometimes the cause is carelessness. Other times the salesperson does not fully understand his or her fiduciary responsibilities. Some salespeople lose sight of other responsibilities when they focus intensely on bringing buyers and sellers together. For example, a salesperson representing a seller might tell a buyer that the seller will accept less than the listing price, which is a breach of the duty of loyalty (discussed a bit later in this chapter). Giving a buyer any specific advice on how much to offer can lead the buyer to believe that the salesperson is an advocate for the buyer. This would create an *implied agency* with the buyer and violate the duties of loyalty and confidentiality to the principal-seller. Because neither party has been informed of the situation or given the opportunity to seek separate representation, the interests of both are jeopardized. This undisclosed dual agency violates licensing laws [see G.S. 93A-6(a)(4)]. It can result in rescission of the sales contract, forfeiture of the commission or the filing of a suit for damages.

For Example Using the previous Roomy Manor example, if Mark doesn't tell Jennifer that he represents the seller of the property, he will be an undisclosed dual agent. Mark has two options. First, knowing Jennifer's comfortable financial situation and intense desire for the property, Mark might choose not to tell Jennifer about the dual-agency situation. Instead, he could tell her that Roomy Manor's owner will accept nothing less than the full asking price. While this will ensure that Mark receives the maximum possible commission, it will also subject him to severe penalties for violating the state's licensing laws. Alternatively, Mark may disclose his relationship with the seller and work out a dual-agency agreement with both parties in which he legally represents both parties' interests.

A more common example of dual agency would be if Mark employed two salespersons, Rob and Susan. Rob is the listing salesperson for Roomy Manor, and Susan meets and begins representing the buyer, Jennifer. Because both Rob and Susan are associated with Mark's real estate brokerage, Mark may be construed as a dual agent and will have to enter into a disclosed dual-agency agreement with the parties.

Disclosed dual agency.

In this case, dual agency is purposely created. In North Carolina, the key to **lawful** dual agency is that *all parties (seller/ buyer, lessor/lesee) must be informed* and must *consent* to the broker representing both of them in the same transaction. In North Carolina, a firm that represents more than one party in the same real estate transaction is a dual agent and must disclose its dual agency to the parties. The written authority for dual agency must be *obtained upon the formation of the relationship, except when an agent is working with a buyer or tenant under an oral agency agreement pursuant to A.0104(a), in which event the express oral authority for dual agency must be* reduced to writing not later than the time that one of the parties represented by the agent makes an offer to purchase, sell, rent, lease, or exchange real estate to another party. Though the possibility of conflict of interest still exists, the disclosure is intended to minimize the risk for the broker and ensure that both principals are aware of its effect on their respective interests.

Designated agency.

Designated agency is sometimes used when a transaction is an in-house sale. It involves appointing one agent of a firm to represent the seller and appointing another agent of the same firm to represent the buyer in the same real estate transaction. However, it must be done with prior express approval of both parties. The firm acts as a dual agent; the individual agents do not. The major advantage of designated agency is that both of the firm's clients (the seller and the buyer) receive a fuller and more direct representation from their respective designated agent.

> *Designated agency occurs in an in-house transaction, when the BIC appoints one agent to represent the buyer and appoints another agent to represent the seller.*

If a firm wants to practice designated agency, the broker-in-charge (BIC) must establish a comprehensive written company policy on designated agency, and this policy must comply with Commission Rules. Firms electing to practice designated agency must specify who within the firm is authorized to appoint designated agents. This person is normally the BIC.

If a firm practices dual agency and designated agency, full written disclosure of this practice should be given to clients and customers at the earliest opportunity. When a firm enters into an agency contract with the seller-client or buyer-client, the client must be given an opportunity to indicate in writing which agency relationship he or she is authorizing. This fulfills the legal requirement for written informed consent. *The authority for designated agency must be reduced to writing not later than the time that the parties are required to reduce their dual agency agreement to writing.*

The BIC must follow current legal restrictions when appointing the designated agent. *If the BIC represents one of the parties as a designated agent, the BIC can appoint only a licensed broker as the designated agent for the other party.* The BIC cannot appoint a licensed salesman as a designated agent if the BIC represents the other party [see Rule A.0104(j)]. The BIC may, however, appoint another licensed broker to represent one party and appoint a licensed salesman to represent the other party.

Commission rules impose another major restriction on the appointment of a designated agent. A real estate agent's duty of confidentiality cannot be breached; to do so would benefit one client to the detriment of the other and would compromise the firm's position as a dual agent. Therefore, if an agent has received *confidential* (and potentially damaging) *information* about one party to the transaction, that agent has an obligation to refuse an appointment as the designated agent of the other party to the transaction. An agent who becomes a designated agent under these circumstances creates potential legal liability for the firm as well as becoming subject to possible disciplinary action by the Commission. Note that while confidential information must be kept confidential, agents must disclose any information required by law to be disclosed, such as material facts about the property.

Some important points about designated agency include the following:

- To become a dual agent, there must be a client relationship with both the seller and the buyer within the same firm.
- There cannot be a designated agency unless there is first a dual agency in existence.
- The rule of confidentiality cannot be broken.
- Designated agency is a form of dual agency that is optional, but it does bring more structure to the transaction.
- To practice designated agency, the firm's policy must authorize it and both parties must give their consent.

Throughout any discussion of agency duties, it is important to remember that an agent's duties to the principal are greater than the agent's duties to the customer (third person). However, a dual agent represents both parties. Therefore, he or she is generally restricted from disclosing to either client information that does not relate directly to the property, such as the personal situation of either party, the financial status of either party, the prices willing to be offered or accepted by either party, any unusual pressure on either party to buy or sell, etc. As mentioned earlier, a dual agent *is required by law* to disclose all material facts about the property to either and both principals.

Agency relationships in real estate rentals. Another type of brokerage contract that creates an agency relationship is the Property Management Agreement, which is entered into between a management firm or broker and a property owner who wishes to hire someone to manage his or her rental properties. *As with all agency agreements involving a property owner, the property management agreement must be in writing from the formation of the relationship.* The property manager/broker becomes the agent and the property owner becomes the principal. The fiduciary—agency—relationship between the property manager/broker and the property owner is the same as that between the broker and the property seller. Any licensed employees of the property manager/broker become subagents of the property owner. Prospective tenants *are* customers (or third parties) of the property manager, *who* owe certain duties *to the tenants* imposed by North Carolina Real Estate Law (*N.C.G.S. Chapter* 93A), fair housing laws (discussed in Chapter 7), and landlord /tenant laws (discussed in Chapter 10). *A property manager of residential property usually will represent only the property owner and will not seek to represent the tenant as well, which would cause the agent to become a dual agent. However, whenever an agent seeks to establish an agency relationship with a tenant thereby making the tenant a client, the*agreement for brokerage services between *the* broker and *the* tenant shall be express and shall be reduced to writing not later than the time any party makes an offer to rent or lease property.

AGENCY DISCLOSURE

To resolve some of the confusion surrounding agency relationships, North Carolina requires that real estate agents must disclose their agency status to both buyers and sellers in every real estate transaction.

A real estate licensee (broker or salesperson) may enter into an oral buyer agency agreement at first substantial contact with a prospective buyer [Rule A.0104 (a)]. At the first substantial contact with a buyer or seller, an agent must provide the buyer or seller with a copy of the Commission-published brochure entitled *Working With Real Estate Agents.* The text of this brochure is shown in Figure 6.3.

In every real estate *sales* transaction the agent shall provide the brochure to a prospective buyer or seller at first substantial contact. The agent must review the brochure with the buyer or seller and make a determination if the agent will act as the agent of the seller or the agent of the buyer. An agency relationship cannot be formed without this review. The nature and obligations of an agency relationship must be clearly explained to the customer so that the customer understands that the agent owes all client-level fiduciary duties only to the client-principal.

Each prospective seller and buyer must be given a copy of the brochure at first substantial contact. The brochure contains information on the various agency relationships such as (1) seller's agent, (2) dual agent, (3) buyer's agent and (4) seller's agent working with a buyer. If the first substantial contact does not occur "face-to-face," then the brochure must be mailed, faxed or e-mailed to the prospective buyer or seller as soon as possible, but in no event later than three (3) calendar days from the date of first substantial contact. Then, the agent must review the contents of the brochure with the prospective seller or buyer at the earliest opportunity thereafter. The brochure can be reformatted to allow for various means of communication, but the text cannot be changed. It must be exactly as printed by the Commission. The brochure is not designed to replace the review and explanation of agency by the agent, but rather to facilitate this explanation. The brochure contains a "tear-off" panel for the buyer or seller to sign, acknowledging receipt and review of the contents by the agent. The agent must keep this panel on file as proof of compliance with Rule A.0104. [See Rule A.0108.]

Rule A.0104(e) also requires a seller's agent or subagent working with a prospective buyer to disclose in writing at first substantial contact their agency status of representing the seller. If first substantial contact occurs other than a face-to-face meeting where it is not practical to provide written disclosure, the broker or salesperson shall immediately disclose by similar means whom he or she represents and shall immediately, but in no event later than three calendar days from the first substantial contact, mail or otherwise transmit a copy of the written disclosure to the buyer. Note that this written disclosure of seller agency or subagency to the prospective buyer now may be accomplished merely by checking the box at the bottom of the tear-off panel of the brochure. (See Figure 6.3.)

An agent who works with and represents a buyer initially under an oral agreement must do so in a *"non-exclusive capacity."* ALL oral buyer agency agreements are non-exclusive! Any buyer agency agreement which seeks to bind the buyer to the agent or firm for a particular time period or which pro-

Figure 6.3   *Text from the Working with Real Estate Agents Brochure*

WORKING WITH REAL ESTATE AGENTS

When buying or selling real estate, you may find it helpful to have a real estate agent assist you. Real estate agents can provide many useful services and work with you in different ways. In some real estate transactions, the agents work for the seller. In others, the seller and buyer may each have agents. And sometimes the same agents work for both the buyer and the seller. It is important for you to know whether an agent is working for you as your agent or simply working with you while acting as an agent of the other party.

This brochure addresses the various types of working relationships that may be available to you. It should help you decide which relationship you want to have with a real estate agent. It will also give you useful information about the various services real estate agents can provide buyers and sellers, and it will help explain how real estate agents are paid.

SELLERS

Seller's Agent

If you are selling real estate, you may want to "list" your property for sale with a real estate firm. If so, you will sign a "listing agreement" authorizing the firm and its agents to represent you in your dealings with buyers as your *seller's agent*. You may also be asked to allow agents from other firms to help find a buyer for your property.

Be sure to read and understand the listing agreement before you sign it.

Duties to Seller: The listing firm and its agents must • promote your best interests • be loyal to you • follow your lawful instructions • provide you with all material facts that could influence your decisions • use reasonable skill, care and diligence, and • account for all monies they handle for you. Once you have signed the listing agreement, the firm and its agents may not give any confidential information about you to prospective buyers or their agents without your permission. But until you sign the listing agreement, you should avoid telling the listing agent anything you would *not* want a buyer to know.

Services and Compensation: To help you sell your property, the listing firm and its agents will offer to perform a number of services for you. These may include • helping you price your property • advertising and marketing your property • giving you all required property disclosure forms for you to complete • negotiating for you the best possible price and terms • reviewing all written offers with you and • otherwise promoting your interests.

For representing you and helping you sell your property, you will pay the listing firm a sales commission or fee. The listing agreement must state the amount or method for determining the commission or fee and whether the firm will allow the firm to share its commission with agents representing the buyer.

Dual Agent

You may even permit the listing firm and its agents to represent you and a buyer at the same time. This "dual agency relationship" is most likely to happen if an agent with your listing firm is working as a *buyer's agent* with someone who wants to purchase your property. If this occurs and you have not already agreed to a dual agency relationship in your listing agreement, your listing agent will ask you to sign a separate agreement or document permitting the agent to act as agent for both you and the buyer.

It may be difficult for a *dual agent* to advance the interests of both the buyer and seller. Nevertheless, a *dual agent* must treat buyers and sellers fairly and equally. Although the *dual agent* owes them the same duties, buyers and sellers can prohibit *dual agents* from divulging certain confidential information about them to the other party.

Some firms also offer a form of dual agency called "designated agency" where one agent in the firm represents the seller and another agent represents the buyer. This option (when available) may allow each "designated agent" to more fully represent each party.

If you choose the "dual agency" option, remember that since a dual agent's loyalty is divided between parties with competing interests, it is especially important that you have a clear understanding of • what your relationship is with the *dual agent* and • what the agent will be doing for you in the transaction.

BUYERS

When buying real estate, you may have several choices as to how you want a real estate firm and its agents to work with you. For example, you may want them to represent only you (as a **buyer's agent**). You may be willing for them to represent both you and the seller at the same time (as a dual agent). Or you may agree to let them represent only the seller (seller's agent or subagent). Some agents will offer you a choice of these services. Others may not.

Buyer's Agent

Duties to Buyer: If the real estate firm and its agents represent you, they must • promote your best interests • be loyal to you • follow your lawful instructions • provide you with all material facts that could influence your decisions • use reasonable skill, care and diligence, and • account for all monies they handle for you. Once you have agreed (either orally or in writing) for the firm and its agents to be your *buyer's agent*, they may not give any confidential information about you to sellers or their agents without your permission. But until you make this agreement with your buyer's agent, you should avoid telling the agent anything you would *not* want a seller to know.

Unwritten Agreements: To make sure that you and the real estate firm have a clear understanding of what your relationship will be and what the firm will do for you, you may want to have a written agreement. However, some firms may be willing to represent and assist you for a time as a *buyer's agent* without a written agreement. But if you decide to make an offer to purchase a particular property, the agent must obtain a written agency agreement. If you do not sign it, the agent can no longer represent and assist you and is no

Continued on the back

Figure 6.3   Text from the Working with Real Estate Agents Brochure (continued)

longer required to keep information about you confidential. Furthermore, if you later purchase the property through an agent with another firm, the agent who first showed you the property may seek compensation from the other firm.

Be sure to read and understand any agency agreement before you sign it.

Services and Compensation: Whether you have a written or unwritten agreement, a *buyer's agent* will perform a number of services for you. These may include helping you • find a suitable property • arrange financing • learn more about the property and • otherwise promote your best interests. If you have a written agency agreement, the agent can also help you prepare and submit a written offer to the seller.

A *buyer's agent* can be compensated in different ways. For example, you can pay the agent out of your own pocket. Or the agent may seek compensation from the seller or listing agent first, but require you to pay if the listing agent refuses. Whatever the case, be sure your compensation arrangement with your *buyer's agent* is spelled out in a buyer agency agreement before you make an offer to purchase property and that you carefully read and understand the compensation provision.

Dual Agent

You may permit an agent or firm to represent you and the seller at the same time. This "dual agency relationship" is most likely to happen if you become interested in a property listed with your *buyer's agent* or the agent's firm. If this occurs and you have not already agreed to a dual agency relationship in your (written or oral) buyer agency agreement, your *buyer's agent* will ask you to sign a separate agreement or document permitting him or her to act as agent for both you and the seller. It may be difficult for a *dual agent* to advance the interests of both the buyer and seller. Nevertheless, a *dual agent* must treat buyers and sellers fairly and equally. Although the *dual agent* owes them the same duties, buyers and sellers can prohibit *dual agents* from divulging certain confidential information about them to the other party.

Some firms also offer a form of dual agency called "designated agency" where one agent in the firm represents the seller and another agent represents the buyer. This option (when available) may allow each "designated agent" to more fully represent each party.

If you choose the "dual agency" option, remember that since a *dual agent's* loyalty is divided between parties with competing interests, it is especially important that you have a clear understanding of
• what your relationship is with the *dual agent* and
• what the agent will be doing for you in the transaction.
This can best be accomplished by putting the agreement in writing at the earliest possible time.

Seller's Agent Working With a Buyer

If the real estate agent or firm that you contact does not offer *buyer agency* or you do not want them to act as your *buyer agent*, you can still work with the firm and its agents. However, they will be acting as the *seller's agent* (or "subagent"). The agent can still help you find and purchase property and provide many of the same services as a *buyer's agent*. The agent must be fair with you and provide you with any "material facts" (such as a leaky roof) about properties.

But remember, the agent represents the seller—not you— and therefore must try to obtain for the seller the best possible price and terms for the seller's property. Furthermore, a *seller's agent* is required to give the seller any information about you (even personal, financial or confidential information) that would help the seller in the sale of his or her property. Agents must tell you *in writing* if they are *sellers' agents* before you say anything that can help the seller. But until you are sure that an agent is not a *seller's agent*, you should avoid saying anything you do *not* want a seller to know. *Sellers' agents* are compensated by the sellers.

The North Carolina Real Estate Commission
P.O. Box 17100 • Raleigh, North Carolina 27619-7100
919/875-3700 • Web Site: www.ncrec.state.nc.us
REC 3.45 5/1/01

00,000 copies of this public document were printed at a cost of $.00 per copy.

WORKING WITH REAL ESTATE AGENTS

This is not a contract

By signing, I acknowledge that the agent named below furnished a copy of this brochure and reviewed it with me.

_____
Buyer or Seller Name (Print or Type)

_____
Buyer or Seller Signature

_____
Buyer or Seller Name (Print or Type)

_____
Buyer or Seller Signature

_____
Date

_____
Firm Name

_____
Agent Name

Disclosure of Seller Subagency

☐ *When showing you property and assisting you in the purchase of a property, the above agent and firm will represent the SELLER. For more information, see "Seller's Agent Working with a Buyer" in the brochure.*

Buyer's Initials Acknowledging Disclosure: _____

Agents must retain this acknowledgment for their files.

hibits the buyer from working with other agents or firms must be in writing from the start. Under the oral buyer agency agreement, a buyer is free to enter into similar agreements with other firms and agents. An oral agreement is considered to be of indefinite duration and can be terminated at the will of either party at any time.

For Example Bull Broker is contacted by a prospective buyer to look at properties for sale. During the initial interview Bull merely hands the brochure to the buyer without any explanation or review and tells the buyer he will represent the buyer as their agent during this transaction. The question is: Has a buyer agency been formed? The answer is no. The brochure must be reviewed and the agent and prospective buyer must determine and agree in what capacity the agent will work with the buyer—whether as a seller's subagent or as a buyer's agent, and if the latter, whether under an oral or written buyer agency agreement.

Rule A.0104 (a) also states, "A broker or salesperson shall not continue to represent a buyer or tenant without a written agreement when such agreement is required by this rule." An agent must enter into a written buyer agency agreement no later than the time an offer to purchase is presented to a seller or the seller's agent and may *not* actually present the offer to the seller's agent unless the buyer-client first has signed a *written* buyer agency agreement. An agent may enter into an oral buyer agency agreement at first substantial contact, but the rule does not prohibit the agent from getting it in writing at first substantial contact. The agent should attempt to get the agency agreement in writing as soon as possible.

For Example Bubba Broker has given the prospective buyer the brochure at first substantial contact, has reviewed it with the buyer and has entered into an oral buyer agency agreement with the buyer. There is a full oral agreement that Bubba will act as the buyer's agent. The buyer finds a home and wants to make an offer. After the offer has been prepared and before presentation to the seller or seller's agent, Bubba attempts to get the buyer agency agreement in writing and signed by the buyer as required by Rule A.0104(a). The buyer refuses to sign the buyer agency agreement. At this time, Bubba can no longer represent the buyer, but can present the offer acting as the seller's subagent. Of course as the seller's subagent, Bubba must share information about the buyer "customer" with the seller-client, and is no longer required to keep information about the buyer confidential.

In the above example the broker must follow very specific conditions in order to present the offer as a seller's agent or subagent:

- The broker must clearly explain to the buyer that the broker will now represent the seller and will have a duty to the now "seller-client" to convey any information, confidential or not, about the now "buyer-customer" that the broker learned during their relationship as buyer agent under the previous oral agreement.
- The broker must officially terminate the oral buyer agency agreement in writing, which should include the former buyer client's consent to do so, and an understanding that confidential information must be revealed.
- The broker must have the consent from the listing firm to act as a seller's subagent and must provide written disclosure of his seller subagency status to the buyer.

Note: prior to switching to seller subagency, the oral buyer agent should consider entering into a written buyer agency agreement limited solely to that property, which few reasonable buyers should refuse.

Because an agent may now work with a buyer under an oral buyer agency agreement, the rule of necessity allows an agent to enter into an oral dual agency agreement which must be put in writing no later than the time an offer is presented. In order to work under an oral dual agency, the dual agency arrangement must have been discussed and the prospective buyer must orally agree for the agent to be a dual agent at the time the oral buyer agency is established. The same applies to designated agency.

The following may be used as a checklist to properly follow disclosure rules:

1. The brochure must be given to prospective sellers and buyers upon first substantial contact in all real estate sales transactions.
2. The agent must review the brochure and a determination of agency status must take place. The buyer/seller must acknowledge receipt by signing the tear-off panel to be retained by the agent.
3. Listing agreements are REQUIRED TO be in writing from the start.
4. The rule ALLOWS for an agent to act as a buyer's agent, a dual agent or a designated agent under an oral agreement, until such time as the agreements must be put in writing, which is not later than the time an offer is going to be presented.
5. Any buyer agency agreement that sets forth exclusivity or a definite period of time must be in writing from the start.

DUTIES AND LIABILITIES OF AGENTS

Agent's Responsibilities to Principal

As mentioned earlier, an agency relationship is a **fiduciary** relationship, one of trust and confidence between the broker and the principal. In a fiduciary relationship, the broker, by law, owes the principal specific duties—the duties of care, obedience, accounting, loyalty and disclosure, easily remembered by the acronym **COALD** (see Figure 6.4). These duties are described below. Note that such duties are not simply moral or ethical obligations; they are the law—the law of agency.

Care, skill and diligence. The broker must exercise a reasonable degree of care, skill and diligence while transacting the business entrusted by the principal. The principal expects the agent's skill and expertise in real estate matters to be superior to that of the average person.

The most fundamental way in which the broker exercises care is to use that skill and knowledge on the principal's behalf. The broker should know all facts that are pertinent to the principal's affairs, such as the physical characteristics of the property being transferred and the type of financing being used.

If the broker represents the seller, care and skill include helping the seller arrive at an appropriate and realistic listing price, discovering facts that affect the seller and disclosing them and properly presenting the contracts that the seller signs. Care and skill also mean making reasonable efforts to market the property, such as advertising and holding open houses, and helping the seller evaluate the terms and conditions of offers to purchase.

A broker who represents the buyer will be expected to help the buyer locate suitable property and evaluate property values, neighborhood and property conditions, financing alternatives and offers and counteroffers with the

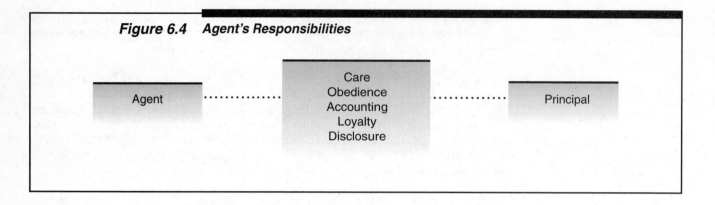

Figure 6.4   Agent's Responsibilities

buyer's interest in mind. A broker who does not make a reasonable effort to properly represent the interests of the principal could be found negligent. The broker is liable to the principal for any loss resulting from negligence or carelessness.

Obedience. The fiduciary relationship obligates the broker to act in good faith at all times, obeying the principal's instructions in accordance with the contract. That obedience is not absolute, however. The broker may not obey any instructions that are unlawful or unethical. For example, the broker may not follow instructions to make the property unavailable to members of a minority group or to conceal a defect in the property. Because illegal acts do not serve the principal's best interest, obeying such instructions violates the broker's duty of loyalty. On the other hand, a broker who exceeds the authority assigned in the contract is liable for any losses that the principal suffers as a result.

Accounting. The broker must be able to report the status of all funds received from, or on behalf of, the principal. Real estate license laws require that brokers give accurate copies of all documents to all parties affected by them and keep copies of such documents on file for three years (see Rule A.0108). In addition, the license laws generally require that the broker deposit immediately all trust funds entrusted to him or her in a special trust account (see Rule A.0107). It is illegal for the broker to commingle such monies with personal funds. *Commingling* is a term used to describe when trust funds and the broker's personal/business funds are placed in the same account.

For Example A broker has accepted an earnest money deposit in connection with an offer to purchase and deposits that money into his business account. The broker receives an earned commission check from another firm and deposits that check into the trust account. Both are examples of commingling, a mixing of trust funds with non-trust funds. Licensing law in North Carolina prohibits commingling.

Loyalty. The broker owes the principal the utmost loyalty. That means placing the principal's interests above those of all others, including the broker's own. The agent must be particularly sensitive to any possible conflicts of interest. *Confidentiality* about the principal's personal affairs is a key element of loyalty. An agent may not, for example, disclose the principal's financial condition. When the principal is the seller, the agent may not reveal such things as the principal's willingness to accept less than the listing price or his or her anxiousness to sell unless the principal has authorized the disclosure. If the principal is the buyer, the agent may not disclose,

for instance, that the buyer will pay more than the offered price if necessary, or that the buyer is under a tight moving schedule or any other fact that might harm the principal's bargaining position. (These are several reasons why undisclosed dual agency could result in rescission, monetary damages, and forfeiture of commission and loss of license.)

Because the agent may not act out of self-interest, the negotiation of a sales contract must be conducted without regard to how much the agent will earn in commission. All states forbid agents to buy property listed with them for their own use or in which they have a personal interest without first disclosing that interest and receiving the principal's consent. An agent must disclose to his/her client any personal or business relationship the agent may have with another party to the transaction, even if it is a former relationship. North Carolina Real Estate License Law and agency law require a buyer's agent to disclose to the buyer-client any personal interest that agent may have in the property. If the licensee is a seller's agent, there is no duty to disclose to the buyer the licensee's personal interest.

For Example Broker Larry's sister owns a piece of property that she bought several years ago with Larry acting as her agent. She now wants to sell it as a For Sale by Owner. She asks Larry to help her sell at the highest possible price, even though the property is not listed with Larry. Larry has a buyer client who is interested in the property and wants to make an offer to purchase. Larry does not reveal his relationship with the seller and tries to get the buyer to make a higher-than-market-value offer. Larry has clearly violated his loyalty to his principal, the buyer.

Disclosure. Along with these four responsibilities goes the duty of disclosure, sometimes called *notice.* It is the broker's duty to keep the principal fully informed at all times of all facts or information the broker obtains that could affect a transaction. A broker who fails to disclose such information, such as the fact that a purchaser does not qualify for a low down payment, may be held liable for any damages that result.

The real estate agent also may be liable for facts he or she *should have known* and revealed to the principal but did not. This duty of *discovery* includes facts favorable or unfavorable to the principal's position, even if the disclosure of those facts would end the transaction.

An agent for the seller has a duty to disclose

- all offers (see Rule A.0106.);
- the identity of the prospective purchasers, including the agent's relationship, if any, to them (such as a relative of the broker being a participating purchaser);
- the ability of the purchaser to complete the sale or offer a higher price;
- any interest the broker has in the buyer (such as the buyer's asking the broker to manage the property after it is purchased); and
- the buyer's intention to resell the property for a profit.

An agent for the buyer must disclose deficiencies of a property as well as sales contract provisions and financing that do not suit the buyer's needs.

The broker should suggest the lowest price that the buyer should pay based on comparable values, regardless of the listing price. The agent should disclose information that could affect the buyer's ability to negotiate the lowest purchase price, such as how long a property has been listed or why the seller is selling.

North Carolina requires that sellers of certain residential properties give the buyer a property disclosure statement. While the real estate agent is not required to fill out the form or give it to the buyer, the agent is required to inform the seller of his or her responsibilities in regard to the property disclosure. Property disclosure is discussed in more detail in Chapter 8.

Agent's Responsibilities to Third Parties

Even though an agent's primary responsibility is to the principal, the agent also has duties to third parties. The duties of the agent to the third party come from three sources: (1) North Carolina license law, (2) the North Carolina Unfair or Deceptive Trade Practices Act and (3) court cases. These duties include

- being honest and fair,
- disclosing all material facts known to the agent that affect the value or desirability of the property and that are not known to the third party and
- complying with North Carolina real estate licensing law and commission rules.

When working with a buyer, a broker (as an agent of the seller) must exercise extreme caution and have knowledge of the laws and ethical considerations that affect this relationship. For example, brokers must be careful about the statements they or their sales staff make about a parcel of real estate. General statements of opinion are permissible as long as they are offered as opinions and without any intent to deceive.

Statements of fact, however, must be accurate. Statements that exaggerate a property's benefits are called **puffing.** Although puffing is legal and a common practice, it must not constitute a misrepresentation of the property. Brokers and salespeople must ensure that none of their statements can be interpreted as involving **fraud.** Fraud is the *intentional* misrepresentation of a material fact in such a way as to harm or take advantage of another person. In addition to false statements about a property, the concept of fraud covers intentional concealment or nondisclosure of important facts. If a contract to purchase real estate is obtained as a result of fraudulent misstatements made by a broker or by that broker's salespeople, the contract may be disaffirmed or renounced by the purchaser. In such a case, the broker will lose a commission. If either party suffers loss because of a broker's misrepresentations, the broker can be held liable for damages. If the broker's misstatements are based on the owner's own inaccurate statements to the broker, however, and the broker had no independent duty to investigate their accuracy, the broker may be entitled to a commission even if the buyer rescinds the sales contract.

Agents must also be careful not to make any misrepresentations or omissions where **material facts** are concerned. Misrepresentation or omission of a material fact by brokers or salespeople is prohibited in North Carolina, and this prohibition includes both "willful" and "negligent" acts. A *willful act* is one that is done intentionally and deliberately, while a *negligent act* is one that is done unintentionally. A *misrepresentation* is communicating false information, while an *omission* is failing to provide or disclose information where there was a duty to provide or disclose such information [see G.S. 93A-6(a)(1)].

Whether a fact is "material" depends on the facts and circumstances of a particular transaction and the application of statutory and/or case law. The North Carolina Real Estate Commission has historically interpreted "material facts" under the Real Estate License Law to include at least:

- *facts about the property itself* (such as a structural defect or defective mechanical systems),
- *facts relating directly to the property* (such as a pending zoning change or planned highway construction in the immediate vicinity) and
- *facts relating directly to the ability of the agent's principal to complete the transaction* (such as a pending foreclosure sale).

Prohibited Conduct   North Carolina real estate licensing law specifically prohibits the following types of acts in the agent's relationship with any party to the transaction [G.S. 93A-6(a)(1)]:

- *Willful misrepresentation:* intentionally misinforming any party involved in a transaction about a material fact
- *Negligent misrepresentation:* unintentionally misinforming any party involved in a transaction about a material fact
- *Willful omission:* intentionally failing to disclose a material fact to any party involved in a transaction
- *Negligent omission:* unintentionally failing to disclose a material fact to any party involved in a transaction

Willful misrepresentation. Willful misrepresentation takes place when agents who have "actual knowledge" of a material fact deliberately misinform a buyer, seller, tenant or landlord concerning such fact. Willful misrepresentation also takes place when an agent who does *not* have actual knowledge of a matter material to the transaction intentionally provides information concerning such matter to a buyer, seller, tenant or landlord without regard for the truthfulness of the information. (See the examples that follow.) This is an act that is intentional on the part of the agent. An agent could also be involved in "indirect misrepresentation", which occurs when an agent misrepresents a material fact to a subagent who in turn passes it on to a third party. If a material fact is misrepresented, courts could provide relief to the injured party in the form of damages or recission of the contract. An agent guilty of misrepresentation could also face disciplinary action by the North Carolina Real Estate Commission.

For Example An agent tells a buyer the cost of utilities is very reasonable without verification from the owner. If the costs are very high, the agent could be guilty of willful misrepresentation.

For Example An agent tells a buyer the foundation of a house is sound and has been properly built, when the agent knows the foundation is substandard and improperly constructed.

For Example A builder explains to an agent that the poor exterior wall insulation resulted from the developer's overall goal of containing cost. When this agent's buyer-client asks about the insulation, the agent replied that the builder was highly reputable and he was certain the insulation met the necessary standards.

For Example A buyer signs a buyer agency agreement with an agent. The buyer wants to purchase property with low taxes. The agent informs the buyer that a particular property has annual taxes of $600 when in fact the agent knows the new assessed value will increase taxes to $1,200.

Negligent misrepresentation. Negligent misrepresentation takes place when agents *unintentionally* misinform a buyer, seller, tenant or landlord concerning a material fact because they do not have actual knowledge of the fact, because they have incorrect information or because of a mistake by the agent. If the agent "should reasonably have known" the truth of the matter that was misrepresented, then the agent may be guilty of "negligent misrepresentation" even though he or she was acting in good faith. The fact that the agent was ignorant about the issue is no excuse. If a buyer relies on the agent's statement, the agent is liable for any damages that may result. If a buyer's agent relies on incorrect information provided by a listing (seller's) agent through the MLS property data, even with disclaimers, the selling agent may be held liable if he or she should reasonably have known the information was incorrect.

For Example A listing agent relies on an appraiser's report that a house has 2,500 square feet of heated living floor space, and enters that information into the MLS property data. However, the house actually has 2,000 square feet. In this case, a prudent and knowledgeable agent should have personally measured the house and accurately calculated the square footage. If the agent relied on the appraiser's report and informed a buyer the house has 2,500 square feet, she has made a negligent misrepresentation.

For Example An agent tells a buyer-client that the home being shown has Levelor blinds throughout, without actually checking the brand name. The blinds are actually cheap imported imitations of Levelor blinds.

Willful omission. Willful omission takes place when agents have "actual knowledge" of a material fact and a duty to disclose such fact to a buyer, seller, tenant or landlord but deliberately fail to disclose such fact.

For Example An agent knows that a highway relocation is pending that would adversely affect value and use of a property a buyer wants to purchase but does not reveal this to the buyer.

For Example An agent lists a property in midwinter knowing that the air-conditioning system does not operate properly but does not reveal that fact to a prospective buyer.

Negligent omission. Negligent omission takes place when agents do *not* have actual knowledge of a material fact but "should reasonably have known" of such fact. If they fail to disclose this fact to a buyer, seller, tenant or landlord, they may be guilty of "negligent omission," even though they acted in good faith in the transaction.

Agents have an obligation to "discover and disclose" material facts about the property that any prudent agent would reasonably have discovered during the transaction. A listing agent would be held more accountable than would a selling agent in discovery and disclosure of defects in the property because of his or her direct fiduciary relationship with the seller and the fact that the listing agent inspected the property and should be more familiar with the property than the selling agent.

For Example An agent has listed a property in a neighborhood where a vacant lot is being considered by the city for installation of a garbage recycling system. The plan has been well publicized in the news media, which also has given much publicity to the fact that the neighbors have filed legal action against the city. The agent does not reveal this information to a buyer and, when questioned, states that he was not aware of these plans.

Frequently, the buyer or the buyer's mortgage lender will request inspections or tests to determine the presence or level of risk. Licensees are urged to obtain advice from state and local authorities responsible for environmental regulation whenever toxic waste dumping, contaminated soil or water, nearby chemical or nuclear facilities, or health hazards such as radon, asbestos and lead paint may be present.

In Practice   The North Carolina Real Estate Commission has published other examples of these prohibited acts in the Study Guide section of *Real Estate Licensing In North Carolina,* to which the student is referred. Students should be thoroughly familiar with these topics.

Stigmatized Properties   In the past few years, brokers have encountered what are called **stigmatized properties,** those properties branded by society as undesirable because of events that occurred there. Such properties are typically marked by a criminal event: a homicide, suicide or other violence; illegal drug or gang-related activity; or other events that render the property socially unmarketable in the community's view.

Under current North Carolina law, the death—even the violent death—or serious illness of a previous owner of a residential property is not a material fact. Thus, it need not be disclosed to a prospective buyer. However, if the prospective buyer specifically asks the agent about the death or illness, the agent must answer truthfully. The one exception to this rule is if the death

or illness is AIDS-related. Because persons with AIDS (or HIV infection) are considered legally handicapped under fair housing laws, an agent cannot disclose this condition, even if asked. Instead, the agent should tell the person who asked the question that the agent is prohibited by law from answering the question.

In Practice   Because real estate licensees have, under the law, enormous exposure to liability, some brokers purchase errors and omissions insurance policies for their firms. Similar to malpractice insurance in the medical field, such policies generally cover liability for errors, mistakes and negligence in the usual listing and selling activities of a real estate office. Individual salespeople, likewise, should be insured. Note that no insurance will protect a licensee from litigation arising from criminal acts. Also, insurance companies normally exclude coverage for violation of civil rights laws. Nor will errors and omission insurance relieve a licensed agent from disciplinary action by the Real Estate Commission.

Liabilities and Consequences of Breach of Duty

Any agent who breaches his or her duties to either the principal or a third party must bear the consequences of that breach. These consequences may include any (or all) of the following:

- Disciplinary action by the North Carolina Real Estate Commission. Any violation of a duty owed to the principal or third parties is grounds for disciplinary action by the Real Estate Commission. If the commission finds that the agent did in fact violate the license law, that agent's license may be revoked or suspended.
- A civil action in court brought by the injured party. If the breach of duty harms either the principal or a third party, the agent may be sued and found liable for the damages caused by the breach. Note that if the agent's improper behavior is deemed to be within the scope of his or her duties, the agent's principal also may be held liable for the damages caused by the agent. The principal can in turn sue the agent for reimbursement for those damages.
- Criminal prosecution brought by the district attorney. A violation of a provision of the real estate law is also a misdemeanor (see G.S. 93A-56). If the agent's breach of duty is also a criminal act, such as fraud or embezzlement, the state's district attorney may bring a criminal action against the agent.

DUTIES AND LIABILITIES OF PRINCIPALS

Duties to Agent

The principal has two basic duties to his or her agent:

1. To act in good faith (to cooperate with the agent and refrain from hindering the agent's efforts to find a buyer). For example, if the principal refuses to let the agent show a home, this is a breach of good faith.
2. To pay the agent the agreed-on compensation when the agent finds a ready, willing and able buyer. Once the agent brings the seller a buyer who is ready, willing and able to purchase the property on the seller's terms, the agent has earned his or her commission, whether or not the seller decides to sell the home.

Duties to Third Parties

Historically, real estate transactions were governed by the doctrine of caveat emptor, or "let the buyer beware." The principal was liable to a buyer only if the principal willfully misrepresented the property. It was up to the buyer to thoroughly examine and research the property, and the buyer was, for all intents and purposes, expected to purchase the property "as is." Property owners had no affirmative duty to reveal defects about the property. This is still true in North Carolina. However, this principle has been gradually eroded by both court decisions and consumer protection laws.

Liabilities and Consequences of Breach of Duty

The principal who violates his or her duties either to the agent or to a third party is liable for the damage caused. The principal may be subject to both a civil lawsuit and criminal prosecution (if so warranted). The principal also may be held liable and accountable for the agent's misconduct, referred to as a **tort,** which is a wrongful act by an agent while representing the principal and *acting within the scope of the employment agreement that created the agency.*

NATURE OF THE BROKERAGE BUSINESS

Regardless of whether he or she is affiliated with a national franchise or marketing organization, a real estate broker is an independent businessperson who sets the policies of his or her own office. A broker engages employees and salespeople, determines their compensation and directs their activities. A broker is free to accept or reject agency relationships with principals. This is an important characteristic of the brokerage business: *a broker has the right to reject agency contracts that, in the broker's judgment, violate the ethics or high standards of the office.* However, once a brokerage relationship has been established, the broker represents the principal and owes that person the duty to exercise care, skill and integrity in carrying out instructions.

Broker-Salesperson Relationship

Although brokerage firms vary widely in size, few brokers today perform their agency duties without the assistance of salespeople. Consequently, much of the business's success hinges on the broker-salesperson relationship.

A *real estate salesperson* is any person licensed to perform real estate activities on behalf of a licensed real estate broker. The broker is fully responsible for the actions performed in the course of the real estate business by all persons licensed under him or her. In turn, *all of a salesperson's activities must be performed in the name of the supervising broker* (see Rule A.0506).

The salesperson can carry out only those responsibilities assigned by the broker with whom he or she is licensed and can receive compensation only from that broker (see Rule A.0109). As an agent of the broker, the salesperson has no authority to make contracts with or receive compensation from any other party, whether the principal, another broker, a buyer or a seller.

Independent contractor versus employee. The agreement between a broker and a salesperson should be set down in a written contract that defines the obligations and responsibilities of the relationship. Generally, the broker is liable for all brokerage acts performed by the salesperson. This is true despite the fact that a salesperson may be hired and considered by a broker for tax purposes as either an employee or an independent contractor. Whether a salesperson is treated as an employee or an independent contractor affects the structure of the salesperson's work responsibilities and the

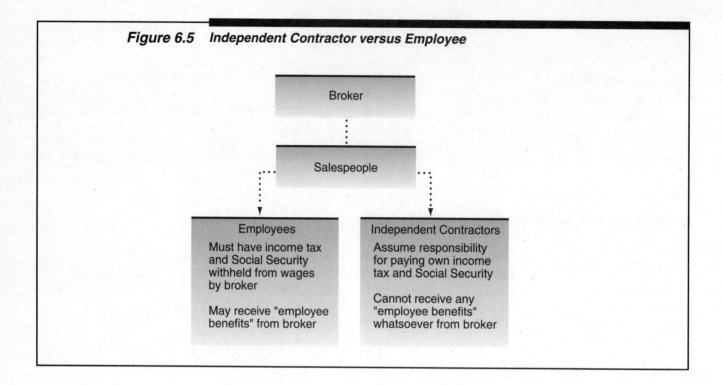

Figure 6.5   Independent Contractor versus Employee

Broker

Salespeople

Employees

Must have income tax and Social Security withheld from wages by broker

May receive "employee benefits" from broker

Independent Contractors

Assume responsibility for paying own income tax and Social Security

Cannot receive any "employee benefits" whatsoever from broker

broker's liability for paying and withholding taxes from the salesperson's earnings (see Figure 6.5).

The nature of the employer-employee relationship allows a broker to exercise certain controls over salespeople who are employees. The broker may require that an **employee** adhere more strictly to regulations concerning such matters as working hours and office routine. As an employer, the broker is required by the federal government to withhold Social Security tax and income tax from wages paid to employees. The broker is also required to pay unemployment compensation tax on wages paid to one or more employees, as defined by state and federal laws. In addition, the broker may provide employees with benefits such as health insurance and profit-sharing plans.

A broker's relationship with an **independent contractor** differs significantly. As an independent contractor, a salesperson operates with more autonomy than an employee, and the broker may not control the salesperson's activities in the same way. Basically, the broker may control what the independent contractor does but not *how* it is done. The independent contractor assumes responsibility for paying his or her own income and Social Security taxes. Also, the independent contractor receives nothing from the broker that could be construed as an employee benefit (such as health insurance).

In Practice   The Internal Revenue Service (IRS) often investigates the independent-contractor-versus-employee situation in real estate offices. Under the "qualified real estate agent" category in the Internal Revenue Code, three requirements can establish independent contractor status: (1) The individual must have a current real estate license. (2) He or she must have a written contract with the broker containing the following clause: "The salesperson will not be treated as an employee with respect to the services performed by such salesperson as a real estate agent for federal tax purposes." (3) Ninety percent or more of the individual's income as a licensee must be based on sales production and not on the number of hours worked. The broker should have a standardized agreement drawn up or reviewed by a lawyer to ensure its compliance with these federal dictates. The broker should also be aware that written agreements mean little to an IRS auditor if the actions of the parties are contrary to the document's provisions.

Antitrust Laws
The real estate industry is subject to federal and state **antitrust laws.** Generally, these laws prohibit monopolies and contracts, combinations and conspiracies that unreasonably restrain trade. The most common antitrust violations are price-fixing, group boycotting and allocation of customers or markets.

Price-fixing is the practice of setting prices for products or services rather than letting competition in the open market establish those prices. In real estate it occurs when brokers agree to set sales commissions, fees or management rates, and it is illegal. Brokers must independently determine commission rates or fees only for their own firms. These decisions must be based on the broker's business judgment and revenue requirements without input from other brokers.

Multiple-listing organizations, Boards of REALTORS® and other professional organizations may not set fees or commission splits. Nor are they allowed to deny membership to brokers based on the fees the brokers charge. Either practice could lead the public to believe that the industry sanctions not only the unethical practice of withholding cooperation from certain brokers but also the illegal practice of restricting open-market competition.

The broker's challenge is to avoid any impression of attempts at price-fixing as well as the actual practice. Hinting in any way to prospective clients that there is a "going rate" of compensation implies that rates are, in fact, standardized. A broker must clarify to clients that the rate stated is only what his or her firm charges. Likewise, discussions of rates among licensees from different firms could be construed as a price-fixing activity and should be avoided scrupulously.

The North Carolina Real Estate Commission is specifically prohibited by law (G.S.93A-3) from making rules and regulations that regulate or dictate commissions, salaries, or fees to be charged by licensees. Commission Rule A.0109(c) states: "The Commission shall not act as a board of arbitration and shall not compel parties to settle disputes concerning such matters as the rate of commission, the division of commissions, pay of salesmen, and similar matters." All commission arrangements between an agent and a principal must be made in a way that shows they have been negotiated between the principal and agent.

Group boycotting occurs when two or more businesses conspire against other businesses or agree to withhold their patronage to reduce competition. It also is illegal under the antitrust laws.

Allocating markets or customers involves an agreement between brokers to divide their markets and refrain from competing with each other for business. Allocations may be made on a geographic basis, with brokers agreeing to specific territories within which they will operate exclusively. The division may occur by markets, such as by price range. These agreements conspire to eliminate competition and are illegal.

The penalties for such acts are severe. For example, under the Sherman Antitrust Act people who are found guilty of fixing prices or allocating markets may be punishable by a maximum $100,000 fine and three years in prison. For corporations, the penalty may be as high as $1 million. In a civil suit a person who has suffered a loss because of the antitrust activities of a guilty party may recover triple the value of the actual damages plus attorney's fees and costs.

SUMMARY

Real estate brokerage is the business of bringing together, for a fee or commission, people who wish to buy, sell, exchange or lease real estate. An important part of real estate brokerage is the law of agency. A real estate broker may be hired by the seller or a buyer to sell or find a particular parcel of real estate. The broker represents the person who hired him and the trend is toward more buyer agents. The person who hires the broker is the principal. The principal and the agent have a fiduciary relationship under which the agent owes the principal the duties of care, obedience, accounting, loyalty and disclosure.

The law of agency governs the principal-agent relationship. Agency relationships may be either express, by the words of the parties or written agreement, or implied, by their actions. In single-agency relationships, the broker/agent represents one party, *either the property owner or the buyer/lessee*, in the transaction. If the agent solicits the assistance of other brokers who cooperate in the transaction, the other brokers are subagents of the principal. Representing two opposing parties in the same transaction is dual agency. Licensees must be careful not to create a dual agency when none was intended. This unintentional or inadvertent dual agency may result in the sales contract's being rescinded and the commission forfeited, or it may result in a lawsuit. Disclosed dual agency requires that both principals be informed and that both consent in writing to the broker's multiple representation. In any case, the prospective parties in the transaction should be informed about the agency alternatives and how client-level versus customer-level services differ.

Real estate agents must disclose their agency status to both buyers and sellers in all real estate sales transactions. This disclosure must be done by giving the buyer or seller the *Working with Real Estate Agents* brochure at first substantial contact. The agent must review and determine with the buyer or seller what the agency relationship will be. An agent with the consent of the buyer may act as a buyer agent, dual agent and/or designated agent under an oral buyer and/or dual agency agreement up until such time as the buyer wishes to make an offer. The buyer or dual agency relationship must be confirmed in writing prior to extending an offer to purchase to the seller or seller's agent. *An agency agreement with a property owner* must be in writing *from the formation of the relationship, namely, at the time the listing is taken or the property management arrangement is made.*

Licensees have certain duties and obligations to their customers as well. Customers are entitled to fair and honest dealings and information that is necessary for them to make informed decisions. This includes disclosing accurate information about property.

A broker may hire sales *agents, whether brokers or salespersons,* to assist in this work. *These agents* work on the broker's behalf as *salaried* employees or an independent contractors.

Many of the general operations of a real estate brokerage are regulated by the real estate license laws. In addition, state and federal antitrust laws prohibit brokers from conspiring to fix prices or allocate customers or markets.

Any violation of agency law is also considered to be a violation of North Carolina Real Estate License Law.

Questions

1. Which of the following statements is true of a real estate broker acting as the agent of the seller?
   a. He or she is obligated to render faithful service to the seller.
   b. He or she can make a secret profit, in addition to the commission.
   c. He or she can agree to a change in price without the seller's approval.
   d. He or she can accept a commission from the buyer without the seller's approval.

2. A broker is entitled to collect a commission from both the seller and the buyer when
   I. the buyer and seller are related.
   II. the broker acts as a disclosed dual agent.
   III. both parties have lawyers.
   a. I only
   b. II only
   c. III only
   d. I and III only

3. The term *fiduciary* refers to
   a. the sale of real property.
   b. principles by which a real estate broker as an agent must conduct his or her business.
   c. one who has legal power to act on behalf of another.
   d. the principal in a principal-agent relationship.

4. While in the employ of a real estate broker, a salesperson has the authority to
   a. act as an agent for the seller.
   b. assume responsibilities assigned by the broker.
   c. accept a commission from another broker.
   d. advertise a property on his or her own behalf.

5. A person who has the authority to enter into contracts concerning all business affairs of another is called a(n)
   a. universal agent.   c. special agent.
   b. secret agent.   d. attorney.

6. The legal relationship between broker and seller is usually a
   a. general agency.
   b. special agency.
   c. secret agency.
   d. universal agency.

7. A real estate broker hired by an owner to sell a parcel of real estate must comply with
   I. any instructions of the buyer.
   II. the doctrine of caveat emptor.
   III. the law of agency.
   a. I only
   b. III only
   c. I and II only
   d. I, II and III

8. McCarthy, a real estate broker, learns that her neighbor Smith wishes to sell his house. McCarthy knows the property well and is able to persuade Jones to make an offer for the property. No listing agreement has been made. McCarthy then asks Smith if she can present an offer to him, and Smith agrees. At this point
   a. Smith is not obligated to pay McCarthy a commission.
   b. Jones is obligated to pay McCarthy for locating the property.
   c. Smith must pay McCarthy a commission.
   d. McCarthy has become a subagent of Jones.

9. A real estate broker who engages salespeople as independent contractors must
   a. withhold income tax from all commissions they earn.
   b. require that they participate in office insurance plans offered to other salespeople hired as employees.
   c. withhold Social Security from all commissions they earn.
   d. refrain from controlling how the salespeople conduct their business activities.

10. Single agency occurs when a real estate agent
    a. represents only one party in a transaction.
    b. represents both the buyer and the seller in a transaction.
    c. chooses to be a dual agent.
    d. has both the listing and the sales sides of a transaction.

11. An agent who breaches his or her fiduciary duties may be subject to
    I. a civil lawsuit.
    II. disciplinary action by the Real Estate Commission.
    III. criminal prosecution.
    a. I only
    b. I and II only
    c. I, II and III
    d. None of the above

12. The principal owes the agent the duty of
    I. good faith.
    II. payment of compensation.
    a. I only
    b. II only
    c. Both I and II
    d. Neither I nor II

13. In North Carolina which of the following statements is true of the doctrine of caveat emptor?
    a. It has been largely replaced by case law and consumer protection laws.
    b. It is still intact for real estate transactions.
    c. It is applicable only if the agent acts as a dual agent.
    d. It means let the seller beware.

14. Under the law of agency, a real estate broker owes all of the following to the principal EXCEPT
    a. care.   c. disclosure.
    b. obedience.   d. advertising.

15. An agency relationship may be terminated by all but which of the following means?
    a. The owner decides not to sell the house.
    b. The broker discovers that the market value of the property is such that he or she will not make an adequate commission.
    c. The owner dies.
    d. The broker secures a ready, willing and able buyer for the seller's property.

16. Maude represents the seller. When should she disclose her agency relationship to the buyer?
    a. After showing the buyer a home he is interested in
    b. When presenting an offer to the seller
    c. When preparing an offer to present to the seller
    d. At first substantial contact

17. A disclosure of agency status should be made by a buyer's agent to the seller
    I. with a written confirmation in the purchase and sale agreement.
    II. at the initial contact with the seller or seller's agent, orally or in writing.
    a. I only
    b. II only
    c. I and II
    d. None of the above

18. Barbara is representing the property seller. She is showing the property to Luis, a prospective buyer. Luis likes the house, but does not want to pay as much as the seller wants. He asks Barbara if the seller would take less than the listing price. Barbara replies that the seller is very anxious to sell and would be "flexible." She encourages Luis to make an offer at $5,000 less than the listing price. Barbara
    a. has done a good job for the seller.
    b. has violated her fiduciary duties to the seller because she disclosed confidential information about the seller to the buyer.
    c. will now be considered a general agent.
    d. has done nothing wrong because she is not making a secret profit from the transaction.

19. Michael is representing the seller, Bart. He shows Bart's house to his cousin, Samantha, who is very interested in buying it. Michael presents Samantha's full-price offer to Bart, who eagerly accepts it. Both Bart and Samantha are very happy with the transaction.
    a. Because both parties are happy with the transaction, it doesn't matter whether Michael disclosed his relationship with Samantha to Bart.
    b. Bart cannot complain about Michael's actions because Samantha's offer was for the full listing price.
    c. Michael has violated his fiduciary duties to Bart by failing to disclose his relationship with Samantha and could be subject to disciplinary action.
    d. Michael has done nothing wrong; he was not required to disclose his relationship with Samantha.

20. The seller tells the listing agent about a latent defect in the property. The listing agent tells the selling agent about the defect, but the selling agent does not inform the buyer. Who is responsible?
    a. The seller
    b. The listing agent
    c. The selling agent
    d. All of the above

21. If a broker's misrepresentation causes loss or injury to a buyer customer, which of the following might be found liable?
    a. Principal
    b. Broker
    c. Both a and b
    d. Neither a nor b

22. Which of the following statements about dual agency is correct?
    I. Dual agency can occur within one firm only after an agent has become a buyer's agent and is showing an in-house listing.
    II. The firm is actually the dual agent.
    a. I only
    b. II only
    c. Both I and II
    d. Neither I nor II

23. In North Carolina, a broker in charge (BIC) must adopt a written policy on practicing designated agency. Which of the following is true concerning designated agency?
    I. The BIC cannot be a designated agent if the other agent in the transaction is a salesperson.
    II. An agent cannot be appointed as a designated agent if he or she has prior confidential knowledge about the other party to the transaction.
    a. I only
    b. II only
    c. Both I and II
    d. Neither I nor II

24. It is discovered after a sale that the land parcel is 10 percent smaller than the owner represented it to be. The broker who passed the erroneous information on to the buyer is
    a. not liable as long as she only repeated the seller's data.
    b. not liable if the misrepresentation was unintentional.
    c. not liable if the buyer actually inspected what she was getting.
    d. liable if the broker knew or should have known of the discrepancy.

7 Fair Housing and Ethical Practices

LEARNING OBJECTIVES

When you've flinished reading this chapter, you should be able to

- **describe** the purpose of federal and state fair housing laws, how they are enforced and their impact on real estate brokers and salespersons.

- **list** the classes of people who are protected against discrimination by various federal and state laws.

- **explain** the purposes of the Americans with Disabilities Act.

- **define** what constitutes sexual harassment.

- **define** these *key terms*:

blockbusting	Fair Housing Act	Office of Fair Housing
Civil Rights Act of 1866	Fair Housing	and Equal
code of ethics	Amendments Act	Opportunity
Department of	Housing and	(OFHEO)
Housing and Urban	Community	protected classes
Development (HUD)	Development Act	redlining
Equal Credit	North Carolina Human	steering
Opportunity Act	Relations	
(ECOA)	Commission	

EQUAL OPPORTUNITY IN HOUSING

The purpose of civil rights laws that affect the real estate industry is to create a marketplace in which all persons of similar financial means have a similar range of housing choices. The goal is to ensure that everyone has the opportunity to live where he or she chooses. Owners, real estate licensees, apartment management companies, real estate organizations, lending agencies, builders and developers must all take a part in creating this single housing market. Federal, state and local fair housing or equal opportunity laws affect every phase of a real estate transaction, from listing to closing.

The U.S. Congress and the Supreme Court have created a legal framework that preserves the Constitutional rights of all citizens. However, while the passage of laws may establish a code for public conduct, centuries of discriminatory practices and attitudes are not so easily changed. Real estate licensees cannot allow their own prejudices to interfere with the ethical and legal conduct of their profession. Similarly, the discriminatory attitudes of property owners or property seekers must not be allowed to affect compliance with the fair housing laws. This is not always easy, and the pressure to avoid offending the person who pays the commission can be intense. However, just remember: *Failure to comply with fair housing laws is both a civil and criminal violation, and it is grounds for disciplinary action against a licensee* (see Rule A.1601).

> "All citizens of the United States shall have the same right in every state and territory as is enjoyed by white citizens thereof to inherit, purchase, lease, sell, hold, and convey real and personal property."—*Civil Rights Act of 1866*

The federal government's effort to guarantee equal housing opportunities to all U.S. citizens began with the passage of the **Civil Rights Act of 1866.** This law prohibits any type of discrimination based on race.

The U.S. Supreme Court's 1896 decision in *Plessy v. Ferguson* established the "separate but equal" doctrine of legalized racial segregation. A series of court decisions and federal laws in the 20 years between 1948 and 1968 attempted to address the inequities in housing that were results of *Plessy.* Those efforts, however, tended to address only certain aspects of the housing market (such as federally funded housing programs). As a result, their impact was limited.

FAIR HOUSING ACT

In 1968, the federal government began to address specific discriminatory practices throughout the real estate industry. Title VIII of the **Civil Rights Act of 1968** (called the *Federal Fair Housing Act*) prohibited discrimination in housing based on race, color, religion or national origin. In 1974, the **Housing and Community Development Act** added sex to the list of **protected classes.** In 1988, the **Fair Housing Amendments Act** included disability and familial status (that is, the presence of children). Today, these laws are known as the federal **Fair Housing Act** (see Figure 7.1). The Fair Housing Act prohibits discrimination on the basis of race, color, religion, sex, handicap, familial status or national origin.

The act also prohibits discrimination against individuals because of their *association* with persons in the protected classes. This law is administered by the **Department of Housing and Urban Development (HUD).** HUD has established rules and regulations that further interpret the practices affected by the law. In addition, HUD distributes an *equal housing opportunity poster* (see Figure 7.2). The poster declares that the office in which it is displayed promises to adhere to the Fair Housing Act and pledges support for affirmative marketing and advertising programs.

In Practice   When HUD investigates a broker for discriminatory practices, it may consider failure to prominently display the equal housing opportunity poster in the broker's place of business as evidence of discrimination.

Table 7.1 describes the activities prohibited by the Fair Housing Act.

Figure 7.1   Federal Fair Housing Laws

Legislation	Race	Color	Religion	National Origin	Sex	Age	Marital Status	Disability	Discrimination	Familial Status	Public Assistance Income
Civil Rights Act of 1866	●										
Fair Housing Act of 1968 (Title VIII)	●	●	●	●					●		
Housing and Community Development Act of 1974					●				●		
Fair Housing Amendments Act of 1988								●	●	●	
Equal Credit Opportunity Act of 1974 (lending)	●	●	●	●	●	●	●		●		●

Figure 7.2   *Equal Housing Opportunity Poster*

U.S. Department of Housing and Urban Development

**EQUAL HOUSING
OPPORTUNITY**

We Do Business in Accordance With the Federal Fair Housing Law

(The Fair Housing Amendments Act of 1988)

It is Illegal to Discriminate Against Any Person Because of Race, Color, Religion, Sex, Handicap, Familial Status, or National Origin

- ■ In the sale or rental of housing or residential lots

- ■ In advertising the sale or rental of housing

- ■ In the financing of housing

- ■ In the provision of real estate brokerage services

- ■ In the appraisal of housing

- ■ Blockbusting is also illegal

Anyone who feels he or she has been discriminated against may file a complaint of housing discrimination:
    1-800-669-9777 (Toll Free)
    1-800-927-9275 (TDD)

**U.S. Department of Housing and Urban Development
Assistant Secretary for Fair Housing and Equal Opportunity
Washington, D.C. 20410**

Previous editions are obsolete

form HUD-928.1A(8-93)

Table 7.1 Fair Housing Act Restrictions

Prohibited by Federal Fair Housing Act	Example
• Refusing to sell, rent or negotiate the sale or rental of housing	Kate owns an apartment building with several vacant units. When an Asian family asks to see one of the units, she tells them to go away.
• Changing terms, conditions or services for different individuals as a means of discriminating	Sarah, a Roman Catholic, calls on a duplex, and the landlord tells her the rent is $400 per month. When she talks to the other tenants, she learns that all the Lutherans in the complex pay only $325 per month.
• Advertising any discriminatory preference or limitation in housing or making any inquiry or reference that is discriminatory in nature	A real estate agent places the following advertisement in a newspaper: "Just Listed! Perfect home for white family, near excellent parochial school!" A developer places this ad in an urban newspaper: "Sunset River Hollow— Dream Homes Just for You!" The ad is accompanied by a photo of several African-American families.
• Representing that a property is not available for sale or rent when in fact it is	Jason, who uses a wheelchair, is told that the house he wants to rent is no longer available. The next day, however, the For Rent sign is still in the window.
• Profiting by inducing property owners to sell or rent on the basis of the prospective entry into the neighborhood of persons of a protected class	Nancy, a real estate agent, sends brochures to homeowners in the predominantly white Ridgewood neighborhood. The brochures, which feature her past success selling homes, include photos of racial minorities, population statistics and the caption, "The Changing Face of Ridgewood."
• Altering the terms or conditions of a home loan, or denying a loan, as a means of discrimination	A lender requires Maria, a divorced mother of two young children, to pay for a credit report. In addition, her father must cosign her application. After talking to a single male friend, Maria learns that he was not required to do either of those things, despite his lower income and poor credit history.
• Denying membership or participation in a multiple-listing service, a real estate organization or another facility related to the sale or rental of housing as a means of discrimination	The Topper County Real Estate Practitioners' Association meets every week to discuss available properties and buyers. None of Topper County's African-American or female agents is allowed to be a member of the association.

Definitions   HUD's regulations provide specific definitions that clarify the scope of the Fair Housing Act.

Housing. The regulations define *housing* as a "dwelling," which includes any building or part of a building designed for occupancy as a residence by one or more families. This includes a single-family house, condominium, cooperative or manufactured housing, as well as vacant land on which any of these structures will be built.

Familial status. Familial status refers to the presence of one or more individuals who have not reached the age of 18 and who live with either a parent or guardian. The term includes a woman who is pregnant. In effect, it means that the Fair Housing Act's protections extend to families with children. Unless a property qualifies as housing for older persons, all properties must be made available to families with children under the same terms and conditions as to anyone else. It is illegal to advertise properties as being for adults only or to indicate a preference for a certain number of children. The number of persons permitted to reside in a property (the occupancy standards) must be based on objective factors such as sanitation or safety. Landlords cannot restrict the number of occupants to eliminate families with children.

FOR EXAMPLE Greg owned an apartment building. One of his elderly tenants, Paul, was terminally ill. Paul requested that no children be allowed in the vacant apartment next door because the noise would be difficult for him to bear. Greg agreed and refused to rent to families with children. Even though Greg only wanted to make things easier for a dying tenant, he was nonetheless found to have violated the Fair Housing Act by discriminating on the basis of familial status.

Disability. A *disability* is a physical or mental impairment. The term includes having a history of, or being regarded as having, an impairment that substantially limits one or more of an individual's major life activities. Persons who have AIDS are protected by the fair housing laws under this classification.

In Practice   The federal fair housing law's protection of disabled persons does not include those who are current users of illegal or controlled substances. Nor are individuals who have been convicted of the illegal manufacture or distribution of a controlled substance protected under this law. However, the law does prohibit discrimination against those who are participating in addiction recovery programs. For instance, a landlord could lawfully discriminate against a cocaine addict but not against a member of Alcoholics Anonymous.

A *disability* is an impairment that substantially limits one or more of a person's major life activities.

It is unlawful to discriminate against prospective buyers or tenants on the basis of disability. Landlords must make reasonable accommodations to existing policies, practices or services to permit persons with disabilities to have equal enjoyment of the premises. For instance, it would be reasonable for a landlord to permit support animals (such as guide dogs) in a normally no-pets building or to provide a designated handicapped parking space in a generally unreserved lot.

People with disabilities must be permitted to make reasonable modifications to the premises at their own expense. Such modifications might include lowering door handles or installing bath rails to accommodate a person in a wheelchair. Failure to permit reasonable modification constitutes discrimination. However, the law recognizes that some reasonable modifications might make a rental property undesirable to the general population. In such a case, the landlord is allowed to require that the property be restored to its previous condition when the lease period ends.

The law does not prohibit restricting occupancy exclusively to persons with handicaps in dwellings that are designed specifically for their accommodation.

For new construction of certain multifamily properties, a number of accessibility and usability requirements must be met under federal law. Access is specified for public and common-use portions of the buildings, and adaptive and accessible design must be implemented for the interior of the dwelling units. Some states have their own laws as well.

Exemptions to the Fair Housing Act

The federal Fair Housing Act provides for certain exemptions. It is important for licensees to know in what situations the exemptions apply. However, licensees should be aware that *no exemptions involve race* and that *no exceptions apply when a real estate licensee is involved in a transaction.*

The sale or rental of a single-family home is exempt when

- the home is owned by an individual who does not own more than three such homes at one time (and who does not sell more than one every two years);
- a real estate broker or salesperson is *not* involved in the transaction; and
- discriminatory advertising is not used.

The rental of rooms or units is exempted in an owner-occupied one- to four-family dwelling.

Dwelling units owned by religious organizations may be restricted to people of the same religion if membership in the organization is not restricted on the basis of race, color or national origin. A private club that is not open to the public may restrict the rental or occupancy of lodgings that it owns to its members as long as the lodgings are not operated commercially.

The Fair Housing Act does not require that housing be made available to any individual whose tenancy would constitute a direct threat to the health or safety of other individuals or that would result in substantial physical damage to the property of others.

Housing for older persons. While the Fair Housing Act protects families with children, certain properties can be restricted to occupancy by elderly persons. Housing intended for persons age 62 or older or housing occupied by at least one person 55 years of age or older per unit (where 80 percent of the units are occupied by individuals 55 or older) is exempt from the familial status protection.

Jones v. Mayer   In 1968, the Supreme Court heard the case of *Jones v. Alfred H. Mayer Company*, 392 U.S. 409 (1968). In its decision, the Court upheld the Civil Rights Act of 1866. This decision is important because although the federal law exempts individual homeowners and certain groups, the 1866 law *prohibits all racial discrimination without exception.* A person who is discriminated against on the basis of race may still recover damages under the 1866 law. *Where race is involved, no exceptions apply.*

The U.S. Supreme Court has expanded the definition of the term *race* to include ancestral and ethnic characteristics, including certain physical, cultural or linguistic characteristics that are commonly shared by a national origin group. These rulings are significant because discrimination on the basis of race, as it is now defined, affords due process of complaints under the provisions of the Civil Rights Act of 1866.

Enforcement of the Fair Housing Act

The federal Fair Housing Act is administered by the **Office of Fair Housing and Equal Opportunity (OFHEO)** under the direction of the secretary of HUD. Any aggrieved person who believes illegal discrimination has occurred may file a complaint with HUD within one year of the alleged act. HUD may also initiate its own complaint. Complaints may be reported to the Office of Fair Housing and Equal Opportunity, Department of Housing and Urban Development, Washington, DC 20410, or to the Office of Fair Housing and Equal Opportunity in care of the nearest HUD regional office. Complaints also may be submitted directly to HUD using an on-line form available on the HUD web site: www.hud.gov/fairhsg1.html.

Upon receiving a complaint, HUD initiates an investigation. Within 100 days of the filing of the complaint, HUD either determines that reasonable cause exists to bring a charge of illegal discrimination or dismisses the complaint. During this investigation period, HUD can attempt to resolve the dispute informally through conciliation. *Conciliation* is the resolution of a complaint by obtaining assurance that the person against whom the complaint was filed (the respondent) will remedy any violation that may have occurred. The respondent further agrees to take steps to eliminate or prevent discriminatory practices in the future. If necessary, these agreements can be enforced through civil action.

The aggrieved person has the right to seek relief through administrative proceedings. Administrative proceedings are hearings held before administrative law judges (ALJs). An ALJ has the authority to award actual damages to the aggrieved person or persons and, if it is believed the public interest will be served, to impose monetary penalties. The penalties range from up to $10,000 for the first offense to $25,000 for a second violation within five years and $50,000 for further violations within seven years. The ALJ also has the authority to issue an injunction to order the offender to either do something (such as rent an apartment to the complaining party) or refrain from doing something (such as acting in a discriminatory manner).

The parties may elect civil action in federal court at any time within two years of the discriminatory act. For cases heard in federal court, unlimited punitive damages can be awarded in addition to actual damages. The court can also issue injunctions. As noted in Chapter 6, errors and omissions insurance carried by licensees normally does not cover losses caused by violations of the fair housing laws.

The *Equal Credit Opportunity Act* prohibits discrimination in granting credit based on:

- race,
- color,
- religion,
- national origin,
- sex,
- marital status,
- age and
- public assistance.

Whenever the attorney general has reasonable cause to believe that any person or group is engaged in a pattern or practice of resistance to the full enjoyment of any of the rights granted by the federal fair housing laws, he or she may file a civil action in any federal district court. Civil penalties may result in an amount not to exceed $50,000 for a first violation and an amount not to exceed $100,000 for second and subsequent violations.

Complaints brought under the Civil Rights Act of 1866 are taken directly to federal courts. The only time limit for action is a state's statute of limitations for *torts*—injuries one individual inflicts on another.

EQUAL CREDIT OPPORTUNITY ACT

The federal **Equal Credit Opportunity Act (ECOA)** protects more classes of persons than the Fair Housing Act. It prohibits discrimination based on race, color, religion, national origin, sex, marital status or age in the granting of credit. It also prevents lenders from discriminating against recipients of public assistance programs such as food stamps and Social Security. As in the Fair Housing Act, the ECOA requires that credit applications be considered only on the basis of income, net worth, job stability and credit rating.

NORTH CAROLINA FAIR HOUSING ACT OF 1983

In 1983, North Carolina passed a fair housing law that is very similar to the federal Fair Housing Act of 1968.

Prohibited Acts North Carolina's Fair Housing Act prohibits the same activities as the federal law (refer to the list of prohibited activities discussed under the federal Fair Housing Act). Thus, one discriminatory act violates both federal and state laws and subjects the violator to both federal and state penalties.

Exemptions While the state law's prohibited activities are similar to the federal law's, the exemptions to the state act contain substantial differences.

> There are substantial differences in exemptions under federal and state laws.

- The federal Fair Housing Act exempts a private owner selling his or her own home without the use of a real estate broker. There is no similar exemption to the state Fair Housing Act. Note that the most restrictive law applies: a person selling his or her own home must not resort to discriminatory practices even though he or she is exempted by federal law (the more restrictive state law applies). The state does, however, exempt the rental of rooms in a private home occupied by the owner.
- The state act exempts the rental of a unit in a one- to four-unit residential building if the owner or one of the owner's family members lives in one of the units. The federal law exempts such a unit only if the owner himself or herself lives in one of the units.
- The state act exempts the rental of rooms in a single-sex dormitory. The federal law does not include this exemption (although it is doubtful that such a practice would be considered a violation of the federal law).

The other exemptions in the federal act are mirrored in the state act.

Enforcement The first place to file a complaint by those who have been injured by discriminatory acts is the **North Carolina Human Relations Commission.**

The commission then begins investigating the complaint and simultaneously tries to resolve the conflict through conference, conciliation or persuasion. If the commission finds there are no reasonable grounds for the complaint, it is dismissed (the injured party may still bring a discrimination suit in state court). However, if there are reasonable grounds to believe unlawful discrimination took place and the commission's informal negotiation process does not work, the commission must then

- dismiss the complaint and issue a right-to-sue letter to the injured party (which entitles the party to bring a court case against the accused at the complainant's own expense) or
- file a lawsuit in state court against the accused.

All lawsuits brought under the North Carolina Fair Housing Act must be brought within 180 days after filing the complaint with the Human Relations Commission.

SEXUAL HARASSMENT

North Carolina has a law (G.S. 14-395) pertaining to sexual harassment by a landlord (lessor) or a lessor's agent of a prospective tenant. This statute defines sexual harassment as *unsolicited overt requests or demands for sexual acts* when (1) submission to such conduct is made a term of the execution or continuation of the lease agreement or (2) submission to or rejection of such conduct by an individual is used to determine whether rights under the lease are accorded.

Sexual harassment has been further defined as any type of sexual behavior that creates an intimidating, hostile or offensive environment. Examples of sexual harassment include

- *verbal harassment*—sexual innuendo, suggestive comments, insults, jokes about sex or gender, sexual propositions and threats;
- *nonverbal harassment*—suggestive or insulting sounds, leering, whistling and obscene gestures;
- *physical harassment*—inappropriate touching, pinching, brushing the body, fondling the body, coerced sexual intercourse and sexual assault.

In Practice   The North Carolina Real Estate Commission can take disciplinary measures against licensees for violating state fair housing laws. Rule A.1601 Fair Housing is quoted: "Conduct by a licensee which violates the provisions of the State Fair Housing Act constitutes improper conduct in violation of G.S. 93A-6(a)(10)."

IMPLICATIONS FOR BROKERS AND SALESPEOPLE

To a large extent, the laws place the burden of responsibility for effecting and maintaining fair housing on real estate brokers and salespeople. Licensees must comply with the laws, which are clear and widely known. The complainant does not have to prove guilty knowledge or specific intent—only the fact that discrimination occurred. In other words, if a licensee violated a fair housing law, that licensee could be found guilty of discrimination even if he or she did not intend to discriminate.

How does a broker go about complying with the laws and making that policy known? HUD offers guidelines for nondiscriminatory language and illustrations for use in real estate advertising. The agency further requires that every broker take affirmative marketing action in the choice of advertising media and in individual canvassing to ensure that all interested individuals have the same range of housing options.

In addition, the National Association of REALTORS® affirms that a broker's position can be emphasized and problems avoided by the prominent display of a sign stating that it is against company policy as well as state and federal laws to offer any information on the racial, ethnic or religious composition of a neighborhood or to place restrictions on listing, showing or providing information on the availability of homes for any of these reasons. If a prospect still expresses a locational preference for housing based on race, the association's guidelines suggest the following response: I cannot give you that kind of advice. I will show you several homes that meet your specifications. You will have to decide which one you want.

There is more to fair housing practices than just following the letter of the law, however. Discrimination involves a sensitive area of human emotions—specifically, fear and the drive for self-preservation based on considerable prejudice and misconception. The broker or salesperson who complies with the law still must interact, in many cases, with a general public whose attitudes cannot be altered by legislation alone. Therefore, a licensee who wishes to comply with the fair housing laws and also succeed in the real estate business must work to educate the public.

For every broker and salesperson, a sincere, positive attitude toward fair housing laws is a good start in dealing with this sensitive issue. It provides an effective model for all who come in contact with the licensee. Active cooperation with local real estate board programs and community committees is also an excellent idea. This evidences the licensee's willingness to serve the community and observe the laws, and it helps to change public attitudes. Both factors can result in good public relations and, ultimately, more business for the licensee.

In Practice   Agents often encounter clients and customers who may want to discriminate on purpose or who may not realize their intentions are actually forms of discrimination. Following are some typical situations with suggested responses.

Situation: A seller-client wants an agent to discriminate against a protected class.

Response: The agent should advise the seller that the act prohibits sellers, when using a broker, to discriminate. Suggested response: "Under North Carolina Fair Housing Act, you have a right to sell to anyone as long as you do not discriminate on the basis of race, color, religion, sex, handicapped or familial status."

Situation: A buyer (client or customer) doesn't want to be shown dwellings in a neighborhood occupied by persons in a protected class.

Response: Collect all information on all properties in all areas that meet the buyer's needs. Have the information available and discuss it with the buyer.

Situation: A buyer wants information about the racial and/or ethnic makeup of a neighborhood in which the buyer is interested.

Response: "We do not keep records or statistics on racial or ethnic population in particular areas. The city planning department, school administrative offices or the census bureau may have that information available."

AMERICANS WITH DISABILITIES ACT

> The *Americans with Disabilities Act* requires *reasonable accommodations* in employment and access to goods, services and public buildings.

Although the *Americans with Disabilities Act (ADA)* is not a housing or credit law, it has a significant effect on the real estate industry. The ADA is important to licensees because it addresses the rights of individuals with disabilities in employment and public accommodations. Real estate brokers are often employers, and real estate brokerage offices are public spaces. The ADA's goal is to enable individuals with disabilities to become part of the economic and social mainstream of society.

Title I of the ADA requires that employers (including real estate licensees) make *reasonable accommodations* that enable an individual with a disability to perform essential job functions. Reasonable accommodations include making the work site accessible, restructuring a job, providing part-time or flexible work schedules and modifying equipment that is used on the job. The provisions of the ADA apply to any employer with 15 or more employees.

Title III of the ADA provides for accessibility to goods and services for individuals with disabilities. While the federal civil rights laws have traditionally been viewed in the real estate industry as housing-related, the practices of licensees who deal with nonresidential property are significantly affected by the ADA. Because people with disabilities have the right to full and equal access to businesses and public services under the ADA, building owners and managers must ensure that any obstacle restricting this right is eliminated. The Americans with Disabilities Act Accessibility Guidelines (ADAAG) contain detailed specifications for designing parking spaces, curb ramps, elevators, drinking fountains, toilet facilities and directional signs to ensure maximum accessibility.

ADA and the Fair Housing Act

The ADA exempts two types of property from its requirements:

1. Property that is covered by the federal Fair Housing Act
2. Property that is exempt from coverage by the federal Fair Housing Act

Some properties, however, are subject to both laws. For example, in an apartment complex, the rental office is a "place of public accommodation." As such, it is covered by the ADA, and must be accessible to persons with disabilities at the owner's expense. Individual rental units would be covered by the Fair Housing Act. If a tenant wished to modify the unit to make it accessible, he or she would be responsible for the cost.

In Practice   Real estate agents need a general knowledge of the ADA's provisions. It is necessary that a broker's workplace and employment policies comply with the law. Also, licensees who are building managers must ensure that the properties are legally accessible. However, ADA compliance questions may arise with regard to a client's property, too. Unless the agent is a qualified ADA expert, it is best to advise commercial clients to seek the services of an attorney, an architect or a consultant who specializes in ADA issues. It is possible that an appraiser may be liable for failing to identify and account for a property's noncompliance.

FAIR HOUSING PRACTICES

For the civil rights laws to accomplish their goal of eliminating discrimination, licensees must apply them routinely. Of course, compliance also means that licensees avoid violating both the laws and the ethical standards of the profession. The following discussion examines the ethical and legal issues that confront real estate licensees.

Blockbusting **Blockbusting** (also known as *panic peddling*) is the act of encouraging people to sell or rent their homes by claiming that the entry of a protected class of people into the neighborhood will have some sort of negative impact on property values. Blockbusting was a common practice during the 1950s and 1960s, as unscrupulous real estate agents profited by fueling "white flight" from cities to suburbs. Any message, however subtle, that property should be sold or rented because the neighborhood is "undergoing changes" is considered blockbusting. It is illegal to assert that the presence of certain persons will cause property values to decline, crime or antisocial behavior to increase and the quality of schools to suffer.

> *Blockbusting:* encouraging the sale or renting of property by claiming that the entry of a protected class of people into the neighborhood will negatively affect property values.

A critical element in blockbusting, according to HUD, is the profit motive. A property owner may be intimidated into selling his or her property at a depressed price to the blockbuster, who in turn sells the property to another person at a higher price. Another term for this activity is *panic selling.* To avoid accusations of blockbusting, licensees should use good judgment when choosing locations and methods for marketing their services and soliciting listings.

Steering **Steering** is the channeling of home seekers to particular neighborhoods. It also includes discouraging potential buyers from considering some areas. In either case, it is an illegal limitation of a purchaser's options.

Steering: channeling home seekers toward or away from particular neighborhoods based on race, religion, national origin or some other consideration.

Steering may be done either to preserve the character of a neighborhood or to change its character intentionally. Many cases of steering are subtle, motivated by assumptions or perceptions about a home seeker's preferences, based on some stereotype. Assumptions are not only dangerous—they are often *wrong.* The licensee cannot *assume* that a prospective home seeker expects to be directed to certain neighborhoods or properties. Steering anyone is illegal.

FOR EXAMPLE An agent lists a home in a predominantly black neighborhood. He places an ad in a publication primarily aimed at black readers, and does not advertise the property in any publication primarily aimed toward whites.

FOR EXAMPLE An agent showing property to a black couple in a predominantly white neighborhood does not use his best efforts to present the offer and get it accepted.

FOR EXAMPLE A broker is marketing homes in a new subdivision and in pictorial ads shows only white families enjoying the amenities.

Advertising

No advertisement of property for sale or rent may include language indicating a preference or limitation. No exception to this rule exists, regardless of how subtle the choice of words. HUD's regulations cite examples that are considered discriminatory (see Figure 7.3). The media used for promoting property or real estate services cannot target one population to the exclusion of others. The selective use of media, whether by language or geography, may have discriminatory impact. For instance, advertising property only in a Korean-language newspaper tends to discriminate against non-Koreans. Similarly, limiting advertising to a cable television channel available only to white suburbanites may be construed as a discriminatory act. However, if an advertisement appears in general-circulation media as well, it may be legal.

Appraising

Those who prepare appraisals or any statements of valuation, whether they are formal or informal, oral or written (including a competitive market analysis), may consider any factors that affect value. However, race, color, religion, national origin, sex, handicap and familial status are not factors that may be considered.

Redlining

Redlining is an illegal practice by lending institutions to deny or discourage loan applications in an area based on its racial composition or deterioration.

The practice of refusing to make mortgage loans or issue insurance policies in specific areas for reasons other than the economic qualifications of the applicants is known as **redlining.** Redlining refers to literally drawing a line around particular areas. This practice is often a major contributor to the deterioration of older neighborhoods. Redlining is frequently based on racial grounds rather than on any real objection to an applicant's credit-worthiness. That is, the lender makes a policy decision that no property in a certain area is qualified for a loan, no matter who wants to buy it, because of the neighborhood's ethnic character. The federal Fair Housing Act prohibits discrimination in mortgage lending and covers not only the actions of primary lenders but also activities in the secondary mortgage market. A lending institution can refuse a loan, but solely on *sound* economic grounds.

	Figure 7.3	HUD's Advertising Guidelines		
CATEGORY	**RULE**	**PERMITTED**	**NOT PERMITTED**
Race Color National Origin	No discriminatory limitation/preference may be expressed	"master bedroom" "good neighborhood"	"white neighborhood" "no French"
Religion	No religious preference/limitation	"chapel on premises" "kosher meals available" "Merry Christmas"	"no Muslims" "nice Christian family" "near great Catholic school"
Sex	No explicit preference based on sex	"mother-in-law suite" "master bedroom" "female roommate sought"	"great house for a man" "wife's dream kitchen"
Handicap	No exclusions or limitations based on handicap	"wheelchair ramp" "walk to shopping"	"no wheelchairs" "able-bodied tenants only"
Familial Status	No preference or limitation based on family size or nature	"two-bedroom" "family room" "quiet neighborhood"	"married couple only" "no more than two children" "retiree's dream house"
Photographs or Illustrations of People	People should be clearly representative and nonexclusive	Illustrations showing ethnic races, family groups, singles, etc.	Illustrations showing groups of all-single people, people of a single ethnicity, or elderly white adults, etc.

The *Home Mortgage Disclosure Act* requires that all institutional mortgage lenders with assets in excess of $10 million and one or more offices in a given geographic area make annual reports. The reports must detail all mortgage loans the institution has made or purchased, broken down by census tract. This law enables the government to detect patterns of lending behavior that might constitute redlining.

Intent and Effect   If an owner or real estate licensee *purposely* sets out to engage in blockbusting, steering or other unfair activities, the intent to discriminate is obvious. However, owners and licensees must examine their activities and policies carefully to determine whether they have *unintentional discriminatory effects.* Whenever policies or practices result in unequal treatment of persons in the protected classes, they are considered discriminatory regardless of any innocent intent. This *effects* test is applied by regulatory agencies to determine whether an individual has been discriminated against.

Threats or Acts of Violence   Being a real estate agent is not generally considered a dangerous occupation. However, some licensees may find themselves the targets of threats or violence merely for complying with fair housing laws. The federal Fair Housing Act of 1968 protects the rights of those who seek the benefits of the open housing law. It also protects owners, brokers and salespersons who aid or encourage the enjoyment of open housing rights. Threats, coercion and intimidation are punishable by criminal action. In such a case, the victim should report the incident immediately to the local police and to the nearest office of the Federal Bureau of Investigation.

PROFESSIONAL ETHICS

Professional conduct involves more than just complying with the law. In real estate, state licensing laws establish those activities that are illegal and therefore prohibited. However, merely complying with the letter of the law may not be enough: licensees may perform *legally*, yet not *ethically*. *Ethics* refers to a system of *moral* principles, rules and standards of conduct. The ethical system of a profession establishes conduct that goes beyond merely complying with the law. These moral principles address two sides of a profession:

1. They establish standards for integrity and competence in dealing with consumers of an industry's services.
2. They define a code of conduct for relations within the industry, among its professionals.

Code of Ethics One way that many organizations address ethics among their members or in their respective businesses is by adopting codes of professional conduct. A **code of ethics** is a written system of standards for ethical conduct. The code contains statements designed to advise, guide and regulate job behavior. To be effective, a code of ethics must be specific by dictating rules that either prohibit or demand certain behavior. Lofty statements of positive goals are not especially helpful. By including sanctions for violators, a code of ethics becomes more effective.

The National Association of REALTORS® (NAR), the largest trade association in the country, adopted a Code of Ethics for its members in 1913. REALTORS® are expected to subscribe to this strict code of conduct. NAR has established procedures for professional standards committees at the local, state and national levels of the organization to administer compliance. Interpretations of the code are known as *Standards of Practice*. The NAR Code of Ethics has proved helpful because it contains practical applications of business ethics. Many other professional organizations in the real estate industry have codes of ethics as well. In addition, many state real estate commissions are required by law to establish codes or canons of ethical behavior for their states' licensees.

SUMMARY

The federal regulations regarding equal opportunity in housing are contained principally in two laws. The Civil Rights Act of 1866 prohibits all racial discrimination, and the Fair Housing Act (Title VIIII of the Civil Rights Act of 1968), as amended, prohibits discrimination on the basis of race, color, religion, sex, handicap, familial status or national origin in the sale, rental or financing of residential property. Discriminatory actions include refusing to deal with an individual or a specific group, changing any terms of a real estate or loan transaction, changing the services offered for any individual or group, creating statements or advertisements that indicate discriminatory restrictions or otherwise attempting to make a dwelling unavailable to any person or group because of race, color, religion, sex, handicap, familial status or national origin. The law also prohibits steering, blockbusting and redlining.

Complaints under the Fair Housing Act may be reported to and investigated by the Department of Housing and Urban Development (HUD). Such complaints may also be taken directly to U.S. district courts. In states and localities that have enacted fair housing legislation that is substantially equivalent to the federal law, complaints are handled by state and local agencies and state courts. Complaints under the Civil Rights Act of 1866 must be taken to federal courts.

State equal opportunity housing laws are found in the North Carolina Fair Housing Act. Its provisions are substantially similar to the federal Fair Housing Act, except in the area of allowable exemptions.

The first place to file a complaint of discrimination in North Carolina is with the North Carolina Human Relations Commission.

A real estate business is only as good as its reputation. Real estate licensees can maintain good reputations by demonstrating good business ability and adhering to ethical standards of business practices. Many licensees subscribe to a code of ethics as members of professional real estate organizations.

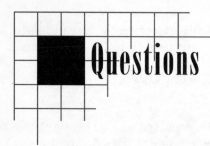

Questions

1. Which of the following acts is permitted under the federal Fair Housing Act?
   a. Advertising property for sale only to a special group
   b. Altering the terms of a loan for a member of a minority group
   c. Refusing to sell a home to an individual because of a poor credit history
   d. Telling an individual for discriminatory reasons that an apartment has been rented when in fact it has not

2. Which of the following statements is true of complaints relating to the Civil Rights Act of 1866?
   a. They must be taken directly to federal court.
   b. They are no longer reviewed in the courts.
   c. They are handled by HUD.
   d. They are handled by state enforcement agencies.

3. The Civil Rights Act of 1866 is unique because it
   a. has been broadened to protect the aged.
   b. adds welfare recipients as a protected class.
   c. contains "choose your neighbor" provisions.
   d. provides no exceptions to racial discrimination.

4. "I hear they're moving in. There goes the neighborhood. Better list with me today!" is an example of
   a. steering.   c. redlining.
   b. blockbusting.   d. testing.

5. The act of channeling homeseekers to a particular area either to maintain or to change the character of the neighborhood is
   a. blockbusting.
   b. redlining.
   c. steering.
   d. permitted under the Fair Housing Act of 1968.

6. A lender's refusal to lend money to potential homeowners attempting to purchase property located in a neighborhood with a predominant minority group is known as
   a. redlining.   c. steering.
   b. blockbusting.   d. qualifying.

7. Which of the following is not permitted under the federal Fair Housing Act and its amendments?
   I. The Harvard Club in New York rents rooms only to graduates of Harvard who belong to the club.
   II. The owner of a 20-unit apartment building rents to women only.
   a. I only
   b. II only
   c. Both I and II
   d. Neither I nor II

8. Under federal law, families with children may be refused rental or purchase in buildings where occupancy is reserved exclusively for those at least how many years old?
   a. 50   c. 62
   b. 60   d. 65

9. Guiding prospective buyers to a particular area because the agent feels they belong there may lead to
   a. blockbusting.   c. steering.
   b. redlining.   d. bird-dogging.

10. An African-American real estate broker's practice of offering a special discount to African-American clients is
    a. satisfactory.
    b. illegal.
    c. legal but ill-advised.
    d. of no consequence.

11. Which of the following statements describe(s) the Supreme Court decision in *Jones v. Alfred H. Mayer Company?*
    I. Racial discrimination is prohibited by any party in the sale or rental of real estate.
    II. Sales by individual residential homeowners are exempt, provided an owner does not employ a broker.
    a. I only
    b. II only
    c. Both I and II
    d. Neither I nor II

12. The federal Fair Housing Amendments Act of 1988 added which of the following as protected classes?
    a. Occupation and source of income
    b. Handicap and familial status
    c. Political affiliation and country of origin
    d. Prison record and marital status

13. The fine for a first violation of the federal Fair Housing Act could be as much as
    a. $500.   c. $5,000.
    b. $1,000.   d. $10,000.

14. The seller who requests prohibited discrimination in the showing of a house should be told
    I. "I'll need those instructions in writing to protect my company."
    II. "I'll do what I can, but I can't guarantee anything."
    III. "We are not allowed to obey such instructions."
    a. I only
    b. II only
    c. III only
    d. I, II or III

15. In North Carolina a person who feels he or she has been discriminated against in housing should
    a. first have the necessary funds for court costs in order to bring a civil action.
    b. first file a complaint with the North Carolina Human Relations Commission.
    c. not pursue it.
    d. first file a complaint with the OFHEO.

16. If a state or local law has been declared substantially equivalent to the federal Fair Housing Act, violations of the fair housing laws are referred to and handled by
    a. federal courts.
    b. local boards of REALTORS®.
    c. state enforcement agencies.
    d. HUD.

17. All of the following are in violation of the Fair Housing Act of 1968 EXCEPT the
    a. refusal of a property manager to rent an apartment to a Catholic couple who are otherwise qualified.
    b. general policy of a loan company to avoid granting home improvement loans to individuals living in transitional neighborhoods.
    c. intentional neglect of a broker to show an Asian family property listings in all-white neighborhoods.
    d. insistence of a widowed woman on renting her spare bedroom only to another widowed woman.

18. Under the provisions of the federal Fair Housing Act of 1968, if a lender refuses to make loans in areas where the population is made up of more than 25 percent African-Americans, the lender is probably guilty of
    a. redlining.
    b. steering.
    c. blockbusting.
    d. nothing (this behavior is not unlawful).

19. A real estate broker wants to end racial segregation. As an office policy, the broker requires that salespersons show prospective buyers from racial or ethnic minority groups only properties that are in certain areas of town where few members of their groups currently live. The broker has prepared a map illustrating the appropriate neighborhoods for each racial or ethnic group. Through this policy, the broker hopes to achieve racial balance in residential housing. Which of the following statements is true regarding this broker's policy?
    a. While the broker's policy may appear to constitute blockbusting, application of the effects test proves its legality.
    b. Because the effect of the broker's policy is discriminatory, it constitutes illegal steering, regardless of the broker's intentions.
    c. The broker's policy clearly shows the intent to discriminate.
    d. While the broker's policy may appear to constitute steering, application of the intent test proves its legality.

20. After a broker takes a listing of a residence, the owner specifies that he will not sell his home to any Asian family. The broker should do which of the following?
    a. Advertise the property exclusively in Asian-language newspapers
    b. Explain to the owner that the instructions violate federal law and that the broker cannot comply with it
    c. Abide by the principal's directions despite the fact that they conflict with the fair housing laws
    d. Require that the owner sign a separate legal document stating the additional instruction as an amendment to the listing agreements

21. A single man with two small children has been told by a real estate agent that homes for sale in a condominium complex are available only to married couples with no children. Which of the following statements is true?
    a. Because a single-parent family can be disruptive if the parent provides little supervision of the children, the condominium is permitted to discriminate against the families under the principle of rational basis.
    b. Condominium complexes are exempt from the fair housing laws and can therefore restrict children.
    c. The man may file a complaint alleging discrimination on the basis of familial status.
    d. Protective covenants in a condominium take precedence over the fair housing laws.

22. The following ad appeared in the newspaper: "For sale: 4 BR brick home; Redwood School District; excellent Elm street location; short walk to St. John's Church and right on the bus line. Move-in conditions. Priced to sell." Which of the following statements is true?
    a. The ad describes the property for sale and is very appropriate.
    b. The fair housing laws do not apply to newspaper advertising.
    c. The ad should state that the property is available to families with children.
    d. The ad should not mention St. John's Church.

8 Basic Contract Law and Agency Contracts

LEARNING OBJECTIVES

When you've finished reading this chapter, you should be able to

- **define** all types of contracts and **give** the requirements for a valid contract.

- **identify** the essential elements of contracts and their legal effect if absent.

- **define** statutes that apply to contract law and the legal remedies on breach of a contract.

- **describe** the different types of agency contracts and the procedures for using agency contracts.

- **define** these *key terms:*

assignment	executed contract	procuring cause
auction	executory contract	protection agreement
bilateral contract	express contract	ready, willing and able
breach of contract	implied contract	buyer
broker protection	legality of object	rescission
clause	legally competent	retainer fee
competitive	parties	reality of consent
(comparative)	liquidated damages	specific performance
market analysis	listing agreement	statute of frauds
(CMA)	multiple-listing service	statute of limitations
consideration	(MLS)	success fee
contract	mutual assent	unenforceable
counteroffer	net listing	contract
earnest money deposit	novation	unilateral contract
employment contract	offer and acceptance	valid contract
exclusive-agency listing	open listing	voidable contract
exclusive-right-to-sell	parol evidence rule	void contract
listing		

CONTRACTS

In the course of their business, brokers and salespeople use many types of contracts and agreements to carry out their responsibilities to sellers, buyers, landlords and tenants, and the general public. Among these are listing contracts, sales contracts, option contracts, land installment contracts and leases. The general body of law that governs the operation of such contract is known as *contract law*. This chapter discusses basic contract law that applies to all types of contracts and the various types of agency contracts.

CONTRACT DEFINITIONS AND CLASSIFICATIONS

A **contract** is a *legally enforceable promise or set of promises between legally competent parties, supported by legal consideration, to do (or refrain from doing) a legal act that must be performed and for which the law provides a remedy if a breach of promise occurs.* A contract must be

- *voluntary*—no one may be forced into a contract.
- *an agreement or a promise*—a contract is essentially a legally enforceable promise.
- *made by legally competent parties*—the parties must be viewed by the law as capable of making a legally binding promise.
- *supported by legal consideration*—a contract must be supported by some valuable thing that induces a party to enter into a contract and that must be legally sufficient to support a contract.
- *about a legal act*—no one may make a legal contract to do something illegal.

Depending on the situation and the nature or language of the agreement, a contract may be express or implied, unilateral or bilateral, executory or executed, valid, unenforceable, voidable or void.

Express and Implied Contracts

Depending on how a contract is created, it may be *express* or *implied.* In an **express contract,** the parties state the terms and show their intentions in words to that effect. An express contract may be either oral or written. In an **implied contract,** the agreement of the parties is demonstrated by their actions or conduct. In a seller-agency relationship, a listing agreement is a written, express contract between the seller and the broker, naming the broker as the fiduciary representative of the seller.

For Example Hugh approaches his neighbor, Bob, and says, "I will paint your house today for $500." Bob replies, "If you paint my house today, I will pay you $500." Hugh and Bob have entered into an express contract.

Ken goes into a restaurant and orders a meal. Ken has entered into an implied contract with the restaurant to pay for the meal, even though payment was not mentioned before the meal was ordered.

Bilateral and Unilateral Contracts

Contracts may also be classified as either *bilateral* or *unilateral.* In a **bilateral contract,** both parties promise to do or refrain from doing something; one promise is exchanged for another ("I will do this, and you will do that"). A real estate sales contract is a bilateral contract because the seller prom-

	Classification of Contract	Legal Effect	Example
Table 8.1 Legal Effects of Contracts			
	Valid	Binding and enforceable on both parties	Agreement complying with essentials of a valid contract
	Void	No legal effect	Contract for an illegal purpose
	Voidable	Valid but may be disaffirmed by one party	Contract with a minor
	Unenforceable	Valid between the parties, but neither may force performance	Certain oral agreements

ises to sell a parcel of real estate and deliver title to the property to the buyer, who promises to pay a certain sum of money for the property.

In a **unilateral contract,** one party makes a promise to induce a second party to do something. The second party is not legally obligated to act; however, if the second party does comply, the first party is obligated to keep the promise ("I will do this if you do that"). For example, if a person runs a newspaper ad offering a reward for the return of a lost pet, that person is promising to pay if the act of returning the pet is fulfilled.

Executed and Executory Contracts

A contract may be classified as either *executed* or *executory*, depending on whether the agreement is performed completely. An **executed contract** is one in which all parties have fulfilled their promises and thus performed the contract. (Do not be confused by the fact that the word *execute* is also used to refer to the signing of a contract.) An **executory contract** exists when something remains to be done by one or both parties. A sales contract, signed and accepted pending closing, is an example of an executory contract.

Validity of Contracts

A contract can be described as *valid, void, voidable* or *unenforceable* (see Table 8.1), depending on the circumstances.

> A contract may be
> - **valid**—has all legal elements; is fully enforceable;
> - **void**—lacks one or all elements; has no legal force or effect;
> - **voidable**—has all legal elements; may be rescinded or disaffirmed; or
> - **unenforceable**—has all legal elements; is enforceable only between the parties.

A **valid contract** complies with all the essential elements of a contract, which will be discussed later in this chapter, and is binding and enforceable on both parties.

A **void contract** is one that has no legal force or effect. It is unenforceable in a court of law because it does not meet the essential elements of a contract. However, a void contract may be fully executed unless one of the parties disaffirms it.

For Example Two persons enter into a "contract" where one party agrees to murder someone if the other party pays him. This calls for an illegal act to take place; therefore, the contract is void at law and could not be enforced in a court of law.

A **voidable contract** is one that seems on the surface to be valid but may be rescinded, or disaffirmed, by one or both parties, based on some legal principle.

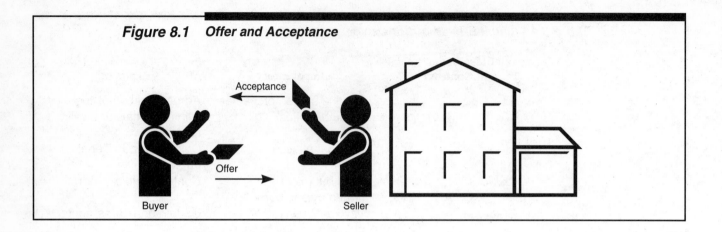

Figure 8.1   *Offer and Acceptance*

If someone makes a contract while drugged or intoxicated, the contract is voidable by that person. A voidable contract will be considered by the courts to be valid if the party who has the option to disaffirm the agreement does not do so within a prescribed period of time. A contract with a minor, for instance, is usually voidable. A contract entered into with a person who is known to be mentally ill is usually voidable during the mental illness. On the other hand a contract entered into with a person who is insane (as determined by the courts) is void.

An **unenforceable contract** has all the elements of a valid contract; however, neither party can sue the other to force performance. Unenforceable contracts are said to be "valid as between the parties" because once the agreement is fully executed and both parties are satisfied, neither has reason to initiate a lawsuit to force performance. For example, an oral agreement for the sale of a parcel of real estate would be unenforceable, because the statute of frauds (discussed later) requires that real estate sales contracts be in writing to be enforceable.

Essential elements of a valid contract. In general, the essentials of a valid contract include the following:

Elements of a contract:

• Legally competent parties
• Mutual assent or deliberate agreement
• Legality of object
• Consideration

- **Legally competent parties:** Both parties to the contract must be of legal age and have sufficient mental capacity. In North Carolina, 18 is the age of contractual capacity. Persons younger than 18 years of age are deemed infants or minors. Generally, minors' contracts are voidable by the minor or may be canceled before or within a reasonable time after the minor reaches age 18. (In other words, an adult cannot hold a minor to a contract, but a minor can hold an adult to a contract.) A salesperson or broker should inquire carefully into the ages of both the purchaser and the seller of real estate. Advanced age, in contrast, may be an indication of a person's incapacity to contract as a result of senility, weakness or other debilities. In questions of legal competency, it may be desirable to refer to the client's lawyer. A party who understands the nature and effect of the contract has sufficient mental capacity. Mental capacity is not the same as medical sanity.

- **Mutual assent or deliberate agreement: Mutual assent** is reached through an offer by one party that is accepted by the other. **Offer and acceptance** means that there must be a "meeting of the minds." Courts look to the objective intent of the parties to determine whether they intended to enter into a binding agreement. The terms of the agreement must be fairly definite and understood by both parties (see Figure 8.1). Furthermore, the acceptance must be actually communicated to the offeror. (The methods of making and receiving offers, the counteroffer, the acceptance and communication will be discussed in detail in Chapter 9.)

- **Legality of object:** To be valid, a contract must not contemplate a purpose that is illegal or against public policy. If a contract calls for immoral performance, discrimination or a criminal act to take place, the contract is void.

- **Consideration:** Courts will not enforce gratuitous (free) promises. **Consideration** is something of legal value (usually one party suffering a legal detriment), bargained for and given in exchange for a promise or an act. Any return promise to perform that has been bargained for and exchanged is legally sufficient to satisfy the consideration element; for example, the purchase price is the consideration in a real estate contract. A binder or earnest money deposit is not consideration and is not an essential element of a contract.

Absence of undue influence, duress, misrepresentation and mistake.

Contracts signed by a person under duress or undue influence are voidable by that person or by a court. Extreme care should be taken when one or more of the parties to a contract are elderly, sick, in great distress or under the influence of alcohol or legal or illegal drugs. To be valid, every contract must be signed as the free and voluntary act of each party. Misrepresentation, fraud or mistake of fact could render a contract voidable by the injured party. In the absence of these factors, **reality of consent** has been reached.

Revocation of an offer.

An offer may be *revoked* by the offeror at any time prior to acceptance if the revocation is communicated directly to the offeree by the offeror. It also can be revoked if the offeree learns of the revocation from a reliable source (such as the listing broker) and observes the offeror acting in a manner that indicates that the offer no longer exists.

Any attempt by the offeree to change the terms proposed by the offeror creates a **counteroffer.** The offeror is relieved of his or her original offer because the offeree has, in effect, rejected it by making a counteroffer. The offeror can accept the offeree's counteroffer or can reject it and, if he or she wishes, make another counteroffer. Any change in the last offer made results in another counteroffer, until one party agrees to the other party's counteroffer and both parties sign the final contract (see Figure 8.2). Counteroffers may be made by "pen and ink" changes or on a completely new offer to purchase and contract form.

An offer or a counteroffer *may be revoked at any time before it has been accepted* (even if the person making the offer or counteroffer agreed to keep the offer open for a set period of time), but the offeree must receive notification of the revocation. The contract should stipulate the manner of acceptance; generally, an offer is not considered accepted until the person making the offer has been *notified of the other party's acceptance.*

When the parties communicate through an agent or at a distance, questions may arise regarding whether an acceptance, a rejection or a counteroffer has effectively taken place. The real estate broker or salesperson should transmit all offers, acceptances or other responses as soon as possible to avoid such

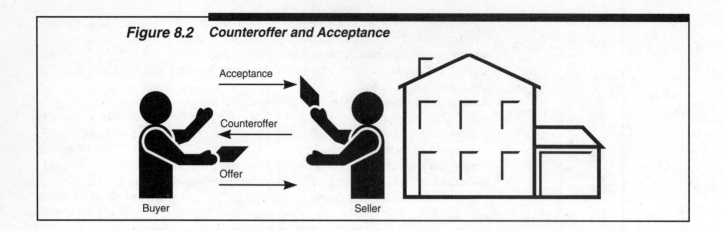

Figure 8.2   *Counteroffer and Acceptance*

Acceptance

Counteroffer

Offer

Buyer   Seller

problems. In North Carolina, these should be delivered as soon as possible, but in no event later than five days after execution [see G.S. 93A-6(a)(13) and Rule A.0106]. Remember that as an agent, a real estate licensee stands in the shoes of his or her principal. Communication of acceptance or revocation to an agent is the same as communication directly to the principal.

For Example A buyer who is represented by an agent has presented an offer to the seller on Monday. On Tuesday, the seller decides to accept the offer. The seller signs the offer to purchase, and on Tuesday night, the seller's agent tells the buyer's agent that the seller has accepted the buyer's offer. Because it is so late, the buyer's agent decides to wait until Wednesday to tell the buyer that the seller has accepted the offer. Early Wednesday morning, the buyer changes his mind and decides to revoke the offer. It is too late. The communication of the seller's acceptance to the buyer's agent is deemed to be communication to the buyer. Because the offer has been accepted and that acceptance has been communicated, the buyer can no longer revoke his offer.

Agreement in writing and signed. Not all contracts must be in writing to be enforceable; however, every state has adopted the common-law doctrine known as the **statute of frauds,** which requires that certain types of contracts be in writing to be enforceable in a court of law.

The North Carolina Statute of Frauds requires that to be enforceable in a court of law, conveyances of interests in real property—such as deeds, contracts for sale, mortgages, options, easements and certain leases (those that are for longer than three years)—must be in writing and signed by the party to be bound or by his or her legally authorized agent. A listing agreement is an employment contract and is not covered by the statute of frauds. However, North Carolina license laws require that listing agreements for sales transactions be in writing (Rule A.0104). The purpose of the statute of frauds is to prevent fraudulent proof of an oral contract.

The **parol evidence rule,** another heritage of the common law, is a rule of evidence that dictates that no oral agreements that contradict the terms of a written contract may be considered in a lawsuit based on the written agreement. The written contract is assumed to be the complete manifestation of the agreement of the parties. The many exceptions to the rule include evidence that a contract was entered into illegally or evidence intended to clarify ambiguous contract terms. The party who drafted the ambiguous terms would most likely be ruled against in a court hearing.

In Practice   If there is any ambiguity in a contract, the courts generally will interpret the agreement against the party who prepared it. For example, if the seller prepares the purchase and sales contract and one of the terms is ambiguous, the court will interpret that term in favor of the buyer.

CONTRACT LAW AND AUCTION SALES

The familiar procedure of a buyer making an offer to purchase, which the real estate agent then presents to the seller for acceptance or rejection, is avoided with an **auction.** Instead of merely presenting the offer to the seller, an auctioneer actually accepts the offer. (The typical real estate agent virtually never has the authority to accept an offer on behalf of the seller.) After the auctioneer accepts the offer, or bid, the buyer and seller formalize their oral agreement with a written document (to satisfy the statute of frauds) [see Rule A.0104(h)]. A real estate auctioneer must have two licenses: (1) a real estate license and (2) an auctioneer's license. The mere crier of sales is exempt from having a real estate license [see G.S. 93A-2(a)].

There are two types of auctions:

1. Auctions with reserve: The seller reserves the right to stop the bidding if it becomes apparent that the high bid will be unacceptable to the seller. The seller must reject all bids before the auction is concluded and the auctioneer accepts a bid.
2. Auctions without reserve: the seller agrees to accept the high bid, no matter what the terms of that bid.

Note that when the seller accepts any bid at any auction, no matter what type, the property is sold. Just because an auction may be with reserve does not mean that the seller can later change his or her mind about accepting a bid.

PERFORMANCE OF CONTRACT

Under any contract, each party has certain rights and duties to fulfill. The question of when a contract must be performed is an important factor. Many contracts call for a specific time at or by which the agreed-on acts must be completely performed. In addition, many contracts provide that "time is of the essence." This means that the contract must be performed within the time limit specified, and any party who has not performed on time is liable for breach of contract. If an offeror includes "time is of the essence" in his or her offer, the offeror can still revoke the offer at any time prior to acceptance.

When a contract does not specify a date for performance, the acts it requires should be performed within a reasonable time (as determined by the court, if a conflict arises). The interpretation of what constitutes a reasonable time will depend on the situation. Generally, if the act can be done immediately—such as a payment of money—it should be performed immediately unless the parties agree otherwise.

In Practice

Despite the best efforts of buyer and seller, it may be impossible to close a transaction on the date stipulated. The seller may not be able to complete necessary repairs before that date. The buyer's lender may be swamped with loan applications and unable to provide funding on the date requested. Buyer and seller can adjust the closing date (or any other contract term) by a modification of the contract—a written addendum signed by all parties. The broker may negotiate the new term(s) but may not sign the modification on behalf of any of the parties. Contingencies must be anticipated so as to allow sufficient time for completion when contracts are executed.

Assignment and Novation

Often, after a contract has been entered into, one party wants to withdraw without actually terminating the agreement. This may be accomplished through either assignment or novation.

Assignment refers to a transfer of rights or duties under a contract. Generally speaking, rights may be assigned to a third party unless the agreement forbids such an assignment. Duties may also be assigned (delegated), but the original obligor remains secondarily liable for them (after the new obligor) unless he or she is specifically released from this responsibility. A contract is generally considered to be assignable unless it states otherwise. The exception to this rule is a contract for personal services, which may not be assigned. Most contracts include a clause that either permits or forbids assignment. An assignment does not terminate the contract.

| *Assignment* = substitution of *parties* |
| *Novation* = substitution of *contracts* |

Novation is another way to avoid the terms of an existing contract without breaching or terminating that contract. *Nova* means new, and *novation* is the substitution of a new contract for an existing agreement with the intent of extinguishing the old contract. The new agreement may be between the same parties, or a new party may be substituted for either (*novation of the parties*). The parties' intent must be to discharge the old obligation. The new agreement must be supported by consideration and must conform with all the essential elements of a valid contract. For example, when a real estate purchaser assumes the seller's existing mortgage loan (see Chapter 12), the lender may release the seller and substitute the buyer as the party primarily liable for the mortgage debt.

Discharge of Contract

A contract may be performed completely, with all terms carried out, or it may be breached (broken) if one of the parties defaults. A contract also may be discharged (canceled) by various other methods. These include the following:

- *Partial performance* of the terms of the contract. This is sometimes referred to as *accord and satisfaction*. When one party accepts something less than agreed on as complete performance, the contract is considered discharged.

- *Substantial performance,* in which one party has substantially performed the contract but does not complete all the details exactly as the contract requires. Such performance—for example, under construction contracts—may be sufficient to force payment, with certain adjustments for any damages suffered by the other party.
- *Impossibility of performance,* in which an act required by the contract cannot be accomplished legally.
- *Mutual agreement* of the parties to cancel.
- *Operation of law,* as in the voiding of a contract by a minor, as a result of fraud or the expiration of the statute of limitations (discussed later in this chapter) or as a result of the alteration of a contract without the written consent of all parties involved. Bankruptcy can also discharge a contractual obligation.

Default—Breach of Contract

A **breach of contract** is a violation, without legal excuse, of any of the terms or conditions of a contract, as when a seller breaches a sales contract by not delivering title to the buyer under the conditions stated in the agreement. The breaching, or defaulting, party has certain burdens, and the nondefaulting party has certain rights.

If a party to a contract defaults, the injured party has several alternatives:

- The injured party may *sue the seller for money (compensatory) damages.* Money damages are awarded to the injured party to compensate him or her for the breach of the contract, not to punish the party who breached the contract. The amount of the money damages should be only what is necessary to "make the party whole"—that is, put the party in the position he or she would have been in if the contract had been performed as agreed. The buyer can be sued for compensatory damages as well if his earnest money is not adequate to cover the seller's losses.
- The injured party may be entitled to collect **liquidated damages.** The term *liquidated damages* is defined as *the amount of money that will compensate the injured party for breach, an amount agreed to by the parties at the time they enter into the contract.* For example, the **earnest money deposit** is often considered liquidated damages in the event the buyer breaches the contract. The seller is entitled to keep the amount of the deposit as compensation for any injuries caused by the breach of contract.
- **Consequential damages** are special damages that might be obtained if the breaching party had intentions of breaking the contract at the time of making the contract.
- The injured party may file a court action, known as a suit for **specific performance,** to force the other party to perform the contract as agreed. Specific performance is ordered only when the subject matter of the contract is not readily available from another source. Because every parcel of real estate is considered unique, a suit for specific performance brought by the buyer or seller under a purchase and sales contract may be successful.
- The injured party may *rescind the contract,* which means the contract is declared invalid and both parties return to the position they were in before they entered into the contract. **Rescission** may be appropriate when facts were misrepresented or one party entered the contract under duress. A right of a rescission may be written into the contract or may be stipulated by law, such as the five-day right of rescission for a

time-share purchase or the seven-day right of rescission for a condominium purchase.

Statute of Limitations   North Carolina law allows a specific time limit during which parties to a contract may bring legal suit to enforce their rights. The **statute of limitations** varies for different legal actions, and any rights not enforced within the applicable time period are lost.

BROKER'S AUTHORITY TO PREPARE DOCUMENTS

A licensed real estate broker or salesperson is not authorized to practice law, in accordance with general statutes [see G.S. 93A-6(a)(11)]. To draft (prepare) legal documents for others is considered to be a practice of law and therefore is prohibited by law in North Carolina. Rule A.0111 of the Real Estate Commission states that an agent "in a real estate transaction shall not draft offers, sales contracts, options, leases, promissory notes, deeds, deeds of trust or other legal instruments by which rights of others are secured". A broker or salesperson may, however, be permitted to fill in the blanks on certain approved preprinted documents (such as sales contracts and leases) when authorized to do so by the parties, provided the licensee does not charge a separate fee for completing such forms.

In Practice   Licensees are permitted to use electronic, computer or word processing equipment to store preprinted approved forms; however, they may not be altered in any way before the form is presented to the parties to the contract. Licensees may however, make written notes, memoranda or correspondence recording negotiations of the parties to the transaction as long as they do not constitute binding agreements. The parties to the instruments may delete or change provisions, but the change or deletion must be marked to so indicate.

Contract forms. *Printed forms* are used for many kinds of contracts because most transactions are similar in nature. The use of printed forms raises three problems: (1) how to *fill in the blanks*, (2) what printed matter is not applicable to a particular sale and is to be *ruled out* by drawing a line through the unwanted words and (3) what additional clauses or agreements (called *riders* or *addenda*) are to be included. All changes and additions should be dated and must be initialed in the margin or on the rider by both parties when the contract is executed.

LISTING CONTRACTS AND PRACTICES

The first type of contract an agent is likely to encounter is the **listing agreement.** As mentioned in Chapter 6, a listing agreement creates a special agency relationship between the principal (usually the seller) and the broker (the agent), wherein the agent is authorized to represent the principal and the principal's property to third parties, including securing and submitting offers for the property.

Why a Listing Agreement?   Just as a supermarket without inventory will have no customers, the real estate broker without inventory will have no customers—and thus no business. To acquire inventory, most brokers obtain listings of properties for sale (although some work with properties for lease, rent, exchange or option).

The listing agreement is an **employment contract** rather than a real estate contract. With a listing agreement, the broker is hired to represent the principal, but real property is not transferred. Listing agreements in sales transactions must be in writing *from the formation of the relationship* [see Rule A.0104(a)]. Every agreement for brokerage services between a broker and an owner of real property must be in writing from the time of its formation. *Under* Commission rules, there can be no verbal/*oral agency agreement with a property owner, whether* a listing contract with a seller *or property management agreement with an owner.*

Under the provisions of North Carolina's real estate license laws, only a broker can act as an agent to list, sell or rent another person's real estate.

Note: Throughout this chapter, unless otherwise stated, the terms *broker, agent* and *firm* are intended to include both the broker and a salesperson working under the broker. However, *only the broker* has the authority to list, lease and sell property and provide other services to a principal.

Broker's Entitlement to a Commission   The broker's compensation is specified in the listing agreement. The most widely used type of compensation is a commission, or brokerage fee, computed as a *percentage of the final accepted sales price.* A flat-fee commission is another way to receive compensation. The commission, usually considered earned when the broker has accomplished the work for which he or she was hired, is due at the closing of the sale or other transaction. Most sales commissions are paid when all terms of the purchase agreement have been fulfilled.

To be entitled to collect a commission, an agent must be licensed, must be employed by the principal under a valid written listing agreement, must be the procuring cause of the sale and must produce a **ready, willing and able buyer.** Licensed salespersons can be paid directly only by their employing brokers, not by a principal. To be considered the **procuring cause** of sale, the broker must have taken action to start (or cause) a chain of events that resulted in the sale. A broker who causes or completes such action without a contract that promises compensation is deemed a volunteer and has no legal claim to compensation.

Once a broker obtains an offer from a ready, willing and able buyer on the seller's terms, the seller is technically liable for the broker's commission. A ready, willing and able buyer is one who is *financially qualified, prepared to buy on the seller's terms and ready to take positive steps toward consummation of the transaction by showing willingness to enter into an enforceable contract.* But even if the transaction is not consummated, the broker still may be entitled to a commission when the seller

- has a change of mind and refuses to sell,
- has a spouse who refuses to sign the deed (if that spouse signed the listing agreement),
- has a title with uncorrected defects,
- commits fraud with respect to the transaction,
- is unable to deliver possession within a reasonable time,

- insists on terms not in the listing (for example, the right to restrict the use of the property) or
- has a mutual agreement with the buyer to cancel the transaction.

In other words, *a broker generally is due a commission if a sale is not consummated because of the principal's default.* Also, even if the buyer backs out without legal cause after the seller has accepted the offer, the broker is entitled to the commission.

The rate of a broker's commission is negotiable in every case. For members of the profession to attempt, however subtly, to impose uniform commission rates is a clear violation of federal antitrust laws. The important point is for broker and client to agree on a rate before the agency relationship is established. If no amount or percentage rate of commission is stated in the listing contract and a legal action results, the court may determine a reasonable commission by evidence of the custom in a particular community. The North Carolina Real Estate Commission is prohibited by law from regulating the amount of commission charged by licensees [see G.S. 93A-3(c)].

Historically, under terms of the traditional agency relationship, the brokerage fee was paid by the seller to the listing broker, who then split that fee with his or her own sales agent who took the listing. If another company found the buyer of the property, the broker also would have to split the fee with that cooperating broker. However, as the practice of buyer agency becomes more widespread, earning compensation becomes a little more confusing.

Naturally, to earn any compensation, the buyer's broker must have an active real estate license and have a valid buyer-agency contract. The terms of that buyer-agency contract will control how much compensation is to be paid to the buyer's agent and which party that compensation will come from. (There are currently no points of law or court cases in North Carolina to provide legal guidance on the question of how to pay a buyer agent.)

Buyer's agents may be compensated by *retainer fees* and *success fees.* The **retainer fee** is typically a small amount of compensation, usually paid up front by the buyer-client when the buyer-agency agreement is signed. This fee is advance compensation for services. The **success fee** is due and payable by the buyer-principal on the signing and acceptance of an offer to purchase property found by the buyer's agent. The buyer-agency agreement normally states that the buyer's agent will first try to recover the success fee from the listing agent (see Figure 8.5, Paragraph 4).

Types of Listing Agreements

The forms of listing agreements, or employment contracts, generally used are (1) open listing, (2) exclusive-agency listing and (3) exclusive-right-to-sell listing.

Open listing. In an **open listing,** the seller retains the right to employ any number of brokers as agents; it is a nonexclusive type listing. The brokers can act simultaneously, and the seller is obligated to pay a commission only to that broker who successfully produces a ready, willing and able buyer. If the seller personally sells the property *without the aid of any of the brokers,* the seller is not obligated to pay any broker a commission; the seller can compete for the commission. If any of the brokers or the owner sells the property, all other open listings on that property will terminate the authority given to those brokers. A broker who was in any way a procuring cause of the transaction, however, may be entitled to a commission if the procuring cause of sale can be proved.

Open listing:

- There are multiple agents.
- Only selling agent is entitled to a commission.
- Seller retains the right to sell independently without obligation.

MATH CONCEPTS

Sharing Commissions

A commission might be shared by many people: the listing broker, the listing salesperson, the selling broker and the selling salesperson. Drawing a diagram can help you determine which person is entitled to receive what amount of the total commission.

Salesperson Eve, while working for broker Harry, took a listing on a $73,000 house at a 6 percent commission rate. Salesperson Ted, while working for broker Mike, found the buyer for the property. If the property sold for the listed price, the listing broker and the selling broker shared the commission equally. If the selling broker kept 45 percent of what he received, how much did salesperson Ted receive? (If the broker retained 45 percent of the total commission that he received, his salesperson would receive the balance: 100% – 45% = 55%.)

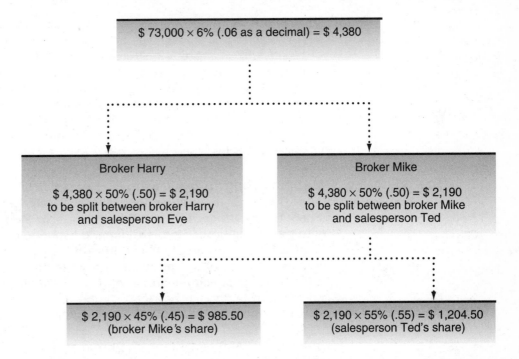

$ 73,000 × 6% (.06 as a decimal) = $ 4,380

Broker Harry

$ 4,380 × 50% (.50) = $ 2,190
to be split between broker Harry
and salesperson Eve

Broker Mike

$ 4,380 × 50% (.50) = $ 2,190
to be split between broker Mike
and salesperson Ted

$ 2,190 × 45% (.45) = $ 985.50
(broker Mike's share)

$ 2,190 × 55% (.55) = $ 1,204.50
(salesperson Ted's share)

Exclusive-agency listing:

- There is one authorized agent.
- Broker receives a commission only if he or she is the procuring cause.
- Seller retains the right to sell without obligation.

Exclusive-agency listing. In an **exclusive-agency listing,** one broker is specifically authorized to act as the exclusive agent of the principal. The *seller* under this form of agreement *retains the right to sell the property by himself or herself,* without obligation to the broker; the seller can compete for the commission. If the seller sells through his or her own efforts, the exclusive agency of the broker is automatically terminated. The seller is obligated to pay a commission to the broker if the broker has been the procuring cause of a sale or if any broker sells the property with or without the authority of the exclusive listing broker.

Exclusive-right-to-sell listing. In an **exclusive-right-to-sell listing,** one broker is appointed as sole agent of the seller and is given the exclusive right, or *authorization,* to represent the property in question. Under this form of listing contract, the seller must pay the broker a *commission regardless of who sells the property* if it is sold while the listing is in effect. In other

Exclusive-right-to-sell listing:

- One authorized agent
- Broker receives a commission regardless of who sells the property.

words, if the seller gives a broker an exclusive-right-to-sell listing but finds a buyer without the broker's assistance, the seller still must pay the broker a commission. In North Carolina, this is the most common form of listing. Please note that the listing contains specific language stating that the broker is entitled to the commission regardless of who actually sells the property. Claiming a commission as the procuring cause of the sale has no legal effect. The term *exclusive right to sell* does not imply that the broker has the authority to enter into a *sales contract* on behalf of the property owner. The listing agreement is not an offer to sell the property, it is an *employment* agreement.

Protection agreement. A **protection agreement** is used to guarantee a broker a commission if a particular property is sold to a particular buyer. It does not create a general listing.

For Example A broker may use a protection agreement when she has a client who is interested in a specific type of property. The broker knows this buyer would be interested in a particular house that is "For Sale by Owner." However, the broker does not want to suggest that the buyer view the house because the broker would lose the opportunity to earn a commission. Instead, the broker might approach the homeowner and ask whether he would agree to pay her a commission if her client decided to purchase the home. Some brokers use a one-party listing agreement in these circumstances, carefully limiting the effectiveness of the listing agreement to the one party the broker has in mind.

Special Listing Provisions

Multiple listing. A *multiple-listing clause* may be included in an exclusive listing. Brokers who are members of a **multiple-listing service (MLS)** agree to pool their listings. The multiple-listing provision gives additional authority to the listing broker to *distribute the listing to other brokers who belong to the MLS.* The contractual obligations among the member brokers of a multiple-listing organization vary widely. Most listing agreements include what is called *an offer of compensation and cooperation.* Under this provision, the commission is divided between the listing broker and the selling broker, regardless of which party the selling broker represents.

Under most MLS contracts, the broker who secures a listing is not only authorized but *obligated* to turn over the listing to the MLS within a definite period of time so that it can be distributed to the other member brokers. The length of time during which the listing broker can offer the property exclusively without notifying the other member brokers varies by REALTOR® board.

A multiple-listing provision offers advantages to both the broker and the seller. Brokers develop a sizable inventory of properties to be sold and are ensured a portion of the commission if they list a property or participate in its sale. Sellers also gain under this form of listing agreement because all members of the multiple-listing organization are eligible to sell their property and are made aware of its availability.

Termination of Listings

A listing agreement may be terminated for any of the following reasons:

- Completion or fulfillment of the purpose for which the agency was created (the best way to terminate a listing)
- Expiration of the terms of the agency
- Mutual agreement to terminate the agency

- Breach by one of the parties, such as abandonment by the agent or revocation by the principal (The breaching party might be liable for damages.)
- By operation of law, as in bankruptcy of the principal (because title to the property would be transferred to a court-appointed receiver)
- Destruction or condemnation of the property
- Death or incapacity of either party (Notice of death is not necessary. Note that if a property is listed with a brokerage firm and the listing agent dies, the listing would not be terminated.)

A listing agreement is a *personal service contract* with the broker (not the individual sales agent), and its success depends on the personal efforts of the broker who is party to the agreement. The broker cannot turn over the listing to another broker. If the broker abandons the listing by failing to work toward its fulfillment or if he or she revokes the agreement, the property owner cannot force the broker to comply with it. The property owner can, however, sue the broker for damages.

The property owner could fail to fulfill the terms of the agreement by refusing to cooperate with reasonable requests of the broker (such as allowing tours of the property by prospective buyers) or by refusing to proceed with a sales contract. If the property owner cancels the listing agreement, he or she could be liable for damages to the broker.

Expiration of listing period. All listings must specify a definite period of time during which the broker is to be employed. *In North Carolina, all written listings must specify a definite termination date* [Rule A.0104](a). The listing form must provide for a definite period of time with an automatic termination date. If the property has not been sold by midnight of the termination date, it is automatically terminated without notification being required of either party.

The Listing Contract Form

A wide variety of listing contract forms is available today. Some brokers draft their own contracts; some use forms prepared by their MLS; some use forms produced by the North Carolina Association of REALTORS®. No matter which form is used, most listing contracts require similar information because the same considerations arise in almost all real estate transactions. A copy of the North Carolina Association of REALTORS® Exclusive Right to Sell Listing Agreement is shown in Figure 8.3.

Description of the premises. All listing agreements should include a clear and precise description of the real estate to be sold. While the legal description does not have to be included for the listing agreement to be valid, it is always wise to do so to avoid confusion and ambiguity.

Note that in addition to the real property, all items of personal property that are to be included in the sale should be described. Most listing agreements include a section that lists the items of personal property that will be left with the real estate when it is sold and the items of real property (fixtures) the seller expects to remove at the time of sale. Each item should be explicitly identified (brand name, serial number, color), even though some items may become points of negotiation should a ready, willing and able buyer be found. Typical items to consider are major appliances, swimming pool and

Figure 8.3   *Exclusive Right to Sell Listing Agreement*

EXCLUSIVE RIGHT TO SELL LISTING AGREEMENT

This EXCLUSIVE RIGHT TO SELL LISTING AGREEMENT ("Agreement") is entered into (Date)_____, between_____ as Seller(s) ("Seller") of the property described below (the "Property"), and_____ as Listing Firm ("Agent").

1.   **REAL PROPERTY.** The real property that is the subject of this Agreement is located in the City of _____, County of _____, State of North Carolina, and is known more particularly and described as: Street Address_____ Zip_____ Legal Description_____ (❑ All ❑ A portion of the property in Deed Reference: Book _____ Page No _____, _____County.)

2.   **FIXTURES.** The following items, if any, are included free of liens: any built-in appliances, light fixtures, ceiling fans, attached floor coverings, blinds, shades, drapery rods and curtain rods, brackets and all related hardware, window and door screens, storm windows, combination doors, awnings, antennas, satellite dishes and receivers, burglar/fire/smoke alarms, pool and spa equipment, solar energy systems, attached fireplace screens, gas logs, fireplace inserts, electric garage door openers with controls, outdoor plants and trees (other than in movable containers), basketball goals, storage sheds, mailboxes, wall and/or door mirrors, and any other items attached or affixed to the Property, EXCEPT the following items:_____ _____

3.   **PERSONAL PROPERTY.** The following personal property is included in the listing price:_____ _____ _____

4.   **LISTING PRICE.** Seller lists the Property at a price of $_____on the following terms: ( ) Cash ( ) Loan Assumption ( ) Conventional ( ) FHA ( ) VA ( ) Seller Financing ( ) Other _____. Seller agrees to sell the Property for the Listing Price or for any other price or on any other terms acceptable to Seller.

5.   **TERM.** In consideration of the Seller agreeing to list the Property for sale and in further consideration of Agent's services and efforts to find a buyer, Agent is hereby granted the exclusive right to sell the Property from (Date) _____ until midnight, (Date)_____.

6.   **AGENCY RELATIONSHIPS.** Seller has received a copy of the "Working With Real Estate Agents" brochure and has reviewed it with Agent. With respect to dual agency *(Check only ONE)*:
    ❑   Seller authorizes the Agent to act as a Dual Agent, representing both the Seller and the Buyer, subject to the terms and conditions of the attached Dual Agency Addendum.
    ❑   Seller desires exclusive representation at all times during this agreement and does NOT authorize Agent to act in the capacity of Dual Agent.

7.   **COOPERATION WITH OTHER AGENTS.** Agent has advised Seller of Agent's general company policy regarding cooperation with subagents, buyer agents or both. Seller authorizes Agent to *(Check ALL applicable authorizations)*:
    ❑   Cooperate with and compensate subagents representing only the Seller
    ❑   Cooperate with and compensate buyer agents representing only the buyer
Cooperating agents must orally disclose the nature of their relationship with a buyer (subagent or buyer agent) to Agent at the time of initial contact with Agent, and confirm that relationship in writing no later than the time an offer to purchase is submitted for the Seller's consideration. **Seller should be careful about disclosing confidential information because agents representing buyers must disclose all relevant information to their clients.**

8.   **AGENT'S COMPENSATION.** Seller agrees to pay Agent a fee of _____ % of the gross sales price of the Property, OR_____, and that such fee shall be deemed earned under any of the following circumstances:

Page 1 of 3

Figure 8.3 Exclusive Right to Sell Listing Agreement (continued)

(a) If a ready, willing and able buyer is procured by Agent, the Seller, or anyone else during the Term of this Agreement at the price and on the terms set forth herein, or at any price and upon any terms acceptable to the Seller;

(b) If the Property is sold, exchanged, conveyed or transferred, or the Seller agrees to sell, exchange, convey or transfer the Property at any price and upon any terms whatsoever, during the Term of this Agreement or any renewal hereof;

(c) If, within _____ days after expiration of the Term of this Agreement (the "Protection Period"), Seller either directly or indirectly sells, exchanges, conveys or transfers, or agrees to sell, exchange, convey or transfer the Property upon any terms whatsoever, to any person with whom Seller, Agent, or any real estate licensee communicated regarding the Property during the Term of this Agreement or any renewal hereof, provided the names of such persons are delivered or postmarked to the Seller within 15 days from date of expiration. HOWEVER, Seller shall NOT be obligated to pay such fee if a valid listing agreement is entered into between Seller and another real estate broker and the Property is sold, exchanged, conveyed or transferred during such Protection Period.

Once earned as set forth above, Agent compensation will be due and payable at the earlier of: (i) closing on the Property; (ii) the Seller's failure to sell the Property (including but not limited to the Seller's refusal to sign an offer to purchase the Property at the price and terms stated herein or on other terms acceptable to the Seller, the Seller's default on an executed sales contract for the Property, or the Seller's agreement with a buyer to unreasonably modify or cancel an executed sales contract for the Property); or (iii) Seller's breach of this Agreement.

9. **AGENT'S DUTIES.** Agent agrees to provide Seller the benefit of Agent's knowledge, experience and advice in the marketing and sale of the Property. Seller understands that Agent makes no representation or guarantee as to the sale of the Property, but Agent agrees to use his best efforts in good faith to find a buyer who is ready, willing and able to purchase the property. Seller acknowledges that Agent is required by law to disclose to potential purchasers of the Property all material facts pertaining to the Property about which the Agent knows or reasonably should know, and that REALTORS® have an ethical responsibility to treat all parties to the transaction honestly. Seller further acknowledges that Agent is being retained solely as a real estate professional, and understands that other professional service providers are available to render advice or services to Seller at Seller's expense, including but not limited to an attorney, insurance agent, tax advisor, surveyor, structural engineer, home inspector, environmental consultant, architect, or contractor. If Agent procures any such services at the request of Seller, Seller agrees that Agent shall incur no liability or responsibility in connection therewith.

In connection with the marketing and sale of the Property, Seller authorizes and directs Agent: (***Check ALL applicable sections***)

❏ to place "For Sale," "Under Contract," "Sale Pending," or other similar signs on the Property (where permitted by law and relevant covenants) and to remove other such signs;

❏ to place a lock box on the Property.

❏ to advertise the Property, including, but not limited to, placing information about the Property on the Internet either directly or through a program of any listing service of which the Agent is a member.

❏ to permit other firms who belong to any listing service of which the Agent is a member to advertise the Property on the Internet in accordance with the listing service rules and regulations.

❏ to submit pertinent information concerning the Property to any listing service of which Agent is a member and to furnish to such listing service notice of all changes of information concerning the Property authorized in writing by Seller. Seller authorizes Agent, upon execution of a sales contract for the Property, to notify the listing service of the pending sale, and upon closing of the sale, to disseminate sales information, including sales price, to the listing service, appraisers and real estate brokers.

Agent shall conduct all brokerage activities in regard to this agreement without respect to the race, color, religion, sex, national origin, handicap or familial status of any buyer, prospective buyer, seller or prospective seller.

10. **SELLER'S DUTIES.** Seller agrees to cooperate with Agent in the marketing and sale of the Property, including but not limited to:

(a) providing to Agent, in a timely manner, accurate information including but not limited to the Residential Property Disclosure Statement (unless exempt), and the Lead-Based Paint or Lead-Based Paint Hazard Addendum with respect to any residential dwelling built prior to 1978;

(b) making the Property available for showing (including working, existing utilities) at reasonable times and upon reasonable notice;

(c) providing Agent as soon as reasonably possible after the execution of this Agreement copies of restrictive covenants, if any, and copies of the bylaws, articles of incorporation, rules and regulations, and other governing documents of the owners' association and/or the subdivision, if applicable.

Page 2 of 3

Agent Initial _____   Seller Initials _____   _____

STANDARD FORM 101
© 7/2002

Figure 8.3   Exclusive Right to Sell Listing Agreement (continued)

If the Property is sold during the period set forth herein, the Seller agrees to execute and deliver a GENERAL WARRANTY DEED conveying fee simple marketable title to the Property, including legal access to a public right of way, free of all encumbrances except ad valorem taxes for the current year, utility easements, rights-of-way, and unviolated restrictive covenants, if any, and those encumbrances that the buyer agrees to assume in the sales contract. Seller represents that the Seller has the right to convey the Property, and that there are currently no circumstances that would prohibit the Seller from conveying fee simple marketable title as set forth in the preceding sentence.

❑ Seller acknowledges receipt of a sample copy of an Offer to Purchase And Contract for review purposes.
❑ Seller acknowledges receipt of a copy of the brochure *Questions and Answers on: Home Inspections*

11. **FLOOD HAZARD INSURANCE.** The Seller ❑ does ❑ does not currently maintain flood hazard insurance on the Property.

12. **SYNTHETIC STUCCO.** To the best of Seller's knowledge, the Property has not been clad previously (either in whole or in part) with an "exterior insulating and finishing system," commonly known as "EIFS" or "synthetic stucco", unless disclosed as follows: (*If the Seller does not wish to disclose, put "No Representation"*): _____
_____.

13. **EARNEST MONEY.** Unless otherwise provided in the sales contract, earnest money deposits paid toward the purchase price shall be held by the Agent, in escrow, until the consummation or termination of the transaction. Any earnest money forfeited by reason of the Buyer's default under a sales contract shall be divided equally between the Agent and Seller. In no event shall the sum paid to the Agent because of a Buyer's default be in excess of the fee that would have been due if the sale had closed as contemplated in the sales contract.

14. **MEDIATION.** If a dispute arises out of or related to this Agreement or the breach thereof, and if the dispute cannot be settled through negotiation, the parties agree first to try in good faith to settle the dispute by mediation before resorting to arbitration, litigation, or some other dispute resolution procedure. If the need for mediation arises, the parties will choose a mutually acceptable mediator and will share the cost of mediation equally.

15. **ADDITIONAL TERMS AND CONDITIONS.** The following additional terms and conditions shall also be a part of this Agreement:_____
_____
_____
_____

16. **ENTIRE AGREEMENT/CHANGES.** This Agreement constitutes the entire agreement between Seller and Agent and there are no representations, inducements, or other provisions other than those expressed herein. All changes, additions, or deletions to this Agreement must be in writing and signed by both Seller and Agent.

Seller and Agent each acknowledge receipt of a signed copy of this Agreement.

THE NORTH CAROLINA ASSOCIATION OF REALTORS®, INC. MAKES NO REPRESENTATION AS TO THE LEGAL VALIDITY OR ADEQUACY OF ANY PROVISION OF THIS FORM IN ANY SPECIFIC TRANSACTION.

Seller_____ SS/TAX ID# _____

Seller_____ SS/TAX ID# _____

Mailing Address _____
Home Phone_____ Work Phone _____ Work Phone _____
Fax _____ E-mail Address _____

Agent (Listing Firm)_____
By: _____Office Phone_____
Fax _____ E-mail Address _____
Office Address_____

Page 3 of 3

STANDARD FORM 101
© 7/2002

spa equipment, fireplace accessories, storage sheds, stacked firewood, stored heating oil and so on.

Listing price. A listing agreement always should state the price the seller wants for his or her property. The other terms of the sale also should be included. For example, whether the price is to be paid in cash or financed is an important term. If the seller's mortgage cannot be assumed or if the seller refuses to offer any type of seller financing, then the seller must be paid in cash. (Note that most buyers must get a mortgage loan in order to pay the seller cash.) Remember, if the broker procures a buyer who is ready, willing and able to purchase on the terms stated in the listing agreement, the broker will be deemed to have earned the commission whether or not the seller accepts the offer.

Note that the listing price is the proposed gross sales price. The seller should understand that any outstanding obligations, such as unpaid real estate taxes, special assessments and mortgage and trust deed debts, remain the seller's responsibility and must be paid from the proceeds of the sale unless otherwise contractually agreed to by the buyer.

Broker's duties. The agreement should state the obligations the broker promises to fulfill. These include but are not limited to advertising, showing the property, submitting the contract to an MLS and accounting for funds received on behalf of the seller.

For example, according to the terms of the contract, will the broker be able to place a sign on the property? Advertise and market the property using the broker's best efforts? Submit the contract to an MLS? Show the property at reasonable times and on reasonable notice to the seller? Place a lockbox on the property and accept earnest money deposits on behalf of the seller? Without written consent of the seller, the broker cannot undertake any such activities.

Brokerage fee. The listing agreement must specify the fee to be paid the broker. The brokerage fee must be freely negotiable between the parties (thus, it cannot be preprinted on a standard form). Real estate agents cannot state or imply that the brokerage fee is set by law or by an MLS or Board of REALTORS®, nor can they state that it is the standard or customary fee.

Brokerage fees can be based on a commission (a percentage of the sales price), a flat fee (a specific sum of money to be paid on the sale of the property) or a net amount. If the listing calls for a net fee, the agreement is referred to as a **net listing.** A net listing provision refers to the amount of money the seller will receive if the property is sold. The seller's property is listed for this net amount, and the broker is free to offer the property for sale at any price higher than the listing price. If the property is sold, the broker receives from the seller any proceeds exceeding the stipulated net amount to be retained by the seller. Although not illegal in North Carolina, *this type of listing is not recommended. The question of fraud frequently is raised because of uncertainty over the sales price set or received by the broker.* The term *net amount* is often misunderstood and disputed.

Override or extender clause. Some listing contracts contain an *override* or *extender clause,* which provides that the property owner will pay the listing broker a commission if, within a specified number of days after the listing expires, the owner sells, rents, leases or options the property to or exchanges the property with someone the owner originally met or made contact with through the broker. (An example of an extender clause can be found in the listing form shown in Figure 8.3.) This clause protects the broker who introduces two parties and thus is the procuring cause of a sale, only to have the parties enter into a contract and complete the transaction after the listing expires. The time for such a clause usually parallels the terms of the listing agreement; for example, a six-month listing would probably carry a **broker protection clause** of six months after the listing's expiration. However, to protect the owner and prevent owner liability for two separate commissions, most of these clauses stipulate that they cannot be enforced if the property is relisted under a new contract, either with the original listing broker or with another broker. To enforce this clause, the listing broker must provide the seller with the names of potential buyers who looked at the property during the listing period.

Agency disclosure. As previously discussed in Chapter 6, the real estate agent must at first substantial contact with a buyer or seller in all real estate sales transactions give and review the brochure and determine agency status. The tear-out panel on the brochure must be appropriately filled out, signed by the buyer/seller, and a copy retained by the agent.

Information Needed When Listing Properties

It is important to obtain as much information as possible concerning a parcel of real estate when taking a listing. It is wise to complete a physical inspection of the property in the presence of the seller and collect all the physical data necessary to submit to the MLS for inclusion in its property data block. Of course, it is important to make sure all the data are accurate. (Puffing is not permitted here as it may be in advertising.) The agent should point out any defects to the seller that may need correcting before the property can be shown. Also during this phase of the listing procedure, the agent should identify all items of personal property the seller may wish to leave behind and identify any fixtures the seller may wish to remove. This process ensures that all possible contingencies are anticipated and provided for, particularly when the listing will be shared with other brokers and salespeople in a multiple-listing agreement.

As part of the MLS agreement, listing brokers are required to use a separate information form, known as a profile or data sheet, for recording many of the property's features. This information generally includes the following (where appropriate):

- Names, addresses and relationship, if any, of the owners
- Legal (or other sufficient) description of the property
- Size of the improvements (square footage)
- Age of the improvements and their type of construction
- Number and dimensions of rooms
- Lot size (frontage and depth)

- Information concerning the facilities, services and institutions (for example, schools, parks and recreational areas, churches, public transportation) available in the neighborhood where the property is located

- Information on any existing loans, including name and address of each lender; type of loan; loan number; loan balance; interest rate; monthly payment and what it includes (principal, interest, real estate tax impounds, hazard insurance impounds, mortgage insurance premiums); whether the loan may be assumed by the buyer and, if so, under what circumstances; whether the loan may be prepaid without penalty; and so forth

- Possibility of seller financing

- Amount of any outstanding special assessments and whether they will be paid by the seller or assumed by the buyer

- Zoning classification of the property

- Current (or most recent year's) property taxes

- Any real property to be removed from the premises by the seller and any personal property to be included in the sale for the buyer (both the listing contract and the subsequent purchase contract should be explicit on these points)

- Any additional information that would make the property more appealing and marketable

- Any required disclosures concerning agency representation, property condition, known defects in the property and the like.

Remember, the real estate broker, as an agent, is responsible for the disclosure of any material information regarding the property. Getting as much initial information from the seller as possible—even if it becomes necessary to ask penetrating and possibly embarrassing questions—will pay off in the long run by saving both principal and agent from potential legal difficulties. The agent must inform the seller of his or her duty to give the buyer a property disclosure statement under the North Carolina Residential Property Disclosure Act, which is discussed later in this chapter. If the property is a residential structure built prior to 1978, the agent must explain the requirement for lead-based paint disclosure. The agent should also gather such pertinent information as legal descriptions. (Most title companies furnish a legal description packet to real estate practitioners.)

Also keep in mind that the agent has a duty to "discover and disclose" material facts, including defects in the property. Thus, it is good business practice to use other sources to verify information provided by the seller. In the listing of industrial, commercial and agricultural properties, pertinent information may be extensive and detailed. An agent experienced in these areas would be best qualified to gather the information in a complete and accurate manner.

The agent should also collect all of the seller's legal documents, such as the deed, and verify the following: (1) the seller's interest in the property, (2) any land-use restrictions that may apply, (3) the size (acreage or square feet) of the land and (4) the square footage of all the buildings.

Calculating Sales Prices, Commissions and Nets to Seller
When a property sells, the sales price equals 100 percent of the money being transferred. Therefore, if a broker is to receive a 6 percent commission, 94 percent will remain for the seller's other expenses and equity. To calculate a commission using a sales price of $80,000 and a commission rate of 6 percent, multiply the sales price by the commission rate:

$$\$80,000 \times 6\% = \$80,000 \times .06 = \$4,800 \text{ commission}$$

To calculate a sales price using a commission of $4,550 and a commission rate of 7 percent (.07 as a decimal), divide the commission by the commission rate:

$$\$4,550 \div 7\% = \$4,550 \div .07 = \$65,000 \text{ sales price}$$

To calculate a commission rate using a commission of $3,200 and a sales price of $64,000, divide the commission by the sales price:

$$\$3,200 \div \$64,000 = .05 \text{ as a decimal} = 5\% \text{ commission rate}$$

To calculate the net to the seller using a sales price of $85,000 and a commission rate of 8 percent (.08 as a decimal), multiply the sales price by 100 percent minus the commission rate:

$$\$85,000 \times (100\% - 8\%) = \$85,000 \times .92 = \$78,200 \text{ net to seller}$$

The same result could be achieved by calculating the commission ($85,000 × .08 = $6,800) and deducting it from the sales price ($85,000 − $6,800 = $78,200). However, this involves unnecessary extra calculations.

Sales price × commission rate = commission
Commission ÷ commission rate = sales price
Commission ÷ sales price = commission rate
Sales price × (100% − commission rate) = net to seller

Pricing the Property

Once a listing is secured and all necessary information obtained, the pricing of the real estate is of primary importance. It is the responsibility of the broker or salesperson to advise and assist, but ultimately it is the *seller* who must determine the listing price for the property. The average seller does not usually have the background to make an informed decision about a fair market price, so real estate agents must be prepared to offer their knowledge, information and expertise in this area. (See page 175 to learn how to determine square footage.)

A broker or salesperson can help the seller determine a listing price for the property by means of a **competitive** (or **comparative**) **market analysis (CMA).** Essentially, a CMA compares the prices of recently sold or listed properties that are similar in location, style and amenities to the subject property. If no such comparisons can be made, or if the seller feels his or her property is unique in some way, a full-scale real estate appraisal—a detailed estimate of a property's value by a professional certified appraiser—may be warranted.

A real estate agent performs a CMA to estimate property value, whereas an appraiser would prepare a detailed full appraisal report.

Whether a CMA or formal appraisal is used, the figure sought is the subject property's market value. *Market value,* as will become clear in Chapter 16, is the most probable price the property will bring in an arm's-length transaction under normal conditions on the open market. A broker performing a CMA will estimate market value as likely to fall within a range (for example, $135,000 to $140,000).

At this point, the agent should also prepare and give the seller an estimate of closing costs, which will help the seller establish the listing price. Although it is the property owner's privilege to set whatever asking price he or she chooses, a broker may reject any listing in which the price is substantially exaggerated. Once the listing price has been established, only this price can be quoted to a prospective buyer unless permission is given by the seller.

All sales agents should make sure the listing contract form is filled in properly and approved by the firm and/or the broker-in-charge. Note that a broker can draft his or her own listing form; a listing form is an employment agreement between the broker and the seller, not a contract between the buyer and the seller. However, the broker-in-charge should have an attorney approve the form. The listing agreement also must comply with Commission rules.

Determining Square Footage

The listing agent is expected to report the square footage of all buildings located on the property being listed. Of primary importance is the residential dwelling. The square footage is normally reported as the "heated living area," that is, the living area heated by the primary heating system. Any deviations, alterations or changes should be given special mention. An agent who reports or communicates the square footage of any building is accountable for accurate measurements and accurate reporting.

North Carolina Real Estate License Law does not require that agents advertise or report the square footage, but if agents do communicate square footage, the Commission expects the information to be verifiable and accurate. There are several guidelines for measuring properties available that agents may use. See Appendix B of this text for the North Carolina Real Estate Commission's "Residential Square Footage Guidelines." Once again the licensing law does not dictate that these guidelines must be used, but if agents do use them it will be in their favor if a party to the transaction challenges their reported square footage. These guidelines contain specific procedures for measuring and reporting square footage, for which an agent would be held accountable by the Commission.

THE NORTH CAROLINA RESIDENTIAL PROPERTY DISCLOSURE ACT

Property Disclosure Statement

North Carolina law requires that the sellers of most residential properties containing one to four units give the buyer a Residential Property Disclosure Statement. The statement must be given to the buyer *no later than the time the buyer makes an offer on the property.* The property disclosure statement may be included in the sales contract, in an addendum to the contract or in a separate document (see Figure 8.4). The form is a state-mandated form and must be used when required. No other form can be substituted. Additional forms may be used, however.

The statement includes disclosures about items relative to the condition of the property about which the owner has actual knowledge, or it may state that the owner makes no representations as to the condition of the property except as otherwise provided in the purchase and sale agreement.

An owner who decides to make "no representations" as to the condition of the property has no duty to disclose those defects, whether or not he or she knows about them.

If the property owner does not deliver the disclosure statement to the buyer prior to or at the time the purchaser makes an offer, the purchaser may cancel any resulting real estate contract. The new revised G.S. 47E-5(b) is partially quoted below.

> The purchaser's right to cancel shall expire if not exercised prior to the following, whichever occurs first:
>
> (1) The end of the third calendar day following the purchaser's receipt of the disclosure statement
> (2) The end of the third calendar day following the date the contract was made
> (3) Settlement or occupancy by the purchaser in the case of a sale or exchange
> (4) Settlement in the case of a purchase pursuant to a lease with option to purchase

If the buyer decides to withdraw the offer, the buyer must give the seller written notice of the withdrawal within the three-day period. When the buyer withdraws the offer, he or she is entitled to a full refund of any earnest money deposit given to the seller.

If, after the seller delivers the disclosure statement to the buyer, the disclosure statement is rendered inaccurate (or discovered to be inaccurate) in a material way, the seller must promptly deliver a corrected disclosure statement to the buyer. If the seller fails to deliver the corrected disclosure statement or fails to make any repairs necessary to make the original disclosure statement correct, the buyer may have a legal remedy for damages.

TYPES OF AGENCY AGREEMENTS

Single Agency   A single agency can be created by the exclusive right-to-sell listing contract or by the exclusive buyer agency agreement. The listing contract has been previously discussed. A discussion of buyer agency agreements follows.

Buyer Agency   **The nonexclusive buyer agency contract.** Under this type of buyer agency contract, the buyer does not have exclusive representation from one particular agent. The potential buyer is free to enter into other buyer agency contracts with other brokers (firms). This also frees the buyer to look for and purchase property through a seller's agent or to purchase property directly from a property owner. Buyer agent compensation under this type of contract may involve a retainer fee or success fee, previously discussed. An oral buyer agency agreement is considered to be "non-exclusive."

Figure 8.4 *Residential Property Disclosure Statement*

STATE OF NORTH CAROLINA
RESIDENTIAL PROPERTY DISCLOSURE STATEMENT
INSTRUCTIONS TO PROPERTY OWNERS

1. G.S. 47E requires owners of residential real estate (single-family homes and buildings with up to four dwelling units) to furnish purchasers a property disclosure statement. This form is the only one approved for this purpose. A disclosure statement must be furnished in connection with the sale, exchange, option and sale under a lease with option to purchase (unless the tenant is already occupying or intends to occupy the dwelling). A disclosure statement is not required for some transactions, including the first sale of a dwelling which has never been inhabited and transactions of residential property made pursuant to a lease with option to purchase where the lessee occupies or intends to occupy the dwelling. For a complete list of exemptions, see G.S. 47E-2.

2. You must check one of the boxes for each of the 20 questions on the reverse side of this form.

    a. If you check "Yes" for any question, you must describe the problem or attach a report from an engineer, contractor, pest control operator or other expert or public agency describing it. If you attach a report, you will not be liable for any inaccurate or incomplete information contained in it so long as you were not grossly negligent in obtaining or transmitting the information.

    b. If you check "No", you are stating that you have no actual knowledge of any problem. If you check "No" and you know there is a problem, you may be liable for making an intentional misstatement.

    c. If you check "No Representation", you have no duty to disclose the conditions or characteristics of the property, even if you should have known of them.

    *   If you check "Yes" or "No" and something happens to the property to make your Statement incorrect or inaccurate (for example, the roof begins to leak), you must promptly give the purchaser a corrected Statement or correct the problem.

3. If you are assisted in the sale of your property by a licensed real estate broker or salesperson, you are still responsible for completing and delivering the Statement to the purchasers; and the broker or salesperson must disclose any material facts about your property which they know or reasonably should know, regardless of your responses on the Statement.

4. You must give the completed Statement to the purchaser no later than the time the purchaser makes an offer to purchase your property. If you do not, the purchaser can, under certain conditions, cancel any resulting contract (See **"Note to Purchasers"** below). You should give the purchaser a copy of the Statement containing your signature and keep a copy signed by the purchaser for your records.

Note to Purchasers: If the owner does not give you a Residential Property Disclosure Statement by the time you make your offer to purchase the property, you may under certain conditions cancel any resulting contract and be entitled to a refund of any deposit monies you may have paid. To cancel the contract, you must personally deliver or mail written notice of your decision to cancel to the owner or the owner's agent within three calendar days following your receipt of the Statement, or three calendar days following the date of the contract, whichever occurs first. However, in no event does the Disclosure Act permit you to cancel a contract after settlement of the transaction or (in the case of a sale or exchange) after you have occupied the property, whichever occurs first.

---

5. In the space below, type or print in ink the address of the property (sufficient to identify it) and your name. Then sign and date.

Property Address: _____

Owner's Name(s): _____

Owner(s) acknowledge having examined this Statement before signing and that all information is true and correct as of the date signed.

Owner Signature: _____ Date _____

Owner Signature: _____ Date _____

Purchaser(s) acknowledge receipt of a copy of this disclosure statement; that they have examined it before signing; that they understand that this is not a warranty by owner or owner's agent; that it is not a substitute for any inspections they may wish to obtain; and that the representations are made by the owner and not the owner's agent(s) or subagent(s). Purchaser(s) are encouraged to obtain their own inspection from a licensed home inspector or other professional.

Purchaser Signature: _____ Date _____

Purchaser Signature: _____ Date _____

REC 4.22
REV 9/02

(OVER)

Page 1 of 2

Figure 8.4 **Residential Property Disclosure Statement (continued)**

Property Address/Description: _____

[Note: In this form, "property" refers only to dwelling unit(s) and not sheds, detached garages or other buildings.]

Regarding the property identified above, do you know of any problem (malfunction or defect) with any of the following:

	Yes*	No	No Representation
1. FOUNDATION, SLAB, FIREPLACES/CHIMNEYS, FLOORS, WINDOWS (INCLUDING STORM WINDOWS AND SCREENS), DOORS, CEILINGS, INTERIOR AND EXTERIOR WALLS, ATTACHED GARAGE, PATIO, DECK OR OTHER STRUCTURAL COMPONENTS including any modifications to them?	☐	☐	☐
a. Siding is ☐ Masonry ☐ Wood ☐ Composition/Hardboard ☐ Vinyl ☐ Synthetic Stucco ☐ Other _____			☐
b. Approximate age of structure? _____			☐
2. ROOF (leakage or other problem)?	☐	☐	☐
a. Approximate age of roof covering? _____			☐
3. WATER SEEPAGE, LEAKAGE, DAMPNESS OR STANDING WATER in the basement, crawl space or slab?	☐	☐	☐
4. ELECTRICAL SYSTEM (outlets, wiring, panel, switches, fixtures etc.)?	☐	☐	☐
5. PLUMBING SYSTEM (pipes, fixtures, water heater, etc.)?	☐	☐	☐
6. HEATING AND/OR AIR CONDITIONING?	☐	☐	☐
a. Heat Source is: ☐ Furnace ☐ Heat Pump ☐ Baseboard ☐ Other_____			☐
b. Cooling Source is: ☐ Central Forced Air ☐ Wall/Window Unit(s) ☐ Other_____			☐
c. Fuel Source is: ☐ Electricity ☐ Natural Gas ☐ Propane ☐ Oil ☐ Other _____			☐
7. WATER SUPPLY (including water quality, quantity and water pressure)?	☐	☐	☐
a. Water supply is: ☐ City/County ☐ Community System ☐ Private Well ☐ Other _____			☐
b. Water pipes are: ☐ Copper ☐ Galvanized ☐ Plastic ☐ Other _____ ☐ Unknown			☐
8. SEWER AND/OR SEPTIC SYSTEM?	☐	☐	☐
a. Sewage disposal system is: ☐ Septic Tank ☐ Septic Tank with Pump ☐ Community System ☐ Connected to City/County System ☐ City/County System available ☐ Straight pipe (wastewater does not go into a septic or other sewer system [note: use of this type of system violates state law]) ☐ Other			☐
9. BUILT-IN APPLIANCES (RANGE/OVEN, ATTACHED MICROWAVE, HOOD/FAN, DISWASHER, DISPOSAL, etc.)?	☐	☐	☐

Also regarding the property identified above, including the lot, other improvements, and fixtures located thereon, do you know of any:

	Yes*	No	No Representation
10. PROBLEMS WITH PRESENT INFESTATION, OR DAMAGE FROM PAST INFESTATION OF WOOD DESTROYING INSECTS OR ORGANISMS which has not been repaired?	☐	☐	☐
11. PROBLEMS WITH DRAINAGE, GRADING OR SOIL STABILITY OF LOT?	☐	☐	☐
12. PROBLEMS WITH OTHER SYSTEMS AND FIXTURES: CENTRAL VACUUM, POOL, HOT TUB, SPA, ATTIC FAN, EXHAUST FAN, CEILING FAN, SUMP PUMP, IRRIGATION SYSTEM, TV CABLE WIRING OR SATELLITE DISH, OR OTHER SYSTEMS?	☐	☐	☐
13. ROOM ADDITIONS OR OTHER STRUCTURAL CHANGES ?	☐	☐	☐
14. ENVIRONMENTAL HAZARDS (substances, materials or products) including asbestos, formaldehyde, radon gas, methane gas, lead-based paint, underground storage tank, or other hazardous or toxic material (whether buried or covered), contaminated soil or water, or other environmental contamination)?	☐	☐	☐
15. COMMERCIAL OR INDUSTRIAL NUISANCES (noise, odor, smoke, etc.) affecting the property?	☐	☐	☐
16. VIOLATIONS OF BUILDING CODES, ZONING ORDINANCES, RESTRICTIVE COVENANTS OR OTHER LAND-USE RESTRICTIONS?	☐	☐	☐
17. UTILITY OR OTHER EASEMENTS, SHARED DRIVEWAYS, PARTY WALLS OR ENCROACHMENTS FROM OR ON ADJACENT PROPERTY?	☐	☐	☐
18. LAWSUITS, FORECLOSURES, BANKRUPTCY, TENANCIES, JUDGMENTS, TAX LIENS, PROPOSED ASSESSMENTS, MECHANICS' LIENS, MATERIALMENS' LIENS, OR NOTICE FROM ANY GOVERNMENTAL AGENCY that could affect title to the property?	☐	☐	☐
19. OWNERS' ASSOCIATION OR "COMMON AREA" EXPENSES OR ASSESSMENTS?	☐	☐	☐
20. FLOOD HAZARD or that the property is in a FEDERALLY-DESIGNATED FLOOD PLAIN?	☐	☐	☐

* If you answered "Yes" to any of the above questions, please explain (Attach additional sheets, if necessary): _____

_____

_____

_____

The exclusive buyer agency contract. Under this type of buyer agency contract one broker (firm) is selected by a potential buyer to represent him or her in the purchase of a property on an exclusive basis. The buyer agrees not to work with any other broker (firm) in the purchase of a property. The employed broker is the *only real estate agent* with whom the buyer can work to locate and purchase property. When the buyer has signed this exclusive buyer agency contract, all agents working for that firm become subagents of that buyer. The buyer, however, may not be restricted from buying directly from a property owner, but language in the contract can still require the buyer to pay the broker a success fee. An exclusive buyer agency agreement must be in writing from the formation of the agency.

Buyer agent's responsibilities. A buyer's agent must

- give the buyer the *Working with Real Estate Agents* brochure.

- ensure that a proper agency contract is entered into;

- explain agency duties and responsibilities;

- properly qualify the prospective buyer-client;

- obtain and verify information about the property;

- disclose agency status to all parties to the transaction;

- discover and disclose material facts about the property;

- assist in the preparation, presentation and negotiation of offers submitted by and on behalf of the buyer-client; and

- assist the buyer-client with preparation for closing the transaction.

Figure 8.5 is an example of an exclusive buyer agency agreement.

Dual Agency   A real estate brokerage firm whose policy is to act as a dual agent, electing to represent both buyers and sellers, must use a written dual agency agreement (no later than the making of an offer) to modify existing relationships that were created when entering into either the exclusive-right-to-sell listing contract or the buyer agency contract.

In Practice   Firms practicing dual agency will normally require that their agents, when entering into either a listing agreement or a buyer's agreement, have the client (buyer or seller) also sign a *dual agency addendum.* This addendum accomplishes the requirement for written informed consent and should be completed when the agency relationship is established. (NCAR Standard Form No. 901 is an appropriate form to use for this purpose. It is not included in this text). The dual agency addendum basically gives a blanket authorization for dual agency, if needed later in the transaction.

The dual agency agreement (see Figure 8.6) will be used to create a dual agency and provide written informed consent if a dual agency addendum has not been previously entered into by the respective clients of the broker. This

Figure 8.5   Exclusive Buyer Agency Agreement

EXCLUSIVE RIGHT TO REPRESENT BUYER
Buyer Agency Agreement
[Consult "Guidelines" (Form 201G) for guidance in completing this form]

STATE OF NORTH CAROLINA, County of _____, Date _____,
_____ ("Buyer"),
hereby employs _____ [Firm Name] as the Buyer's
exclusive agent ("Agent") to assist the Buyer in the acquisition of real property which may include any purchase, option and/or
exchange on terms and conditions acceptable to Buyer.

**Buyer represents that, as of the commencement date of this Agreement, the Buyer is not a party to a buyer representation
agreement with any other Agent. Buyer has received a copy of the "Working with Real Estate Agents" brochure and has
reviewed it with Agent. Buyer further represents that Buyer has disclosed to Agent information about any properties of the
type described in paragraph 1 below that Buyer has visited at any open houses or that Buyer has been shown by any other real
estate agent.**

1. **TYPE OF PROPERTY:** ❑ Residential (improved and unimproved) ❑ Commercial (improved and unimproved)
   ❑ Other _____
   (a) General Location:_____
   (b) Other:_____

2. **DURATION OF AGENCY:** Agent's authority as Buyer's exclusive Agent shall begin _____, and,
subject to paragraph 4, shall expire at midnight, _____.

3. **EFFECT OF AGREEMENT:** Buyer intends to acquire real property of the type described in paragraph 1. *By employing Agent as
Buyer's exclusive Agent, Buyer agrees to conduct all negotiations for such property through Agent, and to refer to Agent all inquiries
received in any form from other agents, salespersons, prospective sellers or any other source, during the time this Agreement is in
effect.*

[Instructions: Initial only ONE]

_____ In the event Buyer wishes to consider a property listed with the Agent's firm, Buyer authorizes Agent to act as a dual
           agent, representing both Buyer and Seller, subject to the terms and conditions of the attached Dual Agency
           Addendum.
_____ Buyer does NOT authorize Agent to act in the capacity of dual agent.

4. **COMPENSATION OF AGENT**
(a) Agent acknowledges receipt of a non-refundable retainer fee in the amount of $_____, which shall ❑   shall not ❑
    be credited toward any compensation due Agent under this Agreement.

(b) Except as otherwise provided below, Agent shall seek compensation from a cooperating listing firm (through the listing firm's
    offer of compensation in MLS or otherwise) or from the seller if there is no listing firm, and Buyer agrees that Agent shall be
    entitled to receive same in consideration for Agent's services hereunder. If Buyer purchases property where no compensation is
    offered   by   either   the   listing   firm   or   the   seller,   then   Buyer   agrees   to   pay   Agent   a   fee   of
    _____
    *(insert dollar amount, percentage of purchase price, or other method of determining Agent's compensation for each type of
    property the Buyer may purchase).* If the compensation offered by the listing firm or seller is less than the compensation inserted
    above, Buyer agrees to pay Agent the difference. **If additional compensation and/or a selling incentive (bonus, trip, money,
    etc.) is offered through the MLS or otherwise, Buyer will permit the Agent to receive it in addition to the compensation set
    forth above.**

North Carolina Association of REALTORS®, Inc.

Buyer Initials _____ _____   Agent Initials _____

STANDARD FORM 201
© 7/2002

Figure 8.5   Exclusive Buyer Agency Agreement (continued)

4. COMPENSATION OF AGENT (continued):

(c) The compensation shall be deemed earned under any of the following circumstances:

    i.   If, during the term of this Agreement, Buyer, any assignee of Buyer or any person/legal entity acting on behalf of Buyer directly or indirectly enters into an agreement to purchase, option, and/or exchange any property of the type described above regardless of the manner in which Buyer was introduced to the property; or

    ii. If, within _____ days after expiration of this Agreement, Buyer enters into a contract to acquire property introduced to Buyer during the term of this Agreement by Agent or any third party, unless Buyer has entered into a valid buyer agency agreement with another real estate agent; or

    iii. If, having entered into an enforceable contract to acquire property during the term of this Agreement, Buyer defaults under the terms of that contract.

(d) The compensation will be due and payable at closing or upon Buyer's default of any purchase agreement. If Buyer defaults, the total compensation that would have been due the Agent will be due and payable immediately in cash from the Buyer. No assignment of rights in real property obtained for Buyer or any assignee of Buyer or any person/legal entity acting on behalf of Buyer pursuant to this Agreement shall operate to defeat any of Agent's rights under this Agreement.

Notice: Buyer understands and acknowledges that there is the potential for a conflict of interest generated by a percentage of price based fee for representing Buyer. The amount, format or rate of real estate commission is not fixed by law, but is set by each broker individually, and may be negotiable between Buyer and Agent.

5. DISCLOSURE OF BUYER'S IDENTITY: Unless otherwise stated in Paragraph 11 below, Agent has Buyer's permission to disclose Buyer's identity.

6. OTHER POTENTIAL BUYERS: Buyer understands that other prospective purchasers represented by Agent may seek property, submit offers, and contract to purchase property through Agent, including the same or similar property as Buyer seeks to purchase. Buyer acknowledges, understands and consents to such representation of other prospective purchasers by Agent through its sales associates.

7. AGENT'S DUTIES: During the term of this Agreement, Agent shall promote the interests of Buyer by: (a) performing the terms of this Agreement; (b) seeking property at a price and terms acceptable to Buyer; (c) presenting in a timely manner all written offers or counteroffers to and from Buyer; (d) disclosing to Buyer all material facts related to the property or concerning the transaction of which Agent has actual knowledge; and (e) accounting for in a timely manner all money and property received in which Buyer has or may have an interest. Unless otherwise provided by law or Buyer consents in writing to the release of the information, Agent shall maintain the confidentiality of all personal and financial information and other matters identified as confidential by Buyer, if that information is received from Buyer during the brokerage relationship. In satisfying these duties, Agent shall exercise ordinary care, comply with all applicable laws and regulations, and treat all prospective sellers honestly and not knowingly give them false information. In addition, Agent may show the same property to other buyers, represent other buyers, represent sellers relative to other properties, or provide assistance to a seller or prospective seller by performing ministerial acts that are not inconsistent with Agent's duties under this Agreement.

8. BUYER'S DUTIES: Buyer shall: (a) work exclusively with Agent during the term of this Agreement; (b) pay Agent, directly or indirectly, the compensation set forth above; (c) comply with the reasonable requests of Agent to supply any pertinent financial or personal data needed to fulfill the terms of this Agreement; (d) be available for reasonable periods of time to examine properties; and (e) pay for all products and/or services required in the examination and evaluation of properties (examples: surveys, water/soil tests, title reports, property inspections, etc.).

9. NON-DISCRIMINATION: *The Agent shall conduct all brokerage activities in regard to this Agreement without respect to the race, color, religion, sex, national origin, handicap or familial status of any buyer, prospective buyer, seller or prospective seller.*

10. OTHER PROFESSIONAL ADVICE: In addition to the services rendered to Buyer by the Agent under the terms of this Agreement, Buyer is advised to seek other professional advice in matters of law, taxation, financing, surveying, wood-destroying insect infestation, structural soundness, engineering, and other matters pertaining to any proposed transaction.

❑ Buyer acknowledges receipt of a copy of the brochure *Questions and Answers on: Home Inspections*

11. ADDITIONAL PROVISIONS: _____
_____
_____ .

Page 2 of 3

Buyer Initials _____   _____   Agent Initials _____

STANDARD FORM 201
© 7/2002

Figure 8.5 Exclusive Buyer Agency Agreement (continued)

12. **ENTIRE AGREEMENT:** This Agreement constitutes the entire agreement between the parties relating to the subject thereof, and any prior agreements pertaining thereto, whether oral or written, have been merged and integrated into this Agreement. No modification of any of the terms of this Agreement shall be valid, binding upon the parties, or entitled to enforcement unless such modification has first been reduced to writing and signed by the parties.

13. **MEDIATION:** If a dispute arises out of or related to this Agreement or the breach thereof, and if the dispute cannot be settled through negotiation, the parties agree first to try in good faith to settle the dispute by mediation before resorting to arbitration, litigation, or some other dispute resolution procedure. If the need for mediation arises, the parties will choose a mutually acceptable mediator and will share the cost of mediation equally.

(NOTE: Buyer should consult with Agent before visiting any resale or new homes or contacting any other real estate agent representing sellers, to avoid the possibility of confusion over the brokerage relationship and misunderstandings about liability for compensation.)

Buyer and Agent each hereby acknowledge receipt of a signed copy of this Agreement.

THE NORTH CAROLINA ASSOCIATION OF REALTORS®, INC. MAKES NO REPRESENTATION AS TO THE LEGAL VALIDITY OR ADEQUACY OF ANY PROVISION OF THIS FORM IN ANY SPECIFIC TRANSACTION.

Buyer _____ SS/TAX ID# _____

Buyer _____ SS/TAX ID# _____

Mailing Address _____

Phone: Home _____ Work _____ Fax _____

E-mail _____

Agent (Firm) _____ Phone _____

By _____

Office Address: _____

Phone _____ Fax _____

E-mail_____

Page 3 of 3

STANDARD FORM 201
© 7/2002

agreement is required when the buyer-client wants to look at property listed with the firm. The dual agency agreement contains the following provisions:

- Names of buyers, sellers and broker (firm)
- Location of the property
- Provisions for agreeing to a dual agency
- Broker's role as a dual agent
- Seller's and buyer's roles
- Provisions for the option of designated agency
- Provisions for compensation
- Statement as to modifying existing agency agreements
- Duration of the dual agency
- Signatures of all parties

SUMMARY

A contract is defined as a legally enforceable promise or set of promises that must be performed and for which the law provides a remedy if a breach occurs.

Contracts may be classified as express or implied; bilateral or unilateral; executed or executory; or, according to their legal enforceability, as valid, void, voidable or unenforceable. The essential elements of a valid contract are legally competent parties, mutual assent, legality of object and consideration. A valid real estate contract must include a description of the property, be in writing and be signed by all parties.

In a number of circumstances, a contract may be canceled before it is performed fully. Furthermore, in many types of contracts, either of the parties may transfer his or her rights and obligations under the agreement by assignment of the contract or novation (substitution of a new contract). The best way to terminate a contract is by full performance.

Contracts frequently used in the real estate business include listings, offers to purchase, installment land contracts and options.

A listing agreement *or property management agreement* is an employment agreement between a broker and a property owner. In the typical real estate transaction, the broker is hired to find *either* a ready, willing and able buyer *or tenant* for the property. *All* agreements *with property owners* must be in writing *from the formation of the relationship* to be valid under Real Estate Commission rules [see Rule A.0104(a)].

The various kinds of listing agreements include open listings, exclusive-agency listings and exclusive-right-to-sell listings. An open listing is one in which, to obtain a commission, the broker must find a buyer before the property is sold by the seller or another broker. Under an exclusive-agency listing, the broker is given the exclusive right to represent the seller, but the seller can avoid paying the broker a commission by selling the property without the broker's help. With an exclusive-right-to-sell listing, the seller employs only one broker and must pay that broker a commission regardless of whether the broker or the seller finds a buyer—provided the buyer is found within the listing period.

Rule A.0104(a) permits licensees to work initially as a buyer or tenant agent under an express *oral* buyer or tenant agency agreement. Minimally, the oral agreement should address issues of compensation and whether the client authorizes dual agency, if the situation arises. All oral buyer/tenant agency agreements are *non-exclusive,* which means the client may work with other agents or independently and the relationship may be terminated by the agent or client with notice at any time. If the agent seeks to restrict the buyer/tenant's ability to work with other agents or to bind the client for a specified period, then the agreement must be in writing from the outset of the restricted relationship. At the latest, an oral buyer/tenant agency agreement must be reduced to writing not later than the time any party to the transaction makes an offer to buy, sell, rent, lease, or exchange property to another. An agent shall *not* continue to represent a client as a buyer or tenant agent if the client refuses to enter into a written agency agreement when required by the rule. Lastly, if an agent works with a buyer (customer) as a *seller's* agent or subagent, then the agent shall disclose his/her seller agency status *in writing* to the buyer *at first substantial contact.*

Figure 8.6 **Dual Agency Agreement**

DUAL AGENCY AGREEMENT

Do NOT use this form if Dual Agency Addenda have been executed by BOTH Seller and Buyer.
(To be signed by Buyer(s) before Offer to Purchase and Contract is signed and to be signed by Seller(s) before offer is reviewed.)
THIS DOCUMENT IS NEITHER AN ADDENDUM TO NOR A PART OF THE OFFER TO PURCHASE AND CONTRACT.

This DUAL AGENCY AGREEMENT ("Agreement") is entered into (Date) _____, among

_____
(hereinafter referred to as "Buyer") and

_____
(hereinafter referred to as "Seller") and

_____ (Real Estate Firm)
(hereinafter referred to as "Broker")

regarding the property located at _____

_____
(hereinafter referred to as the "Property").

The term "Broker" shall sometimes hereinafter include Broker and its individual sales associates, as the sense requires.

1. DUAL AGENCY: Seller and Buyer agree that Broker, acting by and through its individual sales associates, shall serve as both Seller's Agent and Buyer's Agent in the sale of Seller's property to Buyer. In the event Broker serves as a Dual Agent, the parties agree that without permission from the party about whom the information pertains, Broker shall not disclose to the other party the following information:

    (a) That a party may agree to a price, terms or any conditions of sale other than those offered;
    (b) The motivation of a party for engaging in the transaction, unless disclosure is otherwise required by statute or rule; and
    (c) Any information about a party which that party has identified as confidential unless disclosure is otherwise required by statute or rule.

2. BROKER'S DUAL AGENCY ROLE: Because Broker is serving as Agent for both Seller and Buyer in this transaction, Broker shall make every reasonable effort to represent Seller and Buyer in a balanced and fair manner. Broker shall also make every reasonable effort to encourage and effect communication and negotiation between Seller and Buyer. Seller and Buyer understand and acknowledge that:

    (a) Prior to the time this Agreement was entered into, Broker acted as the exclusive Agent of Seller and acted as the exclusive Agent of Buyer.
    (b) In those separate roles Broker may have obtained information which, if disclosed, could harm the bargaining position of the party providing such information to Broker.
    (c) Broker is required by law to disclose to Buyer and Seller any known or reasonably ascertainable material facts.

Seller and Buyer agree that Broker shall not be liable to either party for (1) disclosing material facts required by law to be disclosed; and (2) refusing or failing to disclose other information the law does not require to be disclosed which could harm or compromise one party's bargaining position but could benefit the other party.

3. SELLER'S AND BUYER'S ROLES: Because of Broker's Dual Agency relationship, Seller and Buyer understand and acknowledge that:

    (a) They each have the responsibility of making their own decisions as to what terms are to be included in any purchase and sale agreement between them.

Page 1 of 3

North Carolina Association of REALTORS®, Inc.

Buyer Initials _____ _____ Seller Initials _____ _____

STANDARD FORM 902
© 7/2002

Figure 8.6   *Dual Agency Agreement (continued)*

  (b) They are fully aware of, and understand the implications and consequences of Broker's Dual Agency role as expressed herein to provide balanced and fair representation of Seller and Buyer and to encourage and effect communication between them rather than as an advocate or exclusive Agent or representative.

  (c) They have determined that the benefits of entering into this Dual Agency relationship with Broker, acting as Agent for them both, outweigh any disadvantages or adverse consequences.

  (d) They each may seek independent legal counsel to assist them with the negotiation and preparation of a purchase and sale agreement or with any matter relating to the transaction which is the subject matter of a purchase and sale agreement.

Seller and Buyer agree to indemnify and hold Broker harmless against all claims, damages, losses, expenses or liabilities, other than violations of the North Carolina Real Estate License Law and intentional wrongful acts, arising from Broker's role as a Dual Agent. Seller and Buyer shall each have a duty to protect their own interests and should read this Agreement and any purchase and sale agreement carefully to ensure that they accurately set forth the terms which they want included in said agreements.

4. DESIGNATED AGENT OPTION (Initial only if applicable):

_____ Buyer hereby authorizes the Broker (Firm) to designate an agent(s) to represent the Buyer, to the exclusion of any other licensees associated with the Broker. The agent(s) shall not be so designated and shall not undertake to represent only the interests of the Buyer if the agent(s) has actually received confidential information concerning the Seller in connection with the transaction. The designated agent(s) shall represent only the interests of the Buyer to the extent permitted by law.

_____ Seller hereby authorizes Broker (Firm) to designate an agent(s) to represent the Seller, to the exclusion of any other licensees associated with the Broker. The agent(s) shall not be so designated and shall not undertake to represent only the interests of the Seller if the agent(s) has actually received confidential information concerning the Buyer in connection with the transaction. The designated agent(s) shall represent only the interests of the Seller to the extent permitted by law.

5. COMPENSATION: As compensation for the services rendered under this Agreement, Broker shall be paid a real estate commission by _____ in the amount of _____ as follows: _____

6. PREVIOUS AGENCY AGREEMENTS: The parties agree that this Agreement shall modify any agency agreements previously entered into between Seller and Broker or between Buyer and Broker. If those previous agency agreements contain expiration or termination dates prior to the termination date for this Agreement as set forth below, the expiration or termination dates of the previous agency agreements are hereby extended until the termination of this Agreement. If this Agreement terminates prior to the termination date of any previous agency agreement, the previous agency agreement shall remain in full force and effect in accordance with its terms. In any areas where this Agreement contradicts or conflicts with those agency agreements, this Dual Agency Agreement shall control.

7. DURATION OF DUAL AGENCY: The term of this Agreement shall commence when this document is executed by Seller, Buyer, and Broker and, unless extended by written agreement of all parties, shall automatically terminate upon (a) the closing of the sale of the Property or (b) midnight, _____, whichever occurs first. In the event that Seller and Buyer do not enter into an agreement for the purchase and sale of the Property, or in the event that the purchase and sale transaction described in any agreement between Seller and Buyer is terminated, Broker may terminate its Dual Agency role and this Agreement by mailing written notice thereof to Seller and Buyer. In addition, Buyer may terminate this Agreement at any time prior to the complete execution of an agreement for the purchase and sale of the property by giving Seller and Broker written notice that Buyer is no longer interested in purchasing the property. Seller may terminate this Agreement at any time prior to the complete execution of an agreement for the purchase and sale of the Property by giving Buyer and Broker written notice that Seller is no longer interested in negotiating with Buyer for the purchase and sale of the Property.

8. *The Broker shall conduct all his brokerage activities in regard to this Agreement without respect to the race, color, religion, sex, national origin, handicap or familial status of any buyer, prospective buyer, seller or prospective seller.*

Page 2 of 3

Buyer Initials _____ _____   Seller Initials _____ _____   **STANDARD FORM 902**
© 7/2002

To see the full form, please go to Appendix C.

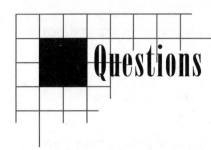

Questions

1. Generally, to be enforceable, contracts for the purchase and sale of real estate
   a. must be signed by only the buyer.
   b. must be signed by only the seller.
   c. may be oral, bound only with a handshake.
   d. must be in writing and signed by the party or parties to be charged.

2. A real estate broker's or salesperson's license gives the licensee the right to
   a. practice law.
   b. "fill in the blanks" on contracts prepared for the broker by a lawyer.
   c. act as a principal to the contract.
   d. act as a notary public.

3. The injured party in a real estate transaction with the right to a suit for specific performance is the
   a. broker and salesperson.
   b. buyer.
   c. title company.
   d. lender.

4. To be enforceable, a contract must be entered into by a(n)
   a. 16-year-old, or younger, male or female.
   b. 18-year-old, or older, male or female.
   c. 21-year-old, or older, male or female.
   d. 25-year-old, or older, male or female.

5. A contract is said to be *bilateral* if
   a. one of the parties is a minor.
   b. the contract has yet to be fully performed.
   c. only one party to the agreement is bound to act.
   d. all parties to the contract are bound to act.

6. During the period of time after a real estate sales contract is signed but before title actually passes, the status of the contract is
   I. voidable.
   II. executory.
   a. I only
   b. II only
   c. Both I and II
   d. Neither I nor II

7. Anita has a contract to buy property but would rather let her friend Laura buy it instead. If the contract allows, Laura can take over Anita's obligation by the process known as
   a. assignment.
   b. substantial performance.
   c. subordination.
   d. mutual consent.

8. A legally enforceable agreement under which two parties agree to do something for each other is known as a(n)
   a. escrow instruction.
   b. promise.
   c. valid contract.
   d. option agreement.

9. Kay drives into a filling station and tops off her gas tank. She is obligated to pay for the fuel through what kind of contract?
   a. Express   c. Oral
   b. Implied   d. Voidable

10. A listing agreement is
    a. a broker's employment contract with salespeople.
    b. a broker's employment contract with a principal.
    c. always an oral agreement.
    d. required by North Carolina license law.

11. Which of the following is a similarity between an exclusive-agency listing and an exclusive-right-to-sell listing?
    a. Under both listings, the seller retains the right to sell the real estate without the broker's help and without paying the broker a commission.
    b. Under both listings, the seller authorizes only one particular salesperson to show the property.
    c. Both listings give the responsibility of representing the seller to one broker only.
    d. Both listings are open listings.

12. All of the following would terminate a listing EXCEPT
    a. expiration of the contract period.
    b. death or incapacity of the broker.
    c. nonpayment of the commission by the seller.
    d. destruction of the improvements on the property.

13. The parties to the listing contract are the
    I. seller and buyer.
    II. seller and broker.
    III. seller and salesperson.
       a. I only
       b. II only
       c. III only
       d. I or III, depending on the type of listing used

14. Which of the following statements is true of a comparative market analysis?
    a. It is exactly the same as an appraisal.
    b. It can help the seller price the property.
    c. By law, it must be completed for each listing taken.
    d. It should not be retained in the property's listing file.

15. A listing taken by a real estate salesperson belongs to the
    a. broker.
    b. seller.
    c. salesperson.
    d. agent and broker equally.

16. All of the following are listing agreements EXCEPT a(n)
    a. open listing.
    b. exclusive-agency listing.
    c. exclusive-right-to-sell listing.
    d. multiple-listing.

17. A seller's residence is listed with a broker, and the seller stipulates that she wants to receive $85,000 from the sale but the broker can sell the property for as much as possible and keep the difference as the commission. The broker agrees. This contract is what type of listing?
    a. Exclusive right to sell
    b. Exclusive agency
    c. Open
    d. Net

18. Seller Richard Munn has his property under an exclusive-agency listing with broker Dodie Baker. If Munn sells his property himself during the term of the listing without Baker's services, he will owe Baker
    a. no commission.
    b. the full commission.
    c. a partial commission.
    d. only reimbursement for broker Baker's costs.

19. Real estate commission rates are set by the
    a. local real estate board.
    b. North Carolina Real Estate Commission.
    c. seller and broker.
    d. MLS.

20. Which of the following statements is(are) true of a sales transaction listing agreement between broker and seller in North Carolina?
    I. It must be in writing.
    II. It may be an oral agreement.
    III. It must be signed by only the broker.
       a. I only
       b. II only
       c. III only
       d. II and III only

21. A listing contract contains a clause that gives the broker the right to collect a commission if the owner sells the property after the listing contract terminates to someone the broker negotiated with. This is what type of clause?
    a. Extender
    b. Subordination
    c. Executory
    d. Bilateral

22. A broker listed a property at an 8 percent commission rate. After the sale closed, the seller discovered that the broker had been listing similar properties at a 6 percent commission rate. Based on this information, which of the following statements is true?
    I. The broker has done nothing wrong.
    II. The seller can cancel the transaction.
    a. I only
    b. II only
    c. Both I and II
    d. Neither I nor II

23. A broker gets a commission if her listed property is sold, no matter who sells it, if the contract is what type of listing agreement?
    a. Net
    b. Open
    c. Exclusive agency
    d. Exclusive right to sell

24. The owners of a parcel of commercial property have executed three open listings with three brokers. All three brokers would like to place a "For Sale" sign on the property. Under these circumstances, which of the following statements is true?
    a. A broker does not have to get the seller's permission before placing a sign on the property.
    b. Only one "For Sale" sign may be placed on the property at one time.
    c. After getting the seller's consent, any or all brokers can place their signs on the property.
    d. The broker who obtained the first open listing must consent to all signs placed on the property.

25. Nick and Kelly sign a contract under which Nick will convey Raptor Manor to Kelly. Nick changes his mind, and Kelly sues for specific performance. What is Kelly seeking in the lawsuit?
    a. Money damages
    b. New contract
    c. Deficiency judgment
    d. Conveyance of the property

9 Sales Contracts and Practices

LEARNING OBJECTIVES

When you've finished reading this chapter, you should be able to

- **determine** when a contract has been formed and **explain** how to handle modifications and counteroffers.

- **describe** all required provisions of a sales contract and be able to **determine** when certain addenda are required.

- **describe** the statute of frauds and its legal effect.

- **explain** the features and uses of the installment land contract and the option to purchase.

- **define** the following *key terms:*

backup offer	"mail-box rule"	optionee
contract of sale	offeree	optionor
counteroffer	offeror	right of first refusal
installment land contract	option	

THE SALES CONTRACT

> The contract of sale is the most important document in the sale of real estate because it sets out the agreement between buyer and seller and establishes each party's legal rights and obligations.

A *real estate sales contract* sets forth all details of the agreement between a buyer and a seller for the purchase and sale of a parcel of real estate. Depending on the state or locality, this agreement may be known as *an offer to purchase, a contract of purchase and sale, a purchase agreement, an earnest money agreement, a deposit receipt* or another variation of these titles. In North Carolina the most common title is "Offer To Purchase and Contract" (see Figure 9.1). The guidelines for completing this form can be found at http://nc.living.net/consumer_information/sf-2g.pdf.

Figure 9.1   Offer to Purchase and Contract

OFFER TO PURCHASE AND CONTRACT

_____, as Buyer,
hereby offers to purchase and _____, as Seller,
upon acceptance of said offer, agrees to sell and convey, all of that plot, piece or parcel of land described below, together with all improvements located thereon and such fixtures and personal property as are listed below (collectively referred to as the "Property"), upon the following terms and conditions:

1. REAL PROPERTY: Located in the City of _____ ,
County of _____, State of North Carolina, being known as and more particularly described as:
Street Address_____ Zip_____
Legal Description:_____
(☐ All ☐ A portion of the property in Deed Reference: Book_____, Page No._____, _____ County.)
NOTE: Prior to signing this Offer to Purchase and Contract, Buyer is advised to review Restrictive Covenants, if any, which may limit the use of the Property, and to read the Declaration of Restrictive Covenants, By-Laws, Articles of Incorporation, Rules and Regulations, and other governing documents of the owners' association and/or the subdivision, if applicable.
2. FIXTURES: The following items, if any, are included in the purchase price free of liens: any built-in appliances, light fixtures, ceiling fans, attached floor coverings, blinds, shades, drapery rods and curtain rods, brackets and all related hardware, window and door screens, storm windows, combination doors, awnings, antennas, satellite dishes and receivers, burglar/fire/smoke alarms, pool and spa equipment, solar energy systems, attached fireplace screens, gas logs, fireplace inserts, electric garage door openers with controls, outdoor plants and trees (other than in movable containers), basketball goals, storage sheds, mailboxes, wall and/or door mirrors, and any other items attached or affixed to the Property, EXCEPT the following items:
_____
_____ .

3. PERSONAL PROPERTY: The following personal property is included in the purchase price:_____
_____ .
4. PURCHASE PRICE: The purchase price is $_____ and shall be paid as follows:
(a) $_____, EARNEST MONEY DEPOSIT with this offer by ☐ cash ☐ personal check ☐ bank check
☐ certified check ☐ other: _____ to be deposited and held in
escrow by _____ ("Escrow Agent") until the sale is closed, at which time it will be credited to Buyer, or until this contract is otherwise terminated. In the event: (1) this offer is not accepted; or (2) any of the conditions hereto are not satisfied, then all earnest monies shall be returned to Buyer. In the event of breach of this contract by Seller, upon Buyer's request, all earnest monies shall be returned to Buyer, but such return shall not affect any other remedies available to Buyer for such breach. In the event this offer is accepted and Buyer breaches this contract, then all earnest monies shall be forfeited upon Seller's request, but receipt of such forfeited earnest monies shall not affect any other remedies available to Seller for such breach.
NOTE: In the event of a dispute between Seller and Buyer over the return or forfeiture of earnest money held in escrow by a broker, the broker is required by state law to retain said earnest money in the broker's trust or escrow account until a written release from the parties consenting to its disposition has been obtained or until disbursement is ordered by a court of competent jurisdiction.
(b) $_____, ADDITIONAL EARNEST MONEY DEPOSIT to be paid to Escrow Agent no later than
_____, TIME BEING OF THE ESSENCE WITH REGARD TO SAID DATE.
(c) $_____, BY ASSUMPTION of the unpaid principal balance and all obligations of Seller on the existing loan(s) secured by a deed of trust on the Property in accordance with the attached Loan Assumption Addendum.
(d) $_____, BY SELLER FINANCING in accordance with the attached Seller Financing Addendum.
(e) $_____, BALANCE of the purchase price in cash at Closing.
5. CONDITIONS: (State N/A in each blank that is not a condition to this contract.)
(a) Buyer must be able to obtain a ☐ FHA ☐ VA (attach FHA/VA Financing Addendum) ☐ Conventional ☐ Other: _____ loan at a ☐ Fixed Rate ☐ Adjustable Rate in the principal amount of _____ (plus any financed VA Funding Fee or FHA MIP) for a term of _____ year(s), at an initial interest rate not to exceed _____ % per annum, with mortgage loan discount points not to exceed _____ % of the loan amount. Buyer shall apply for said loan within _____ days of the Effective Date of this contract. Buyer shall use Buyer's best efforts to secure the lender's customary loan commitment letter on or before _____ and to satisfy all terms and conditions of the loan commitment letter by Closing. After the above letter date, Seller may request in writing from Buyer a copy of the loan commitment letter. If Buyer fails to provide Seller a copy of the loan commitment letter or a written waiver of this loan condition within five days of receipt of Seller's request, Seller may terminate this contract by written notice to Buyer at any time thereafter, provided Seller has not then received a copy of the letter or the waiver.

REALTOR®	**This form jointly approved by:** Page 1 of 4	**STANDARD FORM 2 - T**
	North Carolina Bar Association	© 7/2002
	North Carolina Association of REALTORS®, Inc. EQUAL HOUSING OPPORTUNITY	
	Buyer Initials _____ _____ Seller Initials _____ _____	

Figure 9.1   *Offer to Purchase and Contract (continued)*

(b) There must be no restriction, easement, zoning or other governmental regulation that would prevent the reasonable use of the Property for _____ purposes.

(c) The Property must be in substantially the same or better condition at Closing as on the date of this offer, reasonable wear and tear excepted.

(d) All deeds of trust, liens and other charges against the Property, not assumed by Buyer, must be paid and satisfied by Seller prior to or at Closing such that cancellation may be promptly obtained following Closing. Seller shall remain obligated to obtain any such cancellations following Closing.

(e) Title must be delivered at Closing by GENERAL WARRANTY DEED unless otherwise stated herein, and must be fee simple marketable and insurable title, free of all encumbrances except: ad valorem taxes for the current year (prorated through the date of Closing); utility easements and unviolated restrictive covenants that do not materially affect the value of the Property; and such other encumbrances as may be assumed or specifically approved by Buyer. The Property must have legal access to a public right of way.

6. SPECIAL ASSESSMENTS: Seller warrants that there are no pending or confirmed governmental special assessments for sidewalk, paving, water, sewer, or other improvements on or adjoining the Property, and no pending or confirmed owners' association special assessments, except as follows: _____
_____ .
(Insert "None" or the identification of such assessments, if any.) Seller shall pay all owners' association assessments and all governmental assessments confirmed through the time of Closing, if any, and Buyer shall take title subject to all pending assessments, if any, unless otherwise agreed as follows: _____
_____ .

7. PRORATIONS AND ADJUSTMENTS: Unless otherwise provided, the following items shall be prorated and either adjusted between the parties or paid at Closing: (a) Ad valorem taxes on real property shall be prorated on a calendar year basis through the date of Closing; (b) Ad valorem taxes on personal property for the entire year shall be paid by the Seller unless the personal property is conveyed to the Buyer, in which case, the personal property taxes shall be prorated on a calendar year basis through the date of Closing; (c) All late listing penalties, if any, shall be paid by Seller; (d) Rents, if any, for the Property shall be prorated through the date of Closing; (e) Owners' association dues and other like charges shall be prorated through the date of Closing. Seller represents that the regular owners' association dues, if any, are $_____ per_____ .

8. CLOSING EXPENSES: Buyer shall be responsible for all costs with respect to any loan obtained by Buyer. Buyer shall pay for recording the deed and for preparation and recording of all instruments required to secure the balance of the purchase price unpaid at Closing. Seller shall pay for preparation of a deed and all other documents necessary to perform Seller's obligations under this agreement, and for excise tax (revenue stamps) required by law. If Seller is to pay any of Buyer's expenses associated with the purchase of the Property, the amount thereof shall be $_____ , including any FHA/VA lender and inspection costs that Buyer is not permitted to pay, but excluding any portion disapproved by Buyer's lender.

9. FUEL: Buyer agrees to purchase from Seller the fuel, if any, situated in any tank on the Property at the prevailing rate with the cost of measurement thereof, if any, being paid by Seller.

10. EVIDENCE OF TITLE: Seller agrees to use his best efforts to deliver to Buyer as soon as reasonably possible after the Effective Date of this contract, copies of all title information in possession of or available to Seller, including but not limited to: title insurance policies, attorney's opinions on title, surveys, covenants, deeds, notes and deeds of trust and easements relating to the Property. Seller authorizes (1) any attorney presently or previously representing Seller to release and disclose any title insurance policy in such attorney's file to Buyer and both Buyer's and Seller's agents and attorneys; and (2) the Property's title insurer or its agent to release and disclose all materials in the Property's title insurer's (or title insurer's agent's) file to Buyer and both Buyer's and Seller's agents and attorneys.

11. LABOR AND MATERIAL: Seller shall furnish at Closing an affidavit and indemnification agreement in form satisfactory to Buyer showing that all labor and materials, if any, furnished to the Property within 120 days prior to the date of Closing have been paid for and agreeing to indemnify Buyer against all loss from any cause or claim arising therefrom.

12. PROPERTY DISCLOSURE AND INSPECTIONS:

(a) Property Disclosure:

❑ Buyer has received a signed copy of the N.C. Residential Property Disclosure Statement prior to the signing of this Offer to Purchase and Contract.

❑ Buyer has NOT received a signed copy of the N.C. Residential Property Disclosure Statement prior to the signing of this Offer to Purchase and Contract and shall have the right to terminate or withdraw this contract without penalty prior to WHICHEVER OF THE FOLLOWING EVENTS OCCURS FIRST: (1) the end of the third calendar day following receipt of the Disclosure Statement; (2) the end of the third calendar day following the date the contract was made; or (3) Closing or occupancy by the Buyer in the case of a sale or exchange.

❑ Exempt from N.C. Residential Property Disclosure Statement because (SEE GUIDELINES)
_____ .

❑ The Property is residential and was built prior to 1978 (Attach Lead-Based Paint or Lead-Based Paint Hazards Disclosure Addendum.)

Page 2 of 4

Buyer Initials _____ _____   Seller Initials _____ _____

STANDARD FORM 2 – T
© 7/2002

Figure 9.1   Offer to Purchase and Contract (continued)

(b) **Property Inspection:** Unless otherwise stated herein, Buyer shall have the option of inspecting, or obtaining at Buyer's expense inspections, to determine the condition of the Property. Unless otherwise stated herein, it is a condition of this contract that: (i) the built-in appliances, electrical system, plumbing system, heating and cooling systems, roof coverings (including flashing and gutters), doors and windows, exterior surfaces, structural components (including foundations, columns, chimneys, floors, walls, ceilings and roofs), porches and decks, fireplaces and flues, crawl space and attic ventilation systems (if any), water and sewer systems (public and private), shall be performing the function for which intended and shall not be in need of immediate repair; (ii) there shall be no unusual drainage conditions or evidence of excessive moisture adversely affecting the structure(s); and (iii) there shall be no friable asbestos or existing environmental contamination. Any inspections shall be completed and written notice of necessary repairs shall be given to Seller on or before _____. Seller shall provide written notice to Buyer of Seller's response within _____ days of Buyer's notice. Buyer is advised to have any inspections made prior to incurring expenses for Closing and in sufficient time to permit any required repairs to be completed by Closing.

(c) **Wood-Destroying Insects:** Unless otherwise stated herein, Buyer shall have the option of obtaining, at Buyer's expense, a report from a licensed pest control operator on a standard form in accordance with the regulations of the North Carolina Structural Pest Control Committee, stating that as to all structures, except _____, there was no visible evidence of wood-destroying insects and containing no indication of visible damage therefrom. The report must be obtained in sufficient time so as to permit treatment, if any, and repairs, if any, to be completed prior to Closing. All treatment required shall be paid for by Seller and completed prior to Closing, unless otherwise agreed upon in writing by the parties. The Buyer is advised that the inspection report described in this paragraph may not always reveal either structural damage or damage caused by agents or organisms other than wood-destroying insects. If new construction, Seller shall provide a standard warranty of termite soil treatment.

(d) **Repairs:** Pursuant to any inspections in (b) and/or (c) above, if any repairs are necessary, Seller shall have the option of completing them or refusing to complete them. If Seller elects not to complete the repairs, then Buyer shall have the option of accepting the Property in its present condition or terminating this contract, in which case all earnest monies shall be refunded. Unless otherwise stated herein, any items not covered by (b) (i), b (ii), b (iii) and (c) above are excluded from repair negotiations under this contract.

(e) **Acceptance: CLOSING SHALL CONSTITUTE ACCEPTANCE OF EACH OF THE SYSTEMS, ITEMS AND CONDITIONS LISTED ABOVE IN ITS THEN EXISTING CONDITION UNLESS PROVISION IS OTHERWISE MADE IN WRITING.**

13. **REASONABLE ACCESS:** Seller will provide reasonable access to the Property (including working, existing utilities) through the earlier of Closing or possession by Buyer, to Buyer or Buyer's representatives for the purposes of appraisal, inspection, and/or evaluation. Buyer may conduct a walk-through inspection of the Property prior to Closing.

14. **CLOSING:** Closing shall be defined as the date and time of recording of the deed. All parties agree to execute any and all documents and papers necessary in connection with Closing and transfer of title on or before _____, at a place designated by Buyer. The deed is to be made to _____.

15. **POSSESSION:** Unless otherwise provided herein, possession shall be delivered at Closing. In the event possession is NOT to be delivered at Closing: ☐ a Buyer Possession Before Closing Agreement is attached OR, ☐ a Seller Possession After Closing Agreement is attached.

16. **OTHER PROVISIONS AND CONDITIONS:** (ITEMIZE ALL ADDENDA TO THIS CONTRACT AND ATTACH HERETO.)

17. **RISK OF LOSS:** The risk of loss or damage by fire or other casualty prior to Closing shall be upon Seller. If the improvements on the Property are destroyed or materially damaged prior to Closing, Buyer may terminate this contract by written notice delivered to Seller or Seller's agent and all deposits shall be returned to Buyer. In the event Buyer does NOT elect to terminate this contract, Buyer shall be entitled to receive, in addition to the Property, any of the Seller's insurance proceeds payable on account of the damage or destruction applicable to the Property being purchased.

18. **ASSIGNMENTS:** This contract may not be assigned without the written consent of all parties, but if assigned by agreement, then this contract shall be binding on the assignee and his heirs and successors.

19. **PARTIES:** This contract shall be binding upon and shall inure to the benefit of the parties, i.e., Buyer and Seller and their heirs, successors and assigns. As used herein, words in the singular include the plural and the masculine includes the feminine and neuter genders, as appropriate.

20. **SURVIVAL:** If any provision herein contained which by its nature and effect is required to be observed, kept or performed after the Closing, it shall survive the Closing and remain binding upon and for the benefit of the parties hereto until fully observed, kept or performed.

Page 3 of 4

STANDARD FORM 2 – T
© 7/2002

Buyer Initials _____ _____   Seller Initials _____ _____

Figure 9.1 *Offer to Purchase and Contract (continued)*

21. ENTIRE AGREEMENT: This contract contains the entire agreement of the parties and there are no representations, inducements or other provisions other than those expressed herein. All changes, additions or deletions hereto must be in writing and signed by all parties. Nothing contained herein shall alter any agreement between a REALTOR® or broker and Seller or Buyer as contained in any listing agreement, buyer agency agreement, or any other agency agreement between them.

22. NOTICE AND EXECUTION: Any notice or communication to be given to a party herein may be given to the party or to such party's agent. This offer shall become a binding contract (the "Effective Date") when signed by both Buyer and Seller and such signing is communicated to the offering party. This contract is executed under seal in signed multiple originals, all of which together constitute one and the same instrument, with a signed original being retained by each party and each REALTOR® or broker hereto, and the parties adopt the word "SEAL" beside their signatures below.

Buyer acknowledges having made an on-site personal examination of the Property prior to the making of this offer.

THE NORTH CAROLINA ASSOCIATION OF REALTORS®, INC. AND THE NORTH CAROLINA BAR ASSOCIATION MAKE NO REPRESENTATION AS TO THE LEGAL VALIDITY OR ADEQUACY OF ANY PROVISION OF THIS FORM IN ANY SPECIFIC TRANSACTION. IF YOU DO NOT UNDERSTAND THIS FORM OR FEEL THAT IT DOES NOT PROVIDE FOR YOUR LEGAL NEEDS, YOU SHOULD CONSULT A NORTH CAROLINA REAL ESTATE ATTORNEY BEFORE YOU SIGN IT.

Date: _____   Date: _____

Buyer _____ (SEAL)   Seller _____ (SEAL)

Date: _____   Date: _____

Buyer _____ (SEAL)   Seller _____ (SEAL)

Escrow Agent acknowledges receipt of the earnest money and agrees to hold and disburse the same in accordance with the terms hereof.

Date_____   Firm: _____

                                         By: _____
                                              (Signature)

Selling Agent/Firm/Phone _____

                Acting as ❑ Buyer's Agent   ❑ Seller's (sub)Agent   ❑ Dual Agent

Listing Agent/Firm/Phone _____

                Acting as ❑ Seller's (sub)Agent   ❑ Dual Agent

Page 4 of 4

STANDARD FORM 2 – T
© 7/2002

Whatever the contract is called, when it has been prepared and signed by the purchaser it is an offer to purchase the subject real estate. Later, if the document is accepted and signed by the seller, it becomes, or "ripens into," a *contract of sale.* Any offer-to-purchase form used in North Carolina must meet the provisions and standards of Rule A.0112 of the Real Estate Commission (see Figure 9.2). Other types of sales contracts discussed in this chapter include the installment land contract and the option to purchase contract.

In Practice   Commission Rule A.0112 outlines the provisions that must appear in any offer to purchase and contract used in North Carolina. The Real Estate Commission does not "approve" contract forms. License law strictly prohibits real Estate agents from drafting *sales* contract, that bind other people. The contract forms used in this textbook are NCAR standard forms that have been approved by the North Carolina Bar Association and the North Carolina Association of REALTORS®.

Every sales contract requires at least two parties—a seller (the vendor) and a buyer (the vendee). The same person cannot be both the buyer and seller, because a person cannot legally contract with himself or herself. *The contract of sale is the most important document in the sale of real estate* because it sets out in detail the agreement between the buyer and the seller and establishes their legal rights and obligations. It is more important than the deed itself because *the contract,* in effect, *dictates the contents of the deed.*

Details to be included in a real estate sales contract are price, terms, description of the property, kind and condition of the title, form of deed the seller will deliver, kind of title evidence required, who will provide title evidence and how defects in the title, if any, are to be eliminated. The contract must state all the terms and conditions of the agreement and spell out all contingencies.

In situations where a contract is vague in its terms and one party sues the other based on one of these terms, the courts may refuse to make a contract for the parties. The real estate broker must be aware of the responsibilities and legal rights of the parties to a sale and must see that an adequate contract is prepared. Any error regarding the conditions in a contract could render that contract unenforceable.

Contracts in Writing   The statute of frauds provides that no action may be brought on any contract for the sale of real estate unless the contract is in writing and signed by the parties to be bound by the agreement. The offer to purchase and contract must be in writing to be enforceable.

The Offer and Acceptance   One of the essential elements of a contract being formed (discussed in the previous chapter) was that of *mutual assent* or *deliberate agreement.* To form a valid real estate sales contract there must be an offer made, an acceptance of that offer, and communication of the acceptance to the other party (the offeror).

Figure 9.2   Rule A.0112

A.0112 Offers and Sales Contracts

(a) A broker or salesman acting as an agent in a real estate transaction shall not use a preprinted offer or sales contract form unless the form describes or specifically requires the entry of the following information:

  (1) the names of the buyer and seller;

  (2) a legal description of the real property sufficient to identify and distinguish it from all other property;

  (3) an itemization of any personal property to be included in the transaction;

  (4) the purchase price and manner of payment;

  (5) any portion of the purchase price that is to be paid by a promissory note, including the amount, interest rate, payment terms, whether or not the note is to be secured, and other material terms;

  (6) any portion of the purchase price that is to be paid by the assumption of an existing loan, including the amount of such loan, costs to be paid by the buyer or seller, the interest rate and number of discount points and a condition that the buyer must be able to qualify for the assumption of the loan and must make every reasonable effort to qualify for the assumption of the loan;

  (7) the amount of earnest money, if any, the method of payment, the name of the broker or firm that will serve as escrow agent, an acknowledgment of earnest money receipt by the escrow agent, and the criteria for determining disposition of the earnest money, including disputed earnest money, consistent with Commission Rule .0107 of this Subchapter;

  (8) any loan that must be obtained by the buyer as a condition of the contract, including the amount and type of loan, interest rate and number of discount points, loan term, loan commitment date, and who shall pay loan closing costs; and a condition that the buyer shall make every reasonable effort to obtain the loan;

  (9) a general statement of the buyer's intended use of the property and a condition that such use must not be prohibited by private restriction or governmental regulation;

  (10) the amount and purpose of any special assessment to which the property is subject and the responsibility of the parties for any unpaid charges;

  (11) the date for closing and transfer of possession;

  (12) the signatures of the buyer and seller;

  (13) the date of offer and acceptance;

  (14) a provision that title to the property must be delivered at closing by general warranty deed and must be fee simple marketable title, free of all encumbrances except ad valorem taxes for the current year, utility easements, and any other encumbrances specifically approved by the buyer, or a provision otherwise describing the estate to be conveyed, and encumbrances, and the form of conveyance;

  (15) the items to be prorated or adjusted at closing;

  (16) who shall pay closing expenses;

  (17) the buyer's right to inspect the property prior to closing and who shall pay for repairs and improvements, if any;

  (18) a provision that the property shall at closing be in substantially the same condition as on the date of the offer (reasonable wear and tear excepted), or a description of the required property condition at closing, and

  (19) a provision setting forth the identity of each real estate agent and firm involved in the transaction and disclosing the party each agent and firm represents.

The provisions of this Rule shall apply only to preprinted offer and sales contract forms which a broker or salesman acting as an agent in a real estate transaction proposes for use by the buyer and seller. Nothing contained in this Rule shall be construed to prohibit the buyer and seller in a real estate transaction from altering, amending or deleting any provision in a form offer to purchase or contract; nor shall this Rule be construed to limit the rights of the buyer and seller to draft their own offers or contracts or to have the same drafted by an attorney at law.

Figure 9.2 *Rule A.0112 (continued)*

(b) A broker or salesman acting as an agent in a real estate transaction shall not use a preprinted offer or sales contract form containing the provisions or terms listed in Subparagraphs (b)(1) and (2) of this Rule. A broker, salesman or anyone acting for or at the direction of the broker or salesman shall not insert or cause such provisions or terms to be inserted into any such preprinted form, even at the direction of the parties or their attorneys:

(1) any provision concerning the payment of a commission or compensation, including the forfeiture of earnest money, to any broker, salesman or firm, or

(2) any provision that attempts to disclaim the liability of a broker or salesman for his representations in connection with the transaction.

The Offer. Anyone who makes an offer to purchase property by a contract is known as the **offeror**—the person making the offer. Anyone who receives an offer is known as the **offeree.**

For Example Betty Buyer makes an offer to purchase Sam Seller's house by having her agent, Cooper, prepare a Standard Form 2. Once the form is properly filled out with the terms of Betty's offer, she signs it as the buyer and asks Cooper to present the offer to Sam, through Sam's agent, Cindy. At this point Betty is the offeror and Sam is the offeree.

In the above example a contract is not yet formed; there is merely an offer to buy that has been made by an offeror to an offeree. Those preparing an offer must make certain there are no ambiguities with respect to the language or construction of the offer because the intent of the offer is to bind the parties when it is accepted. An offer must be definite and precise in its terms; it cannot be of an "illusory" nature. Mere advertisements of a property for sale do not constitute an offer, nor does the typical listing contract constitute an offer. Also, preliminary negotiations do not constitute an offer.

Many times an offer may contain conditions and/or contingencies. In other words, the offeror is saying to the offeree, "this is my offer, if the following conditions or contingencies can be met."

For Example Betty Buyer, in the above example, is making an offer of $100,000 contingent on her ability to obtain financing based on an $80,000 loan and other specific loan requirements. If Betty does not qualify for the loan based on contract terms, even after an acceptance, she is relieved from the terms of the contract.

The Acceptance. For an offer to become a binding contract it must be communicated to and accepted by the offeree according to the exact terms and conditions of the offer. An *acceptance* is a promise made by the offeree to fulfill all terms of the offer. If an acceptance of exact terms and conditions takes place and that acceptance is properly communicated back to the offeror, a binding contract is formed. If the offeree changes any of the terms or conditions of the offer, no matter how slight or small, an acceptance does not take place. A counteroffer has been made.

> A counteroffer rejects the original offer and constitutes a new offer, not a revision of the original offer.

The Counteroffer. When the offeree receives the offer and makes a change to that offer, it constitutes a **counteroffer,** which is a rejection of the first offer. When the counteroffer takes place, the original offer cannot be resubmitted. Also, the offeree cannot later change his or her mind and "accept" the original offer. *It has been rejected.*

For Example When Betty made her offer, she entered $100,000 as the offered purchase price. Sam changed the purchase price to $105,000 with a "pen and ink" change, dated and initialed the change and signed the form as the seller. At this time, Sam becomes the offeror, making a new offer back to Betty, who is now the offeree. Once this new offer is communicated to Betty, if she accepts it by initialing and dating the form, she has accepted the offer from Sam. When her acceptance is properly communicated to Sam, a contract has been formed.

If Betty changes the $105,000 to $103,000 and initials and dates the change, a counter-counteroffer has taken place; Betty is once again the offeror and Sam is once again the offeree.

Methods of Communicating Offers and Acceptance

There are various ways that offers and acceptance may be communicated. Probably the most common and the most acceptable way is to communicate in writing; the offeror signs the written offer and communicates it to the offeree, and the offeree signs the written offer, denoting acceptance. When the acceptance is properly communicated, a contract is formed.

Communication of the acceptance may be either oral (by telephone or in person) or by personal delivery of the written acceptance by the offeree or by another person on behalf of the offeree. Communication of an acceptance to either the offeree's or the offeror's agent is the same as communication to the principal.

Traditional, special or electronic mail are acceptable ways to communicate an offer or an acceptance. If an acceptance is placed into the mail service, it is considered as having been delivered when mailed, not necessarily when actually received; this is known as the **"mail-box rule."** The offeror cannot revoke the offer once the acceptance is mailed. The telegraph is another means of communicating an acceptance, although it is seldom used in today's world of real estate business. Facsimiles (fax machine, e-mail, telecopier, etc.) are acceptable means of communicating. The acceptance of the offer takes place when the acceptance is actually received by the offeree's communication device. This form of communicating the offer and acceptance is becoming commonplace in the real estate business.

Termination of Offers

There are several ways to terminate an offer (remember that an offer is not a contract, which may be terminated in different ways). Termination of offers can take place

- if the offeree rejects the offer;
- if the offeree fails to accept within the prescribed time stipuated in the offer;
- within a reasonable time, if the time of acceptance is not prescribed;
- prior to acceptance, if the offeror communicates a revocation of the offer; or
- by the death of the offeror or offeree.

Major Contract Provisions

All real estate sales contracts can be divided into a number of general parts. Although each form of contract will contain these divisions, their location within a particular contract may vary. Generally speaking, the information will include at least the following items:

- Names and marital status of the buyer and seller and the obligations of both parties—the buyer's obligation to purchase the property and the seller's obligation to convey the property. There also should be a statement indicating how the buyer intends to take title.
- Legal description of the property and, if appropriate, the street address.
- Purchase price and how the purchaser intends to pay for the property, including earnest money deposits, additional cash from the purchaser and the conditions of any mortgage financing the purchaser intends to obtain or assume.
- Provision for any contingencies (delays in obtaining financing, inability to obtain financing, purchaser's inability to sell a property to finance the current transaction, seller's inability to acquire another desired property, inability of the seller to clear the title). If a contingency is not met, neither party is bound to carry out the agreement. For example, if the buyer cannot obtain the type of financing described in the agreement, the buyer does not have to proceed with the transaction. If the purchaser makes the sale contingent on selling another home first, the seller may insist on an escape clause. Such a provision allows the seller to look at a more favorable offer, with the original purchaser retaining the right (if challenged) either to firm up the first sales contract by eliminating the contingency or to void the contract.
- Contingency clause providing for completion of the contract should the property be damaged or destroyed between the time the contract is signed and the date of closing. In some instances, destruction of improvements makes performance of a sales contract by the seller impossible.
- Provisions for closing the transaction and transferring possession of the property to the purchaser. A realistic closing date always should be included in the offer to purchase.
- Proration of (adjustment for) real estate taxes, hazard insurance, rents, fuel and other closing costs.
- Provision for title assurance (abstract and legal opinion, certificate of title, title insurance policy, etc.).
- Provision for remedies should either party default on the contract (including liquidated damages and the right to sue for specific performance or damages).
- Signatures of all parties and execution date on which the contract is signed. The signature of a witness is not essential to a valid contract.

Miscellaneous Provisions in a Contract

The following are some of the more common considerations also found in many sales contracts:

- Identification of any personal property to be left on the premises for the purchaser (such as major appliances, lawn and garden equipment). Often, personal property items are sold along with the real estate. These items should be specifically described in the purchase agreement. Custom dictates that when there are many such items, they should be enumerated in a bill of sale, which is evidence of ownership. By describing the personal property in the contract, a broker minimizes any potential conflict between the purchaser and seller as to what constitutes personal property and what constitutes fixtures. It is good practice for a salesperson to bring to the attention of the parties any property that potentially may fall into this difficult classification.

- Identification of any real property to be removed by the seller prior to closing (such as storage sheds).
- Transfer of any applicable warranties on items such as heating and cooling systems or built-in appliances.
- Identification of any leased equipment that must be transferred to the purchaser or returned to the lessor (security systems, cable television boxes, water softeners and the like).
- Type and condition of all utilities.
- Name of appointed closing or settlement agent.
- Creation of closing or settlement instructions.
- Transfer of any impound or escrow account funds.
- Transfer of the homeowner's insurance policy or the issuance of a new one.
- Transfer or payment of any outstanding special assessments.
- Provision by either party for a homeowner warranty program.
- In the event of new FHA or VA financing, a provision that the contract can be voided by the purchaser if the property is appraised for less than the contracted sales price.
- Purchaser's right to a structural engineering report, pest control or insect infestation report or habitability report within a specified number of days.
- Purchaser's right to inspect the property shortly before the closing or settlement (often called the *walk-through*).
- Purchaser's right to have a family member or a lawyer approve the contract within a specified number of days.
- Agreement as to what documents will be provided by each party and when and where they will be delivered.

Addenda

Several addenda may be used with the standard sales contract when appropriate (see Figure 9.3). These addenda address specific issues that may be too complicated to include in the space allowed for "other provisions." The agent should use these approved addenda when dealing with these issues because they increase the chances of proper preparation and negate any suspicion that the agent may be illegally practicing law by drafting a contract. For example, an FHA/VA Financing addendum must be used when the buyer is going to apply for an FHA or a VA loan; a Seller Financing addendum must be used when the seller is providing part or all of the financing; a Buyer Possession before Closing Agreement addendum must be used when the buyer wishes to move onto the property before the closing date; and a Lead-Based Paint Disclosure addendum must be used when required (when the property is a residence built prior to 1978).

Submitting Offers to Seller

Real estate agents are obligated by licensing law to disclose all offers to sellers immediately, but no later than within five days of the offer. Furthermore, listing agents must disclose any additional information they have that may affect a seller's decision to accept an offer. This includes information about the offeror's financial ability to close the transaction, as well as the possibility of other offers that may be presented shortly.

An agent cannot reject an offer on behalf of a seller, nor can an agent screen offers, that is, present only those offers that the agent feels have merit. (All offers must be communicated to the seller.) It is up to the seller to accept or

---

Figure 9.3   ***Addenda Forms Approved by the NCAR and NC Bar***

Contingent Sale Addendum
New Construction Addendum
FHA/VA Financing Addendum
Seller Financing Addendum
Loan Assumption Addendum
Buyer Possession before Closing Agreement Addendum
Seller Possession after Closing Agreement Addendum
Lead-Based Paint Disclosure or Lead-Based Paint Hazard Disclosure Addendum
Radon Inspection Addendum
Additional Provisions Addendum
Backup Offer Addendum

---

reject any offer that is made, however unreasonable that offer is. Agents also must present those offers that may be disadvantageous to them.

For Example   One buyer may offer the seller $90,000 in cash for the seller's home, while another buyer offers the seller $95,000, contingent on obtaining financing. The agent must present both offers as soon as possible, even though if the seller accepts the first offer (because it is in cash), it will mean a smaller commission for the agent.

This agency duty to present all offers is further clarified by Real Estate Commission Rule A.0106, which requires that all licensees deliver a copy of any offer or counteroffer immediately, but no later than five days after execution.

Backup offers.   An agent may receive a **backup offer** on a listed property—an offer that is made after the owner has already signed a contract to sell the property but before the sale has closed. In that case, the agent should inform the offeror that there is an existing contract and inquire whether he or she wishes to withdraw the offer. (Note that according to the Real Estate Commission, agents should discourage a buyer from making a backup offer.) If the offeror still wants to make an offer on the property, the agent must submit the offer to the seller. The agent should advise the seller to seek legal counsel if the seller is interested in the offer. Backup offers that are contingent on the first sale's falling through always should be drafted by an experienced attorney. There is an approved Backup Offer contract addendum (NCAR Standard Form 2A1-T). Note that the agent is required to submit all offers, including backup offers, to the seller immediately.

Handling Contract Modifications and Counteroffers   Frequently, a seller wants certain changes to be made to an offer before accepting it. For example, instead of a $1,000 earnest money deposit, the seller may demand a $5,000 earnest money deposit. As discussed earlier, once the offeree makes any material change in the offer, he or she has *rejected* that offer and created a *counteroffer*. No contract has been formed at this stage. It is up to the original offeror to accept or reject the counteroffer. If the original offeror accepts the counteroffer "with a few changes," another counteroffer has been created and the process begins again.

Negotiations between a buyer and seller may consist of a series of counteroffers before final terms are agreed on. Any changes to the original offer must be made in writing and initialed by both parties. Unfortunately, if all the changes are written into the initial offer, the contract can become virtually unreadable. It is a good idea for the agent to fill in a new standard form with the final terms and have both parties sign and date it. This avoids later confusion over which terms were changed and how.

Furnishing Copies of Offers and Contracts to Buyer and Seller

According to Real Estate Commission Rule A.0106, real estate agents must provide all parties with a copy of any instrument they sign at the time of execution.

For Example When a buyer signs an offer to purchase, the agent must immediately provide the buyer with a copy of that offer. Then if the seller signs the offer, the agent must immediately provide the seller with a copy of that signed offer. And of course, the agent also must give a copy of the offer and contract to purchase—with both signatures—to the buyer.

It is standard practice to fill out six copies of the forms. (Note that a *signed copy becomes an original.*) One copy goes to each of the following: the buyer, the seller, the listing real estate office, the selling real estate office, the closing attorney and the lender.

INSTALLMENT LAND CONTRACT

A real estate sale can be made under an **installment land contract,** sometimes called a *land contract* or *contract for deed.* Under an installment land contract, the seller, also known as the *vendor*, retains legal ownership, while the buyer, known as the *vendee,* secures possession of and an equitable interest in the property. The buyer holds equitable title, and the contract is a cloud on the seller's title.

The buyer usually agrees to give the seller a down payment and pay regular monthly installments of principal and interest over a number of years. The buyer also agrees to pay real estate taxes, insurance premiums, repairs and upkeep on the property. While the buyer obtains possession when the contract is signed by both parties, *the seller is not obligated to execute and deliver a deed to the buyer until a future date, which may not be until all the terms of the contract have been satisfied.*

All installment land contracts must be in writing to be valid and enforceable, as required by the statute of frauds, and must be recorded, as required by the Conner Act (see pages 78-79).

Typical Provisions

Most installment land contracts contain the following provisions:

- Full names of the parties
- Date when the contract is signed
- Legal description of the property to be conveyed
- Contract price of the property conveyed
- Amount of the purchaser's down payment
- Amount and due date of each installment payment
- Interest rate on the unpaid balance and the method of computing the interest

- Seller's promise to deliver a general warranty deed on completion of the contract
- Fact that the purchaser is responsible for the payment of taxes, assessments and other charges against the property from the date of the contract unless agreed to the contrary
- Whether the contract is assignable
- What happens in the event of default

Advantages and Disadvantages

For the seller. The typical land contract is advantageous to the seller for a number of reasons. There is an income tax benefit that comes from receiving the sales price in installments instead of in a lump sum. The seller gets to retain legal title, which makes the seller feel more secure. If the buyer defaults, many land contracts provide forfeiture as a remedy. Forfeiture means that the buyer forfeits all the monthly payments he or she has made as well as his or her rights in the property. Finally, the land contract may be the only way to make property desirable to buyers when interest rates are high or institutional loans are hard to get.

On the other hand, sellers often receive small down payments under a land contract, and a seller may prefer to be "cashed out"—that is, to get immediate cash for his or her equity. For example, the seller may need cash to make a down payment on a new home.

For the buyer. If the buyer has a poor credit rating, a history of foreclosures or bankruptcies, or marginal income, a land contract may be the only way to finance a transaction. The down payment is usually lower than it is in institutional financing arrangements, and the closing costs are usually lower. All these are obvious advantages for the buyer.

However, if the buyer defaults under the land contract, the forfeiture remedy available to the seller is extremely harsh for the buyer. The buyer can lose all the payments made under the contract in addition to the property itself. Also, because the buyer does not get legal title to the property until the end of the contract term, the buyer will find it virtually impossible to use the property as collateral for future financing needs.

OPTION TO PURCHASE REAL ESTATE

An **option** is a *contract by which an* **optionor** *(generally an owner) gives an* **optionee** *(a prospective purchaser or lessee) the right to buy or lease the owner's property at a fixed price within a stated period of time.* An option to purchase has two considerations: the option fee when the option is given, and the agreed-on sales price when the option is exercised. The option fee is nonrefundable if the option is not exercised. The optionee must decide, within the specified time, either to exercise the option right (to buy or lease the property) or to allow the option right to expire. An option is enforceable by only one party—the optionee. (See Figure 9.4 for a sample of an option-to-purchase contract.)

A common application of an option is a lease that includes an option for the tenant to purchase the property. Options on commercial real estate frequently depend on the fulfillment of specific conditions, such as obtaining a zoning change or a building permit. The optionee is usually obligated to exercise the option if the conditions are met.

Figure 9.4 *Option to Purchase*

OPTION TO PURCHASE

Mail/Box after recording to:_____

This instrument was prepared by:_____

Brief description for the Index:_____

_____

This OPTION TO PURCHASE ("Option") is granted on _____ by
_____, the "Seller," to
_____, the "Buyer."
Seller, intending to bind Seller, Seller's heirs, successors and assigns, in consideration of the sum of
_____ Dollars ($_____) (the "Option Money") paid to
Seller by Buyer, receipt of which is acknowledged, grants to the Buyer, Buyer's heirs, successors, assigns or representatives, the exclusive right and option to purchase all of that certain parcel of land, together with all improvements located thereon (collectively, the "Property"), in the City of _____, County of _____,
State of North Carolina, and more particularly described as follows:
Street Address: _____ Zip Code _____
Legal Description: _____
_____ on the terms and conditions set forth below:

1. **Option Period:** This Option shall exist and continue from the date hereof until _____ o'clock ___.M. on _____ ("Option Period"). In order to preserve the full legal rights of Buyer, a notice hereof should be recorded; and this Option (excluding Exhibit A) may be recorded as a legally binding Notice of the Option. **TIME IS OF THE ESSENCE WITH RESPECT TO THE OPTION PERIOD AND EXERCISE.**

2. **Exercise:** At any time during the Option Period, Buyer may exercise this Option by giving Seller a written notice thereof signed by the Buyer, which exercise is effective upon (a) hand delivery, (b) completed facsimile transmission, or (c) prepaid deposit of the notice with an overnight commercial delivery service or in certified mail, return receipt requested, at the following address:

Seller: Seller requests, but does not require, a copy be sent to:

_____   _____
_____   _____
_____   _____

Phone:_____ Fax:_____   Phone:_____ Fax:_____

3. **Contract Upon Exercise:** Upon exercise of this Option, the terms of purchase and sale shall be as set forth on the completed standard "Offer to Purchase and Contract," or standard "Vacant Lot Offer to Purchase and Contract," which is attached as Exhibit A and incorporated herein by reference.

4. **Application of Option Money:** If this Option is exercised, the Option Money shall _____ shall not _____ be applied to the purchase price at Closing. If this Option is not exercised, the Option Money shall be retained by Seller.

Page 1 of 3

This form jointly approved by:
North Carolina Bar Association
North Carolina Association of REALTORS®, Inc.

Seller Initials _____ _____

REALTOR®

STANDARD FORM 8 - T
© 7/2002

Figure 9.4 Option to Purchase (continued)

5. **Entry:** During the Option Period, Buyer and those reasonably designated by Buyer may, with reasonable advance notice to Seller, enter the Property to inspect, survey and appraise the Property. Buyer shall be responsible for the repair of any damage done to the Property during any such entry.

6. **Other Conditions:** _____

_____

_____.

THE NORTH CAROLINA ASSOCIATION OF REALTORS®, INC. AND THE NORTH CAROLINA BAR ASSOCIATION MAKE NO REPRESENTATION AS TO THE LEGAL VALIDITY OR ADEQUACY OF ANY PROVISION OF THIS FORM IN ANY SPECIFIC TRANSACTION. IF YOU DO NOT UNDERSTAND THIS FORM OR FEEL THAT IT DOES NOT PROVIDE FOR YOUR LEGAL NEEDS, YOU SHOULD CONSULT A NORTH CAROLINA REAL ESTATE ATTORNEY BEFORE YOU SIGN IT.

IN WITNESS WHEREOF, the Seller has caused the due execution of the foregoing as of the day and year first above written.

_____   _____ (SEAL)
           (Entity Name)

By:_____   _____ (SEAL)
    Title:_____

_____ (SEAL)

_____ (SEAL)

State of North Carolina - County of _____

I, the undersigned Notary Public of the County and State aforesaid, certify that _____

personally appeared before me this day and acknowledged the due execution of the foregoing instrument for the purposes therein expressed. Witness my hand and Notarial stamp or seal this _____ day of _____, 20_____.

My Commission Expires:_____   _____
                                                                              Notary Public

State of North Carolina - County of _____

I, the undersigned Notary Public of the County and State aforesaid, certify that _____
personally came before me this day and acknowledged that __he is the _____
of _____, a North Carolina or _____ corporation/limited
liability company/general partnership/limited partnership (strike through the inapplicable), and that by authority duly given and as the act of such entity, __he signed the foregoing instrument in its name, on its behalf, as its act and deed. Witness my hand and Notarial stamp or seal, this _____ day of _____, 20_____.

My Commission Expires:_____   _____
                                                                              Notary Public

STANDARD FORM 8 - T
© 7/2002

To see the full form, please go to Appendix C.

Rights of the Parties

For a consideration of a specified amount of money, a present owner (optionor) agrees to give an optionee an irrevocable right to buy the optionor's real estate at a certain price for a limited period of time. At the time the option is signed by the parties, the optionor does not sell, nor does the optionee buy. They merely agree that the optionee will have the right to buy and the owner will be obligated to sell if the optionee decides to exercise the option.

Requirements of Options

All options for real property are required to be in writing under the statute of frauds. Under the Conner Act, an option must be recorded to be enforceable against the claims of third parties.

The option should describe the manner in which the optionee will notify the optionor of his or her decision to exercise the option. Not only should the option spell out the terms under which the optionee can buy the property, it also should describe the major terms of the sale itself, such as the purchase price, financing terms and type of deed that will be used to convey title. The consideration for the option also must be stated clearly. Furthermore, the option should explain whether the price the optionee paid for the option right will be applied toward the purchase price.

Right of First Refusal

An option should not be confused with a **right of first refusal.** A right of first refusal is created when a property owner promises a contracting party that he or she will give that person the first chance to buy the property or to match the bona fide offer of a third party, should the owner decide to sell it. Rights of first refusal are commonly found in leases. The landlord promises the tenant that if the landlord should decide to sell the property, he or she will offer it to the tenant first.

Note that with a right of first refusal, the property owner does not promise to sell the property at all—merely promises that *should* he or she decide to sell, the other party will get the first opportunity to buy. This is different from the option, where the owner promises to sell should the optionee choose to buy.

SUMMARY

An offer to purchase binds a buyer and a seller to a definite sales transaction, as described in detail in the contract. The buyer is bound to purchase the property for the amount stated in the agreement. The seller is bound to deliver a good and marketable title, free from liens and encumbrances (except those allowed by the "subject to" clause of the contract).

The offeror is the person making the offer (could be buyer or seller) and the offeree is the person who is receiving the offer (could be buyer or seller).

If either party to the offer makes a change, it constitutes a counteroffer that rejects the offer.

Modifications to an offer can be done by pen-and-ink changes or the drafting of a complete new offer. Pen-and-ink changes must be initialed and should be dated.

Under an installment land contract, the buyer takes immediate possession of the property and pays off the purchase price over a period of years, and the seller retains legal title until the purchase price is paid in full. The installment land contract serves two legal purposes: (1) it is a contract to convey and (2) it is a financing device.

Under an option agreement, the optionee purchases from the optionor, for a limited time period, the exclusive right to purchase or lease the optionor's property.

Questions

1. The buyer and the seller have entered into a sales contract. While the sale is pending, the listing agent receives another offer for the property.
   a. The agent does not have to present this offer to the seller.
   b. The agent must present this offer to the seller.
   c. The agent has to present this offer to the seller only if its terms are better than the terms of the pending sale.
   d. The agent must tell the offeror that he is prohibited from making an offer while a sale is pending.

2. Which of the following statements is true of an option agreement?
   a. It should not recite a set amount of consideration for purchase of the property.
   b. It is limited to a specified time period.
   c. It has an unlimited time limit.
   d. It is illegal in North Carolina.

3. An agent presented an offer to purchase to the seller. The offer was acceptable to the seller, except that the seller wanted a larger earnest money deposit. To make this change in order to present it to the buyer, the agent
   I. may change the provision in the original offer.
   II. may draw up a new offer.
   III. should tell the buyer orally about the change.
   a. I only
   b. II only
   c. II or III
   d. I or II

4. The buyer's offer is made on the condition that the buyer's present home sells in the next 30 days. This condition is called a(n)
   a. CC&R.   c. unilateral offer.
   b. contingency.   d. option.

5. The buyer's offer is made on the condition that the buyer is able to obtain an 80 percent institutional loan at market interest rates. If the buyer fails to obtain such a loan, the buyer will
   a. have to go ahead with the purchase anyway.
   b. not have to purchase the home, but will forfeit the whole earnest money deposit.
   c. not have to purchase the home, but will forfeit half of the earnest money deposit.
   d. not have to purchase the home and will be entitled to a full refund of his or her earnest money deposit.

6. The seller wants to net $85,000 cash from the sales transaction. The sales commission is 7 percent, the seller's closing costs are $1,000, and the seller's loan payoff figure is $65,000. What must the sales price be to accomplish the seller's goal?
   a. $151,000   c. $161,570
   b. $162,366   d. $155,000

7. Which of the following statements is true when a purchase contract has been signed by the purchaser and then given to the seller's broker with an earnest money deposit check?
   a. This transaction constitutes a valid contract
   b. The purchaser can sue the seller for specific performance
   c. This transaction is considered to be only an offer
   d. The earnest money will be forfeited if the purchaser defaults

8. An offer to purchase real estate can be terminated by all of the following EXCEPT
   a. failure to accept the offer within a prescribed period.
   b. revocation by the offeror communicated to the offeree after acceptance.
   c. conditional acceptance of the offer by the offeree.
   d. death of the offeror or offeree.

9. After an offer is accepted, the seller finds
    out that her broker was also the
    undisclosed agent for the buyer. Which of
    the following statements is true?
    a. The seller can withdraw without
       obligation to broker or buyer.
    b. The seller can withdraw but would be
       subject to liquidated damages.
    c. The seller can withdraw but only with
       the concurrence of the buyer.
    d. The seller would be subject to specific
       performance if she refused to sell.

10. When a buyer and seller have entered into
    a land contract, the buyer acquires an
    immediate interest in the property known
    as
    I. legal title.
    II. equitable title.
    III. statutory title.
       a. I only
       b. II only
       c. I and II only
       d. II and III only

11. Carl and Hannah enter into a real estate
    sales contract. Under the contract terms,
    Carl will pay Hannah $500 a month for ten
    years. Hannah will continue to hold legal
    title to the property. Carl will live on the
    property and pay all real estate taxes,
    insurance premiums and regular upkeep
    costs. What kind of contract do Carl and
    Hannah have?
    a. Option to purchase contract
    b Contract for mortgage
    c. Unilateral contract
    d. Installment land contract

12. The Taylors offer in writing to purchase a
    house owned by the Shorts for $120,000,
    including the draperies, with the offer to
    expire on Saturday at noon. The Shorts
    reply in writing on Thursday, accepting the
    $120,000 offer, but excluding the
    draperies. On Friday, while the Taylors
    consider the counteroffer, the Shorts
    decide to accept the original offer,
    draperies included, and state that in
    writing. At this point, the Taylors
    a. are legally bound to buy the house
       although they have the right to insist
       that the draperies be included.
    b. are not bound to buy.
    c. must buy the house and are not entitled
       to the draperies.
    d. must buy the house, but may deduct
       the value of the draperies from the
       $120,000.

13. Robert signs a contract under which he
    may purchase a house for $80,000 any
    time within the next three months. Robert
    pays the current owner $500 at the time
    the contract is signed. Which of the
    following best describes this contract?
    a. Contingency
    b. Option to purchase
    c. Installment land contract
    d. Sales contract

10 Landlord and Tenant

LEARNING OBJECTIVES

When you've finished reading this chapter, you should be able to

- **identify** and **explain** the characteristics of the four types of nonfreehold estates.

- **explain** the concepts of the Residential Rental Agreements Act and the North Carolina Tenant Security Act.

- **describe** the various types of leases and their purposes; the requirements and general conditions of a valid lease and how a lease may be terminated.

- **explain** the general provisions of leases as they relate to possession, recording, improvements, maintenance, assignment and subleasing, and breach.

- **define** these *key terms:*

covenant of quiet enjoyment	ground lease	net lease
estate at sufferance	holdover tenant	percentage lease
estate at will	index lease	privity of contract
estate for years	landlord	privity of estate
estate from period to period	lease	Residential Rental Agreements Act
fixed rent lease	leasehold estate	sandwich lease
graduated lease	lessee	security deposit
gross lease	lessor	sublease
	month-to-month tenancy	tenant

LEASING REAL ESTATE

A **lease** is a conveyance from a **landlord,** an owner of real estate (known as the **lessor**) to a **tenant** (the **lessee**) that transfers the right of possession and use of the owner's property to the tenant for a specified period of time. A lease is also a contract that generally sets forth the length of time the contract is to run, the amount to be paid by the lessee for the right to use the property and other rights and obligations of the parties.

A lease is said to have a *dual legal personality*—it is a contract and it also conveys an interest in real property. Because of this dual purpose, both the owner and the tenant have certain rights and duties from two sources: (1) **privity of estate** (which comes from traditional property law) and (2) **privity of contract** (which comes from the terms of the contract itself). Privity means the *mutual or successive relationship to the same rights of property.* For example, the lessee has the exclusive right of possession under privity of estate, but the lessor is granted the right to reenter the premises under the terms of the contract.

> A lease covers the conditions upon which a tenant may possess, occupy and use the property.

The landlord grants the tenant the right to occupy the premises and use them for purposes stated in the lease. In return, the landlord retains the right to receive payment for the use of the premises as well as a reversionary right to retake possession after the lease term has expired. The lessor's interest in leased property is called a *leased fee estate plus reversionary right.*

The North Carolina Statute of Frauds requires that a lease be in writing if the term is for longer than three years from the day of execution. Generally, oral leases for less than three years are enforceable. A lease that exceeds three years from the making thereof must be recorded.

In Practice   Even though a particular lease may be enforceable if agreed to orally, such as a lease for one year commencing the day of agreement, it is always better practice to put lease agreements in writing and to have the writing signed by all parties to the agreement. The lease document should be as inclusive as possible, for reasons that will become apparent from reading this chapter.

RESIDENTIAL RENTAL AGREEMENTS ACT

In North Carolina, residential leases and the landlord-tenant relationship are governed by the **Residential Rental Agreements Act.** The primary purpose of this act is to ensure that only habitable residential units are rented. A failure to comply with the terms of this act has potentially serious consequences. The act does not apply to transient quarters such as hotels or motels, nor does it apply to commercial properties.

Obligations of Landlord and Tenant Are Mutually Dependent

The *Residential Rental Agreements Act* makes *the obligations of the landlord and the tenant mutually dependent.* That is, if either the landlord or the tenant fails to fulfill a duty, the other party is no longer responsible for fulfilling his or her equivalent duty. For example, if the landlord fails to provide the tenant with habitable premises, the tenant does not have to remain in the premises for the full lease term.

Landlord's Statutory Duties

The act provides that the landlord's primary duty is to supply "fit" and "habitable" premises to the tenant. This means the premises must be fit for human occupancy. The landlord must comply with current building and housing codes; make all necessary repairs to keep the premises in a habitable condition; keep all common areas safe; and maintain all electrical, plumbing, sanitary, heating, ventilating and other facilities.

If the landlord fails to keep the premises fit, the tenant can invoke the protection of the *common-law doctrine of constructive eviction.* This doctrine gives the tenant the right, in effect, to cancel the remainder of the lease and vacate the premises without penalties. The tenant gives the landlord notice that the premises are uninhabitable. If the situation is not corrected within a reasonable time, the tenant can leave the premises and is no longer responsible for paying rent. In effect, the tenant evicts himself or herself. Of course, the tenant is responsible for paying rent up to and including the last day of occupancy. The tenant security deposit, if any, is to be returned to the tenant.

Law of Negligence

Tenants, or their guests, are sometimes injured on leased property, and the question arises as to whether the landlord can be held accountable for those injuries. The common rule of law holds that the landlord is liable for injuries that occur in common areas—hallways, stairways, elevators, sidewalks and parking lots—when the landlord has negligently failed to maintain safe conditions in those areas. Thus, if a tenant or guest has the right to be on the premises and is injured because of the landlord's failure to maintain the common areas, the injured party may be able to recover damages from the landlord.

However, if the injury occurs in the area exclusively occupied by the tenant—such as an apartment or office space—the results are different. Generally, the landlord is not liable for injuries that occur within the leased premises. The only exception to this rule is if the landlord failed to keep the premises in a habitable condition. Under the Residential Rental Agreements Act, the fact that the landlord failed to maintain the leased premises in a fit and habitable condition can be presented in court as evidence of the landlord's negligence. The negligence could mean that the landlord would be held liable for the injury.

With the increase in crime, the landlord's liability for criminal acts that occur on leased premises or the common areas of rental property has become an issue. In North Carolina, a landlord is not liable for criminal acts committed against his or her tenants unless the landlord knew or should have known of a dangerous situation and did nothing to protect the tenants. For instance, if a "security" rental property is in a high crime area and the landlord knows that the security system is grossly inadequate, the landlord may be liable if a tenant is injured in a mugging in a building hallway.

Tenant's Statutory Duties

The act provides that the tenant's primary duty is to *maintain the dwelling unit.* This means the tenant must keep the occupied premises clean and safe, dispose of all garbage and other waste, keep the plumbing fixtures clean, comply with the obligations imposed on tenants by current housing and building codes, refrain from deliberately or negligently damaging the premises and take responsibility for any damage that does occur.

Tenant Prohibited from Unilaterally Withholding Rent

Under the Residential Rental Agreements Act, tenants do not have the right to withhold rent before they obtain a court order giving them that right. Thus, even when the tenant has a legitimate complaint against the landlord, the tenant cannot decide to withhold all or a portion of the rent as a remedy. Note that this provision does not alter the tenant's right to vacate the premises and stop paying rent on the basis of constructive eviction. If the tenant withholds the rent but retains possession of the property, he or she has violated the rental agreement, giving the landlord the right to evict.

Residential Eviction Remedies

The only possible eviction remedy is that provided for by statute; in other words, a landlord cannot use self-help remedies, no matter how peaceful. For example, the landlord cannot change the locks on the doors to prevent the tenant from entering the premises, cut off the tenant's utilities or seize the tenant's possessions. Instead, the landlord must bring an eviction action in court. A state statute (Article 3 of Chapter 42) has been passed that sets forth public policy against the "self-help" eviction procedure and replaces it with a procedure called *summary ejectment*. This is the only legal way a landlord can evict a tenant.

ACT PROHIBITING RETALIATORY EVICTION

An important provision of this act is known as the *doctrine of retaliatory eviction*. Under this provision, a tenant cannot be evicted because the tenant has asserted a legal right against the landlord. Thus, a tenant cannot be evicted if he or she, in good faith, requests that the landlord make required repairs, becomes involved in a tenants' rights association or complains to a government entity about a landlord's violation of landlord-tenant law. If the landlord tries to evict a tenant within 12 months after the tenant tried to assert a legal right, the tenant can use this doctrine as a defense in the eviction action.

TENANT SECURITY DEPOSIT ACT

The *Tenant Security Deposit Act* regulates the amount of money that can be required as a **security deposit** and what the landlord can do with that deposit. The amount of the security deposit depends on the term of the tenancy. The maximum security deposit is

- two weeks' rent if the tenancy is from week to week,
- one and one-half months' rent if the tenancy is from month to month and
- two months' rent if the tenancy is longer than month to month.

The landlord may do one of two things with the security deposit: (1) the security deposit can be placed in a trust account with an insured North Carolina bank or savings institution or (2) the landlord can obtain a bond as a guarantee for the deposit. The landlord must tell the tenant either the name of the savings institution or the name of the bonding company. (*If a real estate agent is handling the deposit, the agent has only one option: the security deposit must be deposited into a trust account* [see Rule A.0107].)

The Tenant Security Deposit Act provides that a deposit on a residential unit may be used only to reimburse the landlord for nonpayment of rent, damage to the premises, nonfulfillment of the rental period, unpaid bills that may create a lien on the property due to the tenant's occupancy, costs of rerenting after a breach or court costs in connection with an eviction action. If a tenant breaches the lease and abandons the property, the landlord is obligated to diligently attempt to find a new tenant as soon as possible. If the property is rerented, the landlord can withhold only the part of the security deposit that covers the "lost" rent plus costs of rerenting. The remainder of the deposit must be returned to the breaching tenant. If the security deposit does not entirely cover the rent lost due to breach, the landlord may retain the entire deposit.

Damages to the Premises   Even though the tenant security deposit may be retained in whole or in part to pay for damages to the premises, the landlord cannot use the deposit to pay for damages that may be classified under the broad term *ordinary wear and tear*. Real estate law in North Carolina does not define what may constitute ordinary wear and tear versus what may constitute actual damages to the premises. The North Carolina Real Estate Commission has published consumer information on tenant security deposits that provides excellent guidance to landlords, property managers and tenants. Common examples of "ordinary wear and tear" are

- dirty carpet or carpet worn from long use;
- peeling, faded and cracked paint;
- dirty walls and windows;
- leaking plumbing and worn plumbing fixtures; and
- frayed curtains and broken blind strings.

Examples of other damages for which use of the deposit is permitted are

- large holes in the walls;
- crayon marks;
- broken plumbing fixtures, windows and counter tops;
- burned places and stains on carpeting;
- appliances causing extraordinary cleaning due to excessive filth; and
- extraordinary cleaning of the unit due to excessive filth.

CONSTITUTIONAL RIGHTS OF TENANTS IN PUBLIC HOUSING

The tenants of government-subsidized low-income housing have some additional rights. These tenants have an entitlement to continued occupancy and cannot be evicted unless there is "good cause." There must be a finding of fault on the tenant's part, not merely circumstances that are beyond the tenant's control (such as loss of a job). They are entitled to due process.

NORTH CAROLINA VACATION RENTAL ACT

The Vacation Rental Act went into effect January 1, 2000. The new statute establishes uniform rules for landlords, tenants, and their agents involved in the handling of short-term rentals. The act applies to all landlords (using an agent or not) who rent residential property for the purposes of vacation, recreation, or leisure. A licensee may pay a *referral* fee to an unlicensed travel agent *(defined in the statute)* for procuring a tenant *only for vacation rentals according to certain guidelines found in Rule A.0109(e) and* provided that no other acts of real estate requiring a license are performed by the travel agent (motels, hotels, etc. are exempt). The *Vacation Rental* Act calls for the following:

- All rental agreements to be in writing
- Authorizes the landlord to collect payments in advance of the tenancy, but monies must be placed in an escrow account
- Requires the landlord to refund tenant's payments if fit and habitable premises cannot be provided
- Governs the use of monies collected as security deposits
- If the property is sold, the new owner takes title subject to rentals for the next 180 days
- Creates an expedited eviction procedure
- Imposes upon the landlord the duty to provide tenants with fit premises and keep property repaired and safe
- Tenant must also maintain the property and not damage the premises
- If tenants are ordered by authorities to evacuate, the tenant is due a refund of their rent, unless the tenant had been offered insurance to cover the potential risk.

OTHER LANDLORD/TENANT RULES

Landlords must comply with federal and state fair housing laws and must not discriminate unlawfully. (Fair housing rights are discussed in Chapter 7.) Violation of the Residential Rental Agreements Act also constitutes a violation of the *Unfair and Deceptive Business or Trade Act.* The Real Estate Commission also can discipline a licensee for violation of these laws. Landlords must comply with *sexual harassment statutes,* which prohibit unsolicited overt demands for sexual favors when negotiating a lease or determining rights under a lease. Landlords also must comply with the *Americans with Disabilities Act.* (See Chapter 7).

LEASEHOLD (NONFREEHOLD) ESTATES

When a landowner leases his or her real estate to a tenant, the tenant's right to occupy the land for the duration of the lease is called a *leasehold estate.* A leasehold estate is an estate in land that is generally considered personal property.

In the discussion of interests and estates in Chapter 2, freehold estates were differentiated from leasehold estates. Just as there are several types of freehold (ownership) estates, there are also various leasehold estates. The four most important are *estate for years, estate from period to period, estate at will* and *estate (tenancy) at sufferance* (see Table 10.1). One parcel of property can be held in both a nonfreehold and freehold estate at the same time.

Estate for Years (Tenancy for Years)

Estate for years = Any definite period

A leasehold estate that continues for a *definite period of time,* whether for years, months, weeks or even days, is an **estate for years.** An estate for years always has a specific starting and ending time, and it may be for a term of less than one year. It does not automatically renew itself at the end of the lease period. No notice is required to terminate the lease at the end of the lease period. When the lease period expires, the lessee is required to vacate the premises and surrender possession to the lessor. A lease for years may be terminated prior to the expiration date by the mutual consent of both parties, but otherwise neither party may terminate without showing that the lease agreement has been breached. As is characteristic of all leases, a lease, or an estate, for years gives the lessee the right to occupy

Table 10.1 *Leasehold Estates*	
Type of Estate	**Distinguishing Characteristic**
Estate for years	For a definite period of time
Estate from period to period	For a definite period initially, but continues indefinitely until terminated
Estate at will	For an indefinite period of time
Estate at sufferance	Without landlord's consent

and use the leased property—subject, of course, to the terms and covenants contained in the lease agreement itself.

Estate from Period to Period (Periodic Tenancy)

An **estate from period to period,** or a *periodic tenancy,* is created when the landlord and tenant enter into an agreement that continues for a specific period, *being automatically renewed for an indefinite time without a specific ending date.* Rent is payable at definite intervals. Such a tenancy is generally created by agreement or operation of law to run for a certain amount of time, such as week to week, month to month or year to year. A typical residential lease sets up a periodic tenancy. The agreement is automatically renewed for similar succeeding periods until one of the parties gives notice to terminate. In effect, the payment and acceptance of rent extend the lease for another period. In North Carolina, the notice periods are as follows:

- For a week-to-week tenancy, the notice period is two days.
- For a month-to-month tenancy, the notice period is seven days.
- For a year-to-year tenancy, the notice period is one month.

Estate from period to period = Indefinite term; automatically renews.

A **month-to-month tenancy** generally is created when a tenant takes possession with no definite termination date and pays rent monthly. This is usually a valid agreement.

A tenancy from period to period also may be created when a tenant with an estate for years remains in possession, or holds over, after the expiration of the lease term. If no new lease agreement has been made, the landlord may evict the tenant or treat the **holdover tenant** as being under a periodic tenancy. Acceptance of rent is usually considered conclusive proof of the landlord's acquiescence in a periodic tenancy.

Estate at Will

An estate that gives the tenant *the right to possess property with the consent of the landlord for a term of unspecified or uncertain duration* is an **estate at will,** or a tenancy at will. It may be created by express agreement or by operation of law, and during its existence the tenant has all the rights and obligations of a lessor/lessee relationship.

Estate at will = Indefinite term; possession with landlord's consent.

For Example At the end of a lease period, a landlord informs a tenant that in a few months the city is going to demolish the apartment building to make way for an expressway. The landlord gives the tenant the option to occupy the premises until demolition begins. If the tenant agrees to stay, a tenancy at will is created.

An estate at will can be terminated at any time, "at the will" of either party. All that is required is for one party to declare that the tenancy is over. No prior notice is required. However, if the tenancy at will is for agricultural

Table 10.2	Characteristics of Lease Types	
Lease Type	**Used for**	**Lease Characteristic(s)**
Fixed rent lease	Residential leases	Tenant pays a fixed amount of rent
Percentage lease	Commercial leases	Tenants pays a percentage of the gross or net income
Net lease	Commercial leases	Tenant pays all or some of the property charges
Graduated lease	Commercial leases	Tenant pays rent, which increases at predetermined dates
Ground lease	Commercial leases	Tenant typically pays rent on land

land and the tenant has planted crops, the tenant is entitled to return to the premises to harvest those crops under the *doctrine of emblements.*

Estate at Sufferance

An **estate at sufferance,** or a *tenancy at sufferance,* arises when a tenant who lawfully came into possession of real property continues, after his or her rights have expired, to hold possession of the premises *without the consent of the landlord.* An example of an estate at sufferance is when a tenant for years *fails to surrender* possession at the expiration of the lease. The "tenant" has no rights in the property, and the landowner can have him or her removed at any time, without notice. This is not a trespass situation because the tenant originally took possession with the consent of the lessor. This is the lowest estate in real estate.

> *Estate at sufferance =* Tenant's previously lawful possession continued without landlord's consent.

If a tenant has an estate at will or an estate at sufferance and pays the landlord rent monies that the landlord accepts, a periodic tenancy is re-created. Consideration cannot be paid and accepted under either the estate at will or the estate at sufferance.

TYPES OF LEASES

The manner in which rent is determined indicates the type of lease that is in force (see Table 10.2).

Fixed Rent Lease

In a **fixed rent lease,** the tenant's obligation is to pay a *fixed rental,* and the landlord pays all taxes, insurance premiums, mortgage payments, repair costs and the like connected with the property (usually called *property charges*). This type of lease is most often used for residential apartment rentals and is sometimes called a **gross lease.**

Percentage Lease (Retail Lease)

A **percentage lease** provides for rental based on a *percentage of the gross or net income* received by a tenant doing business on the leased property. This type of lease is usually used in the rental of retail business locations.

The percentage lease usually provides for a minimum fixed rental fee plus a percentage of that portion of the tenant's business income that exceeds a stated minimum.

For Example A lease might provide for a minimum monthly rental of $1,500, with a further agreement that the tenant pay an additional amount each month equivalent to 4 percent of all gross sales in excess of $30,000. The percentage charged in such leases varies widely with the nature of the business and is negotiable between landlord and tenant. A tenant's bargaining power is determined by his or her volume of business. Percentages also vary with the location of the property and general economic conditions.

MATH CONCEPTS

Calculating Percentage Lease Rents

Percentage leases usually call for a minimum monthly rent plus a percentage of gross sales income exceeding a stated annual amount. For example, a lease might require minimum rent of $1,300 per month plus 5 percent of the business's sales exceeding $160,000. On an annual sales volume of $250,000, the annual rent would be calculated as follows:

$1,300 per month × 12 months = $15,600
$250,000 − $160,000 = $90,000
$90,000 × .05 (5%) = $4,500
$15,600 base rent + $4,500 percentage rent = $20,100 total rent

Net Lease

A **net lease** provides that in addition to the rent, *the tenant pays all or some of the property charges, including maintenance, property taxes and insurance.* This type of lease is sometimes called a *triple net lease* if the tenant pays *all* of the property charges. The monthly rental paid to the landlord is in addition to these charges and thus is net income for the landlord after operating costs have been paid. Leases for entire commercial or industrial buildings and the land on which they are located, ground leases and long-term leases are usually net leases.

Graduated Lease

A **graduated lease** provides for *increases in rent to occur at set future dates.* Graduated leases are often used in the rental of office space.

For Example A lease may provide for the rent to be $1,000 a month for the first year, $1,200 a month for the second year and $1,400 a month for the third year.

Index Lease

An **index lease** allows *rent to be increased or decreased periodically,* based on changes in a stipulated index, such as the government cost-of-living index or some other index.

Ground Lease (Financing Device)

When a landowner leases land to a tenant who agrees to *erect a building* on the land, the lease is usually referred to as a **ground lease.** Ground leases usually involve separate ownership of land and building. Such a lease must be for a long enough term to make the transaction desirable to the tenant investing in the building. These leases are generally net leases that require the lessee to pay rent as well as real estate taxes, insurance, upkeep and repairs. Such leases often run for terms of 99 years or longer.

Oil and Mineral Lease

When oil companies lease land to explore for oil, gas and other minerals, a special lease agreement must be negotiated. Usually, the landowner receives a cash payment for executing the lease. If minerals are found, the property owner usually receives a portion of the value of the minerals as a royalty. The North Carolina Statute of Frauds states that any mineral lease, regardless of duration, must be in writing to be enforceable.

Full-Service Lease These commercial leases are often used in large office or multitenant buildings such as shopping centers where the tenants share in overall operating expenses for the common areas and the building(s). Usually rent is paid as a base amount plus a share of the complex's operating expenses.

LEASE PROVISIONS

Most leases are complex documents that should be carefully prepared, and both landlords and tenants should not hesitate to seek legal advice if they have questions about the application of certain provisions. Real estate agents are allowed only to fill in preprinted forms. Any additional clauses must be prepared by a lawyer.

Essential Provisions for a Valid Lease The requirements for a valid lease are essentially the same as those for any other contract. Generally, the essentials of a valid lease are as follows:

- *Mutual agreement.* The parties must reach a mutual agreement on all terms of the contract, usually accomplished by means of offer and acceptance.
- *Consideration.* All leases, being contracts, must be supported by valid consideration. In the leasing of real estate, rent is the normal consideration granted for the right to occupy the leased premises.
- *Capacity to contract.* The parties must have the legal capacity to contract. That is, they must be of sound mind and understand what they are agreeing to.
- *Legal objectives.* The objectives of the lease must be legal.

> A valid lease consists of four essential provisions:
>
> - Mutual agreement
> - Considerations
> - Capacity to contract
> - Legal objectives

When the statute of frauds applies, an oral lease is considered to be unenforceable. A description of the leased premises should be stated clearly. If the lease covers land, the legal description of the real estate should be used. If the lease is for part of a building, such as office space or an apartment, that part of the property should be described clearly and carefully. If supplemental space is to be included, the lease should clearly identify it.

Other Common Provisions Many other provisions are commonly found in lease agreements. A copy of North Carolina's Association of REALTORS® Residential Rental Contract is shown in Figure 10.1.

Use of premises. A lessor may restrict a lessee's use of the premises through provisions included in the lease. This is most important in leases for stores or commercial space. For example, a lease may provide that the leased premises are to be used *only* for the purpose of a real estate office *and for no other purpose.* In the absence of such limitations, a lessee may use the premises for any lawful purpose.

Fixtures. Neither the landlord nor the tenant is required to make any improvements to the leased property. In the absence of an agreement to the contrary, the tenant may make improvements with the landlord's permission. Any such alterations generally become the property of the landlord; that is, they become fixtures. However, as discussed in Chapter 2, a tenant may be given the right by the terms of the lease to install trade fixtures or chattel fixtures. It is customary to stipulate that such trade fixtures may be removed by the tenant before the lease expires, provided the tenant restores the premises to their previous condition, normal wear and tear excluded.

Figure 10.1 **Residential Rental Contract**

RESIDENTIAL RENTAL CONTRACT

IN CONSIDERATION of the rent described below and the mutual promises made to each other,_____
_____("Landlord"), by and through
his/her/its agent _____ ("Agent"), leases and rents to _____

("Tenant") and Tenant does hereby lease and rent from Landlord the Premises more particularly described below in accordance with
the following terms and conditions:

1. **The Premises:** Located in the City of _____, County of _____,
State of North Carolina, being known as and more particularly described as:

❑   Street
Address:_____ ❑   Apartment
Complex:_____ Apartment No. _____
❑   Other   Description   (Room,   portion   of   above   address,
etc.):_____

2. **Term:** The term of this lease shall be for _____ (duration) commencing _____ (date) and expiring
_____ (date) (the "Initial Term"). Either Landlord or Tenant may terminate the tenancy at the expiration of the Initial
Term by giving written notice to the other at least _____ days prior to the expiration date of the Initial Term. In the
event such written notice is not given or if the Tenant holds over beyond the Initial Term, the tenancy shall automatically become a
_____ (period) to _____ (period) tenancy upon the same terms and conditions contained herein
and may thereafter be terminated by either Landlord or Tenant giving the other _____ days written notice prior to the last day of
the then current period of the tenancy.

3. **Rent:** Tenant shall pay, without notice, demand or deduction, to Landlord or as Landlord directs _____
(payment period - for example: weekly, monthly, quarterly, annually) rental payments in the amount of
$_____. The first rental payment, which shall be prorated if the Initial Term commences on a day
other than the first day of the applicable rental payment period, shall be due on _____(date).
Thereafter, all rentals shall be paid in advance on or before the _____ day of each subsequent
calendar_____ (payment period - for example: week, month, quarter, year) for the
duration of the tenancy.

4. **Late Payment Fees and Returned Check Fees:** If any rental payment is not received by midnight on the fifth (5th) day
after it is due, Tenant shall pay a late payment fee of _____.
*(NOTE: North Carolina law provides that the late fee may not exceed $15.00 or five percent (5%) of the rental payment, whichever is
greater.) This late payment fee shall be due immediately without demand therefor and shall be added to and paid with the late rental
payment. Tenant also agrees to pay a $_____ processing fee for each check of Tenant that is returned by the financial
institution because of insufficient funds or because the Tenant did not have an account at the financial institution. (NOTE: The
maximum processing fee allowed under North Carolina law is $25.00.)*

5. **Tenant Security Deposit:** Tenant shall deposit with: (check one)
❑ Landlord
❑ Agent

the sum of $_____, as security deposit ("Tenant Security Deposit"), to be administered in accordance
with the North Carolina Tenant Security Deposit Act (N.C.G.S. § 42-50 et. seq.).

North Carolina Association of REALTORS®, Inc.

Tenant Initials _____ _____ Agent Initials _____

STANDARD FORM 410 – T
© 7/2002

Figure 10.1   Residential Rental Contract (continued)

If Landlord holds the Tenant Security Deposit, Landlord will either: (check one)

❑ Deposit the Tenant Security Deposit in a trust account with_____

_____(name of bank or savings institution)

located at_____

_____(address).

OR   ❑   Furnish   a   bond

from_____

_____(name of bonding company)

located at_____

_____(address).

If Agent holds the Tenant Security Deposit, Agent will deposit it in a trust account with _____

_____(name of bank or savings institution)

located at_____

_____(address).

THE TENANT SECURITY DEPOSIT MAY, IN THE DISCRETION OF EITHER THE LANDLORD OR THE AGENT, BE DEPOSITED IN AN INTEREST-BEARING ACCOUNT WITH THE BANK OR SAVINGS INSTITUTION NAMED ABOVE. ANY INTEREST EARNED UPON THE TENANT SECURITY DEPOSIT SHALL ACCRUE FOR THE BENEFIT OF, AND SHALL BE PAID TO, THE LANDLORD, OR AS THE LANDLORD DIRECTS. SUCH INTEREST, IF ANY, MAY BE WITHDRAWN BY LANDLORD OR AGENT FROM SUCH ACCOUNT AS IT ACCRUES AS OFTEN AS IS PERMITTED BY THE TERMS OF THE ACCOUNT.

Upon any termination of the tenancy herein created, the Landlord may deduct from the Tenant Security Deposit amounts sufficient to pay: (1) any damages sustained by the Landlord as a result of the Tenant's nonpayment of rent or nonfulfillment of the Initial Term or any renewal periods, including the Tenant's failure to enter into possession; (2) any damages to the Premises for which the Tenant is responsible; (3) any unpaid bills which become a lien against the Premises due to the Tenant's occupancy; (4) any costs of re-renting the Premises after a breach of this lease by the Tenant; (5) any court costs incurred by the Landlord in connection with terminating the tenancy; and (6) any other damages of the Landlord which may then be a permitted use of the Tenant Security Deposit under the laws of this State. After having deducted the above amounts, the Landlord shall, if the Tenant's address is known to him, refund to the Tenant, within thirty (30) days after the termination of the tenancy and delivery of possession, the balance of the Tenant Security Deposit along with an itemized statement of any deductions. If the Tenant's address is unknown to the Landlord, the Landlord may deduct the above amounts and shall then hold the balance of the Tenant Security Deposit for the Tenant's collection for a six-month period beginning upon the termination of the tenancy and delivery of possession by the Tenant. If the Tenant fails to make demand for the balance of the Tenant Security Deposit within the six-month period, the Landlord shall not thereafter be liable to the Tenant for a refund of the Tenant Security Deposit or any part thereof.

If the Landlord removes Agent or Agent resigns, the Tenant agrees that Agent may transfer any Tenant Security Deposit held by Agent hereunder to the Landlord or the Landlord's designee and thereafter notify the Tenant by mail of such transfer and of the transferee's name and address. The Tenant agrees that such action by Agent shall relieve Agent of further liability with respect to the Tenant Security Deposit. If Landlord's interest in the Premises terminates (whether by sale, assignment, death, appointment of receiver or otherwise), Agent shall transfer the Tenant Security Deposit in accordance with the provisions of North Carolina General Statutes § 42-54.

6. **Tenant's Obligations:** Unless otherwise agreed upon, the Tenant shall:

(a) use the Premises for residential purposes only and in a manner so as not to disturb the other tenants;

(b) not use the Premises for any unlawful or immoral purposes or occupy them in such a way as to constitute a nuisance;

(c) keep the Premises, including but not limited to all plumbing fixtures, facilities and appliances, in a clean and safe condition;

(d) cause no unsafe or unsanitary condition in the common areas and remainder of the Premises used by him;

(e) comply with any and all obligations imposed upon tenants by applicable building and housing codes;

(f) dispose of all ashes, rubbish, garbage, and other waste in a clean and safe manner and comply with all applicable ordinances concerning garbage collection, waste and other refuse;

(g) use in a proper and reasonable manner all electrical, plumbing, sanitary, heating, ventilating, air conditioning, and other facilities and appliances, if any, furnished as a part of the Premises;

(h) not deliberately or negligently destroy, deface, damage or remove any part of the Premises (including all facilities, appliances and fixtures) or permit any person, known or unknown to the Tenant, to do so;

Page 2 of 7

Tenant Initials _____ _____   **STANDARD FORM   410 – T**
Agent Initials _____   © 7/2002

Figure 10.1   Residential Rental Contract (continued)

(i)   be responsible for and liable to the Landlord for all damage to, defacement of, or removal of property from the Premises whatever the cause, except such damage, defacement or removal caused by ordinary wear and tear, acts of the Landlord, his agent, or of third parties not invitees of the Tenant, and natural forces;

(j)   permit the Landlord (and the Landlord hereby reserves the right to) to enter the Premises during reasonable hours for the purpose of (1) inspecting the Premises and the Tenant's compliance with the terms of this lease; (2) making such repairs, alterations, improvements or additions thereto as the Landlord may deem appropriate; and (3) showing the Premises to prospective purchasers or tenants. (The Landlord shall have the right to display "For Sale" or "For Rent" signs in a reasonable manner upon the Premises);

(k)   pay the costs of all utility services to the Premises which are billed directly to the Tenant and not included as a part of the rentals, including, but not limited to, water, electric, telephone, and gas services;

(l)   conduct himself and require all other persons on the Premises with his consent to conduct themselves in a reasonable manner and so as not to disturb other tenants' peaceful enjoyment of the Premises; and

(m)   not abandon or vacate the Premises during the Initial Term or any renewals or extensions thereof. Tenant shall be deemed to have abandoned or vacated the Premises if Tenant removes substantially all of his possessions from the Premises.

(n)   _____

_____

7. **Landlord's Obligations:** Unless otherwise agreed upon, the Landlord shall:

(a)   comply with the applicable building and housing codes to the extent required by such building and housing codes;

(b)   make all repairs to the Premises as may be necessary to keep the Premises in a fit and habitable condition; provided, however, in accordance with paragraph 6.h. and i. above, the Tenant shall be liable to the Landlord for any repairs necessitated by the Tenant's intentional or negligent misuse of the Premises;

(c)   keep all common areas, if any, used in conjunction with the Premises in a clean and safe condition; and

(d)   promptly repair all facilities and appliances, if any, as may be furnished by the Landlord as part of the Premises, including electrical, plumbing, sanitary, heating, ventilating, and air conditioning systems, provided that the Landlord, except in emergency situations, actually receives notification from the Tenant in writing of the needed repairs. In accordance with paragraph 6.h. and i. above, the Tenant shall be liable to the Landlord for any repairs to any facility or appliance necessitated by the Tenant's intentional or negligent misuse or improper operation of them.

8. **Rules and Regulations:** The Tenant, his family, servants, guests and agents shall comply with and abide by all the Landlord's existing rules and regulations and such future reasonable rules and regulations as the Landlord may, at Landlord's discretion, from time to time, adopt governing the use and occupancy of the Premises and any common areas used in connection with them (the "Rules and Regulations"). Landlord reserves the right to make changes to the existing Rules and Regulations and to adopt additional reasonable rules and regulations from time to time; provided however, such changes and additions shall not alter the essential terms of this lease or any substantive rights granted hereunder and shall not become effective until thirty (30) days' written notice thereof shall have been furnished to Tenant. A copy of the existing Rules and Regulations is attached hereto and the Tenant acknowledges that he has read them. The Rules and Regulations shall be deemed to be a part of this lease giving to the Landlord all the rights and remedies herein provided.

9. **Pets:**

❑ Tenant shall not keep or harbor in or about the Premises any animals or pets of any kind including, but not limited to, dogs, cats, birds and marine animals.

❑ Tenant may, upon the payment to Landlord of the sum of $_____ as a non-refundable pet fee, keep as a pet the following:_____ (type of pets permitted). (If this space is left blank, the Tenant may not keep any pets or animals in or about the Premises). If a pet fee is paid pursuant to this paragraph, Tenant acknowledges that the amount is reasonable and agrees that the Landlord shall not be required to refund the pet fee in whole or in part. In the event that a pet or pets are permitted pursuant to the paragraph, Tenant agrees to reimburse Landlord for any primary or secondary damages caused thereby whether the damage is to the Premises or to any common areas used in conjunction with them, and to indemnify Landlord from any liability to third parties which may result from Tenant's keeping of such pet or pets.

The Tenant shall remove any pet previously permitted under this paragraph within_____ hours of written notification from the Landlord that the pet, in the Landlord's sole judgment, creates a nuisance or disturbance or is, in the Landlord's opinion, undesirable. If the pet is caused to be removed pursuant to this paragraph, the Landlord shall not be required to refund the pet fee; however, the Tenant shall be entitled to acquire and keep another pet of the type previously authorized.

Page 3 of 7

Tenant Initials _____ _____
Agent Initials _____

STANDARD FORM 410 – T
© 7/2002

Figure 10.1   Residential Rental Contract (continued)

10. **Alterations**: The Tenant shall not paint or decorate the Premises or make any alterations, additions, or improvements in or to the Premises without the Landlord's prior written consent and then only in a workmanlike manner using materials and contractors approved by the Landlord. All such work shall be done at the Tenant's expense and at such times and in such manner as the Landlord may approve. All alterations, additions, and improvements upon the Premises, made by either the Landlord or Tenant, shall become the property of the Landlord and shall remain upon and become a part of the Premises at the end of the tenancy hereby created.

11. **Permitted Occupants:** The Tenant shall not allow or permit the Premises to be occupied or used as a residence by any person other than Tenant and the following named persons:_____
_____
_____

12. **Rental Application:** In the event the Tenant has submitted a Rental Application in connection with this lease, Tenant acknowledges that the Landlord has relied upon the Application as an inducement for entering into this Lease and Tenant warrants to Landlord that the facts stated in the Application are true to the best of Tenant's knowledge. If any facts stated in the Rental Application prove to be untrue, the Landlord shall have the right to terminate the tenancy and to collect from Tenant any damages resulting therefrom.

13. **Termination for Military Transfer:** If Tenant is a member of the United States Armed Forces who (i) has received permanent change of station orders to move fifty (50) miles or more from the Premises or (ii) is prematurely or involuntarily discharged or relieved from active duty with the United States Armed Forces, Tenant may terminate this lease by written notice of termination to Landlord stating the effective date of such termination, which date shall not be less than thirty (30) days after receipt of notice by Landlord, provided such notice is accompanied by a copy of the official orders of such transfer, discharge or release from active duty or a written verification signed by the Tenant's Commanding Officer. The final rent due by Tenant shall be prorated to such date of termination and shall be payable, together with liquidated damages in the amount of (a) one (1) month's rent for the premises, if less than six (6) months of the term of the lease have elapsed as of the effective date of termination, or (b) the amount of one-half (1/2) of one (1) month's rent, if more than six (6) months but less than nine (9) months of the term of the lease have elapsed as of the effective date of such termination; provided, however, no liquidated damages shall be due unless Tenant has completed less than nine (9) months of the tenancy and Landlord has suffered actual damage due to the loss of the tenancy.

Upon Tenant's compliance with all the requirements of this paragraph, Landlord shall release Tenant from all obligations hereunder and this lease shall terminate. The Tenant Security Deposit shall be returned, subject to the provisions of paragraph 5 above.

14. **Tenant's Duties Upon Termination:** Upon any termination of the Tenancy created hereby, whether by the Landlord or the Tenant and whether for breach or otherwise, the Tenant shall: (1) pay all utility bills due for services to the Premises for which he is responsible and have all such utility services discontinued; (2) vacate the Premises removing therefrom all Tenant's personal property of whatever nature; (3) properly sweep and clean the Premises, including plumbing fixtures, refrigerators, stoves and sinks, removing therefrom all rubbish, trash, garbage and refuse; (4) make such repairs and perform such other acts as are necessary to return the Premises, and any appliances or fixtures furnished in connection therewith, in the same condition as when Tenant took possession of the Premises; provided, however, Tenant shall not be responsible for ordinary wear and tear or for repairs required by law or by paragraph 7 above to be performed by Landlord; (5) fasten and lock all doors and windows; (6) return to the Landlord all keys to the Premises; and (7) notify the Landlord of the address to which the balance of the Security Deposit may be returned. If the Tenant fails to sweep out and clean the Premises, appliances and fixtures as herein provided, Tenant shall become liable, without notice or demand, to the Landlord for a cleaning fee. Such fee shall: (i) reflect the actual costs of cleaning (over and above ordinary wear and tear) and (ii) be deducted from the Security Deposit as provided in paragraph 5 above.

15. **Tenant's Default:** In the event the Tenant shall:

(a) fail to pay the rentals herein reserved as and when they shall become due hereunder; or
(b) fail to perform any other promise, duty or obligation herein agreed to by him or imposed upon him by law and such failure shall continue for a period of five (5) days from the date the Landlord provides Tenant with written notice of such failure,

then in either of such events and as often as either of them may occur, the Landlord, in addition to all other rights and remedies provided by law, may, at its option and with or without notice to Tenant, either (i) terminate this lease or (ii) terminate the Tenant's right to possession of the Premises without terminating this lease. Regardless of whether Landlord terminates this lease or only terminates the Tenant's right of possession without terminating this lease, Landlord shall be immediately entitled to possession of the Premises and the Tenant shall peacefully surrender possession of the Premises to Landlord immediately upon Landlord's demand.

Tenant Initials _____ _____
Agent Initials _____

STANDARD FORM 410 – T
© 7/2002

To see the full form, please go to Appendix C.

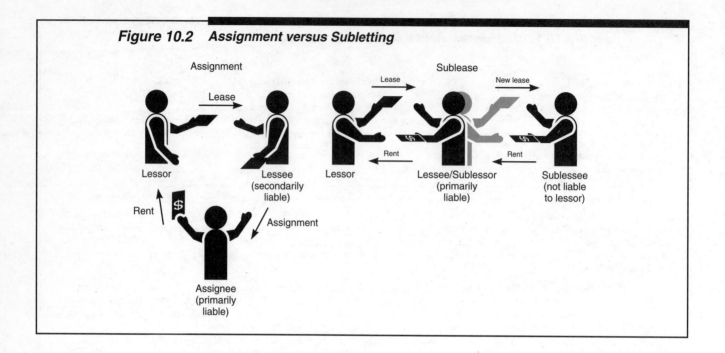

Figure 10.2   Assignment versus Subletting

Repairs (nonresidential property). If the leased property is nonresidential and no lease provision exists to the contrary, landlords are generally not obligated to make any repairs to leased premises except those that are required to make the premises habitable. Tenants typically are required to repair only damage that is caused by their own negligence. And generally the tenant is required to return the premises in the same condition in which they were received, with allowance for ordinary use.

Assignment and subleases. The lessee may assign the lease or may sublease if the lease terms do not prohibit it. A tenant who transfers all of his or her leasehold interests (which include both the entire term of the lease and all premiums) *assigns* the lease. One who transfers less than all of the leasehold interests by leasing them to a new tenant **subleases** (see Figure 10.2). In effect, a sublease is the making of a new lease, wherein the original lessee (tenant) becomes a sublessor and the new tenant becomes a sublessee. In most cases, the sublease or assignment of a lease does not relieve the original lessee of the obligation to make rental payments unless the landlord agrees to waive such liability. When a lease is assigned, the original tenant retains *secondary liability* for paying the rent; when a lease is sublet, the original tenant retains *primary liability* for paying the rent. Most leases prohibit the lessee from assigning or subletting without the lessor's consent. The lessor thus retains control over the occupancy of the leased premises but must not unreasonably withhold consent. The sublessor's (original lessee's) interest in the real estate is known as a **sandwich lease.**

Term of the lease and lease renewal. The *term* of a lease is the period for which the lease will run, and it should be set out precisely. The date of the beginning of the term and the date of its ending should be noted, together with a statement of the total period of the lease; for example, "for a term of three years beginning December 1, 1996, and ending November 30, 1999."

Unless specifically provided for in the lease, a lessee typically has no right to renew a lease. A renewal clause should stipulate when the lessee must notify the lessor that the lease will be renewed, how the lessor must be notified and the length of the new lease period.

Options to purchase. Many leases contain an option that grants the lessee the right to purchase the leased premises. Usually, the price of the property is agreed to in advance, but sometimes the parties agree to abide by an appraiser's estimate of value. Every option should state the purchase price or the exact method the parties will use to determine the purchase price.

Instead of an option, a lease may contain a *right of first refusal* (see Chapter 9).

Landlord's right to enter and the covenant of quiet enjoyment. Once a valid lease has been executed, the lessor, as the owner of the real estate, is usually bound by **the covenant of quiet enjoyment** that is implied by law. Under this covenant, the lessor guarantees that the lessee may take possession of the leased premises and that the landlord will not interfere with the tenant's possession or use of the property. (This right comes from the *privity of estate*.)

The landlord has no right to enter the leased premises during the lease term unless the lease specifically gives the landlord this right (through *privity of contract*). Usually, the landlord is given this right to inspect the property, to make necessary repairs, to show the property to potential tenants and in case of an emergency. Most leases provide that the landlord must give the tenant a certain amount of notice before entering the premises.

Termination of Leases   As with any contract, a lease is discharged when the contract terminates. Termination can occur when all parties have fully performed their obligations under the agreement. The landlord and tenant may agree to cancel the lease, but if the tenant simply abandons the property, the tenant remains liable for the terms of the lease—including the payment of rent. There are several ways in which leases may be terminated:

- The parties to a lease may mutually agree to cancel the lease.
- When the lease term expires, the lease is terminated automatically.
- If one of the parties fails to perform a material obligation, such as if the tenant fails to pay rent or the landlord fails to maintain the premises in a habitable condition, the lease can be terminated.

If the tenant fails to pay rent, the landlord can evict the tenant. If the tenant refuses to leave the premises voluntarily, the landlord must bring an eviction action in court to have the tenant removed.

If the landlord fails to maintain the premises in habitable condition, the tenant is considered *constructively evicted* and may move out and stop paying rent.

- A tenancy may be terminated by operation of law, as in a bankruptcy or condemnation proceeding.

Note that when the owner of leased property dies or the property is sold, *the lease does not terminate.* The heirs of a deceased landlord are bound by the terms of existing valid leases. In addition, if a landlord conveys leased real estate, the new landlord takes the property subject to the rights of the tenants.

Statute of Frauds and Recordation

Any lease that lasts for more than three years from the date of making must be in writing and signed by the landlord to comply with the statute of frauds. For instance, a lease signed on January 1, 1996, and terminating on December 31, 1998, does not have to be in writing. But a lease signed on January 1, 1996, and terminating on January 31, 1999, does have to be in writing.

Under the Conner Act, leases required to be in writing under the statute of frauds must be recorded to be enforceable against third parties. If the lease is not recorded and a third party buys the property, that person is not required to honor the terms of the lease. Failure to observe the statutory requirements in recording a lease does not in any way affect its validity between the parties.

SUMMARY

A lease is an agreement that grants one person the right to use the property of another for a certain period in return for consideration. The lease agreement is a combination of a conveyance creating a leasehold interest in the property and a contract outlining the rights and obligations of the landlord and the tenant.

Any residential lease that violates the Residential Rental Agreements Act is void.

A leasehold estate that runs for a specific length of time creates an estate for years; one that runs for an indefinite number of terms creates a periodic estate (year to year, month to month). An estate at will runs as long as the landlord and tenant agree to it, and an estate at sufferance is possession without the consent of the landlord.

The requirements of a valid lease include mutual assent through offer and acceptance, consideration, capacity to contract and legal objectives. The statute of frauds generally requires that any lease for more than three years from the date of its making must be in writing. Most leases also include clauses relating to rights and obligations of the landlord and tenant such as the use of the premises, subletting and assignment, improvements and repairs and the landlord's right to enter the premises.

Leases may be terminated by the expiration of the lease period, the mutual agreement of the parties or a breach of the lease by either landlord or tenant. It is important to note that in most cases, neither the death of the landlord nor the landlord's sale of the rental property terminates a lease.

There are several basic types of leases, including net leases, gross leases and percentage leases. These leases are classified according to the method used in determining the rental rate of the property.

Questions

1. If a lease is for longer than three years, the lease must be recorded to be
   I. valid between the parties.
   II. enforceable against third parties.
   a. I only
   b. II only
   c. Both I and II
   d. Neither I nor II

2. A landlord may enter leased premises to make repairs if the
   a. landlord knocks first to give notice of intent to enter.
   b. lease gives the landlord this right.
   c. landlord gives 48 hours' notice of intent to enter.
   d. landlord fulfills the covenant of quiet enjoyment.

3. Which of the following statements is true of a tenant from month to month?
   a. The tenant must give notice to the landlord prior to vacating the leased premises.
   b. The tenant need not give notice to the landlord that he or she is vacating the leased premises.
   c. The tenant must give 45 days' notice to the landlord prior to vacating the leased premises.
   d. The tenant can receive his or her security deposit before vacating the leased premises.

4. A lease calls for a minimum rent of $1,200 per month plus 4 percent of the annual gross business exceeding $150,000. This is what type of lease?
   a. Gross   c. Percentage
   b. Graduated   d. Net

5. The requirements of a valid lease include
   a. mutual assent.
   b. consideration.
   c. capacity to contract.
   d. All of the above

6. Which of the following best describes a net lease?
   I. An agreement in which the tenant pays a fixed rent and the landlord pays all taxes, insurance and so forth on the property
   II. A lease in which the tenant pays rent in addition to some or all property charges
   III. A lease in which the tenant pays the landlord a percentage of the monthly income derived from the property
   a. I only
   b. II only
   c. III only
   d. I and II only

7. A percentage lease provides for a
   a. rental of a percentage of the value of a building.
   b. definite periodic rent not exceeding a stated percentage.
   c. definite monthly rent plus a percentage of the tenant's gross receipts in excess of a certain amount.
   d. graduated amount due monthly and not exceeding a stated percentage.

8. A tenant who transfers the remaining term of his or her lease to a third party is
   a. a sublessor.
   b. assigning the lease.
   c. automatically relieved of any further obligation under the lease.
   d. giving the third party a gross lease.

9. If a tenant complains to the authorities about a housing code violation in the building that affects his or her health, the landlord may
   I. correct the violation.
   II. evict the tenant.
   a. I only
   b. II only
   c. Neither I nor II
   d. Both I and II

10. To terminate a month-to-month lease, the lessor must give the lessee notice
    a. seven days prior to the termination date.
    b. 30 days prior to the periodic rent date.
    c. 45 days prior to the termination date.
    d. 60 days prior to the termination date.

11. If a landlord fails to keep the premises in habitable condition, the tenant may
    a. stay in the premises and withhold rent.
    b. withhold rent and deposit it with the clerk of courts.
    c. withhold rent and deposit it in escrow at a bank.
    d. leave the premises and stop paying rent.

12. Special terms in a residential lease can waive the landlord's obligation to keep the
    I. building in habitable condition.
    II. common areas in safe condition.
    a. I only
    b. II only
    c. Both I and II
    d. Neither I nor II

13. A ground lease is usually
    a. short term.
    b. for five to ten years.
    c. for 99 years.
    d. a gross lease.

14. An index lease provides for a
    a. rental of a percentage of the value of a building.
    b. definite periodic rent not exceeding a stated percentage.
    c. definite monthly rent plus a percentage of the tenant's gross receipts in excess of a certain amount.
    d. rental based on a specified index.

15. If a lessor sells the leased premises, the new owner
    I. can negotiate new rental payments with the tenants.
    II. takes the property subject to the terms of the tenants' leases.
    a. I only
    b. II only
    c. Both I and II
    d. Neither I nor II

16. With a month-to-month tenancy, the landlord can require a security deposit equal to
    a. one and one-half month's rent.
    b. two weeks' rent.
    c. two months' rent.
    d. three months' rent.

17. If a tenant breaches his or her duty to pay rent, the landlord may
    a. change the locks and prevent the tenant from entering the premises.
    b. turn off the tenant's utilities.
    c. file an eviction action with the courts.
    d. seize the tenant's possessions.

18. Constructive eviction occurs when the
    a. landlord forceably removes the tenant from the premises after obtaining a court order.
    b. landlord fails to keep the premises in habitable condition.
    c. tenant fails to pay rent on time.
    d. landlord retaliates against the tenant for complaining to a state authority.

19. Which of the following statements is true of a periodic tenancy?
    I. It renews itself automatically unless notice to terminate is given.
    II. It terminates automatically at the expiration of the lease term.
    a. I only
    b. II only
    c. Both I and II
    d. Neither I nor II

20. An estate for years terminates
    a. only with prior notice.
    b. on its second automatic renewal.
    c. after two days notice.
    d. automatically on its expiration date.

21. Dan's landlord has sold his building to the state so that a freeway can be built. Dan's lease has expired, but the landlord is letting him remain until the time the building will be torn down. What is Dan's tenancy called?
    a. Holdover tenancy
    b. Month-to-month tenancy
    c. Tenancy at sufferance
    d. Tenancy at will

22. If the landlord of an apartment building breaches her lease with one of the tenants and the tenant's unit becomes uninhabitable, which of the following would be the most likely result?
    a. Suit for possession
    b. Constructive eviction
    c. Tenancy at sufferance
    d. Covenant of quiet enjoyment

23. What type of lease establishes a set rental payment and requires the lessor to pay for the taxes, insurance and maintenance on the property?
    a. Percentage   c. Expense only
    b. Net   d. Gross

24. Jody has a one-year leasehold interest in Harbor House. The interest automatically renews itself at the end of each year. Jody's interest is referred to as a *tenancy*
    a, for years
    b. from period to period
    c. at will
    d. at sufferance

25. Mary has assigned her apartment lease to Ben, and the landlord has agreed to the assignment. If Ben fails to pay the rent, who is liable?
    a. Ben is primarily liable; Mary is secondarily liable.
    b. Mary is primarily liable; Ben is secondarily liable.
    c, Only Mary is liable.
    d. Only Ben is liable.

26. Which of the following would automatically terminate a residential lease?
    a. Total destruction of the property
    b, Sale of the property
    c. Failure of the tenant to pay rent
    d. Death of the tenant

27. Which of the following transactions would best be described as involving a ground lease?
    a. A landowner agrees to let a tenant drill for oil on a property for 75 years.
    b. With the landowner's permission, a tenant builds a shopping center on a rental property at the tenant's own expense.
    c. A landlord charges a commercial tenant separate amounts for the land and buildings under the lease.
    d. A tenant pays a base amount for the property, plus a percentage of business generated income.

11 Property Management

LEARNING OBJECTIVES

When you've finished reading this chapter, you should be able to

- **explain** the need for property management as an industry specialization and the functions and responsibilities of property managers.

- **identify** the basic elements of a property management agreement.

- **calculate** earned property management fees.

- **explain** how to budget for operating expenses.

- **define** these *key terms:*

life cycle costing	management agreement	property manager tenant improvement

PROPERTY MANAGEMENT

The need for specialized property managers became apparent during the 1930s as lending institutions took possession of numerous foreclosed income properties. Lacking the expertise to administer these properties, they looked to the real estate industry for expert management assistance. In recent years the increased size of buildings; the technical complexities of construction, maintenance and repair; and the trend toward absentee ownership by individual investors and investment groups have led to the expanded use of professional property managers for both residential and commercial properties. Property management has become so important that many brokerage firms maintain separate management departments staffed by carefully selected, well-trained people. A number of corporate and institutional owners of real estate have also established property management departments. Despite this trend, however, some real estate investors still manage their own property and thus must acquire the knowledge and skills of a property manager.

In North Carolina, when a property manager is the owner's *agent,* he or she must have a real estate broker's license. A property manager who is the owner's employee is not required to have a real estate license. G.S. 93A-2(c)(6), quoted below, grants licensing exemptions to certain salaried employees of the managing broker, with limited authority.

Any salaried person employed by a licensed real estate broker, for and on behalf of the owner of any real estate or the improvements thereon, which the licensed broker has contracted to manage for the owner, if the salaried employee is limited in his employment to: exhibiting units on the real estate to prospective tenants; providing the prospective tenants with information about the lease of the units; accepting applications for lease of the units; completing and executing preprinted form leases; and accepting security deposits and rental payments for the units only when the deposits and rental payments are made payable to the owner or the broker employed by the owner. The salaried employee shall not negotiate the amount of security deposits or rental payments and shall not negotiate leases or any rental agreements on behalf of the owner or broker.

FUNCTIONS OF THE PROPERTY MANAGER

> A property manager's primary function is to preserve the value of an owner's investment property while generating income for the owner.

In the simplest terms, a **property manager** is someone who *preserves the value of an investment property while generating income as an agent for the owner.* The agency relationship is created by the *management contract.* The fiduciary relationship that exists between the property manager and the property owner is the same as that which exists between a real estate broker and a seller or buyer, which was discussed in Chapter 6.

The property manager is expected to merchandise the property and control operating expenses so as to maximize income. With this expectation in mind, the property manager chooses the best possible means to carry out an agent's responsibilities and has more authority and discretion than an employee. The manager should maintain and modernize the property to preserve and enhance the owner's capital investment. The manager carries out these objectives by securing suitable tenants, collecting the rents, caring for the premises, budgeting and controlling expenses, hiring and supervising employees, and keeping proper accounts and making periodic reports to the owner. Property managers do not perform functions such as making capital improvements, reinvesting profits, paying the owner's income tax or establishing a depreciation schedule.

Securing Management Business

In today's market, property managers may look to corporate owners, apartment and condominium associations, homeowners' associations, investment syndicates, trusts and absentee owners as possible sources of management business. In securing business from any of these sources, word of mouth is often the best advertising. A manager who consistently demonstrates the ability to increase property income over previous levels should have no difficulty finding new business.

The Property Management Agreement

The first step in taking over the management of any property is to enter into a property **management agreement** with the owner (see Figure 11.1). This agreement creates an agency relationship between the owner and the property manager. A property manager is usually considered to be a *general* *agent,* whereas a real estate broker is usually considered to be a *special agent.* As an agent, the property manager is charged with the same agency responsibilities as the listing broker—care, obedience, accounting, loyalty and disclosure (COALD). (Agency responsibilities are discussed at length in Chapter 6.)

Although an oral property management agreement is enforceable, the management agreement should be in writing and should include the following:

- *Description* of the property.
- *Time period* the agreement covers.
- *Definition of management's responsibilities.* All of the manager's duties should be stated in the contract; exceptions should be noted. Important inclusions are to whom the rent and security deposit are paid; the method used in returning security deposits; and the method of paying mortgages, utilities and other bills.
- *Extent of the manager's authority as an agent.* This provision should state what authority the manager is to have in such matters as hiring, firing and supervising employees; establishing rental rates; making expenditures; and authorizing repairs within the limits set previously with the owner. (Repairs that exceed a certain expense limit may require the owner's written approval.) Making capital improvements would be the owner's responsibility.
- *Reporting.* Agreement should be reached on the frequency and detail of the manager's periodic reports on operations and financial position. These reports enable the owner to monitor the manager's work and serve as a basis for both the owner and the manager to assess trends that can be used in shaping future management policy.
- *Management fee.* The fee can be based on a percentage of gross income or net operating income, a commission on new rentals, a fixed fee or a combination of these. For example, the manager may get 3 percent of all monthly rentals collected. Both the owner and manager must ensure that the agreement is very specific as to how the management fee will be determined.
- *Allocation of costs.* The agreement should state which of the property management expenses, such as fees for custodial and other help, advertising, supplies and repairs, are to be charged to the property's expenses and paid by the owner.

After entering into an agreement with a property owner, a manager handles the property as the owner would. In all activities, the manager's first responsibility is *to realize the highest return on the property that is consistent with the owner's instructions.*

Before contracting to manage any property, the professional property manager should be certain that the building owner has realistic income expectations and is willing to spend money on necessary maintenance. Attempting to meet impossible owner demands by dubious methods can endanger the manager's reputation and make it difficult to obtain future business.

Figure 11.1   *Property Management Agreement*

PROPERTY MANAGEMENT AGREEMENT
Residential Property

THIS PROPERTY MANAGEMENT AGREEMENT, entered into this_____ day of _____ , 20_____
by_____("Owner")
and_____("Agent").

IN CONSIDERATION of the mutual covenants and promises each to the other made herein, the Owner does hereby contract with the Agent exclusively, and the Agent does hereby contract with the Owner, to rent, lease, operate and manage the property more particularly described below and any other property the Owner may assign to Agent from time to time (the "Property") upon the following terms and conditions:

1. **The Property:** Located in the City of _____,
County of_____,
state of North Carolina, being known and more particularly described as:
[ ] Street Address: _____
[ ] Apartment, Townhouse or Condominium Complex(es):_____
[ ] Other description: (Room, portion of the above address, etc.):_____
_____

2. **Duration of Agency:** This Agreement and the agency and employment created shall commence and become effective on
_____ , 20_____ , and shall continue thereafter until terminated as provided herein.

3. **Termination of Agency:** Either the Owner or the Agent may terminate the agency and employment created hereby by giving written notice of his intention to do so_____ days prior to the desired termination date. In the event the Owner terminates within _____ days of the commencement, Owner shall pay to the Agent a termination fee of_____.
No termination fee shall be required of the Owner for termination after the expiration of the number of days above specified and the Agent shall not be entitled to any percentage of any subsequently accruing rentals upon termination. Upon any termination of the Agreement by either the Owner or the Agent, each shall take such steps as are necessary to settle all accounts between them including the following: (1) the Agent shall promptly render to the Owner all rents then on hand after having deducted therefrom any Agent's fees then due and amounts sufficient to cover all other outstanding expenditures of the Agent incurred in connection with operating the Property; (2) the Agent shall render to the Owner records showing all tenants who paid security deposits under leases affecting the Property; (3) the Agent shall deliver to the Owner copies of all tenant's leases and other instruments entered into on behalf of the Owner (Agent may retain copies of such leases and agreements for Agent's records); (4) the Agent shall transfer to the Owner any security deposits held by Agent (5) the Owner shall promptly pay to Agent any fees or amounts due the Agent under the Agreement and shall reimburse the Agent for any expenditures made and outstanding at the time of termination; and (6) the Owner shall notify all current tenants of the termination of the agency status and transfer of such security deposits, if applicable.

4. **Agent's Fee:** The Owner shall pay to the Agent each month during the existence of this Agreement the following: _____
_____
_____
_____

The amounts due the Agent pursuant to this paragraph shall herein be referred to as the Agent's Fee and the Agent may deduct the Agent's Fee monthly from the gross receipts and collections received before remitting the balance of the receipts and collections to the Owner. *Note:* No fees may be deducted from the tenant security deposit until the termination of the tenancy. Thereafter, any fees due the Agent from the Owner may be deducted from any portion of the security deposit due to the Owner.

5. **Agent's Authority:** The owner hereby authorizes and empowers the Agent to perform such acts and take such steps as are necessary, in the Agent's opinion, to operate, manage and lease the Property to the Owner's advantage including, but not limited to:

Page 1 of 4

Figure 11.1 **Property Management Agreement (continued)**

Owner Initial Where Applicable:

_____ Advertising the Property, displaying signs thereon, and renting the Property, including the authority to negotiate, execute, extend and renew leases in the Owner's name for terms not in excess of (_____) _____ year(s) or (_____) _____ month(s);

_____ Instituting and prosecuting such judicial actions and proceedings as may be necessary to recover rents and other sums due the Owner from the tenants or to evict tenants and retain possession, including the authority, in the Agent's discretion, to settle, compromise and release any and all such judicial actions and proceedings;

_____ Collecting all rentals and other charges and amounts due or to become due under all leases covering the Property and giving receipts for the amounts so collected;

_____ Making or causing to be made any repairs which, in the agent's opinion, may be necessary to preserve, maintain and protect the Property; to maintain the facilities and services to the tenants as required by their tenancies; and to comply with any duties or obligations imposed upon the Owner by any local, state or federal law or regulation; including the authority to purchase such supplies and hire such labor as may be necessary in the Agent's opinion to accomplish such repairs;

_____ Performing any duties and exercising any rights conferred upon the Owner as Landlord under any leases entered into in connection with the Property; and

_____
_____
_____

6. **Agent Covenants:** During the duration of this Agreement the Agent agrees:
   (a) To manage and operate the Property to the best of Agent's ability, devoting thereto such time and attention as may be necessary;
   (b) To furnish the services of Agent's organization for renting, leasing, operating and/or managing the Property;
   (c) To solicit tenants and investigate all prospective tenants and to use Agent's best efforts to secure and maintain tenants;
   (d) TO OFFER THE PROPERTY TO THE PUBLIC FOR LEASING IN COMPLIANCE WITH ALL STATE AND FEDERAL HOUSING LAWS, INCLUDING BUT NOT LIMITED TO, ANY FEDERAL AND STATE LAWS AND REGULATIONS PROHIBITING DISCRIMINATION ON THE BASIS OF RACE, COLOR, RELIGION, SEX, NATIONAL ORIGIN, HANDICAP OR FAMILIAL STATUS;
   (e) To collect all monthly rentals and other charges due the Owner from the Property and to make or cause to be made such repairs as he deems appropriate in order to preserve and maintain the Property and to comply with all lease requirements and obligations imposed upon the Owner by North Carolina law (N.C.G.S. § 42-42);
   (f) To answer Tenant requests and complaints and to perform the duties imposed upon the Owner by law or pursuant to the tenant leases covering the Property;
   (g) To render monthly statements of receipts, collections, expenses, charges and disbursements to the Owner and to remit monthly to the Owner the balance of such receipts and collections (unless some other period is agreed upon);
   (h) To furnish Owner with copies of all tenant leases unless this block is checked and initialed by the Owner ❑ _____, in which event the Owner waives the right to receive copies of tenant leases unless Owner specifically requests such copies from the Agent; and
   (i) _____
   _____
   _____.

7. **Owner's Covenants:** During the duration of this Agreement the Owner agrees:
   (a) To advance to the Agent such sums as may be necessary to cover the costs of repairing the Property and maintaining it in a safe, fit and habitable condition as required by North Carolina law (N.C.G.S. § 42-42);
   (b) To reimburse the Agent for any expense actually incurred by him in operating, managing and maintaining the Property, including, but not limited to, advertising expenses, general operating expenses, court costs, attorney's fees and maintenance and supply expenses;

STANDARD FORM 401
© 7/2002

To see the full form, please go to Appendix C.

PROPERTY MANAGEMENT FEE

As mentioned earlier, the property management fee can be based on a percentage of gross or net income, a commission on new rentals, a fixed fee or a combination of these.

For Example Assume a property management agreement provides that the property manager gets 9 percent of all rents collected from a ten-unit apartment building. Two of the units are studio apartments that each rent for $250 a month. Six of the units are one-bedroom apartments that each rent for $325 a month. The remaining two units are two-bedroom apartments that each rent for $400 a month. Because of vacancies and collection losses, the property manager collects the rent for both studio apartments but for only five of the one-bedroom apartments and only one of the two-bedroom units. The property manager's fee is calculated as follows (note that the fee is based on only the amount of money actually collected):

$250 × 2 = $ 500
$325 × 5 = $1,625
$400 × 1 = $ 400
$2,525 total rents collected × .09 percentage of rents collected

$227.25 would be the manager's fee for this month

As with real estate commission rates, all management fees must be negotiable between the parties. It is a violation of federal antitrust laws for property managers to try to establish standard rates for their local areas.

MANAGEMENT CONSIDERATIONS

A property manager must live up to both the letter and the spirit of the management agreement. The owner must be kept well informed on all matters of policy as well as on the financial condition of the property and its operation. A manager must stay in contact with others in the field, thus becoming increasingly knowledgeable and keeping informed on current policies pertaining to the profession.

Budgeting Expenses   Before attempting to rent any property, a property manager should develop a yearly operating budget based on anticipated revenues and expenses and reflecting the long-term goals of the owner. The wise property manager makes his or her projections based on figures for a number of years. In preparing a budget, the manager should begin by allocating money for continuous, fixed expenses—employees' salaries, real estate taxes, property taxes and insurance premiums. Although budgets should be as accurate an estimate of costs as possible, adjustments may be necessary, especially in the case of new properties.

Next, the manager should establish a cash reserve fund for variable expenses such as repairs, decorating and supplies. The amount allocated for the reserve fund can be computed from previous yearly totals of variable expenses.

Capital expenditures. If an owner and a property manager decide that modernization or renovation would enhance the property's value, the manager should budget money to cover the costs of remodeling. The property manager should be thoroughly familiar with the *principle of contribution* (discussed in Chapter 16) or should seek expert advice when estimating any increase in value expected by an improvement. In the case of large-scale construction, the expenses charged against the property's income should be spread over several years.

Life cycle costing. The cost of equipment to be installed in a modernization or renovation must be evaluated over the equipment's entire useful life. This is called **life cycle costing,** a term meaning that both the initial and the operating costs of equipment over its expected life must be measured to compare the total cost of one type of equipment with that of another.

Renting the Property

The role of the property manager should not be confused with that of a broker acting as a leasing agent and concerned solely with renting space. The property manager may use the services of a leasing agent, but that agent does not undertake the full responsibility of maintaining and managing the property. The manager must be concerned with the long-term financial health of the property; the broker is concerned solely with renting space. Note that in renting out residential properties or evicting residential tenants, property managers must be sure to follow the requirements of the Residential Rental Agreements Act (discussed in Chapter 10).

Setting rental rates. In establishing rental rates for a property, a manager must be concerned that, in the long term, the income from the rentable space will cover the property's fixed charges and operating expenses and also provide a fair return on the investment. Consideration must be given to the prevailing rates in comparable buildings and the current level of vacancy in the property to be rented—supply and demand. Once the manager makes a detailed survey of the competitive space available in the neighborhood, rental prices should be adjusted for differences between these neighboring properties and the subject property. Annual rent adjustments are usually warranted. In establishing rental rates, the property manager has four long-term considerations:

1. The rental income must be sufficient to cover the property's fixed charges and operating expenses.
2. The rental income must provide a fair return on the owner's investment.
3. The rental rate should be in line with prevailing rates in comparable buildings. It may be slightly higher or slightly lower, depending on the strength of the property.
4. The current vacancy rate in the property is a good indicator of how great a rent increase is advisable. A building with a low vacancy rate (that is, few vacant units) is a better candidate for an increase than one with a high vacancy rate.

Note that although apartment rental rates are stated in monthly amounts, office and commercial space rentals are usually stated according to the annual or the monthly rate per square foot of space.

If a high level of vacancy exists, an immediate effort should be made to determine why. *A high level of vacancy does not necessarily indicate that rents are too high.* The trouble may be inept management or defects in the property. The manager first should attempt to identify the problem (if any) and correct it, rather than automatically lowering rents. Conversely, *even though a high percentage of occupancy may appear to indicate an effective rental program, it could also mean that rental rates are too low.* With an apartment house or office building, any time the occupancy level exceeds 95 percent, an analysis should be made to be certain that the building rates are not below market.

MATH CONCEPTS

Rental Commissions

Rental commissions are usually based on the annual rent from a property. For example, if an apartment unit rents for $475 per month and the commission payable is 8 percent, the commission is calculated as follows:

$$\$475 \text{ per month} \times 12 \text{ months} = \$5,700$$
$$\$5,700 \times .08 \ (8\%) = \$456$$

Selecting tenants. Generally, the highest rents can be secured from satisfied tenants. A broker may sell a property and then have no further dealings with the purchaser, but much of a building manager's success depends on retaining sound, long-term relationships. The first and most important step is selection. In selecting a prospective commercial or industrial tenant, a manager should be certain that (1) *the size of the space* meets the tenant's requirements (each business "fits the space"), (2) the tenant has the *ability to pay* for the space, (3) the *tenant's business is compatible* with the building and the other tenants' businesses and (4) if the tenant is likely to expand in the future, *expansion space will be available.* Once a prospect becomes a tenant, *the manager must be certain that the tenant remains satisfied in all respects commensurate with fair business dealings.*

Note that in selecting residential tenants, the property manager must comply with all federal and local fair housing laws (discussed in Chapter 7).

Collecting rents. The best way to minimize problems with rent collection is to make a careful selection of tenants in the first place. A property manager's desire for a high level of occupancy should not override good judgment in accepting only those tenants who can be expected to meet their financial obligations to the property owner. The property manager should investigate financial references given by the prospect, by local credit bureaus and, when possible, by the prospective tenant's former landlord.

The terms of rental payment should be spelled out in detail in the lease agreement. A firm and consistent collection plan with a sufficient system of notices and records should be established by the property manager. In cases of delinquency, every attempt must be made to make collections without resorting to legal action. For those cases in which legal recourse is required, the property manager must be prepared to initiate and follow through in conjunction with legal counsel.

It is important that property managers scrupulously follow all state rules and regulations when it comes to collecting and accounting for rents. The Real Estate License Law and the Real Estate Commission's Rules and Regulations require that property managers deposit funds into trust accounts and maintain detailed and accurate trust account records [see Rule A.0107). The North Carolina Tenant Security Deposit Act limits the amount of security deposits for residential property that can be required and mandates how they must be handled (discussed in Chapter 10). The property manager can only collect tenant security deposits if so authorized in the management agreement.

Maintaining the Property

One of the most important functions of a property manager is the supervision of property maintenance. The manager must learn to balance the services provided with the costs they entail so as to satisfy the tenants' needs while minimizing operating expenses.

Efficient property maintenance demands accurate assessment of the needs of the building and the number and kinds of personnel that will meet these needs. Staffing and scheduling requirements will vary with the type, size and regional location of the property, so owner and manager usually agree in advance on maintenance objectives for the property. For one property, the most viable plan may be to operate with a low occupancy level and minimal expenditures for services and maintenance. Another property may be more lucrative if kept in top condition and operated with all possible tenant services because it can then command premium rental rates.

The manager first must protect the physical integrity of the property to ensure that the condition of the building and its grounds is kept at present levels over the long term. For example, preserving the property by repainting the exterior or replacing the heating system will help keep the building functional and decrease routine maintenance costs.

Property maintenance encompasses four areas:

1. Preventive maintenance
2. Repair or corrective maintenance
3. Routine maintenance
4. Construction

Preventive maintenance includes regularly scheduled activities—such as regular painting and periodic lubrication of gears and motors—that will maintain the structure so that the long-range value and physical integrity of the building are preserved. Most authorities agree that preventive upkeep is the most critical but most neglected maintenance responsibility.

Preventive maintenance helps prevent problems and expenses.

Corrective maintenance corrects problems after they've occurred.

Repair or *corrective maintenance* involves the actual repairs that keep the building's equipment, utilities and amenities functioning as contracted for by the tenants. Repairing a boiler, fixing a leaky faucet and mending a broken air-conditioning unit are acts of repair maintenance.

The property manager must also *supervise routine cleaning and repairs* throughout the building, including such day-to-day duties as cleaning common areas; performing minor carpentry and plumbing tasks; and providing regularly scheduled upkeep of heating, air-conditioning and landscaping.

Finally, property maintenance requires new or renovative construction. Especially when handling commercial or industrial space, the property manager often is called on to make **tenant improvements**—alterations to the interior of the building to meet the functional demands of the tenants. These alterations may range from repainting to completely gutting the interior and redefining the space. Tenant improvements are especially important when renting new buildings because the interior is usually left incomplete so that it can be customized for individual tenants.

Supervision of modernization or renovation of buildings that have become functionally obsolete (discussed in Chapter 16) and thus unsuited to today's building needs is also important. The renovation of a building often increases the building's marketability and thus its income potential.

Hiring employees versus contracting for services. One of the major decisions a property manager faces is whether to contract for maintenance services from an outside firm or to hire on-site employees to perform such tasks. This decision should be based on a number of factors, including size of the building and land area, complexity of tenants' requirements and availability of suitable labor.

Handling Environmental Concerns

With the proliferation of federal and state laws and increasing local regulation, environmental concerns have become a major responsibility of the property manager and will require increased management time and attention in the future. Although property managers are not expected to be experts in all of the disciplines necessary to operate a modern building, they are expected to be knowledgeable in many diverse subjects, most of which are technical in nature. Environmental concerns are one such subject.

The property manager must be able to respond to a variety of environmental problems. He or she may manage structures containing asbestos or radon or be called on to arrange an environmental audit of a property. The manager must see that hazardous wastes produced by his or her employer or a building's tenants are properly disposed of. Even the normally nonhazardous waste of an office building must be controlled to avoid violation of laws requiring segregation of types of wastes. In areas where recycling has come into practice, the property manager must provide the facilities and see that tenants sort their trash properly. Note that lead-based paint disclosures are required for residential tenant-occupied property built prior to 1978.

The Americans with Disabilities Act

The *Americans with Disabilities Act (ADA)* has had a significant impact on the responsibilities of the property manager, both in building amenities and in employment issues.

Title I of the ADA provides for the employment of qualified job applicants regardless of their disability. Any employer with 15 or more employees must adopt nondiscriminatory employment procedures. In addition, employers must make reasonable accommodations to enable individuals with disabilities to perform essential job functions.

Property managers must also be familiar with Title III of the ADA, which prohibits discrimination in commercial properties and public accommodations. The ADA requires that managers ensure that people with disabilities have full and equal access to facilities and services. The property manager typically is responsible for determining whether a building meets the ADA's accessibility requirements. The property manager must also prepare a plan for retrofitting a building that is not in compliance when removal of existing barriers is "readily achievable"—that is, can be performed without much difficulty or expense. There are some tax advantages available to help offset the expense of complying with ADA. ADA experts may be consulted, as may architectural designers who specialize in accessibility issues.

To protect owners of existing structures from the massive expense of extensive remodeling, the ADA recommends *reasonably achievable accommodations* to provide access to the facilities and services. New construction and remodeling, however, must meet higher standards of accessibility and usability because it costs less to incorporate accessible features in the design than to retrofit. Though the law intends to provide for people with disabilities, many of the accessible design features and accommodations benefit everyone.

In Practice   The U.S. Department of Justice has ADA specialists available to answer general information questions about compliance issues. The ADA Information Line is at 1-800-514-0301 (TDD 1-800-514-0383).

Existing barriers must be removed when this can be accomplished in a *readily achievable* manner—that is, with little difficulty and at low cost. The following are typical examples of readily achievable modifications:

- Ramping or removing an obstacle from an otherwise accessible entrance
- Lowering wall-mounted public telephones
- Adding raised letters and braille markings on elevator buttons
- Installing auditory signals in elevators
- Reversing the direction in which doors open

Alternative methods can be used to provide reasonable accommodations if extensive restructuring is impractical or if retrofitting is unduly expensive. For instance, installing a cup dispenser at a water fountain that is too high for an individual in a wheelchair may be more practical than installing a lower unit.

In Practice   Federal, state and local laws may provide additional requirements for accommodating people with disabilities. Licensees should be aware of the full range of laws to ensure that their practices are in compliance.

SUMMARY

Property management is a specialized service to owners of income-producing properties in which the managerial function may be delegated to an individual or a firm with particular expertise in the field. The manager, as agent of the owner, becomes the administrator of the project and assumes the executive functions required for the care and operation of the property.

A management agreement establishing the agency relationship between owner and manager must be carefully prepared to define and authorize the manager's duties and responsibilities. The manager's duties include establishing a rental schedule, preparing an operating budget, marketing and renting the property, collecting rents and security deposits, initiating any necessary legal actions, maintaining the property, performing the landlord's duties under the lease, maintaining insurance, maintaining records and reporting to the owner.

Property managers' duties do not normally include reinvesting profits, making capital improvements, establishing a depreciation schedule or paying the owner's income tax.

Projected expenses, combined with the manager's analysis of the condition of the building and the rent patterns in the neighborhood, form the basis on which rental rates for the property are determined. Once a rent schedule is established, the property manager is responsible for soliciting tenants whose needs are suited to the available space and who are financially capable of meeting the proposed rents. Generally, the manager is obligated to collect rents, maintain the building, hire necessary employees, pay taxes for the building and handle tenant problems.

Maintenance includes safeguarding the physical integrity of the property, performing routine cleaning and repairs and making tenant improvements—adapting the interior space and overall design of the property to suit tenants' needs and meet the demands of the market.

The property manager must comply with ADA requirements to ensure that facilities provide for reasonably achievable accommodations.

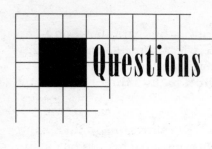

Questions

1. Apartment rental rates are usually expressed
   a. in monthly amounts.
   b. on a per-room basis.
   c. in square feet per month.
   d. in square feet per year.

2. In preparing a budget, the property manager should set up for variable expenses a(n)
   a. control account.
   b. floating allocation.
   c. cash reserve fund.
   d. asset account.

3. An important concern in setting rents is
   I. prevailing rates in the area.
   II. the local apartment owners' association.
   a. I only
   b. II only
   c. Both I and II
   d. Neither I nor II

4. Which of the following might suggest that rents are too low?
   a. Poorly maintained building
   b. Many "For Lease" signs in the area
   c. High occupancy rate
   d. High vacancy level

5. Repairing a boiler is classified as which type of maintenance?
   a. Preventive   c. Routine
   b. Corrective   d. Construction

6. In renting units in an apartment building, a property manager must comply with all of the following EXCEPT
   a. the terms of the management agreement.
   b. the lawful instructions of the owner.
   c. fair housing laws.
   d. the AMA Code of Ethics.

7. All EXCEPT which of the following describe the relationship between a building owner and a property manager?
   a. Agency relationship
   b. Established in a management agreement
   c. Governed by an exclusive-agency agreement
   d. Fiduciary relationship

8. Generally, the provisions of the manager-owner agreement should include all of the following EXCEPT
   a. a definition of the manager's responsibilities.
   b. a listing of previous owners of the property.
   c. the extent of the manager's authority as an agent.
   d. the allocation of costs.

9. When selecting a tenant, consideration should be given to all of the following EXCEPT
   a. size of the space versus the tenant's requirements.
   b. tenant's ability to pay.
   c. racial and ethnic background of the tenant.
   d. compatibility of the tenant's business with other tenants' businesses.

10. A property manager is usually responsible for all of the following EXCEPT
    I. providing a quarterly income statement to the residents of an apartment building.
    II. developing a budget and controlling expenses.
    III. communicating with the owner about physical problems with a building.
    a. I only
    b. II only
    c. I or II only
    d. II and III only

11. Last year your firm managed a 48-unit apartment building. Two units were four-bedroom, penthouse units renting for $1,000 per month. Twenty-five units with three bedrooms and two baths rented for $850 per month. Ten two-bedroom units rented for $750 per month and eleven one-bedroom apartments with balconies rented for $650 per month. The three-bedroom units carried a 5 percent vacancy and credit loss factor; the two-bedroom units carried a 5 percent vacancy and credit loss factor; the one-bedroom units carried a 10 percent vacancy and credit loss factor. The management fee is 12 percent. How much commission did your firm gross last year managing this building?
    a. $53,136
    b. $50,036
    c. $45,480
    d. $51,476

12. When a property manager is establishing a budget for the building, all of the following should be included as an operating expense EXCEPT
    a. heating oil.
    b. cleaning supplies.
    c. foundation repairs.
    d. management fees.

13. In most market areas, rents are determined by
    a. supply and demand factors.
    b. the local apartment owner's association.
    c. HUD.
    d. a tenant's union.

14. A property manager who enters into a management agreement with an owner is usually a
    a. special agent.
    b. general agent.
    c. universal agent.
    d. designated agent.

12 Real Estate Financing: Principles

LEARNING OBJECTIVES

When you've finished reading this chapter, you should be able to

- **distinguish** between title theory and lien theory states.

- **identify** the basic provisions of security and debt instruments and rights and duties of lenders and borrowers.

- **explain** the characteristics of various types of loan payment plans.

- **define** the effect of discount points on yield and **calculate** mathematically how to determine the number of points and the dollar amount of points to be paid by the borrower.

- **define** these *key terms:*

acceleration clause	foreclosure	prepayment penalty
alienation clause	hypothecation	promissory note
beneficiary	interest	satisfaction of
deed of trust	lien theory	mortgage
deficiency judgment	loan origination fee	title theory
discount points	mortgage	usury
due-on-sale clause	negotiable instrument	

BASIC MORTGAGE TERMS AND CONCEPTS

There are two different legal theories about the effect of mortgaging property: the **title theory** and the **lien theory.** Under the *lien theory* (which is the older, more traditional approach), the borrower retains both legal and equitable title to the property. The lender is given the right to have the property sold and the proceeds applied to the debt, should the borrower default under the terms of the mortgage.

Title theory states use the three-party deed of trust instrument (a form of mortgage) as security for the debt. The borrower (grantor) actually conveys legal title to the trustee (third party) to hold for the beneficiary (lender) until the debt is satisfied. The trustee has "power of sale" to sell the property if the debt is not paid. However, the borrower retains equitable title to the property. This means that the borrower has the right to demand the return of the legal title when the debt is repaid. The lender's legal ownership is subject to termination on full payment of the debt or performance of the obligation. *North Carolina follows the title theory.*

> In a lien theory state, the borrower retains both legal and equitable title.
>
> In a title theory state, the borrower (grantor) conveys legal title to a trustee until the debt has been satisfied.

The legal differences between title theory and lien theory are of little significance today. Under both theories, if a borrower defaults, the lender may foreclose the lien, offer the property for sale and apply the funds received from the sale to reduce or extinguish the obligation. As protection to the borrower, most states allow a statutory redemption period during which a defaulted borrower can redeem the property.

Regardless of whether a state follows the title theory or lien theory of mortgages, the security interest that the lender has in the real estate is legally considered personal property. This interest can be transferred only with a transfer of the debt that the mortgage secures.

SECURITY AND DEBT

Generally, any interest in real estate that may be sold may be pledged as security or collateral for a debt. A basic principle of property law—that a person cannot convey greater rights in property than he or she actually has—applies equally to the right to mortgage. So the owner of a fee simple estate can mortgage the fee, and the owner of a leasehold or subleasehold can mortgage that leasehold interest. For example, a large retail corporation renting space in a shopping center may mortgage its leasehold interest to finance remodeling work.

Mortgage Loan Instruments

Two parts to a mortgage loan exist—the debt itself and the security for the debt. When a property is to be mortgaged, the owner must execute, or sign, two separate instruments:

1. The **promissory note,** or *financing instrument,* is the written promise or agreement to repay a debt in definite installments with interest. The mortgagor executes one or more promissory notes to reflect the amount of the debt.
2. The **mortgage/deed of trust,** or *security instrument,* is the document that conveys the property to the lender as security for a debt.

A mortgagor is a borrower who gives a mortgage to a lender (mortgagee) in return for the money. The relationship between mortgagor and mortgagee is shown in Figure 12.1.

Hypothecation is the act of pledging real property as security for payment of a loan without giving up possession of the property. A pledge of security—a mortgage—cannot be effective legally unless there is a debt to secure. *Both the note and the mortgage must be executed to create an enforceable mortgage loan.*

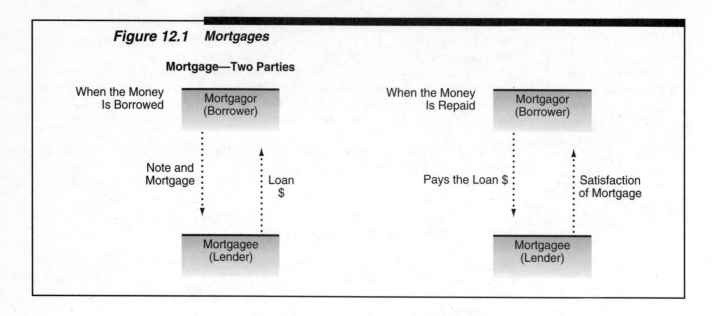

Figure 12.1   Mortgages

Mortgage—Two Parties

Deeds of trust. In some areas of the country, including North Carolina, lenders prefer to use a three-party security instrument known as a *deed of trust,* or trust deed, rather than a mortgage document (see Figure 12.2). In a deed of trust the borrower conveys "naked title" or "bare legal title" (title without the right of possession) to the real estate as security for the loan from the borrower to a third party, called the *trustee.* The trustee then holds title on behalf of the lender, known as the **beneficiary,** who is the legal owner and holder of the note. The wording of the conveyance sets forth actions that the trustee may take if the borrower, known as the *grantor* or *trustor,* defaults under any of the deed of trust terms. The procedure for foreclosing a deed of trust is simpler and faster than the procedure used to foreclose a mortgage, because the deed of trust contains an automatic power-of-sale clause, which in case of the borrower's default, gives the trustee the power to sell the property in a nonjudicial foreclosure. Note that the term *mortgage loan* is commonly used to refer to a loan secured by either a mortgage or deed of trust.

THE PROMISSORY NOTE

When a home purchase is financed with a mortgage loan, the borrower must sign *a promissory note.* The promissory note is legal evidence of the debt between the borrower and lender.

Essential Elements of a Valid Note

The essential elements of a note are (1) term, (2) promise to pay and (3) signature of the borrower(s). A promissory note is a simple document that states the amount of the debt, the time and method of payment and the rate of interest. The note may also refer to or repeat several of the clauses that appear in the mortgage document. The borrower is called the *maker* or *payor* or *obligor,* and the lender is called the *payee.* The note, like the mortgage, should be signed by all parties who have an interest in the property (for example, both spouses should sign the note). (See Figure 12.3 for an example of a promissory note.) Remember that (1) only the borrowers (makers) of the note sign it, (2) it is not recorded (only the security instrument is recorded) and (3) there is only one original that is signed at the closing (although there may be copies given to the various parties).

Essential elements of a note

1. Term
2. Promise to pay
3. Signature of borrowers

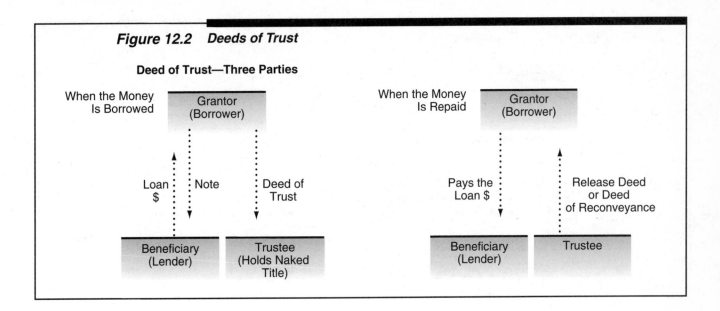

Figure 12.2   Deeds of Trust

A promissory note is usually a **negotiable instrument**—that is, a written promise or order to pay a specific sum of money. An instrument is said to be *negotiable* when its holder, the payee, may transfer the right to receive payment to a third party. This may be accomplished by signing the instrument over to the third party or, in some cases, merely by delivering the instrument to that person. Other examples of negotiable instruments include checks and bank drafts. It is important for the promissory note to be negotiable because lenders often sell their mortgage loans in the secondary mortgage market.

To be negotiable, or freely transferable, an instrument must meet certain requirements of the law. The instrument must be in writing, made by one person to another and signed by the maker. It must contain an unconditional promise to pay a sum of money on demand or at a set date in the future. In addition, the instrument must be payable to the order of a specifically named person or to the bearer (whoever has possession of the note). Instruments that are payable *to order* must be transferred by endorsement; those payable *to bearer* may be transferred by delivery. A nonnegotiable note does not contain *to order* or *to bearer* but is payable to a named person. It is not transferable or assignable. The vast majority of real estate notes are negotiable.

It is important to understand the difference between the negotiability of a *note*—that is, whether a note is transferable from one lender to another— and the negotiability of the *interest rate* of a note. The original parties to the note may negotiate the interest rate of the loan, but once that interest rate is determined, it is binding on the parties to the note, whether or not the note itself is transferred to another party.

Special Note Provisions

Virtually all promissory notes used by institutional lenders contain three additional provisions:

1. **Acceleration clause.** The **acceleration clause** provides that if a borrower defaults, the lender has the right to accelerate the maturity of the debt—to declare the entire debt (plus accrued interest and costs)

Figure 12.3   Promissory Note

SATISFACTION: The debt evidenced by
this Note has been satisfied in full this
_____ day of _____, 19 ____
Signed: _____

PROMISSORY NOTE

_____, N. C.

$ _____

_____, 19 ____

FOR VALUE RECEIVED the undersigned, jointly and severally, promise to pay to _____

_____

_____ or order,

the principal sum of _____

DOLLARS ($ _____), with interest from _____ , at the rate of _____

per cent (_____ %) per annum on the unpaid balance until paid or until default, both principal and interest payable in lawful money of the United States of America, at

the office of _____

or at such place as the legal holder hereof may designate in writing. It is understood and agreed that additional amounts may be advanced by the holder hereof as provided in the instruments, if any, securing this Note and such advances will be added to the principal of this Note and will accrue interest at the above specified rate of interest from the date of advance until paid. The principal and interest shall be due and payable as follows:

If not sooner paid, the entire remaining indebtedness shall become due and payable on _____

If payable in installments, each such installment shall, unless otherwise provided, be applied first to payment of interest then accrued and due on the unpaid principal balance, with the remainder applied to the unpaid principal.

Unless otherwise provided, this Note may be prepaid in full or in part at any time without penalty or premium. Partial prepayments shall be applied to installments due in reverse order of their maturity.

In the event of (a) default in payment of any installment of principal or interest hereof as the same becomes due and such default is not cured within ten (10) days from the due date, or (b) default under the terms of any instrument securing this Note and such default is not cured within fifteen (15) days after written notice to maker, then in either such event the holder may without further notice, declare the remainder of the principal sum, together with all interest accrued thereon and, the prepayment premium, if any, at once due and payable. Failure to exercise this option shall not constitute a waiver of the right to exercise the same at any other time. The unpaid principal of this Note and any part thereof, accrued interest and all other sums due under this Note and the Deed of Trust,

if any, shall bear interest at the rate of _____ per cent (_____ %) per annum after default until paid.

All parties to this Note, including maker and any sureties, endorsers, or guarantors hereby waive protest, presentment, notice of dishonor, and notice of acceleration of maturity and agree to continue to remain bound for the payment of principal, interest and all other sums due under this Note and the Deed of Trust notwithstanding any change or changes by way of release, surrender, exchange, modification or substitution of any security for this Note or by way of any extension or extensions of time for the payment of principal and interest and all such parties waive all and every kind of notice of such change or changes and agree that the same may be made without notice or consent of any of them.

Upon default the holder of this Note may employ an attorney to enforce the holder's rights and remedies and the maker, principal, surety, guarantor and endorsers of this Note hereby agree to pay to the holder reasonable attorney's fees not exceeding a sum equal to fifteen percent (15%) of the outstanding balance owing on said Note, plus all other reasonable expenses incurred by the holder in exercising any of the holder's rights and remedies upon default. The rights and remedies of the holder as provided in this Note and any instrument securing this Note shall be cumulative and may be pursued singly, successively, or together against the property described in the Deed of Trust or any other funds, property or security held by the holder for payment or security, in the sole discretion of the holder. The failure to exercise any such right or remedy shall not be a waiver or release of such rights or remedies or the right to exercise any of them at another time.

This Note is to be governed and construed in accordance with the laws of the State of North Carolina.

This Note is given _____ , and is secured by a

_____ which is a _____ lien upon the property therein described.

IN TESTIMONY WHEREOF, each corporate maker has caused this instrument to be executed in its corporate name by its

_____ President, attested by its

_____ Secretary, and its corporate seal to be hereto affixed, all by order of its Board of Directors first duly given, the day and year first above written.

IN TESTIMONY WHEREOF, each individual maker has hereunto set his hand and adopted as his seal the word "SEAL" appearing beside his name, the day and year first above written.

_____ (SEAL)

_____ (Corporate Name)
By: _____
_____ President
ATTEST: _____

_____ (SEAL)
_____ (SEAL)
_____ (SEAL)

_____ Secretary (Corporate Seal)

_____ (Corporate Name)
By: _____
_____ President
ATTEST: _____

_____ (SEAL)
_____ (SEAL)

_____ Secretary (Corporate Seal)

_____ (SEAL)

due and payable immediately—even though the terms of the mortgage allow the borrower to amortize the debt in regular payments over a period of years. Without the acceleration clause, the lender would have to sue the borrower every time a payment became due and in default.

2. **Prepayment penalty clause.** When a loan is paid in installments over a long term, the total interest paid by the borrower can exceed the principal of the loan. If such a loan is paid off before its full term, the lender collects less interest from the borrower. For this reason, some lenders include a prepayment penalty clause in the promissory note, requiring that the borrower pay a **prepayment penalty** against the unearned portion of the interest for any payments made ahead of schedule. A loan that does not have a prepayment penalty clause will include a prepayment privilege clause, which allows the borrower to prepay a portion or all of the outstanding balance without penalty. Lenders in North Carolina are not permitted to charge a prepayment penalty on any residential loan with an original balance of $150,000 or less. Also, federal law prohibits lenders from charging a prepayment penalty on any FHA-insured loan, any VA-guaranteed loan or any loan that is sold to the Fannie Mae (formerly Federal National Mortgage Association) or Freddie Mac (formerly the Federal Home Loan Mortgage Corporation).

3. **Due-on-sale clause.** Frequently, when a conventional real estate loan is made, the lender wishes to prevent some future purchaser of the property from being able to assume that loan without the lender's permission, particularly at its old rate of interest. For this reason, some lenders include a **due-on-sale clause** (also known as an **alienation clause**) in the note. A due-on-sale clause provides that on sale of the property by the borrower to a buyer who wants to assume the loan, the lender has the choice of either declaring the entire debt to be due and payable immediately or permitting the buyer to assume the loan at current market interest rates. Use of this clause triggers the acceleration clause. The absence of a due-on-sale clause would permit a loan assumption without the lender's prior consent.

Principal and Interest (Debt Service)

A charge for the use of money borrowed (the principal) is called **interest.** Loan payments are usually described as *principal and interest payments* (P&I) *or debt service payments.* Interest may be due either at the end of each payment period (known as payment *in arrears*) or at the beginning of each payment period (payment *in advance*). Whether interest is charged in arrears or in advance is specified in the note. (The interest on the vast majority of mortgage loans is payable in arrears.) In practice, the distinction becomes important if the property is sold before the debt is repaid in full, as will become evident in Chapter 14, "Closing the Real Estate Transaction." Note that the interest charged on real estate loans is *simple interest,* and it is charged only on the outstanding loan balance.

Most mortgage loans are *amortized loans.* That is, as regular payments are made, each payment is broken down and applied first to the interest owed, with the balance applied to the principal amount—over a term of perhaps 15 to 30 years. At the end of the term, the full amount of the principal and all interest due is reduced to zero. Such loans are also called *direct reduction loans.*

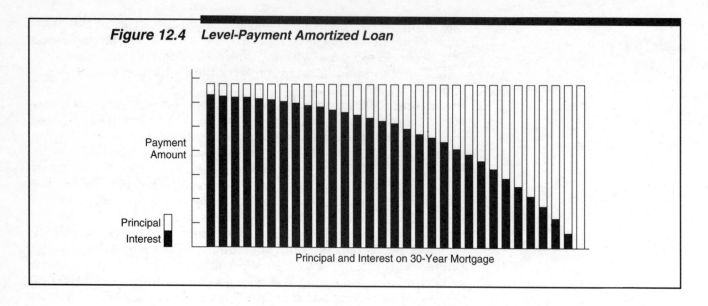

Figure 12.4 *Level-Payment Amortized Loan*

Payment Amount

Principal

Interest

Principal and Interest on 30-Year Mortgage

Each month, in addition to paying P&I, the borrower is normally required by the lender to pay one-twelfth of the annual real property taxes and one-twelfth of the annual homeowner's insurance premium. The payment of these four items is referred to as the PITI. The taxes and insurance portion (TI) of the monthly payment is placed into the lender's escrow account and held until those bills are due. The lender receives the tax and insurance bills and pays those items from its escrow account.

Most amortized mortgage loans are paid in monthly installments; some, however, are payable biweekly, quarterly or semiannually. These payments may be computed based on a number of payment plans, which tend alternately to gain and lose favor with lenders and borrowers as the cost and availability of mortgage money fluctuate. Some of these payment plans are described in the following subsections; one is shown in Figure 12.4.

Fully amortized fixed-rate mortgage. The most frequently used plan, *the fully amortized fixed-rate mortgage*, requires that the mortgagor pay a *constant amount*, usually monthly. This may be referred to as a *level-payment*, simple interest loan. The mortgagee first credits each payment to the interest due and then applies the balance to reduce the principal of the loan. Thus, while each debt service payment remains the same, the portion applied toward repayment of the principal grows and the interest due declines as the unpaid balance of the loan is reduced.

Partially amortized fixed-rate mortgage. With a partially amortized loan, the monthly principal and interest payments are a constant amount, but that amount is not sufficient to completely pay off the loan over the loan term. At maturity, a **balloon payment** will be due to pay the remaining principal. A *balloon payment* is a payment of an amount that is larger than the previous regular payments.

Straight-line amortized mortgage. With *straight-line amortization*, the mortgagor may pay a *different amount for each installment*, with each payment consisting of a fixed amount credited toward the principal plus an additional amount for the interest due on the principal outstanding since the last payment was made.

Calculating Simple Interest

To compute simple interest, use the formula $I = P \times R \times T$, where

$$
\begin{aligned}
I &= \text{interest} \\
P &= \text{principal} \\
R &= \text{rate} \\
T &= \text{time}
\end{aligned}
$$

Apply this formula to a $30,000 loan *(P)* at 8 percent interest *(R)* to be repaid over 15 years *(T)*. To calculate the interest owing for the first month, perform the following calculations:

$$
\begin{aligned}
I &= \$30,000 \times .08 \times 15 \\
I &= \$36,000
\end{aligned}
$$

$36,000 total interest ÷ 15 years = $2,400 yearly interest payment

(**Note:** After the borrower makes the first principal payment, the loan total will be reduced and thus the interest payment also will be reduced.)

$2,400 ÷ 12 months = $200 first monthly interest payment

Interest and Principal Credited from Amortized Payment. Lenders charge borrowers a certain percentage of the principal as interest for each year a debt is outstanding. The amount of interest due on any one payment date is calculated by computing the total yearly interest (based on the unpaid balance) and dividing that figure by the number of payments made each year.

For Example Assume the current outstanding balance of a loan is $70,000. The interest rate is 7½ percent per year, and the monthly P&I payment is $489.30. Based on these facts, the interest and principal due on the next payment would be computed as shown:

$70,000 loan balance × .075 annual interest rate = $5,250 annual interest
$5,250 annual interest ÷ 12 months = $437.50 monthly interest
$489.30 monthly P&I payment – $437.50 monthly interest =
$51.80 monthly principal
$70,000 loan balance – $51.80 monthly principal =
$69,948.20 remaining balance

This process is followed with each payment over the term of the loan. The same calculations are made each month, starting with the declining new balance figure from the previous month.

Interest-only mortgage (term loan). A mortgagor may choose an *interest-only payment plan* that calls for periodic payments of interest only, with the principal to *be paid in full at the end of the loan term.* This is known as an *interest-only,* or a *term, loan.* Generally, such plans are used for construction loans and second mortgages rather than for residential first mortgage loans. Prior to the 1930s, the only form of mortgage loan available was the straight-payment loan, payable after a relatively short term, such as three to five years. The high rate of foreclosure on such loans in the depression years prompted the use of the more manageable amortized loans that are now the norm.

Adjustable-rate mortgage (ARM). Generally, these loans originate at one rate of interest, with the rate fluctuating up or down during the loan term based on the movement of a published index. Because the interest may change, so may the mortgagor's loan payments. Details of how and when the rate of interest on the loan will change are included in the provisions of the note.

Generally, interest rate adjustments are limited to one each year, and a set maximum number of increases may be made over the life of the loan. Certain regulations may enable a lender to adjust the interest rate on a monthly basis. The borrower is usually given the right to repay the loan in full without penalty whenever the interest rate changes. (See the discussion of prepayment penalties earlier in this chapter.)

Common components of an ARM include the following:

- **Note rate (contract rate).** The original rate charged, which is stated in the closing documents, is called the *note rate*.
- **Index.** The interest rate on the outstanding balance of the loan is increased or decreased according to the movements of an index. The most popular index that lending institutions use is the short-term U.S. Treasury bill rate.
- **Margin.** The amount of interest a lender charges over and above the index rate is called the *margin.* For example, if the most recent one-year Treasury bill rate was 3.25 percent, the lender would add a 2 percent margin and charge the borrower a 5.25 percent interest rate on the outstanding loan balance. The amount of the margin remains fixed for the entire life of the loan; it is the movement of the index rate that causes the ARM interest rate to fluctuate.
- **Interest rate caps.** Rate caps limit the amount the interest rate may increase or decrease in any one adjustment period, called the *periodic interest rate cap.* They also limit the amount the interest rate can increase over the entire life of the loan, which is called the *life of loan cap.*
- **Payment cap.** The payment cap, which sets a maximum amount for payments, protects the mortgagor against the possibility of individual payments that he or she cannot afford. With a payment cap, a rate increase can result in negative amortization—an increase in the loan balance. For instance, suppose a borrower's rate increases a full 1 percent. For this borrower a 1 percent rate increase translates into a payment increase of $65 a month. However, the payment cap limits the increase to $45 a month. During that adjustment period the borrower will be paying $20 a month less than the amount required to pay the full principal and interest payment. So each month, $20 is added to the principal balance. This is negative amortization.
- **Adjustment period.** This establishes how often the loan rate may change. Common adjustment periods are every year (a 1-year ARM), every three years (a 3-year ARM) and every five years (a 5-year ARM).
- **Conversion option.** Lenders may offer a conversion option, which permits the mortgage to convert from an adjustable-rate to a fixed-rate loan at certain intervals during the life of the mortgage. The option is subject to certain terms and conditions for the conversion.

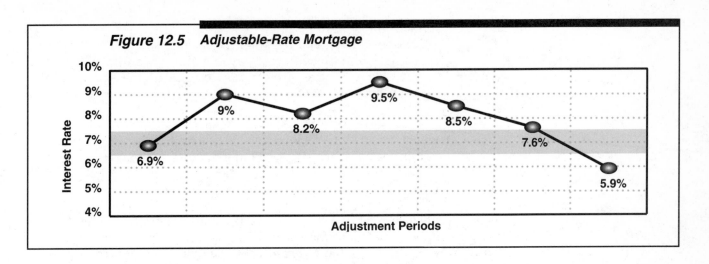

Figure 12.5   Adjustable-Rate Mortgage

Figure 12.5 illustrates the effect interest rate fluctuations and periodic caps have on an adjustable-rate mortgage. Obviously, without rate caps and payment caps, a single mortgage's interest rate could fluctuate wildly over several adjustment periods, depending on the behavior of the index to which it is tied. In Figure 12.5, the borrower's rate ranges from a low of 5.9 percent to a high of 9.5 percent. Such unpredictability makes personal financial planning difficult. On the other hand, if the loan had a periodic rate cap of 7.5 percent, the borrower's rate would never go above that level, regardless of the index's behavior. Similarly, a lender would want a floor to keep the rate from falling below a certain rate (here, 6.5 percent). The shaded area in the figure shows how caps and floors protect against dramatic changes in interest rates.

Graduated payment mortgage (GPM). A *flexible payment plan*, such as a *graduated payment mortgage*, allows a mortgagor to make lower monthly payments for the first few years of the loan (typically the first five years) and larger payments for the remainder of the term, when the mortgagor's income is expected to have increased. The interest on a GPM is fixed throughout the life of the loan. However, in the early years of the loan, the monthly payments are lower than the payments that would be required to fully amortize the loan. This results in negative amortization. As each payment is made, the unpaid interest is added to the principal balance, resulting in an increasing loan balance for the first few years. The monthly payments then increase at stated intervals throughout the loan term, eventually making up for the negative amortization and paying off the loan in full by the end of the loan term. Generally, this type of loan is used to enable first-time buyers and buyers in times of high interest rates to purchase real estate.

Balloon payment loan. When a mortgage loan requires periodic payments that will not fully amortize the amount of the loan by the time the final payment is due, the final payment is an amount that is larger than the previous payments—a balloon payment. Examples would be a "partially amortized loan" and a "term loan."

For Example A loan for $80,000 at 10 percent interest may be computed on a 30-year amortization schedule but paid over a 20-year term, with a final balloon payment due at the end of the 20th year. In this case, each monthly payment would be $792.24 (the amount taken from a 30-year amortization schedule), with a final balloon payment of $56,340 (the amount of principal still owing after 20 years).

Balloon Payment Loan

Consider a loan with the following terms: $80,000 at 8 percent interest, with only interest payable monthly and the loan fully repayable in 15 years. This is how to calculate the amount of the final balloon payment:

$80,000 × .08 = $6,400 annual interest
$6,400 annual interest ÷ 12 months = $533.33 monthly interest payment
$80,000 principal payment + $533.33 monthly interest = $80,533.33
final balloon payment

It is frequently assumed that if payments are made promptly, the lender will extend the balloon payment for another limited term. The lender, however, is in no way legally obligated to grant this extension and can require payment in full when the note is due. The borrower may have to refinance the loan with another lender.

A loan that requires a balloon payment is called a *partially amortized loan* and is quite common in seller financing situations. When sellers finance part or all of the purchase price, they often want to be cashed out—that is, have the seller financing paid off—within three to five years of the sale.

Growing-equity mortgage (GEM). The *growing-equity mortgage,* or *rapid-payoff mortgage,* makes use of a fixed interest rate, but payments of principal are increased according to an index or a schedule. The total payment thus increases, but the borrower's income is expected to keep pace, and the loan is paid off more quickly. (***Note:*** *equity* is the borrower's interest in the property; that is, the value of the property less all outstanding mortgages and other liens.)

Biweekly loans. *Biweekly loans* require that the borrower make a loan payment every two weeks instead of once a month. The amount of the payment is half of what the monthly payment required for 30-year amortization would have been. This payment plan results in the borrower's paying the equivalent of one extra monthly payment a year. (This is because on this payment schedule, the borrower makes 26 biweekly payments—the equivalent of 13 monthly payments.) Because of this, most biweekly loans are paid off in about 20 or 21 years instead of 30 years. Because the loan is paid off earlier, the borrower pays less interest over the life of the loan, and lenders often offer biweekly loans at slightly lower interest rates than standard 30-year loans.

Shared-appreciation mortgage (SAM). Under a *shared-appreciation mortgage,* the lender originates the mortgage at a favorable interest rate (several points below the going rate) in return for a guaranteed share of any gain the borrower realizes when he or she eventually sells the property. This type of loan was originally made to developers of large real estate projects, but in times of expensive mortgage money, it has appeared in the residential finance market. The specific details of the shared-appreciation agreement are set forth in the mortgage or trust deed and note documents.

Usury. The maximum rate of interest charged on loans may be set by state law. Charging illegal interest in excess of this rate is called **usury,** and lenders are penalized for making usurious loans. Usury laws were enacted primarily to protect consumers from unscrupulous lenders that charge unreasonably high interest rates. In some states, a lender that makes a usurious loan is permitted to collect the borrowed money but only at the legal rate of interest. In other states, a usurious lender may lose the right to collect any interest or may lose the entire amount of the loan in addition to the interest. Loans made to corporations are generally exempt from usury laws.

Usury laws are state laws, but federal law preempts state law, and the *Depository Institutions Deregulation and Monetary Control Act* of 1980 specifically exempts from state interest limitations *all* federally related residential first mortgage loans made after March 31, 1980. Federally related loans are those made by federally chartered institutions or those insured or guaranteed by a federal agency. The exemption includes loans used to finance *manufactured housing* (the federal term for *mobile homes*) and the acquisition of stock in a cooperative housing corporation. North Carolina exempts all residential first deeds of trust from usury laws.

Usury laws are complicated, and any licensee who has questions about state or federal usury laws should consult a lawyer.

Discount points. The return or profit on a loan is sometimes called the *yield.* A large part of the yield comes from the interest rate the lender charges on the loan. However, the rate of interest that a lender charges for a mortgage loan might be less than the yield (true rate of return) required by the lender or by an investor who might purchase that loan from the lender. For this reason, the lender can charge **discount points** to make up the difference between the mortgage interest rate and the required investor yield.

> One discount point equals 1 percent of a loan and increases the yield of a loan by ⅛ percent.

The number of points charged varies, depending on the difference between the interest rate and the required yield *and* on the average time the lender expects the loan to be outstanding. While most loans have an average term of 30 years, the average life of all loans is actually 11 to 12 years because loans are usually paid off much sooner, when the borrower sells the property or refinances the loan. Lenders calculate that it takes an average of six to eight discount points to increase the yield 1 percent, with *eight points being the rule of thumb.* Points can be charged on FHA-insured, VA-guaranteed and conventional loans.

For Example Suppose a lender wants to increase its yield on a $100,000 loan by one-half percentage point. If eight points equals a yield increase of one percentage point, to increase the yield by one-half percentage point, the lender would have to charge four points.

The cost to the borrower of a point equals 1 percent of the loan amount and is charged as prepaid interest at the closing. Thus, points charged on a $100,000 loan would be $4,000 ($100,000 × 4%). In this situation, the lender would actually fund $96,000 (the $100,000 principal amount of the loan minus the $4,000 for points), but $100,000 would have to be repaid by the borrower, thereby increasing the investor's yield (a $96,000 loan receiving interest calculated on $100,000).

Discount Points

Depending on the interest rate, it takes between six and eight discount points to change the interest rate 1 percent on a 30-year loan. From the borrower's standpoint, one discount point equals 1 percent of the loan amount. To calculate the net amount of a $75,000 loan after a three-point discount is taken multiply the loan amount by 100 percent minus the discount:

$$
\begin{aligned}
\$75,000 &\times (100\% - 3\%) \\
\$75,000 &\times 97\% \\
\$75,000 &\times .97 = \$72,750
\end{aligned}
$$

Or deduct the dollar amount of the discount from the loan:

$$
\begin{aligned}
\$75,000 &- (\$75,000 \times 3\%) \\
\$75,000 &- (\$75,000 \times .03) \\
\$75,000 &- \$2,250 = \$72,750
\end{aligned}
$$

Investor Yield

From the standpoint of the investor, one discount point received increases the yield on the loan by ⅛ percent. Two points would increase the yield by ¼ percent, four points by ½ percent, six points by ¾ percent and eight points by 1 percent. For example, if a loan carried an interest rate of 9½ percent and a discount of 6 points, the yield to the investor would be calculated as follows:

6 discount points = ¾% increase in yield
9½% interest per the contract + ¾% increase from the discount = 10¼%
yield to the investor

If an investor requires a 10½ percent yield on a loan with a 10⅛ percent interest rate, the number of discount points needed would be calculated as follows:

10½% = 10⁴⁄₈%; 10⁴⁄₈% required yield − 10⅛% interest rate = ⅜% difference;
⅜% = 3 discount points

Discount points should not be confused with the *loan origination fee* charged by most lenders, which is an administrative expense for generating the loan. **Loan origination fees** are not prepaid interest; they are an expense that must be paid to the lender, typically 1 percent of the loan amount regardless of any discount points that might also be charged.

In Practice

Interest payments made under a mortgage loan secured by a first or second home are deductible for federal income tax purposes. This deduction in effect reduces the borrower's total cost of housing for the year. Interest deductions are limited, however, to the interest paid on an initial loan amount or refinancing no greater than the purchase price of the home plus capital improvements, unless the loan proceeds are used for qualified medical or educational purposes. Points (prepaid interest) paid at the time of financing a home purchase are fully deductible for the year paid. Points on a loan to finance property improvements are also fully deductible for the year paid. Points paid on a loan refinancing may be deductible (consult a tax expert). If advance payments of loan principal are made, there is no increase in the deduction. If the entire loan is prepaid, however, any undeducted points may be deducted for that year.

THE MORTGAGE (OR DEED OF TRUST) INSTRUMENT

A mortgage or deed of trust document is typically a little more complicated than a promissory note. The mortgage or deed of trust must refer to the terms of the promissory note and clearly establish through the use of a mortgaging clause that the property is intended to be security for a valid debt. It must identify the lender and the borrower (who must have the capacity to contract) and must include an accurate, adequate description of the property. It must be in writing and signed (and sealed) by all parties who have an interest in the real estate. (The lender does not sign the mortgage or deed of trust.) Finally, the mortgage or deed of trust must be delivered to and accepted by the lender/trustee (see Figure 12.6).

Rights and Duties of the Borrower   The borrower (mortgagor or grantor) is required to fulfill many obligations. These usually include

- payment of the debt in accordance with the terms of the note;
- payment of all real estate taxes on the property given as security;
- maintenance of adequate insurance to protect the lender if the property is destroyed or damaged by fire, windstorm or another hazard;
- maintenance of the property in good repair at all times; and
- lender authorization before making any major alterations or demolishing any building on the mortgaged property.

Failure to meet any of these obligations can result in a borrower's default on the note. When this happens, the loan documents may provide for a grace period (30 days, for example) during which, unless the borrower corrects the default, the lender has the right to foreclose the mortgage or deed of trust after the grace period and collect on the note. The most frequent cause of default is the borrower's failure to meet monthly installments.

The borrower has the right to possess and enjoy the property during the loan term, with no interference from the lender. The borrower also has the right to have title to the property transferred back to him or her when the loan is paid in full. Under the provisions of the mortgage or deed of trust, when the note has been fully paid, the trustee is required to execute a **satisfaction of mortgage,** also known as a *deed of release, reconveyance deed, release of mortgage* or *mortgage discharge*. This document reconveys to the borrower all interest in the real estate that was conveyed to the lender by the original recorded mortgage or deed of trust document. By having this release entered in the public record, the owner shows that the mortgage lien has been removed from the property. In addition, the buyer has the right to redeem the property on default (discussed below, under "Redemption").

Rights of the Lender   A lender has the right to assign the mortgage debt as well as the right to foreclose the mortgage or deed of trust if the borrower defaults. As mentioned earlier, a note is a negotiable instrument; as such, it may be sold to

Figure 12.6   *North Carolina Deed of Trust*

NORTH CAROLINA DEED OF TRUST

SATISFACTION: The debt secured by the within Deed of Trust together with the note(s) secured thereby has been satisfied in full.

This the _____ day of _____, 20___

Signed: _____   _____

_____   _____

Parcel Identifier No. _____   Verified by _____ County on the ____ day of_____, 20___

By: _____

Mail/Box to: _____

This instrument was prepared by: _____

Brief description for the Index: _____

THIS DEED of TRUST made this _____ day of _____, 20___, by and between:

GRANTOR	TRUSTEE	BENEFICIARY

Enter in appropriate block for each party: name, address, and, if appropriate, character of entity, e.g. corporation or partnership.

The designation Grantor, Trustee, and Beneficiary as used herein shall include said parties, their heirs, successors, and assigns, and shall include singular, plural, masculine, feminine or neuter as required by context.

WITNESSETH, That whereas the Grantor is indebted to the Beneficiary in the principal sum of _____

_____ Dollars ($_____),
as evidenced by a Promissory Note of even date herewith, the terms of which are incorporated herein by reference. The final due date for payments of said Promissory Note, if not sooner paid, is_____, 20___.

NC Bar Association Form No. 5 © 1976, Revised © September 1985, 2002   + James Williams & Co., Inc.
Printed by Agreement with the NC Bar Association - 1981   www.JamesWilliams.com

Figure 12.6   North Carolina Deed of Trust (continued)

NOW, THEREFORE, as security for said indebtedness, advancements and other sums expended by Beneficiary pursuant to this Deed of Trust and costs of collection (including attorneys fees as provided in the Promissory Note) and other valuable consideration, the receipt of which is hereby acknowledged, the Grantor has bargained, sold, given and conveyed and does by these presents bargain, sell, give, grant and convey to said Trustee, his heirs, or successors, and assigns, the parcel(s) of land situated in the City of _____, _____ Township, _____ County, North Carolina, (the "Premises") and more particularly described as follows:

TO HAVE AND TO HOLD said Premises with all privileges and appurtenances thereunto belonging, to said Trustee, his heirs, successors, and assigns forever, upon the trusts, terms and conditions, and for the uses hereinafter set forth.

If the Grantor shall pay the Note secured hereby in accordance with its terms, together with interest thereon, and any renewals or extensions thereof in whole or in part, all other sums secured hereby and shall comply with all of the covenants, terms and conditions of this Deed of Trust, then this conveyance shall be null and void and may be canceled of record at the request and the expense of the Grantor.

If, however, there shall be any default (a) in the payment of any sums due under the Note, this Deed of Trust or any other instrument securing the Note and such default is not cured within ten (10) days from the due date, or (b) if there shall be default in any of the other covenants, terms or conditions of the Note secured hereby, or any failure or neglect to comply with the covenants, terms or conditions contained in this Deed of Trust or any other instrument securing the Note and such default is not cured within fifteen (15) days after written notice, then and in any of such events, without further notice, it shall be lawful for and the duty of the Trustee, upon request of the Beneficiary, to sell the land herein conveyed at public auction for cash, after having first giving such notice of hearing as to commencement of foreclosure proceedings and obtained such findings or leave of court as may then be required by law and giving such notice and advertising the time and place of such sale in such manner as may then be provided by law, and upon such and any resales and upon compliance with the law then relating to foreclosure proceedings under power of sale to convey title to the purchaser in as full and ample manner as the Trustee is empowered. The Trustee shall be authorized to retain an attorney to represent him in such proceedings.

The proceeds of the Sale shall after the Trustee retains his commission, together with reasonable attorneys fees incurred by the Trustee in such proceedings, be applied to the costs of sale, including but not limited to, costs of collection, taxes, assessments, costs of recording, service fees and incidental expenditures, the amount due on the Note hereby secured and advancements and other sums expended by the Beneficiary according to the provisions hereof and otherwise as required by the then existing law relating to foreclosures. The Trustee's commission shall be five percent (5%) of the gross proceeds of the sale or the minimum sum of $_____ whichever is greater, for a completed foreclosure. In the event foreclosure is commenced, but not completed, the Grantor shall pay all expenses incurred by Trustee, including reasonable attorneys fees, and a partial commission computed on five per cent (5%) of the outstanding indebtedness or the above stated minimum sum, whichever is greater, in accordance with the following schedule, to-wit: one-fourth (¼) thereof before the Trustee issues a notice of hearing on the right to foreclosure; one-half (½) thereof after issuance of said notice, three-fourths (¾) thereof after such hearing; and the greater of the full commission or minimum sum after the initial sale.

And the said Grantor does hereby covenant and agree with the Trustee as follows:

1. INSURANCE. Grantor shall keep all improvements on said land, now or hereafter erected, constantly insured for the benefit of the Beneficiary against loss by fire, windstorm and such other casualties and contingencies, in such manner and in such companies and for such amounts, not less than that amount necessary to pay the sum secured by this Deed of Trust, and as may be satisfactory to the Beneficiary. Grantor shall purchase such insurance, pay all premiums therefor, and shall deliver to Beneficiary such policies along with evidence of premium payments as long as the Note secured hereby remains unpaid. If Grantor fails to purchase such insurance, pay premiums therefor or deliver said policies along with evidence of payment of premiums thereon, then Beneficiary, at his option, may purchase such insurance. Such amounts paid by Beneficiary shall be added to the principal of the Note secured by this Deed of Trust, and shall be due and payable upon demand of Beneficiary. All proceeds from any insurance so maintained shall at the option of Beneficiary be applied to the debt secured hereby and if payable in installments, applied in the inverse order of maturity of such installments or to the repair or reconstruction of any improvements located upon the Property.

2. TAXES, ASSESSMENTS, CHARGES. Grantor shall pay all taxes, assessments and charges as may be lawfully levied against said Premises within thirty (30) days after the same shall become due. In the event that Grantor fails to so pay all taxes, assessments and charges as herein required, then Beneficiary, at his option, may pay the same and the amounts so paid shall be added to the principal of the Note secured by this Deed of Trust, and shall be due and payable upon demand of Beneficiary.

3. ASSIGNMENTS OF RENTS AND PROFITS. Grantor assigns to Beneficiary, in the event of default, all rents and profits from the land and any improvements thereon, and authorizes Beneficiary to enter upon and take possession of such land and improvements, to rent same, at any reasonable rate of rent determined by Beneficiary, and after deducting from any such rents the cost of reletting and collection, to apply the remainder to the debt secured hereby.

4. PARTIAL RELEASE. Grantor shall not be entitled to the partial release of any of the above described property unless a specific provision providing therefor is included in this Deed of Trust. In the event a partial release provision is included in this Deed of Trust, Grantor must strictly comply with the terms thereof. Notwithstanding anything herein contained, Grantor shall not be

NC Bar Association Form No. 5 © 1976, Revised © September 1985, 2002   + James Williams & Co., Inc.
Printed by Agreement with the NC Bar Association - 1981   www.JamesWilliams.com

To see the full form, please go to Appendix C.

a third party without the permission of the borrower. The lender endorses the note to the third party and also executes an *assignment of mortgage.* The assignee becomes the new owner of the debt and security instrument with all the rights and obligations of the original lender. This assignment must be recorded. On payment in full, or satisfaction of the debt, the assignee is required to execute the satisfaction, or release, of the security instrument (discussed earlier). In the event of a foreclosure, the assignee is required to file the suit. However, the note and mortgage cannot be assigned if the loan is in default.

When a borrower defaults in making payments or fulfilling any of the obligations set forth in the mortgage or deed of trust, the lender can enforce its rights through a **foreclosure.** Such a default may include failure to make payments, destruction of all or part of the property or failure to pay insurance or taxes. Foreclosure is the process of selling the mortgaged real estate to repay the debt from the proceeds of the sale. The foreclosure procedure brings the rights of the parties and all junior lienholders to a conclusion and passes title in the subject property to the highest acceptable bidder at a foreclosure sale. Property thus sold *is free of the mortgage and all junior liens,* but it still may have other encumbrances. Note that the purpose of foreclosure is to cut off the borrower's equity of redemption rights (discussed below).

Methods of foreclosure.

Three general types of foreclosure proceedings exist— judicial, nonjudicial and strict foreclosure. The specific provisions of each method vary from state to state.

1. **Judicial foreclosure.** Mortgages are foreclosed through a court process called *judicial foreclosure.* A judicial foreclosure proceeding provides that the property pledged as security may be sold by court order after the mortgagee has given sufficient public notice. On a borrower's default, the lender may *accelerate* the due date of all remaining monthly payments. The lender's lawyer can then file a suit to foreclose the lien. On presentation of the facts in court, the property is ordered sold. A public sale is advertised and held, and the real estate is sold to the highest acceptable bidder. The new owner receives title to the property by means of a sheriff's deed.

2. **Nonjudicial foreclosure.** A deed of trust does not have to be foreclosed through a court action, so this type of foreclosure is called a *nonjudicial foreclosure* or *foreclosure under power of sale.* Nonjudicial foreclosure is made possible by the *power-of-sale clause* that is found in the deed of trust. The power-of-sale clause gives the trustee the power to sell the property and use the proceeds to repay the debt. (Note that a minihearing is required before the clerk of the court; otherwise, the property cannot be sold.)

   To institute a nonjudicial foreclosure, the trustee or lender must record a notice of default at the county register of deeds office within a designated time period to give notice to the public of the intended auction. Generally, this official notice is accompanied by advertisements published in local newspapers that state the total amount due and the date of the public sale. The trustee then conducts the sale and transfers title to the high bidder by means of a trustee's deed.

3. **Strict foreclosure.** Although the judicial and nonjudicial foreclosure procedures are the prevalent practices today, in a few states it is still

possible for a lender to acquire the mortgaged property by a strict foreclosure process. After appropriate notice has been given to the delinquent borrower and the proper papers have been prepared and filed, the court establishes a specific time period during which the balance of the defaulted debt must be paid in full. If this is not done, the court usually awards full legal title to the lender. *Strict foreclosure is not used in North Carolina.*

Deed in lieu of foreclosure. An alternative to foreclosure is for the lender to accept, or "buy," a *deed in lieu of foreclosure* from the borrower. This is sometimes known as a *friendly foreclosure* because it is accomplished by agreement rather than by civil action. The major disadvantage to this manner of default settlement is that the mortgagee takes the real estate subject to all junior liens; foreclosure eliminates all such liens.

Distribution of proceeds. After the property is sold at the foreclosure sale, the proceeds are distributed in the following order:

1. To pay all costs of the sale, including court costs or trustee fees, legal fees, advertising fees, etc.
2. To pay any outstanding real and personal property taxes or assessments
3. To pay the mortgage or deed of trust debt (assuming this debt has first priority over any other liens)
4. To pay off any other liens in order of priority
5. To pay any surplus to the borrower

Redemption. Defaulting borrowers usually have a chance to redeem their property. In most such cases, redemption takes one of two forms—equitable redemption or statutory redemption.

Historically, the *right of redemption* (also called the *equity of redemption*) is inherited from the old common-law proceedings in which the foreclosure sale ended the *equitable right of redemption.* Carried over to statutory law, this concept provides that if, during the course of a foreclosure proceeding but before the *confirmation of the foreclosure sale,* the borrower pays the lender the total amount due, plus costs, the debt is reinstated as before. The borrower who redeems will be required to repay the accelerated loan in full (see Figure 12.7).

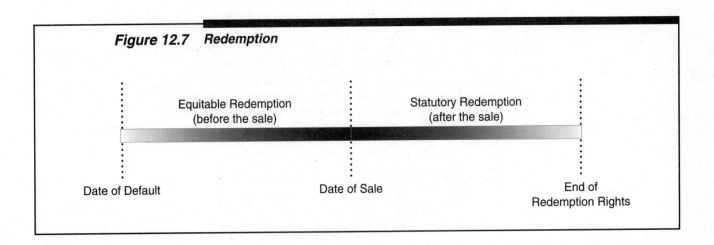

Figure 12.7 **Redemption**

Equitable Redemption
(before the sale)

Statutory Redemption
(after the sale)

Date of Default

Date of Sale

End of
Redemption Rights

The second chance to redeem the property comes after the sale. During this statutory redemption period, a mortgagor can try to raise the necessary funds to redeem the property. In the ten days after the foreclosure sale, the borrower, or others, can submit an "upset bid," a bid to purchase the property for an amount that exceeds the foreclosure sale price by a specific margin. In effect, the borrower forces a resale of the foreclosure property. Note that if the upset bid is accepted, the ten-day redemption period begins again, and someone else may submit an upset bid during that period. If another upset bid is not submitted, the foreclosure sale becomes final and the borrower's right to redeem the property is terminated.

Deficiency judgment. If the foreclosure sale of the real estate secured by a mortgage or trust deed does not produce a sufficient sales price to pay the loan balance in full after deducting expenses and accrued unpaid interest, the lender may be entitled to a *personal judgment* against the maker of the note for the unpaid balance. Such a judgment is called a **deficiency judgment.** It also may be obtained against any endorsers or guarantors of the note and any owners of the mortgaged property who may have assumed the debt by written agreement. If any surplus proceeds from the foreclosure sale exist after real estate taxes, the debt and all junior liens (second mortgage, mechanics' liens and so on) are paid off and expenses and interest are deducted, these proceeds are paid to the borrower. Deficiency judgments are prohibited in certain cases, such as when a purchase-money deed of trust (seller financing) is used. If the seller is holding a purchase-money mortgage/deed of trust, the seller has a special priority in lien payoffs in the foreclosure.

Buying Subject to or Assuming a Seller's Mortgage

When a person purchases real estate that is subject to an outstanding mortgage or deed of trust, the buyer may take the property in one of two ways. The property may be purchased subject to the mortgage, or the buyer may *assume* the mortgage and agree to pay the debt. This technical distinction becomes important if the buyer defaults and the mortgage or deed of trust is foreclosed.

When the property is sold *subject to* the mortgage, the buyer will not be personally obligated to pay the debt in full. The buyer takes title to the real estate knowing that he or she must make payments on the existing loan. On default, the lender forecloses and the property is sold by court order to pay the debt. If the sale does not pay off the entire debt, the purchaser is not liable for the difference. In some circumstances, however, the original seller might continue to be liable, if sale proceeds do not cover the entire debt.

In contrast, a buyer who purchases the property and assumes the seller's debt becomes personally obligated for the payment of the entire debt. If the mortgage is foreclosed and the court sale does not bring enough money to pay the debt in full, a deficiency judgment against the assumptor and the original borrower may be obtained for the unpaid balance of the note. If the original borrower has been released by the assumptor, only the assumptor is liable.

For Example 1. When Jennifer bought her house a short time ago, interest rates were very low. Now Jennifer has been unexpectedly transferred out of the country and needs to sell the house quickly. Because interest rates have risen dramatically since the time of Jennifer's loan, buyers may be attracted by the prospect of assuming her mortgage. Clearly, if a buyer were to take out a mortgage now, the rate would be higher and the cost of home ownership would be increased. By assuming an existing loan with a more favorable interest rate, a buyer can save money.

2. Dylan purchased his house when interest rates were high. In the short time since then, rates have fallen precipitously. If Dylan must sell quickly, he may find that buyers are not interested in assuming a high-interest mortgage. A buyer might purchase Dylan's property subject to the existing mortgage. That is, the buyer would purchase Dylan's equity; Dylan still would be liable for the mortgage, and the bank could foreclose on the property to recover a default. If the foreclosure sale failed to satisfy the debt, Dylan would be liable for the shortfall.

In many cases, a mortgage loan may not be assumed without lender approval. The lending institution requires the assumptor to qualify financially, and many lending institutions charge a transfer fee to cover the costs of changing the records. This charge is usually paid by the purchaser.

SUMMARY

Real estate loans provide the principal source of financing for real estate operations. After a lending institution has received, investigated and approved a loan application, it issues a commitment to make the loan. The borrower is required to execute a note, agreeing to repay the debt, and a mortgage or deed of trust, which secures the note. The security instrument is recorded to give notice to the world of the lender's interest in the property.

Two types of security instruments exist: (1) a mortgage, which involves a borrower (the mortgagor) and a lender (the mortgagee), and (2) a deed of trust, which involves a borrower (the grantor), a lender (the beneficiary) and an independent third party (the trustee). The deed of trust conveys legal title to the property to the trustee, who has the power to sell the property on behalf of the lender if the borrower defaults on the loan.

The note's payment in full entitles the borrower to a satisfaction, or release, of mortgage, which is recorded to clear the lien from the public records. Default by the borrower may result in acceleration of payments, a foreclosure sale and loss of title. Three types of foreclosure sales exist: judicial foreclosure, nonjudicial foreclosure and strict foreclosure.

Questions

1. North Carolina is characterized as a(n)
   a. lien theory state.
   b. title theory state.
   c. intermediate theory state.
   d. state without a theory.

2. Which of the following statements is true of a prepayment penalty in a mortgage instrument?
   a. It usually penalizes early payment of the mortgage.
   b. It is prohibited in all residential and commercial mortgage loans in North Carolina.
   c. It can never be waived, even if the buyer's mortgage is with the same lender as the seller's.
   d. It penalizes the lender when the mortgagor pays off the loan early.

3. Which of the following statements best describes a deed of trust?
   a. It is evidence of a debt.
   b. It uses real estate as security for the repayment of a debt.
   c. It is sometimes called a *promissory note*.
   d. It is evidence of both legal and equitable title.

4. A charge of three discount points on a $120,000 loan is
   a. $450.
   b. $116,400.
   c. $4,500.
   d. $3,600.

5. The person who obtains a real estate loan by signing a deed of trust is called the
   I. trustee.
   II. grantor.
   III. mortgagor.
     a. I only
     b. II only
     c. I and III only
     d. I and II only

6. The borrower under a mortgage is known as the
   a. vendee.
   b. mortgagee.
   c. mortgagor.
   d. beneficiary.

7. Laws that limit the amount of interest that can be charged to the borrower are called
   a. truth-in-lending laws.
   b. usury laws.
   c. the statute of frauds.
   d. RESPA legislation.

8. If a borrower pays $2,700 for points on a $90,000 loan, how many points is the lender charging for this loan?
   a. Two
   b. Three
   c. Five
   d. Six

9. Before the foreclosure sale, the borrower who has defaulted on the loan seeks to pay off the debt plus any accrued interest and costs under the right of
   a. equitable redemption.
   b. defeasance.
   c. usury.
   d. statutory right of redemption.

10. The clause in a note that gives the lender the right to demand that all future installments become due on default is the
    a. escalation clause.
    b. defeasance clause.
    c. alienation clause.
    d. acceleration clause.

11. Which of the following allows a lender to proceed to a foreclosure sale without having to go to court first?
    I. Waiver of redemption right
    II. Power of sale
    III. Alienation clause
      a. I only
      b. II only
      c. III only
      d. I or III only

12. Pledging property for a loan without giving up possession is best described as
    a. hypothecation.
    b. defeasance.
    c. alienation.
    d. novation.

13. Discount points on a mortgage are computed as a percentage of the
    a. selling price.
    b. amount borrowed.
    c. closing costs.
    d. down payment.

14. The clause in a deed of trust that allows the lender to accelerate the loan when the property is transferred is called the
    a. acceleration clause.
    b. prepayment penalty clause.
    c. due-on-sale clause.
    d. defeasance clause.

15. Proceeds from a foreclosure sale first pay
    a. mortgages in the order of recordation.
    b. outstanding property taxes.
    c. junior liens in the order of recordation.
    d. the cost of the sale.

16. In a deed in lieu of foreclosure situation
    a. the lender is obligated to accept the deed.
    b. the lender takes the real estate subject to all junior liens.
    c. a civil action is required.
    d. the lender is eager to become a homeowner.

17. A deficiency judgment on a promissory note may be granted to a
    a. mortgagor.
    b. trustor.
    c. trustee.
    d. mortgagee.

18. Which of the following statements is(are) true if a buyer purchases property subject to the seller's loan and then defaults on the loan?
    I. The buyer is personally liable for the underlying debt.
    II. The seller remains personally liable for the underlying debt.
    a. I only
    b. II only
    c. Both I and II
    d. Neither I nor II

19. A term loan requires that the borrower pay
    a. only the interest during the loan term.
    b. both principal and interest during the loan term.
    c. only the principal during the loan term.
    d. increasing amounts of principal during the loan term.

20. A mortgage that calls for a substantially larger than normal payment at the end of the loan term is what type of loan?
    a. Term
    b. Graduated payment
    c. Balloon
    d. Adjustable rate

21. Interest charges by the lender on a fixed-rate conventional loan are
    a. subject to periodic changes.
    b. almost always simple interest.
    c. usually paid in advance.
    d. All of the above

22. A deficiency judgment is
    a. a court decision declaring that a debt is excused if a foreclosure sale does not satisfy the debt.
    b. a judgment for the balance owing on a debt after the security has been sold to apply toward the debt.
    c. a specific lien.
    d. a general lien with a life of five years.

23. Which of the following types of mortgages features increasing payments with the increases applied directly to the principal?
    a. Shared appreciation
    b. Growing equity
    c. Adjustable rate
    d. Graduated payment

24. A promissory note must be signed by the
    I. borrower.
    II. lender.
    a. I only
    b. II only
    c. Both I and II
    d. Neither I nor II

25. A deed of trust is a
    a. two-party instrument.
    b. three-party instrument.
    c. promissory note.
    d. security instrument that requires a nonjudicial foreclosure.

26. A buyer has purchased a home under an agreement that made the buyer personally obligated to continue making payments under the seller's existing mortgage. If the buyer defaults and the court sale does not satisfy the debt, the buyer will be liable for making up the difference. The buyer has
    a. purchased the home subject to the seller's mortgage.
    b. assumed the seller's mortgage.
    c. benefited from the alienation clause in the seller's mortgage.
    d. benefited from the defeasance clause in the seller's mortgage.

13 Real Estate Financing: Practices

LEARNING OBJECTIVES

When you've finished reading this chapter, you should be able to

- **define** the prevailing criteria for (1) conventional, (2) FHA-insured and (3) VA-guaranteed mortgage loans.

- **identify** other types of financing techniques and special purpose loans.

- **describe** how the secondary mortgage market operates, including the three major agencies, and federal legislation that affects mortgage lending practices.

- **explain** residential lending practices and procedures.

- **define** these *key terms:*

blanket mortgage	open-end mortgage	reverse-annuity
buydown	package loan	mortgage (RAM)
construction loan	primary mortgage	Rural Economic and
conventional loan	market	Community Develop-
Fannie Mae (FNMA)	private mortgage	ment Services
FHA loan	insurance (PMI)	secondary mortgage
Freddie Mac (FHLMC)	purchase-money	market
Ginnie Mae (GNMA)	mortgage	Truth-in-Lending Act
home equity loan	Regulation Z	VA loan
loan-to-value ratio		wraparound loan

TYPES OF MORTGAGES (MORTGAGE LOANS)

The various types of mortgage loans that are available today can be divided roughly into conventional loans and government-sponsored loans.

Conventional Loans   A **conventional loan** is a loan that is not "backed"—that is, insured or guaranteed— by any government agency. In other words, the lender bears all the risk of borrower default when making a conventional loan. Conventional loans are viewed as the most secure loans because their loan-to-value (LTV) ratios are lowest. Mortgage loans are generally classified based on their **loan-to-value ratios.** The LTV is the ratio of debt to value of the property. Value is the sales price or the appraised value, whichever is less. The *lower* the ratio of debt to value, the *higher* the down payment by the borrower. For the lender, the higher down payment means a more secure loan, which minimizes the lender's risk. For instance, if a property is worth $100,000, an 80 percent loan would equal $80,000, and the borrower would make a $20,000 down payment.

Private mortgage insurance. One way a borrower can obtain a mortgage loan with a smaller down payment is under a **private mortgage insurance (PMI)** program. Because the LTV ratio is higher than for other conventional loans, the lender requires additional security to minimize its risk. The borrower purchases insurance from a PMI company as additional security to insure the lender against borrower default. LTVs of up to 95 percent of the appraised value of the property are possible with PMI.

PMI protects a certain percentage of a loan, usually 25 to 30 percent, against borrower default. Normally, the borrower is charged a fee for the first year's premium at closing and a monthly fee while the insurance is in force. Other methods of payment are available, however; the premium may be financed or the fee at closing may be waived in exchange for slightly higher monthly payments. When a borrower has limited funds for investment, these alternative methods of reducing closing costs are very important. Because only a portion of the loan is insured, once the loan is repaid to a certain level (usually 75 or 80 percent of the value of the property), the lender may agree to allow the borrower to terminate the coverage. Practices for termination vary from lender to lender.

In Practice

Effective in July 1999, a federal law required that PMI automatically terminate if a borrower

- has accumulated at least 22 percent equity in the home and
- is current on mortgage payments.

Under the law, a borrower with a good payment history may request that PMI be canceled when he or she has built up equity equal to 20 percent of the purchase price or the appraised value. Lenders are required by the law to inform borrowers of their right to cancel PMI. Before this law was enacted, lenders could (and often did) continue to require monthly PMI payments long after borrowers had built up substantial equity in their homes and the lender no longer risked a loss from the borrower's default.

FHA-Insured Loans

The Federal Housing Administration (FHA) was created in 1934 under the *National Housing Act* to encourage improvement in housing standards and conditions, provide an adequate home-financing system through insurance of housing credit and exert a stabilizing influence on the mortgage market. The FHA was the government's response to the lack of housing, the excessive foreclosures and the collapsed building industry that occurred during the Great Depression.

MATH CONCEPTS

Determining LTV

If a property has an appraised value of $100,000, secured by a $90,000 loan, the LTV is 90 percent:

$$\$90,000 \div \$100,000 = .90, \text{ or } 90\%$$

The FHA, which operates under the Department of Housing and Urban Development (HUD), neither builds homes nor lends money. Rather, *it insures loans on real property made by approved lending institutions.* The FHA does not insure property; it insures lenders against loss in case of borrower default. The common term **FHA loan,** then, refers not to a loan that is made by the agency but to a loan that is insured by it. FHA loans are made by FHA-approved lenders, which are free to set the interest rates on the loans.

The most popular FHA program is Title II, Section 203(b), fixed interest rate loans for 10 to 30 years on one- to four-family residences. The FHA does not fix interest rates on these loans. These rates can be lower than those on conventional loans because the protection of FHA mortgage insurance makes them of less risk to lenders. Technical requirements established under congressional authority must be met before the FHA will issue the insurance. Three of these requirements are as follows:

1. In addition to paying interest, the borrower pays a *one-time mortgage insurance premium for the FHA insurance.* This amount (currently 2 percent of the loan amount) may be paid at closing by the borrower or someone else, or it may be added to the loan amount. (For example, on a $100,000 loan, the one-time premium would equal $2,000, to be either paid in cash at closing or added to the loan amount.) Also, the borrower is charged an annual premium of ½ of 1 percent of the loan amount.
2. The mortgaged real estate must be appraised by an *approved FHA appraiser.* The loan amount generally cannot exceed either of the following: (1) 98.75 percent for loans over $50,000 (for loans less than $50,000, the buyer must contribute 3 percent of the sales price to the downpayment and closing costs) or (2) 97.75 percent of the sales price or appraised value, whichever is less. Note that if the purchase price exceeds the FHA-appraised value, the buyer may pay the difference in cash as part of the down payment. In addition, the FHA has set maximum loan amounts for various regions of the country. Contact your local FHA office for such amounts in your area. FHA regulations require that both buyer and seller sign a statement indicating that they have examined the FHA appraisal.
3. The FHA regulations set standards for type and construction of buildings, quality of neighborhood and credit requirements for borrowers.

Prepayment privileges. When a mortgage loan is insured by the FHA and the real estate given as security is a single-family dwelling or an apartment building with no more than four units, the borrower has the privilege of prepaying the debt without penalty. On the first day of any month before the loan matures, the borrower may pay the entire debt or an amount equal to one or more monthly payments on the principal. The borrower must give the lender written notice of intention to exercise this privilege at least 30 days beforehand; otherwise, the lender has the option of charging up to 30 days' interest in lieu of such notification.

Assumption rules. The assumption rules for FHA-insured loans vary, depending on the date that the loan was originated. For example:

- Loans originated prior to December 1986 generally have no restriction on their assumption. Anyone can assume these loans with no qualifications.
- For loans originated between December 1, 1986, and December 15, 1989, a creditworthiness review of the person proposing to assume is required. If the original loan was for the purchase of a principal residence, this review is required during the first 12 months of the loan's existence. If the original loan was for the purchase of an investment property, the review is required during the first 24 months of the loan. After these time periods have elapsed, anyone can assume these loans with no qualifications.
- For loans originated December 15, 1989, and thereafter, no assumptions are allowed without complete buyer qualification, and investor loans are no longer allowed. All FHA loans made under the 203(b) program are for owner-occupied properties only.

Other FHA loan programs. In addition to loans made under Title II, Section 203(b), FHA loans are granted under the following programs:

- *Title I:* Home improvement loans are covered under this title. Such loans are for relatively low amounts and have repayment terms of no longer than 7 years and 32 days.
- *Title II, Section 234:* Loans made to purchase condominiums are covered under this program, which in most respects is similar to the basic 203(b) program.
- *Title II, Section 245:* Graduated payment mortgages, as discussed in Chapter 12, are allowed under this program. Depending on interest rates, the LTV ratio of such loans might range from 87 to 93 percent.
- *Title II, Section 251:* Adjustable-rate mortgages (ARMs) are allowed under this program. The interest rate cannot change more than 1 percent per year or more than 5 percent over the life of the loan.

Points. The lender of an FHA-insured loan can charge discount points in addition to a 1 percent loan origination fee. The payment of points is a matter of negotiation between the seller and the buyer. However, if the seller pays more than 6 percent of the costs normally paid by the buyer (such as discount points, the loan origination fee, the mortgage insurance premium, buydown fees, prepaid items, impound or escrow amounts and the like), the lender is to treat such payments as sales concessions, and the price of the property for purposes of the loan must be reduced.

Interest rates. Neither HUD nor the FHA regulates the interest rates paid on FHA-insured loans. The rates fluctuate from lender to lender, and the buyer is responsible for obtaining the lowest interest rate possible.

Lead paint notification. HUD now requires that a lead paint notification form be given to residential buyers to sign on or before the date the purchaser executes the sales contract. The FHA requires that the lender be provided with a copy of the notification form at the time of the loan application (see Figure 13.1). In the event the purchaser does not receive and sign the form on or before the date the sales contract is executed, the contract must be reexecuted. This new HUD guideline is required for FHA loans on homes built prior to 1978.

Figure 13.1 Disclosure of Lead-Based Paint and Lead-Based Paint Hazards

LEAD-BASED PAINT OR LEAD-BASED PAINT HAZARD ADDENDUM

It is a condition of this contract that, until midnight of _____ , Buyer shall have the right to obtain a risk assessment or inspection of the Property for the presence of lead-based paint and/or lead-based paint hazards* at Buyer's expense. This contingency will terminate at that time unless Buyer or Buyer's agent delivers to the Seller or Seller's agent a written inspection and/or risk assessment report listing the specific existing deficiencies and corrections needed, if any. If any corrections are necessary, Seller shall have the option of (i) completing them, (ii) providing for their completion, or (iii) refusing to complete them. If Seller elects not to complete or provide for completion of the corrections, then Buyer shall have the option of (iv) accepting the Property in its present condition, or (v) terminating this contract, in which case all earnest monies shall be refunded to Buyer. Buyer may waive the right to obtain a risk assessment or inspection of the Property for the presence of lead-based paint and/or lead based paint hazards at any time without cause.

*Intact lead-based paint that is in good condition is not necessarily a hazard. See EPA pamphlet "Protect Your Family From Lead in Your Home" for more information.

Disclosure of Information on Lead-Based Paint and Lead-Based Paint Hazards

Lead Warning Statement
Every Buyer of any interest in residential real property on which a residential dwelling was built prior to 1978 is notified that such property may present exposure to lead from lead-based paint that may place young children at risk of developing lead poisoning. Lead poisoning in young children may produce permanent neurological damage, including learning disabilities, reduced intelligence quotient, behavioral problems, and impaired memory. Lead poisoning also poses a particular risk to pregnant women. The Seller of any interest in residential real property is required to provide the Buyer with any information on lead-based paint hazards from risk assessments or inspections in the Seller's possession and notify the Buyer of any known lead-based paint hazards. A risk assessment or inspection for possible lead-based paint hazards is recommended prior to purchase.

Seller's Disclosure (initial)
_____ (a) Presence of lead-based paint and/or lead-based paint hazards (check one below):
❑ Known lead-based paint and/or lead-based paint hazards are present in the housing (explain).
_____
_____

❑ Seller has no knowledge of lead-based paint and/or lead-based paint hazards in the housing.
_____ (b) Records and reports available to the Seller (check one below):
❑ Seller has provided the Buyer with all available records and reports pertaining to lead-based paint and/or lead-based paint hazards in the housing (list documents below).
_____
_____

❑ Seller has no reports or records pertaining to lead-based paint and/or lead-based paint hazards in the housing.

Buyer's Acknowledgment (initial)
_____ (c) Buyer has received copies of all information listed above.
_____ (d) Buyer has received the pamphlet *Protect Your Family from Lead in Your Home.*
_____ (e) Buyer has (check one below):
❑ Received a 10-day opportunity (or mutually agreed upon period) to conduct a risk assessment or inspection for the presence of lead-based paint and/or lead-based paint hazards; or
❑ Waived the opportunity to conduct a risk assessment or inspection for the presence of lead-based paint and/or lead-based paint hazards.

Agent's Acknowledgment (initial)
_____ (f) Agent has informed the Seller of the Seller's obligations under 42 U.S.C. 4582(d) and is aware of his/her responsibility to ensure compliance.

Certification of Accuracy
The following parties have reviewed the information above and certify, to the best of their knowledge, that the information provided by the signatory is true and accurate.
Buyer: _____ (SEAL) Date _____
Buyer: _____ (SEAL) Date _____
Agent: _____ Date _____
Seller: _____ (SEAL) Date _____
Seller: _____ (SEAL) Date _____
Agent: _____ Date _____

VA-Guaranteed (GI) Loans

Under the *Servicemen's Readjustment Act of 1944* and subsequent federal legislation, the Department of Veterans Affairs (VA) is authorized to guarantee loans to purchase or construct homes for eligible veterans—those who have served a minimum of 181 days active service since September 16, 1940 (90 days for veterans of World War II, the Korean War and the Vietnam conflict; two full years for those enlisting for the first time after September 7, 1980). The VA also guarantees loans to purchase mobile homes and plots on which to place them. GI loans assist veterans in financing the purchase of homes with little or no down payment at comparatively low interest rates. From time to time, the VA issues rules and regulations setting forth the qualifications, limitations and conditions under which a loan may be guaranteed. (Table 13.1 compares VA and FHA loan programs.)

Like the term *FHA loan, VA loan* is something of a misnomer. Normally, the VA does not lend money itself; it guarantees loans made by lending institutions approved by the agency. The term **VA loan,** then, refers not to a loan that is made by the agency but to one that is guaranteed by it.

There is no VA limit on the amount of the loan a veteran can obtain; this is determined by the lender. The VA does, however, limit the amount of the loan that it will guarantee for the purchase, construction, repair or alteration of a house, condominium or farm residence.

Note that the maximum amount of the guarantee refers to the amount the lender would receive from the VA in case of default and foreclosure if the sale did not bring enough to cover the outstanding balance.

To determine what portion of a mortgage loan the VA will guarantee, the veteran must apply for a *certificate of eligibility.* This certificate does not mean that the veteran will automatically receive a mortgage. It merely sets forth the maximum guarantee the veteran is entitled to.

The VA also will issue a *certificate of reasonable value (CRV)* for the property being purchased, stating its current market value based on a VA-approved appraisal. The CRV places a ceiling on the amount of a VA loan allowed for the property; if the purchase price is greater than the amount cited in the CRV, the veteran may pay the difference in cash or terminate the purchase agreement without penalty. Also, the seller may agree to lower the purchase price to the amount named in the CRV, or both the buyer and the seller may renegotiate the sale and each make a concession on the price.

Ordinarily, a veteran obtains a loan from a VA-approved lending institution; only in locations (such as isolated rural areas) where financing is not reasonably available does the VA actually lend money. The VA does not require a down payment. Although the maximum VA guarantee is currently $50,750, in practice the veteran may be able to obtain a 100 percent loan if the appraised valuation of the property is $203,000 or less and the veteran is entitled to the full $50,750 guarantee.

Maximum loan terms are 30 years for one-family to four-family dwellings and 40 years for farms. Residential property (up to a four-family unit) purchased with a VA loan must be owner-occupied. Interest rates are freely negotiable between the lender and the borrower.

Table 13.1   *Comparison of FHA and VA Loan Programs*

Federal Housing Administration	Department of Veterans Affairs
1. Financing is available to veterans and nonveterans.	1. Financing available only to veterans and certain unremarried widows and widowers.
2. Financing programs are for owner-occupied (1-family to 4-family), residential dwellings.	2. Financing is limited to owner-occupied residential (1-family to 4-family) dwellings; must sign occupancy certificate on two separate occasions.
3. Requires a larger down payment than VA.	
4. Different valuation methods; like VA, there are prescribed valuation procedures for the approved appraisers to follow.	3. Normally does not require down payment.
	4. Methods of valuation differ. VA issues a certificate of reasonable value (CRV).
5. FHA valuation sets the maximum loan FHA will insure but does not limit the sales price.	5. With regard to home loans, the law requires that the VA loan not exceed the appraised value of the home.
6. No prepayment penalty.	6. No prepayment penalty.
7. On default foreclosure and claim, the FHA lender usually gets U.S. debentures.	7. Following default, foreclosure and claim, the lender usually receives cash (if VA elects to take the house).
8. Insures the loan by way of mutual mortgage insurance; premiums paid by buyer or seller. If by buyer, may be paid in cash or added to note.	8. Guarantees loans according to a sliding scale.
9. No secondary financing is permitted until after closing.	9. Secondary financing is permitted in exceptional cases.
10. Buyer pays a 1 percent loan origination fee.	10. Buyer may pay discount points but cannot finance them in the loan; he or she can pay a 1 percent loan origination fee.
11. Loans made prior to 12/1/86 are fully assumable; seller remains liable until the loan is paid off. Loans made between 12/1/86 and 12/15/89 are fully assumable after 12 months on owner-occupied loans; seller remains liable for 5 years. Loans made since 12/15/89 require prior approval of assumptor; seller is released from liability.	11. A funding fee from 1.25 to 3.00 percent must be paid to VA in addition to other fees. It may be paid by the seller or buyer. If paid by the buyer, it may be paid in cash or added to the note. (Note: Cannot exceed $203,000)
	12. VA loan can be assumed by nonveteran without VA approval for loans made prior to 3/1/88; otherwise, approval is required.
	13. For loans originated after 3/1/88, release of liability is automatic if VA approves the assumption.

Assumption rules. VA loans made prior to March 1, 1988, remain freely assumable, but an assumption processing fee is charged. All loans made on or after that date require approval of the buyer and an assumption agreement. Even when a VA loan is assumed, the original veteran borrower remains personally liable for the repayment of the loan unless the VA approves a *release of liability.*

To obtain a release of liability, the veteran must meet three requirements. First, the loan must be up-to-date (there are no past-due payments). Second, the assumptor must have sufficient income and a good enough credit history to qualify for the loan. Third, the assumptor must agree to assume the veteran's obligation for the loan. Note that any release of liability issued by the VA does not release the veteran's liability to the lender. This must be obtained separately from the lender.

Restoration of entitlement. Even though a veteran has used his or her entitlement to purchase a home once, he or she still may be eligible for another VA loan. If the veteran is selling his or her current home, his or her entitlement can be restored. For instance, if the first house is sold and the original VA loan is paid off, the veteran's entitlement will be restored and the veteran will be eligible for another VA home loan that can be used to purchase a replacement home. A veteran's entitlement also can be restored if the veteran sells the home to another veteran who is willing to assume the existing loan and substitute his or her entitlement for the entitlement of the selling veteran.

Prepayment. As with an FHA loan, the borrower under a VA loan can prepay the debt at any time without penalty.

Points. Points are payable by either the veteran borrower or the seller. There is also a funding fee, which the veteran pays the VA at closing. The funding fee is a sliding fee, slated to go up periodically. The VA funding fee is currently 2 percent. In addition to the existing two categories—veterans and National Guard and Reservists—the new requirement includes a third category—veterans who use their entitlement for additional loans, excluding interest rate reduction refinancing loans.

Funding fees are related to down payments as follows:

Down Payment	Veterans	National Guard and Reservists	Veterans with Additional Loans
No down payment	2.00%	2.75%	3.00%
Minimum 5% down payment	1.50%	2.25%	1.50%
10% or higher down payment	1.25%	2.00%	1.25%

VA Funding Fees

As stated above, this increase does not apply to interest rate reduction refinancing loans, which remain at ½ percent, nor does it pertain to direct loans, vendee loans, manufactured loans and loan assumptions, which remain at 1 percent.

| In Practice | Regulations and requirements regarding FHA and VA loans change frequently. Before making an offer based on FHA and/or VA financing, agents working with buyers as clients or customers should always first check with local FHA- and VA-approved lenders as well as with local FHA and VA offices from time to time for current information regarding these government-backed loan programs. Sellers' agents should further check on "hidden fees" that sellers may be required to pay if they accept an offer based on FHA and/or VA financing. |

Rural Economic and Community Development Services

The **Rural Economic and Community Development Services** is a federal agency of the Department of Agriculture. This agency offers programs to help purchase or operate family farms. It also provides loans to help purchase or improve single-family homes in rural areas (generally areas with a population of fewer than 10,000 that are not suburbs of urban areas). Loans are made to low-income and moderate-income families, and the interest rate charged can be as low as 1 percent, depending on the borrower's income. The loan programs fall into two categories: *guaranteed loans*, made and serviced by a private lender and guaranteed by the agency, and *direct loans* from the agency.

The Farm Service Agency (FSA) has farm loan programs designed to help family farmers who are unable to obtain commercial private credit. These farmers may be beginning farmers, those who suffered financial setbacks such as natural disasters or those with limited resources to maintain a profitable operation. Some farmers can satisfy their credit needs through the use of loan guarantees. The money is borrowed from a local agricultural lender that makes and services the loan, and FSA guarantees the lender against default loss up to a maximum of 90 percent. If a farmer cannot qualify for a guaranteed loan, FSA also makes direct loans, which are serviced by FSA. Eligible applicants may obtain a direct loan up to a $200,000 maximum, whereas a guaranteed loan may be as high as $300,000. Both have a maximum repayment period of 40 years.

Other types of loans administered by FSA include Emergency Loss Loans, Rural Youth Loans and Targeted Funds to Beginning Farmers. The FSA also performs loan servicing and supervised credit, meaning it works with each borrower to identify strengths and weaknesses in farm management and production.

The Rural Housing Service Agency, a branch of FSA, administers housing programs for low- to moderate-income rural residents. These types of loans include Direct Single Family Housing Loans, Guaranteed Single Family Housing Loans and Repair Loans and Grants.

The *Direct Single Family Housing Loan* is designed for families with low to very low income (80 percent or less of county median income). These loans can be used to buy, build, improve or repair rural homes. Eligibility requirements include (1) a rural area of less than 10,000 population, (2) families who are without safe and decent housing and (3) families to whom financing is not otherwise available. Availability of funds is based on annual appropriations. Loans may be made up to 100 percent of the appraised value. Interest rates are normally set at market rate, and the term of the loan is typically 33 years, but may be as long as 38 years. Applicants pay some costs, such as the credit report fee, appraisal fee and closing costs, and the applicant must have good credit.

The *Guaranteed Single Family Housing Loan* is designed for moderate-income families who have limited down payment capability. Loans are processed by approved lenders and guaranteed by the U.S. government. Eligibility requirements are similar to the Direct Loan. Maximum loan amounts range from $78,660 to $116,850, depending on the county in which the property is located. Interest rates are negotiable and fixed, with a 30-year loan term.

Repair Loans and Grants are designed for very-low-income individuals (those who earn 50 percent or less of the county median income). Funds can be used for repairs, installation of essential features or to remove health and safety hazards. To qualify, the applicant must (1) live in a rural area of less than 10,000 population, (2) meet the income standards and (3) be unable to get financing elsewhere. Grants are available only if the applicant is at least 62 years old. The interest rate is 1 percent APR (annual percentage rate), terms are up to 20 years and there are no fees. The applicant must have a reasonable credit history.

Other Types of Loans

By altering the terms of the basic mortgage and note, a borrower and a lender can tailor financing instruments to best suit the type of transaction and the financial needs of both parties.

Purchase-money mortgages. A **purchase-money mortgage** is given at the time of purchase to facilitate the sale and refers to the instrument *given by the purchaser to a seller who "takes back" a note and deed of trust for part or all of the purchase price.* It may be a first or second deed of trust, and it becomes a lien on the property when the title passes. In the event of foreclosure on a purchase-money mortgage, this lien takes priority over judgment liens against the borrower and over mechanics' liens. The seller is not entitled to a deficiency judgment.

Package loans. A **package loan** includes not only the real estate but also all fixtures and appliances installed on the premises. In recent years, this type of loan has been used extensively in financing furnished condominium units. Such loans usually include the kitchen range, refrigerator, dishwasher, garbage disposal, washer and dryer, freezer and other appliances, as well as furniture, drapes and carpets. In other words, the lender has "packaged" both real and personal property in the same loan.

Blanket mortgages. A **blanket mortgage** covers *more than one parcel of land* and usually is used to finance subdivision developments (though it can be used to finance the purchase of improved properties as well). These loans usually include a provision, known as *a partial release clause,* that the borrower may obtain the release of any one lot or parcel from the lien by repaying a definite amount of the loan at closing. The lender issues a partial release for each parcel released from the mortgage lien. This release form includes a provision that the lien will continue to cover all other unreleased lots.

Wraparound loans. A **wraparound loan,** also known as an *overriding* or *all-inclusive mortgage*, enables a borrower who is paying off an existing mortgage to obtain additional financing from a second lender or seller. *The new lender, which could be the seller, assumes payment of the existing loan and gives the borrower a new, increased loan at a higher interest rate.* The total amount of the new loan includes the existing loan as well as the additional funds needed by the borrower. The borrower makes payments to the new lender or seller on the larger loan, and the new lender or seller makes payments on the original loan.

For Example Suppose Brown is selling his house for $75,000. He has an outstanding mortgage on the property in the amount of $30,000 at 6 percent interest. The buyer, Morgan, does not want to get an institutional loan, so Brown agrees to extend $65,000 in financing to Morgan at 7 percent interest. Morgan makes a $10,000 down payment, then continues to make monthly payments to Brown. Brown takes a portion of each payment he receives from Morgan, uses it to make the mortgage payment on his $30,000 loan and pockets the rest of the monthly payment.

A wraparound mortgage frequently is used as a method of refinancing real property or financing the purchase of real property when an existing mortgage cannot be prepaid. It also is used to finance the sale of real estate when the buyer wishes to put up a minimum of initial cash for the sale. The buyer takes title subject to the existing mortgage. The buyer also executes a wraparound document to the seller, who collects payments on the new loan and continues to make payments on the old loan. The buyer should require a protective clause in the document granting the right to make payments directly to the original lender in the event of a default on the old loan by the seller.

In Practice   A wraparound loan is possible only if the original loan permits such a refinancing. An acceleration, an alienation or a due-on-sale clause in the original loan documents may prevent a sale under such terms. A real estate licensee should neither encourage nor assist in any financing that violates loan provisions. To do so could result in suspension or revocation of the agent's license.

Open-end mortgages. Open-end mortgages act as a "line of credit," allowing the mortgagee to make additional future advances of funds to the mortgagor, and are generally set up as home equity loans (discussed below). The mortgagee may have a prior lien for the amount of additional future advances if the mortgagee is obligated to make advances, as in construction loans. For unobligated future advances, the lien may be subordinate to other liens that may be created before the additional advancements are made.

Construction loans. A **construction loan** is made to *finance the construction of improvements* on real estate (homes, apartments, office buildings and so forth). Under a construction loan, the lender commits the full amount of the loan but makes *partial installment payments* or draws as the building is being constructed.

Installment payments are made to the *general contractor* for that part of the construction work that has been completed since the previous payment. Prior to each payment, the lender inspects the work. The general contractor must provide the lender with adequate waivers of lien releasing all mechanic's lien rights (see Chapter 2) for the work covered by the payment. This kind of loan generally bears a higher interest rate because of the risks assumed by the lender. These risks include the inadequate releasing of mechanics' liens just referred to, possible delays in completing the building and the financial failure of the contractor or subcontractors. The lender always runs the risk that the loan funds will run out before the construction has been completed. Construction financing is generally *short-term,* or *interim, financing.* The borrower is expected to arrange for a *permanent loan* (also known as an *end loan* or a *take-out loan*) that will repay, or "take out," the construction financing lender when the work is completed. Construction loans normally pose a greater degree of risk to lenders than any other types of loans.

Sale and leaseback. Sale-and-leaseback arrangements are used rather extensively as a means of financing large commercial or industrial plants. The land and building, usually used by the seller for business purposes, are sold to an investor such as an insurance company. The real estate is then leased back by the investor to the seller, who continues to conduct business on the property as a tenant. The buyer becomes the lessor, and the original owner becomes the lessee. This enables a business firm that has money invested in a plant to free that money so it can be used as working capital.

Sale-and-leaseback arrangements are very complex. They involve complicated legal procedures, and their success is usually related to the effects the transaction has on a firm's tax situation. A real estate broker should advise the parties to a sale-and-leaseback arrangement to consult with legal and tax experts when involved in this type of transaction.

Buydowns. A **buydown** is a way to lower the initial interest rate on a mortgage or deed of trust. Perhaps a homebuilder wishes to stimulate sales by offering a lower-than-market rate. Or a first-time residential buyer may have trouble qualifying for a loan at the prevailing rates; relatives or the sellers might want to help the buyer qualify. In any case, a lump sum is paid in cash to the lender at closing. The payment offsets (and so reduces) the interest rate and monthly payments during the mortgage's first few years. Typical buydown arrangements reduce the interest rate by 1 to 3 percent over the first one to three years of the loan term. After that, the rate rises. The assumption is that the borrower's income will also increase and that the borrower will be more able to absorb the increased monthly payments. A common type of buydown is called the *3-2-1 buydown.* The interest rate is bought down by 3 percent in the first year, 2 percent in the second year, and 1 percent in the third year. For the fourth and succeeding years, the interest rate is the note rate.

Home equity loans. *Home equity loans* are a relatively new source of funds for homeowners who wish to finance the purchase of expensive items; consolidate existing installment loans on credit card debt; or pay for medical, educational, home improvement or other expenses. This type of financing has been used increasingly in the past few years, partly because recent tax laws have ended the deductibility of interest on debts not secured by real estate ("consumer interest"). Home equity loans are secured by the borrower's residence, and the interest charged is deductible up to a loan limit of $100,000.

A home equity loan can be taken out as a fixed loan amount or as an equity line of credit. With the home equity line of credit, the lender extends a line of credit that the borrowers can use whenever they want. The borrowers receive their money through checks sent to them, deposits made in a checking or savings account or a book of drafts the borrowers can use, up to their credit limit.

Reverse-annuity mortgages. A **reverse-annuity mortgage (RAM)** is one in which regular monthly payments are made *to the borrower,* based on the equity the homeowner has invested in the property given as security for the loan. A reverse-annuity mortgage allows senior citizens on fixed incomes to realize the equity buildup in their homes without having to sell. The borrower is charged a fixed rate of interest, and the loan is eventually repaid from the sale of the property or from the borrower's estate on his or her death.

Mortgage Priorities   Mortgages and other liens normally have priority in the order in which they have been recorded. A mortgage on land that has no prior mortgage lien on it is a *first mortgage.* When the owner of this land executes another loan for additional funds, the new loan becomes a *second mortgage,* or a *junior mortgage,* when recorded. The second lien is subject to the first lien; the first has prior claim to the value of the land pledged as security. Because second loans represent greater risk to lenders, they are usually issued at higher interest rates.

The priority of mortgage liens may be changed by the execution of a *subordination agreement,* in which the first lender subordinates its lien to that of the second lender. To be valid, such an agreement must be signed by both lenders. Subordination agreements may be contained in the mortgage itself or they may be separate agreements filed for recordation.

SOURCES OF REAL ESTATE FINANCING—THE PRIMARY MORTGAGE MARKET

Few people could afford, or would want, to pay all cash for real estate. Although real estate values may decline for a number of reasons, generally real estate is a much desired asset, and its desirability and scarcity have historically made it an appreciating and profitable investment.

The funds used to finance the purchase of real estate come from a variety of sources that compose the **primary mortgage market**—lenders that supply funds to borrowers as an investment. Lenders may originate loans for the purpose of selling them to other investors as part of what is termed the **secondary mortgage market.**

Currently, the total mortgage debt on residential and commercial property and farms in the United States exceeds $2 trillion. Savings and loan associations hold the majority of the debt. The remainder is held by commercial banks, mutual savings banks, life insurance companies, various federal agencies, mortgage pools or trusts and individuals, real estate investment trusts (REITs), credit unions, noninsured pension funds and others. The primary sources of real estate financing are discussed in this section.

Savings Associations

Savings associations, or thrifts, are some of the most active participants in the home loan mortgage market, specializing in long-term residential loans. A savings association earns money by paying less for the funds it receives than it charges for the loans it makes. Loan income includes more than interest, however; savings associations charge loan origination, loan assumption and other fees. The source of the funds used by savings associations to make home loans is long-term savings—that is, certificates of deposit and other savings vehicles.

Traditionally, savings associations are fairly flexible with regard to their mortgage lending procedures, and they are generally local in nature. In addition, they participate in FHA-insured and VA-guaranteed loans, though only to a limited extent.

All savings associations must be chartered, either by the federal government or by the states in which they are located. *The Financial Institutions Reform, Recovery, and Enforcement Act (FIRREA) of 1989,* enacted in response to the savings and loan association crisis of the 1980s, was intended to ensure the continued viability of the thrift industry. FIRREA restructured the savings and loan association regulatory system as well as the insurance system that protects its depositors. *The Federal Deposit Insurance Corporation (FDIC)* now manages the insurance funds for savings associations and commercial banks. Thrift deposits are insured through the *Savings Association Insurance Fund (SAIF),* and bank deposits are insured through the *Bank Insurance Fund (BIF).*

FIRREA also created the *Office of Thrift Supervision (OTS)* to monitor and regulate the thrift industry and the *Resolution Trust Corporation (RTC)* to liquidate the assets of failed savings associations.

Because of their performance record in the 1980s, thrifts are now subject to stricter capital requirements than before, as well as new housing loan requirements. Effective July 1, 1991, savings associations are required to maintain 70 percent of their loan portfolios in housing-related loans, such as residential mortgage loans, residential construction loans and home equity loans.

Commercial Banks

Commercial banks are an important source of real estate financing. Bank loan departments handle primarily short-term loans such as construction, home improvement and mobile-home loans. This is because a great deal of a commercial bank's funds are *demand funds*—funds that are in short-term accounts such as checking accounts. In some areas, however, commercial banks are originating an increasing number of home mortgages. Like savings associations, banks must be chartered by the state or federal government. Bank deposits are insured by the FDIC. Many banks, owing to excessive lending, became insolvent and merged into stronger, more prudent institutions.

Mutual Savings Banks

Mutual savings banks, which operate like savings and loan associations, are located primarily in northeastern states (none exist in North Carolina). They issue no stock and are mutually owned by their investors. Although mutual savings banks offer limited checking account privileges, they are primarily savings institutions and are highly active in the mortgage market, investing in loans secured by income property as well as residential real estate. In addition, because mutual savings banks usually seek low-risk loan investments, they often prefer to originate FHA-insured or VA-guaranteed loans.

Life Insurance Companies

Insurance companies amass large sums of money from the premiums paid by their policyholders. While a certain portion of this money is held in reserve to satisfy claims and cover operating expenses, much of it is invested in profit-earning enterprises, such as long-term real estate loans.

Most insurance companies like to invest their money in large, long-term loans that finance commercial and industrial properties. They also invest in residential mortgage loans by purchasing large blocks of government-backed loans (FHA-insured and VA-guaranteed loans) from Fannie Mae (formerly the *Federal National Mortgage Association or FNMA*) and other agencies that warehouse such loans for resale in the secondary mortgage market (discussed later in this chapter).

In addition, many life insurance companies seek to further ensure the safety of their investments by insisting on equity positions (known as *equity kickers*) in many projects they finance. A company may require a partnership arrangement with, for example, a project developer or subdivider as a condition of making a loan (called *participation financing*). The recessionary period of the early 1990s was very trying for many insurance companies, as it was for many savings and loan associations and banks.

Mortgage Banking Companies

Mortgage banking companies use money borrowed from other institutions and funds of their own to make real estate loans that may later be sold to investors (with the mortgage companies receiving a fee for servicing the loans). Mortgage bankers are involved in all types of real estate loan activities and often serve as middlemen between investors and borrowers; however, they are not mortgage brokers. Mortgage bankers are subject to considerably fewer lending restrictions than are commercial banks or savings and loans. Mortgage bankers sell most of their loans in the secondary market.

Mortgage Brokers

Mortgage brokers, although not lenders, are often instrumental in obtaining financing. Mortgage brokers are individuals licensed to act as intermediaries in bringing borrowers and lenders together for a commission fee. They locate potential borrowers, process preliminary loan applications and submit the applications to lenders for final approval. Frequently, they work with or for mortgage banking companies in these activities. Unlike mortgage bankers, they never actually originate loans themselves, nor do they get involved in servicing a loan once it is made. Many mortgage brokers are also real estate brokers who offer these financing services in addition to their regular brokerage activities.

Credit Unions

Credit unions are cooperative organizations in which members place money in savings accounts, usually at higher interest rates than other savings institutions offer. In the past, most credit unions made only short-term consumer and home improvement loans, but in recent years they have been branching out to longer-term first and second mortgage and trust deed loans.

Pension Funds   Pension funds have begun to participate actively in financing real estate projects. Most of the real estate activity for pension funds is handled through mortgage bankers and mortgage brokers.

Investment Group Financing   Large real estate projects, including highrise apartment buildings, office complexes and shopping centers, are often financed as joint ventures through group financing arrangements such as syndicates, limited partnerships and REITs.

Individual Lenders   The most common individual lender is the homeseller who offers to finance part or all of the transaction. In fact, sellers are the largest source of junior mortgage money.

GOVERNMENT INFLUENCE IN MORTGAGE LENDING

Aside from FHA-insured and VA-guaranteed loan programs, the federal government influences mortgage lending through the Federal Reserve System (the "Fed") as well as through various federal agencies, such as Rural Economic and Community Development Services. It also deals in the secondary mortgage market through *Ginnie Mae*, *Freddie Mac* and *Fannie Mae*.

Federal Reserve System   Established in 1913 under President Woodrow Wilson, the Fed operates to maintain sound credit conditions, help counteract inflationary and deflationary trends and create a favorable economic climate. The Fed divides the country into 12 Federal Reserve Districts, each served by a Federal Reserve Bank. All nationally chartered banks must join the Fed and purchase stock in its district reserve banks. The Fed regulates the flow of money and interest rates in the marketplace indirectly, through its member banks, by controlling their reserve requirements and discount rates.

Reserve controls. The Fed requires that each member bank keep a certain amount of its assets on hand as reserve funds unavailable for loans or any other use. This requirement was designed primarily to protect customer deposits, but it also provides a means of manipulating the flow of cash in the money market. By increasing its reserve requirements, the Fed in effect limits the amount of money that member banks can use to make loans, thus causing interest rates to increase.

In this manner, the government can slow down an overactive economy by limiting the number of loans that are directed toward major purchases of goods and services. The opposite is also true—by decreasing the reserve requirements, the Fed allows more loans to be made, thus increasing the amount of money circulated in the marketplace and causing interest rates to decline.

Discount rates. Federal Reserve member banks are permitted to borrow money from the district reserve banks to expand their lending operations. The interest rate that the district banks charge for the use of this money is called the *discount rate.* Based on this rate, the member banks determine the percentage rate of interest that they in turn charge their loan customers. Theoretically, when the Federal Reserve discount rate is high, bank interest rates are high; therefore, fewer loans are made and less money circulates in the marketplace. Conversely, a lower discount rate results in lower interest rates, more bank loans and more money in circulation.

Government Influence in the Secondary Market

Mortgage lending takes place in both the primary and secondary mortgage markets. Thus far, this chapter has dealt principally with the primary market, lenders that originate loans. Loans are bought and sold in the secondary mortgage market only after they have been funded. For example, a lender may wish to sell a number of loans to raise immediate funds when it needs more money to meet the mortgage demands in its area. Secondary market activity is especially desirable when money is in short supply because it stimulates the housing construction market as well as the mortgage market.

Generally, when a loan has been sold, the original lender continues to collect the payments from the borrower. The lender then passes the payments along to the investor who has purchased the loan and charges the investor a fee for servicing the loan.

A major source of secondary mortgage market activity is the warehousing agency, which purchases a number of mortgage loans and assembles them into one or more packages of loans for resale to investors. The major warehousing agencies are Fannie Mae, Ginnie Mae and Freddie Mac.

Federal National Mortgage Association. Fannie Mae, formerly the Federal National Mortgage Association **(FNMA)**, is a privately owned corporation that issues its own common stock and provides a secondary market for mortgage loans—conventional as well as FHA and VA loans. (Fannie Mae used to be a government agency, and even though it is now a privately owned corporation, it is still considered a quasi-government agency because it can borrow money from the U.S. Treasury.) Fannie Mae buys a *block* or *pool* of mortgages from a lender in exchange for *mortgage-backed securities* that the lender may keep or sell. The agency guarantees payment of all interest and principal to the holder of the securities. Generally, mortgage bankers are actively involved with Fannie Mae, originating loans and selling them to Fannie Mae while retaining servicing functions. Fannie Mae was instrumental in developing the uniform underwriting guidelines that helped assure investors of the quality of the mortgage-backed securities. These underwriting guidelines are now an accepted part of mortgage loan underwriting procedures and are regularly used to determine a loan applicant's creditworthiness.

Government National Mortgage Association. Ginnie Mae, formerly the Government National Mortgage Association **(GNMA)**, exists as a corporation without capital stock and is a division of HUD. When Fannie Mae changed from a government agency to a private corporation, Ginnie Mae was created to take Fannie Mae's place. Ginnie Mae is designed to administer special-assistance programs and work with Fannie Mae in secondary market activities. Fannie Mae and Ginnie Mae can join forces in times of tight money and high interest rates through their tandem plan. Basically, the *tandem plan* provides that Fannie Mae can purchase high-risk, low-yield (usually FHA) loans at full market rates, with Ginnie Mae guaranteeing payment and absorbing the difference between the low yield and current market prices.

Ginnie Mae also guarantees investment securities issued by private offerors (such as banks, mortgage companies and savings and loan associations) and backed by pools of FHA and VA mortgage loans. The Ginnie Mae pass-through certificate lets small investors buy shares in a pool of mortgages that provides for a monthly "pass-through" of principal and interest payments directly to certificate holders. Such certificates are guaranteed by Ginnie Mae.

Federal Home Loan Mortgage Corporation. **Freddie Mac,** originally the Federal Home Loan Mortgage Corporation **(FHLMC),** provides a secondary market for mortgage loans, primarily conventional loans originated by savings associations. Freddie Mac has the authority to purchase mortgages, pool them and sell bonds in the open market with the mortgages as security. Note, however, that Freddie Mac does not guarantee payment of these mortgages.

Many lenders use the standardized forms and follow the guidelines issued by Freddie Mac because use of these forms is mandatory for lenders that wish to sell mortgages in the agency's secondary mortgage market. The standardized documents include loan applications, credit reports and appraisal forms.

RESIDENTIAL LENDING PRACTICES AND PROCEDURES

All mortgage lenders require that prospective borrowers file an application for credit that provides the lender with the basic information needed to evaluate the acceptability of the proposed loan. The application includes information regarding the purpose, the amount, the rate of interest and the proposed terms of repayment of the loan. This is considered a preliminary offer of a loan agreement; final terms may require lengthy negotiations.

Application for Credit   A prospective borrower must submit personal information to the lender, including employment, earnings, assets and financial obligations. Details of the real estate that will be the security for the loan must be provided, including legal description, improvements, title, survey and taxes. For loans on income property or those made to corporations, additional information is required, such as financial and operating statements, schedules of leases and tenants, and balance sheets.

The lender carefully investigates the application information, studying credit reports and an appraisal of the property before deciding whether to grant the loan. The lender's acceptance of the application is written in the form of a loan commitment, which creates a contract to make a loan and sets forth the details.

In Practice   Because interest rates and loan terms change frequently, check with local sources of real estate financing on a regular basis to learn of specific loan rates and terms. As a licensee, you can better serve your customers and clients if you can knowledgeably refer buyers to local lenders offering the most favorable terms.

Prequalifying Buyers   Every real estate agent should have a basic understanding of the loan standards lenders use as they decide whether to approve a loan. These loan standards, called *underwriting standards* or *qualifying standards,* can then be used by the agent to prequalify the agent's buyers. By prequalifying a buyer, the agent is more likely to avoid the disappointment of a rejected loan application.

MATH CONCEPTS

Determining Maximum Affordability

You can use qualifying ratios to determine the range of housing a prospective buyer can afford. Let's look at an example of the Harrisons, whose monthly income is $3,900. To determine what kind of house they can afford, multiply their monthly income by a given standard ratio, 36 percent, for example.

$$\$3,900 \times .36 = \$1,404$$

Now subtract their recurring expenses, which total $475.

$$\$1,404 - \$475 = \$929$$

The maximum housing payment they can afford under this ratio is $929, including principal, interest, taxes and insurance. Tax and insurance costs will vary according to location, but for purposes of this example, we will assume that 10 percent of the maximum payment is devoted to taxes and insurance. Deduct this 10 percent from the maximum payment.

$$\$929 \times .10 = \$92.90$$
$$\$929 - \$93 \text{ (rounded up)} = \$836$$

The Harrisons can afford to pay $836 a month in principal and interest. If current interest rates are 8 percent, they would qualify for a loan amount of $113,896. (You can use a financial calculator to determine this loan amount, or use a loan factor of 7.34. To use a loan factor, divide the principal and interest payment by the rate factor and multiply by 1,000.) Assuming that the Harrisons have $12,650 for a down payment, they could afford to purchase a home for $126,546.

$$\$113,896 \text{ maximum loan amount} + \$12,650 \text{ down payment} = \$126,546$$

Qualifying standards are fairly complex; however, the basics are easy to understand and remember. The major element of any prequalification procedure is measuring the adequacy of a buyer's income. A lender will never approve a loan if the applicant does not have enough income to meet the monthly loan payments. And until an agent knows how large a loan payment the buyer can afford, the agent will not be able to assist the buyer in selecting an affordable home.

Each of the three major types of loan programs has a different way of measuring the adequacy of a buyer's income.

Conventional loans. Conventional lenders apply two ratios to the buyer's income to measure adequacy: (1) The proposed monthly housing expense can be no more than 28 percent of the borrower's monthly gross income. Note that the proposed monthly housing expense includes principal and interest payments, plus monthly property taxes and hazard insurance payments and homeowner association dues, if applicable. (2) The proposed monthly housing expense plus the buyer's other recurring monthly debts can total no more than 36 percent of the buyer's monthly gross income. Recurring monthly debts include items such as charge card payments, child support payments, personal loan payments and car payments. These qualifying ratios can change, depending on the LTV ratio of the loan. The larger the down payment the borrower makes, the easier it will be to qualify.

For Example The Harrisons are seeking an 80 percent loan. They make $3,900 a month. Their monthly payments include a $300 car payment, a $75 charge card payment and a $100 college loan payment. They want to qualify for an $850 monthly loan payment (including principal, interest, taxes and insurance).

First, add the recurring monthly expenses to the $850 proposed housing expense:

$$\begin{array}{r} \$\ 850 \\ 300 \\ 100 \\ \underline{75} \\ \$1,325 \text{ total monthly expenses} \end{array}$$

If you divide $1,325 by $3,900, you discover that the Harrisons' total monthly expenses equal about 34 percent of their monthly income. Therefore, they would qualify for the proposed loan under the second ratio because 34 percent is less than the maximum 36 percent. If you divide $850 by $3,900, you discover that the Harrisons' proposed housing expense is about 22 percent of their monthly income. This is well within the 28 percent maximum. Because both income standards are met, the Harrisons have a good chance of qualifying for the loan.

Let's assume the Harrisons want a more expensive home that would require a loan of $250,000. How much annual income would the Harrisons need to qualify using the 28/36 ratio if the estimated monthly PITI will be $1,665 and they have other monthly recurring obligations of $2,000? The first step would be to add up all monthly debts, then divide by the 36% ratio to get monthly income required; then multiply by 12 months.

$1,665 + $2,000 = $3,665 divided by .36 = $10,180.56 monthly income × 12 months = $122,166.72 annual income

Let's take an example of determining maximum housing expenses that another couple could have with an annual income of $36,000 and recurring obligations (not including housing expenses) of $400 per month, using the 28/36 percent ratios to qualify under both ratios.

$36,000 annual income divided by 12 months = $3,000 monthly income × .36 = $1,080 maximum recurring obligation, not including housing. Their actual other monthly recurring obligations are $400. $1,080 − $400 = $680 would be their maximum monthly housing expenses.

FHA loans. The FHA also uses the same two ratios to qualify its borrowers; however, the maximum proposed-housing-expense-to-income ratio is 29 percent, and the maximum proposed-total-monthly-expense-to-income ratio is 41 percent. These ratios are calculated in the same manner as the conventional ratios discussed above. The FHA ratios are not dependent on the loan's LTV ratio, as are conventional ratios. They remain constant, regardless of the amount of the down payment. Note that FHA standards are somewhat easier to meet than conventional standards.

VA loans. The VA uses a slightly different method to qualify its borrowers. The VA uses only the total-monthly-expense-to-income ratio, which the VA has set at 41 percent of the borrower's monthly income. Instead of a second ratio, the VA uses the residual-income method. With this qualifying method, buyers must have a certain amount of cash left over after paying their monthly housing expenses and other recurring debts. The VA publishes a table of how much residual income is required for buyers. The amount varies, depending on the number of dependents the buyer has and the geographic region in which the buyer lives. As with the two ratios used by conventional and FHA lenders, VA borrowers must qualify under both the total-monthly-expense-to-income ratio and the residual-income method before the loan will be approved.

For Example   A married couple with two children living in Raleigh with a combined annual gross income of $43,200 want to apply for a $100,000 loan. The VA Cost of Living Table shows the required residual income is $964 for loan amounts above $70,000 for a family of four. Monthly withholding taxes and Social Security taxes are estimated to be $900 per month. Shelter expenses, which include principal, interest, taxes and insurance (PITI), along with maintenance and utilities, are estimated to be $920. Other monthly obligations with six or more monthly payments left total $600.

$$
\begin{array}{rl}
\$3,600 & \text{Monthly gross income} \\
-\ 900 & \text{Taxes and Social Security} \\
-\ 920 & \text{Shelter costs} \\
-\ 600 & \text{Other obligations} \\
\hline
\$1,180 & \text{Residual income}
\end{array}
$$

The actual residual income exceeds the table amount, so the couple qualifies under this method.

Now let's take a look at whether the applicant couple from the previous example meets the 41 percent income ratio test. First add the total monthly obligations together.

$$
\begin{array}{rl}
\$920 & \text{Shelter expense} \\
+600 & \text{Other obligations} \\
\hline
\$1,520 & \text{Total monthly obligations}
\end{array}
$$

Now divide the total monthly obligations by the gross monthly income.

$$\$1,520 \div \$3,600 = .42 = 42\%$$

Because this ratio is more than the 41 percent maximum, the applicant does not qualify under this ratio.

If the applicant's residual income exceeds the required amount by more than 20 percent, the applicant may qualify for the loan, even if the applicant's total-monthly-expense-to-income ratio exceeds the 41 percent maximum.

For Example   The applicant couple's residual income in the previous example was $1,180. They were only required to have $964 in residual income.

$1,180 residual income – $964 required residual income = $216 excess residual income

To find the percentage of excess residual income, divide the excess residual income by the required amount.

$216 excess residual income ÷ $964 required residual income =
.224 or 22% of excess residual income

So even if the applicant couple's income ratio had been higher than 41 percent, they still might have qualified because they had a substantial amount of residual income.

FINANCING LEGISLATION

The federal government regulates the lending practices of mortgage lenders through the Truth-in-Lending Act, the Equal Credit Opportunity Act and the Real Estate Settlement Procedures Act.

Truth-in-Lending Act and Regulation Z

Regulation Z, which was promulgated pursuant to the **Truth-in-Lending Act,** requires that credit institutions inform borrowers of the true cost of obtaining credit so that the borrowers can compare the costs of various lenders and avoid the uninformed use of credit. Regulation Z applies when credit is extended to individuals for personal, family or household uses and when the amount of credit is $25,000 or less. Regardless of the amount, Regulation Z always applies when a credit transaction is secured by a residence.

The regulation requires that the consumer be fully informed of all finance charges as well as the true annual interest rate before a transaction is consummated. The finance charges must include any loan fees, finder's fees, service charges and points, as well as interest. In the case of a mortgage loan made to finance the purchase of a dwelling, the lender also must compute and disclose the *annual percentage rate (APR)* but does not have to indicate the total interest payable during the term of the loan. Also, the lender does not have to include as part of the finance charge such actual costs as title fees, legal fees, appraisal fees, credit report fees, survey fees and closing expenses.

In total, the lender must disclose to the borrower (1) the loan's APR, (2) all finance charges associated with the loan, (3) the total number and amount of all payments and (4) the total amount financed.

Advertising. Regulation Z provides strict regulation of real estate advertisements that include mortgage financing terms. General phrases like "liberal terms available" may be used, but if specifics (called *trigger terms*) are given, they must comply with this regulation. Under the provisions of Regulation Z, the APR—which includes all charges—rather than the interest rate alone must be stated. The total finance charge must be specified as well.

Specific credit terms, such as *down payment, monthly payment, dollar amount of the finance charge* or *term of the loan,* may not be advertised unless the following information is set forth as well: cash price; required down payment; number, amounts and due dates of all payments; and APR. The total of all payments to be made over the term of the mortgage must also be specified unless the advertised credit refers to a first mortgage or deed of trust to finance the acquisition of a dwelling.

Penalties. Regulation Z sets the penalties for noncompliance. The penalty for violation of an administrative order enforcing Regulation Z is $10,000 for each day the violation continues. A fine of up to $10,000 may be imposed for engaging in an unfair or a deceptive practice. In addition, a creditor may be liable to a consumer for twice the amount of the finance charge, for a minimum of $100 and a maximum of $1,000, plus court costs, lawyer's fees and any actual damages. Willful violation is a misdemeanor punishable by a fine of up to $5,000 or one year's imprisonment or both.

Federal Equal Credit Opportunity Act

The federal *Equal Credit Opportunity Act (ECOA),* in effect since 1975, prohibits lenders and others who grant or arrange credit to consumers from discriminating against credit applicants on the basis of race, color, religion, national origin, sex, marital status, age (provided the applicant is of legal age) or dependence on public assistance. In addition, lenders and other creditors must inform all rejected credit applicants, in writing, within 30 days, of the principal reasons why credit was denied or terminated.

Fair Credit Reporting Act

The federal *Fair Credit Reporting Act,* effective since 1970, gives individuals the right to check their own credit reports and demand that mistakes be corrected. Credit bureaus are required to limit the credit information they provide to the previous seven years (except for bankruptcies, which can stay on credit records for ten years). Individuals who have been denied credit based on information found in a credit report can examine their credit report at no charge. Other individuals who want to examine their credit report may have to pay a service fee.

Predatory Lending Act

The Predatory Lending Act is a recent North Carolina law that applies to lenders and addresses permissible fees that may be charged in connection with home loans secured by the first mortgage or first deed of trust. Main provisions include the following:

- To impose restrictions and limitations on high-cost loans
- To revise the permissible fees and charges on certain loans
- To prohibit unfair or deceptive practices by mortgage brokers and lenders
- To provide for public education and counseling about predatory lenders

Real Estate Settlement Procedures Act

The federal *Real Estate Settlement Procedures Act (RESPA)* was created to ensure that the buyer and seller in a residential real estate transaction involving a new first mortgage loan have knowledge of all settlement costs. This important federal law will be discussed in detail in Chapter 14.

SUMMARY

Many types of mortgage loans exist, including conventional loans and those insured by the FHA or guaranteed by the VA. FHA-insured and VA-guaranteed loans must meet certain requirements for the borrower to obtain the benefits of the government backing, which induces the lender to lend its funds. The interest rates for these loans may be lower than those charged for conventional loans. Other types of real estate financing include seller-financed purchase-money mortgages or deeds of trust, blanket mortgages, wraparound mortgages, open-end mortgages, construction loans, sale-and-leaseback agreements, buydowns and home equity loans.

The federal government affects real estate financing money and interest rates through the Federal Reserve Board's discount rate and reserve requirements; it also participates in the secondary mortgage market. Generally, the secondary market is composed of those investors that ultimately purchase and hold the loans as investments. These include insurance companies, investment funds and pension plans. Fannie Mae (Federal National Mortgage Association), Ginnie Mae (Government National Mortgage Association) and Freddie Mac (Federal Home Loan Mortgage Corporation) take an active role in creating a secondary market by regularly purchasing mortgage and deed of trust loans from originators and retaining, or warehousing, them until investment purchasers are available.

Regulation Z, implementing the federal Truth-in-Lending Act, requires that lenders inform prospective borrowers who use their homes as security for credit of all finance charges involved in such a loan. Severe penalties are provided for noncompliance. The federal Equal Credit Opportunity Act prohibits creditors from discriminating against credit applicants on the basis of race, color, religion, national origin, sex, marital status, age or dependence on public assistance. The Real Estate Settlement Procedures Act requires that lenders inform both buyers and sellers in advance of all fees and charges required for the settlement or closing of a residential real estate transaction.

Questions

1. A developer has obtained a large loan to finance the construction of a planned unit development. Which of the following statements is true?
   a. This is a short-term loan, and the developer has arranged for long-term financing to repay it when the construction is completed.
   b. The borrowed money is disbursed in one lump sum after the construction has been completed.
   c. To be sure they are compensated, the lender pays the money borrowed directly to the suppliers and subcontractors.
   d. The developer receives all borrowed money immediately, before any construction is completed.

2. The Carters purchased a residence for $95,000. They made a down payment of $15,000 and agreed to assume the seller's existing mortgage, which had a current balance of $23,000. The Carters financed the remaining $57,000 of the purchase price by executing a mortgage and note to the seller. This type of loan is called a
   a. purchase money mortgage.
   b. package mortgage.
   c. balloon note.
   d. term mortgage.

3. Which of the following best defines the secondary mortgage market?
   I. Lenders that deal exclusively in second mortgages
   II. Market in which loans are bought and sold after they have been originated
   a. I only
   b. II only
   c. I or II only
   d. Neither I nor II

4. A borrower obtains a mortgage loan to make repairs on her home. The loan is not insured or guaranteed by a government agency, and the mortgage document secures the amount of the loan as well as any future funds advanced to the borrower by the lender. This borrower has obtained a
   a. wraparound mortgage.
   b. conventional open-end loan.
   c. land contract.
   d. growing-equity mortgage.

5. Regulation Z requires that lenders
   a. properly inform buyers and sellers of commercial property of all settlement costs in a real estate transaction.
   b. inform prospective borrowers of all charges, fees and interest involved in making a home mortgage loan.
   c. disclose nothing; let the buyer/ mortgagor beware!
   d. study the economic market before they decide what interest rate to charge on residential mortgages.

6. VA mortgages made prior to March 1, 1988, can be
   a. charged a one-time mortgage insurance premium.
   b. charged a prepayment penalty.
   c. made to nonveterans.
   d. freely assumable.

7. Aunt Fran continues to live in the home she purchased 30 years ago, but she now receives monthly checks from her mortgage lender thanks to her
   a. shared-appreciation mortgage.
   b. adjustable-rate mortgage.
   c. reverse-annuity mortgage.
   d. overriding trust deed.

8. The McManns are purchasing an ocean-front summer home in a new resort development. The house is completely equipped, and the McManns have obtained a mortgage loan that covers the purchase price of the residence, including furnishings and appliances. This kind of financing is called a(n)
   a. wraparound loan.
   b. package loan.
   c. blanket loan.
   d. unconventional deed of trust.

9. All of the following are government-owned institutions EXCEPT
   a. Fannie Mae.   c. FHA.
   b. Ginnie Mae.   d. VA.

10. A developer received a loan that covers five parcels of real estate and provides for the release of the mortgage lien on each parcel when certain payments are made on the loan. This type of loan arrangement is called a
    a. purchase-money loan.
    b. blanket loan.
    c. package loan.
    d. wraparound loan.

11. Funds for Federal Housing Administration (FHA) loans are usually provided by
    a. the FHA.
    b. the FDIC.
    c. qualified lenders.
    d. FNMA.

12. Under the provisions of the Truth-in-Lending Act (Regulation Z), the annual percentage rate (APR) of a finance charge includes all of the following components EXCEPT the
    a. discount points.
    b. broker's commission.
    c. loan origination fee.
    d. loan interest rate.

13. No prepayment penalty can be imposed on an FHA-insured 203(b) mortgage on a(n)
    I. single-family home.
    II. chattel.
    III. apartment building of five units or more.
    a. I only
    b. II only
    c. III only
    d. I or II only

14. If buyers were seeking a mortgage on a single-family home, they would be LEAST LIKELY to obtain the mortgage from a
    a. savings and loan association.
    b. commercial bank.
    c. mortgage banker.
    d. life insurance company.

15. Which of the following is NOT a participant in the secondary market?
    I. FHLMC
    II. GNMA
    III. RESPA
    a. I only
    b. II only
    c. III only
    d. II and III only

16. Conventional lenders require that a borrower's proposed-monthly-housing-expense-to-income ratio be no more than
    a. 28 percent.   c. 41 percent.
    b. 36 percent.   d. 22 percent.

17. The Bendermans are applying for a loan that will have a monthly loan payment of $750 (including taxes and insurance). Their recurring monthly expenses equal $500. How much monthly income do they need to qualify for a conventional loan using ratios of 28/36?
    a. $3,472   c $1,923
    b. $2,083   d. $2,679

18. To prequalify a buyer, real estate agents should use the qualifying standards of
    I. lenders.
    II. investors.
    a. I only
    b. II only
    c. Both I and II
    d. Neither I nor II

19. The interest rate on FHA loans is set by
    a. the FHA.
    b. FNMA.
    c. the lender.
    d. the Federal Reserve.

20. Mortgage bankers (companies) deal with
    a. only VA loans.
    b. only FHA loans.
    c. only conventional loans.
    d. all types of long-term mortgage loans.

21. Mortgage bankers (companies) play an important role as a source of real estate financing. Their primary functions include all of the following EXCEPT
    a. servicing mortgage loans they sell to investors.
    b. originating all types of loans.
    c. charging service fees to investors and origination fees to loan applicants.
    d. primarily using their own funds from deposit assets to originate mortgage loans.

22. Which of the following loans gives the lender the greatest degree of risk?
    a. FHA loans
    b. Conventional loans with 95 percent LTV ratios
    c. Construction loans
    d. VA loans with no down payment

23. The main purpose of the Truth-in-Lending Act is to
    a. give a full disclosure of credit charges.
    b. regulate the practice of redlining.
    c. insure that lenders give good-faith estimates of closing costs.
    d. establish legal usury limits.

24. For which type of loan would the buyer have to produce a CRV?
    a. FHA loan
    b. Conventional loan
    c. VA loan
    d. Reverse annuity loan

25. The major difference between a purchase-money mortgage and an installment land contract is
    a. only one can be used for seller financing.
    b. the time at which the buyer gets possession and use of the property.
    c. the time at which delivery of the deed is made.
    d. There is no difference.

26. A buyer purchased a new home for $175,000. The buyer made a down payment of $15,000 and obtained a $160,000 mortgage loan. The builder of the house paid the lender 3 percent of the loan balance for the first year and 2 percent of the loan balance for the second year. This represented total savings for the buyer of $8,000. What type of arrangement does this represent?
    a. Wraparound mortgage
    b. Package mortgage
    c. Blanket mortgage
    d. Buydown mortgage

27. The federal Equal Credit Opportunity Act prohibits lenders from discriminating against potential borrowers on the basis of all of the following EXCEPT
    a. race.
    b. sex.
    c. dependence on public assistance.
    d. amount of income.

28. If a lender agrees to make a loan based on an 80 percent LTV, what is the amount of the loan if the property appraises for $114,500 and the sales price is $116,900?
    a. $83,200   c. $91,600
    b. $91,300   d. $93,520

29. In determining LTV, value is
    a. 80 percent of the sales price or less.
    b. 95 percent of the appraised value.
    c. appraisal value or price, whichever is less.
    d. price or appraisal value, whichever is more.

30. Using the 28/36 rule, how much annual income must one have to qualify for a $120,000 loan at 7 percent for 25 years if the proposed PITI will be $982 and the borrower has other monthly recurring debts of $745?
    a. $57,566   c. $74,014
    b. $42,085   d. $24,833

31. What is the maximum loan a borrower can get using the 28/36 rule if her annual income is $60,000, the mortgage loan factor is $6.67, the estimated monthly taxes and insurance (TI) is $160 and her monthly nonhousing recurring debts total $700?
    a. $185,907.04
    b. $142,929.53
    c. $140,929.53
    d. $91,904

32. If a borrower has an annual gross income of $42,000 and will have monthly recurring debts of $500, not including housing expenses, what will be the maximum monthly housing expenses using the 28/36 rule?
    a. $1,260
    b. $980
    c. $760
    d. $920

Closing the Real Estate Transaction

LEARNING OBJECTIVES

When you've finished reading this chapter, you should be able to

- **describe** closing, the preliminaries that must take place before actual closing and the closing meetings.

- **describe** the steps involved in preparing a closing statement and the steps involved in the transfer of title and funds.

- **list** RESPA requirements.

- **calculate** all types of prorations and prepare a detailed closing statement worksheet.

- **define** these *key terms:*

accrued items	credit	Real Estate Settlement
closing	debit	Procedures Act
closing statement	estoppel certificate	(RESPA)
computerized loan	prepaid items	Uniform Settlement
origination (CLO)	prorations	Statement (HUD-1)
controlled business		
arrangement (CBA)		

PRECLOSING PROCEDURES

Closing is the point at which ownership of a property is transferred in exchange for the sellling price.

Everything a licensee does in the course of a real estate transaction, from soliciting clients to presenting offers and coordinating inspections, leads to one final event: closing. **Closing** is the consummation of the real estate transaction. Closing actually involves three events: (1) the promises made in the sales contract are fulfilled, (2) the mortgage loan funds (if any) are distributed to the buyer and (3) other settlement costs or funds are disbursed. It is the time when the title to the real estate is transferred in exchange for payment of the purchase price. Closing marks the end of any real estate transaction. Before the property changes hands, however, there are important issues that must be resolved.

Buyer's Issues The buyer needs to be sure that the seller is delivering marketable title. The buyer should also ensure that the property is in the promised condition. This involves inspecting

- the title evidence;
- the seller's deed;
- any documents demonstrating the removal of undesired liens and encumbrances;
- the property survey;
- the results of any required inspections, such as termite or structural inspections, or repairs; and
- any leases if there are tenants on the premises.

Unless otherwise stated in the purchase and sales agreement, the buyer has the option of obtaining, at the buyer's expense, a report from a licensed pest control operator on a standard form. The pest inspection report relates whether any evidence of pest (usually termite) infestation or damage exists. Typically, if infestation is found, the seller must pay for the extermination. If pest-caused damage is found and repairs are necessary, the seller usually has three options: (1) completing them, (2) providing for their completion or (3) refusing to complete them. If the seller refuses to complete the repairs, the buyer has two options: (1) accepting the property in its present condition or (2) terminating the contract. (**Note:** If the buyer is obtaining a VA-guaranteed loan, the seller must pay for the pest inspection report.)

Final property inspection. Shortly before the closing takes place, the buyer's agent and the buyer usually make a *final inspection* of the property with the seller's agent (often called the *walk-through*). Through this inspection, the buyer can ensure that necessary repairs have been made, that the property has been well maintained, that all fixtures are in place and that there has been no unauthorized removal or alteration of any part of the improvements.

(**Note:** The request for a preclosing walk-through should be written into the contract to purchase. This clause usually provides that the buyer has an option to a final walk-through inspection within approximately 24 hours prior to actual closing or at a date and time agreed on with the seller. The NCAR standard form Offer to Purchase and Contract has this clause.)

Soil suitability test. If property is unimproved and does not have access to a central sewage disposal system, the buyer should order a *soil suitability test*. This test measures the soil's ability to absorb and drain water. Soil must "perc" properly before approval will be given to install a septic tank system (for on-site sewage disposal). In North Carolina, the buyer customarily pays for this test (formerly called the *percolation test*).

Property survey. A *property survey* gives the purchaser information about the exact location and size of the property. The sales contract specifies who is to pay for the survey. It is usual for the survey to "spot" the location of all buildings, driveways, fences and other improvements located *on* the premises being purchased. Any improvements located on adjoining property that may encroach on the premises being bought also are noted. The survey should describe in detail any existing easements and encroachments. Whether or not the sales contract calls for a survey, lenders frequently require one. The primary reason for the survey is to ensure that nothing has occurred—such as an encroachment—that may make the title unmarketable.

In Practice   Licensees should avoid recommending an individual or a specific source for any inspections or testing services. If the buyer suffers any injury as a result of a provider's negligence, the licensee also may be liable. The better practice is to give clients the names of several professionals who offer high-quality services. Agents should recommend a full set of inspections even if the purchase is made with no financing involved.

Seller's Issues Obviously, the seller's main interest is receiving payment for the property. He or she needs to be sure that the buyer has obtained the necessary financing and has sufficient funds to complete the sale. The seller also needs to be certain that he or she has complied with all the buyer's requirements so the transaction can be completed.

Both parties will want to inspect the closing statement to ensure that all monies involved in the transaction have been accounted for properly. The parties may be accompanied by their attorneys.

In Practice   Depending on local custom, the broker's role at closing can vary from simply being present to conducting the proceedings. A broker's service generally continues after the sales contract is signed—the broker advises the parties in practical matters and makes sure all details are taken care of so that the closing can proceed smoothly. (But remember, a real estate broker is not authorized to give legal advice or otherwise engage in the practice of law.) The broker might make arrangements for such items as title evidence, surveys, appraisals, termite inspections and repairs, or the broker might recommend sources of these services to the parties. At least three sources of each type of professional service should be recommended to give the parties free choice. The broker also is held responsible by the North Carolina Real Estate Commission for the accuracy and delivery of the closing statement either at closing or within five days after closing [see G.S. 93A-6(a)(14)].

Title Procedures Both the buyer and the buyer's lender want assurance that the seller's title complies with the requirements of the sales contract. The buyer usually is required to produce a current title commitment from the title insurance company through the closing attorney. The title commitment is a statement of the status of the seller's title. It discloses all liens, encumbrances, easements, conditions or restrictions that appear on the record and to which the seller's title is subject.

On the date of the closing meeting (the date of delivery of the deed), the buyer has a title commitment that was probably issued several days or weeks before the closing. For this reason, the final opinion of title and the title insurance policy are issued after closing (see Chapter 4).

Unless the buyer is assuming the seller's mortgage loan, the seller's existing loan is paid in full and satisfied on record. The exact amount required to pay the existing loan is provided in a current *payoff statement* from the lender, effective on the date of closing. This payoff statement states the unpaid amount of principal, interest due through the date of payment, the fee for issuing the certificate of satisfaction or release deed, credits (if any) for tax and insurance reserves and the amount of any prepayment penalties. The same procedure is followed for any other liens that must be released before the buyer takes title.

For transactions in which the buyer assumes the seller's existing mortgage loan, the buyer needs to know the exact balance of the loan as of the closing date. In some areas it is customary for the buyer to obtain a mortgage reduction or **estoppel certificate** from the lender that certifies the amount owed on the mortgage loan, the interest rate and the last interest payment made.

Also, the seller may be required to execute an *affidavit of lien waiver* (*affidavit of title*). This is a sworn statement in which the seller assures the title insurance company (and the buyer) that there have been no judgments, bankruptcies or divorces involving the seller since the date of the title examination. The affidavit promises that no unrecorded deeds or contracts were made, no repairs or improvements were made that have not been paid and no defects in the title have arisen that the seller knows of. The seller also affirms that he or she is in possession of the premises. In some areas, this form is required before the title insurance company will issue an owner's policy to the buyer. The affidavit gives the title insurance company the right to sue the seller if his or her statements in the affidavit are incorrect.

CONDUCTING THE CLOSING

In North Carolina, closings are conducted by gathering the parties together and exchanging copies of the documents. This kind of closing is called the *closing meeting* (or a *face-to-face closing*). Current practice in North Carolina is that the buyer is represented by a lawyer. The seller also may be represented by a different lawyer but usually is not. The attorney, normally selected and paid by the buyer, also represents the lender's interest.

A closing involves the resolution of two issues. First, the promises made in the sales contract are fulfilled. Second, the buyer's loan is finalized and the mortgage lender or closing attorney disperses the loan funds. Closings are most often held in the attorney's office; however, they may be held at a number of locations, including the office of the lending institution or the broker. Those attending a typical residential closing may include

- the buyer;
- the seller;
- the real estate salespersons or brokers (both the buyer's and the seller's agents);
- the seller's and the buyer's attorneys;

- representatives of the lending institutions involved with the buyer's new mortgage loan, the buyer's assumption of the seller's existing loan or the seller's payoff of an existing loan; and
- the representative of the title insurance company (although this seldom happens in North Carolina).

Escrow Type Closing

The escrow type closing may be used by the attorney if the parties cannot attend the closing meeting. The parties can agree in advance that the attorney will act as escrow agent, and all funds and paperwork are delivered "into escrow." The designated escrow agent is an impartial third party who conducts the closing. When the deed has been prepared and delivered to the escrow agent, it is considered to have been legally delivered to the buyer under what is called the *relation back doctrine.* This type of closing is seldom used in North Carolina. In other states that practice this type of closing, title insurance companies and lending institutions often act as escrow agents.

Closing Agent or Closing Officer

One person usually conducts the proceedings at a closing and calculates the division of income and expenses between the parties (called *settlement*). For some closings, real estate brokers preside. For others, the closing agent is the buyer's attorney.

The Exchange

When the parties are satisfied that everything is in order, the exchange is made. All pertinent documents then are recorded *in the correct order* to ensure continuity of title. For instance, if the seller is paying off an existing loan and the buyer is obtaining a new loan, the seller's satisfaction of mortgage must be recorded before the seller's deed to the buyer is recorded. The buyer's new mortgage or deed of trust must be recorded *after* the deed, because the buyers cannot pledge the property as security for the loan until they own it. The transaction is "closed" when all documents have been recorded.

IRS Reporting Requirements

Every real estate transaction must be reported to the IRS by the closing agent on Form 1099-S. Information includes the sales price, the amount of property tax reimbursement credited to the seller and the seller's Social Security number. If the closing agent does not notify the IRS, the responsibility for filing the form falls on the mortgage lender, although the brokers or the parties to the transaction ultimately could be held liable.

Lender's Interest in Closing

Whether a buyer is obtaining new financing or assuming the seller's existing loan, the lender wants to protect its security interest in the property. The lender has an interest in making sure that the buyer is getting good, marketable title and that tax and insurance payments are maintained. Lenders want their mortgage liens to have priority over other liens. They also want to ensure that the insurance will be paid up if the property is damaged or destroyed. For this reason a lender generally requires a title insurance policy and a fire and hazard insurance policy (along with a receipt for the premium). In addition, a lender may require additional information: a survey, a termite or other inspection report or a certificate of occupancy (for newly constructed buildings). The lender also may request that a reserve account be established for tax and insurance payments. Lenders sometimes even require representation by their own attorney(s) at closings.

RESPA REQUIREMENTS

The federal **Real Estate Settlement Procedures Act (RESPA)** was enacted to protect consumers from abusive lending practices. RESPA also aids consumers during the mortgage loan settlement process. It ensures that consumers are provided with important, accurate and timely information about the actual costs of settling or closing the transaction. It also eliminates "kickbacks" and other referral fees that tend to inflate the costs of settlement unnecessarily. RESPA prohibits lenders from requiring excessive escrow account deposits.

> **RESPA's Consumer Protections**
>
> - CLO regulation
> - CBA disclosure
> - Settlement cost booklet
> - Good-faith estimate of settlement costs
> - Uniform Settlement Statement
> - Prohibition of kickbacks and unearned fees

RESPA requirements apply when the purchase is financed by a federally related mortgage loan. *Federally related loans* are loans made by banks, savings and loan associations or other lenders whose deposits are insured by federal agencies. The term also covers loans insured by the FHA or guaranteed by the VA; loans administered by HUD; or loans intended to be sold by the lender to Fannie Mae, Ginnie Mae or Freddie Mac. RESPA is administered by HUD.

RESPA regulations apply to first-lien residential mortgage loans made to finance the purchase of one- to four-family homes, cooperatives and condominiums, either for investment or occupancy. RESPA also governs second or subordinate liens for home equity loans. RESPA does not cover a transaction financed solely by a purchase-money mortgage taken back by the seller, an installment contract (contract for deed) or the buyer's assumption of the seller's existing loan. However, if the terms of the assumed loan are modified or if the lender charges more than $50 for the assumption, the transaction will be subject to RESPA.

In Practice   While RESPA's requirements are aimed primarily at lenders, some of its provisions affect real estate brokers and agents as well. Real estate licensees fall under RESPA when they refer buyers to particular lenders, title companies, attorneys or other providers of settlement services. Licensees who offer computerized loan origination (CLO) services also are subject to regulation. Remember: buyers have the right to select their own providers of settlement services.

Controlled Business Arrangements   For the real estate consumer, a service that increases in popularity is "one-stop-shopping." A real estate firm, title insurance company, mortgage broker, home inspection company and even a moving company may agree to offer a package of services to consumers. RESPA permits such a **controlled business arrangement (CBA)** *as long as the consumer is clearly informed of the relationship among the service providers and that other providers are available.* Fees may not be exchanged among the affiliated companies simply for referring business to one another. This may be a particularly important issue for licensees who offer **computerized loan origination (CLO)** services to their clients and customers. While a borrower's ability to "comparison shop" for a loan may be enhanced by a CLO system, his or her range of choices must not be limited. Consumers must be informed of the availability of other lenders.

Disclosure Requirements

Lenders and settlement agents have certain disclosure obligations at the time of loan application and loan closing.

- *Special information booklet:* Lenders must provide a copy of a special informational HUD booklet to every person from whom they receive or for whom they prepare a loan application (except for refinancing). The HUD booklet must be given at the time the application is received or within three days afterward. The booklet provides the borrower with general information about settlement (closing) costs. It also explains the various provisions of RESPA, including a line-by-line explanation of the Uniform Settlement Statement.
- *Good-faith estimate of settlement costs:* No later than three business days after the receipt of the loan application, the lender must provide to all borrowers a good-faith estimate of the settlement costs the borrower is likely to incur. This estimate may be either a specific figure or a range of costs based on comparable past transactions in the area. In addition, if the lender requires that a particular attorney or title company be used to conduct the closing, the lender must state whether it has any business relationship with that firm and must estimate the charges for this service.
- *Uniform Settlement Statement (HUD Form 1):* RESPA requires that a special HUD form (shown in Figure 14.3, page 312) be completed to itemize all charges to be paid by the borrower and seller in connection with settlement. The **Uniform Settlement Statement (HUD-1)** includes all charges that will be collected at closing, whether required by the lender or by a third party. Items paid by the borrower and seller outside closing, not required by the lender, are not included on HUD-1. Charges required by the lender that are paid for before closing are indicated as "paid outside closing" (POC) but are not reflected in the "bottom line" totals of HUD-1. RESPA prohibits a lender from requiring that a borrower deposit amounts in escrow accounts for taxes and insurance that exceed certain limits, to prevent the lender from taking advantage of the borrower. The *seller* is also prohibited from requiring, as a condition of the sale, that the buyer purchase title insurance from a particular company.

The settlement statement must be made available for inspection by the borrower *at or before settlement.* Borrowers have the right to inspect the completed HUD-1, to the extent that the figures are available, *one business day before the closing.* (Sellers are not entitled to this privilege.)

Lenders must retain these statements for two years after the date of closing. In addition, state law requires that licensees retain all records of a transaction for a three-year period (see Rule A.0108). The Uniform Settlement Statement may be altered to allow for local custom, and certain lines may be deleted if they do not apply in the area.

Kickbacks and Referral Fees

RESPA *prohibits the payment of kickbacks,* or *unearned fees,* incident to or as part of a real estate settlement service. It prohibits referral fees *when no services are actually rendered.* The payment or receipt of a fee, kickback or anything of value for referrals for settlement services is prohibited for activities such as making mortgage loans, title searches, title insurance, services rendered by attorneys, surveys, credit reports or appraisals.

Preliminaries to Closing

Preparation for closing involves ordering and reviewing an array of documents. The drafting and preparation of the documents must take place. The closing attorney has the responsibility for ensuring that all legal documents are prepared and properly delivered. Legal documents required to close a residential transaction include items listed below.

Documents provided by the seller include the following:

- The deed (usually prepared by the buyer's attorney, but the seller normally pays this fee)
- Affidavit as to mechanic's lien
- Bill of sale of personal property (If any of the seller's personal property is being transferred to the buyer, ownership can be shown by a bill of sale.)
- Leases and related documents (if the property being transferred is currently leased)
- Statement from the seller's lender (A current loan balance payoff figure must be available as of the day of closing.)
- Proof of repairs or services (If any repairs were necessary, the seller must bring proof to the closing that the repairs have been done.)

Documents provided by the buyer include the following:

- Financing documents (The closing attorney receives a closing package from the lender with instructions on how to prepare the financing documents, including the deed of trust and the promissory note.)
- Title insurance policy (issued after the attorney's opinion of good title)
- Property insurance policy (The buyer is required to bring a current policy to the closing.)
- Wood-destroying insect inspection report (The buyer normally pays for this unless the transaction is financed with a VA loan, in which case the seller pays.)
- Property survey

PREPARATION OF CLOSING STATEMENT

A typical real estate transaction involves expenses for both parties in addition to the purchase price. These include items prepaid by the seller for which he or she must be reimbursed (such as taxes) and items of expense the seller has incurred but for which the buyer will be billed (such as mortgage interest paid in arrears). The financial responsibility for these items must be prorated (or divided) between the buyer and the seller. All expense and prorated items are accounted for on the settlement statement. This is how the exact amount of cash required from the buyer and the net proceeds to the seller are determined (see Figure 14.1). The closing statement worksheet and/or the HUD-1 form are not considered to be legal documents and may be prepared by a licensed real estate agent.

If a real estate licensee prepares the closing statement, the Real Estate Commission will hold that licensee responsible for accuracy and delivery. If another person prepares the statement (attorney, lender, escrow agent, etc.), the Real Estate Commission will hold the broker accountable for accuracy and delivery. The Commission can take appropriate disciplinary action

Figure 14.1	Allocation of Expenses	
Item	**Paid by Seller**	**Paid by Buyer**
Broker's commission	✗ by agreement	✗ by agreement
Attorney's fees	✗ by agreement	✗ by agreement
Recording expenses	✗ to clear title	✗ transfer charges
Excise tax (revenue) stamps	✗	
Title expenses		✗ attorney inspection of title insurance
Loan fees	✗ prepayment penalty	✗ origination fee
Tax and insurance reserves (escrow or impound accounts)		✗
Appraisal fees		✗ if required by lender
Survey fees	✗ if required to pay by sales contract	✗ new mortgage financing

against a broker who fails to provide complete and accurate closing statements and ensure proper delivery [see G.S. 93A-6(a)(14)]. Even though the broker is responsible for accuracy and delivery, the salesperson may attend and participate in the closing.

How the Closing Statement Works

The completion of a **closing statement** involves an accounting of the parties' debits and credits. A **debit** is a charge. That is, it is an amount that a party owes and must pay at the closing. A **credit** is an amount entered in a person's favor—an amount that has already been paid, an amount being reimbursed or an amount the buyer promises to pay in the form of a loan.

> A *debit* is an amount *to be paid by* the buyer or seller; a *credit* is an amount *payable to* the buyer or seller.

To determine the amount the buyer needs at the closing, the buyer's debits are totaled. Any expenses and prorated amounts for items prepaid by the seller are added to the purchase price. Then the buyer's credits are totaled. These include the earnest money (already paid), the balance of the loan the buyer is obtaining or assuming and the seller's share of any prorated items that the buyer will pay in the future (see Figure 14.2). Finally, the total of the buyer's credits is subtracted from the total debits to arrive at the actual amount of cash the buyer must bring to the closing. Usually the buyer brings a cashier's or a certified check.

A similar procedure is followed to determine how much money the seller actually will receive. The seller's debits and credits are totaled separately. The credits include the purchase price plus the buyer's share of any prorated items that the seller has prepaid. The seller's debits include expenses, the seller's share of prorated items to be paid later by the buyer and the balance of any mortgage loan or other lien that the seller is paying off. Finally the total of the seller's debits is subtracted from the total credits to arrive at the amount the seller will receive.

Figure 14.2 Credits and Debits					
Item	Credit to Buyer	Debit to Buyer	Credit to Seller	Debit to Seller	Prorated
Principal amount of new mortgage	X				
Payoff of existing mortgage				X	
Unpaid principal balance if assumed mortgage	X			X	
Accrued interest on existing assumed mortgage	X			X	X
Tenants' security deposits	X			X	
Purchase-money mortgage	X			X	
Unpaid water and other utility bills	X			X	X
Buyer's earnest money	X				
Selling price of property		X	X		
Fuel oil on hand (valued at current market price)		X	X		
Prepaid insurance and tax reserve for mortgage assumed by buyer		X	X		X
Refund to seller of prepaid water charges and similar utility expenses		X	X		X
Prepaid general real estate taxes		X			X
Excise tax (revenue) stamps				X	

Broker's commission. The responsibility for paying the broker's commission was determined by previous agreement. If the broker is the agent for the seller, the seller is responsible for paying the commission. If there is an agency agreement between a broker and the buyer or if two agents are involved, one for the seller and one for the buyer, the commission may be apportioned as an expense between both parties or according to some other arrangement.

Attorney's fees. If either of the parties' attorneys is to be paid from the closing proceeds, that party is charged with the expense in the closing statement. This expense may include fees for the preparation or review of documents or for representing the parties at settlement.

Recording expenses. The *seller* usually pays for recording charges (filing fees) necessary to clear all defects and furnish the purchaser with a marketable title. Items customarily charged to the seller include the recording of release deeds or satisfaction of mortgages, quitclaim deeds, affidavits and satisfaction of mechanic's lien claims. The *purchaser* pays for recording charges that arise from the actual transfer of title. Usually such items include recording the deed that conveys title to the purchaser and the mortgage or deed of trust executed by the purchaser.

Excise tax (revenue) stamps. North Carolina requires a tax in the form of revenue stamps on real estate conveyances. This expense is borne by the seller.

Title expenses. Custom usually requires that the buyer obtain and pay for his or her own title examination.

Evidence of title relied on in the purchase of a parcel of real estate includes a title guaranty or guaranty policy, a fee policy of title insurance or an abstract. Descriptions of these evidences of title are included in Chapter 4.

The title guaranty and fee policy of title insurance are one-time premium charges for insurance that insures the purchaser's title during the period of ownership of real estate. Some lenders request an American Land Title Association (ALTA) policy that insures the mortgagee for the amount of the mortgage loan.

Loan fees. When the purchaser secures a new loan to finance the purchase, the lender ordinarily charges a loan origination fee of 1 to 2 percent of the loan. The fee usually is paid by the purchaser at the time the transaction closes. The lender also may charge discount points. If the buyer assumes the seller's existing financing, there may be an assumption fee. Also, under the terms of some mortgage loans the seller may be required to pay a prepayment charge or penalty for paying off the mortgage loan in advance of its due date.

Tax reserves and insurance reserves (escrow or impound accounts). Most mortgage lenders require that borrowers provide a reserve fund or escrow account to pay future real estate taxes and insurance premiums, especially when the loan-to-value ratio exceeds specified percentages. These payments are often referred to as *prepaids*. The borrower starts the account at closing by depositing funds to cover at least the amount of unpaid real estate taxes from the date of lien to the end of the current month. (The buyer receives a credit from the seller at closing for any unpaid taxes.) Afterward, an amount equal to one month's portion of the estimated taxes is included in the borrower's monthly mortgage payment.

The borrower is responsible for maintaining adequate fire or hazard insurance as a condition of the mortgage loan. Generally, the first year's premium is paid in full at closing. An amount equal to one month's premium is paid after that. The borrower's monthly loan payment includes the principal and interest on the loan plus one-twelfth of the estimated taxes and insurance (PITI). The taxes and insurance are held by the lender in the escrow or impound account until the bills are due. Some lenders also use the escrow account for maintenance fees that are payable on a recurring basis to a homeowner's association.

Appraisal fees. Either the seller or the purchaser pays the appraisal fees, depending on who orders the appraisal. When the buyer obtains a mortgage, it is customary for the lender to require an appraisal. In that case, the buyer bears the cost. If the fee is paid at the time of the loan application, it is reflected on the HUD-1 form as having been *paid outside closing* (POC).

Survey fees. The purchaser who obtains new mortgage financing customarily pays the survey fees.

Additional fees. An FHA borrower owes a lump sum for payment of the mortgage insurance premium (MIP) if it is not being financed as part of the loan. A VA mortgagor pays a funding fee directly to the VA at closing. If a conventional loan carries private mortgage insurance, the buyer prepays one year's insurance premium at closing.

Accounting for Expenses

Expenses paid out of the closing proceeds are debited only to the party making the payment. Occasionally an expense item such as an escrow fee, a settlement fee or a transfer tax may be shared by the buyer and the seller. In that case, each party is debited for his or her share of the expense.

PRORATIONS

Most closings involve a division of financial responsibility between the buyer and seller for such items as loan interest, taxes, rents, and fuel and utility bills. These allowances are called **prorations.** Closing computations typically mean that each party pays for what they used or the time they occupied the property during the appropriate period (month or year). Prorations are necessary to ensure that expenses are divided fairly between the seller and the buyer. For example, the seller may owe current taxes that have not yet been billed; the buyer will want this settled at the closing. If real property taxes have been paid in advance, the seller is entitled to a rebate at the closing. If the buyer assumes the seller's existing mortgage or deed of trust, the seller usually owes the buyer an allowance for accrued interest through the date of closing. The seller is normally responsible for expenses owed on the day of closing, except the buyer's daily interim interest on a new loan, which would be a single entry debit to the buyer.

Accrued items are items to be prorated (such as water bills and interest on an assumed mortgage) that are owed by the seller but will be paid later by the buyer. The seller therefore pays for these items by giving the buyer credit for them at closing. The seller receives a debit for his or her prorated share, and the buyer is given an equal amount as a credit.

Prepaid items are expenses to be prorated, such as real estate taxes already paid by the seller for the current year prior to closing and a homeowner's insurance premium, if the policy is to transferred to the buyer. The item is prorated and the buyer's allocated portion is reflected as a credit to the seller and as a debit to the buyer.

The Arithmetic of Prorating

Accurate prorating involves four considerations:

1. The nature of the item being prorated
2. Whether it is an accrued item that requires the determination of an earned amount
3. Whether it is a prepaid item (such as prepaid real estate taxes) that requires that the unearned amount (that is, a refund to the seller) be determined
4. What arithmetic processes must be used

There are several different ways to prorate items that require a division of funds among the parties (the buyer and the seller). Those listed below are the most common ways to prorate, but tables and computer programs can be used or any other method the buyer and seller may agree to.

360-day year/30-day month method. This method is referred to as the *banker's year/banker's month method* (sometimes as the *statutory method*) and is, perhaps, the easiest to use, but probably not the most accurate. (This is the method used for all prorations in the textbook and on the North Carolina Real Estate State Licensing Examinations.) The year is treated as having 360 days with each month having 30 days.

365-day year method. This method is probably the most accurate and normally will be used in actual real estate closings. If the closing takes place in a leap year, then a 366-day year is used.

Actual-days-in-the-month method. Using this method, the actual days in the month are used. For instance, January would have 31 days and November would have 30 days.

The final proration figure will vary slightly, depending on which computation method is used. (Note that whichever method is used, the seller is responsible for the day of closing on all prorations involving the seller unless otherwise agreed.) The final figure also will vary according to the number of decimal places to which the division is carried. *All of the computations in this chapter are computed by carrying the division to three decimal places.* The third decimal place is rounded off to cents only after the final proration figure is determined.

Accrued Items

When the real estate tax is levied for the calendar year (from January to December) and is payable either during that year or in the following year, the accrued portion is for the period from January 1 through and including the day of closing. If the current tax bill has not yet been issued, the parties must agree on an estimated amount based on the previous year's bill and any known changes in assessment or tax levy for the current year, referred to as the *best estimate* method.

Sample proration calculation. For example, assume a sale is to be closed on April 17 and current real estate taxes of $1,200 are to be prorated accordingly. The accrued period, then, is 107 days (from January 1 through April 17).

January	30
February	30
March	30
April	17
Total	107 days

First determine the prorated cost of the real estate tax per day:

$$\$1,200 \div 360 = \$3.333 \text{ per day}$$

Next, multiply this figure by the accrued period to determine the prorated real estate tax:

$3.333	per day
× 107	days
$356.63	real estate tax

Thus, the accrued real estate tax for 107 days is $356.63. This amount represents the seller's accrued earned tax; it is a *credit to the buyer* and a *debit to the seller* on the closing statement.

In Practice   Many title insurance companies provide proration charts that detail tax factors for each day in the year. To determine a tax proration using one of these charts, multiply the factor given for the closing date by the annual real estate tax.

Prepaid Items   A tax proration could be a *prepaid item*. Because the real estate tax is due and payable on September 1, it may be paid before a closing takes place. Tax prorations calculated for closings taking place later in the year must reflect the fact that the seller has already paid the tax. For example, in the preceding problem, suppose that the taxes already have been paid. The buyer then has to reimburse the seller for the buyer's portion of the taxes; the proration would be *credited to the seller* and *debited to the buyer*.

Sample prepaid item calculation. An example of a prepaid item is the real estate taxes. Assume that closing is to take place on November 13 and the seller has received the annual real estate tax bill of $1,850 and has paid that bill. The seller's liability for taxes is only for the period of January 1 through and including the day of closing, so the seller should get back the buyer's portion of the taxes.

$1,850 ÷ 360	= $5.139 per day
January 1 – November 13 = 313 days × $5.139	= $1,608.507
$1,850.00 – $1,608.51	= $241.49 credit seller/debit buyer

Sample prepaid homeowner's insurance calculation. The closing takes place on June 18, and the sellers had purchased and paid for an annual homeowner's insurance policy on February 1 in the amount of $720. The loan is to be assumed and the insurance policy is to be assigned to the buyers.

$720 ÷ 360   = $2.00 daily premium
February 1 – June 18 = 138 days × $2.00 = $276.00
$720 – $276   = $444 credit seller/debit buyer

General Rules for Prorating

Following are some general guidelines for preparing the closing statement:

- In North Carolina, the seller owns the property on the day of closing, and prorations or apportionments are usually made *through and including the day of closing.*
- Always prorate for the seller first. Once the seller's portion is computed, the buyer's amount will be the same, but an opposite entry: if a debit to the seller, it's a credit to buyer, same amount of money.
- Accrued or prepaid *real estate taxes* are usually prorated at the closing. When the amount of the current real estate tax cannot be determined definitely, the proration is usually based on the last obtainable tax bill.
- *Special assessments* for municipal improvements such as sewers, water mains or streets are usually paid in annual installments over several years, with annual interest charged on the outstanding balance of future installments. The seller normally pays the entire balance due, unless the buyer and seller have agreed otherwise in the sales contract. *The special assessment generally is not prorated at the closing.* The contract of sale must address the manner in which special assessments are to be handled at settlement.
- *Rents* are usually adjusted on the basis of the *actual* number of days in the month of closing in real life situations. It is customary for the seller to receive the rents for the day of closing and to pay all expenses for that day. If any rents for the current month are uncollected when the sale is closed, the buyer often will agree by a separate letter to collect the rents if possible and remit the prorata share to the seller. If the seller is holding a tenant security deposit, it can be transferred to the buyer by a double-entry (debit seller/credit buyer). The tenant security deposit is not prorated.

Sample rent prorations. Assume the monthly rent is $600, closing takes place on June 21 and the seller has received the rent for the month of June (paid in advance).

$600 ÷ 30 days   = $20 per day
21 days (when property owned by seller) × $20 = $420 seller's share
$600 – $420   = $180 buyer's share (debit seller/credit buyer)

Now assume that the monthly rent is $675, closing takes place on June 5, and the seller has not collected the rent prior to closing (paid in arrears). The buyer will collect the entire month's rent of $675.

$675 ÷ 30 days   = $22.50 per day
5 days (when property owned by seller) × $22.50 = $112.50 seller's share (debit buyer/credit seller)

Mortgage loan interest. On almost every mortgage loan the interest is paid *in arrears,* so buyers and sellers must understand that the mortgage payment due on June 1, for example, includes interest due for the month of

May. Thus, if the buyer is getting a new loan, the lender will start charging interest on the day of closing, and will normally collect that amount from the buyer (single entry debit to buyer) on closing. The buyer will not make a monthly payment until the first of the second month. Furthermore, the buyer who assumes a mortgage on May 18 and makes the June payment will be paying for the time the seller occupied the property and should be credited with part of the month's interest.

Sample interest on a new loan (interim interest). Assume that closing is April 12, and the buyer's first mortgage payment will be due on June 1. The loan amount is $95,600 and the interest rate is 6 percent.

$95,600 × .06 interest rate = $5,736 annual interest
$5,736 ÷ 360 days = $15.933 daily interest
19 days × $15.933 = $302.73 interest owed by buyer
(debit buyer)

Note that this is not a prorated item. It is a cost to be paid only by the buyer; therefore, the day of closing belongs to the buyer.

Sample assumed loan interest proration. The loan amount to be assumed is $105,555 at 7 percent interest. The day of closing is May 18. The first step is to calculate the daily amount of interest, then multiply that by the number of days the seller owned the property during that month.

$105,555 × .07 interest rate = $7,388.85 annual interest
$7,388.85 ÷ 360 days = $20.525 daily interest
18 days × $20.525 = $369.45 seller's share of interest
(debit seller/credit buyer)

Security deposits. Security deposits made by tenants to cover the last month's rent of the lease or to cover the cost of repairing damage caused by the tenant are generally transferred by the seller to the buyer (debit seller/ credit buyer), not prorated.

Summary of Items To Be Prorated

Real estate taxes, unpaid	Debit seller/credit buyer
Real estate taxes, prepaid	Credit seller/debit buyer
Rents collected by seller	Debit seller/credit buyer
Rents to be collected by buyer	Credit seller/debit buyer
Interest on assumed loan	Debit seller/credit buyer

Note: A homeowner's insurance policy premium may be prorated if the policy is to be assigned to the buyer, which is extremely rare. Entries would be credit seller/debit buyer for the buyer's prorated share of the premium.

Summary of Other Double Entry Items

Sales price	Credit seller/debit buyer
Assumption of seller's loan	Debit seller/credit buyer
Purchase-money mortgage	Debit seller/credit buyer
Transfer of seller's escrow account	Credit seller/debit buyer
Tenant security deposit, assigned	Debit seller/credit buyer

Fuel oil or gas	Credit seller/debit buyer
Cost of separately sold personal property	Credit seller/debit buyer
Seller's personal property taxes to be paid later by buyer or lender	Debit seller/credit buyer

Normal Single Entry Items to Seller

Seller's personal property taxes to be paid at closing	Debit seller
Pay off seller's existing loan	Debit seller
Deed preparation fee	Debit seller
Revenue stamps	Debit seller
Recordation fee, satisfaction of seller's mortgage	Debit seller
Broker's commission	Debit seller
Delinquent real/personal property taxes	Debit seller
IRS tax liens	Debit seller

Normal Single Entry Items to Buyer

Homeowner's policy, if new	Debit buyer
Loan origination fee	Debit buyer
Financing documents preparation fee	Debit buyer
Deed/mortgage recording fees	Debit buyer
Title insurance premium	Debit buyer
Property survey fee	Debit buyer
Title examination/attorney fee	Debit buyer
Advanced escrow deposits	Debit buyer
Interim interest on buyer's new loan	Debit buyer
Loan discount points	Debit buyer
Earnest money deposit	Credit buyer
New first mortgage loan	Credit buyer
Second/third new mortgage loan	Credit buyer

Note: If taxable personal property (such as a farm tractor) is to be conveyed to the buyer along with real property, the personal property taxes on the item would be prorated per the terms of the new NCAR standard Offer to Purchase and Contract form.

Note: Real property taxes may be handled as a "double-debit" under certain circumstances: (1) agreement of the buyer and seller, (2) seller has received the tax bill, (3) the taxes have not been paid and (4) the taxes are to be paid at closing.

Example: The closing date is December 15, annual taxes are $1,260 and the double-debit method will be used.

$1,260 ÷ 360 days	=	$3.50 daily taxes
January 1 – December 15	=	345 days
345 days × $3.50	=	$1,207.50 debit seller
$1,260 – $1,207.50	=	$52.50 debit buyer

SAMPLE CLOSING STATEMENT

There are many possible formats for settlement computations. The remaining portion of this chapter illustrates a sample transaction using the HUD Uniform Settlement Statement in Figure 14.3 on page 312.

Figure 14.3 **RESPA Uniform Settlement Statement**

A. Settlement Statement

U.S. Department of Housing and Urban Development

OMB Approval No. 2502-0265

B. Type of Loan

1. ☐ FHA 2. ☐ FmHA 3. ☐ Conv. Unins.
4. ☐ VA 5. ☐ Conv. Ins.

6. File Number:	7. Loan Number:	8. Mortgage Insurance Case Number:

C. Note: This form is furnished to give you a statement of actual settlement costs. Amounts paid to and by the settlement agent are shown. Items marked "(p.o.c.)" were paid outside the closing; they are shown here for informational purposes and are not included in the totals.

D. Name & Address of Borrower:	E. Name & Address of Seller:	F. Name & Address of Lender:

G. Property Location:

H. Settlement Agent:

Place of Settlement:

I. Settlement Date:

J. Summary of Borrower's Transaction		K. Summary of Seller's Transaction	
100. Gross Amount Due From Borrower		**400. Gross Amount Due To Seller**	
101. Contract sales price	115,000.00	401. Contract sales price	115,000.00
102. Personal property		402. Personal property	
103. Settlement charges to borrower (line 1400)	5,697.55	403.	
104.		404.	
105.		405.	
Adjustments for items paid by seller in advance		**Adjustments for items paid by seller in advance**	
106. City/town taxes to		406. City/town taxes to	
107. County taxes to		407. County taxes to	
108. Assessments to		408. Assessments to	
109.		409.	
110.		410.	
111.		411.	
112.		412.	
120. Gross Amount Due From Borrower	120,697.55	**420. Gross Amount Due To Seller**	115,000.00
200. Amounts Paid By Or In Behalf Of Borrower		**500. Reductions In Amount Due To Seller**	
201. Deposit or earnest money	23,000.00	501. Excess deposit (see instructions)	
202. Principal amount of new loan(s)	92,000.00	502. Settlement charges to seller (line 1400)	7,560.00
203. Existing loan(s) taken subject to		503. Existing loan(s) taken subject to	
204.		504. Payoff of first mortgage loan	57,964.47
205.		505. Payoff of second mortgage loan	
206.		506.	
207.		507.	
208.		508.	
209.		509.	
Adjustments for items unpaid by seller		**Adjustments for items unpaid by seller**	
210. City/town taxes to		510. City/town taxes to	
211. County taxes 1/1 to 6/15	790.68	511. County taxes 1/1 to 6/15	790.68
212. Assessments to		512. Assessments to	
213.		513.	
214.		514.	
215.		515.	
216.		516.	
217.		517.	
218.		518.	
219.		519.	
220. Total Paid By/For Borrower	115,790.68	**520. Total Reduction Amount Due Seller**	66,315.15
300. Cash At Settlement From/To Borrower		**600. Cash At Settlement To/From Seller**	
301. Gross Amount due from borrower (line 120)	120,697.55	601. Gross amount due to seller (line 420)	115,000.00
302. Less amounts paid by/for borrower (line 220)	(115,790.68)	602. Less reductions in amt. due seller (line 520)	(66,315.15)
303. Cash ☐ From ☐ To Borrower	4,906.89	**603. Cash ☐ To ☐ From Seller**	48,684.85

Section 5 of the Real Estate Settlement Procedures Act (RESPA) requires the following: • HUD must develop a Special Information Booklet to help persons borrowing money to finance the purchase of residential real estate to better understand the nature and costs of real estate settlement services; • Each lender must provide the booklet to all applicants from whom it receives or for whom it prepares a written application to borrow money to finance the purchase of residential real estate; • Lenders must prepare and distribute with the Booklet a Good Faith Estimate of the settlement costs that the borrower is likely to incur in connection with the settlement. These disclosures are manadatory.

Section 4(a) of RESPA mandates that HUD develop and prescribe this standard form to be used at the time of loan settlement to provide full disclosure of all charges imposed upon the borrower and seller. These are third party disclosures that are designed to provide the borrower with pertinent information during the settlement process in order to be a better shopper.

The Public Reporting Burden for this collection of information is estimated to average one hour per response, including the time for reviewing instructions, searching existing data sources, gathering and maintaining the data needed, and completing and reviewing the collection of information.

This agency may not collect this information, and you are not required to complete this form, unless it displays a currently valid OMB control number.

The information requested does not lend itself to confidentiality.

Figure 14.3 RESPA Uniform Settlement Statement (continued)

L. Settlement Charges

			Paid From Borrowers Funds at Settlement	Paid From Seller's Funds at Settlement
700.	Total Sales/Broker's Commission based on price $ 115,000 @ 6.00 % = 6,900.00			
	Division of Commission (line 700) as follows:			
701.	$ to			
702.	$ to			
703.	Commission paid at Settlement			6,900.00
704.				
800.	**Items Payable In Connection With Loan**			
801.	Loan Origination Fee 0.0000 %		920.00	
802.	Loan Discount %		1,840.00	
803.	Appraisal Fee 250.00 to SWIFT APPRAISAL		POC	
804.	Credit Report 60.00 to ACME CREDIT		POC	
805.	Lender's Inspection Fee			
806.	Mortgage Insurance Application Fee to			
807.	Assumption Fee			
808.				
809.				
810.				
811.				
900.	**Items Required By Lender To Be Paid In Advance**			
901.	Interest from 6/15 to 6/30 @$ 25.556 /day		408.90	
902.	Mortgage Insurance Premium for months to			
903.	Hazard Insurance Premium for 1.0 years to HITE INS.		345.00	
904.	years to			
905.				
1000.	**Reserves Deposited With Lender**			
1001.	Hazard insurance 2 months @$ 28.75 per month		57.50	
1002.	Mortgage insurance months @$ per month			
1003.	City property taxes months @$ per month			
1004.	County property taxes 7 months @$ 143.75 per month		1,006.25	
1005.	Annual assessments months @$ per month			
1006.	months @$ per month			
1007.	months @$ per month			
1008.	months @$ per month			
1100.	**Title Charges**			
1101.	Settlement or closing fee to			
1102.	Abstract or title search to			
1103.	Title examination to			
1104.	Title insurance binder to			
1105.	Document preparation to			
1106.	Notary fees to			
1107.	Attorney's fees to		300.00	400.00
	(includes above items numbers:)			
1108.	Title insurance to		540.00	
	(includes above items numbers:)			
1109.	Lender's coverage $ 395.00			
1110.	Owner's coverage $ 145.00			
1111.				
1112.				
1113.				
1200.	**Government Recording and Transfer Charges**			
1201.	Recording fees: Deed $ 10.00 ; Mortgage $ 10.00 ; Releases $ 10.00		20.00	10.00
1202.	City/county tax/stamps: Deed $; Mortgage $			
1203.	State tax/stamps: Deed $ 230.00 ; Mortgage $			230.00
1204.	RECORDING FEES TO CLEAR TITLE			20.00
1205.				
1300.	**Additional Settlement Charges**			
1301.	Survey to		175.00	
1302.	Pest inspection to		85.00	
1303.				
1304.				
1305.				
1400.	Total Settlement Charges (enter on lines 103, Section J and 502, Section K)		5,697.55	7,560.00

**Basic Information
of Offer and Sale**

John and Joanne Iuro listed their home at 3045 North Racine Avenue in Riverdale, North Carolina, with the Open Door Real Estate Company. The listing price was $118,500, and possession could be given within two weeks after all parties had signed the contract. Under the terms of the listing agreement, the sellers agreed to pay the broker a commission of 6 percent of the sales price.

On April 18 the Open Door Real Estate Company submitted a contract offer to the Iuros from Brook Redeman, a bachelor, presently residing at 22 King Court, Riverdale. Redeman offered $115,000, with earnest money/down payment of $23,000 and the remaining $92,000 of the purchase price to be obtained through a new conventional loan. No private mortgage insurance will be necessary because the loan-to-value ratio will not exceed 80 percent. The Iuros signed the contract on April 29. Closing was set for June 15 at the office of the Open Door Real Estate Company, 720 Main Street, Riverdale.

The unpaid balance of the Iuros' mortgage as of June 1 will be $57,700. Payments are $680 per month with interest at 11 percent per annum on the unpaid balance.

The title insurance policy paid by the buyers at the time of closing cost $540, including $395 for lender's coverage and $145 for homeowner's coverage. Recording charges of $20 were paid for the recording of two instruments to clear defects in the sellers' title. State revenue stamps in the amount of $230 ($1 per $500 of sales price or fraction thereof) were affixed to the deed. In addition, the sellers must pay an attorney's fee of $400 for preparation of the deed and for legal representation. This amount will be paid from the closing proceeds.

The buyer must pay an attorney's fee of $300 for examination of the title evidence and legal representation. There is also a $10 fee to record the deed. These amounts also will be paid from the closing proceeds.

Real estate taxes in Riverdale are paid in arrears. Taxes for this year, estimated at last year's figure of $1,725, have not been paid. According to the contract, prorations are to be made on the basis of the 360-day year/30-day month method

**Computing the
Prorations and
Charges**

The following list illustrates the various steps in computing the prorations and other amounts to be included in the settlement to this point.

1. *Closing date:* June 15
2. *Commission:* 6% × $115,000 (sales price) = $6,900
3. *Sellers' mortgage interest:*
   11% × $57,700 (principal due after June 1 payment) = $6,347 interest per year
   $6,347 ÷ 360 days = $17.631 interest per day
   15 days of accrued interest to be paid by the sellers
   15 × $17.631 = $264.465, or $264.47 interest owed by the sellers
   $57,700 + $264.47 = $57,964.47 payoff of sellers' mortgage
4. *Real estate taxes* (estimated at $1,725):
   $1,725 ÷ 360 days = $4.792 per day
   January 1 through June 15 equals 165 days
   165 days × $4.792 = $790.68 debit seller/credit buyer

5. *Revenue stamps* ($1.00 per $500 of consideration or fraction thereof):
$115,000 ÷ $500 = $230
$230 × $1 = $230 stamp tax, debit seller

The sellers' loan payoff is $57,964.47. They must pay an additional $10 to record the mortgage release. The buyer's new loan is from Thrift Federal Savings, 1100 Fountain Plaza, Riverdale, in the amount of $92,000 at 10 percent interest. In connection with this loan, Redeman will be charged $250 to have the property appraised by Swift Appraisal. The Acme Credit Bureau will charge $60 for a credit report. (Because appraisal and credit reports are performed prior to loan approval, they are paid at the time of loan application, whether or not the transaction eventually closes. These items will be noted as *POC*—paid outside closing—on the settlement statement.) In addition, Redeman will pay for interest on his loan for the remainder of the month of closing: 16 days at $25.556 per day, or $408.90. His first full payment (including July's interest) will be due August 1. He must deposit $1,006.25 into a tax reserve account. That is 7/12 of the anticipated county real estate tax of $1,725. A one-year hazard insurance premium at $3 per $1,000 of appraised value ($115,000 ÷ $1,000 × 3 = $345) paid at closing to Hite Insurance Company. An insurance reserve to cover the premium for two months is deposited with the lender. Redeman will have to pay an additional $10 to record the mortgage and $175 for a survey. He will also pay a loan origination fee of $920 and two discount points, plus $85 for a pest inspection.

The Uniform Settlement Statement

The Uniform Settlement Statement is divided into 12 sections. Sections J, K and L contain particularly important information. The borrower's and seller's summaries (J and K) are very similar. In Section J, the buyer/borrower's debits are listed in lines 100 through 112. They are totaled on line 120 (Gross Amount Due From Borrower). The total of the settlement costs itemized in Section L of the statement is entered on line 103 as one of the buyer's charges. The buyer's credits are listed on lines 201 through 219 and totaled on line 220 (Total Paid By/For Borrower). The buyer's credits then are subtracted from the charges to arrive at the cash due from the borrower to close (line 303).

In Section K, the seller's credits are entered on lines 400 through 412 and totaled on line 420 (Gross Amount Due To Seller). The seller's debits are entered on lines 501 through 519 and totaled on line 520 (Total Reduction Amount Due Seller). The total of the seller's settlement charges is on line 502. The debits then are subtracted from the credits to arrive at the cash due the sellers to close (line 603).

Section L is a summary of all the settlement charges for the transaction; the buyer's expenses are listed in one column and the sellers' expenses in the other. If an attorney's fee is listed as a lump sum in line 1107, the settlement should list by line number the services that were included in that total fee.

SUMMARY

Closing a real estate sale involves both title procedures and financial matters. The real estate salesperson or broker is often present at the closing to see that the sale is actually concluded and to account for the earnest money deposit.

Closings must be reported to the IRS on Form 1099-S.

The federal Real Estate Settlement Procedures Act (RESPA) requires disclosure of all settlement costs when a residential real estate purchase is financed by a federally related mortgage loan. RESPA requires that lenders use a Uniform Settlement Statement to detail the financial particulars of a transaction.

The actual amount to be paid by the buyer at the closing is computed by preparation of a closing, or settlement, statement. This lists the sales price, earnest money deposit and all adjustments and prorations due between buyer and seller. The purpose of this statement is to determine the net amount due the seller at closing. The buyer reimburses the seller for prepaid items like unused taxes or fuel oil. The seller credits the buyer for bills the seller owes that will be paid by the buyer (accrued items), such as unpaid water bills.

Questions

1. Which of the following statements is true of real estate closings in North Carolina?
   a. Closings are always conducted by real estate salespeople.
   b. The seller usually pays the expenses for the day of closing.
   c. The buyer must reimburse the seller for accrued but unpaid expenses.
   d. The buyer usually receives the rents for the day of closing.

2. Which of the following documents would a lender generally require at the closing?
   a. Title insurance policy
   b. Market value appraisal
   c. Application
   d. Credit report

3. The RESPA Uniform Settlement Statement must be used to illustrate all settlement charges for
   a. every real estate transaction.
   b. real estate transactions financed by VA and FHA loans only.
   c. residential real estate transactions financed by federally related mortgage loans.
   d. all real estate transactions involving commercial property.

4. Assume annual real estate taxes amount to $1,800 and have been paid in advance for the calendar year. If closing is set for September 15, which of the following is true?
   a. Credit seller $525; debit buyer $1,275
   b. Credit seller $1,275; debit buyer $525
   c. Credit buyer $525; debit seller $1,275
   d. Credit seller $525; debit buyer $525

5. A seller collects rent of $400, payable in advance, from the attic tenant on September 1. Which of the following is true at the closing on September 15?
   a. The seller owes the buyer $400.
   b. The buyer owes the seller $400.
   c. The seller owes the buyer $200.
   d, The buyer owes the seller $200.

6. A building was purchased for $50,000, with 10 percent down and a loan for the balance. If the lender charged the buyer two discount points, how much cash did the buyer need to pay the down payment and loan fees?
   a. $900   c. $5,900
   b. $5,200   d. $6,900

7. At a closing, the seller's lawyer debited the seller and credited the buyer for certain accrued items. These included bills relating to the property
   I. that had already been paid by the seller.
   II. that had yet to be paid by the buyer.
      a. I only
      b. II only
      c. I or II only
      d. Neither I nor II

Questions 8 through 12 pertain to certain items as they would normally appear on a closing statement.

8. The sales price of the property is a
   a. credit to the buyer.
   b. debit to the seller.
   c. credit to the buyer; debit to the seller.
   d. credit to the seller; debit to the buyer.

9. The earnest money left on deposit with the broker is a
   a. credit to the buyer.
   b. debit to the seller.
   c. credit to the buyer; debit to the seller.
   d. credit to the seller; debit to the buyer.

10. Cost of purchasing the fuel oil left in a holding tank on the property is a
    a. credit to the buyer.
    b. debit to the seller.
    c. credit to the buyer; debit to the seller.
    d. credit to the seller; debit to the buyer.

11. The principal amount of the purchaser's new mortgage loan is a
    a. credit to the seller.
    b. credit to the buyer.
    c. debit to the seller.
    d. debit to the buyer.

12. Unpaid real estate taxes, water service, waste disposal service and so forth are
    a. credits to the buyer.
    b. debits to the seller.
    c. credits to the buyer; debits to the seller.
    d. credits to the seller; debits to the buyer.

13. The Real Estate Settlement Procedures Act applies to the activities of
    a. brokers selling commercial and office buildings.
    b. security salespeople selling limited partnerships.
    c. Ginnie Mae or Fannie Mae when purchasing mortgages.
    d. lenders financing the purchase of a borrower's residence.

14. The purpose of RESPA is to ensure that
    I. buyers do not borrow more than they can repay.
    II. real estate brokers are more responsive to buyers' needs.
    III. buyers and sellers know all settlement costs.
       a. I only
       b. III only
       c. I or II only
       d. I, II and III

15. A survey of property is usually paid by
    a. the seller.
    b. the buyer.
    c. both the buyer and the seller, equally.
    d. the real estate appraiser.

16. RESPA was passed to
    a. protect the buyer and the seller.
    b. protect the broker.
    c. protect the lender.
    d. act as consumer protection legislation.

17. When an agent and a broker handle a closing on their own, they must be extremely careful to make sure that all documents and exchanges are correct because the agent and broker are held liable by and responsible to
    a. the seller.
    b. the buyer.
    c. the lender.
    d. the North Carolina Real Estate Commission.

18. Under RESPA, the settlement agent must allow the borrower to examine the closing statement
    I. one day before closing.
    II. with a lawyer present who is paid for by the lender.
    III. at the borrower's request.
       a. I only
       b. II only
       c. III only
       d. I and III only

19. On a settlement statement, the prorations for unpaid real estate taxes paid in arrears would be shown as a
    a. credit to the seller; debit to the buyer.
    b. debit to the seller; credit to the buyer.
    c. credit to both the seller and the buyer.
    d. debit to both the seller and the buyer.

20. In a settlement statement, the selling price will always be a
    I. debit to the buyer
    II. debit to the seller
    III. credit to the buyer
       a. I only
       b. II only
       c. I and II only
       d. II and III only

CLOSING STATEMENT PROBLEM

Use the following information to complete the blank closing statement worksheet and the blank HUD-1 form on pages 321 and 322.

Julie and Vern Marenatha are selling their home to Martha and Joe White for $110,000. The Whites made a $5,000 earnest money deposit, which is being held by the Marenathas' real estate broker in escrow until closing. The Whites are to obtain an 80 percent conventional loan at 10 percent interest and make a 20 percent down payment. The closing date is October 15. The Marenathas agreed to pay their broker a 6 percent commission.

The Marenathas' existing mortgage loan (at 10 percent interest) will have a balance of $82,750 after their October 1 payment. The sellers must also pay accrued interest on their loan payoff at closing. The loan must be paid off at closing. The property taxes for the current year are $1,100 and are unpaid; parties agreed to the double-debit method of proration.

The Whites will pay their mortgage company a $50 credit report fee and a $150 appraisal report fee at closing. The mortgage company is charging a 1 percent loan origination fee and a 1.5 percent loan discount fee. Interim interest on the new loan is to be paid by the Whites at closing. The first loan payment will be due on December 1. The Whites must pay a $345 homeowner's insurance premium, and must deposit an additional $500 into escrow at the closing for property taxes and homeowner's insurance premiums.

Other closing expenses (listed below) will be paid in accordance with custom.

Property survey: $200
Pest inspection report: $75
Title insurance premium: $250
Revenue stamps: $1 per $500 of sales price
Fee to prepare deed: $50
Fee to record deed: $7
Fee to record sellers' satisfaction of mortgage: $7
Fee to record buyers' deed of trust: $7
Buyers' lawyer's fee: $500
(Use a 360-day year and 30-day month to calculate prorations. The seller is responsible for thec- day of closing. Round math to three decimal places until the final answer. See page 463 for answers.)

Closing Statement Worksheet				
	Buyer's Statement		Seller's Statement	
	Debit	Credit	Debit	Credit
Purchase price				
Earnest money				
Principal amount of new loan				
Interim interest				
Payoff of existing loan				
Seller's accrued interest				
Loan origination fee				
Discount points				
Appraisal				
Credit report				
Property survey				
Pest inspection report				
Broker's commission				
Hazard insurance				
Property taxes				
Title insurance premium				
Revenue stamps				
Document (deed) preparation				
Recording fees				
Attorney's fees				
Escrow account deposit				
Subtotals				
Balance due from buyer				
Balance due to seller				
Totals				

Settlement Statement

A. Settlement Statement

U.S. Department of Housing
and Urban Development

OMB Approval No. 2502-0265

B. Type of Loan

| 1. ☐ FHA | 2. ☐ FmHA | 3. ☐ Conv. Unins. | 6. File Number: | 7. Loan Number: | 8. Mortgage Insurance Case Number: |
| 4. ☐ VA | 5. ☐ Conv. Ins. | | | | |

C. Note: This form is furnished to give you a statement of actual settlement costs. Amounts paid to and by the settlement agent are shown. Items marked "(p.o.c.)" were paid outside the closing; they are shown here for informational purposes and are not included in the totals.

D. Name & Address of Borrower:	E. Name & Address of Seller:	F. Name & Address of Lender:

G. Property Location:	H. Settlement Agent:	
	Place of Settlement:	I. Settlement Date:

J. Summary of Borrower's Transaction		K. Summary of Seller's Transaction	
100. Gross Amount Due From Borrower		**400. Gross Amount Due To Seller**	
101. Contract sales price		401. Contract sales price	
102. Personal property		402. Personal property	
103. Settlement charges to borrower (line 1400)		403.	
104.		404.	
105.		405.	
Adjustments for items paid by seller in advance		**Adjustments for items paid by seller in advance**	
106. City/town taxes to		406. City/town taxes to	
107. County taxes to		407. County taxes to	
108. Assessments to		408. Assessments to	
109.		409.	
110.		410.	
111.		411.	
112.		412.	
120. Gross Amount Due From Borrower		**420. Gross Amount Due To Seller**	
200. Amounts Paid By Or In Behalf Of Borrower		**500. Reductions In Amount Due To Seller**	
201. Deposit or earnest money		501. Excess deposit (see instructions)	
202. Principal amount of new loan(s)		502. Settlement charges to seller (line 1400)	
203. Existing loan(s) taken subject to		503. Existing loan(s) taken subject to	
204.		504. Payoff of first mortgage loan	
205.		505. Payoff of second mortgage loan	
206.		506.	
207.		507.	
208.		508.	
209.		509.	
Adjustments for items unpaid by seller		**Adjustments for items unpaid by seller**	
210. City/town taxes to		510. City/town taxes to	
211. County taxes to		511. County taxes to	
212. Assessments to		512. Assessments to	
213.		513.	
214.		514.	
215.		515.	
216.		516.	
217.		517.	
218.		518.	
219.		519.	
220. Total Paid By/For Borrower		**520. Total Reduction Amount Due Seller**	
300. Cash At Settlement From/To Borrower		**600. Cash At Settlement To/From Seller**	
301. Gross Amount due from borrower (line 120)		601. Gross amount due to seller (line 420)	
302. Less amounts paid by/for borrower (line 220)	( )	602. Less reductions in amt. due seller (line 520)	( )
303. Cash ☐ From ☐ To Borrower		**603. Cash** ☐ To ☐ From Seller	

Section 5 of the Real Estate Settlement Procedures Act (RESPA) requires the following: • HUD must develop a Special Information Booklet to help persons borrowing money to finance the purchase of residential real estate to better understand the nature and costs of real estate settlement services; • Each lender must provide the booklet to all applicants from whom it receives or for whom it prepares a written application to borrow money to finance the purchase of residential real estate; • Lenders must prepare and distribute with the Booklet a Good Faith Estimate of the settlement costs that the borrower is likely to incur in connection with the settlement. These disclosures are mandatory.

Section 4(a) of RESPA mandates that HUD develop and prescribe this standard form to be used at the time of loan settlement to provide full disclosure of all charges imposed upon the borrower and seller. These are third party disclosures that are designed to provide the borrower with pertinent information during the settlement process in order to be a better shopper.

The Public Reporting Burden for this collection of information is estimated to average one hour per response, including the time for reviewing instructions, searching existing data sources, gathering and maintaining the data needed, and completing and reviewing the collection of information.

This agency may not collect this information, and you are not required to complete this form, unless it displays a currently valid OMB control number.

The information requested does not lend itself to confidentiality.

Settlement Statement (continued)

L. Settlement Charges

		Paid From Borrowers Funds at Settlement	Paid From Seller's Funds at Settlement
700. Total Sales/Broker's Commission based on price $ @ % =			
Division of Commission (line 700) as follows:			
701. $ to			
702. $ to			
703. Commission paid at Settlement			
704.			
800. Items Payable In Connection With Loan			
801. Loan Origination Fee %			
802. Loan Discount %			
803. Appraisal Fee to			
804. Credit Report to			
805. Lender's Inspection Fee			
806. Mortgage Insurance Application Fee to			
807. Assumption Fee			
808.			
809.			
810.			
811.			
900. Items Required By Lender To Be Paid In Advance			
901. Interest from to @$ /day			
902. Mortgage Insurance Premium for months to			
903. Hazard Insurance Premium for years to			
904. years to			
905.			
1000. Reserves Deposited With Lender			
1001. Hazard insurance months@$ per month			
1002. Mortgage insurance months@$ per month			
1003. City property taxes months@$ per month			
1004. County property taxes months@$ per month			
1005. Annual assessments months@$ per month			
1006. months@$ per month			
1007. months@$ per month			
1008. months@$ per month			
1100. Title Charges			
1101. Settlement or closing fee to			
1102. Abstract or title search to			
1103. Title examination to			
1104. Title insurance binder to			
1105. Document preparation to			
1106. Notary fees to			
1107. Attorney's fees to			
(includes above items numbers:)			
1108. Title insurance to			
(includes above items numbers:)			
1109. Lender's coverage $			
1110. Owner's coverage $			
1111.			
1112.			
1113.			
1200. Government Recording and Transfer Charges			
1201. Recording fees: Deed $; Mortgage $; Releases $			
1202. City/county tax/stamps: Deed $; Mortgage $			
1203. State tax/stamps: Deed $; Mortgage $			
1204.			
1205.			
1300. Additional Settlement Charges			
1301. Survey to			
1302. Pest inspection to			
1303.			
1304.			
1305.			
1400. Total Settlement Charges (enter on lines 103, Section J and 502, Section K)			

15 Basic Residential Construction

LEARNING OBJECTIVES

When you've finished reading this chapter, you should be able to

- **describe** basic architectural types and styles of residential construction.

- **identify** the components of a house foundation and the house framing.

- **describe** all components of residential construction.

- **explain** provisions of North Carolina Building Codes, HUD minimum standards and contractor licensing.

- **define** these *key terms:*

baseboard	HVAC	sheathing
BTU	insulation	shingles
building code	pier	siding
ceiling joist	pitch	sill
floor joist	rafter	slab
footing	ridge board	sole plate
foundation wall	roofing felt	stud
frame	R-value	subfloor
girder		

It is important for real estate agents to have a basic knowledge of residential construction. As agents show homes to prospective buyers, they need to be able to point out basic features and answer basic construction questions. This chapter offers a rudimentary introduction to wood-frame residential construction. Wood-frame construction is popular because it (1) has flexibility of design, (2) costs less, (3) is easy to insulate and (4) takes less time to build.

ARCHITECTURAL TYPES AND STYLES

A few basic architectural styles maintain high levels of popularity, including the one-story, or ranch-style, home; the split-level home; and several types of two-story homes, such as the Cape Cod, colonial and French provincial.

Ranch-style homes offer easy accessibility and maintenance because everything is on one floor. Owners have no need to make frequent trips upstairs or to use high ladders to paint second-story exterior surfaces. Ranch houses are usually moderate-sized and affordable.

The split-level home takes advantage of uneven terrain. And two-story homes offer twice the living area for the cost of the area of only one foundation and roof. With split-level homes, maintenance and access is more difficult than a single-story home because of heights, etc.

Contemporary designs usually combine elements of one-story, two-story or split-level homes with a lot of open space and windows. Contemporary designs are particularly popular in scenic areas.

No one design is inherently superior to another. Whether a buyer prefers a ranch-style to a colonial is simply a matter of individual taste and style. Refer to Figure 15.1 for examples of various architectural styles.

FOUNDATIONS

The foundation of a home must be built on firm soil and constructed with materials that are capable of supporting the weight of the house and resisting damage caused by wood-eating pests.

Basic Components   The basic components of a foundation include the following:

- *Footings.* The foundation rests on **footings,** which are usually made of concrete that is poured into trenches or forms that have been dug or placed beneath the soil line. Footings are typically 16 inches wide and 6 to 8 inches deep. The bottom of each footing must be located below the frost line to avoid the shifting that can be caused when the ground freezes. Footings are the lowest part of construction.
- *Foundation walls.* **Foundation walls** rest on top of the footings and provide a surface upon which the flooring is built. Foundation walls are typically 8 to 12 inches thick.
- *Piers.* **Piers** (columns) may be required to support the flooring between the foundation walls.
- *Concrete slabs.* Concrete **slabs** are sometimes used as the floors of basements, garages or houses.

These basic components of a foundation, as well as other house components, are illustrated in Figure 15.5, page 331.

Termite Protection   Builders must be very careful to protect structures from termite damage. All woody materials must be removed from around the foundation. The soil near the foundation walls and piers is often chemically treated. And any

Figure 15.1 **Architectural Styles**

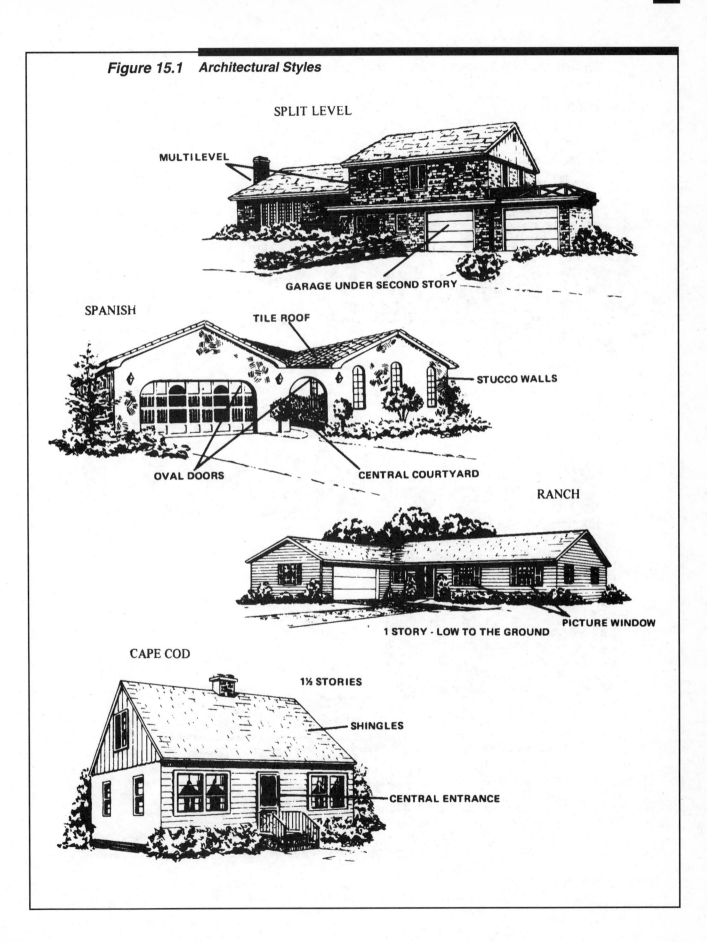

Figure 15.1 *Architectural Styles (continued)*

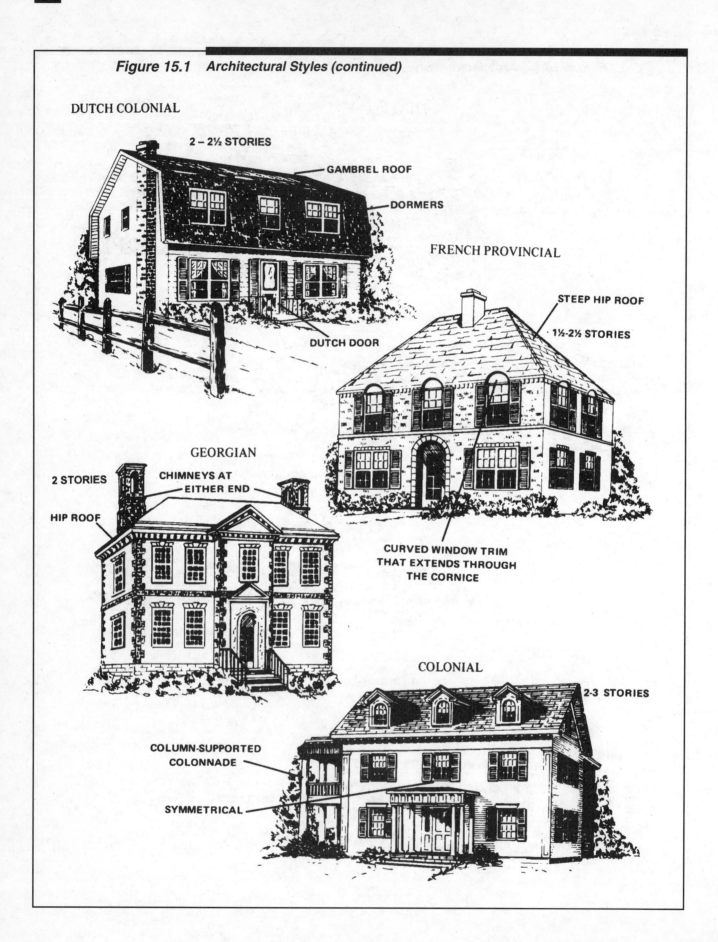

lumber used in the construction that comes in contact with the ground should be pressure-treated. All three measures help prevent infestation and damage caused by termites and other wood-eating insects.

FRAMING

Various dimensions of lumber are used to build the **frame** of a house, which is similar to the skeleton of a body. The elements of the framing consist of the floors, the walls, the ceiling and the roof. See Figure 15.2 and Figure 15.3 for examples of various framing cross-sections.

- *Floor framing.* The floor framing consists of **sills** (the lowest part of framing), pieces of lumber that are placed on top of the foundation walls. **Floor joists** are then attached to the sills at 16-inch or 24-inch intervals. Because the floor joists must support the entire weight of the floor, they typically cannot span the entire width of the structure. Instead, **girders,** which rest on top of piers, are used to support the joists between sills. The **subfloor** is then attached to this system of joists and girders. The subfloor is usually made of sheets of plywood, which are laid on top of the joists and girders. Finally, the subfloor is covered with the floor covering, such as vinyl, carpeting, tile or hardwood strips.
- *Wall framing.* Wall framing consists of **studs,** vertical lumber spaced about 16 inches apart. The **sole plate** connects the studs to the flooring; the top plate connects the studs to the ceiling framing. *Headers,* two pieces of lumber joined together to form a beam, are used to give extra support to wall framing where a window or door will be positioned. This type of framing is called *platform* framing.

  Two other types of framing include *balloon* framing and *post and beam* framing. With balloon framing, a single system of lengthy wall studs is used. The studs run from the foundation up to the ceiling (through both the first and second stories). With post and beam framing, extra-large framing members are used—either 4 × 4 or 6 × 6. These large posts can be placed farther apart than the traditional 16-inch wall studs.
- *Roof framing.* **Ceiling joists,** which are attached to the top plate of the wall, carry the weight of the roof. **Rafters,** the sloping members of the roof frame, connect the ceiling joists and the **ridge boards** (the highest part of the construction). The rafters support the decking or other roofing materials. An alternative method to using ceiling joists, rafters and ridge boards is the *roof truss.* The roof truss is a prefabricated triangular structure that serves the same functions as the ceiling joists, rafters and ridge boards but is easier and quicker to install. The overhang of the roof is called the *eave,* which is made up of the fascia board, the soffit, and the frieze board. Refer to Figure 15.4 for examples of popular types of roof designs.

ELEMENTS OF CONSTRUCTION

Refer to Figure 15.5 for a complete illustration of home construction.

Figure 15.2 **Roof Framing Systems**

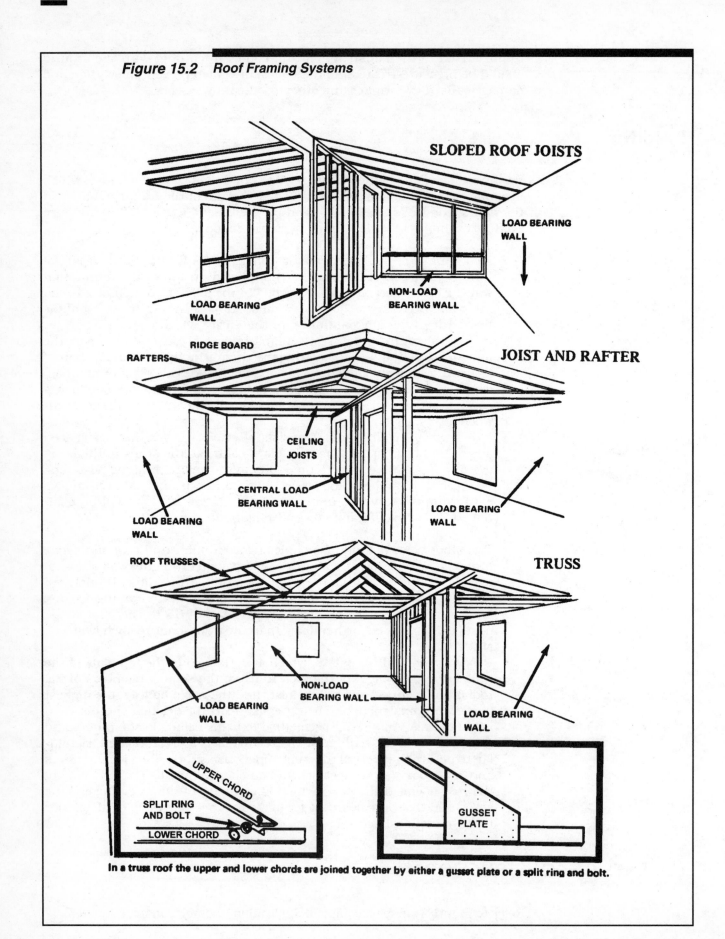

In a truss roof the upper and lower chords are joined together by either a gusset plate or a split ring and bolt.

Figure 15.3 *Exterior Structure Walls and Framing*

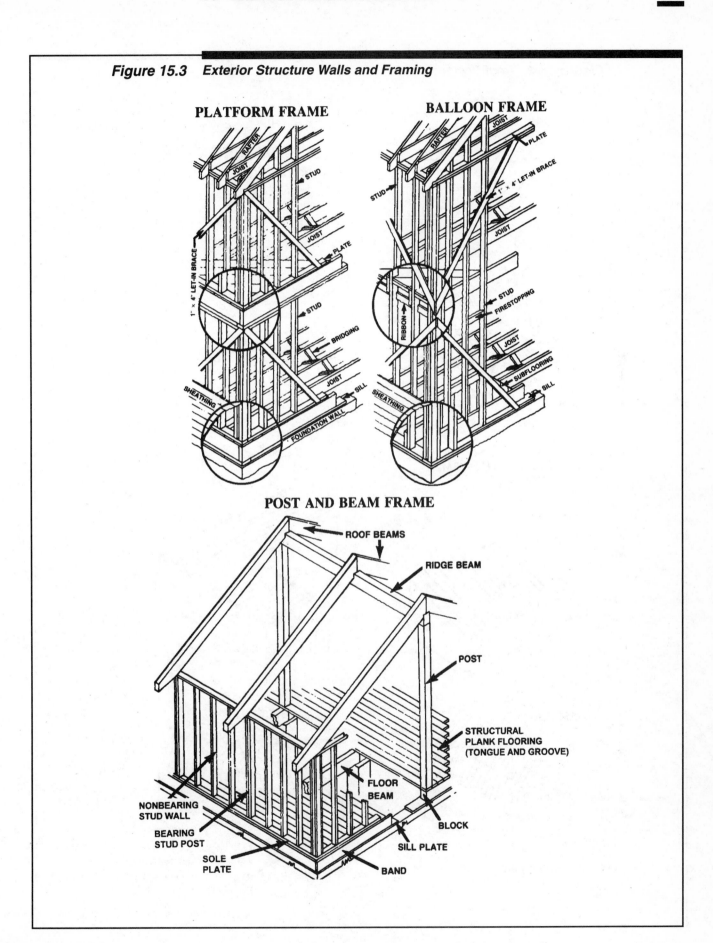

Figure 15.4 *Roof Designs*

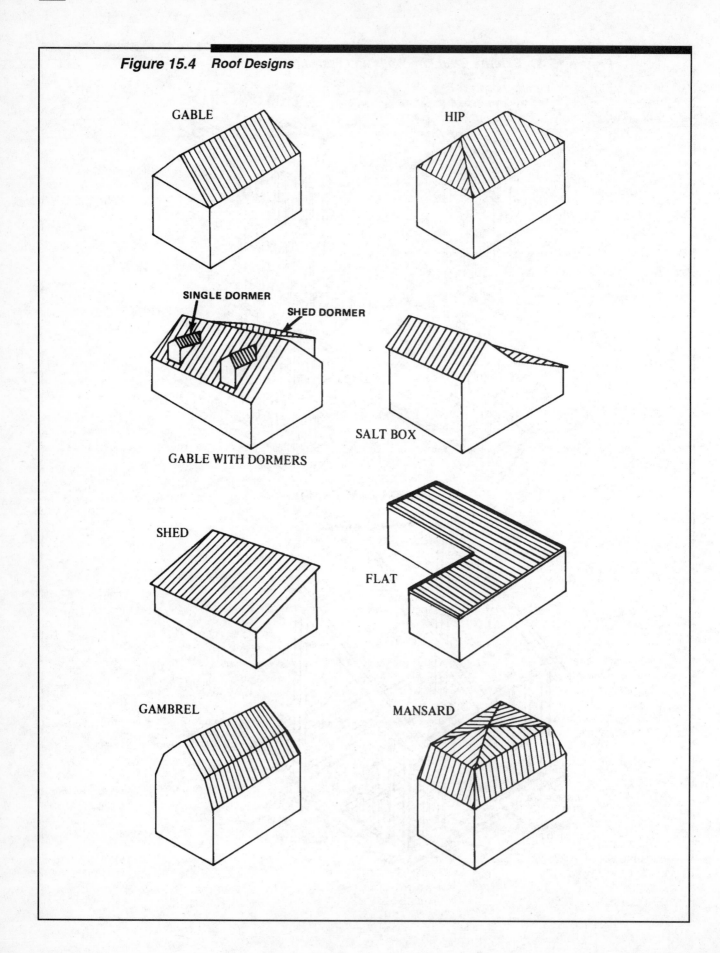

Figure 15.5   **Home Construction**

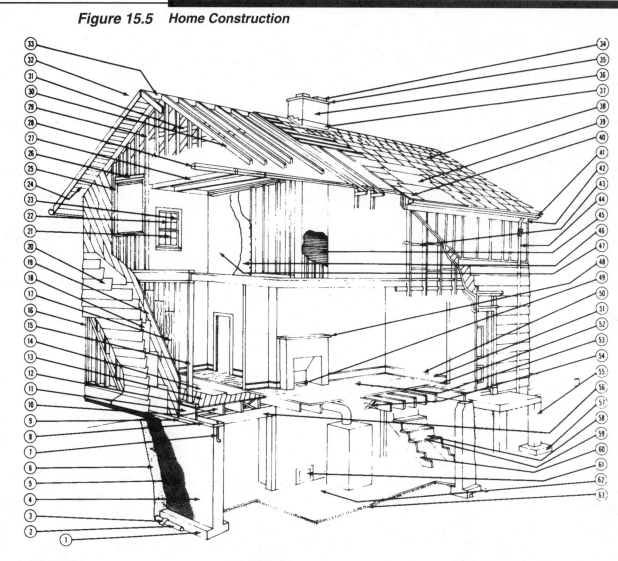

1. FOOTING
2. FOUNDATION DRAIN TILE
3. CRUSHED/WASHED STONE
4. FOUNDATION WALL
5. DAMPPROOFING OR WEATHERPROOFING
6. BACKFILL
7. ANCHOR BOLT
8. SILL PLATE
9. TERMITE SHIELD
10. FLOOR JOIST
11. BAND OR BOX BEAM
12. SOLE PLATE
13. SUBFLOORING
14. BUILDING PAPER
15. WALL STUD
16. CORNER STUDS
17. INSULATION
18. HOUSE WRAP
19. WALL SHEATHING
20. SIDING
21. MULLION

22. MUNTIN
23. WINDOW SASH
24. EAVE (ROOF PROJECTION)
25. WINDOW JAMB TRIM
26. WINDOW HEADER
27. CEILING JOIST
28. TOP AND TIE PLATES
29. GABLE STUD
30. RAFTERS
31. COLLAR TIES
32. GABLE END OF ROOF
33. RIDGE BEAM
34. CHIMNEY FLUES
35. CHIMNEY CAP
36. CHIMNEY
37. CHIMNEY FLASHING
38. ROOFING SHINGLES
39. ROOFING FELT/ICE AND WATER MEMBRANE
40. ROOF SHEATHING
41. EVE TROUGH OR GUTTER
42. FRIEZE BOARD

43. FIRESTOP
44. DOWNSPOUT
45. LATHS
46. PLASTER BOARD
47. PLASTER FINISH
48. MANTEL
49. ASH DUMP
50. BASE TOP MOULDING
51. BASEBOARD
52. SHOE MOULDING
53. FINISH MOULDING
54. CROSS BRIDGING
55. PIER
56. GIRDER
57. FOOTING
58. RISER
59. TREAD
60. STRINGER
61. CLEANOUT DOOR
62. CONCRETE BASEMENT FLOOR
63. CRUSHED/WASHED STONE

Exterior Walls To build the exterior walls, **sheathing** is added to the wall framing. Several types of materials are used for sheathing, including fiber board, foam and plywood. Exterior siding is then added to the sheathing. Exterior siding may be sheets of wood (the most common material), brick veneer, vinyl or aluminum. **Siding** protects the home from the elements and provides a pleasing look.

Windows and Exterior Doors Windows allow for ventilation, light, a view and style. Today, windows are made of insulated glass for energy efficiency.

In addition to providing access, exterior doors add to the style of a home. Exterior doors are usually made of wood, steel or a combination of wood and glass (such as French doors).

Roofing Roofing materials must be able to withstand the elements and provide water protection to the structure. Of course, roofing materials also add to the home's style and character. The most common types of roofing materials are composition **shingles** (made of asphalt and fiberglass), wood shingles or shakes, and layers of **roofing felt** interspersed with tar or asphalt (called a *built-up roof*). The gable roof is the most common. The slope of the roof is measured by the **pitch**, which is the number of inches of rise per foot of horizontal distance. The larger the rise per foot, the steeper the slope.

Insulation **Insulation** is an important factor in any home. Today's energy-conscious consumers are anxious to buy homes that take little energy to heat and cool. Materials used to insulate homes include batts or blankets of insulating materials (which come in sheets) or loose fill insulation (which is blown into open spaces). Any asbestos materials are prohibited.

The insulation value of materials is expressed as an **R-value.** The higher the R-value, the more resistant the material is to the transfer of heat. Building codes require different elements of each home to have different minimum R-values. For example, North Carolina building codes require R-20 insulation in floors, R-16 in walls and R-31 in ceilings.

Interior Finishes Interior finishes are mostly a matter of cost and taste. There is a wide variety of interior finishes—one suited for every budget.

Sheetrock that has been textured and painted is a typical finish for interior walls, as is wood paneling. Ceilings may be finished with sheetrock, acoustical tiles or tongue-and-groove boards. Floors are usually finished with hardwood strips, tiles, carpeting or vinyl. Moldings, such as **baseboards** and casings, are used to finish the seams between the walls and the floors and the areas around doors and windows.

HVAC

Several types of **HVAC** (heating, ventilation and air-conditioning) systems exist. The most common forms include central heating units fueled by gas, oil or electricity; electric baseboard heaters; heat pumps; and forced-air systems (which use a central blower). Solar panels, which provide heat on a year-round basis, have gained in popularity over the last few years but are not as common as gas, oil or electric heating systems. The most efficient type of heat is warm forced air.

BTU

The **BTU,** or British Thermal Unit, is a measure of heat and is used in rating the capacity of air-conditioning and heating equipment. One BTU represents the amount of heat required to raise the temperature of one pound of water one degree Fahrenheit at 39.2 degrees Fahrenheit.

GOVERNMENT REGULATION

North Carolina Uniform Building Code

North Carolina has adopted a uniform **building code** that applies statewide. The code consists of hundreds of pages of requirements on the structure of buildings and their electrical and plumbing systems. Each municipality has a building department that enforces the building code by inspecting buildings during construction. Before a structure can be occupied, the building department must issue a certificate of occupancy, which means that the construction has been completed in a satisfactory manner.

HUD Minimum Standards

Homes that are financed with government loans (such as FHA or VA loans) must meet minimum construction standards set by HUD. Some of these standards may be stricter than the state building codes.

In Practice

North Carolina uniform building codes are subject to change periodically as are HUD minimum standards. An agent working with a buyer who wants to obtain FHA and/or VA financing should always check to ensure that the property meets both standards before an offer to purchase containing provisions for FHA or VA financing is presented to a seller.

Contractor Licensing

In North Carolina, anyone who contracts to construct a building for more than $30,000 must obtain a general contractor's license from the state. Different classifications of licenses exist for different types of construction. For example, single-family home construction requires a residential building classification.

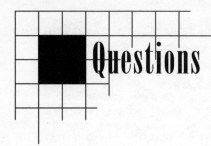

Questions

1. R-value refers to
   a. resistance to the transfer of heat.
   b. resistance to termite infestation.
   c. reduction in construction costs.
   d. a general contractor's license.

2. Pressure-treated lumber is used
   a. to improve the appearance of a home.
   b. to help prevent termite infestation.
   c. to increase the R-value.
   d. for interior wall treatment.

3. The vertical framing member of a wall is a
   a. sole plate.   c. joist.
   b. girder.   d. stud.

4. Based on the cost per square foot of living space, which of the following is the most economical house design?
   a. Split-level   c. Two-story
   b. One-story   d. Modern

5. Which of the following statements is (are) true of exterior siding?
   I. It protects a home from the elements.
   II. It adds to the style of a home.
   a. I only
   b. II only
   c. Both I and II
   d. Neither I nor II

6. The foundation wall rests on top of the
   a. footing.   c. girder.
   b. sill.   d. floor joist.

7. A certificate of occupancy is required
   I. from the local building department.
   II. before anyone can move into a home.
   a. I only
   b. II only
   c. Both I and II
   d. Neither I nor II

8. The lowest part of residential construction is the
   a. sill.
   b. foundation wall.
   c. footing.
   d. ridge board.

9. The highest part of the frame construction is the
   a. sill.   c. ridge board.
   b. rafters.   d. ceiling joists.

10. The following are components of an eave EXCEPT the
    a. soffit.   c. crown molding.
    b. fascia board.   d. frieze board.

Real Property Valuation

LEARNING OBJECTIVES

When you've finished reading this chapter, you should be able to

- **explain** the concepts and types of value, how value may be used, "value-in-exchange" and "value-in-use."

- **give** examples of the basic economic principles of value.

- **explain** the steps in the appraisal process and the three basic valuation approaches used by appraisers.

- **describe** the three types of depreciation and the concepts of "effective age" and "economic life."

- **define** these *key terms:*

age-life method	effective age	replacement cost
appraisal	functional	reproduction cost
capitalization rate	obsolescence	sales comparison
comparative market	gross rent multiplier	approach
analysis	(GRM)	square-foot method
cost approach	highest and best use	unit-in-place method
depreciation	income capitalization	straight-line method
economic life	approach	substitution
economic	physical deterioration	value
(environmental or	quantity-survey	
external)	method	
obsolescence	reconciliation	

APPRAISING

An **appraisal** is an estimate or opinion of value of a specific property as of a specific date. Appraisal reports are relied on in important decisions made by mortgage lenders, investors, public utilities, government agencies, businesses and individuals.

The highest level of appraisal activity is conducted by skilled professionals. However, everyone engaged in the real estate business, even those who are not experts in appraisal, must possess at least a fundamental knowledge of real estate valuation. In the appraisal of residential real estate, a person familiar with the market in a given neighborhood could try to make a quick judgment of market values, but this is not an appraisal and should not be considered particularly reliable and useful.

In North Carolina, to conduct a formal appraisal that will be used in federally related transactions, appraisers must be licensed by the state. Licensed appraisers usually appraise residential properties; certified appraisers typically appraise commercial properties. Note that appraisers are paid a fee, not a commission. The fee is based on the complexity of the appraisal and the length of time necessary to complete it. The fee never should be based on a percentage of the appraised value of the property.

The *Financial Institutions Reform, Recovery and Enforcement Act of 1989 (FIRREA)* was passed by Congress for the primary purpose of overhauling regulations of the thrift industry. However, a major portion of this act was for the regulation of appraisers performing appraisals for federally related loan transactions. This act established many federal agencies charged with the task of setting appraisal standards and minimum qualification requirements. The Appraisal Qualifications Board sets qualification standards and requirements for state-certified appraisers. The Appraisal Standards Board sets minimum standards of practice. In North Carolina, appraisers are licensed and certified through the North Carolina Appraisal Board, after meeting minimum education and experience requirements and passing state examinations. The licensed appraiser need not have a real estate license to perform a real estate appraisal.

VALUE

Value is an abstract word with many acceptable definitions. In a broad sense, **value** may be defined as the relationship between an object desired and a potential purchaser. It is the power of a good or service to command other goods or services in exchange. In terms of real estate appraisal, value may be described as *the present worth of future benefits arising from the ownership of real property.*

For a property to have value in the real estate market, it must have four characteristics, which can be remembered by the acronym DUST:

The four characteristics of value may be remembered by the acronym *DUST: Demand, Utility, Scarcity and Transferability.*

1. *Demand*—the need or desire for possession or ownership backed by the financial means to satisfy that need
2. *Utility*—the capacity to satisfy future owners' needs and desires; how future owners can make good use of the property
3. *Scarcity*—a finite supply
4. *Transferability*—the relative ease of transfer of ownership rights from one person to another; often relates to clear title and satisfactory physical condition

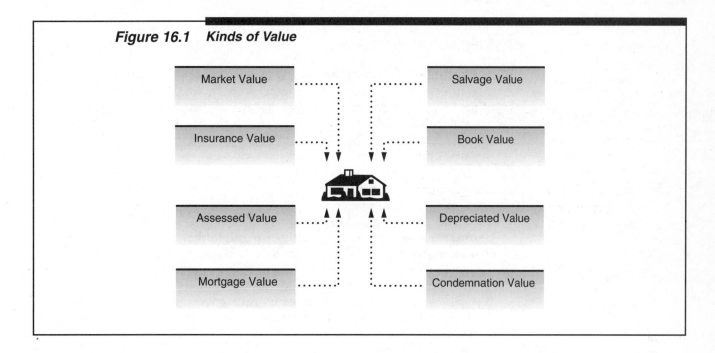

Figure 16.1   Kinds of Value

Market Value	Salvage Value
Insurance Value	Book Value
Assessed Value	Depreciated Value
Mortgage Value	Condemnation Value

Market Value

Even though a given parcel of real estate may have many different kinds of value at the same time (as illustrated in Figure 16.1), generally the goal of an appraiser is to estimate *market value.* The market value of real estate is the most probable price that a property will bring in a competitive and open market, allowing a reasonable time to find a purchaser who buys the property with knowledge of all the uses to which it is adapted and for which it is capable of being used. Included in this definition are the following key points:

- Market value is the *most probable* price a property will bring.
- Payment must be made in *cash* or its equivalent.
- Buyer and seller must act without *undue pressure.*
- A *reasonable length of time* must be allowed for the property to be exposed in the open market.
- Both buyer and seller must be *well informed* of the property's use and potential, including its assets and defects.

> *Market value* is a reasonable *opinion* of a property's value; *market price* is the actual selling price of a property; *cost* may not equal either market value or market price.

Market value versus market price. Market value is an opinion of value based on an analysis of data that may include not only an analysis of comparable sales but also an analysis of potential income and expenses and replacement costs (less depreciation). *Market price*, on the other hand, is what a property *actually* sells for—its sales price. Theoretically, the market price should be the same as the market value. Market price can be taken as accurate evidence of current market value, but only if the conditions essential to market value exist. However, the market price may not be indicative of market value. There are circumstances under which a property may be sold below market value, as when the seller is forced to sell quickly or when a sale is arranged between relatives.

Market value versus cost. An important distinction exists between market value and *cost.* One of the most common misconceptions about valuing property is that cost represents market value. Cost and market value may be equal and often are when the improvements on a property are new. But more often, cost does not equal market value.

For Example Two homes are identical in every respect, except that one is located on a street with heavy traffic and the other is on a quiet residential street. The value of the former may be less than that of the latter, although the cost of each may be exactly the same. Another example is a homeowner who installs a swimming pool at a cost of $15,000; however, the cost of the improvement may not add $15,000 to the value of the property.

Forces and Factors Influencing Property Value

Four forces affect property values:

1. *Social forces.* Social forces that affect values include trends in marriage and divorce rates, family size and longevity.
2. *Economic forces.* Economic forces include income and employment levels, the rate of property taxation, current interest rates and general economic growth.
3. *Political forces.* Political forces include government activities such as zoning and building codes, growth management, environmental legislation and tax structures.
4. *Physical forces.* Physical forces that affect property values include topography, location, climate, size, shape, proximity to major arterials, jobs and public transportation.

Basic Economic Principles of Value

A number of economic principles affect the value of real estate. The most important of these principles are defined in the following paragraphs.

Highest and best use. The most profitable single use to which a property is adapted and for which it is needed, or the use that is likely to be in demand in the reasonably near future, is its **highest and best use.** Highest and best use is noted in every appraisal but also may be the object of a more extensive analysis. For example, a highest-and-best-use study may show that a parking lot in a busy downtown area or a farm surrounded by urbanized land is not the highest and best use of the property. Note that there can be only one highest and best use at any given time. Highest and best use is subject to change—the highest and best use of a property today may not be the highest and best use of the same property five years from now.

Substitution. The principle of **substitution** states that the maximum value of a property tends to be set by the cost of purchasing an equally desirable and valuable substitute property within a reasonable period of time. This principle is the cornerstone of the sales comparison approach to value (discussed in detail later). For example, if house A and house B are equally desirable properties and house A is selling for $60,000 and house B is selling for $70,000, virtually every buyer will choose house A.

Supply and demand. This principle states that the value of a property will increase if the supply decreases and the demand either increases or remains constant—and vice versa. For example, the last lot to be sold in a residential area where the demand for homes is high would probably be worth more than the first lot sold in that area, assuming normal economic conditions exist.

Conformity. This means that maximum value is realized if the use of land conforms to existing neighborhood standards. In residential areas of single-family houses, for example, buildings should be similar in design, construction, size and age. Subdivision restrictions rely on the principle of conformity to ensure maximum future value.

Anticipation. This principle holds that value can increase or decrease in anticipation of some future benefit or detriment affecting the property. For example, the value of a house could be affected by rumors that an adjacent parcel may be converted to some different use in the near future.

Contribution. This principle underlies the process of determining the asking price of a property by making dollar value adjustments to the price of recently sold comparable properties. The value of any component of a property is defined by what its addition contributes to the value of the whole or what its absence detracts from that value. For example, the cost of installing an air-conditioning system and remodeling an older office building may be greater than is justified by the increase in market value (a function of expected net increases) that may result from the improvement to the property. In residential properties an owner sometimes will make a superimprovement such as installing solid mahogany kitchen cabinets. While these cabinets may be quite attractive, the average buyer will not pay for the added cost of this "overimprovement."

Competition. This principle states that profits tend to attract competition. For example, the success of a retail store may motivate investors to open similar stores in the area. This tends to mean less profit for all stores concerned unless the purchasing power in the area increases substantially. Note that excess profit tends to attract ruinous competition.

Change. No physical or economic condition remains constant. Real estate is subject to natural phenomena, such as tornadoes, fires and routine wear and tear of the elements. The real estate business also is subject to the changing demands of its market, as is any business. It is an appraiser's job to study the past to be better able to predict the effects of natural phenomena and the behavior of the marketplace in the future.

THE APPRAISAL PROCESS

The key to an accurate appraisal lies in the methodical collection of data. The appraisal process is an orderly set of procedures used to collect and analyze data to arrive at an ultimate value conclusion. The data are divided into two basic classes:

1. *Specific data,* covering details of the subject property and including comparative data relating to costs, sales, and income and expenses of properties similar to and competitive with the subject property
2. *General data,* covering the nation, region, city and neighborhood. Of particular importance is the neighborhood, where an appraiser finds the physical, economic, social and political influences that directly affect the value and potential of the subject property.

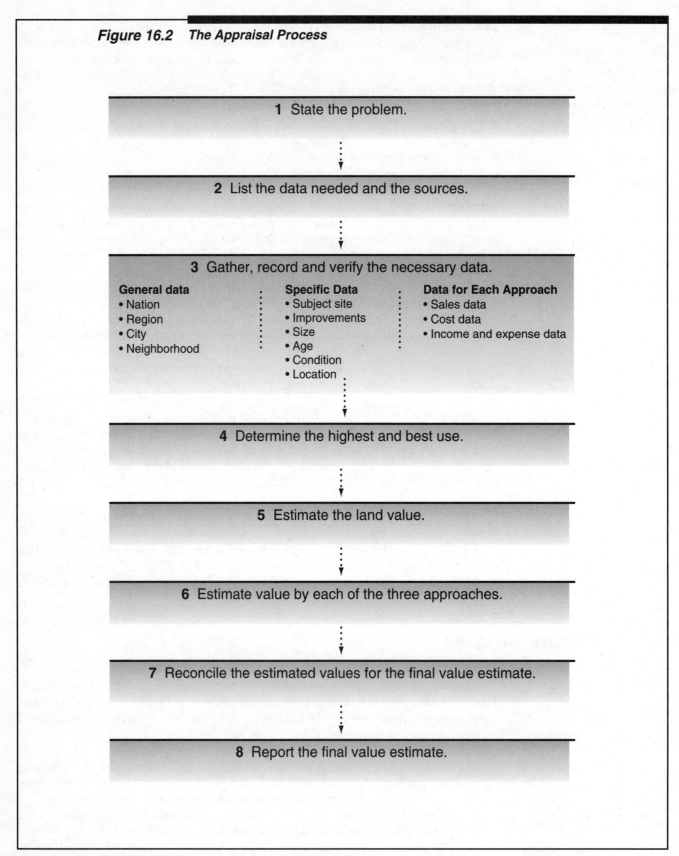

Figure 16.2 *The Appraisal Process*

1 State the problem.

2 List the data needed and the sources.

3 Gather, record and verify the necessary data.

General data	Specific Data	Data for Each Approach
• Nation	• Subject site	• Sales data
• Region	• Improvements	• Cost data
• City	• Size	• Income and expense data
• Neighborhood	• Age	
	• Condition	
	• Location	

4 Determine the highest and best use.

5 Estimate the land value.

6 Estimate value by each of the three approaches.

7 Reconcile the estimated values for the final value estimate.

8 Report the final value estimate.

SOURCE: *California Real Estate Appraisal,* 2nd Edition, by Martha R. Williams. ©1993, 1998, by Longman Group USA, Inc. and Dearborn Financial Publishing, Inc.

The flowchart in Figure 16.2 outlines the steps an appraiser takes in carrying out an appraisal assignment. The numbers in the following list correspond to the numbers on that flowchart.

1. *State the problem.* The kind of value to be estimated must be specified, and the valuation approach(es) most valid and reliable for the kind of property under appraisal must be selected.
2. *List the data needed and the sources.* Based on the approach(es) the appraiser will be using, the types of data needed and the sources to be consulted are listed.
3. *Gather, record and verify the necessary data.* Detailed information concerning the economic, political and social conditions of the nation, region, city and neighborhood and comments on the effects of these data on the subject property must be obtained.
   Specific data about the subject site and improvements must be collected and verified.
   Depending on the appraisal approach(es) used, comparative information relating to sales, income and expenses and to construction costs of comparable properties must be collected. All data should be verified, usually by checking the same information against two different sources. In the case of sales data, one source should be a person directly involved in the transaction.
4. *Determine the highest and best use.* The appraiser analyzes market forces such as competition and current versus potential uses to determine the reasonableness of the property's present use in terms of its profitability.
5. *Estimate the land value.* The features and sales prices of comparable sites are compared with the subject property to determine the value of the land alone. Neither the cost nor the income approach can be used to estimate land value.
6. *Estimate the value by each of the three approaches.* The sales comparison, cost and income capitalization approaches are used to estimate the value of the subject property.
7. *Reconcile the estimated values for the final value estimate.* The appraiser makes a definite statement of conclusions reached, usually in the form of a value estimate of the property.
8. *Report the final value estimate.* After the three approaches have been reconciled and an opinion of value has been reached, the appraiser prepares a formal written report for the client. All information used to estimate the value of a property should be included in this report. The report may take different forms. It may be a narrative report, it may be merely a letter of opinion of value or it may be a form report. The reasons and purpose of the appraisal will sometimes dictate the type of report to be used. A complete appraisal report should
   - identify the real estate and real property interest being appraised;
   - state the purpose and intended use of the appraisal;
   - define the value to be estimated;
   - state the effective date of the value and the date of the report;
   - describe the process of collecting, confirming and reporting the data;
   - list all assumptions and limiting conditions that affect the analysis, opinion and conclusions of value;

- describe the information considered, the appraisal procedures followed and the reasoning that supports the report's conclusions (if an approach was excluded, the report should explain why);
- describe (if necessary or appropriate) the appraiser's opinion of the highest and best use of the real estate;
- describe any additional information that may be appropriate to show compliance with specific guidelines established in the Uniform Standards of Professional Appraisal Practice (USPAP) or to clearly identify and explain any departures from these guidelines; and
- include a signed certification, as required by the Uniform Standards.

In Practice

The role of the appraiser is not to determine value. Rather, an appraiser develops a supportable and objective report about the value of the subject property. The appraiser relies on experience and expertise in valuation theories to evaluate market data. The appraiser does not establish the property's worth; instead, he or she verifies what the market indicates. This is important to remember, particularly when dealing with a property owner who may lack objectivity about the realistic value of his or her property. The lack of objectivity also can complicate a salesperson's ability to list the property within the most probable range of market value. Agents are cautioned against listing property at a price that is so unreasonably high that it is unlikely the property will be shown or sold.

Many lenders and federal agencies have their own form reports. One of the most frequently used is the Fannie Mae Form 1004, *Uniform Residential Appraisal Report*, shown in Figure 16.3. This form is required by many government agencies. The major sections of this form are as follows:

- *Subject:* identification of the property being appraised
- *Neighborhood:* information showing boundaries, characteristics and market conditions
- *Site:* information on lot dimensions, utilities, topography, off-site improvements, easements, flood conditions, etc.
- *Description of improvements:* general descriptions, exterior, interior, foundation, effective age, etc.
- *Comments:* additional features, condition of improvements and adverse environmental conditions
- *Cost approach:* showing applicable estimates derived from the cost approach
- *Sales comparison analysis:* showing three comparables and adjustments and estimated value derived from the sales comparison approach
- *Indicated value by the income approach*
- *Reconciliation:* showing the final estimate of value, the date of the estimate, signatures and license numbers of the appraisers

Figure 16.3 Uniform Residential Appraisal Report

File No. 96-100 Page #1

Summary Appraisal Report
Property Description

UNIFORM RESIDENTIAL APPRAISAL REPORT   File No. 96-100

Property Address 1097 Timbers Crossing	City St. Joseph State MO Zip Code 94334

Legal Description Lot 3, Block G, Harris Billups Estate, Plat Book 8, P. 37 County Buchanan
Assessor's Parcel No. 9223-03-0471   Tax Year 1994   R.E. Taxes $ 1,207.10 Special Assessments $ N/A
Borrower Barr, Frank & Elizabeth   Current Owner Stewart   Occupant [X] Owner [ ] Tenant [ ] Vacant
Property rights appraised [X] Fee Simple [ ] Leasehold   Project Type [ ] PUD [ ] Condominium (HUD/VA only)   HOA $ N/A   /Mo.
Neighborhood or Project Name Harris Billups Estate   Map Reference   Census Tract
Sale Price $ 120,000 Date of Sale   Description and $ amount of loan charges/concessions to be paid by seller None
Lender/Client Barber Savings Association   Address 4390 N. Main St., St. Joseph MO 94330
Appraiser Michelle Tipton   Address 2125 S. Main St., St. Joseph MO 94330

Location	[X] Urban	[ ] Suburban	[ ] Rural	Predominant occupancy	Single family housing		Present land use %		Land use change	
					PRICE $(000)	AGE (yrs)				
Built up	[X] Over 75%	[ ] 25-75%	[ ] Under 25%				One family 85		[X] Not likely [ ] Likely	
Growth rate	[ ] Rapid	[X] Stable	[ ] Slow	[X] Owner	70 Low 00		2-4 family 5		[ ] In process	
Property values	[ ] Increasing	[X] Stable	[ ] Declining	[ ] Tenant	155 High 50		Multi-family 5		To:	
Demand/supply	[ ] Shortage	[X] In balance	[ ] Over supply	[X] Vacant (0-5%)	Predominant		Commercial 5			
Marketing time	[ ] Under 3 mos.	[X] 3-6 mos.	[ ] Over 6 mos.	[ ] Vac.(over 5%)	120 20					

Note: Race and the racial composition of the neighborhood are not appraisal factors.
Neighborhood boundaries and characteristics: Area of mostly single family homes located north of Oak Park Blvd., west of Highway 60, South of Floral Road and east of Dixie Drive.
Factors that affect the marketability of the properties in the neighborhood (proximity to employment and amenities, employment stability, appeal to market, etc.): The subject is located close to neighborhood shopping, parks, public schools and employment centers. The subject's neighborhood exhibits the typical appeal and condition for the area. The presence of 5% commercial utilization is limited to the main thoroughfares and does not adversely affect the subject's value or marketability.

Market conditions in the subject neighborhood (including support for the above conclusions related to the trend of property values, demand/supply, and marketing time -- such as data on competitive properties for sale in the neighborhood, description of the prevalence of sales and financing concessions, etc.): Mortgage money is readily available in the St. Joseph market. Any loan discounts, interest buydowns or concessions do not adversely affect the subject. The subject is located in a family oriented neighborhood whose supply and demand appear to be in balance.

Project Information for PUDs   (If applicable) - - Is the developer/builder in control of the Home Owners' Association (HOA)?   [ ] Yes [ ] No
Approximate total number of units in the subject project   Approximate total number of units for sale in the subject project
Describe common elements and recreational facilities: N/A

Dimensions 80 x 120 (Subject to survey)			Topography	Typical Level
Site area 9600			Size	Typical
	Corner Lot [ ] Yes [X] No		Shape	Rectangular
Specific zoning classification and description Residential (RM-25)			Drainage	Apparently Adequate
Zoning compliance [X] Legal [ ] Legal nonconforming (Grandfathered use) [ ] Illegal [ ] No zoning			View	Residential
Highest & best use as improved: [X] Present use [ ] Other use (explain)			Landscaping	Adequate/ Typical

Utilities	Public	Other	Off-site Improvements	Type	Public	Private		
Electricity	[X]		Street	Asphalt	[X]	[ ]	Driveway Surface	Asphalt
Gas			Curb/gutter	None	[ ]	[ ]	Apparent easements	None observed
Water	[X]		Sidewalk	None	[ ]	[ ]	FEMA Special Flood Hazard Area	[ ] Yes [X] No
Sanitary sewer	[X]		Street lights		[X]	[ ]	FEMA Zone	Map Date
Storm sewer			Alley	None	[ ]	[ ]	FEMA Map No.	

Comments (apparent adverse easements, encroachments, special assessments, slide areas, illegal or legal nonconforming zoning use, etc.): No apparent adverse easements, encroachments or conditions observed.

GENERAL DESCRIPTION		EXTERIOR DESCRIPTION		FOUNDATION		BASEMENT		INSULATION		
No. of Units	1	Foundation	Concrete	Slab	Yes	Area Sq. Ft.	N/A	Roof		[ ]
No. of Stories	1	Exterior Walls	CBS	Crawl Space	No	% Finished		Ceiling		[ ]
Type (Det./Att.)	Detached	Roof Surface	Shingle	Basement	No	Ceiling		Walls		[ ]
Design (Style)	Ranch	Gutters & Dwnspts.	Typical	Sump Pump	N/A	Walls		Floor		[ ]
Existing/Proposed	Yes/No	Window Type	Awning	Dampness	N/A	Floor		None		[ ]
Age (Yrs.)	15	Storm/Screens	No/Yes	Settlement	N/A	Outside Entry		Unknown		[X]
Effective Age (Yrs.)	14 - 17	Manufactured House	No	Infestation	N/A					

ROOMS	Foyer	Living	Dining	Kitchen	Den	Family Rm.	Rec. Rm.	Bedrooms	# Baths	Laundry	Other	Area Sq. Ft.
Basement												N/A
Level 1		X	X	X		X		3	2	X		1950
Level 2												

Finished area above grade contains: 7 Rooms; 3 Bedroom(s); 2 Bath(s); 1,950 Square Feet of Gross Living Area

INTERIOR	Materials/Condition	HEATING		KITCHEN EQUIP.		ATTIC		AMENITIES		CAR STORAGE: 2	
Floors	Carpet/Vinyl/*	Type	Centrl	Refrigerator	[X]	None	[X]	Fireplace(s) #		None	[ ]
Walls	Plaster/Avg	Fuel	Electr	Range/Oven	[X]	Stairs	[ ]	Patio Concrete	[X]	Garage	# of cars
Trim/Finish	Wood/Average	Condition Avg		Disposal	[ ]	Drop Stair	[ ]	Deck	[ ]	Attached	[ ]
Bath Floor	Vinyl/Average	COOLING		Dishwasher	[ ]	Scuttle	[X]	Porch Open	[X]	Detached	[ ]
Bath Wainscot	Ceramic/Avg	Central	X	Fan/Hood	[ ]	Floor	[ ]	Fence	[ ]	Built-In	[ ]
Doors	Wood/Average	Other		Microwave	[ ]	Heated	[ ]	Pool	[ ]	Carport	2
* Average		Condition Avg		Washer/Dryer	[X]	Finished	[ ]			Driveway	Single

Additional features (special energy efficient items, etc.): Typical, ceiling fans (4).

Condition of the improvements, depreciation (physical, functional, and external), repairs needed, quality of construction, remodeling/additions, etc.: The subject shows average condition on the interior and exterior and exhibits the typical appeal for the area. No functional or external obsolescence observed.

Adverse environmental conditions (such as, but not limited to, hazardous wastes, toxic substances, etc.) present in the improvements, on the site, or in the immediate vicinity of the subject property.: No apparent adverse environmental conditions were observed.

Freddie Mac Form 70 6/93   PAGE 1 OF 2   Fannie Mae Form 1004 6/93

Figure 16.3 ***Uniform Residential Appraisal Report (continued)***

UNIFORM RESIDENTIAL APPRAISAL REPORT

File No. 96-100 Page # 2

Valuation Section   File No. 96-100

ESTIMATED SITE VALUE 32,000	= $ 32,000	Comments on Cost Approach (such as, source of cost estimate, site value,
ESTIMATED REPRODUCTION COST-NEW-OF IMPROVEMENTS:		square foot calculation and for HUD, VA and FmHA, the estimated remaining
Dwelling 1,950 Sq. Ft. @$ 58.00 = $ 113,100		economic life of the property): Cost
N/A Sq. Ft. @$ =		estimates derived from Marshall Valuation
Appliances/Patio/Porch = 2,500		Services publications.
Garage/Carport 430 Sq. Ft. @$ 11.00 = 4,730		
Total Estimated Cost New = $ 120,330		
Less Physical Functional External		The subject's land to building ratio is
Depreciation 30,083 = $ 30,083		typical for the area and does not
Depreciated Value of Improvements = $ 90,247		adversely affect the subject value or
"As-is" Value of Site Improvements drive landscp. = $ 2,200		marketability.
INDICATED VALUE BY COST APPROACH = $ 124,447		Est. remaining economic life: 40-45 years

ITEM	SUBJECT	COMPARABLE NO. 1		COMPARABLE NO. 2		COMPARABLE NO. 3	
Address	1097 Timbers Crossin St. Joseph	1255 NE 34 Street		1297 NE 34 Street		1539 NE 38 Street	
Proximity to Subject		1 Block Southwest		1 Block South		5 Blocks Northeast	
Sales Price	$ 120,000	$ 119,000		$ 126,500		$ 121,000	
Price/Gross Living Area	$ 61.54 ⏀	$ 63.47 ⏀		$ 65.89 ⏀		$ 61.58 ⏀	
Data and/or Verification Source	Inspection	MLS		MLS		MLS	
VALUE ADJUSTMENTS	DESCRIPTION	DESCRIPTION	+(-)$ Adjust.	DESCRIPTION	+(-)$ Adjust.	DESCRIPTION	+(-)$ Adjust.
Sales or Financing Concessions		VA	-1,000	Conventional		Conventional	
Date of Sale/Time		8/96		9/96		7/96	
Location	Average	Average		Average		Average	
Leasehold/Fee Simple	Fee Simple	Fee Simple		Fee Simple		Fee Simple	
Site	9600	Corner/Avg		Corner/Avg		Inside/Avg	
View	Residential	Commercial	+2,000	Residential		Residential	
Design and Appeal	Ranch	Ranch/Avg		Ranch/Avg		Ranch/Avg	
Quality of Construction	CBS	CBS		CBS		CBS	
Age	15	16		14		16	
Condition	Average	Average		Average		Average	
Above Grade	Total Bdrms Baths	Total Bdrms Baths		Total Bdrms Baths		Total Bdrms Baths	
Room Count	7 3 2	7 3 2		7 3 2		7 3 2	
Gross Living Area	1,950 Sq. Ft.	1,875 Sq. Ft.	+1,125	1,920 Sq. Ft.		1,965 Sq. Ft.	
Basement & Finished Rooms Below Grade	N/A	None		None		None	
Functional Utility	Average	Average		Average		Average	
Heating/Cooling	Central	Central		Central		Central	
Energy Efficient Items	Typical	Typical		Typical		Typical	
Garage/Carport		Carport (2)		Garage (2)	-5,000	Carport (2)	
Porch, Patio, Deck, Fireplace(s), etc.	Porch Patio	Porch Patio		Porch Patio		Porch Patio	
Fence, Pool, etc.	Average	Average		Fence	-1,000	Average	
Net Adj. (total)		[X]+ [ ]- $ 2,125		[ ]+ [X]- $ 6,000		[X]+ [ ]- $ 0	
Adjusted Sales Price of Comparable		$ 121,125		$ 120,500		$ 121,000	

Comments on Sales Comparison (including the subject property's compatibility to the neighborhood, etc.): All comparables utilized are of similar single family homes located in the same neighborhood as the subject with a range from $120,500 to $121,125. A time adjustment could not be supported by the market.

ITEM	SUBJECT	COMPARABLE NO. 1	COMPARABLE NO. 2	COMPARABLE NO. 3
Date, Price and Data Source, for prior sales within year of appraisal	N/A	N/A	N/A	N/A

Analysis of any current agreement of sale, option, or listing of subject property and analysis of any prior sales of subject and comparables within one year of the date of appraisal: The subject was not listed for sale on the open market.

INDICATED VALUE BY SALES COMPARISON APPROACH		$	121,000
INDICATED VALUE BY INCOME APPROACH (If Applicable) Estimated Market Rent $ 1275 /Mo. x Gross Rent Multiplier 95 = $			121,125

This appraisal is made [X] "as is" [ ] subject to the repairs, alterations, inspections or conditions listed below [ ] subject to completion per plans & specifications.
Conditions of Appraisal: No personal property was included in the estimate of value.

Final Reconciliation: Weight was given to all three approaches, with the most weight given to the market data approach as it best reflects the action of the buyers and sellers.

The purpose of this appraisal is to estimate the market value of the real property that is the subject of this report, based on the above conditions and the certification, contingent and limiting conditions, and market value definition that are stated in the attached Freddie Mac Form 439/FNMA form 1004B (Revised 6/93).
I (WE) ESTIMATE THE MARKET VALUE, AS DEFINED, OF THE REAL PROPERTY THAT IS THE SUBJECT OF THIS REPORT, AS OF September 4, 1996 (WHICH IS THE DATE OF INSPECTION AND THE EFFECTIVE DATE OF THIS REPORT) TO BE $ 121,000

APPRAISER: Michelle Tipton	SUPERVISORY APPRAISER (ONLY IF REQUIRED):	
Signature	Signature	[ ] Did [ ] Did Not
Name Michelle Tipton	Name	Inspect Property
Date Report Signed September 4, 1996	Date Report Signed	
State Certification # St.Cert.Res.REA RD 010092 State MO	State Certification #	State
Or State License # State MO	Or State License #	State

Freddie Mac Form 70 6/93   PAGE 2 OF 2   Fannie Mae Form 1004 6-93

APPROACHES TO VALUE (APPRAISAL METHODS)

To arrive at an accurate estimate of value, three basic approaches, or techniques, are traditionally used by appraisers:

1. The sales comparison approach
2. The cost approach
3. The income capitalization approach

Each method, when completed independently, serves as a check against the others and narrows the range within which the final estimate of value will fall. Generally, each method is considered most reliable for specific types of property.

The Sales Comparison Approach

In the **sales comparison approach,** also known as the *market data approach,* an estimate of value is obtained by comparing the subject property (the property under appraisal) with recently sold comparable properties (properties similar to the subject). This approach is most often used in valuing single-family homes and land. Because no two parcels of real estate are exactly alike, each comparable property must be compared with the subject property, and the sales prices of the comparables must be adjusted for any dissimilar features. The principal factors for which adjustments must be made fall into four basic categories:

The Sales Comparison Approach

1. Date of sale
2. Location
3. Physical features
4. Terms and conditions of sale

---

1. *Date of sale.* An adjustment must be made if economic changes occur between the date of sale of a comparable property and the date of the appraisal.
2. *Location.* An adjustment may be necessary to compensate for locational differences. For example, similar properties might differ in price from neighborhood to neighborhood or even within the same neighborhood.
3. *Physical features.* Physical features that may require adjustment include age of building; size of lot; landscaping; construction; number of rooms; square feet of living space; interior and exterior condition; presence or absence of a garage; a fireplace or an air conditioner; and so forth.
4. *Terms and conditions of sale.* This consideration becomes important if a sale is not financed with a standard mortgage. Be sure that the sale was an "arms-length sale," which means that the property did not sell for an unusually high or low price because of a special relationship between the buyer and seller. An example would be a low-price sale between a parent and child.

Selecting comparables. First and foremost, the comparable selected should be as similar to the subject property as possible, and should have been recently sold (within the past year) in an open and competitive market, under typical market conditions, when the seller and buyer are well informed and not acting under undue pressure. Nontypical conditions may involve seller financing; an estate sale; a foreclosure sale; a buyer under pressure to buy quickly because of school, business or family pressure; and so forth. An important point to remember is this: *the more similar the comparable is, the more recently sold and the fewer adjustments that are required, the more reliable will be the estimate of value.*

After a careful analysis of the differences between comparable properties and the subject property, the appraiser assigns a dollar value to each of these differences. On the basis of his or her knowledge and experience, the appraiser estimates dollar adjustments that reflect actual values assigned in the marketplace. The value of a feature present in the subject property but not in a comparable property is *added to the comparable property's total sales price.* This presumes that, all other features being equal, a property having a feature (such as a fireplace or wet bar) not present in a comparable property would tend to have a higher market value solely because of this feature. (The feature need not be a physical amenity; it may be locational or aesthetic.) Likewise, the value of a feature present in a comparable but not in the subject property is *subtracted from the comparable property's total sales price.* Remember, *all adjustments are made to the sales prices of the comparables, not to that of the subject property.* It must be stressed that a variable is adjusted by value in the marketplace and not by cost. For example, a fireplace may add less value to a dwelling than the actual cost of creating it.

If the comparable property has a feature that is *inferior* to the subject, the appraiser will make a *positive* adjustment to the value of the comparable. Conversely, if the comparable property has a feature that is *superior* to the subject you will make a *negative* adjustment to the value of the comparable. Remember you *never* adjust the value of the subject. Also, never average the adjusted values of the comparable properties.

The adjusted sales prices of the comparables represent the probable value range of the subject property. The appraiser then *correlates* the adjusted sales prices to determine a single market value estimate for the subject property. The correlation is the result of a *weighted averaging process.* The comparable that is most similar to the subject property is given more weight than the other comparables when calculating the single estimate of value.

The sales comparison approach is essential in almost every appraisal of real estate. It is considered the most reliable of the three approaches in appraising residential property, where the amenities (intangible benefits) may be difficult to measure. The most difficult time to employ the sales comparison approach occurs when there are no comparable sales. Agents may want to use the services of a licensed appraiser for any property for which it is difficult to establish an asking price. An example of the sales comparison approach is shown in Table 16.1.

Comparative market analysis (CMA). An informal version of the sales comparison approach is used by brokers and salespeople to help a seller set a price for residential real estate in an active market. This informal version is called a **comparative market analysis,** or *CMA.* While the CMA is a form of appraisal, the licensed real estate agent need not hold an appraiser's license to perform this function while serving a client. However, the North Carolina Real Estate Commission will hold agents accountable for not performing a CMA in a competent manner, and it can take appropriate disciplinary action against the licensee. It is common for agents preparing a CMA to use listed properties and properties whose listings have expired as well as recently sold properties. Listed properties that have not sold generally represent the upper ceiling of value because sales prices tend to be lower than listing prices. Expired listings are useful in showing the seller how unreasonable prices affect sales (generally, listings that have expired were priced too high

Table 16.1   Sales Comparison Approach to Value

| | Subject Property: 155 Potter Dr. | Comparables | | | | |
		A	B	C	D	E
Sales price		$118,000	$112,000	$121,000	$116,500	$110,000
Financing concessions		none	none	none	none	none
Date of sale	none	current	current	current	current	current
Location	good	same	poorer +6,500	same	same	same
Age	6 years	same	same	same	same	same
Size of lot	60' × 135'	same	same	larger −5,000	same	larger −5,000
Landscaping	good	same	same	same	same	same
Construction	brick	same	same	same	same	same
Style	ranch	same	same	same	same	same
No. of rooms	6	same	same	same	same	same
No. of bedrooms	3	same	same	same	same	same
No. of baths	1½	same	same	same	same	same
Sq. ft. of living space	1,500	same	same	same	same	same
Other space (basement)	full basement	same	same	same	same	same
Condition—exterior	average	better −1,500	poorer +1,000	better −1,500	same	poorer +2,000
Condition—interior	good	same	same	better −500	same	same
Garage	2-car attached	same	same	same	same	none +5,000
Other improvements	none	none	none	none	none	none
Net Adjustments		−1,500	+7,500	−7,000	-0-	+2,000
Adjusted Value		$116,500	$119,500	$114,000	$116,500	$112,000

Note: The value of a feature that is present in the subject but not in the comparable property is *added* to the sales price of the comparable. Likewise, the value of a feature that is present in the comparable but not in the subject property is *subtracted*. The adjusted sales prices of the comparables represent the probable range of value of the subject property. From this range, a single market value estimate can be selected. Because the value range of the properties in the comparison chart (excluding comparables B and E) is close, and comparable D required no adjustment, an appraiser might conclude that the indicated market value of the subject is $116,500. However, appraisers use a complex process of evaluating adjustment percentages and may consider other objective factors or subjective judgments based on research.

to sell within the listing period). Once you have listed a property it is a good idea to update the CMA on at least a monthly basis. Make the seller aware of the changes in listing and sales prices in their area. Have the CMA on hand when presenting an offer to purchase from any prospective buyer.

These three types of properties are very helpful when putting together a CMA to help a seller set a listing price. However, bear in mind that an appraiser is allowed to use only actual sales when preparing a sales comparison appraisal. Do not count a listing that is under contract as a "sold" property.

The Cost Approach

The **cost approach** to value is based on the principle of substitution, which states that the maximum value of a property tends to be set by the cost of acquiring an equally desirable and valuable substitute property. The cost approach consists of five steps:

1. Estimate the value of the land as if it were vacant and available to be put to its highest and best use, based on the sales comparison approach, because land cannot be depreciated.

Table 16.2   *Cost Approach to Value*

Subject Property: 155 Potter Dr.

Land Valuation: Size 60′ × 135′ @ $450 per front foot	=		$ 27,000
Plus site improvements: driveway, walks, landscaping, etc.	=		8,000
Total			$ 35,000

Building Valuation: Replacement Cost
    1,500 sq. ft. @ $65 per sq. ft.   = $97,500

Less Depreciation:

Physical depreciation		
Curable		
(items of deferred maintenance)		
exterior painting	$4,000	
Incurable (structural deterioration)	9,750	
Functional obsolescence	2,000	
External depreciation	-0-	
Total		−15,750

Depreciated Value of Building	$ 81,750
Indicated Value by Cost Approach	$116,750

---

2. Separate the land from the improvements, and estimate the current cost of constructing the building(s) and site improvements based, in general, on cost data and experience.
3. Estimate the amount of accrued depreciation of the improvements resulting from physical deterioration, functional obsolescence or locational obsolescence.
4. Deduct the accrued depreciation from the estimated construction cost of the new building(s) and the contributory depreciated value of site improvements.
5. Add the estimated value of the land to the depreciated cost of the building(s) and site improvements to determine the total property value.

Land is always valued as if vacant, and land value is estimated by using the sales comparison approach (step 1); that is, the location and improvements of the subject site are compared with those of similar nearby vacant sites, and adjustments are made for significant differences in size, shape, topography, utilities available, assessments and so on.

There are two ways to look at the construction cost of a building for appraisal purposes (step 2): reproduction cost and replacement cost. **Reproduction cost** is the dollar amount required to construct an exact duplicate of the subject building at current prices. **Replacement cost** is the construction cost, at current prices and using modern materials and methodology, of a property that is not necessarily an exact duplicate but serves the same purpose or function as the original property. Replacement cost is most often used in appraising because it eliminates obsolete features and takes advantage of current construction materials and techniques.

An example of the cost approach to value is shown in Table 16.2.

Determining reproduction or replacement cost. An appraiser using the cost approach computes the reproduction or replacement cost of a building using one of the following methods:

- **Square-foot method.** The cost per square foot of a recently built comparable structure is multiplied by the number of square feet in the subject building. This is the most common method of cost estimation. The example in Table 16.2 uses the square-foot method. For some property, the cost per cubic foot of a recently built comparable structure is multiplied by the number of cubic feet in the subject structure.
- **Unit-in-place method.** The replacement cost of a structure is estimated based on the construction cost per unit of measure of individual building components, including material, labor, overhead and builder's profit. Most components are measured in square feet, although items like plumbing fixtures are estimated by unit cost.
- **Quantity-survey method.** An estimate is made of the quantities of raw materials needed to replace the subject structure (lumber, plaster, brick and so on) as well as of the current price of such materials and their installation costs. These factors are added to indirect costs (building permit, survey, payroll taxes, builder's profit) to arrive at the total replacement cost of the structure. This method is similar to the approach a building contractor takes when preparing a bill for the construction of a building.

Depreciation. In a real estate appraisal, **depreciation** (a loss in value for any reason) refers to any condition that adversely affects the value of an *improvement* to real property. Land does not depreciate because it is here forever and can always be put to its highest and best use when economically and legally feasible to do so. For appraisal purposes (as opposed to depreciation for tax purposes, which will be discussed in Chapter 18), depreciation is divided into three classes according to its cause:

1. **Physical deterioration**—*curable:* Repairs that are physically possible and economically feasible and will result in an increase in appraised value equal to or exceeding their cost fall into this category. Routine maintenance, such as painting and roof replacement, is an example.

1a. **Physical deterioration**—*incurable:* Repairs to major structural components of a building, which deteriorate at different rates, may not be economically feasible and therefore fall into this category. Examples are bearing walls and foundations.

2. **Functional obsolescence**—*curable:* Physical or design features that are no longer considered desirable by property buyers but can be replaced or redesigned at low cost constitute this class of depreciation. For example, outmoded fixtures, such as plumbing, are usually easily replaced. Room function might be redefined at no cost if the basic room layout allows it. A bedroom adjacent to a kitchen, for instance, may be converted to a family room.

2a. **Functional obsolescence**—*incurable:* Currently undesirable physical or design features that cannot be remedied easily are considered functionally obsolete. Many older multistory industrial buildings are considered less suitable than one-story buildings, for example. An office building that cannot be air-conditioned because of the cost of duct installation also suffers from functional obsolescence. A residential example might be a home with five bedrooms but only one bath.

3. **Economic (environmental or external) obsolescence**—*incurable only:* Caused by factors outside the subject property, this type of obsolescence cannot be considered curable. For instance, proximity to a nuisance, such as a polluting factory, is an unchangeable factor that cannot be cured by the owner of the subject property. Economic obsolescence also may be referred to as *locational obsolescence.*

In determining a property's depreciation, most appraisers use the *breakdown method,* in which depreciation is broken down into all three classes, with separate estimates for curable and incurable factors in each class. Depreciation is difficult to measure, and the older the building, the more difficult it is to estimate. The easiest but least precise way to determine depreciation is the **age-life method,** which uses the effective age of a building and its economic (useful) life. When the cost of an asset is depreciated evenly over its useful life, this is called **straight-line depreciation,** as illustrated in the example below. Depreciation is assumed to occur at an even rate over a structure's **economic life,** the period during which it is expected to remain useful for its original intended purpose. (Compare this with a property's *actual life,* the period during which the improvements are expected to remain standing.) To derive the amount of annual depreciation, the property's cost is divided by the number of years of its expected economic life.

For Example A $120,000 property may have a land value of $30,000 and an improvement value of $90,000. If the improvements are expected to last 60 years, the annual straight-line depreciation would be $1,500 ($90,000 ÷ 60 years). Such depreciation can be calculated as an annual dollar amount or as a percentage of the property's replacement cost.

Likewise, you can determine a building's **effective age** by multiplying its economic life by the amount of depreciation the building has already suffered.

For Example If a building has suffered 25 percent depreciation and it has an economic life of 25 years, its effective age is 6.25 years (25 years × .25 = 6.25 years). Regardless of this building's actual age, its effective age would be considered to be about 6 years. Thus it could be considered to have a remaining economic life of 18.75 years.

Much functional obsolescence and all economic obsolescence, however, can be evaluated only by considering the actions of buyers in the marketplace.

Special-purpose properties. The cost approach is most helpful in the appraisal of special-purpose buildings such as schools, churches and public buildings. Such properties are difficult to appraise using other methods because there are seldom any local sales to use as comparables and the properties ordinarily do not generate income.

In the appraisal of special-purpose properties, an inexperienced appraiser may complete only a cost approach analysis and may estimate market value based on the results of that approach alone. But just because a structure was originally constructed for a certain purpose does not mean that it is necessarily the highest and best use for the property. This being the case, a market analysis of other properties having the same projected highest and best use is very important in this type of appraisal. Adjustments must be made for such variables as modification costs, location, time of sale, lot sizes and the like to make valid comparisons between the comparables and the subject property.

The Income Capitalization Approach

The **income capitalization approach** to value, also known as the *income approach,* is based on the present worth of the future rights to income. It assumes that the income derived from a property will control the value of that property. The income approach is used for valuation of income-producing properties—apartment buildings, office buildings, shopping centers and the like. Many properties have potential for producing income but do not because they are owner-occupied. In such cases, the appraiser projects income and expenses based on market studies of similar income-producing properties. In using the income approach to estimate value, an appraiser must work through the following steps:

1. Estimate the annual potential *gross income* using rents from comparable properties, as well as income from other sources such as concessions, laundry facilities and vending machines.
2. Based on market experience, deduct an appropriate allowance for vacancy and rent collection losses to arrive at the *effective gross income.*
3. Based on appropriate operating standards, deduct the annual *operating expenses* of the real estate from the effective gross income to arrive at the annual *net operating income.* Operating expenses include taxes, insurance, maintenance, repairs and reserves for replacement. Management costs are always included as operating expenses, even if the current owner manages the property and does not show a cost for this item. Mortgage payments, however (including principal and interest), are debt service and not considered operating expenses. For example, if a property owner spends $35,000 a year on operating expenses and $25,000 a year on mortgage payments, the $35,000 would be subtracted from effective gross income to determine the property's net income; the $25,000 of mortgage payments (debt service) would not.
4. Estimate the price a typical investor would pay for the income produced by this particular type and class of property. This is done by estimating the rate of return (or yield) that an investor will demand for the investment of capital in this type of building. This rate of return is called the **capitalization** (or "cap") **rate** and is determined by comparing the relationship of net operating income to the sales prices of similar properties that have sold in the current market. For example, a comparable property that produces an annual net income of $15,000 is sold for $187,500. The capitalization rate is $15,000 ÷ $187,500, or 8 percent. If other comparable properties sell at prices that yield substantially the same rate, it may be assumed that 8 percent is the rate that the appraiser should apply to the subject property.
5. Finally, the capitalization rate is applied to the property's annual net income, resulting in the appraiser's estimate of the property value.

With the appropriate capitalization rate and the projected annual net operating income, the appraiser can estimate value by the income approach in the following manner:

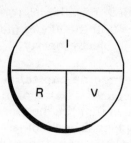

Net Operating Income ÷ Capitalization Rate = Value

Example: $18,000 income ÷ 9% cap rate = $200,000 value

This formula and its variations are important in estimating the value of income property.

$$\frac{\text{Income}}{\text{Rate}} = \text{Value} \qquad \frac{\text{Income}}{\text{Value}} = \text{Rate} \qquad \text{Value} \times \text{Rate} = \text{Income}$$

A very simplified version of the computations used in applying the income capitalization approach is illustrated in Table 16.3.

In Practice   The most difficult step in the income approach to value is determining the appropriate capitalization rate for the property. This rate must be selected to recapture the original investment over the building's economic life, must give the owner an acceptable rate of return on investment and must provide for the repayment of borrowed capital. An income property that carries with it a great deal of risk as an investment generally requires a higher rate of return than does a property considered a safe investment. Capitalization rates for similar properties may be different from block to block within a city owing to varying neighborhood influences.

Gross rent multipliers or gross income multipliers. Certain properties, such as one-family or two-family homes, are not generally purchased as income properties. As a substitute for a more elaborate income analysis, the **gross rent multiplier (GRM)** method may be used in appraising such properties. The GRM relates the sales price of a property to its expected rental income. (Gross *monthly* income is used for residential property; gross *annual* income is used for commercial and industrial property.) The formula is as follows:

$$\frac{\text{Sales Price}}{\text{Rental Income}} = \text{Gross Rent Multiplier}$$

For Example If a property recently sold for $82,000 and its monthly rental income was $650, the GRM for the property would be computed thus:

$$\frac{\$82,000}{\$650} = 126.2 \text{ GRM}$$

Table 16.3   Income Capitalization Approach to Value

Potential Gross Annual Income	$ 0,000
Market rent (100% capacity)	
Income from other sources	+ 600
(vending machines and pay phones)	$ 60,600
Less vacancy and collection losses (estimated) @4%	- 2,424
Effective Gross Income	$ 58,176

Expenses:

Real estate taxes	$9,000	
Insurance	1,000	
Heat	2,800	
Maintenance	6,400	
Utilities, electricity, water, gas	800	
Repairs	1,200	
Decorating	1,400	
Replacement of equipment	800	
Legal and accounting	600	
Advertising	300	
Management	3,000	
Total		$ - 27,300
Annual Net Operating Income		$ 30,876

Capitalization rate = 10% (overall rate)

Capitalization of annual net income: $$\frac{\$30.876}{.10}$$

Indicated Value by Income Approach = $308,760

To establish an accurate GRM, an appraiser should have recent sales and rental data from at least three properties similar to the subject property. The most appropriate GRM can then be applied to the estimated fair market rental of the subject property to arrive at its market value. The formula would then be

Rental Income × GRM = Estimated Market Value

Table 16.4 shows some examples of GRM comparisons.

Table 16.4   Gross Rent Multiplier

Comparable No.	Sales Price	Monthly Rent	GRM
1	$93,600	$650	144
2	78,500	450	174
3	95,500	675	141
4	82,000	565	145
Subject	?	625	?

Note: Based on an analysis of these comparisons, a GRM of 145 seems reasonable for homes in this area. In the opinion of an appraiser, then, the estimated value of the subject property would be $625 × 145, or $90,625.

If a property's income also comes from nonrental sources (such as sales concessions), a *gross income multiplier (GIM)* is used similarly.

Much skill is required to use multipliers accurately because no fixed multiplier exists for all areas or all types of properties. Therefore, many appraisers view the technique simply as a quick, informal way to check the validity of a property value obtained by one of the other appraisal methods. Because the gross multiplier methods are based on gross income rather than net income (they do not take into account operating expenses), the results may not be very accurate.

Reconciliation   If more than one of the three approaches to value are applied to the same property (and appraisers should apply all three methods whenever possible), they will normally produce as many separate indications of value. **Reconciliation** (sometimes called *final reconciliation*) is the art of analyzing and effectively weighing the findings from the different approaches used. To come up with a valid estimate, the appraiser must give more weight to the most appropriate appraisal method for that particular type of property.

Although each approach may serve as an independent guide to value, whenever possible all three approaches should be used as a check on the final estimate of value. The process of reconciliation is more complicated than simply taking the average of the derived value estimates. An average implies that the data and logic applied in each of the approaches are equally valid and reliable and should therefore be given equal weight. In fact, certain approaches are more valid and reliable with some kinds of properties than with others.

Averaging is considered an improper methodology. (In fact, reconciliation never simply entails averaging the three value estimates.) For example, in appraising a home, the income capitalization approach is rarely used, and the cost approach is of limited value unless the home is relatively new; therefore, the sales comparison approach is usually given greatest weight in valuing single-family residences. In the appraisal of income or investment property, the income capitalization approach is normally given the greatest weight. In the appraisal of churches, libraries, museums, schools and other special-use properties that produce little or no income or sales revenue, the cost approach is usually assigned the greatest weight. From this analysis, or reconciliation, a single estimate of market value is produced.

THE PROFESSION OF APPRAISING

In 1932, the American Institute of Real Estate Appraisers was founded. A few years later, another organization, now known as the Society of Real Estate Appraisers, was formed. These two organizations have recently merged. Through the years, a number of other professional appraisal organizations have come into existence; they include the American Society of Appraisers, the National Association of Review Appraisers, the National Association of Independent Fee Appraisers and the American Society of Farm Managers and Rural Appraisers. These organizations have professional designations and strict codes of ethics.

The Appraisal Institute offers two professional designations: RM (Residential Member) and MAI (Member of the Appraisal Institute). The National Association of Independent Fee Appraisers offers the designations IFA (member) and IFAS (senior member). The American Society of Appraisers designation is ASA (senior member).

Through these groups, courses have been established in universities and colleges, and books, journals and other publications devoted to various aspects of appraising have been published. Appraising has become the most specialized branch of real estate. Before awarding their designations, the major recognized appraisal associations require a four-year college degree or the equivalent, plus five years of full-time appraisal experience, in addition to passing an examination and writing acceptable appraisals.

To become state-licensed, appraisers must meet educational, experiential and examination requirements. An application and information book on becoming an appraiser can be obtained by writing to the North Carolina Appraisal Board at P.O. Box 20500, Raleigh, NC 27619-0500. Federally related appraisals must follow the guidelines stated in USPAP (Uniform Standards of Professional Appraisal Practice).

SUMMARY

To appraise real estate is to estimate its value at a given date. Although many types of value exist, the most common objective of an appraisal is to estimate market value—the most probable sales price of a property. Basic to appraising are certain underlying economic principles, such as highest and best use, substitution, supply and demand, balance, conformity, anticipation, contribution, competition and change.

A professional appraiser analyzes a property through three approaches to value. In the sales comparison approach, the value of the subject property is compared with the values of others like it that have sold recently. Because no two properties are exactly alike, adjustments must be made to the comparables' sales prices to account for any differences. With the cost approach, an appraiser calculates the cost of building a similar structure on a similar site. The appraiser then subtracts depreciation (loss in value), which reflects the differences between new properties of this type and the present condition of the subject property. The income capitalization approach is an analysis based on the relationship between the rate of return that an investor requires and the net income that a property produces.

A special, informal version of the income capitalization approach, the gross rent multiplier (GRM), is often used to estimate the value of properties that are not rented but could be. The GRM is computed by dividing the sales price of a property by its gross monthly rent.

Normally, the application of the different approaches results in as many different estimates of value. In the process of reconciliation, the validity and reliability of each approach are weighed objectively to arrive at the single best and most supportable conclusion of value.

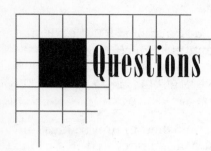

Questions

1. The amount of money a property commands in the marketplace is its
   I. market price.
   II. market value.
   a. I only
   b. II only
   c. Both I and II
   d. Neither I nor II

2. Reconciliation refers to which of the following?
   a. Averaging the results of the sales comparison approach
   b. Separating the value of land from the total value of property to compute depreciation
   c. Analyzing the results obtained by the three different approaches to value to determine a final estimate of value
   d. Process by which an appraiser determines the highest and best use for a parcel of land

3. One method an appraiser uses to determine a building's replacement cost involves the estimated cost of the raw materials needed to build the structure, plus labor and indirect costs. This is called the
   a. square-foot method.
   b. quantity-survey method.
   c. cubic-foot method.
   d. unit-in-place method.

4. If a property's annual net income is $24,000 and it is valued at $300,000, what is its capitalization rate?
   a. 12.5 percent   c. 15 percent
   b. 10.5 percent   d. 8 percent

5. Certain figures must be determined by an appraiser before value can be computed by the income approach. Which one of the following is not required for this process?
   a. Annual net operating income
   b. Capitalization rate
   c. Accrued depreciation
   d. Annual gross income

6. The ceiling, or top limit, of value of an improved parcel of real estate usually is the
   I. sales price paid for a similar property.
   II. cost of buying a lot and erecting a similar building on it.
   a. I only
   b. II only
   c. Both I and II
   d. Neither I nor II

7. The income capitalization approach is given the most weight in the valuation of a(n)
   a. single-family residence.
   b. industrial property.
   c. office building.
   d. school.

8. Capitalization is the process by which annual net operating income is used as the basis to
   a. determine cost.
   b. estimate value.
   c. establish depreciation.
   d. determine potential tax value.

9. From the reproduction or replacement cost of a building, an appraiser deducts depreciation, which represents the
   a. remaining economic life of the building.
   b. remodeling costs to increase rentals.
   c. loss of value due to any cause.
   d. costs to modernize the building.

10. Which of the following factors is not important in comparing properties under the sales comparison approach to value?
    a. Difference in dates of sale
    b. Difference in interior decorating
    c. Difference in appearance and condition
    d. Difference in location

11. The appraised value of a residence with four bedrooms and one bathroom would probably be reduced because of
    a. external obsolescence.
    b. functional obsolescence.
    c. physical deterioration—curable.
    d. physical deterioration—incurable.

12. Depreciation, as used in real estate appraisals, can be caused by any of the following EXCEPT
    a. functional obsolescence.
    b. physical deterioration.
    c. external obsolescence—incurable.
    d. external obsolescence—curable.

13. Which of the following makes use of a rate of investment return?
    a. Sales comparison approach
    b. Cost approach
    c. Income capitalization approach
    d. Gross income multiplier method

14. The elements of value include which of the following?
    a. Competition   c. Anticipation
    b. Scarcity   d. Balance

15. The market value of a parcel of real estate is
    I. an estimate of its future benefits.
    II. the amount of money paid for it.
    III. an estimate of the most probable price it will bring.
    a. I only
    b. III only
    c. I and II only
    d. II or III only

16. Which of the following statements is true of the income capitalization approach to value?
    a. The reproduction or replacement cost of the building must be computed.
    b. The capitalization rate must be estimated.
    c. Depreciation must be determined.
    d. Sales of similar properties must be considered.

17. In the cost approach to value, it is necessary to
    a. determine a dollar value for depreciation.
    b. estimate future expenses and operating costs.
    c. check sales prices of recently sold comparable properties in the area.
    d. reconcile differing value estimates.

18. An appraiser is using the sales comparison method to appraise a property. The subject property has two bedrooms and the comparable property has three bedrooms. The estimated value of the third bedroom is $2,500. The appraiser should
    a. deduct $2,500 from the value of the subject property.
    b. add $2,500 to the value of the subject property.
    c. deduct $2,500 from the value of the comparable property.
    d. add $2,500 to the value of the comparable property.

19. All of the following should be deducted from gross income to arrive at net operating income EXCEPT
    a. utilities.
    b. mortgage payments.
    c. maintenance.
    d. repairs.

20. If the appraiser decides to increase the capitalization rate, the value of the property will
    a. increase.
    b. decrease.
    c. stay the same.
    d. be the same as the capitalization rate.

21. The number of years a property is expected to remain useful for its original purpose is called its
    a. actual life.
    b. economic life.
    c. progressive life.
    d. depreciated life.

22. The formula for estimating value based on the gross rent multiplier is
    a. rental income × gross rent multiplier = estimated market value.
    b. rental income ÷ gross rent multiplier = estimated market value.
    c. estimated market value × rental income = gross rent multiplier.
    d. net operating income × gross rent multiplier = estimated market value.

23. In estimating the value of real estate using the cost approach, the appraiser should
    a. estimate the replacement cost of the improvements.
    b. deduct for depreciation of the land.
    c. determine the original cost and adjust for changes in capitalization rates.
    d. review the sales prices of comparable properties.

24. Under the income approach to estimating the value of real estate, the capitalization rate is the
    a. rate at which the property will increase in value.
    b. rate of return the property will earn as an investment.
    c. rate of capital required to keep the property operating efficiently.
    d. maximum rate of return allowed by usury limits.

25. An example of economic obsolescence is
    a. numerous pillars supporting the ceiling in a store.
    b. roof leaks making the premises unusable and therefore unrentable.
    c. massive cornices in an older structure.
    d. vacant and abandoned buildings in the area.

26. Mary lives in a home located in a suburban community. A new expressway is being built a few blocks away that will reduce the commute time to the urban employment center by 30 minutes. Mary's home is expected to increase in value, based on the principle of
    a. anticipation.
    b. competition.
    c. contribution.
    d. highest and best use.

27. An apartment building generates a monthly gross income of $6,000. Monthly managerial expenses total $1,000. Monthly taxes total $300, monthly debt service totals $2,675. Monthly repairs and maintenance total $1,100. What is the building's monthly net income?
    a. $925   c. $3,600
    b. $1,225   d. $3,900

28. The subject property is a two-story home with three bedrooms, three baths, a family room, a dining room and an attached two-car garage. Which of the following would be a legitimate comparable sale?
    I. Two-story home with 3 bedrooms and 2.5 baths in the same neighborhood that sold 18 months ago
    II. One-story home in a different neighborhood, with 3 bedrooms and 2 baths, a detached one-car garage and no family or dining room
    a. I only
    b. II only
    c. Both I and II
    d. Neither I nor II

29. The subject property has 2,100 square feet, 4 bedrooms, a 2-car garage, no patio, no pool, 2.5 baths and sits on 1 acre. The comparable recently sold for $140,000 and has 1,900 square feet, 3 bedrooms, a 1-car garage, a patio, a pool, 2 baths and sits on 1.5 acres. Market cost data shows the following values: Square foot = $72, 1 bedroom = $2,000, 1-car garage = $1,500, patio = $2,000, pool = $14,000, 1/2 bath = $800, and 1 acre = $30,000. Using this cost data, what is the estimated value of the subject property?
   a. $125,700
   b. $113,700
   c. $127,700
   d. $129,200

30. A broker is asked to estimate the value of a property. She finds four recently sold comparables, A, B, C and D. Comparables A, B and D have positive features worth $3,000, $2,000 and $5,000, respectively, which are not common to the subject property. Comparable C has negative features worth $3,500 that are not common to the subject property. The comparables sold for the following prices: A, $73,000; B, $74,000; C, $62,000; and D, $71,000. What is the range of indicated probable values for the subject property?
   a. $66,000 to $72,000
   b. $65,500 to $66,000
   c. $58,500 to $76,000
   d. $65,500 to $72,000

17 Property Insurance

LEARNING OBJECTIVES

When you've finished reading this chapter, you should be able to

- **describe** the protection afforded by insurance and the characteristics of various types of standard policies.

- **identify** insurance policy terms such as condition, exclusion and endorsement.

- **explain** the following legal issues: (1) insurable interest, (2) coinsurance clause and (3) unoccupied building exclusion.

- **explain** the purpose of the Federal Emergency Management Agency.

- **define** these *key terms:*

basic form	homeowner's	property insurance
bonding	insurance policy	risk management
broad form	liability insurance	subrogation clause
casualty insurance	multiperil policies	surety bonds
coinsurance clause	package insurance	workers'
deductible	premium	compensation acts

BASIC INSURANCE CONCEPTS

Because home ownership represents a large financial investment for most purchasers, homeowners usually protect their investment by taking out insurance on the property. If the property is mortgaged, homeowner's insurance is usually mandatory.

An insurance policy is an agreement between two parties: the insurer and the insured. Insurance represents the transfer of risk. The insurer is the insurance company, which agrees to reimburse the insured, the property owner, for losses caused by a covered event. For example, if a homeowner buys an insurance policy that protects him or her against fire loss and the insured property burns down, the insurer must reimburse the homeowner for the loss, within the limitations of the insurance policy. Insurance companies and insurance policies are regulated by government agencies.

However, the insurance policy is also a contract, subject to all the normal rules of contract law. For example, consideration in the form of *premiums* is required for the insurance contract to be valid. Premiums are considered to be the consumer's cost of coverage. Insurance policies have definite beginning and ending dates.

A **property** or **casualty insurance** policy protects the insured from losses caused by damage to the property and the improvements on that property. A **liability insurance** policy protects the insured from losses caused to third persons or their property. A **package insurance** policy protects the insured from both types of losses.

Three terms are commonly used when describing insurance policies, and it is important to know their definitions.

1. *Condition:* A condition limits or qualifies the duties of the insurance company or the insured (for example, if the policy covers theft, any claim for loss is conditioned on the theft being reported to the police and a police report being filed).
2. *Exclusion:* An exclusion eliminates coverage for a certain item or event (for example, damage caused by flooding may not be covered in the policy).
3. *Endorsement:* An endorsement is an addition to a standard policy that usually increases the amount of insurance coverage (for example, an art collector may obtain an endorsement to receive additional insurance coverage for the collection of fine art in his or her home).

HOMEOWNER'S INSURANCE

Although it is possible for a homeowner to obtain an individual policy for each type of risk, most residential property owners take out insurance in the form of a packaged **homeowner's insurance policy** on their residence. These policies insure holders against the destruction of their property by fire or windstorm, injury to others if it occurs on the property and theft from the premises of any personal property that is owned by the insured or members of the insured's family.

Coverage and Claims The most common homeowner's policy is called a **basic form** (HO-1) and it provides property coverage against:

- fire and lightning,
- glass breakage,
- windstorm and hail,
- explosion,
- riot and civil commotion,
- damage by aircraft,
- damage from vehicles,
- damage from smoke,

- vandalism and malicious mischief,
- theft and
- loss of property removed from the premises when it is endangered by fire or other perils.

The packaged homeowner's policy also includes *liability coverage* for (1) personal injuries to others resulting from the insured's acts of negligence, (2) voluntary medical payments and funeral expenses for accidents sustained by guests or resident employees on the insured's property and (3) physical damage to the property of others caused by the insured. Voluntary medical payments cover injuries to a resident employee but do not cover benefits due under any workers' compensation or occupational disease law.

Selected Legal Issues

Insurable interest. The insured party must have some type of financial interest in the property to recover any losses. The insured person may be the homeowner, the lender or even a property manager. The insured will, however, *never recover more than the actual loss*.

Unoccupied building exclusion. Most policies contain provisions that state that *if the insured building is unoccupied for a certain length of time, the owner may not be able to recover on any losses that may occur.* According to the courts in North Carolina, insurance companies may use 60 days as the vacancy time period. A property owner should make sure the building is not vacant for a longer period than that stated in the insurance policy (for example, 60 days); otherwise, the insured may not be able to recover for any losses.

Interpretation of Policies

The insurance policy is a contract. Most insurance policy contracts are standard forms approved by the North Carolina Insurance Commission. These standard forms have been drafted mostly in favor of the insurer, not the insured. The owner may have to ask a court to interpret any ambiguous clauses.

Characteristics of Homeowners' Policies

Although coverage provided may vary among policies, all homeowners' policies have three common characteristics. First, they all have *fixed ratios of coverage.* That is, each type of coverage in a policy must be maintained at a certain level. The amount of coverage on household contents and other items must be a fixed percentage of the amount of insurance on the building itself. Although the amount of contents coverage may be increased, it cannot be reduced below the standard percentage. In addition, theft coverage may be contingent on the full amount of the contents coverage.

Second, homeowners' policies have an *indivisible premium*, which means the insured receives coverage for all the perils included in the policy for a single rate and may not exclude certain perils from coverage.

Finally, *first-party and third-party insurance* is the liability coverage discussed above. It covers not only damage or loss to the insured's property or its contents but also the insured's legal liability for losses or damages to another's property as well as for injuries suffered by another party while on the insured's property.

The following basic types of insurance policies are identified by number.

- *HO-2.* This **broad form** insurance policy covers more perils than the basic form (including falling objects; weight of ice, snow or sleet; collapse of buildings; malfunctioning heating systems; accidental discharge of water or steam and electrical currents) and is used much more frequently than the basic form.
- *HO-3.* This *all-risk form* insurance policy provides even greater coverage than HO-2. Because it provides the insured with a greater amount of protection, it is the most commonly used policy today.
- *HO-4.* This *tenant's policy* (renter's policy) covers the same perils as HO-2 regarding the insured's personal property. It does not cover the building in which the tenant lives.
- *HO-6.* This policy is designed for the special needs of *condominium owners.*
- *HE-7.* An extended all-risk form providing broad coverage of both real and personal property. The HE-7 is designed for and primarily sold to owners of very expensive property.

Claims   Most homeowner's insurance policies contain a **coinsurance clause.** This provision usually requires that the insured maintain insurance on the property in an amount equal to at least 80 percent of the replacement cost of the dwelling (not including the price of the land). If the owner carries such a policy, a claim may be made for the cost of the repair or replacement of the damaged property without deduction for depreciation.

The formula for calculating the amount of recovery for a claim is as follows:

$$\frac{\text{Amount of insurance carried}}{80\% \text{ replacement value}} \times \text{Claim} = \text{Recovery}$$

For example, assume a homeowner's dwelling has a replacement cost of $100,000 and is damaged by fire. The estimated cost to repair the damaged portion of the dwelling is $71,000. Thus, if the homeowner carries at least $80,000 worth of insurance on the dwelling, the claim against the insurance company can be for the full $71,000.

If the homeowner carries coverage of less than 80 percent of the full replacement cost of the dwelling, the loss will be either settled for the actual cash value (replacement cost less depreciation) or prorated by dividing the percentage of replacement cost actually covered by the policy by the minimum coverage requirement (usually 80 percent). For example, if the building is insured for only 60 percent of its value and suffers a $71,000 loss, the insurance company will pay only $53,250 (60% ÷ 80%, or 75%, of $71,000 = $53,250).

In any event, the *total settlement cannot exceed the face value of the policy.* Because of coinsurance clauses, it is important that homeowners review periodically all policies to be certain that the coverage equals at least 80 percent of the current replacement (new) cost of their home.

Most policies also have a **subrogation clause,** which provides that if the insured collects for damage from the insurance company, any rights the insured may have to sue the person who caused the damage are assigned to the insurance company. A subrogation clause allows the insurance company to pursue legal action to collect the amount paid out from the party at fault and prevents the insured from collecting twice for the same damage.

In Practice   In recent years, builders have been using a synthetic stucco exterior finish on some residential properties. This exterior insulating finishing system (EIFS) is a highly effective moisture barrier that also tends to "seal in" moisture, trapping water in the home's walls and resulting in massive wood rot. Frequently, the effects of the rotting cannot be seen until the damage is extensive and sometimes irreparable. Some insurance companies are now refusing to cover homes with EIFS exteriors, and class action lawsuits have been brought against builders by distressed homeowners.

Federal Flood Insurance Program

The *National Flood Insurance Act of 1968* was authorized by Congress to help owners of property located in flood-prone areas by subsidizing flood insurance. As of 1975, such property owners must obtain flood damage insurance on properties financed by mortgages or other loans, grants or guarantees obtained from federal agencies and federally insured or regulated lending institutions. The program also seeks to improve future management of floodplain areas through land-use and land-control measures.

The Federal Emergency Management Agency (FEMA), which administers the flood insurance program, has maps prepared by the Army Corps of Engineers that identify specific flood-prone areas throughout the country. Property owners in the designated areas who do not obtain flood insurance are unable to obtain federal and federally related financial assistance.

RISK MANAGEMENT FOR PROPERTY MANAGERS

Homeowners are not the only ones who should be concerned about property insurance. Because enormous dollar losses can result from certain occurrences, one of the most critical areas of responsibility for a property manager is the field of insurance. Knowing the purposes of insurance coverage and how to make best use of the many types of insurance available is part of **risk management.**

Risk management involves answering the question "What will happen if something goes wrong?" The perils of any risk must be evaluated in terms of options. In considering the possibility of a loss, the property manager must decide whether it is better to

Handling Risk

- Avoid it
- Retain it
- Control it
- Transfer it

- *avoid it* by removing the source of risk, such as a swimming pool;
- *retain it* to a certain extent by insuring it with a large **deductible** (loss not covered by the insurer);
- *control it* by installing sprinklers, fire doors and other preventive measures; or
- *transfer it* by taking out an insurance policy.

When insurance is considered, a competent, reliable insurance agent should be selected to survey the property and make recommendations. Additional insurance surveys should be obtained if any questions remain. Final decisions, however, must be made by the property owner. A proper decision as to how much and what type of insurance to purchase and where to focus the insurance could save many thousands of dollars, especially in large buildings.

Property managers often are responsible for large sums of funds held in escrow for owners and tenants. Often these funds are administered by the managers or their bookkeepers. **Bonding** should be seriously considered for employees who have such financial responsibilities. Bonding provides a form of "honesty" insurance so that any money lost or embezzled by an employee will be reimbursed by the insurance company.

Types of Insurance Coverage

Many kinds of insurance coverage are available to income-property owners and managers. Listed below are some of the more common types.

- *Fire and hazard.* Fire insurance policies provide coverage against direct loss or damage to property from a fire on the premises. Standard fire coverage can be extended to cover hazards such as windstorm, hail, smoke damage or civil insurrection (like a typical homeowner's policy).
- *Consequential loss, use and occupancy.* Consequential loss insurance, which can include rent loss, covers the loss of revenue to a business if the business's property cannot be used.
- *Contents and personal property.* This type of insurance covers building contents and personal property during periods when neither is actually located on the business premises.
- *Liability.* Public liability insurance covers the risks an owner assumes when the public enters the building. Payments under this coverage are used to settle claims for medical expenses for a person injured in the building as a result of the owner's negligence. Another liability risk is that of medical or hospital payments for injuries sustained by building employees in the course of their employment. These claims are covered by state laws known as **workers' compensation acts.** These laws require that a building owner who is an employer obtain a workers' compensation policy from a private insurance company.
- *Casualty.* Casualty insurance policies include coverage against theft, burglary, vandalism and machinery damage as well as health and accident insurance. Casualty policies are usually written on specific risks, such as theft, rather than being all-inclusive.
- *Surety bonds.* **Surety bonds** cover an owner against financial losses resulting from an employee's criminal acts or negligence while performing assigned duties.

Today, many insurance companies offer **multiperil policies** for apartment and business buildings. These policies offer the property manager an insurance package that includes such standard types of commercial coverage as fire, hazard, public liability and casualty.

Claims

When a claim is made under a policy insuring a building or another physical object, the amount of the claim can be determined using one of two methods: the *depreciated actual value* or *cash value* of the damaged property or the *current replacement cost.* When purchasing insurance, a manager must assess whether the property should be insured at full replacement cost or at depreciated cost. As with the homeowners' policies discussed earlier, commercial policies include *coinsurance clauses* that require that the insured carry fire coverage, usually in an amount equal to 80 percent of the building's replacement value.

In Practice   Agents must be sure that homeowners acquire a homeowner's insurance policy on or before the day of closing. This is required if there will be a mortgage, but it is also strongly advised if this is a cash purchase. Buyers should be reminded that the typical homeowners' insurance policies do not provide coverage for termite damage, breakdown of appliances, flood damage, loss of trees or losses incurred over an extended period of time (such as a leaking roof). Assuming the seller's policy could mean that the buyer does not have a policy that fits his or her needs.

SUMMARY

To protect their investment in real estate, most homeowners purchase insurance. A standard homeowner's insurance policy covers fire, theft and liability and can be extended to cover many types of less common risks. Another type of insurance is available to people who live in apartments and condominiums.

The insured party must have some type of financial interest in the property to recover any losses. The insured will, however, never recover more than the actual loss. Most policies contain provisions that state that if the insured building is unoccupied for a certain length of time, the owner may not be able to recover on any losses that may occur. The insurance policy is a contract. Most insurance policy contracts are standard forms approved by the North Carolina Insurance Commission. These standard forms have been drafted mostly in favor of the insurer, not the insured.

If a homeowner carries insurance issued by more than one company, any benefits paid out are prorated according to the insured amount under each policy.

A subrogation clause enables the insurance company to sue the party responsible for damage to the insured's property.

In addition to homeowner's insurance, the federal government makes flood insurance mandatory for people living in flood-prone areas who wish to obtain federally regulated or federally insured mortgage loans. Most standard homeowner's policies do not cover flood damage.

Most homeowner's policies contain a coinsurance clause that requires that the policyholder maintain insurance in an amount equal to 80 percent of the replacement (new) cost of the home. If this percentage is not met, the policyholder may not be reimbursed for the full repair costs when a loss occurs.

An important duty of a property manager is securing adequate insurance coverage for the premises. The basic types of coverage applicable to commercial structures include fire and hazard insurance on the property and fixtures; consequential loss, use and occupancy insurance to protect the owner against revenue losses; and casualty insurance to provide coverage against such losses as theft, vandalism and destruction of machinery. The manager also should secure both public liability insurance to cover the owner against claims made by people injured on the premises and workers' compensation policies to cover the claims of employees injured on the job.

Questions

1. A typical homeowner's insurance policy covers all of the following EXCEPT
   a. the medical expenses of a person injured in the policyholder's home.
   b. theft.
   c. vandalism.
   d. flood damage.

2. In a homeowner's insurance policy, coinsurance refers to the
   a. specific form of policy purchased by the owner.
   b. stipulation that the homeowner must purchase insurance coverage equal to at least 80 percent of the replacement cost of the structure to be able to collect the full insured amount in the event of a loss.
   c. stipulation that the homeowner must purchase fire insurance coverage equal to at least 70 percent of the replacement cost of the structure to be able to collect the full insured amount in the event of a loss.
   d. specific form of policy purchased when a property is owned by more than one person (i.e., partnership or co-owner).

3. Which of the following statements is true of federal flood insurance?
   a. It is required in certain areas to insure properties financed by federally backed mortgage loans against flood damage.
   b. It is required of all real estate purchasers, no matter where the property is located in North Carolina.
   c. It is never required in North Carolina.
   d. It is paid for by the federal government.

4. A subrogation clause in an insurance policy enables the insurer to
   a. sue the party responsible for damage to the insured's property.
   b. receive 100 percent of replacement cost less depreciation.
   c. receive full cost of the repair or replacement of the damaged property.
   d. protect his or her property in case of a flood.

5. When a property manager chooses an insurance policy with a $150 deductible, the risk management technique being employed is risk
   a. avoidance.
   b. retainment.
   c. control.
   d. transfer.

6. Property manager Carol hires Jerry as the full-time maintenance person for one of the buildings she manages. While repairing a faucet in one of the apartments, Jerry steals a television set. Carol could have protected the owner against this type of loss by purchasing
   a. liability insurance.
   b. workers' compensation insurance.
   c. a surety bond.
   d. casualty insurance.

7. One possible method of determining the amount of a claim under an insurance policy covering damage to a building is the
   I. replacement cost method.
   II. income method.
   a. I only
   b. II only
   c. Both I and II
   d. Neither I nor II

8. Which type of insurance coverage protects the property owner against the claims of employees injured on the job?
   a. Consequential loss
   b. Workers' compensation
   c. Casualty
   d. Surety bond

9. A guest slips on an icy apartment building stair and is hospitalized. A claim against the building owner for medical expenses may be paid under which of the following policies held by the owner?
   a. Workers' compensation
   b. Casualty
   c. Liability
   d. Fire and hazard

10. Which clause in a standard homeowner's insurance policy literally makes the insured share in the loss?
    a. Exclusion clause
    b. Coinsurance clause
    c. Conditions clause
    d. Casualty clause

18 Federal Income Taxation of Real Property Ownership

LEARNING OBJECTIVES

When you've finished reading this chapter, you should be able to

- **identify** the tax benefits of home ownership, including itemized deductions and adjustments that reduce gain.

- **explain** basic tax concepts as they relate to home ownership and when gains may or may not be taxable.

- **explain** the differences in taxation on personal residences and on investment property.

- **calculate** the basis, adjusted basis, amount realized and gains on factual situations.

- **define** these *key terms:*

active income	cost basis	installment sale
adjusted basis	cost recovery	like-kind properties
basis	depreciation	passive investor
boot	gain	tax-deferred exchange
capital gain	income	

INTRODUCTION

All real estate agents should have a general understanding of the tax implications of owning a home. The tax advantages available to homeowners can significantly reduce the out-of-pocket cost of owning a home, and this should be explained to homebuyers, especially first-time homebuyers. However, the discussion and examples used in this chapter are designed to introduce the reader to only general tax concepts—a tax lawyer or certified public accountant (CPA) should be consulted for further details on specific regulations. Real estate agents should never try to give their clients or customers tax advice. Instead, they should indicate that all real estate transactions have tax implications that should be discussed with a competent adviser.

TAX BENEFITS FOR HOMEOWNERS

To encourage home ownership, the federal government allows homeowners certain income tax advantages. Even though the *Tax Reform Act of 1986* greatly restricted or eliminated tax deductions in other areas, benefits for homeowners were kept largely intact.

Tax-Deductible Interest Payments

Homeowners may deduct from their taxable income

- mortgage interest payments on first and second homes. For a principal residence, a second residence or both, the total amount of acquisition debt for which interest can be deducted cannot exceed a total of $1 million. *Acquisition indebtedness* is defined as the debt incurred in acquiring, constructing or substantially improving a principal residence or second residence (or both) of the taxpayer, where the debt is secured by such property. Home equity loans—loans secured by the property and in amounts less than the difference between fair market value and outstanding mortgage loan balance—cannot exceed $100,000. *Home equity indebtedness* is defined as the debt secured by the taxpayer's residence(s) that does not exceed the fair market value of such a residence(s) less the amount of acquisition indebtedness.
- certain loan discount points (those paid when acquiring a residence, not a refinance, are deductible in the year of purchase).
- mortgage prepayment penalties (rare in North Carolina).
- certain loan origination fees may be deductible if they are quoted as a percent of the loan amount and must be paid to obtain the loan. *(Agents and buyers should check with their tax advisers before stating that such fees may or may not be deductible.)*

Real Property Taxes

Real property taxes paid by a homeowner also are deductible. Note that the interest paid on overdue taxes is not deductible.

The mortgage interest deduction combined with the real property tax deduction can mean a substantial annual tax savings for the homeowner.

TAX BENEFITS OF SELLING A PRINCIPAL RESIDENCE

While the two tax benefits discussed above are available to those who currently own their homes, other tax benefits are available to those selling their homes. However, before discussing these tax advantages, some basic tax concepts must be explained.

Basic Tax Concepts

Because the government taxes income, it is worth quickly noting the definition of **income.** Obviously, income includes wages from employment, interest on savings, dividends on stock, pension payments and other commonly accepted forms of income. However, income also includes the gain that a person recognizes when he or she sells a capital asset. If a person sells a painting for $10,000 that was acquired for $5,000, that person has recognized a gain, that is, income, of $5,000, and that income is taxable (unless specifically excluded by the tax code). So it is with the buying and selling of real property.

When a person sells real property for more than he or she paid for it, that person has received a **gain.** A gain from the sale of real property is called a **capital gain.** Capital gains, the profits realized from the sale or exchange of property, are taxed as ordinary income. However, the maximum tax rate that applies to capital gain is 20 percent (not the ordinary 39.6 percent).

The amount of the gain realized from a sale of real property depends on that property's **basis.** The **cost basis** of property is the owner's initial cost for the real estate. The owner of a principal residence can add to the cost basis the cost of any physical capital improvements that add value to the home or prolong its life. This is the property's **adjusted basis.** (Note that the cost of ordinary repairs or maintenance does not increase the adjusted basis.) When the property is sold by the owner, the amount by which the amount realized exceeds the property's adjusted basis is the capital gain taxable as income.

The basis can be adjusted by adding

• closing costs
• capital improvements

Essentially, a homeowner determines his or her adjusted basis by adding:

Purchase price
Closing costs
<u>+ Improvements</u>
Adjusted basis

For Example Suppose Johnson buys a home for $85,000. The closing costs that can be allocated to purchasing the property (but not to obtaining financing) include the lawyer's fees and recording fee, which equal $250. One year later, Johnson spends $2,000 pressure washing and treating her roof. Two years later, Johnson spends $10,000 on an addition to the house. Johnson will calculate her adjusted basis as follows:

$85,000	purchase price
250	closing costs
<u>+10,000</u>	improvements
$95,250	adjusted basis

Notice that the $2,000 spent on the roof is not added to the basis. This is a normal maintenance expense.

To determine the gain that is realized from the sale of a home, the homeowner takes the sales price and deducts the closing costs from that.

Sales price
<u>– Closing costs</u>
Amount realized

For Example Let's continue our previous example. Johnson sells the house for $110,000. Her selling expenses are $5,300. To calculate the amount she realized on the sale, subtract her closing costs from the sales price.

$110,000   sales price
– $5,300   closing costs
$104,700   amount realized

To calculate a homeowner's gain on the sale of a principal residence, simply subtract the adjusted basis from the amount realized on the sale.

Amount realized
– Adjusted basis
Gain

For Example Once again, let's return to Johnson's situation. To calculate her gain on the sale, take the amount realized and subtract her adjusted basis.

$104,700   amount realized
– 95,250   adjusted basis
$ 9,450   gain

Johnson's taxable gain on the sale of her house is $9,450.

Tax-Free Gains from Sale of Principal Residence

Taxpayers who sell their principal residences can take advantage of new tax laws that took effect in May 1997. Under current tax law, capital gains—up to $500,000 for a married couple filing jointly and up to $250,000 for a single person or a married person filing singly—from the sale of a principal residence are excluded from taxation.

There are a few restrictions on this tax benefit: (1) the seller must have occupied the property as his or her primary residence for two of the previous five years and (2) the exclusion is available only once every two years. Because of the first restriction, this exclusion of gain does not apply to vacation properties or second homes.

Under these tax provisions, homeowners with substantial capital gains can downsize into smaller, less-expensive homes without a tax penalty (in most cases). If a seller has gains that exceed the $500,000 or $250,000 limit, those gains will be taxed at the 20 percent capital gains rate.

For Example Suppose the Bowers sold their principal residence, where they have lived for the previous ten years. They originally purchased the house for $98,000, paying $550 in closing costs. They sold it for $179,000, having $15,300 in selling expenses. The gain on the sale can be calculated as follows:

$ 98,000   purchase price
+   550   original closing costs
$ 98,550   adjusted basis

$179,000   sales price
– 15,300   closing costs
$163,700   amount realized

$163,700   amount realized
– 98,550   adjusted basis
$ 65,150   capital gain

Because the amount of their capital gain is well within the $500,000 statutory limits, the Bowers will not owe any taxes on the sale of their home.

Beginning in 2001, if the homeowner has occupied the property as a principal residence for more than five years, the capital gains tax rate may be as low as 18 percent for that portion of the capital gains that is above the statutory limit.

Office in Home

To qualify for tax deductions for an office in the home, the home portion must be used exclusively for business purposes; it must be the taxpayer's principal place of business; it must be where clients, customers or patients are met in the normal course of business; or it must be a separate structure not attached to the dwelling.

TAX BENEFITS OF REAL ESTATE INVESTMENT

One of the main reasons real estate investments were popular—and profitable—in the past was that federal law allowed investors to use losses generated by the investments to shelter income from other sources. The Tax Reform Act of 1986 eliminated some important tax advantages of owning investment real estate, but with professional tax advice investors still may be able to make wise real estate purchases.

Adjusted Basis

As discussed earlier, the adjusted basis in a property is roughly equivalent to the owner's investment in the property. The adjusted basis affects the amount of gain that is realized from the sale of real property. The owner of an investment property calculates his or her basis in that property a little differently from the homeowner. The owner of income property can also add to the cost basis the cost of any physical capital improvements (as opposed to repairs that may be expensed) subsequently made to the property. He or she must subtract from the basis the amount of any depreciation claimed as a tax deduction (discussed later) to arrive at the property's adjusted basis.

Installment Sales

When a seller finances the sale of his or her own property, or when the seller is to receive all or some portion of the sales price in a year or years other than the year of sale, the sale qualifies as an **installment sale.** For instance, a homeseller may agree to finance the sale of the property himself or herself, receiving a 5 percent downpayment, with the balance of the purchase price to be received in monthly payments over a ten-year term. The seller benefits from this type of sale by being able to spread taxation of any gain over the period of years in which the payments are still being received.

With an installment sale, the taxpayer is taxed on a pro rata portion of the total gain as each installment actually is received. For example, if a taxpayer received a gain of $10,000 on a $100,000 contract price, her profit percentage would be 10 percent. If during the tax year she received $5,000 in principal payments, 10 percent of those payments would be taxable that year. Ten percent of $5,000 is $500. She would have to report a taxable gain of $500 in that tax year.

Note that if a homeowner sells his or her principal residence and the gain will exceed the statutory limits of exclusion discussed previously, the homeowner may benefit by selling the principal residence on an installment basis.

Tax benefits of owning a home:

- Tax-deductible interest payments
- Tax-deductible property taxes
- Adjustments to reduce gain liability

Vacation Homes

If a property owner has a vacation home or "second home" and if it is in full use by others, certain expenses may be deductible for tax purposes. But if the owner uses the property for more than 14 days per year or for more than 10 percent of the number of days for which the property is rented, whichever is greater, certain deductions will be disallowed.

Tax-Deferred Exchanges

Real estate investors can *defer* taxation of capital gains by making a property exchange. A **tax-deferred exchange** offers significant tax advantages because no matter how much a property has appreciated since its initial purchase, it may be exchanged for another property and the taxpayer may be able to defer taxes on the entire amount of the gain. Of course, the tax is deferred, not eliminated, so whenever the investor sells the property, the capital gain will be taxable.

The requirements for a tax-deferred exchange are fairly straightforward. First of all, there must be a property transferred and a property received. These properties must be *exchanged*—they cannot be sold. Both the property transferred and the property received must be held for productive use in a trade or business or for investment. (An exchange of principal residences will not qualify for tax-deferral.) Finally, the properties must be **like-kind properties.** Essentially, the like-kind requirement is met when real estate is exchanged for real estate. The real estate does not have to be exchanged for an apartment building to qualify. An apartment building can be exchanged for an office building or gas station, and the exchange will still qualify as like-kind.

Sometimes, a property is exchanged for another property that is worth substantially less money. When this happens, cash or personal property may be included in the transaction to even out the value of the exchange. This cash or personal property is called **boot.** The party receiving boot is taxed on the value of the boot at the time of the exchange.

Generally, the adjusted basis of the exchanged property is the same as the taxpayer's adjusted basis in the original property. For example, if the taxpayer's adjusted basis in the original property is $225,000, the taxpayer's adjusted basis in the new property also will be $225,000. But when boot is given to even out the value of the exchange, the amount of the boot paid is added to the taxpayer's adjusted basis in the new property. The value of the boot received is deducted from the recipient taxpayer's adjusted basis; however, his or her basis is also increased by the amount of taxable gain from the transaction. Because boot is taxable gain, the impact of the receipt of boot on the adjustment basis may be nullified by the same amount of taxable gain.

For Example Investor Anthony owns an apartment building with an adjusted basis of $225,000 and a market value of $375,000. Anthony exchanges this building plus $75,000 cash for a small office building with a market value of $450,000. That building, owned by investor Megan, has an adjusted basis of $175,000. Anthony's basis in the new building will be $300,000 (the $225,000 basis of the building exchanged plus the $75,000 cash boot paid); Anthony has no tax liability on the exchange. Megan must pay tax on the $75,000 boot received and has a basis of $175,000 in the building now owned (the $175,000 basis on the building exchanged, less the $75,000 boot received, plus the $75,000 gain recognized).

Tax-deferred exchanges are governed by strict federal requirements, and competent guidance from a tax professional is essential.

Depreciation

Depreciation, or **cost recovery,** allows an investor to recover the cost of an income-producing asset by taking tax deductions over the period of the asset's useful life. Even though investors usually expect the value of the property to appreciate over time, according to the tax laws all physical structures deteriorate and lose value over time. Cost recovery deductions may be taken only on personal property and improvements to land and only if they are used in a trade or business or for the production of income. Cost recovery deductions cannot be claimed on a principal residence or on land (technically, land never wears out or becomes obsolete).

When depreciation is taken in equal amounts over an asset's useful life, the method used is called *straight-line depreciation.* For certain property purchased before 1987, it was also possible to use an *accelerated cost recovery* system to claim greater deductions in the early years of ownership, gradually reducing the amount deducted in each year of the useful life.

For residential rental property placed in service as of January 1, 1987, the recovery period is set at 27.5 years; for nonresidential property placed in service after May 12, 1993, the recovery period is set at 31.5 years, using only the straight-line depreciation method.

Deducting Losses

In addition to tax deductions for depreciation, investors may be able to deduct losses from their real estate investments. The tax laws are very complex, particularly as a result of the Tax Reform Act of 1986. The amount of loss that may be deducted depends on several factors:

- Whether an investor actively participates in the day-to-day management of the rental property or makes management decisions
- The amount of the loss
- The source of the income against which the loss is to be deducted

Investors who do not actively participate in the management or operation of the real estate are considered **passive investors,** which prevents them from using a loss to offset **active income.** Active income is considered to be wages; income generated from active participation in real estate management; or income from stocks, bonds and the like. The tax code cites specific rules for active and passive income and losses and is subject to changes in the law.

SUMMARY

All real estate agents should have a general understanding of the tax implications of owning real property. Agents should refrain, however, from giving their clients and customers tax advice. One of the income tax benefits available to homeowners allows them to deduct mortgage interest payments (with certain limitations) and property taxes on their federal income tax returns. Income tax on the gain from a sale may be excluded if the homeowner occupied the home for two of the previous five years. Homeowners also may take advantage of an installment sale to generate tax benefits.

Questions

1. In 1998, the Smiths received capital gains of $22,000, which are
   a. deductible only from passive income.
   b. taxed at the regular rate of 40 percent of value.
   c. taxed as ordinary income, but at a lower rate.
   d. subject to the purchase price rule.

2. For tax purposes, the initial cost of an investment property plus the cost of any subsequent improvements to the property, less depreciation (cost recovery deductions), represents the investment's
   a. adjusted basis.   c. basis.
   b. capital gain.   d. salvage value.

3. Which of the following statements is true of capital gains?
   a. They may be realized only from the sale of improvements to real estate, not from the sale of the land itself.
   b. They may be realized only from the sale of the land itself, not from the sale of improvements to the real estate.
   c. Their treatment has changed over the years. An investor should consult both a lawyer and an accountant for detailed and current information.
   d. They must be paid only by those age 55 or older.

4. Federal income tax law allows for
   I. a tax on all capital gains realized from the sale of a residence.
   II. an exclusion of gain in the amount of up to $500,000 from the sale of a personal residence by a married couple filing jointly.
   a. I only
   b. II only
   c. Both I and II
   d. Neither I nor II

5. Federal income tax laws do NOT allow a homeowner to deduct which of the following expenses from his or her taxable income?
   a. Mortgage interest
   b. Real estate taxes
   c. Discount points
   d. Repairs or maintenance

6. The profit a homeowner receives from the sale of the homeowner's principal residence may be
   a. the homeowner's tax basis.
   b. subject to federal income tax.
   c. excluded from taxation up to a statutory limit.
   d. Both b and c

7. Mike Tenenbaum, unmarried, age 38, sells his home of eight years and realizes a $25,000 gain from the sale. Income tax on this profit may be
   a. eliminated by claiming a once-in-a-lifetime exclusion.
   b. excluded from taxation.
   c. eliminated if he donates at least 50 percent of the profit to a charity.
   d. reduced by the amount of mortgage interest paid over the life of the property's ownership.

8. Ada Ryan, age 62, sells the home she has occupied for one of the previous five years and realizes a $52,000 gain from the sale. Income tax on the profit from this sale may be
   a. taxed as capital gains.
   b. postponed by purchasing another residence of equal or greater value within 12 months before or after the sale.
   c. eliminated if she donates at least 50 percent of the profit to a charity.
   d. reduced by the amount of mortgage interest paid over the life of the property's ownership.

9. A homeowner sold his principal residence for $127,500. Selling expenses were $750. The house had been purchased new three years earlier for $75,000. What is the homeowner's gain on this transaction?
    a. $53,250   c. $51,750
    b. $52,500   d. $75,000

10. In question 9, if the property were an investment property, how much of the gain would be subject to income tax?
    a. $51,750   c. $42,300
    b. $52,500   d. $21,000

11. A homeowner bought her house for $72,000. She spent $15,000 on an addition, $3,000 on a new deck, $5,000 on roof repairs and $2,000 on fixing broken windows. Her adjusted basis is
    a. $87,000.   c. $95,000.
    b. $90,000.   d. $97,000.

19 Environmental Issues and the Real Estate Transaction

LEARNING OBJECTIVES

When you've finished reading this chapter, you should be able to

- **identify** the basic environmental hazards an agent should be aware of to protect his or her client's interests.

- **describe** the warning signs, characteristics, causes and solutions of the various environmental hazards most commonly found in real estate transactions.

- **explain** the liability issues arising under environmental protection laws.

- **name** the agencies that administer and enforce environmental laws.

- **define** these *key terms:*

asbestos	electromagnetic fields	radon
capping	(EMFs)	retroactive liability
carbon monoxide (CO)	encapsulation	strict liability
Comprehensive	groundwater	underground storage
Environmental	joint and several	tank (UST)
Response,	liability	urea-formaldehyde
Compensation, and	landfill	UFFI
Liability Act	lead	water table
(CERCLA)		

ENVIRONMENTAL ISSUES

Most states have recognized the need to balance the legitimate commercial use of land with the need to preserve vital resources and protect the quality of their air, water and soil. A growing number of homebuyers base their decisions in part on the desire for fresh air, clean water and outdoor recreational opportunities. Preservation of a state's environment both enhances the quality of life and helps strengthen property values. The prevention and cleanup of pollutants and toxic wastes not only revitalize the land but create greater opportunities for responsible development.

Environmental issues have become an important factor in the practice of real estate. Consumers are becoming more health-conscious and safety-concerned and are enforcing their rights to make informed decisions. Scientists are learning more about our environment, and consumers are reacting by demanding that their surroundings be free of chemical hazards. These developments affect not only sales transactions, but also appraisers, developers, lending institutions and property managers.

Real estate licensees must be alert to the existence of environmental hazards. Although it is important to ensure the health and safety of property users, the burden of disclosure or elimination of hazards is heaviest at the time ownership of property transfers. This creates added liability for real estate practitioners if the presence of a toxic substance causes a health problem. If a property buyer suffers physical harm because of the substance, the licensee can be vulnerable to a personal injury suit in addition to other legal liability. Environmental issues are health issues, and health issues based on environmental hazards have become real estate issues. For this reason, it is extremely important that licensees not only make property disclosures but also see that prospective purchasers get authoritative information about hazardous substances so that they can make informed decisions.

Licensees should be familiar with state and federal environmental laws and the regulatory agencies that enforce them. Licensees are not expected to have the technical expertise necessary to determine whether a hazardous substance is present. However, they must be aware of environmental issues and take steps to ensure that the interests of all parties involved in real estate transactions are protected.

HAZARDOUS SUBSTANCES

Pollution and hazardous substances in the environment are of interest to real estate licensees because they affect the attractiveness, desirability and market value of cities, neighborhoods and backyards. A toxic environment is not a place where anyone would want to live (see Figure 19.1).

Asbestos

Asbestos is a mineral that was once used as insulation because it was resistant to fire and contained heat effectively. Before 1978 (the year when the use of asbestos insulation was banned), asbestos was found in most residential construction. It was a component of more than 3,000 types of building materials. The Environmental Protection Agency (EPA) estimates that about 20 percent of the nation's commercial and public buildings contain asbestos.

Today, we know that inhaling microscopic asbestos fibers can result in a variety of respiratory diseases. The presence of asbestos insulation alone is not necessarily a health hazard. Asbestos is harmful only if it is disturbed or exposed, as often occurs during renovation or remodeling. Asbestos is highly friable; that is, as it ages, asbestos fibers break down easily into tiny filaments and particles. When these particles become airborne, they pose a risk to humans. Airborne asbestos contamination is most prevalent in pub-

> Asbestos insulation can create airborne contaminants that may result in respiratory diseases.

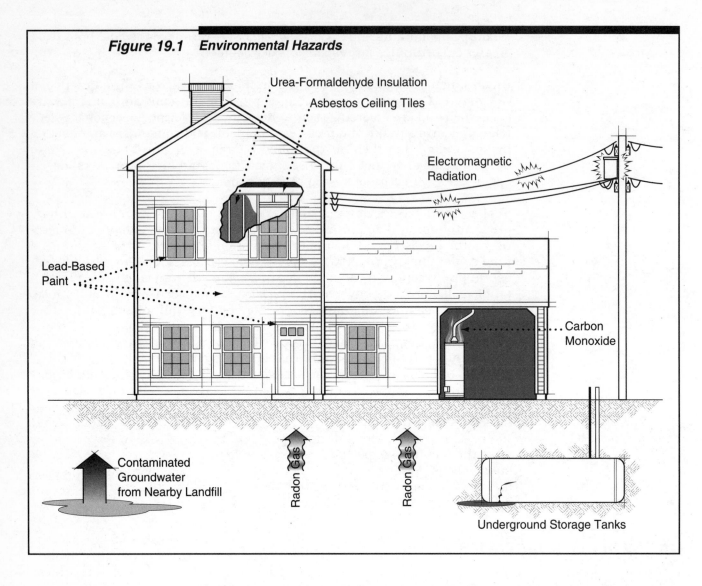

Figure 19.1　Environmental Hazards

Urea-Formaldehyde Insulation

Asbestos Ceiling Tiles

Electromagnetic Radiation

Lead-Based Paint

Carbon Monoxide

Contaminated Groundwater from Nearby Landfill

Radon Gas

Radon Gas

Underground Storage Tanks

lic and commercial buildings, including schools. If the asbestos fibers in the indoor air of a building reach a dangerous level, the building becomes difficult to lease, finance or insure. No safe level of asbestos exposure has been determined.

Asbestos contamination also can be found in residential properties. It was used to cover pipes, ducts, and heating and hot water units. Its fire-resistant properties made it a popular material for use in floor tile, exterior siding and roofing products. Though it may be easy to identify asbestos when it is visible (for instance, when it is wrapped around heating and water pipes), identification may be more difficult when it is behind walls or under floors.

Asbestos is costly to remove because the process requires state-licensed technicians and specially sealed environments. In addition, removal itself may be dangerous: improper removal procedures may further contaminate the air within the structure. The waste generated should be disposed of at a licensed facility, which further adds to the cost of removal. **Encapsulation,** or the sealing off of disintegrating asbestos, is an alternate method of asbestos control that may be preferable to removal in certain circumstances.

However, an owner must periodically monitor the condition of the encapsulated asbestos to make sure it is not disintegrating.

Tests can be conducted to determine the level of airborne asbestos to provide an accurate disclosure in a sales transaction. A more thorough analysis of a building can be performed by an engineer skilled in identifying the presence of materials that contain asbestos. Either of these approaches can satisfy the concerns of a consumer. Appraisers also should be aware of the possible presence of asbestos.

More information on asbestos-related issues is available from the EPA (telephone: 1-202-554-1404). In addition, the EPA has numerous publications that provide guidance, information and assistance with asbestos issues.

Lead-Based Paint and Other Hazards

Lead was used as a pigment and drying agent in alkyd oil-based paint. Lead-based paint may be on any interior or exterior surface, but it is particularly common on doors, windows and other woodwork. The federal government estimates that lead is present in about 75 percent of all private housing built before 1978; that's approximately 57 million homes, ranging from low-income apartments to million-dollar mansions.

An elevated level of lead in the body can cause serious damage to the brain, kidneys, nervous system and red blood cells. The degree of harm is related to the amount of exposure and the age at which a person is exposed. As many as one in every six children may have dangerously high amounts of lead in the blood.

Lead dust can be ingested from the hands by a crawling infant, inhaled by any occupant of a structure or ingested from the water supply because of lead pipes or lead solder. In fact, lead particles can be present elsewhere, too. Soil and groundwater may be contaminated by everything from lead plumbing in leaking landfills to discarded skeet and bullets from an old shooting range. High levels of lead have been found in the soil near waste-to-energy incinerators. Air may be contaminated by leaded gasoline fumes from gas stations or automobile exhausts.

> *Lead* from paint or other sources can result in damage to the brain, nervous system, kidneys and blood.

The use of lead-based paint was banned in 1978. Licensees who are involved in the sale, management, financing or appraisal of properties constructed before 1978 face potential liability for any personal injury that might be suffered by an occupant. Numerous legislative efforts affect licensees, sellers and landlords. There is considerable controversy about practical approaches for handling the presence of lead-based paint. Some suggest that it should be removed; others argue that it should be encapsulated; still others advocate testing to determine the amount of lead present, which then would be disclosed to a prospective owner or resident. In many states, only licensed lead inspectors, abatement contractors, risk assessors, abatement project designers and abatement workers may deal with the removal or encapsulation of lead in a structure.

No federal law requires that homeowners test for the presence of lead-based paint. However, known lead-based paint hazards must be disclosed. In 1996, the EPA and the Department of Housing and Urban Development (HUD) issued final regulations requiring disclosure of the presence of any known lead-based paint hazards to potential buyers or renters. Under the

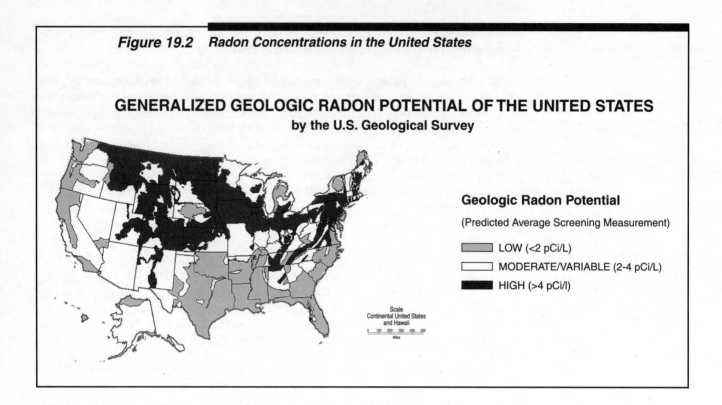

Figure 19.2   *Radon Concentrations in the United States*

GENERALIZED GEOLOGIC RADON POTENTIAL OF THE UNITED STATES
by the U.S. Geological Survey

Geologic Radon Potential

(Predicted Average Screening Measurement)

LOW (<2 pCi/L)

MODERATE/VARIABLE (2-4 pCi/L)

HIGH (>4 pCi/l)

Scale
Continental United States
and Hawaii

0 100 200 300 400 500
Miles

Residential Lead-Based Paint Hazard Reduction Act, persons selling or leasing residential housing constructed before 1978 must disclose the presence of known lead-based paint and provide purchasers or lessees with any relevant records or reports. A lead-based paint disclosure statement must be attached to all sales contracts and leases regarding residential properties built before 1978, and a lead hazard pamphlet must be distributed to all buyers and tenants. Purchasers must be given ten days in which to conduct risk assessments or inspections for lead-based paint or lead-based paint hazards. Purchasers are not bound by any real estate contract until the ten-day period has expired. The regulations specifically require that real estate agents ensure that all parties comply with the law.

EPA guidance pamphlets and other information about lead-based hazards are available from the National Lead Information Center, 800-424-5323.

Radon   **Radon** is a radioactive gas produced by the natural decay of other radioactive substances. Although radon can occur anywhere, some areas are known to have abnormally high amounts. Radon is found in every state, with the highest concentrations in the plains states, the upper Midwest and northeastern United States (see Figure 19.2). If radon dissipates into the atmosphere, it is not likely to cause harm. However, when radon enters buildings and is trapped in high concentrations (usually in basements with inadequate ventilation), it can cause health problems.

Radon is a naturally occurring gas that is a suspected cause of lung cancer.

Opinions differ as to minimum safe levels. But growing evidence suggests that radon may be the most underestimated cause of lung cancer, particularly for children, individuals who smoke and those who spend considerable time indoors.

Because radon is odorless and tasteless, it is impossible to detect without testing. Care should be exercised in the manner in which tests are conducted to ensure that the results are accurate. Radon levels vary, depending on the amount of fresh air that circulates through a house, the weather conditions and the time of year. It is relatively easy to reduce levels of radon by installing ventilation systems or exhaust fans.

Interestingly, the modern practice of creating energy-efficient homes and buildings with practically airtight walls and windows may increase the potential for radon gas accumulation. Once radon accumulates in a basement, efficient heating and ventilation systems can rapidly spread the gas throughout the building.

Home radon-detection kits are available, although more accurate testing can be conducted by radon-detection professionals. The EPA's pamphlet "A Citizen's Guide to Radon" is available from your local EPA office.

Urea-Formaldehyde

Urea-formaldehyde was first used in building materials, particularly insulation, in the 1970s. Gases leak out of the urea-formaldehyde foam insulation **(UFFI)** as it hardens, and they become trapped in the interior of a building. In 1982, the Consumer Product Safety Commission banned the use of UFFI. The ban was reduced to a warning after courts determined that there was insufficient evidence to support a ban. Urea-formaldehyde is known to cause cancer in animals, though the evidence of its effect on humans is inconclusive.

Formaldehyde does cause some individuals to suffer respiratory problems as well as eye and skin irritations. Consumers are becoming increasingly wary of the presence of formaldehyde, particularly if they are sensitive to it.

> *UFFI* is an insulating foam that can release harmful formaldehyde gases.

Because UFFI has received considerable adverse publicity, many buyers express concern about purchasing properties in which it was installed. Tests can be conducted to determine the level of formaldehyde gas in a house. Again, however, care should be exercised to ensure that the results of the tests are accurate and that the source of the gases is properly identified. Elevated levels could be due to a source other than the insulation.

Licensees should be careful that any conditions in an agreement of sale that require tests for formaldehyde are worded properly to identify the purpose for which the tests are being conducted, such as to determine the presence of the insulation or some other source. Appraisers should also be aware of the presence of UFFI.

Carbon Monoxide

Carbon monoxide (CO) is a colorless, odorless gas that occurs as a by-product of burning such fuels as wood, oil and natural gas if combustion is incomplete. Furnaces, water heaters, space heaters, fireplaces and wood stoves all produce CO as a natural result of their combustion of fuel. However, when these appliances function properly and are properly ventilated, their CO emissions are not a problem. When improper ventilation or equipment malfunctions permit large quantities of CO to be released into a residence or commercial structure, it poses a significant health hazard. Its effects are compounded by the fact that CO is so difficult to detect. CO is quickly absorbed by the body. It inhibits the blood's ability to transport oxygen and results in dizziness and nausea. As the concentrations of CO increase, the symptoms become more severe. More than 200 deaths from CO poisoning occur each year.

> *Carbon monoxide* is a by-product of fuel combustion that may result in death in poorly ventilated areas.

Carbon monoxide detectors are available, and their use is mandatory in some areas. Annual maintenance of heating systems also helps avoid CO exposure.

Electromagnetic Fields

Electromagnetic fields (EMFs) are generated by the movement of electrical currents. The use of any electrical appliance creates a small field of electromagnetic radiation: clock radios, blow-dryers, televisions and computers all produce EMFs. The major concern regarding electromagnetic fields involves high-tension power lines. The EMFs produced by these high-voltage lines, as well as by secondary distribution lines and transformers, are suspected of causing cancer, hormonal changes and behavioral abnormalities. There is considerable controversy (and much conflicting evidence) about whether EMFs pose a health hazard. Buyers who are aware of the controversy may, however, be unwilling to purchase property near power lines or transformers. As research into EMFs continues, real estate licensees should stay informed about current findings.

> *EMFs* are produced by electrical currents and may be related to a variety of health complaints.

Groundwater Contamination

Groundwater is the water that exists under the earth's surface within the tiny spaces or crevices in geological formations. Groundwater forms the **water table,** the natural level at which the ground is saturated. This may be near the surface (in areas where the water table is very high) or several hundred feet underground. Surface water also can be absorbed into the groundwater.

Any contamination of the underground water can threaten the supply of pure, clean water for private wells or public water systems. If groundwater is not protected from contamination, the earth's natural filtering systems may be inadequate to ensure the availability of pure water. Numerous state and federal laws have been enacted to preserve and protect the water supply.

Water can be contaminated from a number of sources. Runoff from waste disposal sites, leaking underground storage tanks and pesticides and herbicides are some of the main culprits. Because water flows from one place to another, contamination can spread far from its source. Numerous regulations are designed to protect against water contamination. Once contamination has been identified, its source can be eliminated and the water may eventually become clean. However, the process can be time consuming and extremely expensive.

In Practice

Real estate agents need to be aware of potential groundwater contamination sources both on and off a property. These include underground storage tanks, septic systems, holding ponds, dry wells, buried materials and surface spills. Remember, because groundwater flows over wide areas, the source of contamination may not be nearby.

Underground Storage Tanks

Approximately 3 million to 5 million **underground storage tanks (USTs)** exist in the United States. Underground storage tanks are commonly found on sites where petroleum products are used or where gas stations and auto repair shops are located. They also may be found in a number of other commercial and industrial establishments—including printing and chemical plants, wood treatment plants, paper mills, paint manufacturers, dry cleaners and food processing plants—for storing chemical or other process waste. Military bases and airports also are common sites for underground tanks. In residential areas, they are used to store heating oil.

Some tanks are currently in use, but many are long forgotten. It is an unfortunate fact that it was once common to dispose of toxic wastes by simple burial: out of sight, out of mind. Over time, however, neglected tanks may leak hazardous substances into the environment. This permits contaminants to pollute not only the soil around the tank but also adjacent parcels and groundwater. Licensees should be particularly alert to the presence of fill pipes, vent lines, stained soil and fumes or odors, any of which may indicate the presence of a UST. Detection, removal and cleanup of surrounding contaminated soil can be an expensive operation.

For Example In the 1940s, a gas station in a rural town went out of business. The building fell into disrepair and was torn down. The site was vacant for several years, and its former use was forgotten. A series of commercial ventures were built on the land: a grocery store, a drive-in restaurant, a convenience store. In the late 1980s, residents of the town began noticing strong gasoline fumes in their basements, particularly after a rainstorm. Government investigators concluded that the gasoline tanks buried beneath the former gas station had broken down with age and leaked their contents into the soil. Because the town was located over a large subsurface rock slab, the gasoline could not leach down into the soil, but rather was forced to spread out under the entire town and surrounding farmland. Because the water table floated on the rock slab and the gasoline floated on the water, rains that raised the water table forced the gasoline into the soil near the residents' basements and crawlspaces, resulting in the unpleasant and potentially unhealthy fumes. When the gasoline fumes ignited and destroyed a local manufacturing plant, the residents learned that the problem was not only unpleasant but dangerous, as well.

Recent state and federal laws impose very strict requirements on owners of land on which underground storage tanks are located to detect and correct leaks in an effort to protect the groundwater. The federal UST program is regulated by the EPA. The regulations apply to tanks that contain hazardous substances or liquid petroleum products and that store at least 10 percent of their volume underground. UST owners are required to register their tanks and adhere to strict technical and administrative requirements that govern

- installation,
- maintenance,
- corrosion prevention,
- overspill prevention,
- monitoring and
- record keeping.

Owners also are required to demonstrate that they have sufficient financial resources to cover any damage that might result from leaks.

The following types of tanks are among those that are exempt from federal regulations:

- Tanks that hold less than 110 gallons

- Farm and residential tanks that hold 1,100 gallons or less of motor fuel used for noncommercial purposes
- Tanks that store heating oil burned on the premises
- Tanks on or above the floor of underground areas, such as basements or tunnels
- Septic tanks and systems for collecting stormwater and wastewater

Some states have adopted laws regulating underground storage tanks that are more stringent than the federal laws.

In addition to being aware of possible noncompliance with state and federal regulations, the parties to a real estate transaction should be aware that many older tanks have never been registered. There may be no visible sign of their presence.

Waste Disposal Sites

Americans produce vast quantities of garbage every day. Despite public and private recycling and composting efforts, huge piles of waste materials—from beer cans, junk mail and diapers to food, paint and toxic chemicals—must be disposed of. Landfill operations have become the main receptacles for garbage and refuse. Special hazardous-waste disposal sites have been established to contain radioactive waste from nuclear power plants, toxic chemicals and waste materials produced by medical, scientific and industrial processes.

Perhaps the most prevalent method of common waste disposal is simply to bury it. A **landfill** is an enormous hole, either excavated for the purpose of waste disposal or left over from surface mining operations. The hole is lined with clay or a synthetic liner to prevent leakage of waste material into the water supply. A system of underground drainage pipes permits monitoring of leaks and leaching. Waste is laid on the liner at the bottom of the excavation, and a layer of topsoil is then compacted onto the waste. The layering procedure is repeated again and again until the landfill is full, the layers mounded up sometimes as high as several hundred feet over the surrounding landscape. **Capping** is the process of laying two to four feet of soil over the top of the site and then planting grass or some other vegetation to enhance the landfill's aesthetic value and to prevent erosion. A ventilation pipe runs from the landfill's base through the cap to vent off accumulated natural gases created by the decomposing waste.

Federal, state and local regulations govern the location, construction, content and maintenance of landfill sites. Test wells around landfill operations are installed to constantly monitor the groundwater in the surrounding area, and soil analyses can be used to test for contamination. Completed landfills have been used for such purposes as parks and golf courses. Rapid suburban growth has resulted in many housing developments and office campuses being built on landfill sites. However, buildings constructed on landfills may have problems caused by settling.

For Example A suburban office building constructed on an old landfill site was very popular until its parking lot began to sink. While the structure itself was supported by pylons driven deep into the ground, the parking lot was unsupported. As the landfill beneath it compacted, the wide concrete lot sank lower and lower around the building. Each year, the building's management had to relandscape to cover the exposed foundations. The sinking parking lot eventually severed underground phone and power lines and water mains, causing the tenants considerable inconvenience. Computers were offline for hours, and flooding was frequent on the ground floor. Finally, leaking gases from the landfill began causing unpleasant odors. The tenants moved out and the building was left vacant, a victim of poorly conceived landfill design.

Hazardous and radioactive waste disposal sites are subject to strict state and federal regulation to prevent the escape of toxic substances into the surrounding environment. Some materials, such as radioactive waste, are sealed in containers and placed in "tombs" buried deep underground. The tombs are designed to last thousands of years and are built according to strict federal and state regulations. These disposal sites are usually limited to extremely remote locations, well away from populated areas or farmland.

The *Midwest Interstate Compact on Low-Level Radioactive Waste* is one example of a regional approach to the disposal of hazardous materials. The states of Delaware, Illinois, Indiana, Iowa, Kansas, Kentucky, Maryland, Michigan, Minnesota, Missouri, Nebraska, North Dakota, Ohio, South Dakota, Virginia and Wisconsin have agreed to cooperate in establishing and managing regional low-level radioactive waste sites. This approach allows the participants to share the costs, benefits, obligations and inconveniences of radioactive waste disposal in a fair and reasonable way.

In Practice   Environmental issues have a significant impact on the real estate industry. In 1995, a jury awarded $6.7 million to homeowners whose property values had been lowered because of the defendant tire company's negligent operation and maintenance of a hazardous waste dump site. The 1,713 plaintiffs relied on testimony from economists and a real estate appraiser to demonstrate how news stories about the site had lowered the market values of their homes. Nationwide, some landfill operators now offer price guarantees to purchasers of homes near waste disposal sites. A recent university study found that a home's value increases by more than $6,000 for each mile of its distance from a garbage incinerator.

CERCLA AND ENVIRONMENTAL PROTECTION

The majority of legislation dealing with environmental problems has been instituted within the past two decades. Although the EPA was created at the federal level to oversee such problems, several other federal agencies' areas of concern generally overlap. The federal laws were created to encourage state and local governments to enact their own legislation.

Comprehensive Environmental Response, Compensation, and Liability Act

The **Comprehensive Environmental Response, Compensation, and Liability Act (CERCLA)** was created in 1980. It established a fund of $9 billion, called the *Superfund,* to clean up uncontrolled hazardous waste sites and to respond to spills. It created a process for identifying potentially responsible parties (PRPs) and ordering them to take responsibility for the cleanup action. CERCLA is administered and enforced by the EPA.

Liability. A landowner is liable under CERCLA when a release or a threat of release of a hazardous substance has occurred on his or her property. Regardless of whether the contamination is the result of the landowner's actions or those of others, the owner can be held responsible for the cleanup. This liability includes the cleanup not only of the landowner's property but also of any neighboring property that has been contaminated. A landowner who is not responsible for the contamination can seek reimbursement for the cleanup cost from previous landowners, any other responsible party or the Superfund. However, if other parties are not available, even a landowner who did not cause the problem could be solely responsible for the costs.

Once the EPA determines that hazardous material has been released into the environment, it is authorized to begin remedial action. First, it attempts to identify the PRPs. If the PRPs agree to cooperate in the cleanup, they must agree about how to divide the cost. If the PRPs do not voluntarily undertake the cleanup, the EPA may hire its own contractors to do the necessary work. The EPA then bills the PRPs for the cost. If the PRPs refuse to pay, the EPA can seek damages in court for up to three times the actual cost of the cleanup.

Liability under the Superfund is considered to be strict, joint and several, and retroactive. **Strict liability** means that the owner is responsible to the injured party without excuse. **Joint and several liability** means that each of the individual owners is personally responsible for the total damages. If only one of the owners is financially able to handle the total damages, that owner must pay the total and collect the proportionate shares from the other owners whenever possible. **Retroactive liability** means that the liability is not limited to the current owner, but includes people who have owned the site in the past.

Superfund Amendments and Reauthorization Act. In 1986, the U.S. Congress reauthorized the Superfund. The amended statute contains stronger cleanup standards for contaminated sites and five times the funding of the original Superfund, which expired in September 1985.

The amended act also sought to clarify the obligations of lenders. As mentioned, liability under the Superfund extends to both the present and all previous owners of the contaminated site. Real estate lenders found themselves either as present owners or somewhere in the chain of ownership through foreclosure proceedings.

The amendments created a concept called *innocent landowner immunity*. It was recognized that in certain cases, a landowner in the chain of ownership was completely innocent of all wrongdoing and therefore should not be held liable. The innocent landowner immunity clause established the criteria by which to judge whether a person or business could be exempted from liability. The criteria included the following:

- The pollution was caused by a third party.
- The property was acquired after the fact.
- The landowner had no actual or constructive knowledge of the damage.

- Due care was exercised when the property was purchased (the land-owner made a reasonable search, called an *environmental site assessment*) to determine that no damage to the property existed.
- Reasonable precautions were taken in the exercise of ownership rights.

NORTH CAROLINA ENVIRONMENTAL ISSUES

Lead Hazards

The Consumer Products Safety Commission banned the use of lead-based paint in 1978. If a real estate transaction involves a residential property built prior to 1978, proper disclosures by the seller and/or agent to the buyer or tenant must take place. In North Carolina, this disclosure requirement is met by filling out the Lead-Based or Lead-Based Paint Hazard addendum to the standard offer to purchase and sales contract discussed in Chapter 9.

The Environmental Protection Agency (EPA) and HUD have implemented the EPA and HUD "Real Estate Notification and Disclosure Rule," which addresses topics such as (1) the purpose of the rule; (2) which housing is affected; (3) the seller's, lessor's and agent's responsibilities; (4) purchaser and renter rights; and (5) liability. The purpose of the rule is to ensure that buyers and renters of housing built prior to 1978 receive proper disclosures. Note that lead poisoning may also result from plumbing systems that contain lead pipes. Systems that use lead pipes should be tested frequently.

The North Carolina Law, the *Lead-Based Paint Poisoning Act*, is a law that ensures that there is no lead-based paint in houses connected with HUD-assisted projects.

Petroleum Underground Storage Tank Cleanup Act

The purpose of the *Leaking Petroleum Underground Storage Tank Cleanup Act* is to regulate underground storage tanks' discharge of any hazardous substance, including gas and oil. *Owners of properties with tanks that may be leaking face the heavy financial burden of cleanup costs, even though they themselves did not install the tanks.* This act covers both residential and commercial properties.

Coastal Area Management Act

The *Coastal Area Management Act (CAMA)* is designed to protect, preserve and give management guidelines in coastal areas. It places a severe limitation on developments in the coastal estuarine system. A majority of coastal areas in North Carolina, such as wetlands and marshes, have been declared areas of environmental concern. Any proposed development or changes in these areas, such as building, dredging, filling or digging, clearing or bulkheading, first must be approved through a permit process. Property owners in violation of CAMA will face serious legal problems and penalties.

Dredge and Fill Act

The *Dredge and Fill Act* provides that before participating in any dredging or filling that may affect vegetation or aquatic conditions in North Carolina waters or marshlands, the property owner must obtain a permit from the Coastal Resources Commission.

Sediment Pollution Control Act

The *Sediment Pollution Control Act* was enacted to handle problems that occur as a result of sedimentation in state waters. Sedimentation may have natural causes, such as erosion, or manmade causes, such as the deposit of soil or other materials into water. Any type of development, construction or any other activity that may disturb vegetation or topography and cause sedimentation is illegal and subject to the act. The act calls for erosion control devices, the development of sedimentation plans and the creation of natural buffer zones. The law is enforced by the North Carolina Department of Environment, Health and Natural Resources.

LIABILITY OF REAL ESTATE PROFESSIONALS

Environmental law is a relatively new phenomenon. Although federal and state laws have defined many of the liabilities involved, common law is being used for further interpretation. The real estate professional and all others involved in a real estate transaction must be aware of both actual and potential liability.

Sellers, as mentioned earlier, often carry the most exposure. Innocent landowners might be held responsible, even though they did not know about the presence of environmental hazards. Purchasers may be held liable, even if they didn't cause the contamination. Lenders may end up owning worthless assets if owners default on the loans rather than undertaking expensive cleanup efforts. Real estate licensees could be held liable for improper disclosure; therefore, it is necessary to be aware of the potential environmental risks from neighboring properties such as gas stations, manufacturing plants or even funeral homes.

Additional exposure is created for individuals involved in other aspects of real estate transactions. For example, real estate appraisers must identify and adjust for environmental problems. Adjustments to market value typically reflect the cleanup cost plus a factor of the degree of panic and suspicion that exist in the current market. Although the sales price can be affected dramatically, it is possible that the underlying market value would remain relatively equal to others in the neighborhood. The real estate appraiser's greatest responsibility is to the lender, which depends on the appraiser to identify environmental hazards. Although the lender may be protected under certain conditions through the 1986 amendments to the Superfund Act, it must be aware of any potential problems and may require additional environmental reports.

Insurance carriers also might be affected in the transactions. Mortgage insurance companies protect lenders' mortgage investments and might be required to carry part of the ultimate responsibility in cases of loss. More important, hazard insurance carriers might be directly responsible for damages if such coverage was included in the initial policy.

Discovery of Environmental Hazards

Real estate licensees are not expected to have the technical expertise necessary to discover the presence of environmental hazards. However, because they are presumed by the public to have special knowledge about real estate, licensees must be aware both of possible hazards and of where to seek professional help.

Obviously, the first step for a licensee is to ask the owner. The owner already may have conducted tests for carbon monoxide or radon. He or she also may be aware of a potential hazardous condition. An environmental hazard can actually be turned into a marketing plus if the owner already has done the detection and abatement work. Potential buyers can be assured that an older home is no longer a lead paint or an asbestos risk.

The most appropriate people on whom a licensee can rely for sound environmental information are scientific or technical experts. Environmental auditors can provide the most comprehensive studies. Their services are usually relied on by developers and purchasers of commercial and industrial properties. An environmental audit includes the property's history of use and the results of extensive and complex tests of the soil, water, air and structures. Trained inspectors conduct air-sampling tests to detect radon, asbestos or EMFs. They can test soil and water quality and can inspect for lead-based paints (lead inspections required by the Residential Lead-Based Paint Hazard Reduction Act must be conducted by certified inspectors). While environmental auditors may be called on at any stage in a transaction, they are most frequently brought in as a condition of closing. Not only can such experts detect environmental problems, they can usually offer guidance about how best to resolve the conditions.

Disclosure of Environmental Hazards
State laws address the issue of disclosure of known material facts regarding a property's condition. These same rules apply to the presence of environmental hazards. A real estate licensee may be liable if he or she should have known of a condition, even if the seller neglected to disclose it. Property condition disclosures are discussed in Chapter 8.

SUMMARY

Environmental issues are important to real estate licensees because they may affect real estate transactions by raising issues of health risk or cleanup costs. Some of the principal environmental toxins include asbestos, lead, radon and urea-formaldehyde insulation.

Licensees who are involved with the sale, management, financing or appraisal of properties constructed before 1978 should be aware of potential lead-based paint in the structures. Other hazards include asbestos, urea-formaldehyde foam insulation (UFFI), radon and electromagnetic fields (EMFs).

Landfills are the most common method of disposing of solid waste materials by layering them between several feet of soil. Improperly constructed or maintained landfills may present a danger to groundwater.

CERCLA established the Superfund to finance the cleanup of hazardous waste disposal sites. Under the Superfund, liability for those found to have created unlawful hazardous waste sites is strict, joint and several, and retroactive.

North Carolina has several environmental protection laws, including the Leaking Petroleum Underground Storage Tank Cleanup Act, the Coastal Area Management Act, the Dredge and Fill Act, and the Sediment Pollution Control Act.

Questions

1. Asbestos is most dangerous when it
   a. is used as insulation.
   b. crumbles and becomes airborne.
   c. gets wet.
   d. is wrapped around heating and water pipes.

2. Encapsulation refers to the
   a. process of sealing a landfill with three to four feet of topsoil.
   b. way in which asbestos insulation is applied to pipes and wiring systems.
   c. method of sealing disintegrating asbestos.
   d. way in which asbestos becomes airborne.

3. Jerry is a real estate salesman. He shows a pre-World War I house to Tom, a prospective buyer. Tom has two toddlers and is worried about potential health hazards. Which of the following is true?
   a. There is a risk that urea-foam insulation was used in the original construction.
   b. Because Jerry is a licensed real estate salesman, he can offer to inspect for lead and remove any lead risks.
   c. Because the house was built before 1978, there is a good likelihood of the presence of lead-based paint.
   d. Lead poisoning may occur only when lead paint chips are chewed and swallowed.

4. Which of the following is true regarding asbestos?
   a. The removal of asbestos can cause further contamination of a building.
   b. Asbestos causes health problems only when it is eaten.
   c. The level of asbestos in a building is affected by weather conditions.
   d. HUD requires all asbestos-containing materials to be removed from all residential buildings.

5. Which of the following best describes the water table?
   a. Natural level at which the ground is saturated
   b. Level at which underground storage tanks may be safely buried
   c. Measuring device used by specialists to measure groundwater contamination
   d. Always underground

6. All of the following are true of electromagnetic fields EXCEPT that electromagnetic fields are
   a. a suspected but unproven cause of cancer, hormonal abnormalities and behavioral disorders.
   b. generated by all electrical appliances.
   c. present only near high-tension wires or large electrical transformers.
   d. caused by the movement of electricity.

7. Which of the following describes the process of creating a landfill site?
   a. Waste is liquefied, treated and pumped through pipes to "tombs" under the water table.
   b. Waste and topsoil are layered in a pit, mounded up, then covered with dirt and plants.
   c. Waste is compacted and sealed into a container, then placed in a "tomb" designed to last several thousand years.
   d. Waste is buried in an underground concrete vault.

8. Liability under the Superfund is
   a. limited to the owner of record.
   b. joint and several and retroactive, but not strict.
   c. voluntary.
   d. strict, joint and several, and retroactive.

9. All of the following have been proven to pose health hazards, EXCEPT
   a. asbestos fibers.
   b. carbon monoxide.
   c. electromagnetic fields.
   d. urea-formaldehyde.

10. Which of the following environmental hazards poses a risk due to particles or fibers in the air?
    a. Carbon monoxide   c. UFFI
    b. Radon   d. Asbestos

11. Under the Federal Lead-Based Paint Hazard and Reduction Act, which of the following statements is true?
    a. All residential housing built prior to 1978 must be tested for the presence of lead-based paint before being listed for sale or rent.
    b. A disclosure statement must be attached to all sales contracts and leases involving residential properties built prior to 1978.
    c. A lead hazard pamphlet must be distributed to all prospective buyers, but not to tenants.
    d. Purchasers of housing built before 1978 must be given five days to test the property for the presence of lead-based paint.

12. Radon poses the greatest potential health risk to humans when it is
    a. contained in insulation material used during the 1970s.
    b. found in high concentrations of unimproved land.
    c. trapped and concentrated in inadequately ventilated areas.
    d. emitted by malfunctioning or inadequately ventilated appliances.

20 Real Estate Mathematics

LEARNING OBJECTIVES

When you've finished reading this chapter, you should be able to

- **apply** formulas used to compute area, percentages, fractions and be able to make necessary conversions.

- **calculate** the loan-to-value ratio, the interest rate on a loan, prorations and PITI.

- **determine** different commission amounts.

- **explain** the difference between gross and net profit.

- **define** these *key terms:*

  amortization   percentage

INTRODUCTION

Real estate involves working with numbers, from calculating commissions to determining loan payments to figuring out property taxes. Therefore, a real estate professional must have a working knowledge of math. This chapter focuses on the basic principles of math that a residential real estate licensee will use when working with a client or customer. The North Carolina Real Estate Commission's published syllabus on the Salesperson Fundamental Prelicensing course lists the particular subject areas of real estate math in which the prelicensing state exam applicant must be able to demonstrate a high level of proficiency. Even though there are many math examples and working solutions throughout this textbook, this chapter is designed to provide some basic math applications and give the student practice in problem solving through mathematical calculation. There are numerous practice problems for students to sharpen their skills for real estate applied math.

BASICS

Most real estate professionals use calculators or computers to assist them with math computations. Additionally, calculators are permitted when taking the state licensing exam. (See *Real Estate Licensing In North Carolina,* published by the Real Estate Commission, for detailed information on calculators.) A basic calculator that adds, subtracts, multiplies and divides is sufficient for most purposes. Financial calculators can offer additional functions, such as determining monthly loan payment amounts. Because each brand of calculator tends to be slightly different, be sure to refer to the user's manual for your calculator to understand how to use it properly.

Decimals   Calculators state numbers in decimal form. Therefore, to use a calculator, all numbers must be expressed the same way. The use of a calculator will often result in numerous digits following a decimal point.

For Example   100 divided by 30 = 3.3333333

Use normal rounding off at 3 decimal places before going to the next calculation: 3.3333333 would round down to 3.333.

> *Example:*   800 divided by 30 = 26.666666, which rounds up to 26.667

If the fourth digit is less than 5, drop the fourth and any following digits. If the fourth digit is 5 or more, round up.

Converting Fractions to Decimals   To convert a fraction to a decimal, divide the numerator (top number) by the denominator (bottom number).

> *Examples:*   ½ = 1 ÷ 2 = 0.5
> ¾ = 3 ÷ 4 = 0.75
> 5/8 = 5 ÷ 8 = 0.625
> 9/3 = 9 ÷ 3 = 3
> 5 and ¼ = 5 + (1 ÷ 4) = 5 + 0.25 = 5.25

PERCENTAGES

Many real estate calculations use percentages. For example a real estate broker's commission is usually stated as a percentage of the sales price. A **percentage** is a portion of a whole amount. The whole or total always represents 100 percent. For instance, 20 percent means 20 parts of the possible 100 parts that comprise the whole.

> *Example:*   20% = 20 parts of 100

Working with Percentages When working with percentages, the percent must first be converted to a decimal. To do this, move the decimal two places to the *left* and *drop* the percent sign.

> *Example:*   20% ➔ 0.20

Another way to convert a percent to a decimal is to *divide* the percent by 100 and *drop* the percent sign.

> *Example:*   20% ➔ 20 ÷ 100 ➔ 0.20

Most calculators will automatically change a number stated as a percent into a decimal (usually by entering the percentage number and then pressing the percent key), so that it can be used in a calculation.

Working with Decimals Percents are sometimes stated as decimals. To find the percent, you need to do the reverse of what was just explained above. To do this, move the decimal two places to the *right* and *add* the percent sign.

> *Example:*   0.20 ➔ 20%

Another way to convert a decimal to a percent is to *multiply* the decimal by 100 and *add* the percent sign.

> *Example:*   .20 ➔ 0.20 × 100 ➔ 20%

Approaching a Percentage Problem Keep in mind that there are always three components to a percentage problem. The first is the rate, or percentage. The second is the whole amount, or the number that you are usually trying to find a percentage of. And the third is the part of the whole number. If you are given two of these components, you can calculate the third.

$$\text{Rate} = \text{Part} \div \text{Whole}$$

$$\text{Whole} = \text{Part} \div \text{Rate} \qquad \text{Part} = \text{Rate} \times \text{Whole}$$

Calculating the Part of a Whole To calculate the part of a whole number, you multiply the whole by the rate, or the percent stated as a decimal.

> *Example:*   A broker is going to receive a commission of 20% of the sales price on a parcel of land. If the land sells for $230,000, what commission will the broker receive?

(Note that 20 percent is the rate, expressed as a percent; $230,000 is the whole. We are trying to find the commission, which is the part.)

> Step 1. Convert the percent to a decimal.
>
> 20% ➔ 20 ÷ 100 ➔ 0.20
>
> Step 2. Multiply the whole (here, sales price) by the decimal.
>
> $230,000 × 0.20 = $46,000

The broker will receive a $46,000 commission.

Calculating the Rate   Just as the part of a whole number can be calculated if we know the whole and the rate, the rate can be calculated if we know the part and the whole. To calculate the rate, you divide the part by the whole.

> *Example:*   Suppose we knew that a broker received a $46,000 commission on the sale of land for which the sales price was $230,000. What percentage rate of the whole did the broker receive?

(Note that $230,000 is the whole, and $46,000 is the part; we are trying to find the rate.)

Step 1. Divide the part by the whole.

$$\$46,000 \div \$230,000 = \$0.200$$

Step 2. Convert the decimal to a percent.

$$0.20 \rightarrow 0.20 \times 100 \rightarrow 20\%$$

The broker received a 20 percent commission.

Calculating the Whole or Total Amount   The whole or total amount can be found when we know the part and the rate. To calculate the whole amount, you divide the part by the rate.

> *Example:*   Suppose we knew that a broker received a $46,000 commission on the sale of land, and that the commission rate was 20 percent. What did the land sell for?

(Note that $46,000 is the part and 20 percent is the rate, expressed as a percent; we are trying to find the whole.)

Step 1. Convert the percentage to a decimal.

$$20\% \rightarrow 0.20 \div 100 \rightarrow 0.20$$

Step 2. Divide the part by the rate.

$$\$46,000 \div 0.20 = \$230,000$$

The land sold for $230,000.

Summary   The following formulas summarize the concept of working with percentage problems.

$$\text{Part} = \text{Whole} \times \text{Rate}$$
$$\text{Rate} = \text{Part} \div \text{Whole}$$
$$\text{Whole} = \text{Part} \div \text{Rate}$$

USING PERCENTS

The following is a summary of some of the most common uses of percentages in real estate.

Broker's Commission A broker's commission is usually set as a percentage of the sales price. Further, a salesperson's share of the commission is usually set as a percentage of the broker's commission.

> *Example:* A seller listed a home for $200,000 and agreed to pay the broker a commission of 5 percent. The home sold four weeks later for 90 percent of the list price. The listing broker paid the salesperson 50 percent of her share of the commission. How much commission did the salesperson receive?

Sales price = 90% of $200,000 = 0.90 × 200,000 = $180,000
Broker's commission = 5% of $180,000 = 0.05 × 180,000 = $9,000
Salesperson's commission = 50% of $9,000 = 0.50 × 9,000 = $4,500

Loan-to-Value Ratio Lenders typically are concerned about the amount of money they are lending out for the purchase of property, compared with the value of the property. They obviously would like the value to be greater than the loan amount, in case they need to foreclose on the property and have it sold to pay off the outstanding loan amount. In analyzing the relationship between the loan amount and the value of the property, lenders compute a percentage that is referred to as the *loan-to-value (LTV) ratio.* This ratio is calculated by dividing the loan amount by the value of the property.

> *Example 1:* A borrower is taking out a $150,000 loan to buy a $187,500 property. What is the LTV ratio? (The part [loan amount] and the whole [property value] are given, and we are trying to find the rate.)

LTV (rate) = part ÷ whole = $150,000 ÷ $187,500 = 0.80 = 80%

> *Example 2:* A buyer wants to purchase a $200,000 home, and the lender tells the buyer he can get a 90 percent LTV (sales price × LTV = loan amount).

$200,000 × 0.90 = $180,000 loan amount: $20,000 down payment

Interest Interest is the cost associated with borrowing money. It is usually stated as a percentage of the amount of money borrowed. The percentage is referred to as the *interest rate,* which is an annual rate. The amount of interest paid (a part) is determined by multiplying the loan amount (whole) by the interest rate.

> *Example 1:* A lender charges 7.5 percent interest a year. If a borrower takes out a loan for $335,000, how much interest will the borrower pay in the first year?)

Interest = 7.5% of $335,000 = 0.075 × $335,000 = $25,125 annual interest.

Example 2:   The annual interest on a loan of $100,000 is $9,000. What is the interest rate?

$9,000 interest ÷ $100,000 loan amount = 0.09 = 9% rate

Example 3:   If the annual interest is $7,200 and the interest rate is 9 percent, what is the loan amount?

$7,200 ÷ 0.09 = $80,000 loan amount

Loan Discount Points   Points are monies charged by a lender for making a loan at a rate lower than the current market rate. It takes 1 discount point to effectively increase the yield by ⅛ of 1 percent. This is known as the lender's *Rule of Thumb*. For each ⅛ percent increase in yield, the lender charges one discount point. One point equals 1 percent of the loan amount. The cost to the borrower of one point equals 1 percent of the loan amount.

Example 1:   The market interest rate is 7.5 percent, but the buyer wants to get a 7 percent loan. The difference is 1/2 percent. The lender would charge 4 points to effectively increase the yield by 1/2 percent.

Example 2:   A lender charges 4 points to make a mortgage loan. The buyer plans on buying a $200,000 house, and needs to take out a loan for 80 percent of the purchase price. How many points will the buyer have to pay?

Loan Amount = 80% of $200,000 = 0.80 × 200,000 = $160,000
Points = 4% of $160,000 = 0.04 × 160,000 = $6,400

Example 3:   Market rates are 7½ percent, the borrower wants a 7 percent loan. Enough points will be charged to increase the yield by ½ percent; ½ percent = ⅘ percent; 4 points would be charged.

MEASUREMENTS

To determine the area of a parcel of land or space in a house, real estate professionals must know how to use and calculate measurements.

Linear Measurements   Linear measurement is a measurement along a straight line. It is usually used to determine the length of something, such as the length of a lot line or width of a room. To convert an inch into a decimal part of a foot, divide the inches by 12.

Example: A measurement of 10 feet (') 7 inches (") would be converted to 10 + (7 ÷ by 12 = 0.583) = 10.583'.

> **Common Types of Linear Measurements**
>
> Inch
> Foot (12 inches)
> Yard (3 feet)
> Rod (16.5 feet)
> Mile (5,280 feet)

Area Measurements   Area is the two-dimensional surface of an object. Area is quoted in square units, or in acres.

> **Common Types of Area Measurements**
>
> Square feet
> Square yard (9 square feet)
> **Acre (43,560 square feet)**
> Square mile (640 square acres)

Converting one unit of measurement to another. One unit of measurement can easily be converted to another unit of measurement (known to an unknown). If the known unit is smaller than the unknown unit (for instance, when you know the number of feet and are trying to calculate the number of yards), you divide the known unit by how many known units there are in the unknown unit (such as 3 feet in a yard). If the known unit is larger than the unknown unit (for instance, when you know the number of inches and are trying to calculate the number of feet), you multiply the known unit by how many known units there are in the unknown unit (such as 12 inches to a foot).

> Put to memory:
>
> 43,560 sq. ft. = 1 acre
> 1 acre contains
> 43,560 square feet

> *Example 1:* A lot is 150 feet deep and 300 feet wide. How many square feet in the lot?
>
> 150' × 300' = 45,000 sq. ft.

> *Example 2:* How many acres in the lot in Example 1?
>
> 45,000 sq. ft. ÷ 43,560 sq. ft. = 1.033 acres

> *Example 3:* A room consists of 18 square yards. How many square feet is that?

Number of sq. yd. × number of sq. ft. per yd. (there are 9 sq. ft. in a sq. yd.) = 18 × 9 = 162 sq. ft.

Conversion of square feet to acres. Divide the number of square feet by 43,560. To convert acreage into square feet, multiply the number of acres by 43,560.

> *Example 1:* A lot is 660' by 330'. How many acres are in the lot?
>
> 660' × 330' = 217,800 sq. ft. ÷ 43,560 = 5 acres

> *Example 2:* There are 7.2 acres in a parcel. How many square feet does the parcel contain?
>
> 7.2 acres × 43,560 = 313,632 sq. ft.

Conversion of measurements into value. Divide the value or dollar amount by the unit of measurement.

> *Example:*   A parcel of land just sold for $100,000. It was 250' by 250'. How much did it sell for per square foot? ($100,000 ÷ 62,500 = $1.60 per square foot [250' × 250' = 62,500 sq. ft.]) How much did it sell for per acre? (62,500 ÷ 43,560 = 1.43 acres; $100,000 ÷ 1.43 = $69,930.07 per acre) How much did it sell for per front foot? ($100,000 ÷ 250' = $400 per front foot) **Note:** The first measurement given is always the frontage.

Calculating the area of a square or rectangle. Squares and rectangles are four-sided objects. All four sides of a square are the same length. Opposite sides of a rectangle are the same length.

To determine the area of a square or a rectangle, *multiply the length by the width.*

> *Example 1:*   A room is 10 feet wide and 13 feet long (rectangle). How many square feet?
>
> length × width = 10' × 13' = 130 sq. ft.

> *Example 2:*   A lot is 120 feet wide and 175 feet deep (rectangle). How many square feet? How many acres?
>
> length × width = 120' × 175' = 21,000 sq. ft.
> 21,000 sq. ft. ÷ 43,560 (because there are 43,560 sq. ft. in an acre) = 0.4821 acre

Calculating the area of a triangle. A triangle is a three-sided object. The three sides of a triangle can be the same length or different lengths. If a triangle has a right angle at one corner (90 degrees, known as a *right triangle*), one side of the right angle is referred to as the base, and the other side is referred to as the height. Calculating the area of this type of triangle involves *multiplying the base times the height and then dividing by two. A right triangle is really nothing more than half of a square or rectangle.*

> *Example:*   A right-angle triangle has a base of 50 feet and a height of 20 feet. What is the square footage?
>
> (base × height) ÷ 2 = (50' × 20') ÷ 2 = 1,000 sq. ft. ÷ 2 = 500 sq. ft.

Calculating the area of an irregular shape. To calculate the area of an irregular shape, divide the shape into regular shapes such as squares, rectangles and triangles. Calculate the area of each regular shape and add the areas together.

Using Measurements   **Square footage of a room.** Very often, a real estate professional will be asked about the square footage or area of a room. The best way to approach this is by thinking of a room as the area of a rectangle or square. Therefore, to find the square footage, multiply the length in feet by the width in feet.

Example: A room is 20 feet wide and 14 feet long (rectangle). How many square feet?

length × width = 20′ × 14′ = 280 sq. ft.

Size of a lot. It is easy to calculate the area of a lot shaped like a rectangle or square. Simply multiply the meaure of the front lot line in feet by that of the depth of the lot in feet (same as length × width). For irregularly shaped lots, you would need to divide the lot into regular shapes, calculate the area of each shape and add together. The area of a lot is typically expressed in acres, or for smaller lots in square feet.

Example: John Farmer has a piece of land that is 110′ wide and 420 feet long. He is interested in subdividing it into four equal lots. If he can do this, how many acres will there be per lot?

area of parcel = length × width = 110′ wide × 420′ long = 46,200 sq. ft.
46,200 sq. ft. ÷ 43,560 (because there are 43,560 sq. ft. in an acre) =
1.06 acres
1.06 acres ÷ 4 lots = 0.2652 acre or *about ¼ of an acre each*

SPECIFIC MATH APPLICATIONS

Real Property Taxation (Chapter 2)   Owners of real property in North Carolina are required to pay annual property taxes based on an assessed value of the property and an annual tax rate.

Parts of the problem:

1. The annual tax rate
2. The assessed value
3. The annual taxes

Formulas:

1. To determine the annual taxes: the tax rate times the assessed value
2. To determine the assessed value: the annual taxes divided by the tax rate
3. To determine the tax rate: the annual taxes divided by the assessed value

Note: The tax rate is expressed as a dollar amount per $100 of assessed value. If the tax rate is $1.67/$100, that means the property owner will pay $1.67 for each $100 of assessed value. The assessed value can be divided by 100, and the result multiplied by $1.67 to get the annual taxes. Or

Convert the $1.67 to a percent (1.67% = 0.0167) and multiply by the assessed value (0.0167 × assessed value).

Example 1:   If the tax rate is $1.67/$100 and the assessed value is $120,000, the annual taxes are $2,004.

$1.67 ÷ $100 = 0.0167 × $120,000 = $2,004 annual taxes, or
$120,000 ÷ 100 = $1,200 × $1.67 = $2,004.

Example 2:   If the annual taxes are $1,800 and the assessed value
is $110,000, the tax rate is 0.0164 = $1.64/$100.

$1,800 ÷ $110,000 = 0.0163636, rounded to 0.0164 = $1.64/$100

Example 3:   If the tax rate is $1.20/$100 and the annual taxes are
$1,200. The assessed value is $100,000.

$1,200 ÷ 0.012 = $100,000 assessed value.

Brokerage Commissions, Commission Splits: In-House and Cooperating (Chapter 8)

Even though previously mentioned as part of the section on percentages, commissions and commission splits need to be further discussed. Agents and their clients agree on a commission in the employment agreement. It is normally determined as a percentage of the final accepted sales price.

Parts of commission math problems include: (1) the sales price, (2) the commission rate, (3) commission earned, (4) in-house splits and (5) splits with cooperating brokers.

Formulas: earned commission = sales price × the commission rate
Rate = commission ÷ the sales price
Sales price = commission ÷ rate

In-house commission splits. The sales agents work for the brokerage firm. Their employment agreements establish commission splits.

Example: Two agents working for ABC Realty are on an in-house 50/50 split. One sells a house for $120,000 at a 6 percent commission. The gross commission is $7,200 ($120,000 × 0.06 = $7,200) If one agent listed and the other sold the property, their earned commission is $3,600, and ABC Realty's share is $3,600. That is, if Lucy listed the property and Sam, another agent within ABC Realty, sold it, $3,600 would go to ABC Realty, Lucy would earn $1,800 and Sam would earn $1,800.

Cooperating brokerage splits. If one company lists the property and another firm sells the property, normally through a multiple-listing service (MLS), the gross commission will be split between the two firms, based on a previous agreement. The commission will be split between the two firms and then between the firms and their agents.

Example: Sharon, the listing agent with ABC Realty, listed a home for $200,000 at a commission rate of 6%. Harold, an agent working for XYZ Realty, sold the home for the listed price. The co-op split is 50/50. ($200,000 × 0.06 = $12,000 gross commission × 0.50 = $6,000; $6,000 goes to ABC and $6,000 goes to XYZ.) If Sharon is on an in-house 50/50 split, she earns $3,000, her firm earns $3,000. If Harold is on a 70/30 in-house split, that is, 70 percent to Harold and 30 percent to the firm, he earns $4,200 ($6,000 × 0.70) and XYZ earns $1,800 ($6,000 × 0.30).

Profit and Loss Math; Percent of Gross and Net Profit; Seller's Net (Chapter 8)

Profit and loss. When real property is sold, a profit and/or a loss may occur. Many times sellers are concerned about the profit they may earn or, if a low price is accepted, a loss they may incur. The agent must understand the concepts of profit and loss math and how it applies to real estate transactions.

If the problem gives the value (present or original) and asks for a percent of loss or a percent of profit, the math is quite simple. Divide the amount of profit (or loss) by the original value, and that gives the percent of profit or loss.

Example 1:   A house recently sold for $120,000, and was originally purchased for $100,000. The profit is 20 percent. ($120,000 present value − $100,000 original value = $20,000 amount of profit ÷ original value of $100,000 = 0.20, or 20%)

Example 2:   A house was purchased for $100,000 a few years ago and just sold at $90,000. The loss is 10 percent. ($100,000 present value − $90,000 original value = $10,000 loss ÷ original value of $100,000 = 0.10, or 10%)

If a problem gives the original or present value, gives the percentage of profit or loss in the problem, then asks for the present or original value, the math becomes a bit more complicated. Some rules to remember:

1. When a problem gives the "original value" and asks for "present value," you *multiply* by the percentage of profit or loss.
2. When the problem gives the "present value" and asks for the "original value," you *divide* by the percentage of profit or loss.
3. If a profit occurs, add; if a loss occurs, subtract. Treat the value given in the problem as the 100 percent figure.

Example 1:   A house recently sold for $120,000 at a 13 percent profit. What was the original value?

$120,000 = 100% + 13% = 113% = 1.13
$120,000 ÷ 1.13 = $106,194.69 original value

Example 2:   A house recently sold for $96,000 at a 10 percent loss. What was the original value?

$$\$96,000 = 100\% - 10\% = 90\% = 0.090$$
$$\$96,000 \div 0.90 = \$106,666.66 \text{ original value}$$

Example 3:   A house cost $230,000 four years ago and just sold at a 9 percent profit. What was the sales price?

$$\$230,000 = 100\% + 9\% \text{ profit} = 109\% = 1.09$$
$$\$230,000 \times 1.09 = \$250,700 \text{ sales price (present value)}$$

Example 4:   A house cost $180,000 four years ago and just sold at an 11 percent loss. What did it sell for?

$$\$180,000 = 100\% - 11\% \text{ loss} = 89\% = 0.89$$
$$\$180,000 \times 0.89 = \$160,200 \text{ sales price (present value)}$$

Gross profit vs. net profit. *Gross profit* is nothing more than the present value less the original value, and the difference equals the amount of gross profit. The amount of gross profit divided by the original value equals the percent of gross profit.

Example: The original value of a house was $80,000, and it recently sold for $100,000. The gross profit is 25%. ($100,000 – $80,000 = $20,000 amount of gross profit ÷ $80,000 original value = 25%)

To find *net profit,* take into consideration the closing costs the buyer had to pay when the house was purchased and the selling expenses that had to be paid when it was sold.

Example: (using the figures in the preceding example): When the owners bought the house for $80,000, they had to pay $1,000 in closing costs, making the original cost $81,000. When they later sold for $100,000, they had to pay $7,000 in selling expenses. Their net profit is 14.8 percent. ($80,000 + $1,000 = $81,000 original value; $100,000 – $7,000 = $93,000 present value; $93,000 – $81,000 = $12,000 amount of net profit; $12,000 net profit ÷ $81,000 original value = 0.148 = 14.8 percent net profit)

Determining minimum sales price to get the seller a net amount.
Often on a listing appointment the seller will want to know what the house must sell for in order for the seller to "net" (realize a profit of) a certain amount. The agent should be able to calculate a probable sales price. This is also known as a *net to seller problem.* This question asks what the projected sales price should be. Students can check their work by taking one of the answers giving the proposed sales price and deducting the sales expenses. The resulting amount should equal the amount that the seller wishes to net.

Parts of the problem: (1) seller's desired net; (2) the commission to be paid; (3) closing costs to be paid by the seller.

Step 1. Add the seller's net to all closing costs, including any loan payoff.

Step 2.   Subtract the given commission rate from 100 percent.

Step 3.   Divide Step 1 by Step 2.

Example: A seller wants to net $120,000 from the sale of his home. The closing costs are estimated to be $1,200 and the agreed-on commission is 7 percent. There is an existing loan of $40,000 that must be paid off at closing. What must the house sell for if the seller is to receive his $120,000 "net"?

Step 1. $120,000 net + $1,200 closing costs + $40,000 loan payoff = $161,200

Step 2.   100% – 7% = 93% = 0.93

Step 3. $161,200 ÷ 0.93 = $173,333.33 is the lowest acceptable sales price needed to get the desired net for the seller.

Real Estate Financing Calculations (Chapters 12 and 13)

Agents must be familiar with calculations involving principal and interest, computation of monthly payments (PITI), mortgage debt reduction (amortization), total interest paid over the life of the loan, loan origination fees, discount points, loan-to-value ratios and how to compute total loan fees. Agents also must be able to give buyers a general idea of about how much they will be able to borrow based on standard qualifying ratios.

Amortization (debt liquidation). *Amortization* is the process of paying off a home loan by making periodic (monthly) payments of principal (P) and interest (I). Amortization literally means to "kill the debt." A monthly PI payment can be easily computed by using a mortgage payment constant chart (amortization chart) (see Table 20.1). The chart is based on a $1,000 loan. The interest rate and the term dictate the loan factor, which is the amount in dollars needed to amortize a $1,000 loan. Looking at the chart, if a person borrowed $1,000 for 30 years at 7 percent the monthly payment would be $6.65. To compute a monthly PI payment: You want to borrow $75,000 at 7 percent for 30 years. $75,000 ÷ $1,000 = 75 × $6.65 = $498.75 PI

Principal, interest, taxes, insurance (PITI). The borrower is probably going to be required by the lender to place into escrow one-twelfth of the annual property taxes and one-twelfth of the homeowner's annual insurance premium each month, along with the PI payment. The PITI can be computed by adding monthly debt service to the tax and insurance monthly escrow payments.

Example: The borrower wants to borrow $130,000 at 7.5 percent for 30 years. The loan factor is $6.99. The estimated annual taxes are $1,200, and the estimated annual insurance premium is $360. The monthly PITI is $1,038.70.

$130,000 ÷ 1,000 = 130 × $6.99 = $908.70 PI.
$1,200 ÷ 12 months = $100 T
$360 ÷ 12 months = $30.00 I
$908.70 PI + $100 T + $30 I = $1,038.70 PITI.

Table 20.1 Mortgage Factor Chart

Equal Monthly Payment to Amortize a Loan of $1,000

<table>
<tr><td rowspan="2">How To Use This Chart</td><td>Rate</td><td>Term 10 Years</td><td>Term 15 Years</td><td>Term 20 Years</td><td>Term 25 Years</td><td>Term 30 Years</td></tr>
<tr><td>4</td><td>10.13</td><td>7.40</td><td>6.06</td><td>5.28</td><td>4.78</td></tr>
</table>

	Rate	Term 10 Years	Term 15 Years	Term 20 Years	Term 25 Years	Term 30 Years
	4	10.13	7.40	6.06	5.28	4.78
	4⅛	10.19	7.46	6.13	5.35	4.85
	4¼	10.25	7.53	6.20	5.42	4.92
	4⅜	10.31	7.59	6.26	5.49	5.00
	4½	10.37	7.65	6.33	5.56	5.07
	4⅝	10.43	7.72	6.40	5.63	5.15
	4¾	10.49	7.78	6.47	5.71	5.22
	4⅞	10.55	7.85	6.54	5.78	5.30
	5	10.61	7.91	6.60	5.85	5.37
	5⅛	10.67	7.98	6.67	5.92	5.45
	5¼	10.73	8.04	6.74	6.00	5.53
	5⅜	10.80	8.11	6.81	6.07	5.60
	5½	10.86	8.18	6.88	6.15	5.68
	5⅝	10.92	8.24	6.95	6.22	5.76
	5¾	10.98	8.31	7.03	6.30	5.84
	5⅞	11.04	8.38	7.10	6.37	5.92
	6	11.10	8.44	7.16	6.44	6.00
	6⅛	11.16	8.51	7.24	6.52	6.08
	6¼	11.23	8.57	7.31	6.60	6.16
	6⅜	11.29	8.64	7.38	6.67	6.24
	6½	11.35	8.71	7.46	6.75	6.32
	6⅝	11.42	8.78	7.53	6.83	6.40
	6¾	11.48	8.85	7.60	6.91	6.49
	6⅞	11.55	8.92	7.68	6.99	6.57
	7	11.61	8.98	7.75	7.06	6.65
	7⅛	11.68	9.06	7.83	7.15	6.74
	7¼	11.74	9.12	7.90	7.22	6.82
	7⅜	11.81	9.20	7.98	7.31	6.91
	7½	11.87	9.27	8.05	7.38	6.99
	7⅝	11.94	9.34	8.13	7.47	7.08
	7¾	12.00	9.41	8.20	7.55	7.16
	7⅞	12.07	9.48	8.29	7.64	7.25
	8	12.14	9.56	8.37	7.72	7.34
	8⅛	12.20	9.63	8.45	7.81	7.43
	8¼	12.27	9.71	8.53	7.89	7.52
	8⅜	12.34	9.78	8.60	7.97	7.61
	8½	12.40	9.85	8.68	8.06	7.69
	8⅝	12.47	9.93	8.76	8.14	7.78
	8¾	12.54	10.00	8.84	8.23	7.87
	8⅞	12.61	10.07	8.92	8.31	7.96
	9	12.67	10.15	9.00	8.40	8.05
	9⅛	12.74	10.22	9.08	8.48	8.14
	9¼	12.81	10.30	9.16	8.57	8.23
	9⅜	12.88	10.37	9.24	8.66	8.32
	9½	12.94	10.45	9.33	8.74	8.41
	9⅝	13.01	10.52	9.41	8.83	8.50
	9¾	13.08	10.60	9.49	8.92	8.60
	9⅞	13.15	10.67	9.57	9.00	8.69
	10	13.22	10.75	9.66	9.09	8.78
	10⅛	13.29	10.83	9.74	9.18	8.87
	10¼	13.36	10.90	9.82	9.27	8.97
	10⅜	13.43	10.98	9.90	9.36	9.06
	10½	13.50	11.06	9.99	9.45	9.15
	10⅝	13.57	11.14	10.07	9.54	9.25
	10¾	13.64	11.21	10.16	9.63	9.34

How To Use This Chart

To use this chart, start by finding the appropriate interest rate. Then follow that row over to the column for the appropriate loan term. This number is the *interest rate factor* required each month to amortize a $1,000 loan. To calculate the principal and interest (PI) payment, multiply the interest rate factor by the number of 1,000s in the total loan.

For example, if the interest rate is 10 percent for a term of 30 years, the interest rate factor is 8.78. If the total loan is $100,000, the loan contains 100 1,000s. Therefore

$100 \times 8.78 = \$878$ PI

To estimate a mortgage loan amount using the amortization chart, divide the PI payment by the appropriate interest rate factor. Using the same facts as in the first example:

$\$878 \div 8.78 = \$100$
1,000's, or $100,000

Total interest paid over the life of the loan. On a fixed-rate mortgage loan the monthly PI payment will remain constant. Multiply the monthly PI payment by the number of payments made over the life of the loan and subtract the original principal to find the total interest paid. If the monthly payment is $498.75 over the 30-year $75,500 loan, the total interest paid over the life of the loan is $104,050. ($498.75 × 360 payments = $179,550 PI – $75,500 P = $104,050 I).

Mortgage debt reduction (amortization). The monthly PI payment will do two things. The principal portion will reduce the debt by the amount of monthly principal paid, and the interest portion will supply the lender's yield on the loan.

> *Example:*   The monthly PI payment is $498.75 with the loan amount of $75,500 at 7 percent. After the first month's payment, the loan amount is reduced to $75,441.67. ($75,500 × .07 = $5,285 annual interest ÷ 12 months = $440.42 monthly interest; $498.75 PI – $440.42 I = $58.33 P; $75,500 – $58.33 = $75,441.67 loan amount after one month's payment)

Loan origination fees, discount points and assumption fees. Lenders charge various fees to the borrower when processing a loan application. The origination fee is normally 1 percent of the loan amount, and discount points (previously discussed) may be charged to increase the yield. In the event of a loan assumption, the lender normally will charge an assumption fee, quoted as a percentage of the amount to be assumed.

> *Example:*   The loan amount is $90,500. The lender will charge a 1 percent loan origination fee. Market interest rates are 7.25 percent, but the buyer wants to get a rate of 7 percent, which the lender has agreed to as long as the buyer pays appropriate discount points. The total amount of fees to be paid by the buyer is $2,715. ($90,500 × 0.01 = $905 origination fee; 7.25% – 7% = 0.25% = 2 points; $90,500 × 0.02 = $1,810 discount points; $905 + $1,810 = $2,715)

Equity. Equity is defined as the difference between the value of the property and the debts on the property. As time goes by, the value increases and the debt is reduced, which creates an increase in equity over a period of time.

Value – Debt = Equity

> *Example:*   A buyer purchases a home for $100,000 and receives an $80,000 loan. ($100,000 value – $80,000 debt = $20,000 original equity)
>
> To find the *percent of equity increase,* divide the amount of increase in equity by the original equity.

Example: Over time the value of the above home increases to $130,000 and the debt is reduced to $70,000. What is the percent of equity increase? ($130,000 value − $70,000 debt = $60,000 new equity) The increase in equity is $40,000. ($60,000 new − $20,000 original) To compute the percentage of equity increase, divide the amount of increase in equity by the original equity. ($40,000 ÷ $20,000 = 2. = 200%)

Qualifying the buyer. This was discussed previously in Chapter 13. There will be some practice math questions on this subject at the end of this chapter.

Prorations (Chapter 14) *Prorate* means *to divide proportionately.* In real estate, prorations are used to divide income and expenses of a property between buyer and seller at closing. Refer to Chapter 14 for an introduction of when and how prorations are used at closing and for math examples.

Calculating prorations. In most cases when calculating prorations there are three steps to follow.

Step 1. Find the daily amount.

Real estate taxes: annual taxes are $1,080 ÷ 360 days = $3 per day

Step 2. Count the number of days the seller has owned the property for the proration period, including the day of closing.

Closing is April 15: Jan. 1 to Apr. 15 = 105 days

Step 3. Multiply Step 1 by Step 2

$3 per day × 105 days = $315 debit seller/credit buyer

Note: If a prorated item has been prepaid by the seller prior to closing, a fourth step must be added in which the seller must be credited for the over-paid amount, which will be debited to the buyer.

Subtract the seller's actual liability from what seller has prepaid and credit the seller, debit the buyer.

Closing is November 19, annual real estate taxes are $1,080 and seller has paid the taxes prior to closing. ($1,080 ÷ 360 days = $3 per day; Jan. 1 - Nov. 19 = 319 days × $3 = $957 "seller share" of taxes; seller paid $1,080 − $957 = $123 credit seller/debit buyer.)

These same steps will be followed when prorating rents, interest on an assumed loan and insurance premiums.

Difference between debit and credit. To calculate a proration problem, you need to know how expenses and income are posted on the closing statement. A *debit takes money* from a person. A *credit gives money* to a person. When the prorated item involves both the buyer and seller, there always will be a double entry. If the seller owes the buyer, the prorated amount will be debited to the seller and credited to the buyer. If the buyer owes the seller, the prorated item will be debited to the buyer and credited to the seller.

A word of caution! *If the math application is done correctly and the student is not knowledgeable about the proper entries to be made on the closing statement, the math question will probably be missed. You must know when items will be debited and credited to the parties!*

Appraisal Calculations (Chapter 16)

Math calculations were discussed in Chapter 16, to the extent required. There are some practice math problems on this subject at the end of this chapter.

Income Tax Calculations Related to Home Ownership (Chapter 18)

Math calculations on this subject were previously discussed in chapter 18 to the extent required. There are some practice problems on this subject at the end of this chapter.

SUMMARY

Real estate professionals can expect to encounter math-type problems in their day-to-day activities. Calculators and computers greatly help with any needed computations, so licensees should become familiar with operating a calculator and/or computer. When using a calculator, all numbers must first be converted to decimal form.

The three most common types of math computations that come up in residential real estate are (1) working with percentages, (2) figuring measurements and (3) estimating prorations.

A *percentage* is a portion of a whole number stated as a percent. The whole or total always represents 100 percent. To calculate the part of the whole number, you multiply the whole by the percent rate stated as a decimal. Percents are used in calculating commissions, property and conveyance taxes, financing points and interest, and appreciation and depreciation.

Measurements are used to determine the area of a parcel of land or space in a house. Linear measurements, such as feet, are single-dimension measurements that are used to measure the length of the perimeter of a room or lot. Area measurements, such as square feet, are two-dimension measurements that can be used to measure the floor area of a room or acreage of a lot.

Prorations are used to divide income and expenses of a property between buyer and seller at closing. The manner and process of proration depends on local customs. In general, when calculating prorations, you need to know to whom the proration is to be debited and credited, the number of days owed, and the amount of the expense or income per day. Items such as property taxes, rent, insurance, and fuel oil are typically prorated, along with interest on an assumed loan and homeowners' association dues.

Questions

1. Bob is buying a house for $123,000. His lender will give him a mortgage loan for 95 percent of the purchase price. How much down payment must Bob come up with?
   a. $1,230
   b. $6,150
   c. $12,300
   d. $116,000

2. Two brokers split a 6 percent commission equally on a $73,000 home. The selling salesperson, Joe, was paid 70 percent of his broker's share. The listing salesperson, Janice, was paid 30 percent of her broker's share. How much did Janice receive?
   a. $657
   b. $4,380
   c. $1,533
   d. $1,314

3. Carly is taking out a $356,000 loan to pay for a property she is buying that is worth $1,200,000. What is the loan-to-value ratio?
   a. 3.37%
   b. 29.67%
   c. 29.8%
   d. 30.23%

4. A house recently sold for $135,000 at a commission rate of 6.5 percent. The MLS service got 5 percent of the commission as a listing fee. The listing broker got 40 percent of the commission with 55 percent going to the selling broker. You, the selling agent were on an in-house split of 60 percent to you, 40 percent to your broker. What was your earned commission?
   a. $2,750.96
   b. $2,106.00
   c. $2,895.75
   d. $1,930.50

5. A recent sale generated a gross commission of $2,000. Salesperson Al received 2 percent of the *sales price,* the broker received 5 percent of the sales price and salesperson Betty received 3 percent of the sales price. How much in dollars did Al, the broker and Betty, respectively, receive for this transaction?
   a. $400, $1,000, $600
   b. $200, $800, $1,000
   c. $500, $1,000, $500
   d. None of the above

6. A residential lot in Mecklenburg County is presently assessed by the county tax assessor's office at $75,000, and the tax rate is $1.678/$100 of assessed value. If the property owner constructs a house on the lot that is assessed at $250,000 upon completion, what is the property owner's new monthly tax liability?
   a. $5,453.50
   b. $4,195.33
   c. $2,261.20
   d. $454.46

7. Sam bought a parcel of land containing 350 acres and 1,300 feet of road frontage. Margaret wants to buy the neighboring tract that has the same depth but has 6,000 feet of road frontage. How many acres are in the tract of land that Margaret wants to buy?
   a. 1,615.4 acres
   b. 1,430 acres
   c. 1,815.3 acres
   d. Cannot figure without the depth

8. A parcel of land is 660' by 660', and a small stream equally divides the parcel into two lots. How many acres are contained in each lot?
   a. 10
   b. 2.5
   c. 5
   d. 0.5

9. Charles bought a cabin in the mountains five years ago for $20,000. Its value went up, and today he sold it for $25,000. What percent profit did he make on his investment?
   a. 20%
   b. 25%
   c. 33%
   d. 80%

10. Tom bought five lots several months ago for $20,000 each. During the next few months he had the lots surveyed and divided the land into 9 lots, which he later sold for $17,000 each. What was his percent profit?
    a. 65%
    b. 47%
    c. 53%
    d. 33%

11. You are on a listing appointment and the sellers tell you they would like to net $135,000 from the sale of their home. You estimate they will have to pay $950 in miscellaneous closing costs, and you will charge them a 6.5 percent commission to sell the property. They also have a loan payoff of $53,500. What must the property sell for to ensure they receive their desired net?
    a. $201,764.25
    c. $201,604.27
    b. $145,401.06
    d. $202,620.32

Based on the following scenario, answer questions 12 through 14.

Gary bought a house for $180,000 with an 85 percent LTV ratio. The term of the loan is 30 years at a 7 percent rate of interest. It will take a loan factor of 6.65 to amortize the loan. The annual real property taxes are estimated to be $996, and the annual premium for the homeowner's policy is estimated at $480.

12. What is the monthly PITI?
    a. $1,140.45
    c. $1,320.00
    b. $1,100.45
    d. $1,017.22

13. What will be the total amount of interest paid over the life of the loan if payments are made for the full 30-year term?
    a. $366,282
    c. $213,282
    b. $153,000
    d. $321,300

14. What will be the principal amount owing after the first month's payment has been made?
    a. $152,875.05
    c. $153.000.00
    b. $152,775.07
    d. $152,323.33

15. Bill and Betty just received $25,000 profit from the sale of their home. They are in the process of buying a new home for $185,500 with an 80 percent LTV ratio. The lender is charging the normal loan origination fee and is lending the money at 1.5 discount points. Bill and Betty must pay an attorney $400 to handle the closing, and they also must pay for the revenue stamps. How much money will the lender be paid in fees?
    a. $1,484
    c. $3,710
    b. $2,226
    d. $41,581

16. Using the same information as in question 15, how much cash do Bill and Betty need to close the transaction?
    a. $1,484
    c. $3,710
    b. $2,226
    d. $41,581

17. Lynn bought a home five years ago for $105,000 with a 90 percent LTV ratio. She is now selling the home for 20 percent more than it cost. Her loan has been reduced by 8 percent. What is her percent of equity increase?
    a. 2.72%
    c. 272%
    b. 27.2%
    d. 372%

18. A husband and wife apply for an $80,000 conventional mortgage loan on a house valued at $85,000. The lender estimates that the couple's housing expenses will be $895 per month, and they have other recurring debts of $425 per month. The couple's combined annual gross income is $40,800. Under which of the following expense-to-income ratios will the lender find the couple to be qualified, based on the 28/36 ratios?
    I. Housing-expense-to-gross-income ratio
    II. Recurring-obligations-to-gross-income ratio
    a. I only
    b. II only
    c. Both I and II
    d. Neither I or II

19. Using the 28/36 ratios, how much annual income must the borrower have to qualify for a $98,000 loan at 8 percent for 30 years if the proposed PI payment will be $719.32, taxes and insurance will be $135 per month and the borrower's other monthly recurring debts total $500?
    a. $45,144.00
    c. $58,042.00
    b. $36,613.71
    d. $28,478.32

20. What is the maximum amount a buyer can borrow using the 28/36 ratio if her annual income is $53,000, her monthly taxes and insurance are estimated to be $150 per month, the mortgage factor is $8.0462 and her nonhousing recurring debts total $650?
    a. $175,000.00
    c. $182,000.00
    b. $135,053.00
    d. $98,182.99

21. Joan wants to buy a house for $96,000. Her annual income is $38,500. The amount she wishes to borrow will generate a monthly PI payment of $700. What are the maximum nonhousing debts she can have to qualify under the 28/36 ratio?
    a. $700   c. $557
    b. $455   d. $480

22. You are purchasing a four-unit apartment building and going to close on November 14. Each apartment rents for $575 per month. On November 1, one apartment is vacant and the other tenants have paid the November rent. Compute the rent proration through the day of closing, and indicate proper entries on a closing statement.
    a. $805 credit seller/debit buyer
    b. $805 debit seller/credit buyer
    c. $920 credit seller/debit buyer
    d. $920 debit seller/credit buyer

23. The buyer is going to assume the seller's 7 percent loan with a loan balance of $82,000 as of the day of closing, which will be August 11. Of the following, which would be the correct closing statement entries?
    a. $82,000 debit seller/credit buyer and $175.38 debit seller/credit buyer
    b. $82,000 credit seller/debit buyer and $175.38 credit seller/debit buyer
    c. $82,000 debit seller/credit buyer
    d. $175.38 debit seller/credit buyer

24. Closing will take place on November 15. Annual real estate taxes are $1,260 and have been paid by the seller. Of the following, which would be the appropriate closing statement entries?
    a. $1,102.50 debit seller/credit buyer
    b. $157.50 credit seller/debit buyer
    c. $1,102.50 credit seller/debit buyer
    d. $157.50 debit seller/credit buyer

Use the following information to answer questions 25 and 26.

Closing will take place on February 15. The following items have been agreed on by both buyer and seller and are included in the accepted offer to purchase and contract. Determine the net due the seller and the cash needed by the buyer. (Use the 360-day method of prorations and round off at three decimals.)

Sales price:	$150,000
Commission:	7.5%
Buyer's new loan:	$90,000 at 7%
Buyer to pay interim interest:	
Buyer's earnest money deposit:	$3,000
Buyer's origination fee:	1%
Buyer's discount points:	1%
Seller's loan payoff:	$50,000
Unpaid real estate taxes:	$1,260
Other miscellaneous closing costs:	
Deed preparation:	$150
Revenue stamps:	
Title insurance premium:	$185
New homeowner's policy:	$380
Attorney fees:	$550

25. How much did the seller net?
    a. $60,037.50   c. $88,442.50
    b. $88,142.50   d. $88,300.00

26. How much cash does the buyer need at closing?
    a. $60,195.00   c. $59,137.50
    b. $60,020.00   d. $60,037.50

27. The subject property to be appraised is a 3-bedroom brick ranch with 3,000 square feet. It does not have a garage but does have a patio. Comparable 1 is a 3-bedroom brick ranch that recently sold for $100,000. It has 2,800 square feet, a garage and a patio. Comparable 2, a 3-bedroom brick ranch, recently sold for $110,000. It also has a garage and a patio and 3,000 square feet. Comparable 3, a 3-bedroom brick ranch, recently sold for $86,000, has 2,600 square feet, no garage, but does have a patio. Using the sales comparison approach, abstract the cost data, make appropriate adjustments and estimate the value of the subject property.
    a. $94,000   c. $109,000
    b. $114,000   d. $106,000

Use the following information to answer questions 28 through 31.

When you bought your home, you paid $120,000 for it plus $1,600 in closing costs. During ownership you added $16,000 worth of capital improvements. Later when you sold the home for $165,000, you paid a 7 percent commission and other closing costs of $1,300. Answer the following questions.

28. What was your basis?
    a. $120,000
    b. $137,600
    c. $152,150
    d. $14,550

29. What was your adjusted basis?
    a. $120,000
    b. $137,600
    c. $152,150
    d. $14,550

30. What was your amount realized?
    a. $120,000
    b. $137,600
    c. $152,150
    d. $44,550

31. What was your gain?
    a. $120,000
    b. $137,600
    c. $152,150
    d. $14,550

APPENDIX A

Real Estate License Law, Commission Rules, and Trust Account Guidelines

In 1957, the North Carolina General Assembly enacted into law, to be effective July 1, 1957, the *Real Estate Licensing Act,* codified as Chapter 93A of the General Statutes of North Carolina. This law created the North Carolina Real Estate Commission and empowered it to write and enforce reasonable rules and regulations concerning the business activities of real estate licensees. The Commission has the authority to approve real estate prelicensing schools and also publishes prelicensing course syllabi. The Real Estate Commission also publishes and updates as required a booklet entitled *Real Estate Licensing in North Carolina.* The real estate licensing applicant is required to be knowledgeable about certain portions of General Statute 93A and Commission Rules, which are contained in this appendix. *The study of this material should take place directly from the materials in this appendix.*

NORTH CAROLINA REAL ESTATE LICENSE LAW

Codified as Chapter 93A of the General Statutes of North Carolina

Article 1.
Real Estate Brokers and Salespersons.

Article 2.
Real Estate Recovery Fund.

Article 3.
Private Real Estate Schools.

Article 4.
Time Shares

Article 5.
Real Estate Appraisers.
[Repealed]

Please note: Certain "gender neutral" terms used in the Real Estate License Law as reprinted in this booklet are subject to final revision by the Revisor of Statutes.

Real Estate License Law

[Codified as Chapter 93A of the General Statutes of North Carolina]

ARTICLE 1.
REAL ESTATE BROKERS AND SALESPERSONS.

93A-1. License required of real estate brokers and real estate salespersons.

From and after July 1, 1957, it shall be unlawful for any person, partnership, corporation, limited liability company, association, or other business entity in this State to act as a real estate broker or real estate salesperson, or directly or indirectly to engage or assume to engage in the business of real estate broker or real estate salesperson or to advertise or hold himself or herself or themselves out as engaging in or conducting such business without first obtaining a license issued by the North Carolina Real Estate Commission (hereinafter referred to as the Commission), under the provisions of this Chapter. A license shall be obtained from the Commission even if the person, partnership, corporation, limited liability company, association, or business entity is licensed in another state and is affiliated or otherwise associated with a licensed real estate broker or salesperson in this State.

93A-2. Definitions and exceptions.

(a) A real estate broker within the meaning of this Chapter is any person, partnership, corporation, limited liability company, association, or other business entity who for a compensation or valuable consideration or promise thereof lists or offers to list, sells or offers to sell, buys or offers to buy, auctions or offers to auction (specifically not including a mere crier of sales), or negotiates the purchase or sale or exchange of real estate, or who leases or offers to lease, or who sells or offers to sell leases of whatever character, or rents or offers to rent any real estate or the improvement thereon, for others.

(a1) The term broker-in-charge within the meaning of this Chapter shall mean a real estate broker who has been designated as the broker having responsibility for the supervision of real estate salespersons engaged in real estate brokerage at a particular real estate office and for other administrative and supervisory duties as the Commission shall prescribe by rule.

(b) The term real estate salesperson within the meaning of this Chapter shall mean and include any person who under the supervision of a real estate broker designated as broker-in-charge of a real estate office, for a compensation or valuable consideration is associated with or engaged by or on behalf of a licensed real estate broker to do, perform or deal in any act, acts or transactions set out or comprehended by the foregoing definition of real estate broker.

(c) The provisions of this Chapter shall not apply to and shall not include:

(1) Any person, partnership, corporation, limited liability company, association, or other business entity who, as owner or lessor, shall perform any of the acts aforesaid with reference to property owned or leased by them, where the acts are performed in the regular course of or as incident to the management of that property and the investment therein.

(2) Any person acting as an attorney-in-fact under a duly executed power of attorney from the owner authorizing the final consummation of performance of any contract for the sale, lease or exchange of real estate.

(3) The acts or services of an attorney-at-law.

(4) Any person, while acting as a receiver, trustee in bankruptcy, guardian, administrator or executor or any person acting under order of any court.

(5) Any person, while acting as a trustee under a trust agreement, deed of trust or will, or his or her regular salaried employees.

(6) Any salaried person employed by a licensed real estate broker, for and on behalf of the owner of any real estate or the improvements thereon, which the licensed broker has contracted to manage for the owner, if the salaried employee is limited in his or her employment to: exhibiting units on the real estate to prospective tenants; providing the prospective tenants with information about the lease of the units; accepting applications for lease of the units; completing and executing preprinted form leases; and accepting security deposits and rental payments for the units only when the deposits and rental payments are made payable to the owner or the broker employed by the owner. The salaried employee shall not negotiate the amount of security deposits or rental payments and shall not negotiate leases or any rental agreements on behalf of the owner or broker.

(7) Any owner who personally leases or sells his or her own property.

(8) Any housing authority organized in accordance with the provisions of Chapter 157 of the General Statutes and any regular salaried employees of the housing authority when performing acts authorized in this Chapter as to any property owned or leased by the housing authority. This exception shall not apply to any person, partnership, corpo-

ration, limited liability company, association, or other business entity that contracts with a housing authority to sell or manage property owned or leased by the housing authority.

93A-3. Commission created; compensation; organization.

(a) There is hereby created the North Carolina Real Estate Commission, hereinafter called the Commission. The Commission shall consist of nine members, seven members to be appointed by the Governor, one member to be appointed by the General Assembly upon the recommendation of the President Pro Tempore of the Senate in accordance with G.S. 120-121, and one member to be appointed by the General Assembly upon the recommendation of the Speaker of the House of Representatives in accordance with G.S. 120-121. At least three members of the Commission shall be licensed real estate brokers or real estate salespersons. At least two members of the Commission shall be persons who are not involved directly or indirectly in the real estate or real estate appraisal business. Members of the Commission shall serve three-year terms, so staggered that the terms of three members expire in one year, the terms of three members expire in the next year, and the terms of three members expire in the third year of each three-year period. The members of the Commission shall elect one of their members to serve as chairman of the Commission for a term of one year. The Governor may remove any member of the Commission for misconduct, incompetency, or willful neglect of duty. The Governor shall have the power to fill all vacancies occurring on the Commission, except vacancies in legislative appointments shall be filled under G.S. 120-122.

(b) Members of the Commission shall receive as compensation for each day spent on work for the Commission the per diem, subsistence and travel allowances as provided in G.S. 93B-5. The total expense of the administration of this Chapter shall not exceed the total income therefrom; and none of the expenses of said Commission or the compensation or expenses of any office thereof or any employee shall ever be paid or payable out of the treasury of the State of North Carolina; and neither the Commission nor any officer or employee thereof shall have any power or authority to make or incur any expense, debt or other financial obligation binding upon the State of North Carolina. After all expenses of operation, the Commission may set aside an expense reserve each year not to exceed ten percent (10%) of the previous year's gross income; then any surplus shall go to the general fund of the State of North Carolina.

(c) The Commission shall have power to make reasonable bylaws, rules and regulations that are not inconsistent with the provisions of this Chapter and the General Statutes; provided, however, the Commission shall not make rules or regulations regulating commissions, salaries, or fees to be charged by licensees under this Chapter.

(c1) The provisions of G.S. 93A-1 and G.S. 93A-2 notwithstanding, the Commission may adopt rules to permit a real estate broker to pay a fee or other valuable consideration to a travel agent for the introduction or procurement of tenants or potential tenants in vacation rentals as defined in G.S. 42A-4. Rules adopted pursuant to this subsection may include a definition of the term 'travel agent', may regulate the conduct of permitted transactions, and may limit the amount of the fee or the value of the consideration that may be paid to the travel agent. However, the Commission may not authorize a person or entity not licensed as a broker or salesperson to negotiate any real estate transaction on behalf of another.

(c2) The Commission shall adopt a seal for its use, which shall bear thereon the words "North Carolina Real Estate Commission." Copies of all records and papers in the office of the Commission duly certified and authenticated by the seal of the Commission shall be received in evidence in all courts and with like effect as the originals.

(d) The Commission may employ an Executive Director and professional and clerical staff as may be necessary to carry out the provisions of this Chapter and to put into effect the rules and regulations that the Commission may promulgate. The Commission shall fix salaries and shall require employees to make good and sufficient surety bond for the faithful performance of their duties. The Commission may, when it deems it necessary or convenient, delegate to the Executive Director, legal counsel for the Commission, or other Commission staff, professional or clerical, the Commission's authority and duties under this Chapter, but the Commission may not delegate its authority to make rules or its duty to act as a hearing panel in accordance with the provisions of G.S. 150B-40(b).

(e) The Commission shall be entitled to the services of the Attorney General of North Carolina, in connection with the affairs of the Commission or may on approval of the Attorney General, employ an attorney to assist or represent it in the enforcement of this Chapter, as to specific matters, but the fee paid for such service shall be approved by the Attorney General. The Commission may prefer a complaint for violation of this Chapter before any court of competent jurisdiction, and it may take the necessary legal steps through the proper legal offices of the State to enforce the provisions of this Chapter and collect the penalties provided therein.

(f) The Commission is authorized to expend expense reserve funds as defined in G.S. 93A-3(b) for the purpose of conducting education and information programs relating to the real estate brokerage business for the information, education, guidance and protection of the general public, licensees, and applicants for license. The education and information programs may include preparation, printing and distribution of publications and articles and the conduct of conferences, seminars, and lectures.

93A-4. Applications for licenses; fees; qualifications; examinations; privilege licenses; renewal or reinstatement of license; power to enforce provisions.

(a) Any person, partnership, corporation, limited liability company, association, or other business entity hereafter desiring to enter into business of and obtain a license as a real estate broker or real estate salesperson shall make written application for such license to the Commission in the form and manner prescribed by the Commission. Each applicant for a license as a real estate broker or real estate salesperson shall be at least 18 years of age. Each applicant for a license as a real estate salesperson shall, within three years preceding the date application is made, have satisfactorily completed, at a school approved by the Commission, a real estate fundamentals course consisting of at least 67 hours of classroom instruction in subjects determined by the Commission, or shall possess real estate education or experience in real estate transactions which the Commission shall find equivalent to the course. Each applicant for a license as a real estate broker shall, within three years preceding the date the application is made, have satisfactorily completed, at a school approved by the Commission, an education program consisting of at least 60 hours of classroom instruction in subjects determined by the Commission, which shall be in addition to the course required for a real estate salesperson license, or shall possess real estate education or experience in real estate transactions which the Commission shall find equivalent to the education program. Each applicant for a license as a real estate broker or real estate salesperson shall be required to pay a fee, fixed by the Commission but not to exceed thirty dollars ($30.00).

(b) Except as otherwise provided in this Chapter, any person who submits an application to the Commission in proper manner for a license as real estate broker or a license as real estate salesperson shall be required to take an oral or written examination. The Commission may allow an applicant to elect to take the examination by computer as an alternative to the written or oral examination and may require the applicant to pay the Commission or a provider contracted by the Commission the actual cost of administering the computerized examination. The cost of the computerized examination shall be in addition to any other fees the applicant is required to pay under subsection (a) of this section. The examination shall determine the applicant's qualifications with due regard to the paramount interests of the public as to the applicant's competency. A person holding a real estate salesperson license in this State and applying for a real estate broker license shall not be required to take an additional examination under this subsection.

An applicant for licensure under this Chapter shall satisfy the Commission that he or she possesses the competency, honesty, truthfulness, integrity, and general moral character necessary to protect the public interest and promote public confidence in the real estate brokerage business. If the results of any required competency examination and investigation of the applicant's moral character shall be satisfactory to the Commission, then the Commission shall issue to the applicant a license, authorizing the applicant to act as a real estate broker or real estate salesperson in the State of North Carolina, upon the payment of privilege taxes now required by law or that may hereafter be required by law.

(c) All licenses issued by the Commission under the provisions of this Chapter shall expire on the 30th day of June following issuance or on any other date that the Commission may determine and shall become invalid after that date unless reinstated. A license may be renewed 45 days prior to the expiration date by filing an application with and paying to the Executive Director of the Commission the license renewal fee. The license renewal fee is thirty dollars ($30.00) unless the Commission sets the fee at a higher amount. The Commission may set the license renewal fee at an amount that does not exceed fifty dollars ($50.00). The license renewal fee may not increase by more than five dollars ($5.00) during a 12-month period. The Commission may adopt rules establishing a system of license renewal in which the licenses expire annually with varying expiration dates. These rules shall provide for prorating the annual fee to cover the initial renewal period so that no licensee shall be charged an amount greater than the annual fee for any 12-month period. All licenses reinstated after the expiration date thereof shall be subject to a late filing fee of five dollars ($5.00) in addition to the required renewal fee. In the event a licensee fails to obtain a reinstatement of such license within 12 months after the expiration date thereof, the Commission may, in its discretion, consider such person as not having been previously licensed, and thereby subject to the provisions of this Chapter relating to the issuance of an original license, including the examination requirements set forth herein. Duplicate licenses may be issued by the Commission upon payment of a fee of five dollars ($5.00) by the licensee. Commission certification of a licensee's license history shall be made only after the payment of a fee of ten dollars ($10.00).

(d) The Commission is expressly vested with the power and authority to make and enforce any and all reasonable rules and regulations connected with license application, examination, renewal, and reinstatement as shall be deemed necessary to administer and enforce the provisions of this Chapter. The Commission is further authorized to adopt reasonable rules and regulations necessary for the approval of real estate schools, instructors, and textbooks and rules that prescribe specific requirements pertaining to instruction, administration, and content of required education courses and programs.

(e) Nothing contained in this Chapter shall be construed as giving any authority to the Commission nor any licensee of the Commission as authorizing any licensee to engage in the practice of law or to render any legal service as specifically set out in G.S. 84-2.1 or any other legal service not specifically referred to in said section.

93A-4A. Continuing education.

(a) The Commission shall establish a program of continuing education for real estate brokers and salespersons. A person licensed as a real estate broker or salesperson must present evidence to the Commission upon the second license renewal following initial licensure, and every renewal thereafter, that during the 12 months preceding the annual license expiration date the person has completed eight classroom hours of real estate instruction in courses approved by the Commission.

(a1) In addition to the requirements of subsection (a) of this section, the Commission may require real estate brokers-in-charge to complete a special course of study, not to exceed six classroom hours every three years, in subjects prescribed by the Commission.

(b) The Commission shall establish procedures allowing for a deferral of continuing education for brokers and salespersons while they are not actively engaged in real estate brokerage.

(c) The Commission may adopt any reasonable rules not inconsistent with this Chapter to give purpose and effect to the continuing education requirement, including rules that govern:

(1) The content and subject matter of continuing education courses.

(2) The curriculum of courses required.

(3) The criteria, standards, and procedures for the approval of courses, course sponsors, and course instructors.

(4) The methods of instruction.

(5) The computation of course credit.

(6) The ability to carry forward course credit from one year to another.

(7) The deferral of continuing education for brokers and salespersons not engaged in brokerage.

(8) The waiver of or variance from the continuing education requirement for hardship or other reasons.

(9) The procedures for compliance and sanctions for noncompliance.

(d) The Commission may establish a nonrefundable course application fee to be charged to a course sponsor for the review and approval of a proposed continuing education course. The fee shall not exceed one hundred twenty-five dollars ($125.00) per course. The Commission may charge the sponsor of an approved course a nonrefundable fee not to exceed seventy-five dollars ($75.00) for the annual renewal of course approval.

The Commission may also require a course sponsor to pay a fee for each licensee completing an approved continuing education course conducted by the sponsor. The fee shall not exceed five dollars ($5.00) per licensee.

The Commission shall not charge a course application fee, a course renewal fee, or any other fee for a continuing education course sponsored by a community college, junior college, college, or university located in this State and accredited by the Southern Association of Colleges and Schools.

(e) The Commission may award continuing education credit for an unapproved course or related educational activity. The Commission may prescribe procedures for a licensee to submit information on an unapproved course or related educational activity for continuing education credit. The Commission may charge a fee to the licensee for each course or activity submitted. The fee shall not exceed fifty dollars ($50.00).

93A-5. Register of applicants; roster of brokers and salespersons; financial report to Secretary of State.

(a) The Executive Director of the Commission shall keep a register of all applicants for license, showing for each the date of application, name, place of residence, and whether the license was granted or refused. Said register shall be prima facie evidence of all matters recorded therein.

(b) The Executive Director of the Commission shall also keep a current roster showing the names and places of business of all licensed real estate brokers and real estate salespersons, which roster shall be kept on file in the office of the Commission and be open to public inspection.

(c) On or before the first day of September of each year, the Commission shall file with the Secretary of State a copy of the roster of real estate brokers and real estate salespersons holding certificates of license, and at the same time shall also file with the Secretary of State a report containing a complete statement of receipts and disbursements of the Commission for the preceding fiscal year ending June 30 attested by the affidavit of the Executive Director of the Commission.

93A-6. Disciplinary action by Commission.

(a) The Commission shall have power to take disciplinary action. Upon its own initiative, or on the complaint of any person, the Commission may investigate the actions of any person or entity licensed under this Chapter, or any other person or entity who shall assume to act in such capacity. If the Commission finds probable cause that a licensee has violated any of the provisions of this Chapter, the Commission may hold a hearing on the allegations of misconduct.

The Commission shall have power to suspend or revoke at any time a license issued under the provisions of this Chapter, or to reprimand or censure any licensee, if, following a hearing, the Commission adjudges the licensee to be guilty of:

(1) Making any willful or negligent misrepresentation or any willful or negligent omission of material fact.

(2) Making any false promises of a character likely to influence, persuade, or induce.

(3) Pursuing a course of misrepresentation or making of false promises through agents, salespersons, advertising or otherwise.

(4) Acting for more than one party in a transaction without the knowledge of all parties for whom he or she acts.

(5) Accepting a commission or valuable consideration as a real estate salesperson for the performance of any of the acts specified in this Article or Article 4 of this Chapter, from any person except his or her broker-in-charge or licensed broker by whom he or she is employed.

(6) Representing or attempting to represent a real estate broker other than the broker by whom he or she is engaged or associated, without the express knowledge and consent of the broker with whom he or she is associated.

(7) Failing, within a reasonable time, to account for or to remit any moneys coming into his or her possession which belong to others.

(8) Being unworthy or incompetent to act as a real estate broker or salesperson in a manner as to endanger the interest of the public.

(9) Paying a commission or valuable consideration to any person for acts or services performed in violation of this Chapter.

(10) Any other conduct which constitutes improper, fraudulent or dishonest dealing.

(11) Performing or undertaking to perform any legal service, as set forth in G.S. 84-2.1, or any other acts constituting the practice of law.

(12) Commingling the money or other property of his or her principals with his or her own or failure to maintain and deposit in a trust or escrow account in an insured bank or savings and loan association in North Carolina all money received by him or her as a real estate licensee acting in that capacity, or an escrow agent, or the temporary custodian of the funds of others, in a real estate transaction; provided, these accounts shall not bear interest unless the principals authorize in writing the deposit be made in an interest bearing account and also provide for the disbursement of the interest accrued.

(13) Failing to deliver, within a reasonable time, a completed copy of any purchase agreement or offer to buy and sell real estate to the buyer and to the seller.

(14) Failing, at the time the transaction is consummated, to deliver to the seller in every real estate transaction, a complete detailed closing statement showing all of the receipts and disbursements handled by him or her for the seller or failing to deliver to the buyer a complete statement showing all money received in the transaction from the buyer and how and for what it was disbursed.

(15) Violating any rule or regulation promulgated by the Commission.

The Executive Director shall transmit a certified copy of all final orders of the Commission suspending or revoking licenses issued under this Chapter to the clerk of superior court of the county in which the licensee maintains his or her principal place of business. The clerk shall enter these orders upon the judgment docket of the county.

(b) Following a hearing, the Commission shall also have power to suspend or revoke any license issued under the provisions of this Chapter or to reprimand or censure any licensee when:

(1) The licensee has obtained a license by false or

fraudulent representation;

(2) The licensee has been convicted or has entered a plea of guilty or no contest upon which final judgment is entered by a court of competent jurisdiction in this State, or any other state, of the criminal offenses of: embezzlement, obtaining money under false pretense, fraud, forgery, conspiracy to defraud, or any other offense involving moral turpitude which would reasonably affect the licensee's performance in the real estate business;

(3) The licensee has violated any of the provisions of G.S. 93A-6(a) when selling, leasing, or buying his or her own property;

(4) The broker's unlicensed employee, who is exempt from the provisions of this Chapter under G.S. 93A-2(c)(6), has committed, in the regular course of business, any act which, if committed by the broker, would constitute a violation of G.S. 93A-6(a) for which the broker could be disciplined; or

(5) The licensee, who is also a State-licensed or State-certified real estate appraiser pursuant to Chapter 93E of the General Statutes, has violated any provisions of Chapter 93E of the General Statutes and has been reprimanded or has had his or her appraiser license or certificate suspended or revoked by the Appraisal Board.

(c) The Commission may appear in its own name in superior court in actions for injunctive relief to prevent any person from violating the provisions of this Chapter or rules promulgated by the Commission. The superior court shall have the power to grant these injunctions even if criminal prosecution has been or may be instituted as a result of the violations, or whether the person is a licensee of the Commission.

(d) Each broker shall maintain complete records showing the deposit, maintenance, and withdrawal of money or other property owned by his or her principals or held in escrow or in trust for his or her principals. The Commission may inspect these records periodically, without prior notice and may also inspect these records whenever the Commission determines that they are pertinent to an investigation of any specific complaint against a licensee.

(e) When a person or entity licensed under this Chapter is accused of any act, omission, or misconduct which would subject the licensee to disciplinary action, the licensee, with the consent and approval of the Commission, may surrender his or her or its license and all the rights and privileges pertaining to it for a period of time established by the Commission. A person or entity who surrenders his or her or its license shall not

thereafter be eligible for or submit any application for licensure as a real estate broker or salesperson during the period of license surrender.

93A-6.1. Commission may subpoena witnesses, records, documents, or other materials.

(a) The Commission, Executive Director, or other representative designated by the Commission may issue a subpoena for the appearance of witnesses deemed necessary to testify concerning any matter to be heard before or investigated by the Commission. The Commission may issue a subpoena ordering any person in possession of records, documents, or other materials, however maintained, that concern any matter to be heard before or investigated by the Commission to produce the records, documents, or other materials for inspection. Upon written request, the Commission shall revoke a subpoena if it finds that the evidence, the production of which is required, does not relate to a matter in issue, or if the subpoena does not describe with sufficient particularity the evidence, the production of which is required, or if for any other reason in law the subpoena is invalid. If any person shall fail to fully and promptly comply with a subpoena issued under this section, the Commission may apply to any judge of the superior court resident in any county where the person to whom the subpoena is issued maintains a residence or place of business for an order compelling the person to show cause why he or she should not be held in contempt of the Commission and its processes. The court shall have the power to impose punishment for acts that would constitute direct or indirect contempt if the acts occurred in an action pending in superior court.

(b) The Commission shall be exempt from the requirements of Chapter 53B of the General Statutes with regard to subpoenas issued to compel the production of a licensee's trust account records held by any financial institution. Notwithstanding that exemption, the Commission shall serve, pursuant to G.S. 1A-1, Rule 4(j) of the N.C. Rules of Civil Procedure or by certified mail to the licensee's last known address, a copy of the subpoena and notice that the subpoena has been served upon the financial institution. Service of the subpoena and notice on the licensee shall be made within 10 days following service of the subpoena on the financial institution holding the trust account records.

93A-7. Power of courts to revoke.

Whenever any person, partnership, association or corporation claiming to have been injured or damaged by the gross negligence, incompetency, fraud, dishonesty or misconduct on the part of any licensee following the calling or engaging in the business herein described and shall file suit upon such claim against such licensee in any court of record in this State and shall recover judgment thereon, such court may as part of its judgment or decree in such case, if it deem it a proper case in which so to do, order a written copy of the transcript of record in said case to be forwarded by the clerk of court to the chairman of the said Commission with a recommendation that the licensee's certificate of license be revoked.

93A-8. Penalty for violation of Chapter.

Any person violating the provisions of this Chapter shall upon conviction thereof be deemed guilty of a Class 1 misdemeanor.

93A-9. Licensing nonresidents.

An applicant from another state, which offers licensing privileges to residents of North Carolina, may be licensed by conforming to all the provisions of this Chapter and, in the discretion of the Commission, such other terms and conditions as are required of North Carolina residents applying for license in such other state; provided that the Commission may exempt from the examination prescribed in G.S. 93A-4 a broker or salesperson duly licensed in another state if a similar exemption is extended to licensed brokers and salespersons from North Carolina.

93A-10. Nonresident licensees; filing of consent as to service of process and pleadings.

Every nonresident applicant shall file an irrevocable consent that suits and actions may be commenced against such applicant in any of the courts of record of this State, by the service of any process or pleading authorized by the laws of this State in any county in which the plaintiff may reside, by serving the same on the Executive Director of the Commission, said consent stipulating and agreeing that such service of such process or pleadings on said Executive Director shall be taken and held in all courts to be valid and binding as if due service had been made personally upon the applicant in this State. This consent shall be duly acknowledged, and, if made by a corporation, shall be authenticated by its seal. An application from a corporation shall be accompanied by a duly certified copy of the resolution of the board of directors, authorizing the proper officers to execute it. In all cases where process or pleadings shall be served, under the provisions of this Chapter, upon the Executive Director of the Commission, such process or pleadings shall be served in duplicate, one of which shall be filed in the office of the Commission and the other shall be forwarded immediately by the Executive Director of the Commission, by registered mail, to the last known business address of the nonresident licensee against which such process or pleadings are directed.

93A-11. Reimbursement by real estate independent contractor of brokers' workers' compensation.

(a) Notwithstanding the provisions of G.S. 97-21 or any other provision of law, a real estate broker may include in the governing contract with a real estate salesperson whose nonemployee status is recognized pursuant to section 3508 of the United States Internal Revenue Code, 26 U.S.C. § 3508, an agreement for the salesperson to reimburse the broker for the cost of covering that salesperson under the broker's workers' compensation coverage of the broker's business.

(b) Nothing in this section shall affect a requirement under any other law to provide workers' compensation coverage or in any manner exclude from coverage any person, firm, or corporation otherwise subject to the provisions of Article 1 of Chapter 97 of the General Statutes.

Sections 93A-12 through 93A-15: Reserved for future codification purposes.

ARTICLE 2.
REAL ESTATE RECOVERY FUND.

ARTICLE 3.
PRIVATE REAL ESTATE SCHOOLS.

Interested persons may obtain a copy of Article 2 or 3 by making written request to the North Carolina Real Estate Commission.

ARTICLE 4.
TIME SHARES.

93A-39. Title.

This Article shall be known and may be cited as the "North Carolina Time Share Act."

93A-40. Registration required of time share projects; real estate salespersons license required.

(a) From and after July 1, 1984, it shall be unlawful for any person in this State to engage or assume to engage in the business of a time share salesperson without first obtaining a real estate broker or salesperson license issued by the North Carolina Real Estate Commission under the provisions of Article I of this Chapter, and it shall be unlawful for a time share developer to sell or offer to sell a time share located in this State without first obtaining a certificate of registration for the time share project to be offered for sale issued by the North Carolina Real Estate Commission under the provisions of this Article.

(b) A person responsible as general partner, corporate officer, joint venturer or sole proprietor who intentionally acts as a time share developer, allowing the offering of sale or the sale of time shares to a purchaser, without first obtaining registration of the time share project under this Article shall be guilty of a Class I felony.

93A-41. Definitions.

When used in this Article, unless the context otherwise requires, the term:

(1) "Commission" means the North Carolina Real Estate Commission;

(2) "Developer" means any person or entity which creates a time share or a time share project or program, purchases a time share for purpose of resale, or is engaged in the business of selling its own time shares and shall include any person or entity who controls, is controlled by, or is in common control with the developer which is engaged in creating or selling time shares for the developer, but a person who purchases a time share for his or her occupancy, use, and enjoyment shall not be deemed a developer;

(3) "Enrolled" means paid membership in exchange programs or membership in an exchange program evidenced by written acceptance or confirmation of membership;

(4) "Exchange company" means any person operating an exchange program;

(5) "Exchange program" means any opportunity or procedure for the assignment or exchange of time shares among purchasers in the same or other time share project;

(5a) "Independent escrow agent" means a licensed attorney located in this State or a financial institution located in this State;

(6) "Managing agent" means a person who undertakes the duties, responsibilities, and obligations of the management of a time share program;

(7) Person" means one or more natural persons, corporations, partnerships, associations, trusts, other entities, or any combination thereof;

(7a) "Project broker" means a natural person licensed as a real estate broker and designated by the developer to supervise brokers and salespersons at the time share project;

(8) "Purchaser" means any person other than a developer or lender who owns or acquires an interest or proposes to acquire an interest in a time share;

(9) "Time share" means a right to occupy a unit or any of several units during five or more separated time periods over a period of at least five years, including renewal options, whether or not coupled with a freehold estate or an estate for years in a time share project or a specified portion thereof, including, but not limited to, a vacation license, prepaid hotel reservation, club membership, limited partnership, vacation bond, or a plan or system where the right to use is awarded or apportioned on the basis of points, vouchers, split, divided, or floating use;

(9a) "Time share instrument" means an instrument transferring a time share or any interest, legal or beneficial, in a time share to a purchaser, including a contract, installment contract, lease, deed, or other instrument;

(10) "Time share program" means any arrangement for time shares whereby real property has been made subject to a time share;

(11) "Time share project" means any real property that is subject to a time share program;

(11a) "Time share registrar" means a natural person who is designated by the developer to record or cause time share instruments and lien releases to be recorded and to fulfill the other duties imposed by this Article;

(12) "Time share salesperson" means a person who sells or offers to sell on behalf of a developer a time share to a purchaser; and

(13) "Time share unit" or "unit" means the real property or real property improvement in a project which is divided into time shares and designated for separate occupancy and use.

93A-42. Time shares deemed real estate.

(a) A time share is deemed to be an interest in real estate, and shall be governed by the law of this State relating to real estate.

(b) A purchaser of a time share may in accordance with G.S. 47-18 register the time share instrument by which he or she acquired his or her interest and upon such registration shall be entitled to the protection provided by Chapter 47 of the General Statutes for the recordation of other real property instruments. A time share instrument transferring or encumbering a time share shall not be rejected for recordation because of the nature or duration of that estate, provided all other requirements necessary to make an instrument recordable are complied with.

(c) The developer shall record or cause to be recorded a time share instrument:

(1) Not less than six days nor more than 45 days following the execution of the contract of sale by the purchaser; or

(2) Not later than 180 days following the execution of the contract of sale by the purchaser, provided that all payments made by the purchaser shall be placed by the developer with an independent escrow agent upon the expiration of the 10-day escrow period provided by G.S. 93A-45(c).

(d) The independent escrow agent provided by G.S.

93A-42(c)(2) shall deposit and maintain the purchaser's payments in an insured trust or escrow account in a bank or savings and loan association located in this State. The trust or escrow account may be interest-bearing and the interest earned shall belong to the developer, if agreed upon in writing by the purchaser; provided, however, if the time share instrument is not recorded within the time periods specified in this section, then the interest earned shall belong to the purchaser. The independent escrow agent shall return all payments to the purchaser at the expiration of 180 days following the execution of the contract of sale by the purchaser, unless prior to that time the time share instrument has been recorded. However, if prior to the expiration of 180 days following the execution of the contract of sale, the developer and the purchaser provide their written consent to the independent escrow agent, the developer's obligation to record the time share instrument and the escrow period may be extended for an additional period of 120 days. Upon recordation of the time share instrument, the independent escrow agent shall pay the purchaser's funds to the developer. Upon request by the Commission, the independent escrow agent shall promptly make available to the Commission inspection of records of money held by him or her.

(e) In no event shall the developer be required to record a time share instrument if the purchaser is in default of his or her obligations.

(f) Recordation under the provisions of this section of the time share instrument shall constitute delivery of that instrument from the developer to the purchaser.

93A-43. Partition.

When a time share is owned by two or more persons as tenants in common or as joint tenants either may seek a partition by sale of that interest but no purchaser of a time share may maintain an action for partition by sale or in kind of the unit in which such time share is held.

93A-44. Public offering statement.

Each developer shall fully and conspicuously disclose in a public offering statement:

(1) The total financial obligation of the purchaser, which shall include the initial purchase price and any additional charges to which the purchaser may be subject;

(2) Any person who has or may have the right to alter, amend or add to charges to which the purchaser may be subject and the terms and conditions under which such charges may be imposed;

(3) The nature and duration of each agreement between the developer and the person managing the time share program or its facilities;

(4) The date of availability of each amenity and facility of the time share program when they are not completed at the time of sale of a time share;

(5) The specific term of the time share;

(6) The purchaser's right to cancel within five days of execution of the contract and how that right may be exercised under G.S. 93A-45;

(7) A statement that under North Carolina law an instrument conveying a time share must be recorded in the Register of Deeds Office to protect that interest; and

(8) Any other information which the Commission may by rule require.

The public offering statement shall also contain a one page cover containing a summary of the text of the statement.

93A-45. Purchaser's right to cancel; escrow; violation.

(a) A developer shall, before transfer of a time share and no later than the date of any contract of sale, provide a prospective purchaser with a copy of a public offering statement containing the information required by G.S. 93A-44. The contract of sale is voidable by the purchaser for five days after the execution of the contract. The contract shall conspicuously disclose the purchaser's right to cancel under this subsection and how that right may be exercised. The purchaser may not waive this right of cancellation. Any oral or written declaration or instrument that purports to waive this right of cancellation is void.

(b) A purchaser may elect to cancel within the time period set out in subsection (a) by hand delivering or by mailing notice to the developer or the time share salesperson. Cancellation under this section is without penalty and upon receipt of the notice all payments made prior to cancellation must be refunded immediately.

(c) Any payments received by a time share developer or time share salesperson in connection with the sale of the time share shall be immediately deposited by such developer or salesperson in a trust or escrow account in an insured bank or savings and loan association in North Carolina and shall remain in such account for 10 days or cancellation by the purchaser, whichever occurs first. Payments held in such trust or escrow accounts shall be deemed to belong to the purchaser and not the developer. In lieu of such escrow requirements, the Commission shall have the authority to accept, in its discretion, alternative financial assurances adequate to protect the purchaser's interest during the contract cancellation period, including but not limited to a surety bond, corporate bond, cash deposit or irrevocable letter of credit in an amount equal to the escrow requirements.

(d) If a developer fails to provide a purchaser to whom a time share is transferred with the statement as required by subsection (a), the purchaser, in addition to any rights to damages or other relief, is entitled to receive from the developer an amount equal to ten percent (10%) of the sales price of the time share not to exceed three thousand dollars ($3,000). A receipt signed by the purchaser stating that he or she has received the statement required by subsection (a) is prima facie evidence of delivery of such statement.

93A-46. Prizes.

An advertisement of a time share which includes the offer of a prize or other inducement shall fully comply with the provisions of Chapter 75 of the General Statutes.

93A-47. Time shares proxies.

No proxy, power of attorney or similar device given by the purchaser of a time share regarding the management of the time share program or its facilities shall exceed one year in duration, but the same may be renewed from year to year.

93A-48. Exchange programs.

(a) If a purchaser is offered the opportunity to subscribe to any exchange program, the developer shall, except as provided in subsection (b), deliver to the purchaser, prior to the execution of (i) any contract between the purchaser and the exchange company, and (ii) the sales contract, at least the following information regarding such exchange program:

(1) The name and address of the exchange company;

(2) The names of all officers, directors, and shareholders owning five percent (5%) or more of the outstanding stock of the exchange company;

(3) Whether the exchange company or any of its officers or directors has any legal or beneficial interest in any developer or managing agent for any time share project participating in the exchange program and, if so, the name and location of the time share project and the nature of the interest;

(4) Unless the exchange company is also the developer a statement that the purchaser's contract with the exchange company is a contract separate and distinct from the sales contract;

(5) Whether the purchaser's participation in the exchange program is dependent upon the continued affiliation of the time share project with the exchange program;

(6) Whether the purchaser's membership or participation, or both, in the exchange program is voluntary or mandatory;

(7) A complete and accurate description of the terms and conditions of the purchaser's contractual relationship with the exchange company and the procedure by which changes thereto may be made;

(8) A complete and accurate description of the procedure to qualify for and effectuate exchanges;

(9) A complete and accurate description of all limitations, restrictions, or priorities employed in the operation of the exchange program, including, but not limited to, limitations on exchanges based on seasonality, unit size, or levels of occupancy, expressed in boldfaced type, and, in the event that such limitations, restrictions, or priorities are not uniformly applied by the exchange program, a clear description of the manner in which they are applied;

(10) Whether exchanges are arranged on a space available basis and whether any guarantees of fulfillment of specific requests for exchanges are made by the exchange program;

(11) Whether and under what circumstances an owner, in dealing with the exchange company, may lose the use and occupancy of his or her time share in any properly applied for exchange without his or her being provided with substitute accommodations by the exchange company;

(12) The expenses, fees or range of fees for participation by owners in the exchange program, a statement whether any such fees may be altered by the exchange company, and the circumstances under which alterations may be made;

(13) The name and address of the site of each time share project or other property which is participating in the exchange program;

(14) The number of units in each project or other property participating in the exchange program which are available for occupancy and which qualify for participation in the exchange program, expressed within the following numerical groupings, 1-5, 6-10, 11-20, 21-50 and 51, and over;

(15) The number of owners with respect to each time share project or other property which are eligible to participate in the exchange program expressed within the following numerical groupings, 1-100, 101-249, 250-499, 500-999, and 1,000 and over, and a statement of the criteria used to determine those owners who are currently eligible to participate in the exchange program;

(16) The disposition made by the exchange company of time shares deposited with the exchange program by owners eligible to participate in the exchange program and not used by the exchange company in effecting exchanges;

(17) The following information which, except as provided in subsection (b) below, shall be independently audited by a certified public accountant in accordance with the standards of the Accounting Standards Board of the American Institute of Certified Public Accountants and reported for each year no later than July 1, of the succeeding year:

a. The number of owners enrolled in the exchange program and such numbers shall disclose the relationship between the exchange company and owners as being either fee paying or gratuitous in nature;

b. The number of time share projects or other properties eligible to participate in the exchange program categorized by those having a contractual relationship between the developer or the association and the exchange company and those having solely a contractual relationship between the exchange company and owners directly;

c. The percentage of confirmed exchanges, which shall be the number of exchanges confirmed by the exchange company divided by the number of exchanges properly applied for, together with a complete and accurate statement of the criteria used to determine whether an exchange requested was properly applied for;

d. The number of time shares or other intervals for which the exchange company has an outstanding obligation to provide an exchange to an owner who relinquished a time share or interval during the year in exchange for a time share or interval in any future year; and

e. The number of exchanges confirmed by the exchange company during the year; and

(18) A statement in boldfaced type to the effect that the percentage described in subparagraph (17)c. of subsection (a) is a summary of the exchange requests entered with the exchange company in the period reported and that the percentage does not indicate a purchaser's/owner's probabilities of being confirmed to any specific choice or range of choices, since availability at individual locations may vary.

The purchaser shall certify in writing to the receipt of the information required by this subsection and any other information which the Commissioners may by rule require.

(b) The information required by subdivisions (a), (2), (3), (13), (14), (15), and (17) shall be accurate as of December 31 of the year preceding the year in which the information is delivered, except for information delivered within the first 180 days of any calendar year which shall be accurate as of December 31 of the year two years preceding the year in which the information is delivered to the purchaser. The remaining information required by subsection (a) shall be accurate as of a date which is no more than 30 days prior to the date on which the information is delivered to the purchaser.

(c) In the event an exchange company offers an exchange program directly to the purchaser or owner, the exchange company shall deliver to each purchaser or owner, concurrently with the offering and prior to the execution of any contract between the purchaser or owner and the exchange company the information set forth in subsection (a) above. The requirements of this paragraph shall not apply to any renewal of a contract between an owner and an exchange company.

(d) All promotional brochures, pamphlets, advertisements, or other materials disseminated by the exchange company to purchasers in this State which contain the percentage of confirmed exchanges described in (a)(17)c. must include the statement set forth in (a)(18).

93A-49. Service of process on exchange company.

Any exchange company offering an exchange program to a purchaser shall be deemed to have made an irrevocable appointment of the Commission to receive service of lawful process in any proceeding against the exchange company arising under this Article.

93A-50. Securities laws apply.

The North Carolina Securities Act, Chapter 78A, shall also apply, in addition to the laws relating to real estate, to time shares deemed to be investment contracts or to other securities offered with or incident to a time share; provided, in the event of such applicability of the North Carolina Securities Act, any offer or sale of time shares registered under this Article shall not be subject to the provisions of G.S. 78A-24 and any real estate broker or salesperson registered under Article 1 of this Chapter shall not be subject to the provisions of G.S. 78A-36.

93A-51. Rule-making authority.

The Commission shall have the authority to adopt rules and regulations that are not inconsistent with the provisions of this Article and the General Statutes of North Carolina. The Commission may prescribe forms and procedures for submitting information to the Commission.

93A-52. Application for registration of time share project; denial of registration; renewal; reinstatement; and termination of developer's interest.

(a) Prior to the offering in this State of any time share located in this State, the developer of the time share project shall make written application to the Commission for the registration of the project. The application shall be accompanied by a fee in an amount fixed by the Commission but not to exceed fifteen hundred dollars ($1500), and shall include a description of the project, copies of proposed time share instruments including public offering statements, sale contracts, deeds, and other documents referred to therein, information pertaining to any marketing or managing entity to be employed by the developer for the sale of time shares in a time share project or the management of the project, information regarding any exchange program available to the purchaser, an irrevocable appointment of the Commission to receive service of any lawful process in any proceeding against the developer or the developer's salespersons arising under this Article, and such other information as the Commission may by rule require.

Upon receipt of a properly completed application and fee and upon a determination by the Commission that the sale and management of the time shares in the time share project will be directed and conducted by persons of good moral character, the Commission shall issue to the developer a certificate of registration authorizing the developer to offer time shares in the project for sale. The Commission shall within 15 days after receipt of an incomplete application, notify the developer by mail that the Commission has found specified deficiencies, and shall, within 45 days after the receipt of a properly completed application, either issue the certificate of registration or notify the developer by mail of any specific objections to the registration of the project. The certificate shall be prominently displayed in the office of the developer on the site of the project.

The developer shall promptly report to the Commission any and all changes in the information required to be submitted for the purpose of the registration. The developer shall also immediately furnish the Commission complete information regarding any change in its interest in a registered time share project. In the event a developer disposes of, or otherwise terminates its interest in a time share project, the developer shall certify to the Commission in writing that its interest in the time share project is terminated and shall return to the Commission for cancellation the certificate of registration.

(b) In the event the Commission finds that there is substantial reason to deny the application for registration as a time share project, the Commission shall notify the applicant that such application has been denied and shall afford the applicant an opportunity for a hearing before the Commission to show cause why the application should not be denied. In all proceedings to deny a certificate of registration, the provisions of Chapter 150B of the General Statutes shall be applicable.

(c) The acceptance by the Commission of an application for registration shall not constitute the approval of its contents or waive the authority of the Commission to take disciplinary action as provided by this Article.

(d) All certificates of registration granted and issued by the Commission under the provisions of this Article shall expire on the 30th day of June following issuance thereof, and shall become invalid after such date unless reinstated. Renewal of such certificate may be effected at any time during the month of June preceding the date of expiration of such registration upon proper application to the Commission and by the payment of a renewal fee fixed by the Commission but not to exceed one thousand five hundred dollars ($1,500) for each time share project. The developer shall, when making application for renewal, also provide a copy of the report required in G.S. 93A-48. Each certificate reinstated after the expiration date thereof shall be subject to a late filing fee of fifty dollars ($50.00) in addition to the required renewal fee. In the event a time share developer fails to reinstate the registration within 12 months after the expiration date thereof, the Commission may, in its discretion, consider the time share project as not having been previously registered, and thereby subject to the provisions of this Article relating to the issuance of an original certificate. Duplicate certificates may be issued by the Commission upon payment of a fee of one dollar ($1.00) by the registrant developer. Except as prescribed by Commission rules, all fees paid pursuant to this Article shall be nonrefundable.

93A-53. Register of applicants; roster of registrants; registered projects; financial report to Secretary of State.

(a) The Executive Director of the Commission shall keep a register of all applicants for certificates of registration, showing for each the date of application, name, business address, and whether the certificate was granted or refused.

(b) The Executive Director of the Commission shall also keep a current roster showing the name and address of all time share projects registered with the Commission. The roster shall be kept on file in the office of the Commission and be open to public inspection.

(c) On or before the first day of September of each year, the Commission shall file with the Secretary of State a copy of the roster of time share projects registered with the Commission and a report containing a complete statement of income received by the Commission in connection with the registration of time share projects for the preceding fiscal year ending June 30th attested by the affidavit of the Executive Director of the Commission. The report shall be made a part of those annual reports required under the provisions of G.S. 93A- 5.

93A-54. Disciplinary action by Commission.

(a) The Commission shall have power to take disciplinary action. Upon its own motion, or on the verified complaint of any person, the Commission may investigate the actions of any time share salesperson, developer, or project broker of a time share project registered under this Article, or any other person or entity who shall assume to act in such capacity. If the Commission finds probable cause that a time share salesperson, developer, or project broker has violated any of the provisions of this Article, the Commission may hold a hearing on the allegations of misconduct.

The Commission shall have the power to suspend or revoke at any time a real estate license issued to a time share salesperson or project broker, or a certificate of registration of a time share project issued to a developer; or to reprimand or censure such salesperson, developer, or project broker; or to fine such developer in the amount of five hundred dollars ($500.00) for each violation of this Article, if, after a hearing, the Commission adjudges either the salesperson, developer, or project broker to be guilty of:

(1) Making any willful or negligent misrepresentation or any willful or negligent omission of material fact about any time share or time share project;

(2) Making any false promises of a character likely to influence, persuade, or induce;

(3) Pursuing a course of misrepresentation or making of false promises through agents, salesperson, advertising or otherwise;

(4) Failing, within a reasonable time, to account for all money received from others in a time share transaction, and failing to remit such monies as may be required in G.S. 93A- 45 of this Article;

(5) Acting as a time share salesperson or time share developer in a manner as to endanger the interest of the public;

(6) Paying a commission, salary, or other valuable consideration to any person for acts or services performed in violation of this Article;

(7) Any other conduct which constitutes improper, fraudulent, or dishonest dealing;

(8) Performing or undertaking to perform any legal service as set forth in G.S. 84-2.1, or any other acts not specifically set forth in that section;

(9) Failing to deposit and maintain in a trust or escrow account in an insured bank or savings and loan association in North Carolina all money received from others in a time share transaction as may be required in G.S. 93A-45 of this Article or failing to place with an independent escrow agent the funds of a time share purchaser when required by G.S. 93A-42(c);

(10) Failing to deliver to a purchaser a public offering statement containing the information required by G.S. 93A-44 and any other disclosures that the Commission may by regulation require;

(11) Failing to comply with the provisions of Chapter 75 of the General Statutes in the advertising or promotion of time shares for sale, or failing to assure such compliance by persons engaged on behalf of a developer;

(12) Failing to comply with the provisions of G.S. 93A-48 in furnishing complete and accurate information to purchasers concerning any exchange program which may be offered to such purchaser;

(13) Making any false or fraudulent representation on an application for registration;

(14) Violating any rule or regulation promulgated by the Commission;

(15) Failing to record or cause to be recorded a time share instrument as required by G.S. 93A-42(c), or failing to provide a purchaser the protection against liens required by G.S. 93A-57(a); or

(16) Failing as a time share project broker to exercise reasonable and adequate supervision of the conduct of sales at his or her project or location by the brokers and salespersons under his or her control.

(a1) The clear proceeds of fines collected pursuant to subsection (a) of this section shall be remitted to the Civil Penalty and Forfeiture Fund in accordance with G.S. 115C-457.2.

(b) Following a hearing, the Commission shall also have power to suspend or revoke any certificate of registration issued under the provisions of this Article or to reprimand or censure any developer when the registrant has been convicted or has entered a plea of guilty or no contest upon which final judgment is entered by a court of competent jurisdiction in this State, or any other state, of the criminal offenses of: embezzlement, obtaining money under false pretense, fraud, forgery, conspiracy to defraud, or any other offense involving moral turpitude which would reasonably affect the developer's performance in the time share business.

(c) The Commission may appear in its own name in superior court in actions for injunctive relief to prevent any person or entity from violating the provisions of this Article or rules promulgated by the Commission. The superior court shall have the power to grant these injunctions even if criminal prosecution has been or may be instituted as a result of the violations, or regardless of whether the person or entity has been registered by the Commission.

(d) Each developer shall maintain or cause to be maintained complete records of every time share transaction including records pertaining to the deposit, maintenance, and withdrawal of money required to be held in a trust or escrow account, or as otherwise required by the Commission, under G.S. 93A-45 of this Article. The Commission may inspect these records periodically without prior notice and may also inspect these records whenever the Commission determines that they are pertinent to an investigation of any specific complaint against a registrant.

(e) When a licensee is accused of any act, omission, or misconduct under this Article which would subject the licensee to disciplinary action, the licensee may, with the consent and approval of the Commission, surrender his or her or its license and all the rights and privileges pertaining to it for a period of time to be established by the Commission. A licensee who surrenders his or her or its license shall not be eligible for, or submit any application for, licensure as a real estate broker or salesperson or registration of a time share project during the period of license surrender. For the purposes of this section, the term licensee shall include a time share developer.

93A-55. Private enforcement.

The provisions of the Article shall not be construed to limit in any manner the right of a purchaser or other person injured by a violation of this Article to bring a private action.

93A-56. Penalty for violation of Article.

Except as provided in G.S. 93A-40(b) and G.S. 93A-58, any person violating the provisions of this Article shall be guilty of a Class 1 misdemeanor.

93A-57. Release of liens.

(a) Prior to any recordation of the instrument transferring a time share, the developer shall record and furnish notice to the purchaser of a release or subordination of all liens affecting that time share, or shall provide a surety bond or insurance against the lien from a company acceptable to the Commission as provided for liens on real estate in this State, or such underlying lien document shall contain a provision wherein the lienholder subordinates its rights to that of a time share purchaser who fully complies with all of the provisions and terms of the contract of sale.

(b) Unless a time share owner or a time share owner who is his or her predecessor in title agree otherwise with the lienor, if a lien other than a mortgage or deed of trust becomes effective against more than one time share in a time share project, any time share owner is entitled to a release of his or her time share from a lien upon payment of the amount of the lien attributable to his or her time share. The amount of the payment must be proportionate to the ratio that the time share owner's liability bears to the liabilities of all time share owners whose interests are subject to the lien. Upon receipt of payment, the lien holder shall promptly deliver to the time share owner a release of the lien covering that time share. After payment, the managing agent may not assess or have a lien against that time share for any portion of the expenses incurred in connection with that lien.

93A-58. Registrar required; criminal penalties; project broker.

(a) Every developer of a registered project shall, by affidavit filed with the Commission, designate a natural person to serve as time share registrar for its registered projects. The registrar shall be responsible for the recordation of time share instruments and the release of liens required by G.S. 93A-42(c) and G.S. 93A-57(a). A developer may, from time to time, change the designated time share registrar by proper filing with the Commission and by otherwise complying with this subsection. No sales or offers to sell shall be made until the registrar is designated for a time share project.

The registrar has the duty to ensure that the provisions of this Article are complied with in a time share project for which he or she is registrar. No registrar shall record a time share instrument except as provided by this Article.

(b) A time share registrar shall be guilty of a Class I felony if he or she knowingly or recklessly fails to record or cause to be recorded a time share instrument as required by this Article.

A person responsible as general partner, corporate officer, joint venturer or sole proprietor of the developer of a time share project shall be guilty of a Class I felony if he or she intentionally allows the offering for sale or the sale of time share to purchasers without first designating a time share registrar.

(c) The developer shall designate for each project and other locations where time shares are sold or offered for sale a project broker. The project broker shall act as supervising broker for all persons licensed as salespersons at the project or other location and shall directly, personally, and actively supervise all persons licensed as brokers or salespersons at the project or other location in a manner to reasonably ensure that the sale of time shares will be conducted in accordance with the provisions of this Chapter.

93A-59. Preservation of time share purchaser's claims and defenses.

(a) For one year following the execution of an instrument of indebtedness for the purchase of a time share, the purchaser of a time share may assert against the seller, assignee of the seller, or other holder of the instrument of indebtedness, any claims or defenses available against the developer or the original seller, and the purchaser may not waive the right to assert these claims or defenses in connection with a time share purchase. Any recovery by the purchaser on a claim asserted against an assignee of the seller or other holder of the instrument of indebtedness shall not exceed the amount paid by the purchaser under the instrument. A holder shall be the person or entity with the rights of a holder as set forth in G.S. 25-3-301.

(b) Every instrument of indebtedness for the purchase of a time share shall set forth the following provision in a clear and conspicuous manner:

"NOTICE: FOR A PERIOD OF ONE YEAR FOLLOWING THE EXECUTION OF THIS INSTRUMENT OF INDEBTEDNESS, ANY HOLDER OF THIS INSTRUMENT OF INDEBTEDNESS IS SUBJECT TO ALL CLAIMS AND DEFENSES WHICH THE PURCHASER COULD ASSERT AGAINST THE SELLER OF THE TIME SHARE. RECOVERY BY THE PURCHASER SHALL NOT EXCEED AMOUNTS PAID BY THE PURCHASER UNDER THIS INSTRUMENT."

Sections 93A-60 through 93A-69: Reserved for future codification purposes.

Article 5.
Real Estate Appraisers.
[Repealed]

NORTH CAROLINA REAL ESTATE COMMISSION RULES

CHAPTER 93A

Statutory Authority: Sections 93A-3(c), 93A-4(d), 93A-33, and 93A-51 of the
North Carolina Real Estate License Law; and the North Carolina Administrative Procedures Act.

NORTH CAROLINA ADMINISTRATIVE CODE
TITLE 21
OCCUPATIONAL LICENSING BOARDS
CHAPTER 58
REAL ESTATE COMMISSION

CHAPTER 58
REAL ESTATE COMMISSION
Subchapter 58A
Real Estate Brokers and Salespersons

SECTION A.0100
GENERAL BROKERAGE

A.0101 Proof of Licensure

(a) The annual license renewal pocket card issued by the Commission to each licensee shall be retained by the licensee as evidence of licensure. Each licensee shall carry his or her pocket card on his or her person at all times while engaging in real estate brokerage and shall produce the card as proof of licensure whenever requested.

(b) The principal broker of a firm shall retain the firm's renewal pocket card at the firm and shall produce it upon request as proof of firm licensure as required by Rule .0502(i)(3).

(c) Every licensed real estate business entity or firm shall prominently display its license certificate or facsimile thereof in each office maintained by the entity or firm. A broker-in-charge shall also prominently display his or her license certificate in the office where he or she is broker-in-charge.

A.0102 Branch Office (Repealed)

A.0103 Licensee Name and Address

Upon initial licensure and at all times thereafter, every licensee shall assure that the Commission has on record the licensee's current personal name, firm name, trade name, residence address and firm address. Every licensee shall notify the Commission in writing of each change of personal name, firm name, trade name, residence address and firm address within ten days of said change. All addresses shall be sufficiently descriptive to enable the Commission to correspond with and locate the licensee.

A.0104 Agency Agreements and Disclosure

(a) Every agreement for brokerage services in a real estate transaction shall be in writing. Every agreement for brokerage services between a broker and an owner of the property to be the subject of a transaction must be in writing from the time of its formation. Every agreement for brokerage services between a broker and a buyer or tenant shall be express and shall be reduced to writing not later than the time one of the parties makes an offer to purchase, sell, rent, lease, or exchange real estate to another. However, every agreement between a broker and a buyer or tenant which seeks to bind the buyer or tenant for a period of time or to restrict the buyer's or tenant's right to work with other agents or without an agent shall be in writing from its for-

mation. A broker or salesperson shall not continue to represent a buyer or tenant without a written agreement when such agreement is required by this rule. Every written agreement for brokerage services of any kind in a real estate sales transaction shall provide for its existence for a definite period of time and shall provide for its termination without prior notice at the expiration of that period, except that an agency agreement between a landlord and broker to procure tenants for the landlord's property may allow for automatic renewal so long as the landlord may terminate with notice at the end of any contract period and any subsequent renewals.

(b) Every listing agreement, written buyer agency agreement or other written agreement for brokerage services in a real estate sales transaction shall contain the following provision: The broker shall conduct all his brokerage activities in regard to this agreement without respect to the race, color, religion, sex, national origin, handicap or familial status of any buyer, prospective buyer, seller or prospective seller. The provision shall be set forth in a clear and conspicuous manner which shall distinguish it from other provisions of the agreement. For the purposes of this Rule, the term, familial status, shall be defined as it is in G.S. 41A-3(1b).

(c) In every real estate sales transaction, a broker or salesperson shall, at first substantial contact directly with a prospective buyer or seller, provide the prospective buyer or seller with a copy of the publication "Working with Real Estate Agents," review it with him or her, and determine whether the agent will act as the agent of the buyer or seller in the transaction. If the first substantial contact with a prospective buyer or seller occurs by telephone or other electronic means of communication where it is not practical to provide the "Working with Real Estate Agents" publication, the broker or salesperson shall at the earliest opportunity thereafter, but in no event later than three days from the date of first substantial contact, mail or otherwise transmit a copy of the publication to the prospective buyer or seller and review it with him or her at the earliest practicable opportunity thereafter.

(d) A real estate broker or salesperson representing one party in a transaction shall not undertake to represent another party in the transaction without the written authority of each party. Such written authority must be obtained upon the formation of the relationship except when a buyer or tenant is represented by a broker without a written agreement in conformity with the requirements of subsection (a) of this rule. Under such circumstances, the written authority for dual agency must be reduced to writing not later than the time that one of the parties represented by the broker or salesperson makes an offer to purchase, sell, rent, lease, or exchange real estate to another party.

(e) In every real estate sales transaction, a broker or salesperson working directly with a prospective buyer as a seller's agent or subagent shall disclose in writing to the prospective buyer at the first substantial contact with the prospective buyer that the broker or salesperson represents the interests of the seller. If the first substantial contact occurs by telephone or by means of other electronic communication where it is not practical to provide written disclosure, the broker or salesperson shall immediately disclose by similar means whom he represents and shall immediately, but in no event later than three days from the date of first substantial contact, mail or otherwise transmit a copy of the written disclosure to the buyer.

(f) In every real estate sales transaction, a broker or salesperson representing a buyer shall, at the initial contact with the seller or seller's agent, disclose to the seller or seller's agent that the broker or salesperson represents the buyer's interests. In addition, in every real estate sales transaction other than auctions, the broker or salesperson shall, no later than the time of delivery of an offer to the seller or seller's agent, provide the seller or seller's agent with a written confirmation disclosing that he represents the interests of the buyer. The written confirmation may be made in the buyer's offer to purchase.

(g) The provisions of Paragraphs (c), (d) and (e) of this Rule shall not apply to real estate licensees representing sellers in auction sales transactions.

(h) A broker or salesperson representing a buyer in an auction sale transaction shall, no later than the time of execution of a written agreement memorializing the buyer's contract to purchase, provide the seller or seller's agent with a written confirmation disclosing that he represents the interests of the buyer. The written confirmation may be made in the written agreement.

(i) A firm which represents more than one party in the same real estate transaction is a dual agent and, through the brokers and salespersons associated with the firm, shall disclose its dual agency to the parties.

(j) When a firm represents both the buyer and seller in the same real estate sales transaction, the firm may, with the prior express approval of its buyer and seller clients, designate one or more individual brokers or salespersons associated with the firm to represent only the interests of the seller and one or more other individual brokers and salespersons associated with the firm to represent only the interests of the buyer in the transaction. The authority for designated agency must be reduced to writing not later than the time that the parties are required to reduce their dual agency agreement to writing in accordance with subsection (d) of this

rule. An individual broker or salesperson shall not be so designated and shall not undertake to represent only the interests of one party if the broker or salesperson has actually received confidential information concerning the other party in connection with the transaction. A broker-in-charge shall not act as a designated agent for a party in a real estate sales transaction when a salesperson under his or her supervision will act as a designated agent for another party with a competing interest.

(k) When a firm acting as a dual agent designates an individual broker or salesperson to represent the seller, the broker or salesperson so designated shall represent only the interest of the seller and shall not, without the seller's permission, disclose to the buyer or a broker or salesperson designated to represent the buyer:

(1) that the seller may agree to a price, terms, or any conditions of sale other than those established by the seller;

(2) the seller's motivation for engaging in the transaction unless disclosure is otherwise required by statute or rule; and

(3) any information about the seller which the seller has identified as confidential unless disclosure of the information is otherwise required by statute or rule.

(l) When a firm acting as a dual agent designates an individual broker or salesperson to represent the buyer, the broker or the salesperson so designated shall represent only the interest of the buyer and shall not, without the buyer's permission, disclose to the seller or a broker or salesperson designated to represent the seller:

(1) that the buyer may agree to a price, terms, or any conditions of sale other than those offered by the buyer;

(2) the buyer's motivation for engaging in the transaction unless disclosure is otherwise required by statute or rule; and

(3) any information about the buyer which the buyer has identified as confidential unless disclosure of the information is otherwise required by statute or rule.

(m) A broker or salesperson designated to represent a buyer or seller in accordance with Paragraph (j) of this Rule shall disclose the identity of all of the brokers and salespersons so designated to both the buyer and the seller. The disclosure shall take place no later than the presentation of the first offer to purchase or sell.

(n) When an individual broker or salesperson represents both the buyer and seller in the same real estate sales transaction pursuant to a written agreement authorizing dual agency, the parties may provide in the written agreement that the broker or salesperson shall not disclose the following information about one party to the other without permission from the party about whom the information pertains:

(1) that a party may agree to a price, terms or any conditions of sale other than those offered;

(2) the motivation of a party for engaging in the transaction, unless disclosure is otherwise required by statute or rule; and

(3) any information about a party which that party has identified as confidential, unless disclosure is otherwise required by statute or rule.

A.0105 Advertising

(a) Blind Ads. A licensee shall not advertise the sale, purchase, exchange, rent or lease of real estate, for another or others, in a manner indicating the offer to sell, purchase, exchange, rent, or lease is being made by the licensee's principal only. Every such advertisement shall clearly indicate that it is the advertisement of a broker or brokerage firm and shall not be confined to publication of only a post office box number, telephone number, or street address.

(b) Registration of Assumed Name. In the event that any licensee shall advertise in any manner using a firm name or an assumed name which does not set forth the surname of the licensee, the licensee shall first file the appropriate certificate with the office of the county register of deeds in compliance with G.S. 66-68 and notify the Commission in writing of the use of such a firm name or assumed name.

(c) Authority to Advertise.

(1) A salesperson shall not advertise the sale, purchase, exchange, rent or lease of real estate for another or others without his or her broker's consent and without including in the advertisement the name of the broker or firm with whom the salesperson is associated.

(2) A licensee shall not advertise or display a "for sale" or "for rent" sign on any real estate without the consent of the owner or his or her authorized agent.

(d) Business names. A licensee shall not include the name of a salesperson or an unlicensed person in the name of a sole proprietorship, partnership or non-corporate business formed for the purpose of real estate brokerage.

A.0106 Delivery of Instruments

(a) Except as provided in Paragraph (b) of this Rule, every broker or salesperson shall immediately, but in no event later than five days from the date of execution, deliver to the parties thereto copies of any required written agency agreement, contract, offer, lease, or option affecting real property.

(b) A broker or salesperson may be relieved of his or her duty under Paragraph (a) of this Rule to deliver copies of leases or rental agreements to the property owner, if the broker:

(1) obtains the express written authority of the property owner to enter into and retain copies of leases or rental agreements on behalf of the property owner;

(2) executes the lease or rental agreement on a pre-printed form, the material terms of which may not be changed by the broker without prior approval by the property owner except as may be required by law;

(3) promptly provides a copy of the lease or rental agreement to the property owner upon reasonable request; and

(4) delivers to the property owner within 45 days following the date of execution of the lease or rental agreement, an accounting which identifies the leased property and which sets forth the names of the tenants, the rental rates and rents collected.

A.0107 Handling and Accounting of Funds

(a) All monies received by a licensee acting in his or her fiduciary capacity shall be deposited in a trust or escrow account maintained by a broker not later than three banking days following receipt of such monies except that earnest money deposits paid by means other than currency which are received on offers to purchase real estate and tenant security deposits paid by means other than currency which are received in connection with real estate leases shall be deposited in a trust or escrow account not later than three banking days following acceptance of such offer to purchase or lease; the date of acceptance of such offer to purchase or lease shall be set forth in the purchase or lease agreement. All monies received by a salesperson shall be delivered immediately to the broker by whom he or she is employed.

(b) In the event monies received by a licensee while acting in a fiduciary capacity are deposited in a trust or escrow account which bears interest, the broker having custody over such monies shall first secure from all parties having an interest in the monies written authorization for the deposit of the monies in an interest-bearing account. Such authorization shall specify how and to whom the interest will be disbursed, and, if contained in an offer, contract, lease, or other transaction instrument, such authorization shall be set forth in a clear and conspicuous manner which shall distinguish it from other provisions of the instrument.

(c) Closing statements shall be furnished to the buyer and the seller in the transaction at the closing or not more than five days after closing.

(d) Trust or escrow accounts shall be so designated by the bank or savings and loan association in which the account is located, and all deposit tickets and checks drawn on said account as well as the monthly bank statement for the account shall bear the words "Trust Account" or "Escrow Account."

(e) A licensee shall maintain and retain records sufficient to identify the ownership of all funds belonging to others. Such records shall be sufficient to show proper deposit of such funds in a trust or escrow account and to verify the accuracy and proper use of the trust or escrow account. The required records shall include but not be limited to:

(1) bank statements.

(2) canceled checks which shall be referenced to the corresponding journal entry or check stub entries and to the corresponding sales transaction ledger sheets or for rental transactions, the corresponding property or owner ledger sheets. Checks shall clearly identify the payee and shall bear a notation identifying the purpose of the disbursement. When a check is used to disburse funds for more than one sales transaction, owner, or property, the check shall bear a notation identifying each sales transaction, owner, or property for which disbursement is made, including the amount disbursed for each, and the corresponding sales transaction, property, or owner ledger entries. When necessary, the check notation may refer to the required information recorded on a supplemental disbursement worksheet which shall be cross-referenced to the corresponding check. In lieu of retaining canceled checks, a licensee may retain digitally imaged copies of the canceled checks provided that such images are legible reproductions of the front and back of the original instruments with no more than four (4) instruments per page and no smaller images than 2.25 x 5.0 inches, and provided that the licensee's bank retains the original checks on file for a period of at least five (5) years and makes them available to the licensee and the Commission upon request.

(3) deposit tickets. For a sales transaction, the deposit ticket shall identify the purpose and remitter of the funds deposited, the property, the parties involved, and a reference to the corresponding sales transaction ledger entry. For a rental transaction, the deposit ticket shall identify the purpose and remitter of the funds deposited, the tenant, and the corresponding property or owner ledger entry. For deposits of funds belonging to or collected on behalf of a property owner association, the deposit ticket shall identify the property or property interest for which the payment is made, the property or interest owner, the remitter, and the purpose of the payment. When a single deposit ticket is used to deposit funds collected for more than one sales transaction, property owner, or property, the required information shall be recorded on the ticket for each sales transaction, owner, or property, or the ticket may refer to the same information recorded on a supplemental deposit worksheet which shall be cross-referenced to the corresponding deposit ticket.

(4) a payment record sheet for each property or interest for which funds are collected and deposited into a property owner association trust account as required by Subsection (i) of this Rule. Payment record sheets shall identify the amount, date, remitter, and purpose of payments received, the amount and nature of the obligation for which payments are made, and the amount of any balance due or delinquency.

(5) a separate ledger sheet for each sales transaction and for each property or owner of property managed by the broker identifying the property, the parties to the transaction, the amount, date, and purpose of the deposits and from whom received, the amount, date, check number, and purpose of disbursements and to whom paid, and the running balance of funds on deposit for the particular sales transaction or, in a rental transaction, the particular property or owner of property. Monies held as tenant security deposits in connection with rental transactions may be accounted for on a separate tenant security deposit ledger for each property or owner of property managed by the broker. For each security deposit the tenant security deposit ledger shall identify the remitter, the date the deposit was paid, the amount, the tenant, landlord, and subject property. For each disbursement of tenant security deposit monies, the ledger shall identify the check number, amount, payee, date, and purpose of the disbursement. The ledger shall also show a running balance. When tenant security deposit monies are accounted for on a separate ledger as provided herein, deposit tickets, canceled checks and supplemental worksheets shall reference the corresponding tenant security deposit ledger entries when appropriate.

(6) a journal or check stubs identifying in chronological sequence each bank deposit and disbursement of monies to and from the trust or escrow account, including the amount and date of each deposit and an appropriate reference to the corresponding deposit ticket and any supplemental deposit worksheet, and the amount, date, check number, and purpose of disbursements and to whom paid. The journal or check stubs shall also show a running balance for all funds in the account.

(7) copies of contracts, leases and management agreements.

(8) closing statements and property management statements.

(9) covenants, bylaws, minutes, management agreements and periodic statements relating to the management of a property owner association.

(10) invoices, bills, and contracts paid from the trust account, and any documents not otherwise described

herein necessary and sufficient to verify and explain record entries.

Records of all receipts and disbursements of trust or escrow monies shall be maintained in such a manner as to create a clear audit trail from deposit tickets and canceled checks to check stubs or journals and to the ledger sheets. Ledger sheets and journals or check stubs must be reconciled to the trust or escrow account bank statements on a monthly basis. To be sufficient, records of trust or escrow monies must include a worksheet for each such monthly reconciliation showing the ledger sheets, journals or check stubs, and bank statements to be in agreement and balance.

(f) All trust or escrow account records shall be made available for inspection by the Commission or its authorized representatives in accordance with Rule 58A .0108.

(g) In the event of a dispute between the seller and buyer or landlord and tenant over the return or forfeiture of any deposit other than a residential tenant security deposit held by a licensee, the licensee shall retain said deposit in a trust or escrow account until the licensee has obtained a written release from the parties consenting to its disposition and or until disbursement is ordered by a court of competent jurisdiction. If it appears to a broker holding a disputed deposit that a party has abandoned his or her claim, the broker may disburse the money to the other claiming parties according to their written agreement provided that the broker first makes a reasonable effort to notify the party who has apparently abandoned his or her claim and provides that party with an opportunity to renew his or her claim to the disputed funds. Tenant security deposit monies shall be disposed of in accordance with the requirements of N.C.G.S. 42-50 through 56 and N.C.G.S. 42A-18.

(h) A broker may transfer earnest money deposits in his or her possession collected in connection with a sales transaction from his or her trust account to the closing attorney or other settlement agent not more than ten days prior to the anticipated settlement date. A licensee shall not disburse prior to settlement any earnest money in his or her possession for any other purpose without the written consent of the parties.

(i) The funds of a property owner association, when collected, maintained, disbursed or otherwise controlled by a licensee, are trust monies and shall be treated as such in the manner required by this Rule. . Such funds must be deposited into and maintained in a trust or escrow account or accounts dedicated exclusively for funds belonging to a single property owners association and may not be commingled with funds belonging to other property owner associations or other persons or parties. A licensee who undertakes to act as manager of a property owner association or as the custodian of funds belonging to a property owner association shall provide the association with periodic statements which report the balance of association funds in the licens-

ee's possession or control and which account for the funds the licensee has received and disbursed on behalf of the association. Such statements must be made in accordance with the licensee's agreement with the association, but in no event shall the statements be made less frequently than every 90 days.

(j) Every licensee shall safeguard the money or property of others coming into his or her possession in a manner consistent with the requirements of the Real Estate License Law and the rules adopted by the Commission. A licensee shall not convert the money or property of others to his or her own use, apply such money or property to a purpose other than that for which it was paid or entrusted to him or her, or permit or assist any other person in the conversion or misapplication of such money or property.

(k) In addition to the records required by subdivision (e) of this rule, a licensee acting as agent for the landlord of a residential property used for vacation rentals shall create and maintain a subsidiary ledger sheet for each property or owner of such properties onto which all funds collected and disbursed are identified in categories by purpose. On a monthly basis, the licensee shall reconcile the subsidiary ledger sheet to the corresponding property or property owner ledger sheet.

A.0108 Retention of Records

Licensees shall retain records of all sales, rental, and other transactions conducted in such capacity, whether the transaction is pending, completed or terminated prior to its successful conclusion. The licensee shall retain such records for three years after all funds held by the licensee in connection with the transaction have been disbursed to the proper party or parties or until the successful or unsuccessful conclusion of the transaction, whichever occurs later. Such records shall include contracts of sale, written leases, agency contracts, options, offers to purchase, trust or escrow records, earnest money receipts, disclosure documents, closing statements and any other records pertaining to real estate transactions. All such records shall be made available for inspection by the Commission or its authorized representatives without prior notice.

A.0109 Brokerage Fees and Compensation

(a) A licensee shall not receive, either directly or indirectly, any commission, rebate or other valuable consideration of more than nominal value from a vendor or a supplier of goods and services for an expenditure made on behalf of the licensee's principal in a real estate transaction without the written consent of the licensee's principal.

(b) A licensee shall not receive, either directly or indirectly, any commission, rebate or other valuable consideration of more than nominal value for services which the licensee recommends, procures, or arranges relating to a real estate transaction for any party, without full disclosure to such party; provided, however, that nothing in this Rule shall be construed to permit a licensee to accept any fee, kickback or other valuable consideration that is prohibited by the Real Estate Settlement Procedures Act of 1974 (12 USC 2601 et. seq.) or any rules and regulations promulgated by the United States Department of Housing and Urban Development pursuant to such Act.

(c) The Commission shall not act as a board of arbitration and shall not compel parties to settle disputes concerning such matters as the rate of commissions, the division of commissions, pay of salespersons, and similar matters.

(d) A licensee shall not undertake in any manner, any arrangement, contract, plan or other course of conduct, to compensate or share compensation with unlicensed persons or entities for any acts performed in North Carolina for which licensure by the Commission is required.

(e) A broker may pay or promise to pay consideration to a travel agent in return for procuring a tenant for a vacation rental as defined by the Vacation Rental Act if:

(1) the travel agent only introduces the tenant to the broker, but does not otherwise engage in any activity which would require a real estate license;

(2) the introduction by the travel agent is made in the regular course of the travel agent's business; and

(3) the travel agent has not solicited, handled or received any monies in connection with the vacation rental.

For the purpose of this rule, a travel agent is any person or entity who is primarily engaged in the business of acting as an intermediary between persons who purchase air, land, and ocean travel services and the providers of such services. A travel agent is also any other person or entity who is permitted to handle and sell tickets for air travel by the Airlines Reporting Corporation (ARC). Payments authorized hereunder shall be made only after the conclusion of the vacation rental tenancy. Prior to the creation of a binding vacation rental agreement, the broker shall provide a tenant introduced by a travel agent a written statement advising him to rely only upon the agreement and the broker's representations about the transaction. The broker shall keep for a period of three years records of a payment made to a travel agent including records identifying the tenant, the travel agent and their addresses, the property and dates of the tenancy, and the amount paid.

A.0110 Broker-in-Charge

(a) Every real estate firm shall designate a broker to serve as the broker-in-charge at its principal office and a broker to serve as broker-in-charge at any branch office. No broker shall be broker-in-charge of more than one office or branch office. If a firm shares office space with one or more other firms, one broker may serve as broker-in-charge of each firm at that location. No office or branch office of a firm shall have more than one designated broker-in-charge. A broker who is a sole proprietor shall designate himself or herself as a broker-in-charge if the broker engages in any transaction where the broker is required to deposit and maintain monies belonging to others in a trust account, engages in advertising or promoting his or her services as a broker in any manner, or has one or more brokers or salespersons affiliated with him or her in the real estate business. Each broker-in-charge shall make written notification of his or her status as broker-in-charge to the Commission on a form prescribed by the Commission within 10 days following the broker's designation as broker-in-charge. The broker-in-charge shall assume the responsibility at his or her office for:

(1) the retention and display of current license renewal pocket cards by all brokers and salespersons employed at the office for which he or she is broker-in-charge; the proper display of licenses at such office in accordance with Rule .0101 of this Section; and assuring that each licensee employed at the office has complied with Rules .0503, .0504 and .0506 of this Subchapter;

(2) the proper notification to the Commission of any change of business address or trade name of the firm and the registration of any assumed business name adopted by the firm for its use;

(3) the proper conduct of advertising by or in the name of the firm at such office;

(4) the proper maintenance at such office of the trust or escrow account of the firm and the records pertaining thereto;

(5) the proper retention and maintenance of records relating to transactions conducted by or on behalf of the firm at such office, including those required to be retained pursuant to Rule .0108 of this Section;

(6) the proper supervision of salespersons associated with or engaged on behalf of the firm at such office in accordance with the requirements of Rule .0506 of this Subchapter;

(7) the verification to the Commission of the experience of any salesperson at such office who may be applying for licensure as a broker; and

(8) the proper supervision of all brokers and salespersons employed at the office for which he or she is broker-in-charge with respect to adherence to agency agreement and disclosure requirements.

(b) When used in this Rule, the term:

(1) "Branch Office" means any office in addition to the principal office of a broker which is operated in connection with the broker's real estate business; and

(2) "Office" means any place of business where acts are performed for which a real estate license is required.

(c) A broker-in-charge must continuously maintain his or her license on active status.

(d) Each broker-in-charge shall notify the Commission in writing of any change in his or her status as broker-in-charge within 10 days following the change. Upon written request of a salesperson within five years after termination of his or her association with a broker-in-charge, the broker-in-charge shall provide the salesperson, in a form prescribed by the Commission, an accurate written statement regarding the number and type of properties listed, sold, bought, leased, or rented for others by the salesperson while under the supervision of the broker-in-charge.

(e) A licensed real estate firm which demonstrates on a form prescribed by the Commission that it has qualified for licensure solely for the purpose of receiving compensation for brokerage services furnished by its principal broker through another firm, and that no person is affiliated with it other than its principal broker, shall not be required to designate a broker-in-charge.

(f) Every broker-in-charge shall complete the Commission's broker-in-charge course at least once every five years following the effective date of this Rule. Every broker designated as a broker-in-charge after October 1, 2000 shall complete the Commission's broker-in-charge course within 120 days following designation and at least once every five years thereafter for so long as he or she remains broker-in-charge. If a broker who is a designated broker-in-charge fails to complete the broker-in-charge course within the prescribed time period, the broker-in-charge status of that broker shall be immediately terminated, and the broker must complete the broker-in-charge course before he or she may again be designated as a broker-in-charge.

A.0111 Drafting Legal Instruments

(a) A broker or salesperson acting as an agent in a real estate transaction shall not draft offers, sales contracts, options, leases, promissory notes, deeds, deeds of trust or other legal instruments by which the rights of others are secured; however, a broker or salesperson may complete preprinted offer, option contract, sales contract and lease forms in real estate transactions when authorized or directed to do so by the parties.

(b) A broker or salesperson may use electronic, computer, or word processing equipment to store preprinted offer and sales contract forms which comply with Rule .0112, as well as preprinted option and lease forms, and may use such equipment to complete and print offer, contract and lease documents. Provided, however, a broker or salesperson may not alter the form before it is presented to the par-

ties. If the parties propose to delete or change any word or provision in the form, the form must be marked to indicate the change or deletion made. The language of the form shall not be modified, rewritten, or changed by the broker or salesperson or their clerical employees unless directed to do so by the parties.

(c) Nothing contained in this rule shall be construed to prohibit a broker or salesperson from making written notes, memoranda or correspondence recording the negotiations of the parties to a real estate transaction when such notes, memoranda or correspondence do not themselves constitute binding agreements or other legal instruments.

A.0112 Offers and Sales Contracts

(a) A broker or salesperson acting as an agent in a real estate transaction shall not use a preprinted offer or sales contract form unless the form describes or specifically requires the entry of the following information:

(1) the names of the buyer and seller;

(2) a legal description of the real property sufficient to identify and distinguish it from all other property;

(3) an itemization of any personal property to be included in the transaction;

(4) the purchase price and manner of payment;

(5) any portion of the purchase price that is to be paid by a promissory note, including the amount, interest rate, payment terms, whether or not the note is to be secured, and other material terms;

(6) any portion of the purchase price that is to be paid by the assumption of an existing loan, including the amount of such loan, costs to be paid by the buyer or seller, the interest rate and number of discount points and a condition that the buyer must be able to qualify for the assumption of the loan and must make every reasonable effort to quality for the assumption of the loan;

(7) the amount of earnest money, if any, the method of payment, the name of the broker or firm that will serve as escrow agent, an acknowledgment of earnest money receipt by the escrow agent, and the criteria for determining disposition of the earnest money, including disputed earnest money, consistent with Commission Rule .0107 of this Subchapter;

(8) any loan that must be obtained by the buyer as a condition of the contract, including the amount and type of loan, interest rate and number of discount points, loan term, loan commitment date, and who shall pay loan closing costs; and a condition that the buyer shall make every reasonable effort to obtain the loan;

(9) a general statement of the buyer's intended use of

the property and a condition that such use must not be prohibited by private restriction or governmental regulation;

(10) the amount and purpose of any special assessment to which the property is subject and the responsibility of the parties for any unpaid charges;

(11) the date for closing and transfer of possession;

(12) the signatures of the buyer and seller;

(13) the date of offer and acceptance;

(14) a provision that title to the property must be delivered at closing by general warranty deed and must be fee simple marketable title, free of all encumbrances except ad valorem taxes for the current year, utility easements, and any other encumbrances specifically approved by the buyer, or a provision otherwise describing the estate to be conveyed, and encumbrances, and the form of conveyance;

(15) the items to be prorated or adjusted at closing;

(16) who shall pay closing expenses;

(17) the buyer's right to inspect the property prior to closing and who shall pay for repairs and improvements, if any;

(18) a provision that the property shall at closing be in substantially the same condition as on the date of the offer (reasonable wear and tear excepted), or a description of the required property condition at closing; and

(19) a provision setting forth the identity of each real estate agent and firm involved in the transaction and disclosing the party each agent and firm represents.

The provisions of this rule shall apply only to preprinted offer and sales contract forms which a broker or salesperson acting as an agent in a real estate transaction proposes for use by the buyer and seller. Nothing contained in this Rule shall be construed to prohibit the buyer and seller in a real estate transaction from altering, amending or deleting any provision in a form offer to purchase or contract; nor shall this Rule be construed to limit the rights of the buyer and seller to draft their own offers or contracts or to have the same drafted by an attorney at law.

(b) A broker or salesperson acting as an agent in a real estate transaction shall not use a preprinted offer or sales contract form containing the provisions or terms listed in Subparagraphs (b)(1) and (2) of this Rule. A broker, salesperson or anyone acting for or at the direction of the broker or salesperson shall not insert or cause such provisions or terms to be inserted into any such preprinted form, even at the direction of the parties or their attorneys:

(1) any provision concerning the payment of a commission or compensation, including the forfeiture of earnest money, to any broker, salesperson or firm; or

(2) any provision that attempts to disclaim the liability of a broker or salesperson for his or her representations in connection with the transaction.

A.0113 Reporting Criminal Convictions

Any broker or salesperson who is convicted of any felony or misdemeanor or who has disciplinary action taken against him or her in connection with any other professional license shall file with the Commission a written report of such conviction within 60 days of the final judgment or final order in the case. A form for this report is available from the Commission.

A.0114 Residential Property Disclosure Statement

(a) Every owner of real property subject to a transfer of the type contemplated by G.S. 47E-1, 47E-2, and 47E-3, shall complete the following residential property disclosure statement and furnish a copy of the complete statement to a purchaser in accordance with the requirements of G.S. 47E-4. The form shall bear the seal of the North Carolina Real Estate Commission and shall read as follows:

STATE OF NORTH CAROLINA
RESIDENTIAL PROPERTY DISCLOSURE STATEMENT
INSTRUCTIONS TO PROPERTY OWNERS

1. G.S. 47E requires owners of residential real estate (single-family homes and buildings with up to four dwelling units) to furnish purchasers a property disclosure statement. This form is the only one approved for this purpose. A disclosure statement must be furnished in connection with the sale, exchange, option and sale under a lease with option to purchase (unless the tenant is already occupying or intends to occupy the dwelling). A disclosure statement is not required for some transactions, including the first sale of a dwelling which has never been inhabited and transactions of residential property made pursuant to a lease with option to purchase where the lessee occupies or intends to occupy the dwelling. For a complete list of exemptions, see G.S. 47E-2.

2. You must check one of the boxes for each of the 20 questions on the reverse side of this form.

    a. If you check "Yes" for any question, you must describe the problem or attach a report from an engineer, contractor, pest control operator or other expert or public agency describing it. If you attach a report, you will not be liable for any inaccurate or incomplete information contained in it so long as you were not grossly negligent in obtaining or transmitting the information.

    b. If you check "No", you are stating that you have no actual knowledge of any problem. If you check "No" and you know there is a problem, you may be liable for making an intentional misstatement.

    c. If you check "No Representation", you have no duty to disclose the conditions or characteristics of the property, even if you should have known of them.

    *   If you check "Yes" or "No" and something happens to the property to make your Statement incorrect or inaccurate (for example, the roof begins to leak), you must promptly give the purchaser a corrected Statement or correct the problem.

3. If you are assisted in the sale of your property by a licensed real estate broker or salesperson, you are still responsible for completing and delivering the Statement to the purchasers; and the broker or salesperson must disclose any material facts about your property which they know or reasonably should know, regardless of your responses on the Statement.

4. You must give the completed Statement to the purchaser no later than the time the purchaser makes an offer to purchase your property. If you do not, the purchaser can, under certain conditions, cancel any resulting contract (See **"Note to Purchasers"** below). You should give the purchaser a copy of the Statement containing your signature and keep a copy signed by the purchaser for your records.

Note to Purchasers: If the owner does not give you a Residential Property Disclosure Statement by the time you make your offer to purchase the property, you may under certain conditions cancel any resulting contract and be entitled to a refund of any deposit monies you may have paid. To cancel the contract, you must personally deliver or mail written notice of your decision to cancel to the owner or the owner's agent within three calendar days following your receipt of the Statement, or three calendar days following the date of the contract, whichever occurs first. However, in no event does the Disclosure Act permit you to cancel a contract after settlement of the transaction or (in the case of a sale or exchange) after you have occupied the property, whichever occurs first.

---

5. In the space below, type or print in ink the address of the property (sufficient to identify it) and your name. Then sign and date.

    Property Address: _____

    Owner's Name(s): _____
    Owner(s) acknowledge having examined this Statement before signing and that all information is true and correct as of the date signed.

    Owner Signature: _____ Date _____

    Owner Signature: _____ Date _____
    Purchaser(s) acknowledge receipt of a copy of this disclosure statement; that they have examined it before signing; that they understand that this is not a warranty by owner or owner's agent; that it is not a substitute for any inspections they may wish to obtain; and that the representations are made by the owner and not the owner's agent(s) or subagent(s). Purchaser(s) are encouraged to obtain their own inspection from a licensed home inspector or other professional.

    Purchaser Signature: _____ Date _____

    Purchaser Signature: _____ Date _____

Property Address/Description: _____

[Note: In this form, "property" refers only to dwelling unit(s) and not sheds, detached garages or other buildings.]

Regarding the property identified above, do you know of any problem (malfunction or defect) with any of the following:

	Yes*	No	No Representation
1. FOUNDATION, SLAB, FIREPLACES/CHIMNEYS, FLOORS, WINDOWS (INCLUDING STORM WINDOWS AND SCREENS), DOORS, CEILINGS, INTERIOR AND EXTERIOR WALLS, ATTACHED GARAGE, PATIO, DECK OR OTHER STRUCTURAL COMPONENTS including any modifications to them?	☐	☐	☐
a. Siding is ☐ Masonry ☐ Wood ☐ Composition/Hardboard ☐ Vinyl ☐ Synthetic Stucco ☐ Other _____			☐
b. Approximate age of structure? _____			☐
2. ROOF (leakage or other problem)?	☐	☐	☐
a. Approximate age of roof covering? _____			☐
3. WATER SEEPAGE, LEAKAGE, DAMPNESS OR STANDING WATER in the basement, crawl space or slab?	☐	☐	☐
4. ELECTRICAL SYSTEM (outlets, wiring, panel, switches, fixtures etc.)?	☐	☐	☐
5. PLUMBING SYSTEM (pipes, fixtures, water heater, etc.)?	☐	☐	☐
6. HEATING AND/OR AIR CONDITIONING?	☐	☐	☐
a. Heat Source is: ☐ Furnace ☐ Heat Pump ☐ Baseboard ☐ Other_____			☐
b. Cooling Source is: ☐ Central Forced Air ☐ Wall/Window Unit(s) ☐ Other_____			☐
c. Fuel Source is: ☐ Electricity ☐ Natural Gas ☐ Propane ☐Oil ☐ Other _____			☐
7. WATER SUPPLY (including water quality, quantity and water pressure)?	☐	☐	☐
a. Water supply is: ☐ City/County ☐ Community System ☐ Private Well ☐ Other _____			☐
b. Water pipes are: ☐ Copper ☐ Galvanized ☐ Plastic ☐ Other _____ ☐Unknown			☐
8. SEWER AND/OR SEPTIC SYSTEM?	☐	☐	☐
a. Sewage disposal system is: ☐ Septic Tank ☐ Septic Tank with Pump ☐ Community System ☐ Connected to City/County System ☐ City/County System available ☐ Straight pipe (wastewater does not go into a septic or other sewer system [note: use of this type of system violates state law]) ☐ Other _____			☐
9. BUILT-IN APPLIANCES (RANGE/OVEN, ATTACHED MICROWAVE, HOOD/FAN, DISHWASHER, DISPOSAL, etc.)?	☐	☐	☐

Also regarding the property identified above, including the lot, other improvements, and fixtures located thereon, do you know of any:

	Yes*	No	No Representation
10. PROBLEMS WITH PRESENT INFESTATION, OR DAMAGE FROM PAST INFESTATION OF WOOD DESTROYING INSECTS OR ORGANISMS which has not been repaired?	☐	☐	☐
11. PROBLEMS WITH DRAINAGE, GRADING OR SOIL STABILITY OF LOT?	☐	☐	☐
12. PROBLEMS WITH OTHER SYSTEMS AND FIXTURES: CENTRAL VACUUM, POOL, HOT TUB, SPA, ATTIC FAN, EXHAUST FAN, CEILING FAN, SUMP PUMP, IRRIGATION SYSTEM, TV CABLE WIRING OR SATELLITE DISH, OR OTHER SYSTEMS?	☐	☐	☐
13. ROOM ADDITIONS OR OTHER STRUCTURAL CHANGES?	☐	☐	☐
14. ENVIRONMENTAL HAZARDS (substances, materials or products) including asbestos, formaldehyde, radon gas, methane gas, lead-based paint, underground storage tank, or other hazardous or toxic material (whether buried or covered), contaminated soil or water, or other environmental contamination)?	☐	☐	☐
15. COMMERCIAL OR INDUSTRIAL NUISANCES (noise, odor, smoke, etc.) affecting the property?	☐	☐	☐
16. VIOLATIONS OF BUILDING CODES, ZONING ORDINANCES, RESTRICTIVE COVENANTS OR OTHER LAND-USE RESTRICTIONS?	☐	☐	☐
17. UTILITY OR OTHER EASEMENTS, SHARED DRIVEWAYS, PARTY WALLS OR ENCROACHMENTS FROM OR ON ADJACENT PROPERTY?	☐	☐	☐
18. LAWSUITS, FORECLOSURES, BANKRUPTCY, TENANCIES, JUDGMENTS, TAX LIENS, PROPOSED ASSESSMENTS, MECHANICS' LIENS, MATERIALMENS' LIENS, OR NOTICE FROM ANY GOVERNMENTAL AGENCY that could affect title to the property?	☐	☐	☐
19. OWNERS' ASSOCIATION OR "COMMON AREA" EXPENSES OR ASSESSMENTS?	☐	☐	☐
20. FLOOD HAZARD or that the property is in a FEDERALLY-DESIGNATED FLOOD PLAIN?	☐	☐	☐

* If you answered "Yes" to any of the above questions, please explain (Attach additional sheets, if necessary): _____

_____

_____

_____

(b) The form described in Paragraph (a) of this Rule may be reproduced, but the form shall not be altered or amended in any way.

SECTION A.0200
GENERAL PROVISIONS
(Repealed)

SECTION A.0300
APPLICATION FOR LICENSE

A.0301 Form

An individual or business entity who wishes to file an application for a broker or salesperson license shall make application on a form prescribed by the Commission and can obtain the required form upon request to the Commission. In general, the application form for an individual calls for information such as the applicant's name and address, the applicant's social security number, satisfactory proof of the applicant's identity, places of residence, education, prior real estate licenses, and such other information necessary to identify the applicant and determine the applicant's qualifications and fitness for licensure. The application form for a business entity is described in Rule .0502 of this Section.

A.0302 Filing and Fees

(a) All applications for a real estate license must be properly completed and must be submitted to the Commission's office accompanied by the appropriate application fee. Examination scheduling of qualified applicants who are required to pass the real estate licensing examination shall be accomplished in accordance with Rule .0401 of this Section.

(b) The license application fee shall be $30.00. Applicants electing to take the licensing examination by computer must pay, in addition to the license application fee, the examination fee charged by the Commission's authorized testing service.

(c) An applicant shall update information provided in connection with an application or submit a newly completed application form without request by the Commission to assure that the information provided in the application is current and accurate. Failure to submit updated information prior to the issuance of a license may result in disciplinary action against a licensee in accordance with G.S. §93A-6(b)(1). In the event that the Commission requests an applicant to submit updated information or to provide additional information necessary to complete the application and the applicant fails to submit such information within 90 days following the Commission's request, the Commission shall cancel the applicant's application. An applicant whose license application has been canceled and who wishes to obtain a real estate license must start the licensing process over by submitting a written application to the Commission upon a prescribed form and paying all required fees.

A.0303 Payment of Application Fees

Payment of application fees shall be made to the Commission in the form and manner acceptable to the Commission. Once an application has been filed and processed, the application fee may not be refunded. Payment of fees for taking the license examination by computer shall be made directly to the Commission's authorized testing service in the form and manner acceptable to the testing service.

A.0304 Experience Qualifications for Applicants

Experience obtained by a salesperson or broker applicant in violation of law or rule may not be recognized by the Commission as fulfilling the requirements for licensure when the applicant is requesting the Commission to waive the prescribed education requirement based wholly or in part on equivalent experience obtained by the applicant.

SECTION A.0400
EXAMINATIONS

A.0401 Time and Place for Examinations

(a) Licensing examinations for applicants found by the Commission to be qualified for the examination shall be scheduled as follows:

(1) An applicant who elects to take the licensing examination by computer shall be provided a notice of examination eligibility that shall be valid for a period of 90 days and for a single administration of the licensing examination. Upon receipt of a notice of examination eligibility from the Commission or from the Commission's authorized computer testing service, the applicant shall schedule the examination by contacting the testing service in accordance with procedures established by the testing service. The testing service will schedule applicants for examination at their choice of one of the Commission's established testing locations and will notify applicants of the time and place of their examinations.

(2) An applicant who elects to take the licensing examination by the paper and pencil method shall be scheduled for examination based on the date of application filing, the applicant's requested testing location and the Commission's published list of testing locations, schedule of examination dates and examination filing deadlines. For the purpose of meeting any examination filing deadline date, the completed application must be either received in the Commission's office or postmarked not later than the date in question. Applicants shall be given written notice of when and where to appear for examination.

(b)   Scheduled examinations may be postponed as follows:

(1)   An examination for an applicant who has been scheduled for the computerized examination may be postponed provided the applicant makes the request for postponement directly to the Commission's authorized computer testing service in accordance with procedures established by the testing service. An applicant's computerized examination shall not be postponed beyond the 90 day period for which the applicant's notice of examination eligibility is valid.

(2)   An examination for an applicant who has been scheduled to take the examination by the paper and pencil method may be postponed provided the applicant makes the request for postponement directly to the Commission so that the request is received prior to the scheduled examination date. A scheduled examination date for a paper and pencil examination may only be postponed until one of the next two following scheduled examination dates.

A request to postpone a scheduled licensing examination without starting the licensing process over by filing another application and paying all required fees shall be granted only once unless the applicant satisfies the requirements for obtaining an excused absence stated in Paragraph (c) of this Rule.

(c)   An applicant may be granted an excused absence from a scheduled examination if the applicant provides evidence that the absence was the direct result of an emergency situation or condition which was beyond the applicant's control and which could not have been reasonably foreseen by the applicant. A request for an excused absence must be promptly made in writing and must be supported by appropriate documentation verifying the reason for the absence. The following restrictions shall also apply to requests for excused absences:

(1)   Requests for excused absences from a scheduled computerized examination must be submitted directly to the computer testing service in accordance with procedures established by the testing service. A request for an excused absence from a computerized examination shall be denied if the applicant cannot be rescheduled and examined prior to expiration of the applicant's 90 day period of examination eligibility.

(2)   Requests for excused absences from a scheduled paper and pencil examination must be submitted directly to the Commission. An applicant whose absence from a scheduled paper and pencil examination is excused may be rescheduled for one of the next two following scheduled examination dates. A request for an excused absence from a scheduled paper and pencil examination received more than 15 days after the examination date shall be denied unless the applicant was unable to file a timely request due to the same circumstances that prevented the applicant from taking the examination. An applicant shall be limited to three excused absences from a paper and pencil examination without filing another application and fee.

A.0402 Subject Matter and Passing Scores

(a)   The real estate licensing examination shall test applicants on the following general subject areas:

(1)   real estate law;

(2)   real estate brokerage law and practices;

(3)   the Real Estate License Law, rules of the Commission, and the Commission's trust account guidelines;

(4)   real estate finance;

(5)   real estate valuation (appraisal);

(6)   real estate mathematics; and

(7)   related subject areas.

(b)   In order to pass the real estate licensing examination, an applicant must attain a score at least equal to the passing score established by the Commission in compliance with psychometric standards for establishing passing scores for occupational licensing examinations as set forth in the "Standards for Educational and Psychological Testing" jointly promulgated by the American Educational Research Association, the American Psychological Association, and the National Council on Measurement in Education. Passing applicants will receive only a score of "pass"; however, failing applicants will be informed of their actual score. A passing examination score obtained by a license applicant shall be recognized as valid for a period of one year from the date of examination, during which time the applicant must fully satisfy any remaining requirements for licensure that were pending at the time of examination; provided that the running of the one-year period shall be tolled by issuance of a notice to the applicant, pursuant to Rule .0501(c) of this Section, that his or her moral character is in question, and shall resume running when the applicant's application is either approved for license issuance, denied or withdrawn. The application of an applicant with a passing examination score who fails to satisfy all remaining requirements for licensure within one year shall be canceled and the applicant shall be required to reapply and satisfy all requirements for licensure, including retaking and passing the license examination, in order to be eligible for licensure.

A.0403 Re-applying for Examination

(a)   The license application of an individual found by the Commission to be qualified for the licensing examination shall be immediately canceled upon the occurrence of any of the following events:

(1) the applicant fails to pass a licensing examination;

(2) the applicant fails to appear for and take any examination for which the applicant has been scheduled without having the applicant's examination postponed or absence excused in accordance with Rule .0401(b) and (c) of this Section; or

(3) the applicant allows the 90 day period of eligibility for examination by computer as provided for in Rule .0401(a) of this Section to expire without the applicant taking and passing the examination.

(b) An individual whose license application has been canceled and who wishes to obtain a real estate license must start the licensing process over by submitting a written application to the Commission upon a prescribed form and paying all required fees. Subsequent examinations shall be scheduled in accordance with Rule .0401 of this Section.

A.0404 Cheating and Related Misconduct

Applicants shall not cheat or attempt to cheat on an examination by any means, including both giving and receiving assistance, and shall not communicate in any manner for any purpose with any person other than an examination supervisor during an examination. Applicants shall not disrupt the quiet and orderly administration of an examination in any manner. Violation of this Rule shall be grounds for dismissal from an examination, invalidation of examination scores, and denial of a real estate license, as well as for disciplinary action if the applicant is a licensed salesperson.

A.0405 Confidentiality of Examinations

Licensing examinations are the exclusive property of the Commission and are confidential. No applicant or licensee shall obtain, attempt to obtain, receive or communicate to other persons examination questions. Violation of this Rule shall be grounds for denial of a real estate license if the violator is an applicant and disciplinary action if the violator is a licensee.

A.0406 Examination Review

(a) An applicant who fails an examination may review the examination as provided in Paragraphs (b) and (c) of this Rule. Applicants who pass an examination may not review the examination. Applicants who review an examination may not be accompanied by any other person at a review session, nor may any other person review an examination on behalf of an applicant.

(b) An applicant who fails an examination taken by computer may review the examination at the testing center immediately following completion of the examination and receipt of the applicant's examination results but prior to leaving the testing center. An applicant eligible for examination review who fails to review the examination at the testing center immediately following completion of the examination will be deemed to have waived the right to review the examination.

(c) An applicant who fails an examination taken by the paper and pencil method may review the examination at such times and places as are scheduled by the Executive Director provided the applicant makes a request to review the examination not later than the request deadline date established by the Executive Director for a scheduled examination review date. Failure to request an appointment to review an examination by the request deadline date shall constitute a waiver of the right to review such examination. An applicant who has taken the examination by the paper and pencil method may be granted an excused absence from a scheduled examination review if the applicant provides evidence satisfactory to the Commission that the absence was the direct result of an emergency situation or condition which was beyond the applicant's control and which could not have been reasonably foreseen. A request for an excused absence must be promptly made in writing and must be supported by appropriate documentation verifying the reason for the absence. A request for an excused absence received more than 15 days after the scheduled examination review will be denied unless the applicant was unable to file a timely request due to the same circumstances that prevented the applicant from attending the examination review. An applicant who fails to appear for a scheduled examination review and who does not obtain an excused absence in accordance with this Rule shall be deemed to have waived the right to review the examination.

SECTION A.0500
LICENSING

A.0501 Character

(a) At a meeting of the Commission following each licensing examination, the applicants who have passed the examination shall be considered for licensing. When the moral character of an applicant is in question, action by the Commission will be deferred until the applicant has affirmatively demonstrated that he or she possesses the requisite truthfulness, honesty and integrity.

(b) When the moral character of an applicant is in question, the Commission shall notify the applicant and the applicant shall be entitled to demonstrate his or her character and fitness for licensure at a hearing before the Commission according to the provisions of G.S. 150B.

(c) Notice to the applicant that his or her moral character is in question shall be in writing, sent by certified mail, return receipt requested, to the address shown upon the application. The applicant shall have 60 days from the date of receipt of this notice to request a hearing before the Commission. Failure to request a hearing within this time shall constitute a waiver of the applicant's right to a hearing on his or her application for licensing, and the application shall be deemed denied. Nothing in this Rule shall be interpreted to prevent an applicant from re-applying for licensure.

A.0502 Business Entities

(a) Every business entity other than a sole proprietorship shall apply for and obtain from the Commission a firm license prior to engaging in business as a real estate broker. An entity which changes its business form shall be required to submit a new application immediately upon making the change and to obtain a new license. Incomplete applications shall not be acted upon by the Commission. Application forms for partnerships, corporations, limited liability companies, associations and other business entities required to be licensed as brokers shall be available upon request to the Commission and shall set forth the name of the entity, the name under which the entity will do business, the address of its principal office, and a list of all brokers and salespersons associated with the entity.

(b) The application of any partnership, including a general partnership, limited partnership and limited liability partnership, shall also call for a full description of the organization of the applicant and persons affiliated with the applicant, including a copy of its written partnership agreement or if no written agreement exists, a written description of the rights and duties of the several partners; a copy of any Certificate of Limited Partnership as may be required by law; past conviction of criminal offenses of any general or limited partner; past revocation, suspension, or denial of a business or professional license of any general or limited partner; and the name and residence address of each general and limited partner.

(c) The application of a limited liability company shall also call for a full description of the organization of the applicant and persons affiliated with the applicant, including a copy of its Articles of Organization evidencing its authority to engage in the business of real estate brokerage; past conviction of criminal offenses of any manager or member; past revocation, suspension, or denial of a business or professional license of any manager or member; and the name and residence address of each manager or member.

(d) The application of a corporation shall also call for a full description of the organization of the applicant and persons affiliated with the applicant, including a copy of its Articles of Incorporation evidencing its authority to engage in the business of real estate brokerage; past conviction of criminal offenses of any corporate director, officer, employee or shareholder who owns ten percent or more of the outstanding shares of any class; past revocation, suspension, or denial of a business or professional license to any director, officer, employee or shareholder who owns ten percent or more of the outstanding shares of any class; the name and residence address of each director and officer of the corporation; and the name and address of each person, partnership, corporation, or other entity owning ten percent or more of the outstanding shares of any class.

(e) The application of any other business entity shall also call for a full description of the organization of the applicant and persons affiliated with the applicant, including a copy of its organizational documents evidencing its authority to engage in real estate brokerage; past conviction of criminal offenses of any principal in the company; past revocation, suspension or denial of a business or professional license of any principal; and the name and residence address of each principal. For purposes of this Paragraph, the term "principal" shall mean any person or entity who owns the business entity to any extent, or who is an officer, director, manager, member, partner or who holds any other comparable position.

(f) A foreign business entity shall further qualify by filing with its application for license a copy of any certificate of authority to transact business in this state issued by the North Carolina Secretary of State which may be required by law and a consent to service of process and pleadings which shall be accompanied by a duly certified copy of the resolution of the general partners, managers or board of directors authorizing the proper partner, manager or officer to execute said consent.

(g) After filing a written application with the Commission and upon a showing that at least one principal of said business entity holds a broker license on active status and in good standing and will serve as principal broker of the entity, the entity shall be licensed provided it appears that the applicant entity employs and is directed by personnel possessed of the requisite truthfulness, honesty, and integrity. The principal broker of a partnership of any kind must be a general partner of the partnership, the principal broker of a limited liability company must be a manager of the company, and the principal broker of a corporation must be an officer of the corporation. A licensed business entity may serve as the principal broker of another licensed business entity if the principal broker-entity has as its principal broker a natural person who is himself licensed as a broker. The natural person who is principal broker shall assure the performance of the principal broker's duties with regard to both entities.

(h) The licensing of a business entity shall not be construed to extend to the licensing of its partners, managers, members, directors, officers, employees or other persons acting for the entity in their individual capacities regardless of whether they are engaged in furthering the business of the licensed entity.

(i) The principal broker of a business entity shall assume responsibility for:

> (1) designating and assuring that there is at all times a broker-in-charge for each office and branch office of the entity at which real estate brokerage activities

are conducted;

(2) renewing the real estate broker license of the entity;

(3) retaining the firm's renewal pocket card at the firm and producing it as proof of firm licensure upon request and maintaining a photocopy of the firm license certificate and pocket card at each branch office thereof;

(4) notifying the Commission of any change of business address or trade name of the entity and the registration of any assumed business name adopted by the entity for its use; and

(5) notifying the Commission in writing of any change of his or her status as principal broker within ten days following the change.

(j) Every licensed business entity and every entity applying for licensure shall conform to all the requirements imposed upon it by the North Carolina General Statutes for its continued existence and authority to do business in North Carolina. Failure to conform to such requirements shall be grounds for disciplinary action or denial of the entity's application for licensure. Upon receipt of notice from an entity or agency of this state that a licensed entity has ceased to exist or that its authority to engage in business in this state has been terminated by operation of law, the Commission shall cancel the license of the entity.

A.0503 License Renewal; Penalty for Operating While License Expired

(a) All real estate licenses issued by the Commission under G.S. 93A, Article 1 shall expire on the 30th day of June following issuance. Any licensee desiring renewal of a license shall apply for renewal within 45 days prior to license expiration by submitting a renewal application on a form prescribed by the Commission and submitting with the application the required renewal fee of thirty-five dollars ($35.00).

(b) Any person desiring to renew his or her license on active status shall, upon the second renewal of such license following initial licensure, and upon each subsequent renewal, have obtained all continuing education required by G.S. 93A-4A and Rule .1702 of the Subchapter.

(c) A person renewing a license on inactive status shall not be required to have obtained any continuing education in order to renew such license; however, in order to subsequently change his or her license from inactive status to active status, the licensee must satisfy the continuing education requirement prescribed in Rule .1703 of the Subchapter.

(d) Any person or firm which engages in the business of a real estate broker or salesperson while his, her, or its license is expired is subject to the penalties prescribed in G.S. 93A.

A.0504 Active and Inactive License Status

(a) Except for licenses that have expired or that have been revoked, suspended or surrendered, all licenses issued by the Commission shall be designated as being either on active status or inactive status. The holder of a license on active status may engage in any activity requiring a real estate license and may be compensated for the provision of any lawful real estate brokerage service. The holder of a license on inactive status may not engage in any activity requiring a real estate license, including the referral for compensation of a prospective seller, buyer, landlord or tenant to another real estate licensee or any other party. A licensee holding a license on inactive status must renew such license and pay the prescribed license renewal fee in order to continue to hold such license. The Commission may take disciplinary action against a licensee holding a license on inactive status for any violation of G.S. 93A or any rule promulgated by the Commission, including the offense of engaging in an activity for which a license is required while a license is on inactive status.

(b) Upon initial licensure, a salesperson's license shall be assigned by the Commission to inactive status and the license of a broker or firm shall be assigned to active status. A license shall be assigned by the Commission to inactive status upon the written request of the licensee. A salesperson's license shall be assigned by the Commission to inactive status when the salesperson is not under the active, personal supervision of a broker-in-charge. A firm's license shall be assigned by the Commission to inactive status when the firm does not have a principal broker. A broker or salesperson shall also be assigned to inactive status if, upon the second renewal of his or her license following initial licensure, or upon any subsequent renewal, he or she has not satisfied the continuing education requirement described in Rule .1702 of this Subchapter.

(c) A salesperson with an inactive license who desires to have such license placed on active status must comply with the procedures prescribed in Rule .0506(b) of this Section.

(d) A broker with an inactive license who desires to have such license placed on active status shall file with the Commission a request for license activation on a form prescribed by the Commission containing identifying information about the broker, a statement that the broker has satisfied the continuing education requirements prescribed by Rule .1703 of this Subchapter, the date of the request, and the signature of the broker. Upon the mailing or delivery of this form, the broker may engage in real estate brokerage activities requiring a license; however, if the broker does not receive from the Commission a written acknowledgment of the license activation within 30 days of the date shown on the form, the broker shall immediately terminate his or her real estate brokerage activities pending receipt of the written acknowledgment from the Commission. If the broker is notified that he or she is not eligible for license activation due to a continuing education deficiency, the broker must terminate all real estate brokerage activities until such time as the continuing education deficiency is satisfied and a new request for license activation is submitted to the Commission.

(e) A firm with an inactive license which desires to have its license placed on active status shall file with the Commission a request for license activation on a form prescribed by the Commission containing identifying information about the firm and its principal broker. If the principal broker has an inactive license, he or she must satisfy the requirements of Paragraph (d) of this Rule. Upon the mailing or delivery of the completed form by the principal broker, the firm may engage in real estate brokerage activities requiring a license; however, if the firm's principal broker does not receive from the Commission a written acknowledgment of the license activation within 30 days of the date shown on the form, the firm shall immediately terminate its real estate brokerage activities pending receipt of the written acknowledgment from the Commission. If the principal broker is notified that the firm is not eligible for license activation due to a continuing education deficiency on the part of the principal broker, the firm must terminate all real estate brokerage activities until such time as the continuing education deficiency is satisfied and a new request for license activation is submitted to the Commission.

A.0505 Reinstatement of Expired License, Revoked, Surrendered or Suspended License

(a) Licenses expired for not more than 12 months may be reinstated upon proper application and payment of the thirty-five dollar ($35.00) renewal fee plus five dollar ($5.00) late filing fee. In order to reinstate such license on active status, the applicant shall also present evidence satisfactory to the Commission of having obtained such continuing education as is required by Rule .1703 of this Subchapter to change an inactive license to active status. A person reinstating such a license on inactive status shall not be required to have obtained any continuing education in order to reinstate such license; however, in order to subsequently change his or her reinstated license from inactive status to active status, the licensee must satisfy the continuing education requirement prescribed in Rule .1703 of this Subchapter, and be supervised by a broker-in-charge in compliance with the requirements of Rule .0506 of this Section.

(b) Reinstatement of licenses expired for more than 12 months may be considered upon proper application and payment of a thirty dollar ($30.00) fee. Applicants must satisfy the Commission that they possess the current knowledge, skills and competence, as well as the truthfulness, honesty and integrity, necessary to function in the real estate business in a manner that protects and serves the public interest. To demonstrate current knowledge, skills and competence, the Commission may require such applicants to

complete real estate education or pass the license examination or both.

(c) Reinstatement of a revoked license may be considered upon proper application and payment of a thirty dollar ($30.00) fee. Applicants must satisfy the same requirements as those prescribed in Paragraph (b) of this Rule for reinstatement of licenses expired for more than 12 months.

(d) Reinstatement of a license surrendered under the provisions of G.S. 93A-6(e) may be considered upon termination of the period of surrender specified in the order approving the surrender and upon proper application and payment of a thirty dollar ($30.00) fee. Applicants must satisfy the same requirements as those prescribed in Paragraph (b) of this Rule for reinstatement of licenses expired for more than 12 months.

(e) When a license is suspended by the Commission, the suspended license shall be restored at the end of the period of active suspension; however, in order for the license to be restored on active status, the licensee shall be required to also demonstrate that the licensee has satisfied the continuing education requirement for license activation prescribed by Rule .1703 of this Subchapter and is supervised by a broker-in-charge in compliance with the requirements of Rule .0506 of this Section, if applicable.

A.0506 Salesperson to be Supervised by Broker

(a) A salesperson may engage in or hold himself or herself out as engaging in activities requiring a real estate license only while his or her license is on active status and he or she is supervised by the broker-in-charge of the real estate firm or office where the salesperson is associated. A salesperson may be supervised by only one broker-in-charge at a time.

(b) Upon a salesperson's association with a real estate broker or brokerage firm, the salesperson and the broker-in-charge of the office where the salesperson will be engaged in the real estate business shall immediately file with the Commission a salesperson supervision notification on a form prescribed by the Commission containing identifying information about the salesperson and the broker-in-charge, a statement from the broker-in-charge certifying that he or she will supervise the salesperson in the performance of all acts for which a license is required, the date that the broker-in-charge assumes responsibility for such supervision, and the signatures of the salesperson and broker-in-charge. If the salesperson is on inactive status at the time of associating with a broker or brokerage firm, the salesperson and broker-in-charge shall also file, along with the salesperson supervision notification, the salesperson's request for license activation on a form prescribed by the Commission containing identifying information about the salesperson, the salesperson's statement that he or she has satisfied the continuing education requirements prescribed by Rule .1703 of this Subchapter, the date of the request, and the signatures of the salesperson and the salesperson's proposed broker-in-charge. Upon the mailing or delivery of the required form(s), the salesperson may engage in real estate brokerage activities requiring a license under the supervision of the broker-in-charge; however, if the salesperson and broker-in-charge do not receive from the Commission a written acknowledgment of the salesperson supervision notification and, if appropriate, the request for license activation, within 30 days of the date shown on the form, the broker-in-charge shall immediately terminate the salesperson's real estate brokerage activities pending receipt of the written acknowledgment from the Commission. If the salesperson and broker-in-charge are notified that the salesperson is not eligible for license activation due to a continuing education deficiency, the broker-in-charge shall cause the salesperson to immediately cease all activities requiring a real estate license until such time as the continuing education deficiency is satisfied and a new salesperson supervision notification and request for license activation is submitted to the Commission.

(c) A broker-in-charge who certifies to the Commission that he or she will supervise a licensed salesperson shall actively and personally supervise the salesperson in a manner which reasonably assures that the salesperson performs all acts for which a real estate license is required in accordance with the Real Estate License Law and Commission rules. A supervising broker who fails to supervise a salesperson as prescribed in this Rule may be subject to disciplinary action by the Commission.

(d) Upon the termination of the supervisory relationship between a salesperson and his or her broker-in-charge, the salesperson and the broker-in-charge shall provide written notification of the date of termination to the Commission not later than 10 days following said termination.

A.0507 Payment of License Fees

Checks, credit cards, and other forms of payment given the Commission for fees due which are returned unpaid shall be considered cause for license denial, suspension, or revocation.

A.0508 Duplicate License Fee (Repealed)

A.0509 Duplicate License Fee

A licensee may, by filing a prescribed form and paying a five dollar ($5.00) fee to the Commission, obtain a duplicate real estate license or pocket card to replace an original license or pocket card which has been lost, damaged or destroyed or if the name of the licensee has been lawfully changed.

A.0510 Cancellation of Salesperson License upon Broker Licensure

When a person holding a salesperson license is issued a broker license, the person's salesperson license shall be automatically canceled.

SECTION A.0600
REAL ESTATE COMMISSION HEARINGS

A.0601 Complaints/Inquiries/Motions/Other Pleadings

(a) There shall be no specific form required for complaints. To be sufficient, a complaint shall be in writing, identify the respondent licensee and shall reasonably apprise the Commission of the facts which form the basis of the complaint.

(b) When investigating a complaint, the scope of the Commission's investigation shall not be limited only to matters alleged in the complaint. In addition, a person making a complaint to the Commission may change his or her complaint by submitting the changes to the Commission in writing.

(c) When a complaint has not been submitted in conformity with this rule, the Commission's legal counsel may initiate an investigation if the available information is sufficient to create a reasonable suspicion that any licensee or other person or entity may have committed a violation of the provisions of the Real Estate License Law or the rules adopted by the Commission.

(d) There shall be no specific forms required for answers, motions, or other pleadings relating to contested cases before the Commission, except they shall be in writing. To be sufficient, the document must reasonably apprise the Commission of the matters it alleges or answers. To be considered by the Commission, every answer, motion, request or other pleading must be submitted to the Commission in writing or made during the hearing as a matter of record.

(e) During the course of an investigation of a licensee, the Commission, through its legal counsel or other staff, may send the licensee a Letter of Inquiry requesting the licensee to respond. The Letter of Inquiry, or attachments thereto, shall set forth the subject matter being investigated. Upon receipt of the Letter of Inquiry, the licensee shall respond within 14 calendar days. Such response shall include a full and fair disclosure of all information requested. Licensees shall include with their written response copies of all documents requested in the Letter of Inquiry.

(f) Hearings in contested cases before the Commission shall be conducted according to the provisions of Article 3A of Chapter 150B of the General Statutes of North Carolina.

(g) Persons who make complaints are not parties to contested cases, but may be witnesses.

A.0616 Procedures For Requesting Hearings When Applicant's Character Is In Question

(a) When the moral character of an applicant for licensure or approval is in question, the applicant shall not be licensed or approved until the applicant has affirmatively demonstrated that the applicant possesses the requisite truthfulness, honesty and integrity. For the purposes of this rule, applicant means any person or entity making application for licensure as a real estate broker or salesperson or for licensure or approval as a prelicensing or continuing education instructor, director, coordinator, school, or sponsor. When the applicant is an entity, it shall be directed and controlled by persons who are truthful and honest and who possess integrity.

(b) When the character of an applicant is in question, the Commission shall defer action upon the application until the applicant is notified by letter. The letter informing the applicant that his or her moral character is in question shall be sent by certified mail, return receipt requested, to the address shown upon the application. The applicant shall have 60 days from the date of receipt of this letter to request a hearing before the Commission. If the applicant fails to request a hearing within this time or if a properly addressed letter is returned to the Commission undelivered, applicant s right to a hearing shall be considered waived and the application shall be deemed denied. If the applicant makes a timely request for a hearing in accordance with the provisions of this rule, the Commission shall provide the applicant with a Notice of Hearing and hearing as required by Article 3A of Chapter 150B of the North Carolina General Statutes.

(c) Nothing in this Rule shall be interpreted to prevent an unsuccessful applicant from reapplying for licensure or approval if such application is otherwise permitted by law.

SECTION A.0700
PETITIONS FOR RULES

SECTION A.0800
RULE MAKING

SECTION A.0900
DECLARATORY RULINGS

SECTION A.1000
SCHOOLS
(Transferred to C.0100)

SECTION A.1100
REAL ESTATE PRE-LICENSING COURSES
(Transferred/Repealed. Transfers are at C.0300 Prelicensing and Pre-certification Courses)

SECTION A.1200
CERTIFICATION OF REAL ESTATE INSTRUCTORS
(Repealed)

SECTION A.1300
PRIVATE REAL ESTATE SCHOOLS
(Transferred/Repealed. Transfers are at C.0200)

SECTION A.1400
REAL ESTATE RECOVERY FUND

SECTION A.1500 FORMS (Repealed)

Interested persons may obtain a copy of Sections A.0600 through A.1500 by making written request to the North Carolina Real Estate Commission.

SECTION A.1600
DISCRIMINATORY PRACTICES PROHIBITED

A.1601 Fair Housing

Conduct by a licensee which violates the provisions of the State Fair Housing Act constitutes improper conduct in violation of G.S. 93A-6(a)(10).

SECTION A.1700
MANDATORY CONTINUING EDUCATION

A.1701 Purpose and Applicability

This Section describes the continuing education requirement for real estate brokers and salespersons authorized by G.S. 93A-4A, establishes the continuing education requirement to change a license from inactive status to active status, establishes attendance requirements for continuing education courses, establishes the criteria and procedures relating to obtaining an extension of time to complete the continuing education requirement, establishes the criteria for obtaining continuing education credit for an unapproved course or related educational activity, and addresses other similar matters.

A.1702 Continuing Education Requirement

(a) In order to renew a broker or salesperson license on active status, the person requesting renewal of a license shall, upon the second renewal of such license following initial licensure, and upon each subsequent annual renewal, have completed, within one year preceding license expiration, eight classroom hours of real estate continuing education in courses approved by the Commission as provided in Subchapter 58E. Four of the required eight classroom hours must be obtained each license period by completing a mandatory update course developed annually by the Commission. The remaining four hours must be obtained by completing one or more Commission-approved elective courses described in Rule .0305 of Subchapter 58E. The licensee bears the responsibility for providing, upon request of the Commission, evidence of continuing education course completion satisfactory to the Commission.

(b) No continuing education shall be required to renew a broker or salesperson license on inactive status; however, to change a license from inactive status to active status, the licensee must satisfy the continuing education requirement described in Rule .1703 of this Section.

(c) No continuing education shall be required for a licensee who is a member of the North Carolina General Assembly to renew his or her license on active status.

(d) The terms "active status" and "inactive status" are defined in Rule .0504 of this Subchapter. For continuing education purposes, the term "initial licensure" shall include the first time that a license of a particular type is issued to a person, and reinstatement of an expired or revoked license.

A.1703 Continuing Education for License Activation

(a) A broker or salesperson requesting to change an inactive license to active status on or after the licensee's second license renewal following his or her initial licensure shall be required to demonstrate completion of continuing education as described in Paragraph (b) or (c) of this Rule, whichever is appropriate.

(b) If the inactive licensee's license has properly been on active status at any time since the preceding July 1, the licensee is considered to be current with regard to continuing education and no additional continuing education is required to activate the license.

(c) If the inactive licensee's license has not properly been on active status since the preceding July 1 and the licensee has a deficiency in his or her continuing education record for the previous license period, the licensee must make up the deficiency and fully satisfy the continuing education requirement for the current license period in order to activate the license. Any deficiency may be made up by completing, during the current license period or previous license period, approved continuing education elective courses; however, such courses will not be credited toward the continuing education requirement for the current license period. When crediting elective courses for purposes of making up a continuing education deficiency, the maximum number of credit hours that will be awarded for any course is four hours. When evaluating the continuing education record of a licensee with a deficiency for the previous license period to determine the licensee's eligibility for active status, the licensee shall be deemed eligible for active status if the licensee has fully satisfied the continuing education requirement for the current license period and has taken any two additional continuing education courses since the beginning of the previous license period, even if the licensee had a continuing education deficiency prior to the beginning of the previous license period.

A.1704 No Credit for Prelicensing Courses

No credit toward the continuing education requirement shall be awarded for completing a real estate prelicensing course.

A.1705 Attendance and Participation Requirements

In order to receive any credit for satisfactorily completing an approved continuing education course, a licensee must attend at least 90 percent of the scheduled classroom hours for the course, regardless of the length of the course, and must comply with student participation standards described in Rule .0511 of Subchapter 58E. No credit shall be awarded for attending less than 90 percent of the scheduled classroom hours.

A.1706 Repetition of Courses

A continuing education course may be taken only once for continuing education credit within a single license period.

A.1707 Elective Course Carry-Over Credit

A maximum of four hours of continuing education credit for an approved elective course taken during the current license period may be carried over to satisfy the continuing education elective requirement for the next following license period if the licensee receives no continuing education elective credit for the course toward the elective requirement for the current license period or the previous license period. However, if a continuing education elective course is used to wholly or partially satisfy the elective requirement for the current or previous license period, then any excess hours completed in such course which are not needed to satisfy the four-hour elective requirement for that license period may not be carried forward and applied toward the elective requirement for the next following license period.

A.1708 Equivalent Credit

(a) A licensee may request that the Commission award continuing education credit for a course taken by the licensee that is not approved by the Commission, or for some other real estate education activity, by making such request on a form prescribed by the Commission and submitting a nonrefundable evaluation fee of thirty dollars ($30.00) for each request for evaluation of a course or real estate education activity. In order for requests for equivalent credit to be considered and credits to be entered into a licensee's continuing education record prior to the June 30 license expiration date, such requests and all supporting documents must be received by the Commission on or before June 10 preceding expiration of the licensee's current license, with the exception that requests from instructors desiring equivalent credit for teaching Commission-approved continuing education courses must be received by June 30. Any equivalent continuing education credit awarded under this Rule shall be applied first to make up any continuing education deficiency for the previous license period and then to satisfy the continuing education requirement for the current license period; however, credit for an unapproved course or educational activity, other than teaching an approved elective course, that was completed during a previous license period may not be applied to a subsequent license period.

(b) The Commission may award continuing education elective credit for completion of an unapproved course which the Commission finds equivalent to the elective course component of the continuing education requirement set forth in Section .0300 of Subchapter 58E. Completion of an unapproved course may serve only to satisfy the elective requirement and cannot be substituted for completion of the mandatory update course.

(c) Real estate education activities, other than teaching a Commission-approved course, which may be eligible for credit include, but are not limited to: developing a Commission-approved elective continuing education course, authorship of a published real estate textbook; and authorship of a scholarly article, on a topic acceptable for continuing education purposes, which has been published in a professional journal such as a law journal or professional college or university journal or periodical. The Commission may award continuing education elective credit for activities which the Commission finds equivalent to the elective course component of the continuing education requirement set forth in Section .0300 of Subchapter 58E. No activity other than teaching a Commission-developed mandatory update course shall be considered equivalent to completing the mandatory update course.

(d) The Commission may award credit for teaching the Commission-developed mandatory update course and for teaching an approved elective course. Credit for teaching an approved elective course shall be awarded only for teaching a course for the first time. Credit for teaching a Commission-developed mandatory update course may be awarded for each licensing period in which the instructor teaches the course. The amount of credit awarded to the instructor of an approved continuing education course shall be the same as the amount of credit earned by a licensee who completes the course. Licensees who are instructors of continuing ed-

ucation courses approved by the Commission shall not be subject to the thirty dollar ($30.00) evaluation fee when applying for continuing education credit for teaching an approved course. No credit toward the continuing education requirement shall be awarded for teaching a real estate pre-licensing course.

(e) A licensee completing a real estate appraisal pre-licensing, precertification or continuing education course approved by the North Carolina Appraisal Board may obtain real estate continuing education elective credit for such course by submitting to the Commission a written request for equivalent continuing education elective credit accompanied by a nonrefundable processing fee of twenty dollars ($20.00) and a copy of the certificate of course completion issued by the course sponsor for submission to the North Carolina Appraisal Board.

A.1709 Extensions of Time to Complete Continuing Education

A licensee on active status may request and be granted an extension of time to satisfy the continuing education requirement for a particular license period if the licensee provides evidence satisfactory to the Commission that he or she was unable to obtain the necessary education due to an incapacitating illness or other circumstance which existed for a substantial portion of the license period and which constituted a severe and verifiable hardship such that to comply with the continuing education requirement would have been impossible or unreasonably burdensome. The Commission shall in no case grant an extension of time to satisfy the continuing education requirement for reasons of business or personal conflicts. The Commission also shall not grant such an extension of time when, in the opinion of the Commission, the principal reason for the licensee's inability to obtain the required education in a timely manner was unreasonable delay on the part of the licensee in obtaining such education. If an extension of time is granted, the licensee shall be permitted to renew his or her license on active status but the license shall be automatically changed to inactive status at the end of the extension period unless the licensee satisfies the continuing education requirement prior to that time. If an extension of time is not granted, the licensee may either satisfy the continuing education requirement prior to expiration of the license period or renew his or her license on inactive status. The length of any extension of time granted and the determination of the specific courses which shall be accepted by the Commission as equivalent to the continuing education the licensee would have been required to have completed had the licensee not been granted the extension is wholly discretionary on the part of the Commission. The licensee's request for an extension of time must be submitted on a form prescribed by the Commission.

A.1710 Denial or Withdrawal of Continuing Education Credit

(a) The Commission may deny continuing education credit claimed by a licensee or reported by a course sponsor for a licensee, and may withdraw continuing education credit previously awarded by the Commission to a licensee upon finding that:

(1) The licensee or course sponsor provided incorrect or incomplete information to the Commission concerning continuing education completed by the licensee;

(2) The licensee failed to comply with either the attendance requirement established by Rule .1705 of this Section or the student participation standards set forth in Rule .0511 of Subchapter 58E; or

(3) The licensee was mistakenly awarded continuing education credit due to an administrative error.

(b) When continuing education credit is denied or withdrawn by the Commission under Paragraph (a) of this Rule, the licensee remains responsible for satisfying the continuing education requirement. However, when an administrative error or an incorrect report by a course sponsor results in the denial or withdrawal of continuing education credit for a licensee, the Commission may, upon request of the licensee, grant the licensee an extension of time to satisfy the continuing education requirement.

(c) A licensee who obtains or attempts to obtain continuing education credit through misrepresentation of fact, dishonesty or other improper conduct shall be subject to disciplinary action pursuant to G.S. 93A-6.

A.1711 Continuing Education Required of Nonresident Licensees

(a) Real estate brokers and salespersons licensed in North Carolina but residing in another state at the time they apply for license renewal who wish to renew their licenses on active status may fully satisfy the continuing education requirement by any one of the following means:

(1) A nonresident licensee may, at the time of license renewal, hold a real estate license on active status in another state and certify on a form prescribed by the Commission that the licensee holds such license.

(2) A nonresident licensee may, within one year preceding license expiration, complete the Commission-prescribed Update course plus four classroom hours of instruction in Commission-approved continuing education elective courses.

(3) A nonresident licensee may, within one year preceding license expiration, complete eight classroom hours in courses approved for continuing education credit by the real estate licensing agency in the licensee's state of residence or in the state where the course was taken. To obtain credit for a continuing education course completed in another state and not approved by the Commission, the licensee must submit a written request for continuing education credit accompanied by a nonrefundable processing fee of twenty dollars ($20.00) per request and evidence satisfactory to the Commission that the course was completed and that the course was approved for continuing education credit by the real estate licensing agency in the licensee's state of residence or in the state where the course was taken.

(4) A nonresident licensee may obtain eight hours equivalent credit for a course or courses not approved by the Commission or for related educational activities as provided in Rule .1708 of this Section. The maximum amount of continuing education credit the Commission will award a nonresident licensee for an unapproved course or educational activity is eight hours.

(b) When requesting to change an inactive license to active status, or when applying for reinstatement of a license expired for not more than 12 months, a nonresident broker or salesperson may fully satisfy the continuing education requirements described in Rules .0505 and .1703 of this Subchapter by complying with any of the options described in Paragraph (a) of this Rule.

(c) No carry-over credit to a subsequent license period shall be awarded for a course taken in another state that has not been approved by the North Carolina Real Estate Commission as an elective course.

Subchapter 58B
Time Shares

SECTION B.0100
TIME SHARE PROJECT REGISTRATION

B.0101 Application for Registration

(a) Every application for time share project registration shall be filed at the Commission's office upon a form prescribed by the Commission. Every such application shall contain or have appended thereto:

(1) information concerning the developer's title or right to use the real property on which the project is located, including a title opinion provided by an independent attorney performed within 30 days preceding the date of application;

(2) information concerning owners of time shares at the project other than the developer;

(3) a description of the improvements and amenities located at the project, including a description of the number and type of time share units;

(4) a description of the time share estate to be sold or conveyed to purchasers;

(5) information concerning the developer and his or her financial ability to develop the project (including the developer's most recent audited financial statement, any loan commitments for completion of the proposed time share project, a projected budget for the construction, marketing and operation of the time share project until control by purchasers is asserted, and details of any source of funding for the time share project other than consumer sales proceeds), and information concerning the marketing and managing entities and their relationship to the developer;

(6) the developer's name and address, past real estate development experience and such other information necessary to determine the moral character of those selling and managing the project;

(7) copies of all documents to be distributed to time share purchasers at the point of sale or immediately thereafter; and

(8) such information as may be required by G.S. 93A-52.

The form shall also describe the standards for its proper completion and submission.

(b) In accordance with G.S. 93A-52, an application for time share registration shall be considered to be properly completed when it is wholly and accurately filled out and when all required documents are appended to it and appear to be in compliance with the provisions of the Time Share

Act, and, where the project is a condominium, the Condominium Act or Unit Ownership Act.

(c) An entity which owns time shares at a time share project where there are one or more existing registered developers may also apply to the Commission for registration of its time shares, provided that the entity does not control a registered developer, is not controlled by a registered developer, and is not in common control of the project with a registered developer.

B.0102 Registration Fee

(a) Every application for time share project registration must be accompanied by a certified check made payable to the North Carolina Real Estate Commission. For the initial registration of any time share project, or for a subsequent registration of a time share project by a developer proposing to sell or develop time shares equivalent to at least 20 per cent of the original time share project, the fee is $1,000.00. For a subsequent registration of a previously or presently registered time share project by a developer proposing to sell or develop time shares equivalent to less than 20 per cent of the original time share project, the fee is $800.00. For an initial or subsequent time share project consisting of a single family dwelling unit or a single dwelling unit in a multiple dwelling unit property and in which 10 or less time shares will be or have been created, the fee is $600.00. For any time share registration by a homeowner association for the purpose of re-selling time shares in its own project which it has acquired in satisfaction of unpaid assessments by prior owners, the fee is $400.00.

(b) Applications for registration not accompanied by the appropriate fee shall not be considered by the Commission.

(c) In the event a properly completed application filed with the Commission is denied for any reason, or if an incomplete application is denied by the Commission or abandoned by the developer prior to a final decision by the Commission, the amount of two hundred fifty dollars ($250.00) shall be retained by the Commission from the application fee and the balance refunded to the applicant developer.

B.0103 Renewal of Time Share Project Registration

(a) Every developer desiring the renewal of a time share project registration shall apply for the same in writing upon a form prescribed by the Commission during the month of June. Every such renewal application shall be accompanied by a certified check made payable to the North Carolina Real Estate Commission in the amount of seven hundred fifty dollars ($750.00). To renew the time share project registration, the properly completed renewal application accompanied by the prescribed fee must be received at the Commission's office prior to the expiration of the certificate of registration.

(b) Applications for the renewal of a time share project registration shall be signed by the developer, by two executive officers of the developer, or by the developer's attorney at law and shall certify that the information contained in the registration filed with the Commission is accurate and current on the date of the renewal application. Making a false certification on a time share project registration renewal application shall be grounds for disciplinary action by the Commission.

B.0104 Amendments to Time Share Project Registration

(a) A developer shall notify the Commission immediately, but in no event later than 15 days, after any material change in the information contained in the time share project registration.

(b) A material change shall be any change which reflects a difference in:

(1) the nature, quality or availability of the purchaser's ownership or right to use the time share;

(2) the nature, quality or availability of any amenity at the project;

(3) the developer's title, control or right to use the real property on which the project is located;

(4) the information concerning the developer, the managing or marketing entities, or persons connected therewith, previously filed with the Commission;

(5) the purchaser's right to exchange his or her unit; however, a change in the information required to be disclosed to a purchaser by G.S. 93A-48 shall not be a material change; or

(6) the project or time share as originally registered which would be significant to a reasonable purchaser.

(c) Amendments to time share project registrations shall be submitted in the form of substitute pages for material previously filed with the Commission. New or changed information shall be conspicuously indicated by underlining in red ink. Every amendment submitted shall be accompanied by a cover letter signed by the developer or the developer's attorney containing a summary of the amendment and a statement of reasons for which the amendment has been made. The cover letter shall state:

(1) the name and address of the project and its registration number;

(2) the name and address of the developer;

(3) the document or documents to which the amendment applies;

(4) whether or not the changes represented by the amendment required the assent of the time share owners and, if so, how the assent of the time share owners was obtained; and

(5) the recording reference in the office of the register of deeds for the changes, if applicable.

Developers of multiple projects must submit separate amendments and cover letters for each project for which amendments are submitted.

(d) The Commission may, in its discretion, require the developer to file a new time share project registration application in the place of an amendment form. Such refiling shall be without fee.

B.0105 Notice of Termination

(a) A developer of a registered time share project which, for any reason, terminates its interest, rights, ownership or control of the project or any significant part thereof shall immediately notify the Commission in writing on a form prescribed by the Commission for that purpose. Notice of termination to the Commission shall include the date of termination, the reasons therefor, the identity of the developer's successor, if any, and a report on the status of time share sales to purchasers on the date of termination.

(b) Upon receipt of a properly executed notice of termination of the developer's interest in a time share project, the Commission shall enter a notation of cancellation of registration in the file of the project, and shall notify the developer of cancellation. A developer's failure to give notice of termination as provided herein shall not prevent cancellation of the project's registration under G.S. 93A-52

SECTION B.0200
PUBLIC OFFERING STATEMENT

B.0201 General Provisions

(a) Information contained in a public offering statement shall be accurate on the day it is supplied to a purchaser. Before any public offering statement is supplied to a purchaser, the developer shall file a copy of the statement with the Commission.

(b) In addition to the information required to be contained in a public offering statement by G.S. 93A-44, every public offering statement shall disclose to the purchaser of a time share complete and accurate information concerning:

(1) the real property type of the time share program, whether tenancy-in-common, condominium or other, and a description of the estate the purchaser will own, the term of that estate and the remainder interest, if any, once the term has expired;

(2) the document creating the time share program, a statement that it is the document which governs the

program and a reference to the location where the purchaser may obtain or examine a copy of the document;

(3) whether or not the property is being converted to a time share from some other use and, if so, a statement to that effect and disclosure of the prior use of the property;

(4) the maximum number of time shares in the project, each recreational and other commonly used facility offered, and who or what will own each facility, if the project is to be completed in one development or construction phase;

(5) if the project is planned in phased construction or development, the complete plan of phased offerings, including the maximum number of time shares which may be in the project, each recreational and other commonly used facility, who or what will own each facility, and the developer's representations regarding his or her commitment to build out the project;

(6) the association of owners or other entity which will ultimately be responsible for managing the time share program, the first date or event when the entity will convene or commence to conduct business, each owner's voting right, if any, and whether and for how long the developer, as time share owner, will control the entity;

(7) the location where owners may inspect the articles and bylaws of the owners association, or other organizational documents of the entity and the books and records it produces;

(8) whether the entity has lien rights against time share owners for failure to pay assessments;

(9) whether or not the developer has entered into a management contract on behalf of the managing entity, the extent to which the managing entity's powers are delegated to the manager and the location where a copy of the management contract may be examined;

(10) whether or not the developer will pay assessments for time shares which it owns and a statement that the amount of assessments due the managing entity from owners will change over time, as circumstances may change;

(11) whether or not the developer sponsors or will sponsor a rental or resale program and, if so, a summary of the program or programs; and

(12) the developer's role at the project, if the developer is a separate entity from any other registered developer of the time share project.

(c) The inclusion of false or misleading statements in a public offering statement shall be grounds for disciplinary action by the Commission.

B.0202 Public Offering Statement Summary

Every public offering statement shall contain a one page cover prescribed by the Commission and completed by the developer entitled Public Offering Statement Summary. The Public Offering Statement Summary shall read as follows:

PUBLIC OFFERING STATEMENT SUMMARY

NAME OF PROJECT:

NAME AND REAL ESTATE LICENSE NUMBER OF SALESPERSON:

This Public Offering Statement contains information which deserves your careful study, as you decide whether or not to purchase a time share.

The Public Offering Statement includes general information about the real estate type, the term, and the size of this time share project. It also includes a general description of the recreational and other facilities existing now, or to be provided in the future. The Public Offering Statement will tell you how maintenance and management of the project will be provided and how the costs of these services will be charged to purchasers. From the Public Offering Statement, you will also learn how the project will be governed and whether purchasers will have a voice in that government. You will also learn that a time share instrument will be recorded to protect your real estate interest in your time share.

The Public Offering Statement contains important information, but is not a substitute for the detailed information contained in the contract of purchase and the legal documents which create and affect the time share program at this project.

Please study this Public Offering Statement carefully. Satisfy yourself that any questions you may have are answered before you decide to purchase. If a salesperson or other representative of the developer has made a representation which concerns you, and you cannot find that representation in writing, ask that it be pointed out to you.

NOTICE

UNDER NORTH CAROLINA LAW, YOU MAY CANCEL YOUR TIME SHARE PURCHASE WITHOUT PENALTY WITHIN FIVE DAYS AFTER SIGNING YOUR CONTRACT. TO CANCEL YOUR TIME SHARE PURCHASE, YOU MUST MAIL OR HAND DELIVER WRITTEN NOTICE OF YOUR DESIRE TO CANCEL YOUR PURCHASE TO (name and address of project). IF YOU CHOOSE TO MAIL YOUR CANCELLATION NOTICE, THE NORTH CAROLINA REAL ESTATE COMMISSION RECOMMENDS THAT YOU USE REGISTERED OR CERTIFIED MAIL AND THAT YOU RETAIN YOUR POSTAL RECEIPT AS PROOF OF THE DATE YOUR NOTICE WAS MAILED. UPON CANCELLATION, ALL PAYMENTS WILL BE REFUNDED TO YOU.

B.0203 Receipt for Public Offering Statement

(a) Prior to the execution of any contract to purchase a time share, a time share developer or a time share salesperson shall obtain from the purchaser a written receipt for the public offering statement, which shall display, directly over the buyer signature line in type in all capital letters, no smaller than the largest type on the page on which it appears, the following statement: DO NOT SIGN THIS RECEIPT UNLESS YOU HAVE RECEIVED A COMPLETE COPY OF THE PUBLIC OFFERING STATEMENT TO TAKE WITH YOU.

(b) Receipts for public offering statements shall be maintained as part of the records of the sales transaction.

SECTION B.0300
CANCELLATION

B.0301 Proof of Cancellation

(a) The postmark date affixed to any written notice of a purchaser's intent to cancel his or her time share purchase shall be presumed by the Commission to be the date the notice was mailed to the developer. Evidence tending to rebut this presumption shall be admissible at a hearing before the Commission.

(b) Upon receipt of a purchaser's written notice of his or her intent to cancel his or her time share purchase, the developer, or his or her agent or representative, shall retain the notice and any enclosure, envelope or other cover in the developer's files at the project, and shall produce the file upon the Commission's request.

(c) When there is more than one registered developer at a time share project and a purchaser gives written notice of his or her intent to cancel his or her time share purchase that is received by a developer or sales staff other than the one from whom his or her time share was purchased, the developer or sales staff receiving such notice shall promptly deliver it to the proper developer who shall then honor the notice if it was timely sent by the purchaser.

SECTION B.0400
TIME SHARE SALES OPERATIONS

B.0401 Retention of Time Share Records

A time share developer and a time share salesperson shall retain or cause to be retained for a period of three years complete records of every time share sale, rental, or exchange transaction made by or on behalf of the developer. Records required to be retained shall include but not be limited to offers, applications and contracts to purchase, rent or exchange time shares; records of the deposit, maintenance and disbursement of funds required to be held in trust; receipts; notices of cancellation and their covers if mailed; records regarding compensation of salespersons; public offering statements; and any other records pertaining to time share transactions. Such records shall be made available to the Commission and its representatives upon request.

B.0402 Time Share Agency Agreements and Disclosure

Time share sales transactions conducted by licensees on behalf of a time share developer are subject to 21 NCAC 58A .0104.

SECTION B.0500
HANDLING AND ACCOUNTING OF FUNDS

B.0501 Time Share Trust Funds

(a) Except as otherwise permitted by G.S. 93A-45(c), all monies received by a time share developer or a time share salesperson in connection with a time share sales transaction shall be deposited into a trust or escrow account not later than three banking days following receipt and shall remain in such account for ten days from the date of sale or until cancellation by the purchaser, whichever first occurs.

(b) All monies received by a person licensed as a salesperson in connection with a time share transaction shall be delivered immediately to his or her project broker.

(c) When a time share purchaser timely cancels his or her time share purchase, the developer shall refund to the purchaser all monies paid by the purchaser in connection with the purchase. The refund shall be made no later than 30 days following the date of execution of the contract. Amounts paid by the purchaser with a bank card or a credit card shall be refunded by a cash payment or by issuing a credit voucher to the purchaser within the 30-day period.

(d) Every project broker shall obtain and keep a written representation from the developer as to whether or not lien-free or lien-subordinated time share instruments can be recorded within 45 days of the purchaser's execution of the time share purchase agreement. When a lien-free or lien-subordinated instrument cannot be recorded within said time period, on the business day following the expiration of the ten day time share payment escrow period, a project broker shall transfer from his or her trust account all purchase deposit funds or other payments received from a purchaser who has not canceled his or her purchase agreement, to the independent escrow agent in a check made payable to the independent escrow agent. Alternatively, the check may be made payable to the developer with a restrictive endorsement placed on the back of the check providing "For deposit to the account of the independent escrow agent for the (name of time share project) only."

SECTION B.0600
PROJECT BROKER

B.0601 Designation of Project Broker

The developer of a registered time share project shall designate for each project subject to the developer's control a project broker by filing with the Commission an affidavit on the form prescribed. The developer may from time to time change the designated project broker by filing a new designation form with the Commission within ten days following the change.

B.0602 Duties of the Project Broker

(a) The broker designated by the developer of a time share project to be project broker shall assume responsibility for:

(1) The display of the time share project certificate registration and the license certificates of the real estate salespersons and brokers associated with or engaged on behalf of the developer at the project;

(2) The determination of whether each licensee employed has complied with Rules .0503 and .0506 of Subchapter 58A;

(3) The notification to the Commission of any change in the identity or address of the project or in the identity or address of the developer or marketing or managing entities at the project;

(4) The deposit and maintenance of time share purchase or rental monies in a trust or escrow account until proper disbursement is made; and

(5) The proper maintenance of accurate records at the project including all records relating to the handling of trust monies at the project, records relating to time share sales and rental transactions and the project registration and renewal.

(b) The project broker shall review all contracts, public offering statements and other documents distributed to the purchasers of time shares at the project to ensure that the documents comport with the requirements of the Time Share Act and the rules adopted by the Commission, and to ensure that true and accurate documents have been given to the purchasers.

(c) The project broker shall not permit time share sales to be conducted by any person not licensed as a broker or salesperson, and shall not delegate or assign his or her supervisory responsibilities to any other person, nor accept control of his or her supervisory responsibilities by any other person.

(d) The project broker shall notify the Commission in writing of any change in his or her status as project broker within ten days following the change.

SECTION B.0700—
TIME SHARE FORMS

B.0701 Forms for Time Share Projects

B.0701 is not reprinted in this booklet but is available upon written request to the North Carolina Real Estate Commission.

Subchapter 58C
Real Estate Prelicensing Education

Rules for Subchapter 58C are not reprinted in this booklet but are available upon written request to the North Carolina Real Estate Commission.

Subchapter 58D
Real Estate Appraisers
(Repealed)

Subchapter 58E
Real Estate Continuing Education

Rules for Subchapter 58E are not reprinted in this booklet but are available upon written request to the North Carolina Real Estate Commission.

TRUST ACCOUNT GUIDELINES

I. INTRODUCTION

"Trust" is perhaps the one word which best describes the relationship of the real estate licensee to his or her clients and customers. The seller trusts the licensee to promote his or her best interests in the sale of the property. The investor trusts the licensee/rental manager to manage his or her property and protect the investment. The buyer trusts the licensee to provide complete and accurate information concerning the property which he or she is considering buying. But perhaps nowhere is the licensee's position of trust more clearly illustrated than in his or her role as custodian of the funds of others; i.e., "trust money."

The following information is provided for the purpose of assisting North Carolina real estate licensees in understanding and carrying out their duties and responsibilities as trustees for the funds of others. It is important that both licensees and persons studying for real estate licenses carefully study this material, and that practicing licensees review and evaluate their current procedures in light of this information.

While no single treatment of this subject can possibly answer all questions or address all situations that the licensee may encounter, nevertheless, an attempt has been made to deal with those questions that arise most frequently and to address those situations most often encountered during the course of "typical" real estate transactions. In addition, the specialized areas of property owner association management and rental management have been given separate treatment where it was deemed necessary.

Licensees are reminded that questions or problems involving the handling or accounting of trust money should be directed to the Real Estate Commission office in Raleigh.

II. LEGAL REQUIREMENTS

For most people, a home represents the largest single investment (the most expensive purchase) they will ever make. Rental payments and security deposits represent a substantial financial investment on the part of tenants. Consequently, during the course of real estate transactions, sizable sums of money change hands, a great deal of which passes through the hands of the real estate licensee. Recognizing the very serious consequences of the licensee's actions as a trustee for these funds, the Real Estate License Law (N.C.G.S. 93A) includes a number of provisions designed to govern the activities of real estate licensees acting in the capacity of trustee.

In general, these provisions require licensees to deposit trust monies in an escrow or trust account maintained by a broker (separate from the broker's general or operating account); to maintain complete records of deposits and withdrawals; and to make a final accounting to the persons for whom the broker is holding the funds. Specifically, Section 93A6(a) of the License Law empowers the Real Estate Commission with the ability to suspend or revoke any real estate license or to reprimand or censure any licensee where the licensee is deemed to be guilty of:

(7) Failing, within a reasonable time, to account for or to remit any moneys coming into his or her possession which belong to others.

(12) Commingling the money or other property of his or her principals with his or her own or failure to maintain and deposit in a trust or escrow account in an insured bank or savings and loan association in North Carolina all money received by him or her as a real estate licensee acting in that capacity, or an escrow agent, or the temporary custodian of the funds of others, in a real estate transaction; provided, these accounts shall not bear interest unless the principals authorize in writing the deposit be made in an interest bearing account and also provide for the disbursement of the interest accrued.

(14) Failing, at the time the transaction is consummated, to deliver to the seller in every real estate transaction, a complete detailed closing statement showing all of the receipts and disbursements handled by him or her for the seller or failing to deliver to the buyer a complete statement showing all money received in the transaction from the buyer and how and for what it was disbursed.

Also,

(d) Each broker shall maintain complete records showing the deposit, maintenance, and withdrawal of money or other property owned by his principals or held in escrow or in trust for his principals. The Commission may inspect these records periodically, without prior notice and may also inspect these records whenever the Commission determines that they are pertinent to an investigation of any specific complaint against a licensee.

With regard to monies received in time share sales transactions, Section 93A45 of the License Law requires that:

(c) Any payments received by a time share developer or time share salesperson in connection with the sale of the time share shall be immediately deposited by such developer or salesperson in a trust or escrow account in an insured bank or savings and loan association in North Carolina and shall remain in such account for 10 days or cancellation by the purchaser, whichever occurs first. Payments held in such trust or escrow accounts shall be deemed to belong to the purchaser and not the developer.

In addition, the Real Estate Commission has adopted rules to enable it to administer the statutes. Specifically, these rules are:

A. 0107 Handling and Accounting of Funds

(a) All monies received by a licensee acting in his or her fiduciary capacity shall be deposited in a trust or escrow account maintained by a broker not later than three banking days following receipt of such monies except that earnest money deposits paid by means other than currency which are received on offers to purchase real estate and tenant security deposits paid by means other than currency which are received in connection with real estate leases shall be deposited in a trust or escrow account not later than three banking days following acceptance of such offer to purchase or lease; the date of acceptance of such offer to purchase or lease shall be set forth in the purchase or lease agreement. All monies received by a salesperson shall be delivered immediately to the broker by whom he or she is employed.

(b) In the event monies received by a licensee while acting in a fiduciary capacity are deposited in a trust or escrow account which bears interest, the broker having custody over such monies shall first secure from all parties having an interest in the monies written authorization for the deposit of the monies in an interest-bearing account. Such authorization shall specify how and to whom the interest will be disbursed, and, if contained in an offer, contract, lease, or other transaction instrument, such authorization shall be set forth in a clear and conspicuous manner which shall distinguish it from other provisions of the instrument.

(c) Closing statements shall be furnished to the buyer and the seller in the transaction at the closing or not more than five days after closing.

(d) Trust or escrow accounts shall be so designated by the bank or savings and loan association in which the account is located, and all deposit tickets and checks drawn on said account as well as the monthly bank statement for the account shall bear the words "Trust Account" or "Escrow Account."

(e) A licensee shall maintain and retain records sufficient to identify the ownership of all funds belonging to others. Such records shall be sufficient to show proper deposit of such funds in a trust or escrow account and to verify the accuracy and proper use of the trust or escrow account. The required records shall include but not be limited to:

(1) bank statements.

(2) canceled checks which shall be referenced to the corresponding journal entry or check stub entries and to the corresponding sales transaction ledger sheets or for rental transactions, the corresponding property or owner ledger sheets. Checks shall clearly identify the payee and shall bear a notation identifying the purpose of the disbursement. When a check is used to disburse funds for more than one sales transaction, owner, or property, the check shall bear a notation identifying each sales transaction, owner, or property for which disbursement is made, including the amount disbursed for each, and the corresponding sales transaction, property, or owner ledger entries. When necessary, the check notation may refer to the required information recorded on a supplemental disbursement worksheet which shall be cross-referenced to the corresponding check. In lieu of retaining canceled checks, a licensee may retain digitally imaged copies of the canceled checks provided that such images are legible reproductions of the front and back of the original instruments with no more than four (4) instruments per page and no smaller images than 2.25 x 5.0 inches, and provided that the licensee's bank retains the original checks on file for a period of at least five (5) years and makes them available to the licensee and the Commission upon request.

(3) deposit tickets. For a sales transaction, the deposit ticket shall identify the purpose and remitter of the funds deposited, the property, the parties involved, and a reference to the corresponding sales transaction ledger entry. For a rental transaction, the deposit ticket shall identify the purpose and remitter of the funds deposited, the tenant, and the corresponding property or owner ledger entry. For deposits of funds belonging to or collected on behalf of a property owner association, the deposit ticket shall identify the property or property interest for which the payment is made, the property or interest owner, the remitter, and the purpose of the payment. When a single deposit ticket is used to deposit funds collected for more than one sales transaction, property owner, or property, the required information shall be recorded on the ticket for each sales transaction, owner, or property, or the ticket may refer to the same information recorded on a supplemental deposit worksheet which shall be cross-referenced to the corresponding deposit ticket.

(4) a payment record sheet for each property or interest for which funds are collected and deposited into a property owner association trust account as required by Subsection (i) of this Rule. Payment record sheets shall identify the amount, date, remitter, and purpose of payments received, the amount

and nature of the obligation for which payments are made, and the amount of any balance due or delinquency.

(5) a separate ledger sheet for each sales transaction and for each property or owner of property managed by the broker identifying the property, the parties to the transaction, the amount, date, and purpose of the deposits and from whom received, the amount, date, check number, and purpose of disbursements and to whom paid, and the running balance of funds on deposit for the particular sales transaction or, in a rental transaction, the particular property or owner of property. Monies held as tenant security deposits in connection with rental transactions may be accounted for on a separate tenant security deposit ledger for each property or owner of property managed by the broker. For each security deposit the tenant security deposit ledger shall identify the remitter, the date the deposit was paid, the amount, the tenant, landlord, and subject property. For each disbursement of tenant security deposit monies, the ledger shall identify the check number, amount, payee, date, and purpose of the disbursement. The ledger shall also show a running balance. When tenant security deposit monies are accounted for on a separate ledger as provided herein, deposit tickets, canceled checks and supplemental worksheets shall reference the corresponding tenant security deposit ledger entries when appropriate.

(6) a journal or check stubs identifying in chronological sequence each bank deposit and disbursement of monies to and from the trust or escrow account, including the amount and date of each deposit and an appropriate reference to the corresponding deposit ticket and any supplemental deposit worksheet, and the amount, date, check number, and purpose of disbursements and to whom paid. The journal or check stubs shall also show a running balance for all funds in the account.

(7) copies of contracts, leases and management agreements.

(8) closing statements and property management statements.

(9) covenants, bylaws, minutes, management agreements and periodic statements relating to the management of a property owner association.

(10) invoices, bills, and contracts paid from the trust account, and any documents not otherwise described herein necessary and sufficient to verify and explain record entries.

Records of all receipts and disbursements of trust or escrow monies shall be maintained in such a manner as to create a clear audit trail from deposit tickets and canceled checks to check stubs or journals and to the ledger sheets. Ledger sheets and journals or check stubs must be reconciled to the trust or escrow account bank statements on a monthly basis. To be sufficient, records of trust or escrow monies must include a worksheet for each such monthly reconciliation showing the ledger sheets, journals or check stubs, and bank statements to be in agreement and balance.

(f) All trust or escrow account records shall be made available for inspection by the Commission or its authorized representatives in accordance with Rule 58A .0108.

(g) In the event of a dispute between the seller and buyer or landlord and tenant over the return or forfeiture of any deposit other than a residential tenant security deposit held by a licensee, the licensee shall retain said deposit in a trust or escrow account until the licensee has obtained a written release from the parties consenting to its disposition and or until disbursement is ordered by a court of competent jurisdiction. If it appears to a broker holding a disputed deposit that a party has abandoned his or her claim, the broker may disburse the money to the other claiming parties according to their written agreement provided that the broker first makes a reasonable effort to notify the party who has apparently abandoned his or her claim and provides that party with an opportunity to renew his or her claim to the disputed funds. Tenant security deposit monies shall be disposed of in accordance with the requirements of N.C.G.S. 42-50 through 56 and N.C.G.S. 42A-18.

(h) A broker may transfer earnest money deposits in his or her possession collected in connection with a sales transaction from his or her trust account to the closing attorney or other settlement agent not more than ten days prior to the anticipated settlement date. A licensee shall not disburse prior to settlement any earnest money in his or her possession for any other purpose without the written consent of the parties.

(i) The funds of a property owner association, when collected, maintained, disbursed or otherwise controlled by a licensee, are trust monies and shall be treated as such in the manner required by this Rule. Such funds must be deposited into and maintained in a trust or escrow account or accounts dedicated exclusively for funds belonging to a single property owner association and may not be commingled with funds belonging to other property owner associations or other persons or parties. A licensee who undertakes to act as manager of a property owner association or as the custodian of funds belonging to a property owner association shall provide the association with periodic statements which report the balance of association funds in the licensee's possession or control and which account for the funds the licensee has received and disbursed on behalf of the association. Such statements must be made in accordance with the licensee's agreement with the association, but in no event shall the statements be made less frequently than every 90 days.

(j) Every licensee shall safeguard the money or property of others coming into his or her possession in a manner consistent with the requirements of the Real Estate License Law and the rules adopted by the Commission. A licensee shall not convert the money or property of others to his or her own use, apply such money or property to a purpose other than that for which it was paid or entrusted to him or her, or permit or assist any other person in the conversion or misapplication of such money or property.

(k) In addition to the records required by subdivision (e) of this rule, a licensee acting as agent for the landlord of a residential property used for vacation rentals shall create and maintain a subsidiary ledger sheet for each property or owner of such properties onto which all funds collected and disbursed are identified in categories by purpose. On a monthly basis, the licensee shall reconcile the subsidiary ledger sheet to the corresponding property or property owner ledger sheet.

B. 0501 Time Share Trust Funds

(a) Except as otherwise permitted by G.S. 93A45(c), all monies received by a time share developer or a time share salesperson in connection with a time share sales transaction shall be deposited into a trust or escrow account not later than three banking days following receipt and shall remain in such account for ten days from the date of sale or until cancellation by the purchaser, whichever first occurs.

(b) All monies received by a person licensed as a salesperson in connection with a time share transaction shall be delivered immediately to his or her project broker.

(c) When a time share purchaser timely cancels his or her time share purchase, the developer shall refund to the purchaser all monies paid by the purchaser in connection with the purchase. The refund shall be made no later than 30 days following the date of execution of the contract. Amounts paid by the purchaser with a bank card or a credit card shall be refunded by a cash payment or by issuing a credit voucher to the purchaser within the 30 day period.

(d) Every project broker shall obtain and keep a written representation from the developer as to whether or not lien-free or lien-subordinated time share instruments can be recorded within 45 days of the purchaser's execution of the time share purchase agreement. When a lien-free or lien-subordinated instrument cannot be recorded within said time period, on the business day following the expiration of the ten day time share payment escrow period, a project broker shall transfer from his or her trust account all purchase deposit funds or other payments received from a purchaser who has not canceled his or her purchase agreement, to the independent escrow agent in a check made payable to the independent escrow agent. Alternatively, the check may be made payable to the developer with a restrictive endorsement placed on the back of the check providing "For deposit to the account of the independent escrow agent for the (name of time share project) only."

The Commission considers violations of these laws and rules to be a particularly serious matter. In fact, more licensees are disciplined for trust money or trust account violations than for any other single type of offense.

III. TRUST MONEY

Definition

In the context of real estate transactions, "trust money" is most commonly money belonging to others received by a real estate licensee who is acting as an agent in a real estate transaction. Certain monies, such as tenant security deposits and time share down payment monies are trust money simply because the law declares them to be. Also, a licensee who acts as the temporary custodian of money belonging to others must hold that money in trust even if the circumstances are only collateral to the licensee's role as an agent in a real estate related matter. For example, a licensee who collects money on behalf of a property owner associations must deposit that money into a properly designated trust or escrow account.

The most common examples of trust money are earnest money deposits, down payments, tenant security deposits, rents, homeowner association dues and assessments, and money received from final settlements. In the case of resort and other short-term rentals, trust money would also include advance reservation deposits and the state (and local, if applicable) sales taxes on the gross receipts from such rentals.

Except for a deposit of $100 or less to protect the trust account from bank fees, it is inappropriate for a licensee to mix trust money he or she holds for others with his or her own money or money in which he or she has a personal financial interest. This impermissible mixing of trust money is referred to as commingling. For example, it would be commingling if a broker were to deposit and maintain his or her own commission money in his or her trust account.

When a licensee commingles the money he or she holds for others with his or her own in the same bank account, he or she creates doubt whether the account is, in fact, a trust account. These doubts may deprive the account of the special status given to trust accounts and may place money belonging to the licensee's customers and clients in jeopardy.

IV. TRUST ACCOUNTS

Definition/Purpose

A "trust account" (or "escrow account") is simply a bank account into which trust money (and only trust money) is deposited. It must be a separate custodial account which provides for withdrawal of funds on demand (without prior notice).

By depositing trust money in a trust account and keeping accurate records that identify each depositor (buyer, seller, landlord, tenant, etc.), the depositors are protected from the funds being "frozen" (attached) should the broker/trustee become involved in legal action or become incapacitated or die. Also, deposits are insured by the Federal Deposit Insurance Corporation (FDIC), up to $100,000 per each individual for whom funds are deposited. For example, if a broker is holding $60,000 in his or her trust account for one client, and $50,000 for another, both clients' deposits will be fully insured, assuming neither has other money on deposit in personal accounts in the same bank which would raise the total of his or her money in the bank over $100,000. (Funds in excess of $100,000 for one individual at the same bank are not insured, whether the funds are in one account or spread among several accounts.) Furthermore, by placing these funds in a separate account, brokers are less likely to confuse the trust money with their personal or business funds and inadvertently use trust money (which belongs to others) for personal or business purposes.

Opening the Account

Trust accounts must be opened and maintained in either an insured bank or savings and loan association in North Carolina. A broker who is not using his or her real estate license is not required to open or maintain a trust account. Likewise, if a practicing broker does not collect or otherwise handle the funds of others, no trust account is required. Only when the broker or a licensee associated with the broker or under the broker's supervision takes possession of trust money must the broker open and properly maintain a trust account.

When a broker holds trust money in sales or rental transactions, only one trust account is required, and all earnest money deposits, tenant security deposits, rents, and other trust money can be deposited into this one common account. However, brokers who are active in both sales and rental management often find it helpful to use more than one trust account. For example, they may wish to keep a "general sales trust account" for earnest money deposits, settlement proceeds, etc., and a "rental trust account" for tenant security deposits, rents, and related receipts. Although it is not required, many brokers involved in rental management elect to maintain an additional "security deposit trust account" for the purpose of separating tenant security deposits from rents and other related receipts.

Brokers who manage a property owner association must deposit and maintain that association's trust funds in a trust or escrow account dedicated exclusively for funds of that association. A property owner association's trust funds must not be commingled with the funds belonging to another property owner association or with the funds belonging to third parties (earnest money deposits, security deposits, rents, etc. belonging to third parties). Brokers may open more than one trust account for a property owner association. A salesperson coming into control of the trust funds of an association must deposit and maintain that association's trust funds in a trust account maintained by a broker.

Broker-Owner Trust Monies

Brokers who sell or lease their own property must not commingle funds received in connection with these properties with funds they hold in trust for others. Earnest money, tenant security deposits and other funds required to be held in trust in connection with broker-owned property must be held in a separate trust account.

For example, if a broker does business as a sole proprietorship, and also owns several rental houses, the broker must not deposit either the rents or the tenant security deposits for the rental properties he or she owns into his or her sole proprietorship trust account since it contains other clients' funds. This would constitute commingling. Instead, because the Tenant Security Deposit Act requires all residential landlords to keep the tenant's security deposit in a trust account, the broker should set up a separate trust account for the security deposits from his or her own tenants.

Only when the owner of the rental property and the owner of the real estate company are separate legal identities may the broker deposit trust monies from the rental property into the real estate company trust account. Thus, for example, if the broker's real estate company is a corporation and the rental property is owned by the broker individually, then the corporation may manage the individual broker's rental property and may deposit both rental receipts and tenant security deposits into the corporate trust account(s) established for third party clients of the corporation.

A broker who is uncertain whether money from personally-owned rental properties can be deposited into his or her trust account should maintain a separate trust account in order to assure compliance and avoid commingling.

A trust account must be designated as a "Trust Account" or "Escrow Account" by the bank (or savings and loan association) in which the account is located, and all bank statements, deposit tickets and checks drawn on the account must bear the words, "Trust Account" or "Escrow Account."

Trust accounts are subject to the same service charges as regular checking accounts. Whenever possible, brokers should arrange for the depository to either bill them for these expenses or charge these expenses to the broker's personal or general operating account. However, if such arrangements cannot be made, the broker may deposit and maintain in his or her trust account a maximum of $100.00 of his or her personal funds (or such other amount as may be required) to cover such charges. A broker who keeps $100 of his or her own money in the trust account must be careful to properly enter and identify personal funds on the deposit ticket and on a personal funds ledger sheet in his or her trust account records. Thereafter, the broker must record any bank charges as they occur in his or her trust account journal or check stub running balance and post the bank charges on the personal funds ledger sheet.

Interest-Bearing Trust Accounts

Trust money may be deposited in an interest-bearing trust account ONLY under the following conditions: (1) the broker must obtain from the persons for whom he or she is holding the funds written authorization to deposit the funds into an interest-bearing account; (2) the authorization must clearly specify how and to whom the interest will be disbursed; and (3) if the authorization is contained in an offer, contract, lease or other transaction instrument, it must be set forth in a manner which shall draw attention to the authorization and distinguish it from other provisions of the instrument (for example, italics, boldface type, underlining, a blank _____ to be filled in with the name of the party to whom the interest will be paid, or some similar means).

Inasmuch as trust money must be deposited in a demand account in an insured bank or savings and loan association, the investment of such funds in any type of security, including government bonds, would be prohibited. The investment of trust money in most certificates of deposit is also prohibited. Trust money may be maintained in a certificate of deposit with an insured bank or savings and loan association only if the certificate of deposit is insured and the terms governing it permit withdrawal of the trust money on demand and without any penalty that would reduce the principal amount of the trust money invested in this manner. Trust monies may not be deposited in sweep accounts or invested in repurchase agreements.

V. DEPOSITING TRUST MONEY

Who Should Deposit?

When listing property for sale or lease, a provision should be included in the listing or rental management agreement naming the broker as trustee or escrow agent for the purpose of receiving and holding trust money. Likewise, offers to purchase, sales agreements, leases, etc. should specify in whose account the trust money will be held so that all persons who have an interest in the funds will know whom to hold responsible for their safekeeping.

Unless the parties have agreed otherwise, trust money received by a licensee working with a buyer in a co-brokered sales transaction should be immediately delivered to the listing broker for deposit into the listing broker's trust account. In general, all trust money received by an individual licensee who is associated with or employed by a broker or brokerage firm should, of course, be deposited in the trust account of the employing broker or firm. All trust money received by a real estate salesperson must be immediately delivered to the salesperson's supervising broker.

A broker may transfer possession of trust money to a bookkeeper, secretary, or some other clerical employee for that person to deposit the funds in a trust account; however, the broker will still be held responsible for the care and custody of such funds. Brokers should closely and diligently supervise the acts of these persons. Periodic audits and bonding of such persons is recommended.

When to Deposit?

Earnest money received on offers to purchase and tenant security deposits received in connection with leases must be deposited in a trust account not later than three banking days following acceptance of the offer to purchase or lease; however, cash deposits must be deposited not later than three banking days following receipt of such deposits. The date of acceptance must be shown in the purchase or lease agreement. Rents, settlement proceeds, and other trust money must be deposited in a trust account not later than three banking days following receipt of the funds.

VI. DISBURSING TRUST MONEY

Permitted Uses/Access

The instrument creating the trust (sales contract, rental management agreement, lease, etc.) should clearly state to whom and under what conditions the trust money will be disbursed (especially in the event the transaction is not consummated). Brokers may disburse trust money only for the purpose(s) set forth in this instrument; for example, brokers may not use trust money to pay for credit reports, surveys, appraisal fees, or other transaction expenses without the consent of both the buyer and the seller, or the landlord and tenant.

Access to trust money should be limited and carefully controlled. Although a broker may authorize a secretary, a bookkeeper, or some other person who is not a party to the transaction to sign checks withdrawing trust money, the broker will not escape liability and responsibility for the misuse of the funds by such persons. Again, brokers are advised to closely supervise these persons, and periodic audits and bonding of such persons are recommended.

When to Disburse?

Sales Transactions:

In "sales transactions," brokers will normally disburse trust money upon the happening of one of the following events:

(1) Upon revocation or rejection of an offer. A buyer (offeror) may revoke an offer to purchase at any time prior to being notified of the acceptance of the offer. If the buyer revokes his or her offer or if the offer is rejected by the seller (offeree), then the broker should return the earnest money to the buyer. However, if the earnest money is in the form of a personal check which has already been deposited by the broker, the broker should not refund the deposit until the check has cleared.

(2) Upon termination of a transaction. If, for some reason, a transaction is not consummated and there is no dispute between the parties as to the disposition of the trust money, then the broker should disburse the money according to the provisions of the sales agreement. However, in the event of a dispute between the buyer and seller over the funds (or if the broker has reason to believe that such a dispute may arise), then the broker must attempt to obtain a written release from the parties consenting to its disposition, and failing this, the broker must retain the funds in his or her trust account until the dispute is litigated by the parties and disbursement is ordered by a court of competent jurisdiction.

(3) Upon closing of a transaction. At the successful conclusion of a real estate transaction, any funds pertaining to the transaction which are on deposit in the broker's trust account should be paid to and subsequently disbursed by the person designated to close the transaction (usually an attorney or lending officer).

Occasionally, however, the broker will actually conduct the closing and disburse the funds. In such cases, brokers should not transfer trust money from their trust account to their general business account for final disbursement, because this would result in a commingling of trust money and non-trust money during that period of time in which the trust money is in the business account. Trust money should be disbursed directly from the trust account to the persons entitled to such funds.

Furthermore, brokerage fees, including interest earned on interest-bearing accounts, or commissions (when earned), should be disbursed promptly (within 30 days) from the trust account to the broker's general business account, with each check clearly indicating the specific transaction to which it applies. When a broker retains deposit money in his or her trust account in order to pay all or a part of the commission or fees owed to him or other licensees involved, he or she should pay the money from his or her trust account into his or her general business account and make further payments from that account. Brokers should not, of course, withdraw from the trust account any portion of their earned commissions prior to closing without the express consent of all parties to the transaction.

Lease Transactions:

In "lease transactions," that is, transactions involving the leasing or renting of real estate for others, the leasing agent or rental manager must deposit all rental income and tenant security deposits in his or her trust account; likewise, all disbursements required in connection with the property must be made directly from the trust account to the person(s) entitled to such funds. In general, disbursements of rental income are made to pay the operating expenses of the leased property (utilities, maintenance, mortgage payments, administrative costs, etc.) with the balance being remitted to the property owner. The scope and extent of the rental manager's authority to expend funds on behalf of the owner should be expressly stated in the Rental Management Agreement.

The rental manager must pay these operating expenses in a timely manner; however, disbursements must not at any time exceed the amount of funds on hand for that particular property owner. For example, if the manager has collected only $300 in rent from property owned by Mr. A, he or she cannot disburse $400 from his or her trust account to repair Mr. A's roof. Although the total of all funds in the trust account may be sufficient to cover the $400 expenditure, such payment would, of course, result in the disbursement of funds belonging to other persons to pay for Mr. A's roof.

The Rental Management Agreement should specify the procedure to follow in situations where expenses exceed receipts for a particular owner. For example, the agreement may authorize the broker to hold a certain sum of money in reserve, or the manager may agree to pay such expenses from his or her general operating account and then be reimbursed as rents are collected. The rental manager should not, however, place any of his or her own funds into his or her trust account to offset such "deficit spending," because this would, of course, constitute a commingling of the rental manager's funds with funds which he or she is holding for others.

Regarding the disposition of tenant security deposits, the rental manager or leasing agent should be aware that such deposits may be used only for certain specified purposes, and if not used, the deposit must be promptly refunded to the tenant (certainly within 30 days after termination of the tenancy). Chapter 42, Article 6 of the North Carolina General Statutes, entitled "Tenant Security Deposit Act," with which brokers acting in the capacity of rental managers, leasing agents, etc. should be thoroughly familiar, sets forth the permitted uses of the deposit. These permitted uses are nonpayment of rent, actual damage to the premises, excluding ordinary wear and tear, nonfulfillment of the rental period, unpaid bills which become a lien on the property, the reasonable costs of re-renting the premises after breach of the lease by the tenant, costs of removal and storage of tenant's property after a summary ejectment proceeding and court costs in connection with terminating the tenancy. Brokers must remain aware that security deposits are the property of the tenants, not the owners, during the duration of the tenancy.

Rental management fees, including interest earned by the broker, should be disbursed promptly (within 30 days) from the trust account to the broker's general business account, and division of earned fees among the broker's agents should be handled through the general business account.

VII. RECORDKEEPING AND ACCOUNTING

Retention of Records

Brokers are required to maintain complete records of all trust account receipts and disbursements, including bank statements, canceled checks, deposit tickets, closing statements, rental management reports and agreements, copies of offers (both accepted and rejected), copies of contracts, leases and rental management agreements, property owner association management agreements, covenants, by-laws, minutes, periodic statements and other transaction records. Rule A.0107(e) requires brokers to maintain copies of these documents as well as other detailed books and records. The use and maintenance of separate ledger sheets comparable to those illustrated in the "Guidelines" is required. In the event a branch office maintains a separate trust account, a separate bookkeeping system should be maintained in such office.

Trust Account Journal

Pursuant to Rule A.0107(e)(5), the broker's trust account records must include a journal or check stubs. The journal records in chronological sequence trust money received and disbursed by the broker on behalf of all parties. The bookkeeping entries recorded in the journal must include the following information: 1) the amount and date of each bank deposit and an appropriate reference to the corresponding deposit ticket and any supplemental deposit worksheet (the Commission recommends sequentially numbering deposit tickets and noting the number on the journal and the supplemental deposit worksheet); 2) the amount, date, check number and purpose of disbursements and to whom paid; and 3) a running balance for all funds in the trust account (the running balances must be recorded after each deposit and disbursement entry).

Trust Account Ledgers

In a real estate sales transaction where a broker receives trust funds, ledger sheets record in chronological sequence trust money received (earnest money deposits, closing proceeds, etc.) and disbursed by the broker for each sales transaction. In the case of rental management, ledger sheets record in chronological sequence trust money received (rents, security deposits, etc.) and disbursed by the broker for a particular property or property owner. Each ledger sheet must identify the seller or landlord's name, the buyer or tenant's name and the property address of the property sold or managed by the broker. The bookkeeping entries to each ledger sheet must include: 1) the amount, date, and purpose of the bank deposits and from whom received; 2) the amount, date, check number and purpose of disbursements and to whom paid; and 3) a running balance of funds on deposit for the particular sales transaction or, in a rental transaction, the particular property or property owner.

Security Deposit Ledgers

The receipt of a tenant security deposit and any corresponding disbursement of the security deposit for a property managed by a broker may be recorded on a separate ledger sheet apart from the ledger sheet that records the income and expenses on behalf of the property or property owner. This ledger sheet must identify the property owner's name, the tenant's name, and the property address. The bookkeeping entries posted to this security deposit ledger sheet must include the same information as described above under "Trust Account Ledgers."

Payment Record Sheets

In a property owner association transaction where a broker receives trust funds, a payment record sheet for each property or property interest records in chronological sequence the accrual of assessments or monies due and any corresponding receipt of monies. Each payment record sheet must identify 1) the amount, date, remitter and purpose of payments received, 2) the amount and nature of the obligation, and 3) the amount of balance due. Essentially, a payment record sheet is an accounts receivable ledger maintained on an accrual account basis and maintained by property or property interest.

Timeliness

It must be emphasized that all receipts and disbursements must be recorded in the journal and posted to the applicable ledger sheet in a timely manner. Also, reconciliation worksheets should be prepared within a reasonable time frame after receipt of the trust account bank statement. A broker's failure to follow these accounting and bookkeeping principles increases the risk of errors and the misapplication of trust money.

Trust Account Deposit Tickets

A broker should maintain as part of his or her trust account records a bank-validated deposit ticket for each bank deposit. This bank-validated deposit ticket is the broker's record evidencing deposit of trust funds into the trust account. In a sales transaction, the bank-validated deposit ticket must identify 1) the purpose (earnest money deposit) and the remitter of funds deposited; 2) the property; 3) the parties involved (buyer and seller); and 4) a reference to the corresponding sales transaction ledger sheet. If the remitter and the buyer are the same, then only one name would be required to identify both the remitter and buyer.

In a rental transaction, the bank-validated deposit ticket must identify 1) the purpose (rent, security deposit, etc.) and the remitter of funds deposited; 2) the tenant; and 3) the corresponding property or owner ledger sheet. If the remitter and the tenant are the same, then only one name would be required to identify both the remitter and the tenant.

In a property owner association transaction, the bank-validated deposit ticket must identify 1) the property or property interest (example: time share interest) for which the payment is deposited, 2) the property or interest owner, 3) the remitter, and 4) the purpose of the payment.

Trust Account Checks

Original canceled checks must be obtained from the bank for all broker trust accounts. They must be retained as part of the broker's trust account records. In lieu of canceled checks, a broker may retain digitally imaged copies of the canceled checks. The front and back of the imaged copies of the original canceled checks must be legible with no more than four checks per page. The image of each check must be no smaller than 2.25 x 5.0 inches. Also, the bank must retain the original canceled checks for a period of at least 5 years and provide the checks upon request. Canceled checks can be retained on a computer CD ROM (produced by the bank) as long as the checks can be reproduced as described above.

When preparing a check disbursing trust monies from a trust account, the broker must include on the face of the check a reference to the corresponding journal entry or check stub entry. The check number and date on the check are sufficient to reference the corresponding journal entry as long as the check is easily traceable to the entry recording the check in the journal.

Also, the check must reference the corresponding sales transaction ledger sheets or for rental transactions, the corresponding property or owner ledger sheets. In a sales transaction, identifying the buyer, seller and property address on the check is sufficient to reference a check to the sales transaction ledger. For a rental transaction, identifying the property address on the check is sufficient to reference a check to a property ledger sheet or an owner's name is sufficient to reference a check to an owner ledger sheet.

The purpose of the disbursement must be identified on the face of the check or on the corresponding supplemental disbursement worksheet.

Supplemental Worksheets

A bank deposit ticket may include monies from more than one real estate transaction and it may be impractical to identify on it all the monies deposited into the trust account on a deposit ticket. When a single deposit ticket is used for multiple transactions, the broker may create a supplemental deposit worksheet and record on it the information necessary to properly trace the deposited monies. For example, rents collected in cash from various tenants could be recorded on a single deposit ticket as currency and deposited in a lump sum amount. The required identifying information must then be recorded on a supplemental deposit worksheet referencing the deposit ticket. To reference the worksheet to the deposit ticket, the broker must at least record the date and the total amount of the deposit on the worksheet. The Commission recommends sequentially numbering the deposit tickets and recording that number on the worksheet, journal, and ledger sheets as well as the date and the amount.

Likewise, a check may represent disbursements applicable to more than one sales transaction, property, or property owner ledger sheet and it may be impractical to identify all the corresponding ledger sheets on the check itself. For example, one check may be written to disburse rental management fees applicable to various properties. In such an instance, a supplemental disbursement worksheet referencing the corresponding check (date, check number, payee and amount) must be prepared for the check showing the identity of the monies disbursed out of the trust account as outlined above under "Trust Account Checks".

Reconciliation/Trial Balance

Rule A.0107(e) further requires that brokers report all receipts and disbursements of trust monies in such a manner as to create a clear audit trail from deposit tickets and canceled checks to check stubs or journals and to the ledger sheets. A broker must reconcile ledger sheets and his or her journal or check stubs to the trust account bank statements on a monthly basis. The broker must create a worksheet (Trial Balance) for each such monthly reconciliation and must retain the worksheet (Trial Balance) as part of his or her trust account records.

The trial balance must identify each ledger (e.g. buyer and seller, property address, tenant, etc.) and show the ledger balances as of the date of the trial balance. A trial balance is simply a list of all funds in the trust or escrow account and the identification of the owners of those funds. The month-end bank statement balance must be reconciled to the checkbook and/or journal balance (i.e. running balance of funds on deposit) taking into consideration outstanding checks and deposits. The checkbook and/or journal balance should equal (be balanced with) the total outstanding liability as shown on the ledgers (individual transaction ledgers).

Trust account records must be retained by brokers for at least three years after all the funds held by the licensee in connection with the transaction have been disbursed or until the successful or unsuccessful conclusion of the transaction, whichever occurs later. The trust account records must be made available for inspection by the Commission or its authorized representatives without prior notice. [NOTE: The Real Estate Commission employs Trust Account Auditors to make "spot inspections" of trust accounts and to assist in the investigation of complaints alleging improper handling of trust money.]

Computers

The Commission receives numerous inquiries concerning the format of bookkeeping systems, especially computerized bookkeeping systems. The Commission cannot endorse or recommend a specific computer product for brokers to use. The basic requirements for the computerized bookkeeping system are the same as those requirements for a manual system. The broker-in-charge is encouraged to review these requirements prior to investing in a computerized bookkeeping system that may not comply with Commission guidelines.

Certain software vendors have submitted to the Commission their bookkeeping software systems for evaluation of compliance with the Commission's Rules and Trust Account Guidelines. A list of the softwares evaluated and found to substantially comply can be found on the Commission's web site at ncrec.state.nc.us.

Accounting to Principals

Brokers must account for all trust money which they receive and disburse during the course of a real estate transaction. In the rental management area, this accounting would be in the form of a "rental management report", in sales transactions, a "closing statement" and in property owner association management, a "periodic statement" is used.

Although no specific form or format is required, the rental management report, the closing statement and the periodic statement must set forth in a clear and concise fashion a complete accounting of all funds received and disbursed by the broker.

Rental Management Reports:

The "rental management report" is simply a periodic accounting to the owner of all funds received and paid out in connection with the owner's property. The major item of income is, of course, rent, and the major expense items include utilities, maintenance expenses, and administrative costs. It is the responsibility of the broker/rental manager to see that the property owner receives this income and expense report at such times as are required by the management agreement (usually monthly) and that the report covers all receipts and disbursements handled by the rental manager on behalf of the owner. The broker/rental manager must also make a full accounting to the tenant, within 30 days of the termination of the tenancy, regarding the tenant's security deposit (See G.S. 4252).

Closing Statements:

The "closing statement" is used in sales transactions to show all receipts and disbursements that the broker has handled for the seller, and all money that the broker has received from the buyer and how much money was disbursed. While it is the broker's responsibility to see that the buyer and seller receive a copy of this statement(s) at the closing of the transaction (or not more than five days after closing), the broker is not required to personally prepare the closing statements. He or she may instead elect to adopt the statements prepared by the person who closed the transaction (usually an attorney or lending officer) provided such statements account for all funds received and disbursed in the transaction; however, the broker will be held responsible for the accuracy of closing statements he or she provides to the parties, regardless of who prepares such closing statements.

Periodic Statements:

Licensees who manage a property owner association or who are the custodian of funds of an association must provide to that association periodic statements of not only the balance of the trust funds in the licensee's control but also an accounting of the trust funds received and disbursed on behalf of the association. The periodic statements must be provided by the licensee to the property owner association in accordance with the property management agreement, but in no event less frequently than every 90 days. The property owner association balance sheet and income statement of the funds in the licensee's control is sufficient to account to the association as periodic statements.

YOUR REALTY COMPANY, INC.

TRUST ACCOUNT JOURNAL

NC Insured Bank A/C# 123-456-7890

DATE	DESCRIPTION	NUM		DEPOSITS	CHECKS	BALANCE
1/03/0X	DEPOSIT	0X-1 (A)	√	$3,600.00		$3,600.00
1/04/0X	DEPOSIT	0X-2	√	$2,300.00		$5,900.00
1/11/0X	Ajax Plumbing - 143 N. Blvd - Repairs	101	√		$75.00	$5,825.00
1/20/0X	Gerald Howard - 143 N. Blvd Net Jan Rent to Owner	102			$465.00	$5,360.00
1/21/0X	Your Realty Company, Inc. 1/0X Mgt Fees	103	√		$115.00	$5,245.00
1/22/0X	Jack Thomas - NSF - 1362 Main St	DM (B)	√		$2,500.00	$2,745.00
1/30/0X	F. Lee Bailey, Attorney 119 Maple Closing	104			$1,000.00	$1,745.00
1/31/0X	DEPOSIT	0X-3		$2,500.00		$4,245.00
1/31/0X	NC Insured Bank Check Printing Charges	DM	√		$25.00	$4,220.00

(A) - **Referenced to sequentially numbered deposit tickets**
(B) - **Debit Memo**
√ - **Cleared Bank**

DEPOSIT TICKET

YOUR REALTY COMPANY, INC.
TRUST ACCOUNT
DATE _____ 1/3/0X _____

0X-1

	DOLLARS	CENTS
CURRENCY		
COINS		
CHECKS		
1. Your Realty Co, Inc.	$100	00
2. Personal Funds		
3.		
4. Jones to Wood - EMD	$1,000	00
5. 119 Maple St		
6.		
7. Clay to Thomas	$2,500	00
8. EMD - 1362 Main		
9. Street		
TOTAL	$3,600	00

DEPOSIT TICKET

YOUR REALTY COMPANY, INC.
TRUST ACCOUNT
DATE _____ 1/31/0X _____

0X-3

	DOLLARS	CENTS
CURRENCY		
COINS		
CHECKS		
1. Thomas - 1362 Main	$2,500	00
2. Street - Redeposit		
3. EMD - NSF Check		
4. Clay, Seller		
5.		
6.		
7.		
8.		
9.		
TOTAL	$2,500	00

DEPOSIT TICKET

YOUR REALTY COMPANY, INC.
TRUST ACCOUNT

DATE _____1/4/0X_____

0X-2

	DOLLARS	CENTS
CURRENCY SDW (C)	$2,300	00
COINS		
CHECKS		
1.		
2.		
3.		
4.		
TOTAL	$2,300	00

(C) - Referenced to supplemental deposit worksheet for deposit ticket #2.

SUPPLEMENTAL DEPOSIT WORKSHEET
Deposit Ticket #2   (D)
1/4/0X

REMITTER/BUYER/TENANT	PROPERTY	PURPOSE	AMOUNT
Clark	143 North Boulevard	Security Deposit	$600.00
Clark	143 North Boulevard	Jan Rent	$600.00
Stephens	2500 Johnson Street	Security Deposit	$550.00
Stephens	2500 Johnson Street	Jan Rent	$550.00
	TOTAL		$2,300.00

(D)-Supplemental deposit worksheet cross-referenced back to deposit ticket #2.

LEDGERS

NAME: Your Realty Company, Inc. - Personal Funds				ACCOUNT NO.		
ADDRESS:				SHEET NO.		
DATE		ITEMS		DEPOSITS	CHECKS	BALANCE
1/03	OX	Your Realty Company Inc. Personal Funds	OX-1	$100.00		$100.00
1/31	OX	NC Insured Bank Check Printing Charges	DM		$25.00	$75.00

NAME: Jones (Seller) to Wood (Buyer)				ACCOUNT NO.		
ADDRESS: 119 Maple St				SHEET NO.		
DATE		ITEMS		DEPOSITS	CHECKS	BALANCE
1/03	OX	John Wood EMD	OX-1	$1,000.00		$1,000.00
1/30	OX	F. Lee Bailey, Attorney Closing	104		$1,000.00	$0.00

NAME: Clay (Seller) to Thomas (Buyer)				ACCOUNT NO.		
ADDRESS: 1362 Main Street				SHEET NO.		
DATE		ITEMS		DEPOSITS	CHECKS	BALANCE
1/03	OX	Jack Thomas EMD	OX-1	$2,500.00		$2,500.00
1/22	OX	Jack Thomas NSF	DM		$2500.00	$0.00
1/31	OX	Jack Thomas Redeposit NSF EMD Check	OX-3	$2,500.00		$2,500.00

LEDGERS

NAME: Gerald Howard, Owner - - Clark, Tenant				ACCOUNT NO.		
ADDRESS: 143 North Boulevard				SHEET NO.		
DATE		ITEMS		DEPOSITS	CHECKS	BALANCE
1/04	0X	Charles Clark Security Deposit	0X-2	$600.00		$600.00
1/04	0X	Charles Clark Jan Rent	0X-2	$600.00		$1,200.00
1/11	0X	Ajax Plumbing Repairs	101		$75.00	$1,125.00
1/20	0X	Gerald Howard Net Jan Rent To Owner	102		$465.00	$660.00
1/21	0X	Your Realty Co., Inc. Jan Management Fee	103		$60.00	$600.00

NAME: Allan Ward, Owner - - Stephens, Tenant				ACCOUNT NO.		
ADDRESS: 2500 Johnson Street				SHEET NO.		
DATE		ITEMS		DEPOSITS	CHECKS	BALANCE
1/04	0X	Blake Stephens Security Deposit	0X-2	$550.00		$550.00
1/04	0X	Blake Stephens Jan Rent	0X-2	$550.00		$1,100.00
1/21	0X	Your Realty Co., Inc. Jan Management Fee	103		$55.00	$1,045.00

YOUR REALTY COMPANY   103
TRUST ACCOUNT
ANYTOWN, NC 12345

                                                        1/21/0X

   Your Realty Company, Inc. $ 115.^{00}

   One hundred fifteen and ^{00}/100 ------------------------Dollars

   1/0X Mgt Fees - SCW   John Broker

   6625 54218974932478 56784   89745662147

SUPPLEMENTAL CHECK WORKSHEET
1/21/0X - CHECK #103 - YOUR REALTY CO., INC.   (E)

PROPERTY	PURPOSE	AMOUNT
143 North Boulevard	1/0X Management Fees	$60.00
2500 Johnson Street	1/0X Management Fees	$55.00
		$115.00

(E) - Date and check number provide cross-reference to corresponding check.

Bank Account Reconciliation
Your Realty Company, Inc.

Period Ending _1/31/0X_

Ending Balance from Bank Statement   A. $ _3,185.00_

List Deposits in Transit $ _2,500.00_
    (Deposits posted to the journal
    that have not cleared the bank)

Total Deposits in Transit   +   B. $ _2,500.00_

List Outstanding Checks
    (Checks posted to the journal that
    have not cleared the bank)

Check	Date	Amount
_102_	_1/20/0X_	$ _465.00_
_104_	_1/30/0X_	$ _1,000.00_
		$

Total Outstanding Checks   -   C. $ _1,465.00_

Reconciled Bank Balance   D. $ _4,220.00_

YOUR REALTY COMPANY, INC.
TRIAL BALANCE

NC INSURED BANK A/C# _123-456-789_

DATE: _1/31/0X_

OWNER	PROPERTY	AMOUNT
Your Realty Company, Inc.		$75.00
Clay	1362 Main Street	$2,500.00
Howard	143 North Boulevard	$600.00
Ward	2500 Johnson Street	$1,045.00
TOTAL		$4,220.00

NOTE
THE TOTAL ON THE TRIAL BALANCE EQUALS THE RECONCILED BANK BALANCE ON THE BANK RECONCILIATION AND THE JOURNAL RUNNING BALANCE AS OF 1/31/00.

LICENSE LAW AND RULE COMMENTS

Comments on Selected Provisions of the North Carolina Real Estate License Law and Real Estate Commission Rules

INTRODUCTION

These comments on selected North Carolina Real Estate License Law and Real Estate Commission Rules provisions are intended to assist real estate licensees, prelicensing course students and others in understanding the License Law and Commission rules. The comments are organized in a topic format that often differs from the sequence in which the topics are addressed in the License Law and Commission rules. The topics selected for comment here are of particular importance and/or are likely to be frequently encountered in the usual course of real estate practice. The appropriate references to the License Law and Commission rules are provided beside each listed topic.

LICENSE REQUIREMENT

General [G.S. 93A-1 and 93A-2]

Anyone who for compensation transacts real estate business in this state as an agent for another must have a North Carolina real estate broker or salesperson license. This requirement applies to any person or entity who directly or indirectly engages in the business of a real estate broker or salesperson while physically in the state of North Carolina. A real estate licensee is commonly referred to as a real estate "agent," although the latter does not actually appear in the License Law.

The primary difference between a salesperson license and a broker license is that a broker may operate as an unsupervised independent agent while a salesperson must work under the supervision of a broker who has been designated with the Real Estate Commission as "broker-in-charge" of a real estate office.

A broker-in-charge is a broker who has been designated with the Commission as the broker having responsibility for the supervision of salespersons engaged in real estate brokerage at a particular real estate office and for other administrative and supervisory duties prescribed by Commission rule.

Note that a real estate "licensee" is NOT automatically a "REALTOR®." A licensed real estate agent is a REALTOR® only if he/she belongs to the National Association of REALTORS®, a private trade association.

Licensing of Business Entities [G.S. 93A-1 and 2; Rule A.0502]

In addition to individuals (persons), "business entities" also must be licensed in order to engage in the real estate business. Any corporation, partnership, limited liability company, association or other business entity (other than a sole proprietorship) must obtain a separate real estate firm broker license.

Activities Requiring a License [G.S. 93A-2]

Persons and business entities who for compensation perform the activities listed below as an agent for others are considered to be performing brokerage activities and must have a real estate license. There is no exemption for engaging a limited number of transactions. A person or entity who performs a brokerage service in even one transaction must be licensed. Similarly, no fee or other compensation is so small as to exempt one from the application of the statute when acting for another in a real estate transaction. Brokerage activities include:

1. Listing (or offering to list) real estate for sale or rent, including any act performed by a real estate licensee in connection with obtaining and servicing a listing agreement. Examples of such acts include, but are not limited to, soliciting listings, providing information to the property owner, and preparing listing agreements or property management agreements.

2. Selling or buying (or offering to sell or buy) real estate, including any act performed by a real estate licensee in connection with assisting others in selling or buying real estate. Examples of such acts include, but are not limited to, advertising listed property for sale, "showing" listed property to prospective buyers, providing information about listed property to prospective buyers, negotiating a sale or purchase of real estate, and assisting with the completion of contract offers and counteroffers using preprinted forms and communication of offers and acceptances.

3. Leasing or renting (or offering to lease or rent) real estate, including any act performed by real estate licensees in connection with assisting others in leasing or renting real estate. Examples of such acts include, but are not limited to, advertising listed property for rent, "showing" listed rental property to prospective tenants, providing information about listed rental property to prospective tenants, negotiating lease terms, and assisting with the completion of lease offers and counteroffers using preprinted forms and communication of offers and acceptances.

4. Conducting (or offering to conduct) a real estate auction. (Mere criers of sale are excluded.) NOTE: An auctioneer's license is also required to auction real estate.

5. Selling, buying, leasing, assigning or exchanging any interest in real estate, including a leasehold interest, in connection with the sale or purchase of a business.

6. Referring a party to a real estate licensee, if done for compensation. Any arrangement or agreement between a licensee and an unlicensed person that calls for the licensee to compensate the unlicensed person in any way for finding, introducing or referring a party to the licensee has been determined by North Carolina's courts to be prohibited under the License Law. Therefore, no licensee may pay a finder's fee, referral fee, "bird dog" fee or similar compensation to an unlicensed person.

Unlicensed Employees — Permitted Activities

The use of unlicensed assistants and other unlicensed office personnel in the real estate industry is very widespread and the Commission is frequently asked by licensees what acts such persons may lawfully perform. To provide guidance to licensees regarding this matter, the Commission has prepared the following list of acts that an unlicensed assistant or employee may lawfully perform so long as the assistant or employee is salaried or hourly paid and is not paid on a per-transaction basis.

An unlicensed, salaried employee MAY:

1. Receive and forward phone calls and electronic messages to licensees.

2. Submit listings and changes to a multiple listing service, but only if the listing data or changes are compiled and provided by a licensee.

3. Secure copies of public records from public repositories (i.e., register of deeds office, county tax office, etc.).

4. Place "for sale" or "for rent" signs and lock boxes on property at the direction of a licensee.

5. Order and supervise routine and minor repairs to listed property at the direction of a licensee.

6. Act as a courier to deliver or pick up documents.

7. Schedule appointments for showing property listed for sale or rent.

8. Communicate with licensees, property owners, prospects, inspectors, etc. to coordinate or confirm appointments.

9. Show rental properties managed by the employee's employing broker to prospective tenants and complete and execute preprinted form leases for the rental of such properties.

10. Type offers, contracts and leases from drafts of preprinted forms completed by a licensee.

11. Record and deposit earnest money deposits, tenant security deposits and other trust monies, and otherwise maintain records of trust account receipts and disbursements, under the close supervision of the office broker-in-charge, who is legally responsible for handling trust funds and maintaining trust accounts.

12. Assist a licensee in assembling documents for closing.

13. Compute commission checks for licensees affiliated with a broker or firm and act as bookkeeper for the firm's bank operating accounts.

Exemptions [G.S. 93A-2]

The following persons and organizations are specifically exempted from the requirement for real estate licensure:

1. **Property owners** when selling or leasing their own property. This includes both individual property owners personally selling or leasing their property and business entities selling or leasing real estate owned by the business entity. To qualify under this exemption, the person or entity must be the actual title holder or share title with an undivided interest.

[Note: The Commission takes the position that the *bona fide* officers and employees of a **corporation** need not be licensed to sell or lease real estate belonging to the corporation. This is because corporations have a separate legal identity and can only function through its officers and employees, thus such officers and employees must be exempt when selling or leasing the corporation's property in order to give effect to the corporation exemption. However, the officers and employees of other business entities are considered to be exempt only if they personally are title owners of the property to be sold or leased. Thus, a partner in a general partnership is exempt as an owner when selling or leasing partnership-owned real estate, but an officer or employee of the partnership who is not also a partner is not exempt.]

---

2. Persons acting as **attorneys-in-fact** under a power of attorney in consummating performance under a contract for the sale, lease or exchange of real estate. (Note: This limited exemption applies only to the final completion of a transaction already commenced. The licensing requirement may not be circumvented by obtaining a power of attorney.)

3. **Attorneys-at-law** when performing real estate activities in the normal course of providing legal services to their clients, such as when administering an estate or trust. Attorneys may NOT otherwise engage in real estate brokerage practice without a real estate license.

4. **Persons acting under court order** (e.g., receivers, trustees in bankruptcy, guardians or personal representatives)

5. **Trustees** acting under a trust agreement, deed of trust or will.

6. Certain **salaried employees of broker-property managers.** (See G.S. 93A-2(c)(6) for details.)

NOTE: Although there is no specific statutory exemption for real estate **appraisers**, persons who appraise real estate for compensation are not required to have a real estate license to conduct such appraisals. However, such persons are required to be licensed or certified as a real estate appraiser by the North Carolina Appraisal Board.

THE REAL ESTATE COMMISSION

Composition [G.S. 93A-3(a)]

The Real Estate Commission consists of nine (9) members who serve three-year terms. Seven members are appointed by the Governor and two are appointed by the General Assembly upon the recommendations of the Speaker of the House of Representatives and the President Pro Tempore of the Senate. At least three (3) members must be licensed brokers or salespersons. At least two (2) members must be "public members" who are NOT involved directly or indirectly in the real estate brokerage or appraisal businesses.

Purpose and Powers [G.S. 93A-3(a), (c) and (f); G.S. 93A-6(a) and (b);G.S. 93A-4(d) and 93A-4A]

The principal purpose of the Real Estate Commission is to protect the interests of members of the general public in their dealings with real estate brokers and salespersons. This is accomplished through the exercise of the following statutory powers granted to the Commission:

1. Licensing real estate brokers, salespersons and brokerage firms, and registering time share projects.

2. Establishing and administering a prelicensing education program for prospective licensees and a continuing education program for licensees.

3. Providing education and information relating to the real estate brokerage business for licensees and the general public.

4. Regulating the business activities of brokers, salespersons and brokerage firms, including disciplining licensees who violate the License Law or Commission rules.

It should be noted that the Commission is specifically prohibited, however, from regulating commissions, salaries or fees charged by real estate licensees and from arbitrating disputes between parties regarding matters of contract such as the rate and/or division of commissions, pay of salespersons or similar matters. [See G.S. 93A-3(c) and Rule A.0109.]

Disciplinary Authority [G.S. 93A-6(a)-(c)]

The Real Estate Commission is authorized to take a variety of disciplinary actions against licensees who the Commission finds guilty of violating the License Law or Commission rules while acting as real estate licensees. These are: reprimand, censure, license suspension and license revoca-

tion. The License Law also permits a licensee under certain circumstances to surrender his/her license with the consent of the Commission. Disciplinary actions taken against licensees are regularly reported in the Commission's quarterly newsletter which is distributed to all licensees and also may be reported in local and regional newspapers.

It should be noted that licensees may be disciplined by the Commission for committing acts prohibited by the License Law when selling, leasing, or buying real estate for themselves, as well as for committing such acts in transactions handled as agents for others. [G.S. 93A-6(b)(3)]

The Commission also has the power to seek in its own name injunctive relief in superior court to prevent any person (licensees and others) from violating the License Law or Commission rules. A typical example of where the Commission might pursue injunctive relief in the courts is where a person engages in real estate activity without a license or during a period when the person's license is suspended, revoked or expired. [G.S. 93A-6(c)]

Any violation of the License Law or Commission rules is a criminal offense (misdemeanor) and may be prosecuted in a court of law. However, a finding by the Commission that a licensee has violated the License Law or Commission rules does not constitute a criminal conviction. [G.S. 93-8]

PROHIBITED ACTS BY LICENSEES

G.S. 93A-6 provides a list of prohibited acts which may result in disciplinary action against licensees. Discussed below are the various prohibited acts, except for those related to handling and accounting for trust funds, which are discussed in the Commission's "Trust Account Guidelines," and the failure to deliver certain instruments to parties in a transaction, which is discussed in the subsequent section on "General Brokerage Provisions."

Important Note

The provisions of the License Law relating to misrepresentation or omission of a material fact, conflict of interest, licensee competence, handling of trust funds, and improper, fraudulent or dishonest dealing generally apply independently of other statutory law or case law such as the law of agency. Nevertheless, another law may have an effect on the application of a License Law provision. For example, the requirements of the N.C. Tenant Security Deposit Act relating to the accounting to a tenant for a residential security deposit within 30 days after termination of a tenancy amplify the general License Law provisions (and Commission rules) requiring licensees to account for such funds within a reasonable time. Thus, in this instance, a violation of the Tenant Security Deposit Act's provisions would also be considered by the Commission to be a violation of the License Law.

Similarly, the law of agency and the law of contracts, which are derived from case law, may be taken into consideration when applying the provisions of the License Law. Thus, a licensee's agency status and role in a transaction might affect the licensee's duties under the license law. Examples of how an agent's duties under the License Law may be affected by the application of other laws are included at various points in this section on "Prohibited Acts by Licensees."

Misrepresentation or Omission [G.S. 93A-6(a)(1)]

Misrepresentation or omission of a material fact by brokers or salespersons is prohibited, and this prohibition includes both "willful" and "negligent" acts. A "willful" act is one that is done intentionally and deliberately, while a "negligent" act is one that is done unintentionally. A "misrepresentation" is communicating false information, while an "omission" is failing to provide or disclose information where there is a duty to provide or disclose such information.

For purposes of applying G.S. 93A-6(a)(1), whether a fact is "material" depends on the facts and circumstances of a particular transaction and the application of statutory and/or case law. The Commission has historically interpreted "material facts" under the Real Estate License Law to at least include:

Facts about the property itself (such as a structural defect or defective mechanical systems);

Facts relating directly to the property (such as a pending zoning change or planned highway construction in the immediate vicinity); and

Facts relating directly to the ability of the agent's principal to complete the transaction (such as a pending foreclosure sale).

Regardless of whom the agent represents, these facts must be disclosed to both the agent's principal and to third parties the agent deals with on the principal's behalf. In addition, an agent has a duty to disclose to his principal any information that may affect the principal's rights and interests or influence the principal's decision in the transaction.

Note, however, that G.S. 39-50 and 42-14.2 specifically provide that the fact that a property was occupied by a person who died or had a serious illness while occupying the property is NOT a material fact. Thus, agents do not need to voluntarily disclose such a fact. If a prospective buyer or tenant specifically asks about such a matter, the agent may either decline to answer or respond honestly. If, however, a prospective buyer or tenant inquires as to whether a previous owner or occupant had AIDS, the agent is prohibited by fair housing laws from answering such an inquiry because persons with AIDS are considered to be "handicapped" under such laws.

This introductory information should assist in understanding G.S. 93A-6(a)(1), which establishes four separate (although closely related) categories of conduct which are prohibited. These are discussed below, and a few examples of prohibited conduct are provided for each category.

Willful Misrepresentation — Where an agent who has "actual knowledge" of a material fact deliberately misinforms a buyer, seller, tenant or landlord concerning such fact. Also, where an agent who does NOT have actual knowledge of a matter material to the transaction provides incorrect information concerning such matter to a buyer, seller, tenant or landlord without regard for the actual truth of the matter (i.e., where an agent intentionally provides information without knowing whether or not it is true and the information provided is in fact not true).

Note: The following examples of willful misrepresentation apply regardless of the agent's status (seller's agent or buyer's agent) or role (listing agent or selling agent).

Example: An agent knows that a listed house has a severe flooding problem during heavy rains. In response to a question from a prospective buyer who is being shown the house during dry weather, the agent states that there is no flooding problem.

Example: An agent knows that the heat pump at a listed house is inoperative, but tells a prospective buyer that all mechanical systems and appliances are in good condition.Example: An agent knows that the approximate market value of a house is $80,000, but tells the property owner that the house is worth $90,000 in order to obtain a listing.

Example: An agent is completely unfamiliar with the features or condition of a listed property; however, the agent informs a prospective buyer that the plumbing is in good working order without first checking with the owner. (The agent in such instance is acting without regard for the truth of the matter being represented. If the plumbing in fact needs significant repair, then the agent may be guilty of willful misrepresentation.)

Example: Without checking with the owner, an agent tells a prospective buyer of a listed house that heating and cooling costs are "very reasonable." (Because the agent acted without regard for the truth of the matter, he may be guilty of willful misrepresentation if heating and cooling costs are in fact extraordinarily high.)

Negligent Misrepresentation — Where an agent unintentionally misinforms a buyer, seller, tenant or landlord concerning a material fact either because he does not have actual knowledge of the fact, because he has incorrect information, or because of a mistake by the agent. If the agent "should reasonably have known" the truth of the matter that was misrepresented, then the agent may be guilty of "negligent misrepresentation" even though he was acting in good faith.

Negligent misrepresentation by real estate agents occurs frequently in real estate transactions. The most common situation results from the recording of incorrect information in an MLS® computer or book due to the negligence of the listing agent. When a prospective buyer is subsequently provided the incorrect information from the MLS® by the agent working with the buyer, a negligent misrepresentation occurs.

A listing agent is generally held to a higher standard with regard to negligent misrepresentation of material facts about a listed property to a buyer than is a selling agent who is acting as a seller's subagent. This is because (1) The listing agent is in the best position to ascertain facts about the property, (2) the listing agent is expected to take reasonable steps to assure that property data included with the listing is correct and (3) it is considered reasonable for a selling agent to rely on the accuracy of the listing data in most instances. However, a buyer's agent may in some cases be held to a higher standard than a seller's subagent because of the buyer's agent's duties to the buyer under the law of agency and the buyer's agent's special knowledge of the buyer's particular situation and needs.

Example: An agent has previously sold several lots in a subdivision under development and all those lots passed a soil suitability test for an on-site septic system. The agent then sells Lot 35 without checking as to whether this lot satisfies the soil test; however, the agent informs the buyer that Lot 35 will support an on-site septic system when in fact the contrary is true. (The agent was at least negligent in not checking the soil test result on Lot 35 and guilty of negligent misrepresentation. This result is not affected by the agent's agency status or role in the transaction.)

Example: An owner tells a listing agent with ABC Realty that his house has 1850 heated square feet. Without personally verifying the square footage, the agent records 1850 square feet on the listing form. The listing is placed in the local MLS and the MLS book is distributed showing the house as having 1850 square feet. The house is subsequently sold by a sales agent with XYZ Realty who tells the buyer that according to the MLS data, the house has 1850 square feet. The buyer later discovers that the house actually has only 1750 square feet. (In this situation, the listing agent did not make a direct misrepresentation to the buyer; however, he initiated the chain of communication which led to the buyer being misinformed, and thus indirectly misrepresented a material fact. Further, his failure to verify the square footage constituted negligence. Therefore, the listing agent is guilty of a negligent misrepresentation. Although the selling agent directly communicated the incorrect information to the buyer, he probably acted reasonably in relying on the data in the MLS book. In this case, if the selling agent had no reason to doubt the MLS data, the selling agent is not guilty of a negligent misrepresentation. Note, however, that if the square

footage discrepancy had been sufficiently large that a reasonably prudent selling agent should have known the listed data was incorrect, then the selling agent would also have been guilty of negligent misrepresentation. The result in this particular example is not affected by the selling agent's agency status (seller's subagent or buyer's agent), although this might be a factor in other situations.

Willful Omission — Where the agent has "actual knowledge" of a material fact and a duty to disclose such fact to a buyer, seller, tenant, or landlord, but he deliberately fails to disclose such fact.

Example: An agent knows that a zoning change is pending which would adversely affect the value of a listed property, but fails to disclose such information to a prospective buyer. The agent has committed a willful omission and this result is not affected by the agent's agency status or role in the transaction.

[Note: Information about a zoning change (or planned highway) that would enhance the value of a seller's property must also be disclosed to the seller, even if the agent is a buyer's agent.]

Example: An agent knows that the city has just decided to extend water and sewer lines to a subdivision that has been plagued for years by serious water quality and sewage disposal problems. This will result in a substantial increase in the value of homes in the subdivision. The agent, who is working with a buyer to purchase a house in the subdivision, does not inform the seller of the city's recent decision. The agent has committed a willful omission and this result is not affected by the agent's agency status or role in the transaction.

Example: An agent knows that a listed house has a major defect (e.g., crumbling foundation, no insulation, malfunctioning septic tank, leaking roof, termite infestation, etc.) but fails to disclose such information to a prospective buyer. The agent has committed a willful omission and this result is not affected by the agent's agency status or role in the transaction.

Example: A selling agent working with a buyer as a subagent of the seller learns that the buyer is willing to pay more than the price in the buyer's offer, but fails to disclose this information to the seller (or listing agent) when presenting the offer. The selling agent has committed a willful omission. If, however, the selling agent were acting as a buyer's agent, then the result would be different because the agent does not represent the seller.

Example: A buyer's agent becomes aware that the seller with whom his buyer is negotiating is under pressure to sell quickly and may accept much less than the listing price. Believing such information should always be kept confidential, the buyer's agent does not provide the buyer with this information. The buyer's agent is guilty of a willful omission. An agent must disclose to his principal any information that might affect the principal's decision in the transaction.

Example: Suppose in the immediately preceding example that the seller's property is listed with the firm of the buyer's agent and the firm's policy is to practice dual agency in in-house sales situations where it represents both the seller and the buyer. In this situation, the buyer's agent would not be considered to have committed a willful omission under the License Law by not disclosing the information about the seller's personal situation to the buyer. Note: This assumes however that the buyer's agent properly disclosed his status as a buyer's agent to the seller or seller's agent upon "initial contact," that dual agency was properly authorized in writing by both the seller and buyer prior to showing the seller's property to the buyer and that the dual agency agreement provided for this limitation on disclosure. This position on the application of the License Law has been adopted by the Real Estate Commission to promote fairness and equity in transactions involving dual agency.

Negligent Omission — Where an agent does NOT have actual knowledge of a material fact, but he "should reasonably have known" of such fact, then he may be guilty of "negligent omission" if he fails to disclose this fact to a buyer, seller, tenant or landlord, even though he acted in good faith in the transaction.

The prohibition against negligent omission creates a "duty to discover and disclose" material facts which a reasonably prudent agent would typically have discovered in the course of the transaction. A listing agent is typically in a much better position than a selling agent to discover material facts relating to a listed property and thus, will be held to a higher standard than will a selling agent acting as a seller's subagent. On the other hand, a buyer's agent in some circumstances may be held to a higher standard than a seller's subagent because of the buyer's agent's duties to the buyer under the law of agency, particularly if the buyer's agent is aware of a buyer's special needs with regard to a property. Again we see how the agency relationships between agents and principals to a transaction and the agent's role in the transaction can affect a licensee's duties and responsibilities under the License Law.

Instances of negligent omission occur much less frequently than instances of negligent misrepresentation. This is because most facts about a listed property are recorded on a detailed property data sheet from which information is taken for inclusion in MLS computers/books. If incorrect information taken from an MLS computer/book is passed on to a prospective purchaser, then a "misrepresentation,"

rather than an "omission," has occurred. Nevertheless, there are examples of negligent omission which can be cited.

Example: A listing agent lists for sale a house located adjacent to a street that is about to be widened into a major thoroughfare. The thoroughfare project has been very controversial and highly publicized. The city recently finalized its decision to proceed with the project and the plans for the street widening are recorded in the city planner's office. A buyer, working with a selling agent, makes an offer to buy the house. The listing agent does not disclose the street widening plans to the buyer or selling agent and claims later that he was not aware of the plans. In this situation, both the listing and selling agents are probably guilty of a negligent omission because each "should reasonably have known" of the street widening plans, clearly a material fact, and should have disclosed this fact to the buyer. This result is not affected by whether the selling agent is a buyer agent or seller's subagent.

Example: A seller has a 30,000 square foot commercial property for sale which cannot be expanded under local zoning laws. The buyer is looking for property in the 25,000 - 30,000 square foot range, but has told his buyer's agent that he needs a property where he can expand to 50,000 square feet or more in the future. The seller does not think to advise the buyer's agent that the property cannot be expanded, and the buyer's agent makes no inquiry about it although he is aware of the buyer's special needs. The buyer's agent is guilty of a negligent omission for failing to discover and disclose a special circumstance that he knew was important to his client.

Example: When listing a house, a listing agent is told by the seller that one area of the roof leaks badly when it rains, but the moisture so far is being contained in the attic. The listing agent forgets to note this on the MLS data sheet and forgets to disclose the leaking roof problem to prospective buyers and selling agents. The listing agent is guilty of a negligent omission. Because his failure to disclose the leaking roof problem was unintentional, the listing agent is not guilty of a willful omission; however, his forgetfulness resulting in his failure to disclose the defect constitutes a negligent omission.

Making False Promises [G.S. 93A-6(a)(2)]

Real estate brokers and salespersons are prohibited from "making any false promises of a character likely to influence, persuade or induce." It is unimportant whether or not the broker or salesperson originally intended to honor his promise; failure to honor a promise is sufficient to constitute a violation of this provision. The promise may relate to any matter which might influence, persuade or induce a person to perform some act which he might not otherwise perform.

Example: An agent promises a prospective apartment tenant that the apartment he is considering renting will be repainted before the tenant moves in. The agent then fails to have the work done after the lease is signed.

Example: An agent promises a property owner that if he lists his house for sale with the agent's firm, then the firm will steam-clean all the carpets and wash all the windows. The firm then fails to have the work done after the listing contract is signed.

Other Misrepresentations [G.S. 93A-6(a)(3)]

Real estate brokers and salespersons are prohibited from pursuing a course of misrepresentation (or making of false promises) through other agents or salespersons or through advertising or other means.

Example: In marketing subdivision lots for a developer, a broker regularly advertises that the lots for sale are suitable for residential use when in fact the lots will not pass a soil suitability test for on-site sewage systems.

Example: A broker is marketing a new condominium complex which is under construction. Acting with the full knowledge and consent of the broker, the broker's agents regularly inform prospective buyers that units will be available for occupancy on June 1, when in fact the units won't be available until at least September 1.

Conflict of Interest [G.S. 93A-6(a)(4) and (6); Rule A.0104(d)]

G.S. 93A-6(a)(4) prohibits a real estate agent from "acting for more than one party in a transaction without the knowledge of all parties for whom he or she acts." Commission Rule A.0104(d) takes this a step further by providing that a broker or brokerage firm representing one party in a transaction shall not undertake to represent another party in the transaction without the express written authority (i.e., authorization of dual agency) of each party (subject to one exception, explained in the dual agency section). A typical violation of this provision occurs when the agent has only one principal in a transaction but acts in a manner which benefits another party without the principal's knowledge. In such a situation, the agent violates the duty of loyalty and consent owed to his principal.

Example: A house is listed with Firm X. When showing the house to a prospective buyer not represented by Firm X, an agent of Firm X advises the buyer to offer substantially less than the listing price because the seller must move soon and is very anxious to sell the property fast. The agent and Firm X are contractually obligated to represent only the seller. By advising the prospective buyer as indicated in this example, the agent is acting to benefit the buyer without the seller's knowledge and consent. This act violates both the License Law and the Law of Agency.

Example: An agent with Firm Y assists her sister in purchasing a house listed with Firm X without advising Firm X or the seller of her relationship with the buyer. The agent is "officially" acting as a subagent of the seller in the transaction. In this situation, there is an inherent conflict of interest on the part of the agent. If the agent does not disclose her relationships to both parties, then the agent violates both the License Law and Law of Agency. In fact, since her allegiance lies with her sister, the agent should instead act as a buyer's agent from the outset. The same would be true if the buyer were a close friend or business associate of the agent, or in any way enjoyed a special relationship to the agent which would clearly influence the agent to act in behalf of the buyer rather than the seller.

G.S. 93A-6(a)(4) also prohibits any "self-dealing" on the part of an agent. For example, if an agent attempts to make a secret profit in a transaction where he is supposed to be representing a principal, then the agent violates this "conflict of interest" provision.

Example: An agent lists a parcel of undeveloped property which is zoned for single-family residential use. The agent knows that this property is about to be rezoned for multi-family residential use, which will greatly increase the property's value. Rather than informing the seller of this fact, the agent offers to buy the property at the listed price, telling the seller that he wants to acquire the property as a long-term investment. The deal closes. Several months later, after the rezoning has been accomplished, the agent sells the property at a substantial profit.

G.S. 93A-6(a)(6) prohibits a licensee from "representing or attempting to represent a real estate broker other than the broker by whom he or she is engaged or associated, without the express knowledge and consent of the broker with whom he or she is associated." While brokers may work for or be associated with more than one real estate company, so long as they have the express consent of all brokers-in-charge, salespersons may never engage in brokerage activities for more than one company at a time.

Improper Brokerage Commission [G.S. 93A-6(a)(5) and (9)]

A broker or salesperson may NOT pay a commission or valuable consideration to any person for acts or services performed in violation of the License Law. [G.S. 93A-6(a)(9)] This provision flatly prohibits a broker or salesperson from paying an unlicensed person for acts which require a real estate license. Following are examples of prohibited payments:

Example: The payment by brokers of commissions to previously licensed sales associates who failed to properly renew their licenses (for any acts performed after their licenses had expired). [Note that payment could properly be made for commissions earned while the license was on active status, even if the license is inactive or expired at time of payment. The key is, was the license on active status at the time all services were rendered which generated the commission?]

Example: The payment of a commission, salary or fee by brokers to unlicensed employees or independent contractors (e.g., secretaries, "trainees" who haven't passed the license examination, etc.) for performing acts or services requiring a real estate license.

Example: The payment by brokers or salespersons of a "finder's fee," "referral fee," "bird dog fee," or any other valuable consideration to unlicensed persons who find, introduce, or bring together parties to a real estate transaction. This is true even if the ultimate consummation of the transaction is accomplished by a licensed broker or salesperson and even if the act is performed without expectation of compensation. Thus, a broker or salesperson may NOT compensate a friend, relative, former client or any other unlicensed person for "referring" a prospective buyer, seller, landlord or tenant to such broker or salesperson. This prohibition extends to "owner referral" programs at condominium or time share complexes and "tenant referral" programs at apartment complexes.

In addition, a licensed salesperson may NOT accept any compensation for brokerage services from anyone other than his employing broker or brokerage firm. Consequently, a broker may not pay a commission or fee directly to a salesperson of another broker or firm. Any such payment must be made through the salesperson's employing broker or firm. [G.S. 93A-6(a)(5)]

Unworthiness and Incompetence [G.S. 93A-6(a)(8)]

This broad provision authorizes the Real Estate Commission to discipline any broker or salesperson who, based on the agent's conduct and consideration of the public interest, is found to be unworthy or incompetent to work in the real estate business. A wide range of conduct may serve as the basis for a finding of unworthiness or incompetence, including conduct which violates other specific provisions of the License Law or Commission rules. Here are a few examples of improper conduct which do not specifically violate another License Law provision but which might support a finding of unworthiness or incompetence.

1. Failure to properly complete (fill in) real estate contracts or to use contract forms which are legally adequate.

2. Failure to diligently perform the services required under listing contracts or property management contracts.

3. Failure to provide accurate closing statements to sellers and buyers or accurate income/expense reports to property owners.

Improper Dealing [G.S. 93A-6(a)(10)]

This broad provision prohibits a real estate agent from engaging in "any other conduct [not specifically prohibited elsewhere in the License Law] which constitutes improper, fraudulent or dishonest dealing." The determination as to whether particular conduct constitutes "improper, fraudulent or dishonest dealing" is made by the Real Estate Commission on a case-by-case basis. Therefore, a broad range of conduct might be found objectionable under this provision, depending on the facts in a case.

One category of conduct which violates this provision is any breach of the duty to exercise skill, care, and diligence in behalf of a client under the Law of Agency. (Note that other breaches of Agency Law duties constituting either a "misrepresentation or omission," a "conflict of interest" or a "failure to properly account for trust funds" are covered by other specific statutory provisions.)

Another category of conduct which violates this provision is any violation of the State Fair Housing Act. This is mentioned separately under the "Discriminatory Practices" heading.

Example: A broker is personally conducting the closing of a real estate sale he has negotiated. The seller does not show up for the closing. In order to avoid a delay in closing the transaction, the broker forges the seller's signature on a deed to the property and proceeds with the closing in the seller's absence.

Example: An agent assists a prospective buyer in perpetrating a fraud in connection with a mortgage loan application by preparing two contracts — one with false information for submission to the lending institution, and another which represents the actual agreement between seller and buyer. (This practice is commonly referred to as "dual contracting" or "contract kiting.")

Example: A broker lists a property for sale and agrees in the listing contract to place the listing in the local MLS, to advertise the property for sale, and to use his best efforts in good faith to find a buyer. The broker places a "For Sale" sign on the property, but fails to place the property in the MLS for more than 30 days and fails to otherwise advertise the property during the listing period. (The broker has failed to exercise reasonable skill, care and diligence in behalf of his client as required by the listing contract and the Law of Agency.)

Example: An agent is aware that the owners of a house listed with his company are out of town for the weekend, yet the agent gives a prospective buyer the house keys and allows such prospect to look at the listed house without accompanying the prospect. (The agent has failed to exercise reasonable skill, care and diligence in behalf of his client.)

Discriminatory Practices [G.S. 93A-6(a)(10); Rule A.1601]

Any conduct by a broker or salesperson which violates the provisions of the State Fair Housing Act is considered by the Commission to constitute "improper conduct" and to be a violation of the License Law.

Practice of Law [G.S. 93A-4(e); G.S. 93A-6(a)(11); Rule A.0111]

Brokers and salespersons may not perform for others any legal service described in G.S. 84-2.1 or any other legal service. Following are several examples of real estate-related legal services which brokers and salespersons may NOT provide.

1. Drafting legal documents such as deeds, deeds of trust, leases and real estate sales contracts for others. Although brokers and salespersons may "fill in" or "complete" preprinted real estate contract forms which have been drafted by an attorney, they may NOT under any circumstances complete or fill in deed or deed of trust forms.

2. Abstracting or rendering an opinion on legal title to real property.

3. Providing "legal advice" of any nature to clients and customers, including advice concerning the nature of any interest in real estate or the means of holding title to real estate. (Note: Although providing advice concerning the legal ramifications of a real estate sales contract is prohibited, merely "explaining" the provisions of such a contract is not only acceptable, but highly recommended.)

Other Prohibited Acts [G.S. 93A-6(b)]

In addition to those prohibited acts previously discussed, G.S. 93A-6(b) prescribes several other specific grounds for disciplinary action by the Commission, including:

1. Where a licensee has obtained a license by false or fraudulent representation (e.g., falsifying documentation of prelicensing education, failing to disclose prior criminal convictions, etc.).

2. Where a licensee has been convicted of, or pled guilty or no contest to, certain types of criminal offenses.

3. Where a broker's unlicensed employee, who is exempt from licensing under G.S. 93A-2(c)(6) (property management exception), has committed an act which, if committed by the broker, would have constituted a violation of the License Law.

4. Where a licensee who is also a State-licensed or State-certified real estate appraiser has violated any of the provisions of the North Carolina Real Estate Appraisers Act and been disciplined by the N.C. Appraisal Board.

Lastly, be aware that under (b)(3), licensees may be disciplined for violating any of the 15 provisions under subsection (a) when selling, buying, or leasing their own property.

GENERAL BROKERAGE PROVISIONS

Discussed below are selected Commission rules related to general brokerage.

Agency Agreements and Disclosure [Rule A.0104]

Provided below is a brief summary of the various provisions of the Commission's rule regarding agency agreements and disclosure. For a much more in-depth discussion of this rule and its application, the reader is referred to the Commission's *North Carolina Real Estate Manual.*

Agency Agreements: As revised effective September 1, 2002, Rule A.0104(a) now requires all agency agreements for brokerage services (in both sales and lease transactions) to be in writing. Previously, only agency agreements in sales transactions were required to be in writing. Revised paragraph (a) now:

• Requires written agreements with property owners (whether sellers or lessors, commercial or residential) from the inception of the relationship;

• Allows express **oral** buyer/tenant agency agreement from the outset of the relationship which must be reduced to *writing no later than the time any party to the transaction wants to extend an offer.* As a practical matter, this oral agreement needs to address all key aspects of the relationship, including agent compensation, authorization for dual agency, etc.

(**Note:** agreement must be in writing from the outset if it seeks to limit the buyer/tenant's right to work with other agents or binds the client to the agent for any definite time period. In other words, an oral buyer/tenant agency agreement is non-exclusive and must be terminable by the client at any time.)

Further, every written agency agreement of any kind must also:

• Provide for its existence for a definite period of time and terminate without prior notice at the expiration of that period. [Exception: an agency agreement between a broker and a landlord to procure tenants for the landlord's property may allow for automatic renewal so long as the landlord may terminate with notice at the end of any contract or renewal period.]

• Contain the Rule A.0104(b) non-discrimination (fair housing) provision, namely: "The broker shall conduct all his brokerage activities in regard to this agreement without respect to the race, color, religion, sex, national origin, handicap or familial status of any buyer, prospective buyer, seller or prospective seller." (This provision must be set forth in a clear and conspicuous manner which shall distinguish it from other provisions of the agency agreement.)

Working with a buyer under an express oral buyer agency agreement became possible with the July 1, 2001 revisions to Rule A.0104 which were intended to address the problem of buyers being reluctant to sign a written buyer agency agreement at the outset of their relationship with a buyer agent. The idea underlying these earlier revisions was to allow an agent to work temporarily with a prospective buyer as a buyer's agent under an oral agreement while the agent established a rapport with the buyer that would make the buyer feel more comfortable with signing a written buyer agency agreement.

Although the rule now allows oral buyer/tenant agency agreements until the point in time when any party is ready to present an offer, it nevertheless is highly advisable that agents have such agreements reduced to writing and signed by the buyer/tenant at the earliest possible time in order to avoid misunderstanding and conflict between the buyer/ tenant and agent. Recall also that the agent must obtain a written buyer agency agreement from the buyer not later than the time either party to the transaction extends an offer to the other. If the buyer will not sign a written buyer agency agreement prior to an offer being presented, then the agent may not continue to work with the buyer as a buyer's agent. Moreover, the agent may not begin at this point to work with the buyer as a seller's subagent unless the agent (1) fully advises the buyer of the consequences of the agent switching from buyer's agent to seller's agent (including the fact that the agent would have to disclose to the seller any information, including "confidential" information about the buyer, that might influence the seller's decision in the transaction), (2) obtains the buyer's consent, and (3) obtains the consent of the seller and listing firm, which is the seller's agent.

Agency Disclosure Requirement: While Rule A.0104(a) now requires all agency agreements, whether for lease or sales transactions, to be in writing, the Rule A.0104(c) disclosure requirement still applies only to sales transactions. It requires licensees to provide prospective buyers and sellers, at first substantial contact, with a copy of the *Working with Real Estate Agents* brochure, to review the brochure with them and then reach an agreement regarding their agency relationship. Note that the obligation under this rule is not satisfied merely by handing the prospective seller or buyer the brochure to read. The agent is required to review the contents of the brochure with the prospective buyer or seller and then reach agreement with the prospective buyer or seller as to whether the agent will work with the buyer or seller as his/her agent or as the agent of the other party. In the case of a prospective **seller**, the agent may either (1) act as the seller's agent, which is the typical situation and which requires a written agreement from the outset of their relationship, or (2) work with the seller as a buyer's agent if the agent already represents a prospective buyer. In the case of a prospective **buyer**, the agent may either (1) act as the buyer's agent under either an oral or written agree-

ment as addressed in Rule A.0104(a), or (2) work with the buyer as a seller's agent, disclosure of which must be in writing from the outset.

The *Working with Real Estate Agents* brochure replaced the former "Description of Agent Duties and Relationships" language found in all agency agreements effective July 1, 2001.

Disclosure of Agency Status by Sellers' Agents and Subagents to Prospective Buyers: Paragraph (e) of Rule A.0104, like (c), requires a seller's agent or subagent in sales transactions to disclose his/her agency status in writing to a prospective buyer at the "first substantial contact" with the buyer. It is recommended that sellers' agents make this required written disclosure using the form provided for this purpose in the *Working with Real Estate Agents* brochure that must be provided to buyers (as well as to sellers) at first substantial contact. This form has a place for the buyer to acknowledge receipt of the brochure and disclosure of agency status, thereby providing the agent with written evidence of having provided the brochure and disclosure. The disclosure may, however, be made using a different form — the most important point is that the disclosure be made in writing in a timely manner. The reason for this requirement is that buyers tend to assume that an agent they contact to work with them in locating a property for purchase is "their" agent and working primarily in their interest. This may or may not be the case in reality. The purpose of the disclosure requirement is to place prospective buyers on notice that the agent they are dealing with is NOT "their" agent before the prospective buyer discloses to the agent information which the buyer would not want a seller to know because it might compromise the buyer's bargaining position.

Most frequently, **"first substantial contact"** will occur at the first "face-to-face" meeting with a prospective buyer. However, the point in time that "first substantial contact" with a prospective buyer occurs will vary depending on the particular situation and may or may not be at the time of the first or initial contact with the prospective buyer. Many first contacts are by telephone and do not involve discussions which reach the level that would require disclosure, although some initial phone contacts, especially those with out-of-town buyers, could reach this level. "First substantial contact" occurs at the point in time when a discussion with a prospective buyer begins to focus on the buyer's specific property needs and desires or on the buyer's financial situation. Typically, that point in time is reached when the agent is ready to solicit information from the prospective buyer that is needed to identify prospective properties to show the buyer. Therefore, an agent planning to work with a prospective buyer as a seller's agent or subagent should assure that disclosure of his/her agency status is made in writing to the prospective buyer prior to obtaining from the prospective buyer any personal or confidential information that the buyer would not want a seller to know. A few examples of such personal or confidential information include: The maximum price a buyer is willing to pay for a property; the buyer's ability to pay more than the price offered by the buyer; or the fact that a buyer has a special interest in purchasing the seller's property rather than some other similar property. In any event, the disclosure must be made prior to discussing with the prospective buyer his/her specific needs or desires regarding the purchase of a property. As a practical matter, this means the disclosure will always need to be made prior to showing a property to a prospective buyer. The best policy is to simply make the disclosure at the earliest possible time.

If first substantial contact occurs by telephone or by means of other electronic communication where it is not practical to provide written disclosure, the agent shall immediately disclose by similar means whom he/she represents and shall immediately, but in no event later than three days from the date of first substantial contact, mail or otherwise transmit a copy of the written disclosure to the buyer.

Disclosure of Agency Status by Buyers' Agents to Sellers or Sellers' Agents: Paragraph (f) of Rule A.0104 requires a buyer's agent to disclose his/her agency status to a seller or seller's agent at the "initial contact" with the seller or seller's agent. "Initial contact" will typically occur when a buyer's agent telephones or otherwise contacts the listing firm to schedule a showing. The initial disclosure may be oral, but a written confirmation of the previous oral disclosure must be made (except in auction sale transactions) no later than the time of delivery of an offer to purchase. The written confirmation may be (and usually is) included in the offer to purchase. In fact, Commission Rule A.0112(a)(19) requires that any preprinted offer to purchase and contract form used by an agent include a provision providing for confirmation of agency status by each real estate agent (and firm) involved in the transaction.

Consent to Dual Agency: Paragraph (d) of Rule A.0104 requires generally that an agent must obtain the written authority of all parties prior to undertaking to represent those parties as a dual agent. It is important to note that this requirement applies to all real estate transactions (sales and lease/rentals), not just to sales transactions. [In sales transactions, this written authority to act as a dual agent is usually limited to "in-house" sales transactions and is usually included in the listing and buyer agency contracts. If those contracts do not grant such authority, then the agent must have both the seller and buyer consent to the dual agency prior to beginning to act as a dual agent for both parties.]

Paragraph (d) of Rule A.0104 currently requires written authority for dual agency from the formation of the relationship except situations where a buyer/tenant is represented by an agent working under an oral agency agreement as permitted by A.0104(a), in which case written authority for dual agency must be obtained no later than the time one of the parties represented by the agent working as a dual agent

makes an offer to purchase, sell, rent, lease, or exchange real estate to the other party. Thus, it is permissible for the agent to operate for a limited period of time under an oral dual agency agreement. It is very important to remember that G.S. 93A-6(a)(4) still requires agents to obtain the consent of all parties prior to beginning to act as a dual agent for those parties. Therefore, it is essential that agents electing to operate as a dual agent for a limited period of time without obtaining this authority in writing still explain fully the consequences of their acting as a dual agent and obtain the parties' oral consent.

As a practical matter in sales transactions, agents will frequently have already obtained written authority to act as a dual agent for in-house sales transactions at the time the initial written listing or buyer agency agreement is executed. However, under Paragraph (a) of Rule A.0104, many buyer's agents may elect to work with their buyer clients for a period of time under an oral buyer agency agreement. Paragraph (d) permits such buyer's agents to also operate for a limited period of time as a dual agent in order to deal with situations where a buyer client is interested in a property listed with the agent's firm. Note that, although an oral dual agency agreement for a limited period of time is permitted by Commission rules, it is strongly recommended that agents have any dual agency agreement in writing from the outset of the dual agency arrangement. This will provide the agent with some evidence that the matter of dual agency was discussed with the parties and that they consented to it. Such evidence could prove quite useful if a party later asserts that the agent did not obtain their consent for dual agency in a timely manner.

Auction Sales: Paragraph (g) of Rule A.0104 provides that the provisions of Paragraphs (c), (d) and (e) of the Rule shall not apply to real estate licensees representing sellers in auction sales transactions. Note that in auction sales, the real estate agents involved almost invariably work only as seller's agents and this fact is considered to be self-evident. Thus, there is no need for agents to distribute and review the *Working with Real Estate Agents* brochure, no need for disclosure of agency status by the seller's agents, and no dual agency. For the unusual situation where a buyer may be represented by an agent in an auction sale transaction, Paragraph (h) of Rule A.0104 provides that such a buyer's agent shall, no later than the time of execution of a written agreement memorializing the buyer's contract to purchase, provide the seller or seller's agent with a written confirmation that he/she represents the buyer.

Dual Agency Status of Firm: Paragraph (i) of Rule A.0104 codifies in the Commission's rules the common law rule that a firm which represents more than one party in the same real estate sales transaction is a dual agent, and further states that the firm, through the brokers and salespersons affiliated with the firm, shall disclose its dual agency to the parties. This rule provision does not establish any additional requirement for licensees and is intended merely to clarify that the Commission follows the common law rule. In other words, dual agency is not limited to those situations where an individual agent is working with both a buyer client and seller client (or lessor and commercial tenant) in the same transaction. If one agent of a firm is working with a buyer client of the firm and another agent of the same firm is working with a seller client of the firm in a transaction involving the sale of the seller client's property to the buyer client, then the firm is a dual agent (as it also holds the agency agreements). However, a firm functions through its employees, namely, its associated agents; thus, under the common law, whenever the firm is a dual agent of certain parties in a transaction, all licensees affiliated with that firm are also dual agents of those parties in that transaction.

Designated Agency: Paragraphs (j) - (m) of Rule A.0104 authorize real estate firms to engage in a form of dual agency practice referred to in the rule as "designated agency" in certain sales transactions involving in-house dual agency. "Designated agency" is an optional method of practicing dual agency that may be adopted by a real estate firm if the firm establishes a policy consistent with the Commission's designated agency rules. Designated agency involves appointing or "designating" an individual agent(s) in a firm to represent only the interests of the seller and another individual agent(s) to represent only the interests of the buyer when a firm has an in-house dual agency situation.

The principal advantage of the designated agency approach over the "standard" dual agency approach is that each of a firm's clients (seller and buyer) receive fuller representation by their designated agent. In the typical dual agency situation, client advocacy is essentially lost because the dual agent may not seek an advantage for (i.e, "advocate" for) one client to the detriment of the other client. The dual agent must remain completely neutral and impartial at all times. Designated agency returns "advocacy" to the services provided by the respective designated agents and allows them to more fully represent their respective clients.

Authority to practice designated agency must be in writing no later than the time a written dual agency agreement is required under A.0104(d). Additional required procedures for practicing designated agency are clearly spelled out in Paragraphs (j) - (m) and are not discussed further here. For more detailed coverage of dual and designated agency, the reader is once again referred to the Commission's *North Carolina Real Estate Manual*.

Dual Agency by Individual Agent: Paragraph (n) of Rule A.0104 authorizes individual brokers or salespersons representing both the buyer and seller in the same real estate sales transaction pursuant to a written dual agency agreement to include in the agreement a provision authorizing the broker or salesperson not to disclose certain "confidential" information about one party to the other party without permission from the party about whom the informa-

tion pertains. This provision is intended to allow individual dual agents to treat confidential information about their clients in a manner similar to that allowed for firms practicing designated agency.

Advertising [Rule A.0105]

The rule prohibits "blind ads;" rather, all advertising must indicate that it is the advertisement of a broker or brokerage firm. Be aware that A.0105(c)(1) prohibits salespersons from advertising "without his or her broker's consent" and must include the broker's name in the advertising. Lastly, licensees may not advertise under an assumed name without registering the assumed name with the applicable County Register of Deeds office and no business entity (other than a corporation) may include in its name the name of an unlicensed person or salesperson. [See A.0105(b) and (d)].

Delivery of Instruments [G.S. 93A-6(a)(13) and (14); Rules A.0106 and A.0107(c)]

Among other things, this rule requires agents to "immediately, but in no event later than five days from the date of execution, deliver to the parties thereto copies of any ... offer..." [Emphasis added.] This does NOT mean that agents may in every case wait up to five days to present an offer to a seller. Rather, it means that an agent must immediately, as soon as possible, present to the seller any offer received by the agent. If the agent is the "selling agent," then the offer should be immediately presented to the "listing agent" who should, in turn, immediately present the offer to the seller. The "five day" provision is included only to allow for situations where the seller is not immediately available (e.g., seller is out of town), and represents an outside time limit within which offers must always be presented. In all cases where the seller is available, the offer should be presented as soon as possible.

The same rule also means that a prospective buyer who signs an offer must immediately be provided a copy of such offer. (A photocopy is acceptable for this purpose.) Do NOT wait until after the offer is accepted (or rejected) by the seller.

In addition, this rule means that an offer must be immediately presented to a seller even if there is a contract pending on the property. Of course, in this instance, it is essential that the agent also advise the seller that serious legal problems could result from the seller's acceptance of such offer and that the seller should contact an attorney if he is interested in treating the offer as a "back-up" offer or in attempting to be released from the previously signed contract.

Retention of Records [Rule A.0108]

Note that as of September 1, 2002, licensees are required to maintain and retain various documents pertaining to their brokerage transactions for three years from the successful or unsuccessful conclusion of the transaction or the disbursement of all trust monies pertaining to that transaction, whichever occurs later. Thus, a licensee holding a disputed earnest money deposit which isn't finally disbursed until July, 2004 from a transaction that terminated without closing in September, 2002, would be required to retain the A.0108 transaction file documents until July, 2007.

Brokerage Fees and Compensation [Rule A.0109]

This rule prohibits a broker or salesperson from receiving any form of valuable consideration from a vendor or supplier of goods or services in connection with an expenditure made on behalf of his principal in a real estate transaction without first obtaining the written consent of the principal.

> **Example:** A broker manages several rental units for various owners and routinely employs Ajax Cleaning Service to clean the units after the tenants leave. The broker pays Ajax a $50 per unit fee for its services out of rental proceeds received and deposited in his trust account. Ajax then "refunds" to the broker $10 for each $50 fee it receives, but the property owners are not aware that the broker receives this payment from Ajax in addition to his regular brokerage fee. The broker in this situation is making a secret profit without the property owners' knowledge and is violating the rule.

This rule also prohibits a broker or salesperson from receiving any form of valuable consideration for recommending, procuring, or arranging services for a party to a real estate transaction without full disclosure to such party. The party for whom the services are recommended, procured, or arranged does not have to be the agent's principal.

> **Example:** An agent sells a listed lot to a buyer who wants to build a house on the lot. Without the buyer's knowledge, the agent arranges with ABC Homebuilders for ABC to pay the agent a 3% referral fee if the agent recommends ABC to the buyer and the buyer employs ABC to build his house. The agent then recommends ABC to the buyer, ABC builds the buyer's house for $100,000 and ABC secretly pays the agent $3,000 for his referral of the buyer. The agent has violated this rule. (Note that the buyer in this situation likely paid $3,000 more for his house than was necessary because it is very likely the builder added the agent's referral fee to the price he charged the buyer for building the house. The main point here is that the buyer had the right to know that the agent was not providing disinterested advice when recommending the builder.)

> **Example:** A selling agent in a real estate transaction, while acting as a subagent of the seller, recommends to a buyer who has submitted an offer that the buyer apply to Ready Cash Mortgage Company for his mortgage loan. The agent knows that Ready Cash will pay him a "referral fee" of $100 for sending him the buyer's business if the loan is made to the buyer, but the agent does not

disclose this fact to the buyer. If the agent subsequently accepts the referral fee from the lender, he will have violated this rule. (The buyer has the right to know that the agent's recommendation is not a disinterested one.)

While A.0109(d) continues to absolutely prohibit licensees from sharing compensation with any unlicensed person for acts which require a real estate license, paragraph (e), which was added to Rule A.0109 effective September 1, 2002, allows one narrow, limited exception, namely: licensees may now pay referral fees to travel agents who contact them to book vacation rentals only, so long as well-defined procedures are followed.

Broker-in-Charge [Rule A.0110]

Every firm is required to designate a broker to serve as broker-in-charge at each office. The broker-in-charge is the person the Commission will hold responsible for the supervision and management of an office. The eight specific responsibilities of a broker-in-charge are enumerated in Paragraph (a). Effective October 1, 2000, all brokers-in-charge are required to take the Commission's broker-in-charge course once every five years; brokers newly designated as a broker-in-charge must take the broker-in-charge course within 120 days of being designated, unless they already have taken the course (which also counts as elective continuing education credit) within the preceding five years.

Drafting Legal Instruments [Rule A.0111]

This rule prohibits licensees from drafting legal instruments, e.g., contracts, deeds, deeds of trust, etc., but does allow them to fill in the blanks on preprinted sales contract forms, which is not construed to be the unauthorized practice of law.

Offers and Sales Contracts [Rule A.0112]

This rule specifies what minimum terms must be contained in any preprinted offer or sales contract form a licensee, acting as an agent, proposes for use by a party in a real estate transaction.

Reporting Criminal Convictions [Rule A.0113]

Licensees are required to report to the Commission any criminal convictions or any disciplinary action taken against them by any other professional board within sixty (60) days of the final judgment or order in the case. This reporting requirement is ongoing in nature.

Residential Property Disclosure Statement [Rule A.0114]

State law requires that most residential property owners complete a disclosure form to give to prospective purchasers. The form seeks to elicit information about the condition of the property by asking various questions, to which owners may answer "yes," "no," or "no representation." Failure to provide a buyer with this form may allow the buyer to cancel the contract by notifying the seller in writing within three calendar days of contract acceptance.

HANDLING TRUST FUNDS

See the "Trust Account Guidelines" contained in this booklet for complete coverage of this important topic. Licensees and applicants should have a thorough knowledge and understanding of the "Trust Account Guidelines."

Questions

1. The North Carolina Real Estate Commission shall, after a hearing, suspend or revoke the license of a licensee who
   a. has violated any of the provisions of the North Carolina license law.
   b. is not a REALTOR®.
   c. has violated the state motor vehicle law.
   d. is older than age 70.

2. Which of the following statements is true of a person in the business of renting and managing rental apartments for others?
   a. He or she is exempt from the North Carolina real estate license law.
   b. He or she must hold a North Carolina securities license.
   c. He or she must hold a North Carolina real estate license.
   d. He or she must hold a North Carolina vendor's license.

3. A real estate license must be renewed every
   a. year.
   b. two years.
   c. three years.
   d. five years.

4. A licensee can have his or her North Carolina real estate license revoked for
   a. placing a "For Sale" sign on a property without the owner's consent.
   b. advertising in local newspapers.
   c. belonging to a local trade association.
   d. buying a property listed by another broker after having disclosed to the seller, in writing, that the licensee holds a North Carolina real estate license.

5. A salesperson can have his or her license suspended or revoked for
   a. advertising properties in another county.
   b. listing property anywhere in North Carolina.
   c. paying a finder's fee to an unlicensed person.
   d. turning all trust funds over to the broker immediately on receipt instead of depositing them into a trust account.

6. In North Carolina, which of the following statements is true of the real estate license of a person who willingly disregards or violates any of the provisions of the North Carolina Real Estate License Law?
   a. It will be suspended or revoked.
   b. It may not be reissued for at least two months.
   c. It must be suspended for no more than six months.
   d. It may be reinstated immediately upon payment of a fine.

7. The broker-in-charge of any real estate office in North Carolina must
   I. be bonded.
   II. display their license and the firm's license.
   III. be either Realtists or REALTORS®.
      a. I only
      b. II only
      c. III only
      d. I and II only

8. In North Carolina, a real estate broker must
   a. list properties.
   b. include his or her name in advertisements of a client's property.
   c. belong to a local trade association.
   d. hold open houses.

9. Which of the following statements is true of a real estate licensee who is not a lawyer and engages in any activity that constitutes the practice of law?
   a. He or she may charge a fee for preparing deeds.
   b. He or she is in violation of the North Carolina real estate license law.
   c. He or she may legally do so only in the area of real estate law.
   d. He or she is not acting illegally.

10. Each time-share developer in the state registers its project with the
    a. recorder in the county where the project is located.
    b. clerk of courts in the county where the project is located.
    c. office of the secretary of state of North Carolina.
    d. Real Estate Commission.

11. In North Carolina, a person who sells time-shares must be
    a. a notary public.
    b. licensed as a real estate broker.
    c. licensed as an auctioneer.
    d. licensed as a real estate broker or salesperson.

12. All North Carolina licensees are bound by the
    I. Code of Ethics.
    II. REALTORS® Standards of Practice.
    III. North Carolina real estate law.
    a. I only
    b. II only
    c. III only
    d. I, II and III

13. Which of the following statements is(are) true regarding time-shares?
    I. They are considered personal property.
    II. They are considered real property.
    a. I only
    b. II only
    c. I and II, depending on who sells them
    d. Neither I nor II (They are considered hybrid property.)

14. Appointments to the North Carolina Real Estate Commission are made by the
    a. Governor
    b. President Pro Tempore of the State Senate
    c. Speaker of the State House of Representatives
    d. All the above

15. The members of the North Carolina Real Estate Commission serve terms of how many years?
    a. One
    b. Two
    c. Three
    d. Four

16. Each time-share developer must deposit all money received from purchasers in
    I. its business account immediately on receipt.
    II. an escrow account for ten days.
    a. I only
    b. II only
    c. Both I and II
    d. Neither I nor II

17. In North Carolina, the real estate salesperson's license expires
    a. automatically after two years.
    b. on June 30 each year.
    c. exactly one year from the date the license was issued.
    d. one year from the end of the month in which the license was issued.

18. In North Carolina, a written complaint against a licensee should be sent to the
    a. governor.
    b. director of commerce.
    c. superintendent.
    d. North Carolina Real Estate Commission.

19. A broker must deposit all rents collected for others into a trust account
    a. within three banking days after receipt.
    b. that is always an interest-bearing account.
    c. unless directed otherwise by one of the parties to the transaction.
    d. that is reconciled on a weekly basis.

20. All listing and buyer agency agreements for a sales transaction must
    I. be in writing.
    II. have a definite termination date.
    a. I only
    b. II only
    c. Both I and II
    d. Neither I nor II

21. Earnest money deposits other than cash must be deposited into the broker's trust account
    a. within 24 hours of their receipt.
    b. only if the seller authorizes the broker to do so.
    c. no later than three banking days following the acceptance of the offer to purchase.
    d. no later than three banking days after their receipt.

22. All listing and buyer agency agreements must
    I. contain a clause stating that the listed property will be listed to all buyers, regardless of protected class.
    II. contain a description of an agent's duties and relationships as written by the Commission.
    a. I only
    b. II only
    c. Both I and II
    d. Neither I nor II

23. A broker's trust account must
    I. be a separate custodial account.
    II. provide for withdrawal on demand.
    III. be opened in an insured bank or savings and loan association in North Carolina.
    a. I only
    b. II only
    c. Both I and II
    d. I, II and III

24. A broker has authorized his bookkeeper to withdraw funds from his trust account. The bookkeeper embezzles some of the funds.
    a. Only the bookkeeper is liable for the misuse of the funds, because the broker delegated this responsibility.
    b. The broker is always responsible for the misuse of trust funds.
    c. No one is liable for the misuse of the funds; the owner of the funds is out of luck.
    d. The Commission will issue a letter to the owner of the trust funds, explaining the problem, and relieving the broker of responsibility.

APPENDIX B

Residential Square Footage Guidelines

INTRODUCTION

It is often said that the three most important factors in making a homebuying decision are "location," "location," and "location." Other than "location," the single most-important factor is probably the size or "square footage" of the home. Not only is it an indicator of whether a particular home will meet a homebuyer's space needs, but it also affords a convenient (though not always accurate) method for the buyer to estimate the value of the home and compare it with other properties.

Although real estate agents are not required by the Real Estate License Law or Real Estate Commission rules to report the square footage of properties offered for sale (or rent), when they do report square footage, it is essential that the information they give prospective purchasers be accurate. At a minimum, information concerning square footage should include the amount of *living area* in the dwelling. The following guidelines and accompanying illustrations are designed to assist real estate brokers and salespersons in measuring, calculating and reporting (both orally and in writing) the *living area* contained in detached and attached single-family residential buildings. When reporting square footage, real estate agents should carefully follow these *Guidelines* or any other standards that are comparable to them, including those approved by the American National Standards Institute, Inc. (ANSI) which are recognized by the North Carolina Real Estate Commission as comparable standards.* Agents should be prepared to identify, when requested, the standard used.

LIVING AREA CRITERIA

Living area (sometimes referred to as "heated living area" or "heated square footage") is space that is intended for human occupancy and is:

1. Heated by a conventional heating system or systems (forced air, radiant, solar, etc.) that are permanently installed in the dwelling—not a portable heater—which generates heat sufficient to make the space suitable for year-round occupancy;

2. Finished, with walls, floors and ceilings of materials generally accepted for interior construction (e.g., painted drywall/sheet rock or panelled walls, carpeted or hardwood flooring, etc.) and with a ceiling height of at least seven feet, except under beams, ducts, etc. where the height must be at least six feet four inches *[Note: In rooms with sloped ceilings (e.g., finished attics, bonus rooms, etc.) you may also include as living area the portion of the room with a ceiling height of at least five feet if at least one-half of the finished area of the room has a ceiling height of at least seven feet.];* and

3. Directly accessible from other living area (through a door or by a heated hallway or stairway).

---

*The following materials were consulted in the development of these *Guidelines*:
The *American National Standard for Single-Family Residential Buildings:
Square Footage-Method for Calculating* approved by the American National Standards Institute, Inc.;
House Measuring & Square Footage published by the Carolina Multiple Listing Services, Inc.; and
materials compiled by Bart T. Bryson, MAI, SRA, and Mary L. D'Angelo.

Real estate appraisers and lenders generally adhere to more detailed criteria in arriving at the *living area* or "gross living area" of residential dwellings. This normally includes distinguishing "above grade" from "below-grade" area, which is also required by many multiple listing services. "Above-Grade" is defined as space on any level of a dwelling which has *living area* and no earth adjacent to any exterior wall on that level. "Below-Grade" is space on any level which has *living area,* is accessible by interior stairs, and has earth adjacent to any exterior wall on that level. If earth is adjacent to any portion of a wall, the entire level is considered "below-grade." Space that is "at" or "on grade" is considered "above-grade."

While real estate agents are encouraged to provide the most complete information available about properties offered for sale, the *Guidelines* recognize that the separate reporting of "above-grade" and "below-grade" area can be impractical in the advertising and marketing of homes. For this reason, *real estate agents are permitted under these Guidelines to report square footage of the dwelling as the total "living area"* without a separate distinction between "above-grade" and "below-grade" areas. However, to help avoid confusion and concern, agents should alert purchasers and sellers that the appraisal report may reflect differences in the way *living area* is defined and described by the lender, appraiser, and the *North Carolina Building Code* which could affect the amount of *living area* reported.

Determining whether an area is considered *living area* can sometimes be confusing. Finished rooms used for general living (living room, dining room, kitchen, den, bedrooms, etc.) are normally included in *living area.* For other areas in the dwelling, the determination may not be so easy. *For example, the following areas are considered **living area** if they meet the criteria (i.e., heated, finished, directly accessible from living area):*

- *Attic*, but note in the listing data that the space is located in an attic (Fig. 2). *[Note: If the ceiling is sloped, remember to apply the "ceiling height" criteria.]*

- *Basement (or "Below-Grade")*, but note in the listing data that the space is located in a basement or "below-grade" (Fig. 1). *[Note: For reporting purposes, a "basement" is defined as an area below the entry level of the dwelling which is accessible by a **full** flight of stairs and has earth adjacent to some portion of at least one wall above the floor level.]*

- *Bay Window*, if it has a floor, a ceiling height of at least seven feet, and otherwise meets the criteria for living area (Fig. 2).

- *Bonus Room (e.g., Finished Room over Garage)* (Fig. 3). *[Note: If the ceiling is sloped, remember to apply the "ceiling height" criteria.]*

- *Breezeway* (enclosed).

- *Chimney*, if the chimney base is inside *living area*. If the chimney base is outside the *living area* but the hearth is in the *living area*, include the hearth in the *living area* but not the chimney base (Fig. 1).

- *Closets*, if they are a functional part of the *living area.*

- *Dormers* (Fig. 6).

- *Furnace (Mechanical) Room* Also, in order to avoid excessive detail, if the furnace, water heater, etc. is located in a small closet in the *living area*, include it in *living area* even if it does not meet other *living area* criteria (Fig. 4).

- *Hallways*, if they are a functional part of the *living area*.

- *Laundry Room/Area* (Fig. 6).

- *Office* (Fig. 1).

- *Stairs*, if they meet the criteria and connect to *living area* (Fig. 1, 2, 3, 4, 5, 6). Include the stairway with the area from which it descends, **not to exceed the area of the opening in the floor**. If the opening for the stairway exceeds the length and width of the stairway, deduct the excess open space from the upper level area. Include as part of the lower level area the space beneath the stairway, regardless of its ceiling height.

- *Storage Room* (Fig. 6).

OTHER AREA

Note in the listing data and advise purchasers of any space that does not meet the criteria for *living area* but which contributes to the value of the dwelling; for example, unfinished basements, unfinished attics (with permanent stairs), unfinished bonus rooms, shops, decks, balconies, porches, garages and carports.

HELPFUL HINTS

Concealed in the walls of nearly all residential construction are pipes, ducts, chases, returns, etc. necessary to support the structure's mechanical systems. Although they may occupy *living area*, to avoid excessive detail, do **not** deduct the space from the *living area*.

When measuring and reporting the *living area* of homes, be alert to any remodeling, room additions (e.g., an enclosed porch) or other structural modifications to assure that the space meets all the criteria for *living area*. **Pay particular attention to the heating criteria, because the heating system for the original structure may not be adequate for the increased square footage.** Although agents are not required to determine the adequacy of heating systems, they should at least note whether there are heat vents, radiators or other heat outlets in the room before deciding whether to include space as *living area*.

When an area that is not part of the *living area* (e.g., a garage) shares a common wall with the *living area*, treat the common wall as the exterior wall for the *living area*; therefore, the measurements for the *living area* will include the thickness of the common wall, and the measurements for the other area will not.

Interior space that is open from the floor of one level to the ceiling of the next higher level is included in the square footage for the lower level only. However, any area occupied by interior balconies, lofts, etc. on the upper level or stairs that extend to the upper level is included in the square footage for the upper level.

MEASURING

The amount of *living area* and "other area" in dwellings is based upon **exterior measurements**. A one-hundred-foot-long tape measure is recommended for use in measuring the exterior of dwellings, and a thirty-foot retractable tape for measuring interior and hard-to-reach spaces. A tape measure that indicates linear footage in "tenths of a foot" will greatly simplify your calculations. For best results, take a partner to assist you in measuring. But if you do not have someone to assist you, a screwdriver or other sharp tool can be used to secure the tape measure to the ground.

Begin at one corner of the dwelling and proceed with measuring each exterior wall. **Round off your measurements to the nearest inch** (or tenth-of-a-foot if your tape indicates footage in that manner). Make a sketch of the structure. Write down each measurement as you go, and record it on your sketch. A clipboard and graph paper are helpful in sketching the dwelling and recording the measurements. Measure *living area* and "other area," but identify them separately on your sketch. Look for offsets (portions of walls that "jut out"), and adjust for any "overlap" of exterior walls (Fig. 3) or "overhang" in upper levels (Fig. 5).

When you cannot measure an exterior surface (such as in the case of attics and below-grade areas), measure the perimeter walls of the area from the inside of the dwelling. Remember to add **six inches** for each exterior wall and interior wall that you encounter in order to arrive at the exterior dimensions (Fig. 2, 3, 4, 6).

Measure all sides of the dwelling, making sure that the overall lengths of the front and rear sides are equal, as well as the ends. Then inspect the interior of the dwelling to identify spaces which cannot be included in *living area*. You may also find it helpful to take several photographs of the dwelling for later use when you return to your office.

CALCULATING SQUARE FOOTAGE

From your sketch of the dwelling, identify and separate *living area* from "other area." If your measurements are in inches (rather than tenths-of-a-foot), convert your figures to a decimal as follows:

1" = .10 ft.	7" = .60 ft.
2" = .20 ft.	8" = .70 ft.
3" = .25 ft.	9" = .75 ft.
4" = .30 ft	10" = .80 ft.
5" = .40 ft.	11" = .90 ft.
6" = .50 ft.	12" = 1.00 ft.

Calculate the *living area* (and other area) by multiplying the length times the width of each rectangular space. Then add your subtotals and round off your figure for total square footage to the nearest **square foot**. Double-check your calculations. When in doubt, re-check them and, if necessary, re-measure the house.

ATTACHED DWELLINGS

When measuring an "attached" single-family home (e.g., townhouse, duplex, condominium, etc.), use the same techniques just described. If there is a common wall, measure to the inside surface of the wall and add **six inches**. [*Note: In the case of condominiums, do not include the thickness of exterior or common walls.*] Do not include any "common areas" (exterior hallways, stairways, etc.) in your calculations.

PROPOSED CONSTRUCTION

For proposed construction, your square footage calculations will be based upon dimensions described in blueprints and building plans. When reporting the projected square footage, be careful to disclose that you have calculated the square footage based upon plan dimensions. Therefore, the square footage may differ in the completed structure. Do not rely on any calculations printed on the plans.

AGENTS' RESPONSIBILITIES
(Effective May 9, 2001)

Real estate agents are expected to be able to accurately calculate the square footage of most dwellings. When reporting square footage, whether to a party to a real estate transaction, another real estate agent, or others, a real estate agent is expected to provide accurate square footage information that was compiled using these *Guidelines* or comparable standards. While an agent is expected to use reasonable skill, care and diligence when calculating square footage, it should be noted that the Commission does not expect absolute perfection. Because all properties are unique and no guidelines can anticipate every possibility, minor discrepancies in deriving square footage are not considered by the Commission to constitute negligence on the part of the agent. Minor variations in tape readings and small differences in rounding off or conversion from inches to decimals, when multiplied over distances, will cause reasonable discrepancies between two competent measurements of the same dwelling. In addition to differences due to minor variations in measurement and calculation, discrepancies between measurements may also be attributable to reasonable differences in interpretation. For instance, two agents might reasonably differ about whether an addition to a dwelling is sufficiently finished under these *Guidelines* to be included within the measured living area. Differences

which are based upon an agent's thoughtful judgment reasonably founded on these or other similar guidelines will not be considered by the Commission to constitute error on the agent's part. Deviations in calculated square footage of less than five percent will seldom be cause for concern.

As a general rule, the most reliable way for an agent to obtain accurate square footage data is by personally measuring the dwelling unit and calculating the square footage. It is especially recommended that *listing agents* use this approach for dwellings that are not particularly unusual or complex in their design.

As an alternative to personally measuring a dwelling and calculating its square footage, an agent may rely on the square footage reported by other persons when it is reasonable under the circumstances to do so. Generally speaking, an agent working with a buyer (either as a buyer's agent or as a seller's agent) may rely on the listing agent's square footage representations except in those unusual instances when there is an error in the reported square footage that should be obvious to a reasonably prudent agent. For example, a buyer's agent would not be expected to notice that a house advertised as containing 2200 square feet of living area in fact contained only 2000 square feet. On the other hand, that same agent, under most circumstances, would be expected to realize that a house described as containing 3200 square feet really contained only 2300 square feet of living area. If there is such a "red flag" regarding the reported square footage, the agent working with the buyer should promptly point out the suspected error to the buyer and the listing agent. The listing agent should then verify the square footage and correct any error in the information reported.

It is also appropriate for an agent to rely upon measurements and calculations performed by other professionals with greater expertise in determining square footage. A new agent who may be unsure of his or her own calculations should seek guidance from a more experienced agent. As the new agent gains experience and confidence, he or she will become less reliant on the assistance of others. In order to ensure accuracy of the square footage they report, even experienced agents may wish to rely upon a competent state-licensed or state-certified appraiser or another agent with greater expertise in determining square footage. For example, an agent might be confronted with an unusual measurement problem or a dwelling of complex design. The house described in Figure 8 in these *Guidelines* is such a property. When an agent relies upon measurements and calculations personally performed by a competent appraiser or a more expert agent, the appraiser or agent must use these *Guidelines* or other comparable standards and the square footage reported must be specifically determined in connection with the current transaction. An agent who relies on another's measurement would still be expected to recognize an obvious error in the reported square footage and to alert any interested parties.

Some sources of square footage information are by their very nature unreliable. For example, an agent should **not** rely on square footage information determined by the property owner or included in property tax records. An agent should also **not** rely on square footage information included in a listing, appraisal report or survey prepared in connection with an earlier transaction.

In areas where the prevailing practice is to report square footage in the advertising and marketing of homes, agents whose policy is **not** to calculate and report square footage must disclose this fact to prospective buyer and seller clients before entering into agency agreements with them.

ILLUSTRATIONS

For assistance in calculating and reporting the area of homes, refer to the following illustrations showing the *living area* shaded. To test your knowledge, an illustration and blank "Worksheet" for a home with a more challenging floor plan has also been included. (A completed "Worksheet" for the Practice Floor Plan can be found on page 23.) In reviewing the illustrations, assume that for those homes with basements, attics, etc., the exterior measurements shown have been derived from interior measurements taking into account walls and partitions. (*see page 4*). Where there is a common wall between *living area* and other area (*see page 3*) the measurements shown in the illustrations include the thickness of the common wall in *living area* except in the condominium example where wall thickness is not included.

ONE STORY WITH BASEMENT AND CARPORT

(Figure 1)

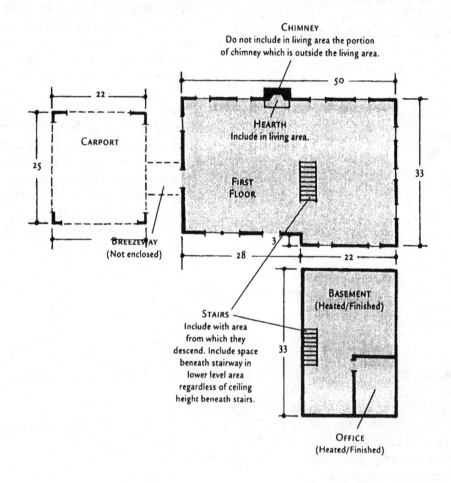

CHIMNEY
Do not include in living area the portion
of chimney which is outside the living area.

HEARTH
Include in living area.

FIRST FLOOR

50

33

CARPORT

22

25

BREEZEWAY
(Not enclosed)

28

3

22

BASEMENT
(Heated/Finished)

33

STAIRS
Include with area
from which they
descend. Include space
beneath stairway in
lower level area
regardless of ceiling
height beneath stairs.

OFFICE
(Heated/Finished)

ONE STORY WITH BASEMENT AND CARPORT WORKSHEET

LIVING AREA			
AREA	DIMENSIONS	SUBTOTAL	TOTAL
1st Floor	50 x 30	1,500	
	3 x 22	+ 66	1,566
Basement	22 x 33		726
Total			2,292

OTHER AREA			
AREA	DIMENSIONS	SUBTOTAL	TOTAL
Carport	22 x 25		550

REPORT: ONE-STORY DETACHED HOUSE WITH 2,292 SQUARE FEET OF LIVING AREA OF WHICH 726 SQUARE FEET ARE IN A FINISHED BASEMENT, PLUS A 550-SQUARE-FOOT CARPORT.

TWO STORY WITH OPEN FOYER AND FINISHED ATTIC

(Figure 2)

ATTIC
Add 1 ft. (6" for each exterior side wall) to inside measurements.
Thus, 19' inside measurement equals 20' exterior measurement.
In this example, do NOT add for front and rear walls since the allowable
square footage (5' ceiling height) does not extend to the kneewalls.

STAIRWAY WITH OPEN AREA
1. Calculate area of
open space (10' x 12' = 120 sf).
2. Subtract from second floor area
(1,200-120=1,080 sf).
3. Add stairway (6' x 4' = 24
+ 1,080 = 1,104 sf).

3RD FLOOR ATTIC
(Heated/Finished)

3 FT. KNEEWALL
In rooms with sloped ceilings, do not include any area with a ceiling height of less than 5 ft.

BAY WINDOW
(Floored)
Include in living area
if it is floored and has
ceiling height of at
least 7 ft.
1. Calculate area
of triangles (3' x 4'÷ 2
= 6 sf x 2 = 12 sf).
2. Add area of
triangles (12 sf)
to remaining area
of bay window (6' x 4'
= 24 sf) = 36 sf.

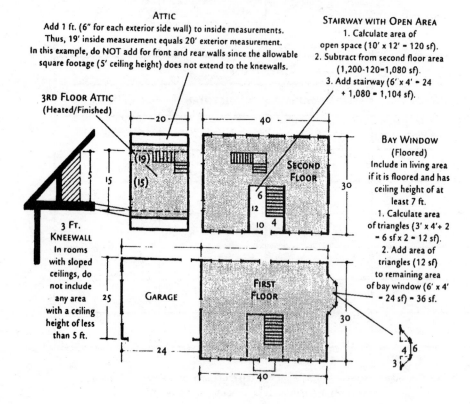

TWO STORY WITH OPEN FOYER AND FINISHED ATTIC WORKSHEET

LIVING AREA			
AREA	DIMENSIONS	SUBTOTAL	TOTAL
1st Floor	40 x 30	1,200	
Bay Window		36	1,236
2nd Floor	40 x 30	1,200	
	10 x 12	− 120	
	4 x 6	+ 24	1,104
Fin. Attic	20 x 15		<u>300</u>
Total			2,640
OTHER AREA			
AREA	DIMENSIONS	SUBTOTAL	TOTAL
Garage	25 x 24		600

REPORT: TWO-STORY DETACHED HOUSE WITH 2,640 SQUARE FEET OF LIVING AREA OF WHICH 300 SQUARE FEET ARE IN A FINISHED ATTIC, PLUS A 600-SQUARE-FOOT GARAGE.

TWO STORY WITH "BONUS ROOM" OVER GARAGE

(Figure 3)

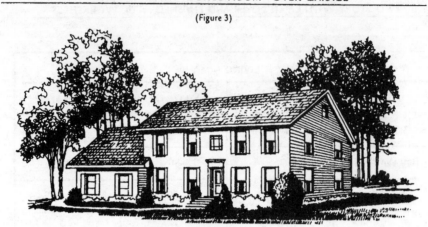

BONUS ROOM

If the "Bonus Room" is accessible from living area through a door,
hallway or stairway, include in living area; otherwise, report as other area.

In rooms with sloped ceilings, add 6" for each knee wall at least 5' in height.

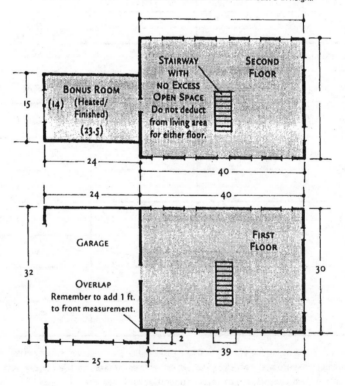

TWO STORY WITH "BONUS ROOM" OVER GARAGE WORKSHEET

LIVING AREA			
AREA	**DIMENSIONS**	**SUBTOTAL**	**TOTAL**
1st Floor	40 x 30		1,200
2nd Floor	40 x 30		1,200
Bonus Room	15 x 24		<u>360</u>
Total			2,760

OTHER AREA			
AREA	**DIMENSIONS**	**SUBTOTAL**	**TOTAL**
Garage	24 x 32	768	
	1 x 2	+ 2	770

REPORT: TWO-STORY DETACHED HOUSE WITH 2,760 SQUARE FEET OF LIVING AREA OF WHICH 360 SQUARE FEET
ARE IN A "BONUS ROOM" OVER THE GARAGE, PLUS A 770-SQUARE-FOOT GARAGE.

SPLIT FOYER

(Figure 4)

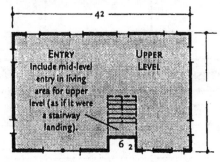

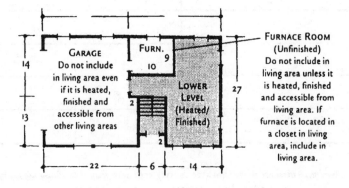

SPLIT FOYER WORKSHEET

LIVING AREA			
AREA	DIMENSIONS	SUBTOTAL	TOTAL
Upper Level	27 x 42	1,134	
	6 x 2	– 12	1,122
Lower Level	22 x 27	594	
	6 x 2	– 12	
	13 x 2	– 26	
	9 x 10	– 90	<u>466</u>
Total			1,588
OTHER AREA			
AREA	DIMENSIONS	SUBTOTAL	TOTAL
Garage	27 x 20	540	
	2 x 13	+ 26	566
Furnace Room	9 x 10		90

REPORT: SPLIT-FOYER DETACHED HOUSE WITH 1,588 SQUARE FEET OF LIVING AREA,
PLUS A 566-SQAURE-FOOT GARAGE AND 90-SQUARE-FOOT FURNACE ROOM.

SPLIT (TRI-) LEVEL WITH OVERHANG

(Figure S)

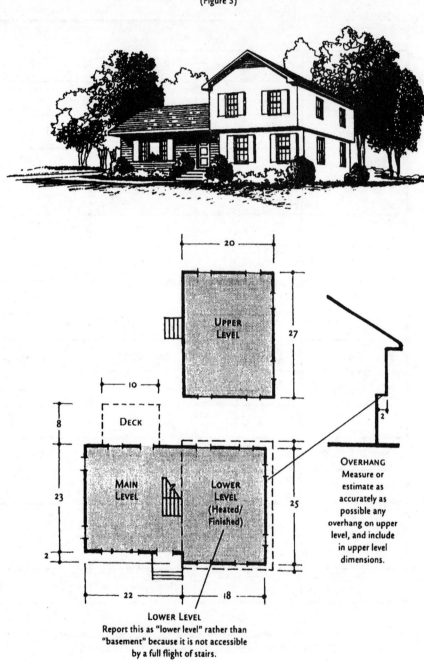

OVERHANG
Measure or estimate as accurately as possible any overhang on upper level, and include in upper level dimensions.

LOWER LEVEL
Report this as "lower level" rather than "basement" because it is not accessible by a full flight of stairs.

Split (Tri-) Level With Overhang Worksheet

LIVING AREA			
AREA	DIMENSIONS	SUBTOTAL	TOTAL
Main Level	22 x 23		506
Lower Level	18 x 25		450
Upper Level	27 x 20		<u>540</u>
Total			1,496

OTHER AREA			
AREA	DIMENSIONS	SUBTOTAL	TOTAL
Deck	8 x 10		80

REPORT: SPLIT-LEVEL DETACHED HOUSE WITH 1,496 SQUARE FEET OF LIVING AREA, PLUS AN 80-SQUARE-FOOT DECK.

ONE AND ONE-HALF STORY

(Figure 6)

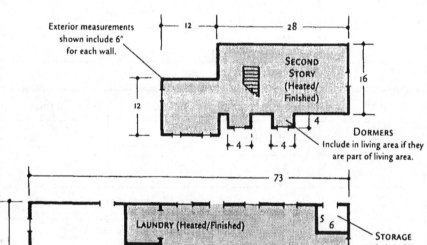

Exterior measurements shown include 6" for each wall.

SECOND STORY (Heated/Finished)

12   28   16   12   4   4   4

DORMERS
Include in living area if they are part of living area.

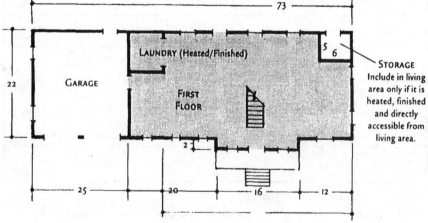

73

LAUNDRY (Heated/Finished)

5 6

GARAGE

22

FIRST FLOOR

2

25   20   16   12

STORAGE
Include in living area only if it is heated, finished and directly accessible from living area.

ONE AND ONE-HALF STORY WORKSHEET

LIVING AREA			
AREA	DIMENSIONS	SUBTOTAL	TOTAL
1st Floor	48 x 22	1,056	
	16 x 2	+ 32	
	5 x 6	− 30	1,058
2nd Floor	16 x 28	448	
	4 x 4	+ 16	
	4 x 4	+ 16	
	12 x 12	+ 144	<u>624</u>
Total			1,682
OTHER AREA			
AREA	DIMENSIONS	SUBTOTAL	TOTAL
Garage	22 x 25		550
Storage	5 x 6		30

REPORT: ONE AND ONE-HALF STORY DETACHED HOUSE WITH 1,682 SQUARE FEET OF LIVING AREA, PLUS A 550-SQUARE-FOOT GARAGE.

CONDOMINIUM

(Figure 7)

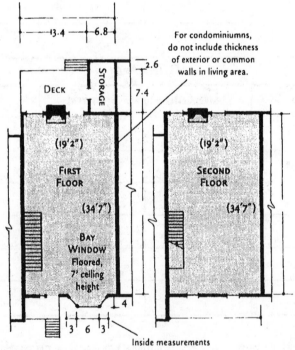

CONDOMINIUM WORKSHEET

LIVING AREA			
AREA	DIMENSIONS	SUBTOTAL	TOTAL
1st Floor	34.6 x 19.2	664.3	
Bay Window		36.0	700
2nd Floor	34.6 x 19.2	664.3	664
Total			1,364
OTHER AREA			
AREA	DIMENSIONS	SUBTOTAL	TOTAL
Deck	13.4 x 7.4	99.2	99
Storage	10 x 6.8		68

REPORT: TWO-STORY CONDOMINIUM WITH 1,364 SQUARE FEET OF LIVING AREA, PLUS A 99 SQUARE FOOT DECK.

PRACTICE FLOOR PLAN

(Figure 8)

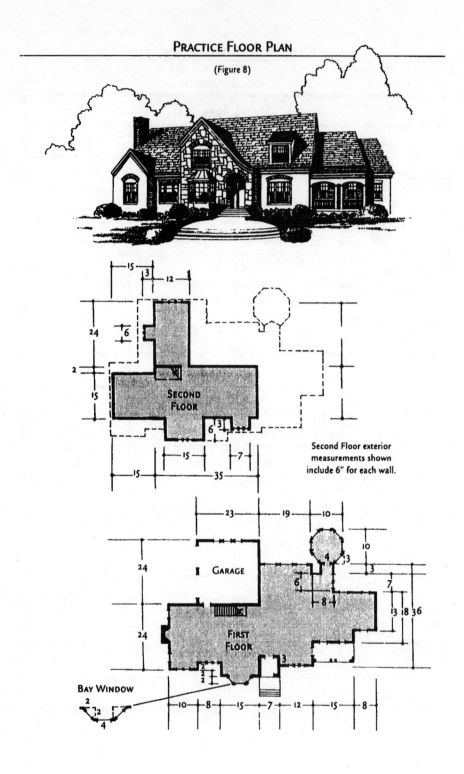

Second Floor exterior measurements shown include 6" for each wall.

Practice Floor Plan Worksheet

LIVING AREA			
AREA	DIMENSIONS	SUBTOTAL	TOTAL
OTHER AREA			
AREA	DIMENSIONS	SUBTOTAL	TOTAL

REPORT:

PRACTICE FLOOR PLAN

(Zoned to facilitate calculations)

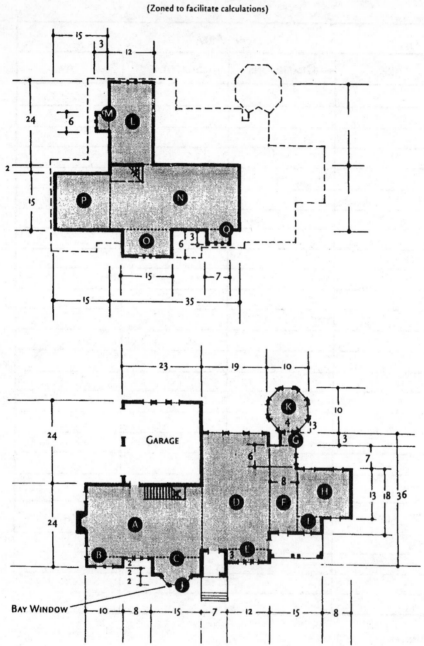

BAY WINDOW

PRACTICE FLOOR PLAN WORKSHEET

LIVING AREA			
AREA	DIMENSIONS	SUBTOTAL	TOTAL
1st Floor A	22 x 33	726	
1st Floor B	2 x 10	20	
1st Floor C	4 x 15	60	
1st Floor D	19 x 33	627	
1st Floor E	3 x 12	36	
1st Floor F	8 x 25	200	
1st Floor G	4 x 3	12	
1st Floor H	15 x 13	195	
1st Floor I	7 x 5	35	
Bay Window J		12	
Oct. Window K		82	2,005
2nd Floor L	24 x 12	288	
2nd Floor M	3 x 6	18	
2nd Floor N	17 x 35	595	
2nd Floor O	15 x 6	90	
2nd Floor P	15 x 15	225	
2nd Floor Q	3 x 7	21	1,237
Total			3,242
OTHER AREA			
AREA	DIMENSIONS	SUBTOTAL	TOTAL
Garage	24 x 23		552

REPORT: ONE AND ONE-HALF STORY DETACHED HOUSE WITH 3,242 SQUARE FEET OF LIVING AREA, PLUS A 552-SQUARE-FOOT GARAGE.

APPENDIX C

North Carolina Real Estate Forms

Dual Agency Agreement (1 of 3)

DUAL AGENCY AGREEMENT

Do NOT use this form if Dual Agency Addenda have been executed by BOTH Seller and Buyer.
(To be signed by Buyer(s) before Offer to Purchase and Contract is signed and to be signed by Seller(s) before offer is reviewed.)
THIS DOCUMENT IS NEITHER AN ADDENDUM TO NOR A PART OF THE OFFER TO PURCHASE AND CONTRACT.

This DUAL AGENCY AGREEMENT ("Agreement") is entered into (Date) _____, among

_____
(hereinafter referred to as "Buyer") and

_____
(hereinafter referred to as "Seller") and

_____ (Real Estate Firm)
(hereinafter referred to as "Broker")

regarding the property located at _____

_____ (hereinafter referred to as the "Property").

The term "Broker" shall sometimes hereinafter include Broker and its individual sales associates, as the sense requires.

1. DUAL AGENCY: Seller and Buyer agree that Broker, acting by and through its individual sales associates, shall serve as both Seller's Agent and Buyer's Agent in the sale of Seller's property to Buyer. In the event Broker serves as a Dual Agent, the parties agree that without permission from the party about whom the information pertains, Broker shall not disclose to the other party the following information:

    (a) That a party may agree to a price, terms or any conditions of sale other than those offered;
    (b) The motivation of a party for engaging in the transaction, unless disclosure is otherwise required by statute or rule; and
    (c) Any information about a party which that party has identified as confidential unless disclosure is otherwise required by statute or rule.

2. BROKER'S DUAL AGENCY ROLE: Because Broker is serving as Agent for both Seller and Buyer in this transaction, Broker shall make every reasonable effort to represent Seller and Buyer in a balanced and fair manner. Broker shall also make every reasonable effort to encourage and effect communication and negotiation between Seller and Buyer. Seller and Buyer understand and acknowledge that:

    (a) Prior to the time this Agreement was entered into, Broker acted as the exclusive Agent of Seller and acted as the exclusive Agent of Buyer.
    (b) In those separate roles Broker may have obtained information which, if disclosed, could harm the bargaining position of the party providing such information to Broker.
    (c) Broker is required by law to disclose to Buyer and Seller any known or reasonably ascertainable material facts.

Seller and Buyer agree that Broker shall not be liable to either party for (1) disclosing material facts required by law to be disclosed; and (2) refusing or failing to disclose other information the law does not require to be disclosed which could harm or compromise one party's bargaining position but could benefit the other party.

3. SELLER'S AND BUYER'S ROLES: Because of Broker's Dual Agency relationship, Seller and Buyer understand and acknowledge that:

    (a) They each have the responsibility of making their own decisions as to what terms are to be included in any purchase and sale agreement between them.

North Carolina Association of REALTORS®, Inc.

Buyer Initials _____ _____ Seller Initials _____ _____

STANDARD FORM 902
© 7/2002

Dual Agency Agreement (2 of 3)

(b) They are fully aware of, and understand the implications and consequences of Broker's Dual Agency role as expressed herein to provide balanced and fair representation of Seller and Buyer and to encourage and effect communication between them rather than as an advocate or exclusive Agent or representative.

(c) They have determined that the benefits of entering into this Dual Agency relationship with Broker, acting as Agent for them both, outweigh any disadvantages or adverse consequences.

(d) They each may seek independent legal counsel to assist them with the negotiation and preparation of a purchase and sale agreement or with any matter relating to the transaction which is the subject matter of a purchase and sale agreement.

Seller and Buyer agree to indemnify and hold Broker harmless against all claims, damages, losses, expenses or liabilities, other than violations of the North Carolina Real Estate License Law and intentional wrongful acts, arising from Broker's role as a Dual Agent. Seller and Buyer shall each have a duty to protect their own interests and should read this Agreement and any purchase and sale agreement carefully to ensure that they accurately set forth the terms which they want included in said agreements.

4. DESIGNATED AGENT OPTION (Initial only if applicable):

_____ Buyer hereby authorizes the Broker (Firm) to designate an agent(s) to represent the Buyer, to the exclusion of any other licensees associated with the Broker. The agent(s) shall not be so designated and shall not undertake to represent only the interests of the Buyer if the agent(s) has actually received confidential information concerning the Seller in connection with the transaction. The designated agent(s) shall represent only the interests of the Buyer to the extent permitted by law.

_____ Seller hereby authorizes Broker (Firm) to designate an agent(s) to represent the Seller, to the exclusion of any other licensees associated with the Broker. The agent(s) shall not be so designated and shall not undertake to represent only the interests of the Seller if the agent(s) has actually received confidential information concerning the Buyer in connection with the transaction. The designated agent(s) shall represent only the interests of the Seller to the extent permitted by law.

5. COMPENSATION: As compensation for the services rendered under this Agreement, Broker shall be paid a real estate commission by _____ in the amount of _____
_____ as follows:
_____
_____

6. PREVIOUS AGENCY AGREEMENTS: The parties agree that this Agreement shall modify any agency agreements previously entered into between Seller and Broker or between Buyer and Broker. If those previous agency agreements contain expiration or termination dates prior to the termination date for this Agreement as set forth below, the expiration or termination dates of the previous agency agreements are hereby extended until the termination of this Agreement. If this Agreement terminates prior to the termination date of any previous agency agreement, the previous agency agreement shall remain in full force and effect in accordance with its terms. In any areas where this Agreement contradicts or conflicts with those agency agreements, this Dual Agency Agreement shall control.

7. DURATION OF DUAL AGENCY: The term of this Agreement shall commence when this document is executed by Seller, Buyer, and Broker and, unless extended by written agreement of all parties, shall automatically terminate upon (a) the closing of the sale of the Property or (b) midnight, _____, whichever occurs first. In the event that Seller and Buyer do not enter into an agreement for the purchase and sale of the Property, or in the event that the purchase and sale transaction described in any agreement between Seller and Buyer is terminated, Broker may terminate its Dual Agency role and this Agreement by mailing written notice thereof to Seller and Buyer. In addition, Buyer may terminate this Agreement at any time prior to the complete execution of an agreement for the purchase and sale of the property by giving Seller and Broker written notice that Buyer is no longer interested in purchasing the property. Seller may terminate this Agreement at any time prior to the complete execution of an agreement for the purchase and sale of the Property by giving Buyer and Broker written notice that Seller is no longer interested in negotiating with Buyer for the purchase and sale of the Property.

8. *The Broker shall conduct all his brokerage activities in regard to this Agreement without respect to the race, color, religion, sex, national origin, handicap or familial status of any buyer, prospective buyer, seller or prospective seller.*

Buyer Initials _____ _____   Seller Initials _____ _____   **STANDARD FORM 902**
© 7/2002

Dual Agency Agreement (3 of 3)

THIS IS INTENDED TO BE A LEGALLY BINDING DUAL AGENCY AGREEMENT THAT MAY ULTIMATELY RESTRICT YOUR LEGAL RIGHTS OR REMEDIES. IF YOU DO NOT UNDERSTAND THIS AGREEMENT OR FEEL THAT IT DOES NOT PROVIDE FOR YOUR LEGAL NEEDS, YOU SHOULD CONSULT AN ATTORNEY BEFORE YOU SIGN IT.

Buyer, Seller and Broker each hereby acknowledges receipt of a signed copy of this Dual Agency Agreement.

THE NORTH CAROLINA ASSOCIATION OF REALTORS®, INC. MAKES NO REPRESENTATION AS TO THE LEGAL VALIDITY OR ADEQUACY OF ANY PROVISION OF THIS FORM IN ANY SPECIFIC TRANSACTION.

_____   _____   _____   _____
Buyer   Date   Seller   Date

_____   _____   _____   _____
Buyer   Date   Seller   Date

_____   _____
Broker (Selling Firm)   Broker (Listing Firm)

_____   _____   _____   _____
By: Selling Sales Associate   Date   By: Listing Sales Associate   Date

STANDARD FORM 902
© 7/2002

Option to Purchase (1 of 3)

OPTION TO PURCHASE

Mail/Box after recording to:_____

This instrument was prepared by:_____

Brief description for the Index:_____

This OPTION TO PURCHASE ("Option") is granted on _____ by _____, the "Seller," to _____, the "Buyer." Seller, intending to bind Seller, Seller's heirs, successors and assigns, in consideration of the sum of _____ Dollars ($_____) (the "Option Money") paid to Seller by Buyer, receipt of which is acknowledged, grants to the Buyer, Buyer's heirs, successors, assigns or representatives, the exclusive right and option to purchase all of that certain parcel of land, together with all improvements located thereon (collectively, the "Property"), in the City of _____, County of _____, State of North Carolina, and more particularly described as follows:

Street Address: _____ Zip Code _____

Legal Description: _____

_____ on the terms and conditions set forth below:

1. **Option Period:** This Option shall exist and continue from the date hereof until _____ o'clock ____.M. on _____ ("Option Period"). In order to preserve the full legal rights of Buyer, a notice hereof should be recorded; and this Option (excluding Exhibit A) may be recorded as a legally binding Notice of the Option. **TIME IS OF THE ESSENCE WITH RESPECT TO THE OPTION PERIOD AND EXERCISE.**

2. **Exercise:** At any time during the Option Period, Buyer may exercise this Option by giving Seller a written notice thereof signed by the Buyer, which exercise is effective upon (a) hand delivery, (b) completed facsimile transmission, or (c) prepaid deposit of the notice with an overnight commercial delivery service or in certified mail, return receipt requested, at the following address:

Seller: Seller requests, but does not require, a copy be sent to:

_____   _____

_____   _____

_____   _____

Phone:_____ Fax:_____   Phone:_____ Fax:_____

3. **Contract Upon Exercise:** Upon exercise of this Option, the terms of purchase and sale shall be as set forth on the completed standard "Offer to Purchase and Contract," or standard "Vacant Lot Offer to Purchase and Contract," which is attached as Exhibit A and incorporated herein by reference.

4. **Application of Option Money:** If this Option is exercised, the Option Money shall _____ shall not _____ be applied to the purchase price at Closing. If this Option is not exercised, the Option Money shall be retained by Seller.

Page 1 of 3

This form jointly approved by:
North Carolina Bar Association
North Carolina Association of REALTORS®, Inc.

STANDARD FORM 8 - T
© 7/2002

Seller Initials _____ _____

Option to Purchase (2 of 3)

5. **Entry:** During the Option Period, Buyer and those reasonably designated by Buyer may, with reasonable advance notice to Seller, enter the Property to inspect, survey and appraise the Property. Buyer shall be responsible for the repair of any damage done to the Property during any such entry.

6. **Other Conditions:** _____
_____
_____.

THE NORTH CAROLINA ASSOCIATION OF REALTORS®, INC. AND THE NORTH CAROLINA BAR ASSOCIATION MAKE NO REPRESENTATION AS TO THE LEGAL VALIDITY OR ADEQUACY OF ANY PROVISION OF THIS FORM IN ANY SPECIFIC TRANSACTION. IF YOU DO NOT UNDERSTAND THIS FORM OR FEEL THAT IT DOES NOT PROVIDE FOR YOUR LEGAL NEEDS, YOU SHOULD CONSULT A NORTH CAROLINA REAL ESTATE ATTORNEY BEFORE YOU SIGN IT.

IN WITNESS WHEREOF, the Seller has caused the due execution of the foregoing as of the day and year first above written.

_____ (SEAL)
       (Entity Name)

By:_____ (SEAL)
   Title:_____

_____ (SEAL)

_____ (SEAL)

_____

State of North Carolina - County of _____

I, the undersigned Notary Public of the County and State aforesaid, certify that _____
_____
personally appeared before me this day and acknowledged the due execution of the foregoing instrument for the purposes therein expressed. Witness my hand and Notarial stamp or seal this _____ day of _____, 20_____.

My Commission Expires:_____   _____
                                                             Notary Public

_____

State of North Carolina - County of _____

I, the undersigned Notary Public of the County and State aforesaid, certify that _____
personally came before me this day and acknowledged that __he is the _____
of _____, a North Carolina or _____ corporation/limited liability company/general partnership/limited partnership (strike through the inapplicable), and that by authority duly given and as the act of such entity, __he signed the foregoing instrument in its name, on its behalf, as its act and deed. Witness my hand and Notarial stamp or seal, this _____ day of _____, 20_____.

My Commission Expires:_____   _____
                                                             Notary Public

STANDARD FORM 8 - T
© 7/2002

Option to Purchase (3 of 3)

State of North Carolina - County of _____

I, the undersigned Notary Public of the County and State aforesaid, certify that _____

_____

_____ .

Witness my hand and Notarial stamp or seal, this _____ day of _____, 20_____ .

My Commission Expires:_____

Notary Public

The foregoing Certificate(s) of _____

_____ is/are certified to be correct. This instrument and this certificate are duly

registered at the date and time and in the Book and Page shown on the first page hereof.

_____ Register of Deeds for _____ County

By:_____ Deputy/Assistant - Register of Deeds

Page 3 of 3

STANDARD FORM 8 - T
© 7/2002

Residential Rental Contract (1 of 7)

RESIDENTIAL RENTAL CONTRACT

IN CONSIDERATION of the rent described below and the mutual promises made to each other,_____
_____ ("Landlord"), by and through
his/her/its agent _____ ("Agent"), leases and rents to _____
_____
("Tenant") and Tenant does hereby lease and rent from Landlord the Premises more particularly described below in accordance with
the following terms and conditions:

    1. **The Premises:** Located in the City of _____, County of _____,
State of North Carolina, being known as and more particularly described as:

❑   Street
Address:_____❑   Apartment
Complex:_____ Apartment No. _____
     ❑   Other   Description   (Room,   portion   of   above   address,
etc.):_____

    2. **Term:** The term of this lease shall be for _____ (duration) commencing _____ (date) and expiring
_____ (date) (the "Initial Term"). Either Landlord or Tenant may terminate the tenancy at the expiration of the Initial
Term by giving written notice to the other at least _____ days prior to the expiration date of the Initial Term. In the event
such written notice is not given or if the Tenant holds over beyond the Initial Term, the tenancy shall automatically become a
_____ (period) to _____ (period) tenancy upon the same terms and conditions contained herein
and may thereafter be terminated by either Landlord or Tenant giving the other _____ days written notice prior to the last day of
the then current period of the tenancy.

    3. **Rent:** Tenant shall pay, without notice, demand or deduction, to Landlord or as Landlord directs _____
(payment period - for example: weekly, monthly, quarterly, annually) rental payments in the amount of
$_____. The first rental payment, which shall be prorated if the Initial Term commences on a day
other than the first day of the applicable rental payment period, shall be due on _____ (date).
Thereafter, all rentals shall be paid in advance on or before the _____ day of each subsequent
calendar_____ (payment period - for example: week, month, quarter, year) for the
duration of the tenancy.

    4. **Late Payment Fees and Returned Check Fees:** If any rental payment is not received by midnight on the fifth (5th) day
after it is due, Tenant shall pay a late payment fee of _____.
(NOTE: North Carolina law provides that the late fee may not exceed $15.00 or five percent (5%) of the rental payment, whichever is
greater.) *This late payment fee shall be due immediately without demand therefor and shall be added to and paid with the late rental
payment. Tenant also agrees to pay a $_____ processing fee for each check of Tenant that is returned by the financial
institution because of insufficient funds or because the Tenant did not have an account at the financial institution.* (NOTE: The
maximum processing fee allowed under North Carolina law is $25.00.)

    5. **Tenant Security Deposit:** Tenant shall deposit with: (check one)
❑   Landlord
❑   Agent

the sum of $_____, as security deposit ("Tenant Security Deposit"), to be administered in accordance
with the North Carolina Tenant Security Deposit Act (N.C.G.S. § 42-50 et. seq.).

North Carolina Association of REALTORS®, Inc.

STANDARD FORM 410 – T
© 7/2002

Tenant Initials _____ _____   Agent Initials _____

Residential Rental Contract (2 of 7)

If Landlord holds the Tenant Security Deposit, Landlord will either: (check one)
❑ Deposit the Tenant Security Deposit in a trust account with_____
_____(name of bank or savings institution)
located at_____
_____(address).

OR ❑   Furnish   a   bond
from_____
_____(name of bonding company)
located at_____
_____(address).

If Agent holds the Tenant Security Deposit, Agent will deposit it in a trust account with _____
_____(name of bank or savings institution)
located at_____
_____(address).

THE TENANT SECURITY DEPOSIT MAY, IN THE DISCRETION OF EITHER THE LANDLORD OR THE AGENT, BE DEPOSITED IN AN INTEREST-BEARING ACCOUNT WITH THE BANK OR SAVINGS INSTITUTION NAMED ABOVE. ANY INTEREST EARNED UPON THE TENANT SECURITY DEPOSIT SHALL ACCRUE FOR THE BENEFIT OF, AND SHALL BE PAID TO, THE LANDLORD, OR AS THE LANDLORD DIRECTS. SUCH INTEREST, IF ANY, MAY BE WITHDRAWN BY LANDLORD OR AGENT FROM SUCH ACCOUNT AS IT ACCRUES AS OFTEN AS IS PERMITTED BY THE TERMS OF THE ACCOUNT.

Upon any termination of the tenancy herein created, the Landlord may deduct from the Tenant Security Deposit amounts sufficient to pay: (1) any damages sustained by the Landlord as a result of the Tenant's nonpayment of rent or nonfulfillment of the Initial Term or any renewal periods, including the Tenant's failure to enter into possession; (2) any damages to the Premises for which the Tenant is responsible; (3) any unpaid bills which become a lien against the Premises due to the Tenant's occupancy; (4) any costs of re-renting the Premises after a breach of this lease by the Tenant; (5) any court costs incurred by the Landlord in connection with terminating the tenancy; and (6) any other damages of the Landlord which may then be a permitted use of the Tenant Security Deposit under the laws of this State. After having deducted the above amounts, the Landlord shall, if the Tenant's address is known to him, refund to the Tenant, within thirty (30) days after the termination of the tenancy and delivery of possession, the balance of the Tenant Security Deposit along with an itemized statement of any deductions. If the Tenant's address is unknown to the Landlord, the Landlord may deduct the above amounts and shall then hold the balance of the Tenant Security Deposit for the Tenant's collection for a six-month period beginning upon the termination of the tenancy and delivery of possession by the Tenant. If the Tenant fails to make demand for the balance of the Tenant Security Deposit within the six-month period, the Landlord shall not thereafter be liable to the Tenant for a refund of the Tenant Security Deposit or any part thereof.

If the Landlord removes Agent or Agent resigns, the Tenant agrees that Agent may transfer any Tenant Security Deposit held by Agent hereunder to the Landlord or the Landlord's designee and thereafter notify the Tenant by mail of such transfer and of the transferee's name and address. The Tenant agrees that such action by Agent shall relieve Agent of further liability with respect to the Tenant Security Deposit. If Landlord's interest in the Premises terminates (whether by sale, assignment, death, appointment of receiver or otherwise), Agent shall transfer the Tenant Security Deposit in accordance with the provisions of North Carolina General Statutes § 42-54.

6. **Tenant's Obligations:** Unless otherwise agreed upon, the Tenant shall:
(a) use the Premises for residential purposes only and in a manner so as not to disturb the other tenants;
(b) not use the Premises for any unlawful or immoral purposes or occupy them in such a way as to constitute a nuisance;
(c) keep the Premises, including but not limited to all plumbing fixtures, facilities and appliances, in a clean and safe condition;
(d) cause no unsafe or unsanitary condition in the common areas and remainder of the Premises used by him;
(e) comply with any and all obligations imposed upon tenants by applicable building and housing codes;
(f) dispose of all ashes, rubbish, garbage, and other waste in a clean and safe manner and comply with all applicable ordinances concerning garbage collection, waste and other refuse;
(g) use in a proper and reasonable manner all electrical, plumbing, sanitary, heating, ventilating, air conditioning, and other facilities and appliances, if any, furnished as a part of the Premises;
(h) not deliberately or negligently destroy, deface, damage or remove any part of the Premises (including all facilities, appliances and fixtures) or permit any person, known or unknown to the Tenant, to do so;

Tenant Initials _____ _____   **STANDARD FORM 410 – T**
Agent Initials _____   © 7/2002

Residential Rental Contract (3 of 7)

    (i) be responsible for and liable to the Landlord for all damage to, defacement of, or removal of property from the Premises whatever the cause, except such damage, defacement or removal caused by ordinary wear and tear, acts of the Landlord, his agent, or of third parties not invitees of the Tenant, and natural forces;

    (j) permit the Landlord (and the Landlord hereby reserves the right to) to enter the Premises during reasonable hours for the purpose of (1) inspecting the Premises and the Tenant's compliance with the terms of this lease; (2) making such repairs, alterations, improvements or additions thereto as the Landlord may deem appropriate; and (3) showing the Premises to prospective purchasers or tenants. (The Landlord shall have the right to display "For Sale" or "For Rent" signs in a reasonable manner upon the Premises);

    (k) pay the costs of all utility services to the Premises which are billed directly to the Tenant and not included as a part of the rentals, including, but not limited to, water, electric, telephone, and gas services;

    (l) conduct himself and require all other persons on the Premises with his consent to conduct themselves in a reasonable manner and so as not to disturb other tenants' peaceful enjoyment of the Premises; and

    (m) not abandon or vacate the Premises during the Initial Term or any renewals or extensions thereof. Tenant shall be deemed to have abandoned or vacated the Premises if Tenant removes substantially all of his possessions from the Premises.

    (n) _____

_____

_____

    7. **Landlord's Obligations:** Unless otherwise agreed upon, the Landlord shall:

    (a) comply with the applicable building and housing codes to the extent required by such building and housing codes;

    (b) make all repairs to the Premises as may be necessary to keep the Premises in a fit and habitable condition; provided, however, in accordance with paragraph 6.h. and i. above, the Tenant shall be liable to the Landlord for any repairs necessitated by the Tenant's intentional or negligent misuse of the Premises;

    (c) keep all common areas, if any, used in conjunction with the Premises in a clean and safe condition; and

    (d) promptly repair all facilities and appliances, if any, as may be furnished by the Landlord as part of the Premises, including electrical, plumbing, sanitary, heating, ventilating, and air conditioning systems, provided that the Landlord, except in emergency situations, actually receives notification from the Tenant in writing of the needed repairs. In accordance with paragraph 6.h. and i. above, the Tenant shall be liable to the Landlord for any repairs to any facility or appliance necessitated by the Tenant's intentional or negligent misuse or improper operation of them.

    8. **Rules and Regulations:** The Tenant, his family, servants, guests and agents shall comply with and abide by all the Landlord's existing rules and regulations and such future reasonable rules and regulations as the Landlord may, at Landlord's discretion, from time to time, adopt governing the use and occupancy of the Premises and any common areas used in connection with them (the "Rules and Regulations"). Landlord reserves the right to make changes to the existing Rules and Regulations and to adopt additional reasonable rules and regulations from time to time; provided however, such changes and additions shall not alter the essential terms of this lease or any substantive rights granted hereunder and shall not become effective until thirty (30) days' written notice thereof shall have been furnished to Tenant. A copy of the existing Rules and Regulations is attached hereto and the Tenant acknowledges that he has read them. The Rules and Regulations shall be deemed to be a part of this lease giving to the Landlord all the rights and remedies herein provided.

    9. **Pets:**

    ❑ Tenant shall not keep or harbor in or about the Premises any animals or pets of any kind including, but not limited to, dogs, cats, birds and marine animals.

    ❑ Tenant may, upon the payment to Landlord of the sum of $_____ as a non-refundable pet fee, keep as a pet the following:_____ (type of pets permitted). (If this space is left blank, the Tenant may not keep any pets or animals in or about the Premises). If a pet fee is paid pursuant to this paragraph, Tenant acknowledges that the amount is reasonable and agrees that the Landlord shall not be required to refund the pet fee in whole or in part. In the event that a pet or pets are permitted pursuant to the paragraph, Tenant agrees to reimburse Landlord for any primary or secondary damages caused thereby whether the damage is to the Premises or to any common areas used in conjunction with them, and to indemnify Landlord from any liability to third parties which may result from Tenant's keeping of such pet or pets.

    The Tenant shall remove any pet previously permitted under this paragraph within_____ hours of written notification from the Landlord that the pet, in the Landlord's sole judgment, creates a nuisance or disturbance or is, in the Landlord's opinion, undesirable. If the pet is caused to be removed pursuant to this paragraph, the Landlord shall not be required to refund the pet fee; however, the Tenant shall be entitled to acquire and keep another pet of the type previously authorized.

Tenant Initials _____ _____

Agent Initials _____

STANDARD FORM 410 – T

© 7/2002

Residential Rental Contract (4 of 7)

10. **Alterations**: The Tenant shall not paint or decorate the Premises or make any alterations, additions, or improvements in or to the Premises without the Landlord's prior written consent and then only in a workmanlike manner using materials and contractors approved by the Landlord. All such work shall be done at the Tenant's expense and at such times and in such manner as the Landlord may approve. All alterations, additions, and improvements upon the Premises, made by either the Landlord or Tenant, shall become the property of the Landlord and shall remain upon and become a part of the Premises at the end of the tenancy hereby created.

11. **Permitted Occupants:** The Tenant shall not allow or permit the Premises to be occupied or used as a residence by any person other than Tenant and the following named persons:_____

_____

12. **Rental Application:** In the event the Tenant has submitted a Rental Application in connection with this lease, Tenant acknowledges that the Landlord has relied upon the Application as an inducement for entering into this Lease and Tenant warrants to Landlord that the facts stated in the Application are true to the best of Tenant's knowledge. If any facts stated in the Rental Application prove to be untrue, the Landlord shall have the right to terminate the tenancy and to collect from Tenant any damages resulting therefrom.

13. **Termination for Military Transfer:** If Tenant is a member of the United States Armed Forces who (i) has received permanent change of station orders to move fifty (50) miles or more from the Premises or (ii) is prematurely or involuntarily discharged or relieved from active duty with the United States Armed Forces, Tenant may terminate this lease by written notice of termination to Landlord stating the effective date of such termination, which date shall not be less than thirty (30) days after receipt of notice by Landlord, provided such notice is accompanied by a copy of the official orders of such transfer, discharge or release from active duty or a written verification signed by the Tenant's Commanding Officer. The final rent due by Tenant shall be prorated to such date of termination and shall be payable, together with liquidated damages in the amount of (a) one (1) month's rent for the premises, if less than six (6) months of the term of the lease have elapsed as of the effective date of termination, or (b) the amount of one-half (1/2) of one (1) month's rent, if more than six (6) months but less than nine (9) months of the term of the lease have elapsed as of the effective date of such termination; provided, however, no liquidated damages shall be due unless Tenant has completed less than nine (9) months of the tenancy and Landlord has suffered actual damage due to the loss of the tenancy.

Upon Tenant's compliance with all the requirements of this paragraph, Landlord shall release Tenant from all obligations hereunder and this lease shall terminate. The Tenant Security Deposit shall be returned, subject to the provisions of paragraph 5 above.

14. **Tenant's Duties Upon Termination:** Upon any termination of the Tenancy created hereby, whether by the Landlord or the Tenant and whether for breach or otherwise, the Tenant shall: (1) pay all utility bills due for services to the Premises for which he is responsible and have all such utility services discontinued; (2) vacate the Premises removing therefrom all Tenant's personal property of whatever nature; (3) properly sweep and clean the Premises, including plumbing fixtures, refrigerators, stoves and sinks, removing therefrom all rubbish, trash, garbage and refuse; (4) make such repairs and perform such other acts as are necessary to return the Premises, and any appliances or fixtures furnished in connection therewith, in the same condition as when Tenant took possession of the Premises; provided, however, Tenant shall not be responsible for ordinary wear and tear or for repairs required by law or by paragraph 7 above to be performed by Landlord; (5) fasten and lock all doors and windows; (6) return to the Landlord all keys to the Premises; and (7) notify the Landlord of the address to which the balance of the Security Deposit may be returned. If the Tenant fails to sweep out and clean the Premises, appliances and fixtures as herein provided, Tenant shall become liable, without notice or demand, to the Landlord for a cleaning fee. Such fee shall: (i) reflect the actual costs of cleaning (over and above ordinary wear and tear) and (ii) be deducted from the Security Deposit as provided in paragraph 5 above.

15. **Tenant's Default:** In the event the Tenant shall:

(a) fail to pay the rentals herein reserved as and when they shall become due hereunder; or
(b) fail to perform any other promise, duty or obligation herein agreed to by him or imposed upon him by law and such failure shall continue for a period of five (5) days from the date the Landlord provides Tenant with written notice of such failure,

then in either of such events and as often as either of them may occur, the Landlord, in addition to all other rights and remedies provided by law, may, at its option and with or without notice to Tenant, either (i) terminate this lease or (ii) terminate the Tenant's right to possession of the Premises without terminating this lease. Regardless of whether Landlord terminates this lease or only terminates the Tenant's right of possession without terminating this lease, Landlord shall be immediately entitled to possession of the Premises and the Tenant shall peacefully surrender possession of the Premises to Landlord immediately upon Landlord's demand.

Page 4 of 7

Tenant Initials _____ _____   **STANDARD FORM 410 – T**
Agent Initials _____   © 7/2002

Residential Rental Contract (5 of 7)

In the event Tenant shall fail or refuse to surrender possession of the Premises, Landlord shall, in compliance with Article 2A of Chapter 42 of the General Statutes of North Carolina, reenter and retake possession of the Premises only through a summary ejectment proceeding. In the event Landlord terminates this lease, all further rights and duties hereunder shall terminate and Landlord shall be entitled to collect from Tenant all accrued but unpaid rents and any damages resulting from the Tenant's breach. In the event Landlord terminates the Tenant's right of possession without terminating this lease, Tenant shall remain liable for the full performance of all the covenants hereof, and Landlord shall use reasonable efforts to re-let the Premises on Tenant's behalf. Any such rentals reserved from such re-letting shall be applied first to the costs of re-letting the Premises and then to the rentals due hereunder. In the event the rentals from such re-letting are insufficient to pay the rentals due hereunder in full, Tenant shall be liable to the Landlord for any deficiency. In the event Landlord institutes a legal action against the Tenant to enforce the lease or to recover any sums due hereunder, Tenant agrees to pay Landlord reasonable attorney's fees in addition to all other damages. Note: No fees may be deducted from the Tenant Security Deposit until the termination of the tenancy. Thereafter, any fees due the Agent from the Landlord may be deducted from any portion of the Security Deposit due to the Landlord.

16. **Landlord's Default; Limitation of Remedies and Damages**: Until the Tenant notifies the Landlord in writing of an alleged default and affords the Landlord a reasonable time within which to cure, no default by the Landlord in the performance of any of the promises or obligations herein agreed to by him or imposed upon him by law shall constitute a material breach of this lease and the Tenant shall have no right to terminate this lease for any such default or suspend his performance hereunder. In no event and regardless of their duration shall any defective condition of or failure to repair, maintain, or provide any area, fixture or facility used in connection with recreation or recreational activities, including but not limited to swimming pools, club houses, and tennis courts, constitute a material breach of this lease and the Tenant shall have no right to terminate this lease or to suspend his performance hereunder. In any legal action instituted by the Tenant against the Landlord, the Tenant's damages shall be limited to the difference, if any, between the rent reserved in this lease and the reasonable rental value of the Premises, taking into account the Landlord's breach or breaches, and in no event, except in the case of the Landlord's willful or wanton negligence, shall the Tenant collect any consequential or secondary damages resulting from the breach or breaches, including but not limited to the following items: damage or destruction of furniture or other personal property of any kind located in or about the Premises, moving expenses, storage expenses, alternative interim housing expenses, and expenses of locating and procuring alternative housing.

17. **Removal, Storage and Disposition of Tenant's Personal Property:**
    (a) Ten days after being placed in lawful possession by execution of a writ of possession, the Landlord may throw away, dispose of, or sell all items of personal property remaining on the Premises. During the 10-day period after being placed in lawful possession by execution of a writ of possession, the Landlord may move for storage purposes, but shall not throw away, dispose of, or sell any items of personal property remaining on the Premises unless otherwise provided for in Chapter 42 of the North Carolina General Statutes. Upon the Tenant's request prior to the expiration of the 10-day period, the Landlord shall release possession of the property to the Tenant during regular business hours or at a time agreed upon. If the Landlord elects to sell the property at public or private sale, the Landlord shall give written notice to the Tenant by first class mail to the Tenant's last known address at least seven days prior to the day of the sale. The seven-day notice of sale may run concurrently with the 10-day period which allows the Tenant to request possession of the property. The written notice shall state the date, time, and place of the sale, and that any surplus of proceeds from the sale, after payment of unpaid rents, damages, storage fees, and sale costs, shall be disbursed to the Tenant, upon request, within 10 days after the sale, and thereafter be delivered to the government of the county in which the rental property is located. Upon the Tenant's request prior to the day of sale, the Landlord shall release possession of the property to the Tenant during regular business hours or at a time agreed upon. The Landlord may apply the proceeds of the sale to the unpaid rents, damages, storage fees, and sale costs. Any surplus from the sale shall be disbursed to the Tenant, upon request, within 10 days of the sale and shall thereafter be delivered to the government of the county in which the rental property is located.
    (b) If the total value of all property remaining on the Premises at the time of execution of a writ of possession in an action for summary ejectment is less than one hundred dollars ($100.00), then the property shall be deemed abandoned five days after the time of execution, and the Landlord may throw away or dispose of the property. Upon the Tenant's request prior to the expiration of the five-day period, the Landlord shall release possession of the property to the Tenant during regular business hours or at a time agreed upon.

18. **Bankruptcy:** If any bankruptcy or insolvency proceedings are filed by or against the Tenant or if the Tenant makes any assignment for the benefit of creditors, the Landlord may, at his option, immediately terminate this Tenancy, and reenter and repossess the Premises, subject to the provisions of the Bankruptcy Code (11 USC Section 101, et. seq.) and the order of any court having jurisdiction thereunder.

Page 5 of 7

Tenant Initials _____ _____
Agent Initials _____

STANDARD FORM 410–T
© 7/2002

Residential Rental Contract (6 of 7)

---

19. **Tenant's Insurance; Release and Indemnity Provisions:** The Tenant shall be solely responsible for insuring any of his personal property located or stored upon the Premises upon the risks of damage, destruction, or loss resulting from theft, fire, storm and all other hazards and casualties. Regardless of whether the Tenant secures such insurance, the Landlord and his agents shall not be liable for any damage to, or destruction or loss of, any of the Tenant's personal property located or stored upon the Premises regardless of the cause or causes of such damage, destruction, or loss, unless such loss or destruction is attributable to the intentional acts or willful or wanton negligence of the Landlord. The Tenant agrees to release and indemnify the Landlord and his agents from and against liability for injury to the person of the Tenant or to any members of his household resulting from any cause whatsoever except only such personal injury caused by the negligent, or intentional acts of the Landlord or his agents.

20. **Agent:** The Landlord and the Tenant acknowledge that the Landlord may, from time to time in his discretion, engage a third party ("the Agent") to manage, supervise and operate the Premises or the complex, if any, of which they are a part. If such an Agent is managing, supervising and operating the Premises at the time this lease is executed, his name will be shown as "Agent" on the first page hereof. With respect to any Agent engaged pursuant to this paragraph, the Landlord and the Tenant hereby agree that: (1) Agent acts for and represents Landlord in this transaction; (2) Agent shall have only such authority as provided in the management contract existing between the Landlord and Agent; (3) Agent may perform without objection from the Tenant, any obligation or exercise any right of the Landlord imposed or given herein or by law and such performance shall be valid and binding, if authorized by the Landlord, as if performed by the Landlord; (4) the Tenant shall pay all rentals to the Agent if directed to do so by the Landlord; (5) except as otherwise provided by law, the Agent shall not be liable to the Tenant for the nonperformance of the obligations or promises of the Landlord contained herein; (6) nothing contained herein shall modify the management contract existing between the Landlord and the Agent; however, the Landlord and the Agent may from time to time modify the management agreement in any manner which they deem appropriate; (7) the Landlord, may, in his discretion and in accordance with any management agreement, remove without replacing or remove and replace any agent engaged to manage, supervise and operate the Premises.

21. **Form**: The Landlord and Tenant hereby acknowledge that their agreement is evidenced by this form contract which may contain some minor inaccuracies when applied to the particular factual setting of the parties. The Landlord and Tenant agree that the courts shall liberally and broadly interpret this lease, ignoring minor inconsistencies and inaccuracies, and that the courts shall apply the lease to determine all disputes between the parties in the manner which most effectuates their intent as expressed herein. The following rules of construction shall apply: (1) handwritten and typed additions or alterations shall control over the preprinted language when there is an inconsistency between them; (2) the lease shall not be strictly construed against either the Landlord or the Tenant; (3) paragraph headings are used only for convenience of reference and shall not be considered as a substantive part of this lease; (4) words in the singular shall include the plural and the masculine shall include the feminine and neuter genders, as appropriate; and (5) the invalidity of one or more provisions of this lease shall not affect the validity of any other provisions hereof and this lease shall be construed and enforced as if such invalid provision(s) were not included.

22. **Amendment of Laws**: In the event that subsequent to the execution of this lease any state statute regulating or affecting any duty or obligation imposed upon the Landlord pursuant to this lease is enacted, amended, or repealed, the Landlord may, at his option, elect to perform in accordance with such statute, amendment, or act of repeal in lieu of complying with the analogous provision of this lease.

23. **Eminent Domain and Casualties:** The Landlord shall have the option to terminate this lease if the Premises, or any part thereof, are condemned or sold in lieu of condemnation or damaged by fire or other casualty.

24. **Inspection of Premises:**
❑ Tenant acknowledges that Tenant has inspected the Premises and completed a Move-in Inspection Form. Landlord has accepted the form as completed.
❑ Tenant has the right to inspect the Premises and complete the Move-in Inspection Form prior to occupying the Premises.

25. **Other Terms and Conditions:**
(a) ❑ (Check if applicable) The Premises were built prior to 1978. (Attach Standard Form # 430, "Disclosure of Information on Lead-Based Paint and Lead-Based Paint Hazards.")
(b) If there is an Agent involved in this transaction, Agent hereby discloses to Tenant that Agent is acting for and represents Landlord.
(c) The following additional terms and conditions shall also be a part of this lease:
_____
_____
_____
(d) Itemize all addenda to this Contract and attach hereto: _____
_____

Tenant Initials _____ _____   **STANDARD FORM 410–T**
Agent Initials _____   © 7/2002

Residential Rental Contract (7 of 7)

26. **Smoke Detectors:** Pursuant to North Carolina General Statutes Section 42-42, the Landlord shall provide operable smoke detectors, either battery-operated or electrical, having an Underwriters' Laboratories, Inc., listing or other equivalent national testing laboratory approval, that are installed in accordance with either the standards of the national Fire Protection Association or the minimum protection designated in the manufacturer's instructions. The Landlord shall repair or replace the smoke detectors provided the Landlord is notified in writing by the Tenant. The Landlord shall place new batteries in any battery-operated smoke detectors at the beginning of the Initial Term of the Tenancy; **the Tenant shall replace the batteries as needed during the Tenancy.**

27. **Notice:** Any notices required or authorized to be given hereunder or pursuant to applicable law shall be mailed or hand delivered to the following addresses:
Tenant: the address of the Premises
Landlord: the address to which rental payments are sent.

28. **Assignment:** The Tenant shall not assign this lease or sublet the Premises in whole or part.

29. **Waiver:** No waiver of any breach of any obligation or promise contained herein shall be regarded as a waiver of any future breach of the same or any other obligation or promise.

30. **Execution; Counterparts:** When Tenant signs this lease, he acknowledges he has read and agrees to the provisions of this lease. This lease is executed in _____ (number) counterparts with an executed counterpart being retained by each party hereto.

31. **Entire Agreement:** This Agreement contains the entire agreement of the parties and there are no representations, inducements or other provisions other than those expressed in writing. All changes, additions or deletions hereto must be in writing and signed by all parties.

TENANT: LANDLORD:

_____(SEAL)   _____(SEAL)

_____(SEAL)   _____(SEAL)

Date: _____   By:_____, AGENT

                                          _____(SEAL)

                                          Date: _____

STANDARD FORM 410 – T
© 7/2002

Property Management Agreement (1 of 4)

PROPERTY MANAGEMENT AGREEMENT
Residential Property

THIS PROPERTY MANAGEMENT AGREEMENT, entered into this_____ day of _____, 20_____
by_____ ("Owner")
and_____ ("Agent").

IN CONSIDERATION of the mutual covenants and promises each to the other made herein, the Owner does hereby contract with the Agent exclusively, and the Agent does hereby contract with the Owner, to rent, lease, operate and manage the property more particularly described below and any other property the Owner may assign to Agent from time to time (the "Property") upon the following terms and conditions:

   1. **The Property:** Located in the City of _____,
County of_____,
state of North Carolina, being known and more particularly described as:
[ ] Street Address: _____
[ ] Apartment, Townhouse or Condominium Complex(es):_____
[ ] Other description: (Room, portion of the above address, etc.):_____
_____

   2. **Duration of Agency:** This Agreement and the agency and employment created shall commence and become effective on
_____, 20_____ , and shall continue thereafter until terminated as provided herein.

   3. **Termination of Agency:** Either the Owner or the Agent may terminate the agency and employment created hereby by giving written notice of his intention to do so_____ days prior to the desired termination date. In the event the Owner terminates within _____ days of the commencement, Owner shall pay to the Agent a termination fee of_____.
No termination fee shall be required of the Owner for termination after the expiration of the number of days above specified and the Agent shall not be entitled to any percentage of any subsequently accruing rentals upon termination. Upon any termination of the Agreement by either the Owner or the Agent, each shall take such steps as are necessary to settle all accounts between them including the following: (1) the Agent shall promptly render to the Owner all rents then on hand after having deducted therefrom any Agent's fees then due and amounts sufficient to cover all other outstanding expenditures of the Agent incurred in connection with operating the Property; (2) the Agent shall render to the Owner records showing all tenants who paid security deposits under leases affecting the Property; (3) the Agent shall deliver to the Owner copies of all tenant's leases and other instruments entered into on behalf of the Owner (Agent may retain copies of such leases and agreements for Agent's records); (4) the Agent shall transfer to the Owner any security deposits held by Agent (5) the Owner shall promptly pay to Agent any fees or amounts due the Agent under the Agreement and shall reimburse the Agent for any expenditures made and outstanding at the time of termination; and (6) the Owner shall notify all current tenants of the termination of the agency status and transfer of such security deposits, if applicable.

   4. **Agent's Fee:** The Owner shall pay to the Agent each month during the existence of this Agreement the following: _____
_____
_____
_____

The amounts due the Agent pursuant to this paragraph shall herein be referred to as the Agent's Fee and the Agent may deduct the Agent's Fee monthly from the gross receipts and collections received before remitting the balance of the receipts and collections to the Owner. *Note:* No fees may be deducted from the tenant security deposit until the termination of the tenancy. Thereafter, any fees due the Agent from the Owner may be deducted from any portion of the security deposit due to the Owner.

   5. **Agent's Authority:** The owner hereby authorizes and empowers the Agent to perform such acts and take such steps as are necessary, in the Agent's opinion, to operate, manage and lease the Property to the Owner's advantage including, but not limited to:

North Carolina Association of REALTORS®, Inc.

Owner Initials _____ _____   Agent Initials _____

STANDARD FORM 401
© 7/2002

Property Management Agreement (2 of 4)

Owner Initial Where Applicable:

_____ Advertising the Property, displaying signs thereon, and renting the Property, including the authority to negotiate, execute, extend and renew leases in the Owner's name for terms not in excess of (_____) _____year(s) or (_____) _____month(s);

_____ Instituting and prosecuting such judicial actions and proceedings as may be necessary to recover rents and other sums due the Owner from the tenants or to evict tenants and retain possession, including the authority, in the Agent's discretion, to settle, compromise and release any and all such judicial actions and proceedings;

_____ Collecting all rentals and other charges and amounts due or to become due under all leases covering the Property and giving receipts for the amounts so collected;

_____ Making or causing to be made any repairs which, in the agent's opinion, may be necessary to preserve, maintain and protect the Property; to maintain the facilities and services to the tenants as required by their tenancies; and to comply with any duties or obligations imposed upon the Owner by any local, state or federal law or regulation; including the authority to purchase such supplies and hire such labor as may be necessary in the Agent's opinion to accomplish such repairs;

_____ Performing any duties and exercising any rights conferred upon the Owner as Landlord under any leases entered into in connection with the Property; and

_____

_____

_____

6. **Agent Covenants:** During the duration of this Agreement the Agent agrees:

(a) To manage and operate the Property to the best of Agent's ability, devoting thereto such time and attention as may be necessary;

(b) To furnish the services of Agent's organization for renting, leasing, operating and/or managing the Property;

(c) To solicit tenants and investigate all prospective tenants and to use Agent's best efforts to secure and maintain tenants;

(d) TO OFFER THE PROPERTY TO THE PUBLIC FOR LEASING IN COMPLIANCE WITH ALL STATE AND FEDERAL HOUSING LAWS, INCLUDING BUT NOT LIMITED TO, ANY FEDERAL AND STATE LAWS AND REGULATIONS PROHIBITING DISCRIMINATION ON THE BASIS OF RACE, COLOR, RELIGION, SEX, NATIONAL ORIGIN, HANDICAP OR FAMILIAL STATUS;

(e) To collect all monthly rentals and other charges due the Owner from the Property and to make or cause to be made such repairs as he deems appropriate in order to preserve and maintain the Property and to comply with all lease requirements and obligations imposed upon the Owner by North Carolina law (N.C.G.S. § 42-42);

(f) To answer Tenant requests and complaints and to perform the duties imposed upon the Owner by law or pursuant to the tenant leases covering the Property;

(g) To render monthly statements of receipts, collections, expenses, charges and disbursements to the Owner and to remit monthly to the Owner the balance of such receipts and collections (unless some other period is agreed upon);

(h) To furnish Owner with copies of all tenant leases unless this block is checked and initialed by the Owner ❏ _____, in which event the Owner waives the right to receive copies of tenant leases unless Owner specifically requests such copies from the Agent; and

(i) _____

_____

_____.

7. **Owner's Covenants:** During the duration of this Agreement the Owner agrees:

(a) To advance to the Agent such sums as may be necessary to cover the costs of repairing the Property and maintaining it in a safe, fit and habitable condition as required by North Carolina law (N.C.G.S. § 42-42);

(b) To reimburse the Agent for any expense actually incurred by him in operating, managing and maintaining the Property, including, but not limited to, advertising expenses, general operating expenses, court costs, attorney's fees and maintenance and supply expenses;

STANDARD FORM 401
© 7/2002

Property Management Agreement (3 of 4)

(c) NOT TO TAKE ANY ACTION OR ADOPT ANY POLICY THE EFFECT OF WHICH WOULD BE TO PREVENT THE AGENT FROM OFFERING THE PROPERTY FOR RENTAL IN COMPLIANCE WITH ALL APPLICABLE FEDERAL AND STATE LAWS AND REGULATIONS, INCLUDING, BUT NOT LIMITED TO, THOSE LAWS AND REGULATIONS PROHIBITING DISCRIMINATION ON THE BASIS OF RACE, COLOR, RELIGION, SEX, NATIONAL ORIGIN, HANDICAP OR FAMILIAL STATUS IN THE LEASING OF THE PROPERTY;

(d) To carry, at his expense, comprehensive general public liability insurance against any and all claims or demands whatever arising out of, or in any way connected with, the operation, leasing and maintenance of the Property, which policies shall be written so as to protect the Agent in the same manner as the Owner and which shall be in the minimum amounts of $_____ for each injury or death of one person in each accident or occurrence, $_____ for injuries to or death of more than one person in each accident or occurrence, and $_____ for property damage in each accident or occurrence;

(e) To defend, indemnify and save the Agent harmless from any and all damages, claims, suits or costs, whether for personal injury or otherwise, arising out of the Agent's management of the Property whether such claims are filed or damages incurred before or after the termination of this Agreement; and

(f) _____
_____.

8. **Tenant Security Deposits:** The Agent may, in Agent's discretion, either (1) require tenants of the Property to make a security deposit in an amount as permitted by law to secure the tenants' obligations under leases of the Property (such security deposits shall hereinafter be referred to as "Tenant Security Deposits") or (2) to forego the requirement that Tenant Security Deposits be made. If the Agent requires such Tenant Security Deposits, they shall be placed in a trust account in the _____ (Owner's or Agent's) name in a North Carolina bank or savings and loan association. The Agent shall be authorized to make withdrawals therefrom for the purpose of returning and accounting for them to the tenants. THE AGENT MAY IN AGENT'S DISCRETION PROVIDE IN THE LEASES THAT THE TENANT SECURITY DEPOSITS MAY BE PLACED IN AN INTEREST-BEARING ACCOUNT. IF THE LEASES PERMIT THE PLACEMENT OF TENANT SECURITY DEPOSITS IN AN INTEREST-BEARING ACCOUNT, THE LEASES SHALL SPECIFY WHETHER SUCH INTEREST SHALL BE PAYABLE TO THE OWNER OR TO THE TENANT AS THE AGENT, IN AGENT'S DISCRETION, DEEMS APPROPRIATE. IF THE LEASE PROVIDES THAT SUCH INTEREST IS PAYABLE TO THE TENANT, THE AGENT SHALL ACCOUNT FOR THE INTEREST IN THE MANNER SET FORTH IN SUCH LEASE. IF THE LEASE PROVIDES THAT SUCH INTEREST IS PAYABLE TO THE OWNER OR AS THE OWNER DIRECTS, THEN AS BETWEEN THE OWNER AND THE AGENT, SUCH INTEREST SHALL BELONG TO _____ (Owner or Agent). IF THE INTEREST IS TO BE PAID TO AGENT, THE AGENT MAY REMOVE SUCH INTEREST FROM THE ACCOUNT AT ALL TIMES AND WITH SUCH FREQUENCY AS IS PERMITTED UNDER THE TERMS OF THE ACCOUNT.

9. **Existing Tenant Security Deposits:** Upon the commencement of this Agreement the Owner shall deliver to the Agent a list showing the current tenants of the Property who previously made Tenant Security Deposits under existing leases of the Property and the amounts they deposited. Simultaneously therewith, the Owner shall either: (1) place the Tenant Security Deposits held under existing leases in a trust account in the _____ (Owner's or Agent's) name and authorize the Agent to make withdrawals therefrom for the purpose of returning them to the current tenants as required by their leases or by law or (2) supply the Agent with evidence of a surety bond from a North Carolina insurance company securing the Owner's obligation to return the Tenant Security Deposits to the proper tenants as required by law. In the event the Owner elects to furnish a surety bond pursuant to this paragraph, Owner shall thereafter advance to the Agent such sums as may be necessary from time to time to allow the Agent to return the deposits to the existing tenants as required by their leases or by law.

10. **Late Payment Fees; Returned Check Fees:** If the tenant leases provide for late payment fees and/or returned check fees, such fees, when collected by Agent, shall belong to _____ (Owner or Agent).

11. **Notices:** Any notices required or permitted to be given hereunder shall be written and shall be mailed by certified mail by each party to the following address:

Property Management Agreement (4 of 4)

12. **Form:** The Owner and Agent hereby acknowledge that their Agreement is evidenced by this form contract which may contain some minor inaccuracies when applied to the particular circumstances of the parties. The Owner and Agent agree that the courts shall liberally and broadly interpret this Agreement, ignoring minor inconsistencies and inaccuracies, and that the courts shall apply the Agreement to determine all disputes between the parties in the manner which most effectuates their intent as expressed herein. The following rules of construction shall be applied: (1) handwritten and typed additions or alterations shall control over the preprinted language when there is an inconsistency between them; (2) the Agreement shall not be strictly construed against either the Owner or the Agent; (3) paragraph headings are used only for convenience of reference and shall not be considered as a substantive part of this Agreement; (4) words in the singular shall include the plural and the masculine shall include the feminine and neuter genders, as appropriate; (5) no waiver of any breach of any obligation or promise contained herein shall be regarded as a waiver of any future breach of the same or any other obligation or promise; and (6) the invalidity of one or more provisions of this Agreement shall not affect the validity of any other provisions hereof and this Agreement shall be construed and enforced as if such invalid provisions were not included.

THE NORTH CAROLINA ASSOCIATION OF REALTORS®, INC. MAKES NO REPRESENTATION AS TO THE LEGAL VALIDITY OR ADEQUACY OF ANY PROVISION OF THIS FORM IN ANY SPECIFIC TRANSACTION.

IN WITNESS WHEREOF, the parties hereto have set their hands and seals the day and year first above written.

AGENT:_____(SEAL)

OWNER:_____(SEAL)

STANDARD FORM 401
© 7/2002

North Carolina Deed of Trust (1 of 4)

NORTH CAROLINA DEED OF TRUST

SATISFACTION: The debt secured by the within Deed of Trust together with the note(s) secured thereby has been satisfied in full.

This the _____ day of _____, 20____

Signed:_____   _____

_____   _____

Parcel Identifier No._____   Verified by _____ County on the ____ day of_____, 20__

By:_____

Mail/Box to: _____

This instrument was prepared by:_____

Brief description for the Index: _____

THIS DEED of TRUST made this _____ day of _____, 20____, by and between:

GRANTOR	TRUSTEE	BENEFICIARY

Enter in appropriate block for each party: name, address, and, if appropriate, character of entity, e.g. corporation or partnership.

The designation Grantor, Trustee, and Beneficiary as used herein shall include said parties, their heirs, successors, and assigns, and shall include singular, plural, masculine, feminine or neuter as required by context.

WITNESSETH, That whereas the Grantor is indebted to the Beneficiary in the principal sum of _____
_____ Dollars ($_____),
as evidenced by a Promissory Note of even date herewith, the terms of which are incorporated herein by reference. The final due date for payments of said Promissory Note, if not sooner paid, is_____, 20___.

NC Bar Association Form No. 5 © 1976, Revised © September 1985, 2002   + James Williams & Co., Inc.
Printed by Agreement with the NC Bar Association - 1981   www.JamesWilliams.com

North Carolina Deed of Trust (2 of 4)

NOW, THEREFORE, as security for said indebtedness, advancements and other sums expended by Beneficiary pursuant to this Deed of Trust and costs of collection (including attorneys fees as provided in the Promissory Note) and other valuable consideration, the receipt of which is hereby acknowledged, the Grantor has bargained, sold, given and conveyed and does by these presents bargain, sell, give, grant and convey to said Trustee, his heirs, or successors, and assigns, the parcel(s) of land situated in the City of _____, _____ Township, _____ County, North Carolina, (the "Premises") and more particularly described as follows:

TO HAVE AND TO HOLD said Premises with all privileges and appurtenances thereunto belonging, to said Trustee, his heirs, successors, and assigns forever, upon the trusts, terms and conditions, and for the uses hereinafter set forth.

If the Grantor shall pay the Note secured hereby in accordance with its terms, together with interest thereon, and any renewals or extensions thereof in whole or in part, all other sums secured hereby and shall comply with all of the covenants, terms and conditions of this Deed of Trust, then this conveyance shall be null and void and may be canceled of record at the request and the expense of the Grantor.

If, however, there shall be any default (a) in the payment of any sums due under the Note, this Deed of Trust or any other instrument securing the Note and such default is not cured within ten (10) days from the due date, or (b) if there shall be default in any of the other covenants, terms or conditions of the Note secured hereby, or any failure or neglect to comply with the covenants, terms or conditions contained in this Deed of Trust or any other instrument securing the Note and such default is not cured within fifteen (15) days after written notice, then and in any of such events, without further notice, it shall be lawful for and the duty of the Trustee, upon request of the Beneficiary, to sell the land herein conveyed at public auction for cash, after having first giving such notice of hearing as to commencement of foreclosure proceedings and obtained such findings or leave of court as may then be required by law and giving such notice and advertising the time and place of such sale in such manner as may then be provided by law, and upon such and any resales and upon compliance with the law then relating to foreclosure proceedings under power of sale to convey title to the purchaser in as full and ample manner as the Trustee is empowered. The Trustee shall be authorized to retain an attorney to represent him in such proceedings.

The proceeds of the Sale shall after the Trustee retains his commission, together with reasonable attorneys fees incurred by the Trustee in such proceedings, be applied to the costs of sale, including but not limited to, costs of collection, taxes, assessments, costs of recording, service fees and incidental expenditures, the amount due on the Note hereby secured and advancements and other sums expended by the Beneficiary according to the provisions hereof and otherwise as required by the then existing law relating to foreclosures. The Trustee's commission shall be five percent (5%) of the gross proceeds of the sale or the minimum sum of $ _____ whichever is greater, for a completed foreclosure. In the event foreclosure is commenced, but not completed, the Grantor shall pay all expenses incurred by Trustee, including reasonable attorneys fees, and a partial commission computed on five per cent (5%) of the outstanding indebtedness or the above stated minimum sum, whichever is greater, in accordance with the following schedule, to-wit: one-fourth (¼) thereof before the Trustee issues a notice of hearing on the right to foreclosure; one-half (½) thereof after issuance of said notice, three-fourths (¾) thereof after such hearing; and the greater of the full commission or minimum sum after the initial sale.

And the said Grantor does hereby covenant and agree with the Trustee as follows:

1. INSURANCE. Grantor shall keep all improvements on said land, now or hereafter erected, constantly insured for the benefit of the Beneficiary against loss by fire, windstorm and such other casualties and contingencies, in such manner and in such companies and for such amounts, not less than that amount necessary to pay the sum secured by this Deed of Trust, and as may be satisfactory to the Beneficiary. Grantor shall purchase such insurance, pay all premiums therefor, and shall deliver to Beneficiary such policies along with evidence of premium payments as long as the Note secured hereby remains unpaid. If Grantor fails to purchase such insurance, pay premiums therefor or deliver said policies along with evidence of payment of premiums thereon, then Beneficiary, at his option, may purchase such insurance. Such amounts paid by Beneficiary shall be added to the principal of the Note secured by this Deed of Trust, and shall be due and payable upon demand of Beneficiary. All proceeds from any insurance so maintained shall at the option of Beneficiary be applied to the debt secured hereby and if payable in installments, applied in the inverse order of maturity of such installments or to the repair or reconstruction of any improvements located upon the Property.

2. TAXES, ASSESSMENTS, CHARGES. Grantor shall pay all taxes, assessments and charges as may be lawfully levied against said Premises within thirty (30) days after the same shall become due. In the event that Grantor fails to so pay all taxes, assessments and charges as herein required, then Beneficiary, at his option, may pay the same and the amounts so paid shall be added to the principal of the Note secured by this Deed of Trust, and shall be due and payable upon demand of Beneficiary.

3. ASSIGNMENTS OF RENTS AND PROFITS. Grantor assigns to Beneficiary, in the event of default, all rents and profits from the land and any improvements thereon, and authorizes Beneficiary to enter upon and take possession of such land and improvements, to rent same, at any reasonable rate of rent determined by Beneficiary, and after deducting from any such rents the cost of reletting and collection, to apply the remainder to the debt secured hereby.

4. PARTIAL RELEASE. Grantor shall not be entitled to the partial release of any of the above described property unless a specific provision providing therefor is included in this Deed of Trust. In the event a partial release provision is included in this Deed of Trust, Grantor must strictly comply with the terms thereof. Notwithstanding anything herein contained, Grantor shall not be

NC Bar Association Form No. 5 © 1976, Revised © September 1985, 2002   + James Williams & Co., Inc.
Printed by Agreement with the NC Bar Association - 1981   www.JamesWilliams.com

North Carolina Deed of Trust (3 of 4)

entitled to any release of property unless Grantor is not in default and is in full compliance with all of the terms and provisions of the Note, this Deed of Trust, and any other instrument that may be securing said Note.

5. WASTE. The Grantor covenants that he will keep the Premises herein conveyed in as good order, repair and condition as they are now, reasonable wear and tear excepted, and will comply with all governmental requirements respecting the Premises or their use, and that he will not commit or permit any waste.

6. CONDEMNATION. In the event that any or all of the Premises shall be condemned and taken under the power of eminent domain, Grantor shall give immediate written notice to Beneficiary and Beneficiary shall have the right to receive and collect all damages awarded by reason of such taking, and the right to such damages hereby is assigned to Beneficiary who shall have the discretion to apply the amount so received, or any part thereof, to the indebtedness due hereunder and if payable in installments, applied in the inverse order of maturity of such installments, or to any alteration, repair or restoration of the Premises by Grantor.

7. WARRANTIES. Grantor covenants with Trustee and Beneficiary that he is seized of the Premises in fee simple, has the right to convey the same in fee simple, that title is marketable and free and clear of all encumbrances, and that he will warrant and defend the title against the lawful claims of all persons whomsoever, except for the exceptions hereinafter stated. Title to the property hereinabove described is subject to the following exceptions:

8. SUBSTITUTION OF TRUSTEE. Grantor and Trustee covenant and agree to and with Beneficiary that in case the said Trustee, or any successor trustee, shall die, become incapable of acting, renounce his trust, or for any reason the holder of the Note desires to replace said Trustee, then the holder may appoint, in writing, a trustee to take the place of the Trustee; and upon the probate and registration of the same, the trustee thus appointed shall succeed to all rights, powers and duties of the Trustee.

☐ **THE FOLLOWING PARAGRAPH, 9. SALE OF PREMISES, SHALL NOT APPLY UNLESS THE BLOCK TO THE LEFT MARGIN OF THIS SENTENCE IS MARKED AND/OR INITIALED.**

9. SALE OF PREMISES. Grantor agrees that if the Premises or any part thereof or interest therein is sold, assigned, transferred, conveyed or otherwise alienated by Grantor, whether voluntarily or involuntarily or by operation of law [other than: (i) the creation of a lien or other encumbrance subordinate to this Deed of Trust which does not relate to a transfer of rights of occupancy in the Premises; (ii) the creation of a purchase money security interest for household appliances; (iii) a transfer by devise, descent, or operation of law on the death of a joint tenant or tenant by the entirety; (iv) the grant of a leasehold interest of three (3) years or less not containing an option to purchase; (v) a transfer to a relative resulting from the death of a Grantor; (vi) a transfer where the spouse or children of the Grantor become the owner of the Premises; (vii) a transfer resulting from a decree of a dissolution of marriage, legal separation agreement, or from an incidental property settlement agreement, by which the spouse of the Grantor becomes an owner of the Premises; (viii) a transfer into an inter vivos trust in which the Grantor is and remains a beneficiary and which does not relate to a transfer of rights of occupancy in the Premises], without the prior written consent of Beneficiary, Beneficiary, at its own option, may declare the Note secured hereby and all other obligations hereunder to be forthwith due and payable. Any change in the legal or equitable title of the Premises or in the beneficial ownership of the Premises, including the sale, conveyance or disposition of a majority interest in the Grantor if a corporation or partnership, whether or not of record and whether or not for consideration, shall be deemed to be the transfer of an interest in the Premises.

10. ADVANCEMENTS. If Grantor shall fail to perform any of the covenants or obligations contained herein or in any other instrument given as additional security for the Note secured hereby, the Beneficiary may, but without obligation, make advances to perform such covenants or obligations, and all such sums so advanced shall be added to the principal sum, shall bear interest at the rate provided in the Note secured hereby for sums due after default and shall be due from Grantor on demand of the Beneficiary. No advancement or anything contained in this paragraph shall constitute a waiver by Beneficiary or prevent such failure to perform from constituting an event of default.

11. INDEMNITY. If any suit or proceeding be brought against the Trustee or Beneficiary or if any suit or proceeding be brought which may affect the value or title of the Premises, Grantor shall defend, indemnify and hold harmless and on demand reimburse Trustee or Beneficiary from any loss, cost, damage or expense and any sums expended by Trustee or Beneficiary shall bear interest as provided in the Note secured hereby for sums due after default and shall be due and payable on demand.

12. WAIVERS. Grantor waives all rights to require marshaling of assets by the Trustee or Beneficiary. No delay or omission of the Trustee or Beneficiary in the exercise of any right, power or remedy arising under the Note or this Deed of Trust shall be deemed a waiver of any default or acquiescence therein or shall impair or waive the exercise of such right, power or remedy by Trustee or Beneficiary at any other time.

13. CIVIL ACTION. In the event that the Trustee is named as a party to any civil action as Trustee in this Deed of Trust, the Trustee shall be entitled to employ an attorney at law, including himself if he is a licensed attorney, to represent him in said action and the reasonable attorney's fee of the Trustee in such action shall be paid by the Beneficiary and added to the principal of the Note secured by this Deed of Trust and bear interest at the rate provided in the Note for sums due after default.

14. PRIOR LIENS. Default under the terms of any instrument secured by a lien to which this Deed of Trust is subordinate shall constitute default hereunder.

15. OTHER TERMS.

NC Bar Association Form No. 5 © 1976, Revised © September 1985, 2002   + James Williams & Co., Inc.
Printed by Agreement with the NC Bar Association - 1981   www.JamesWilliams.com

North Carolina Deed of Trust (4 of 4)

IN WITNESS WHEREOF, the Grantor has duly executed the foregoing as of the day and year first above written.

_____   _____(SEAL)
(Entity Name)

By:_____   _____(SEAL)
Title:_____

By:_____   _____(SEAL)
Title:_____

By:_____   _____(SEAL)
Title:_____

_____(SEAL)

_____(SEAL)

_____(SEAL)

USE BLACK INK ONLY

SEAL-STAMP

State of North Carolina - County of _____

I, the undersigned Notary Public of the County and State aforesaid, certify that _____ _____ personally appeared before me this day and acknowledged the due execution of the foregoing instrument for the purposes therein expressed. Witness my hand and Notarial stamp or seal this _____ day of _____, 20__.

My Commission Expires:_____   _____
                                        Notary Public

SEAL-STAMP

State of North Carolina - County of _____

I, the undersigned Notary Public of the County and State aforesaid, certify that _____ _____ personally came before me this day and acknowledged that _he is the _____ of _____, a North Carolina or _____ corporation/limited liability company/general partnership/limited partnership (strike through the inapplicable), and that by authority duly given and as the act of each entity, _he signed the forgoing instrument in its name on its behalf as its act and deed. Witness my hand and Notarial stamp or seal this _____ day of _____, 20__.

My Commission Expires:_____   _____
                                        Notary Public

SEAL-STAMP

State of North Carolina - County of _____

I, the undersigned Notary Public of the County and State aforesaid, certify that _____ _____ _____

Witness my hand and Notarial stamp or seal this _____ day of _____, 20__.

My Commission Expires:_____   _____
                                        Notary Public

The foregoing Certificate(s) of _____ is/are certified to be correct. This instrument and this certificate are duly registered at the date and time and in the Book and Page shown on the first page hereof.

_____   Register of Deeds for _____ County

By:_____   Deputy/Assistant - Register of Deeds

NC Bar Association Form No. 5 © 1976, Revised © September 1985, 2002   * James Williams & Co., Inc.
Printed by Agreement with the NC Bar Association - 1981   www.JamesWilliams.com

Sample North Carolina Real Estate Licensing Examination

The following sample exam contains the types of questions examinees might find on their licensing examination. These questions are meant to provide prospective licensees with additional practice in preparing for the examination. Note that proration calculations are based on a 30-day month unless otherwise stated.

REAL ESTATE LAW

1. Which of the following methods of describing land is NOT used in North Carolina?
   I. Metes and bounds
   II. Rectangular survey
      a. I only
      b. II only
      c. Both I and II
      d. Neither I nor II

2. Real estate taxes for the current year may be paid without penalty
   a. at any time.
   b. by September 1 of the current tax year.
   c. before the end of the current tax year.
   d. up to two years after the tax bill is issued.

3. A description of property that reads "Beginning at the large oak tree on the northern line of State Road 18, approximately one mile west to the intersection of State Road and the Great Southern Railroad right-of-way, north approximately 15′ along the old drainage ditch . . ." is a
   I. legal description that could be used in North Carolina.
   II. metes-and-bounds description.
      a. I only
      b. II only
      c. Both I and II
      d. Neither I nor II

4. To be valid in North Carolina, a deed must include the
   I. grantor's seal.
   II. grantee's signature.
      a. I only
      b. II only
      c. Both I and II
      d. Neither I nor II

5. Thompson is openly occupying her neighbor's property. Thompson has no claim to the neighbor's title, so she would have to occupy the property for how many years to establish adverse possession?
   a. 7   c. 15
   b. 10   d. 20

6. Which of the following deeds contains no warranties at all and may convey no title at all, depending on the grantor's interest in the property when the deed is executed?
   a. Warranty deed   c. Sheriff's deed
   b. Quitclaim deed   d. Deed of trust

7. Jones paid $75,000 for the Blacks' home. He took out a new mortgage loan for $65,000. How much was the excise tax?
   a. $150   c. $75
   b. $130   d. $65

8. The North Carolina law that provides that a contract to sell land is not protected against a third party unless recorded is called the
   a. Marketable Title Act.
   b. Conner Act.
   c. Equitable Title Act.
   d. North Carolina Fair Housing Act.

9. The deed that contains five or more covenants is the
   a. general warranty deed.
   b. quitclaim deed.
   c. deed of trust.
   d. grant deed.

10. Hannah grants a life estate to her grandson and stipulates that on the grandson's death, the title to the property will pass to her son-in-law. This second estate is known as an estate
    a. in remainder.   c. at sufferance.
    b. in reversion.   d. for years.

11. A tenancy for years is a tenancy
    a. with the consent of the landlord.
    b. that expires on a specific date.
    c. created by the death of the owner.
    d. created by a testator.

12. Killigan built a structure that has six stories. Several years later, an ordinance was passed in that area banning any building higher than four stories. Killigan's building is an example of a
    I. nonconforming use.
    II. conditional use.
        a. I only
        b. II only
        c. Both I and II
        d. Neither I nor II

13. According to the Conner Act, an oral lease for longer than three years is
    a. a long-term lease.
    b. renewable.
    c. illegal.
    d. unenforceable.

14. Police power includes all of the following except
    a. zoning.
    b. deed restrictions.
    c. building codes.
    d. subdivision regulations.

15. A defect in or a cloud on title to property may be cured by
    a. obtaining quitclaim deeds from all interested parties.
    b. recording the title.
    c. paying cash for the property at closing.
    d. bringing an action to repudiate the title.

16. What is the difference between a general lien and a specific lien?
    I. A general lien cannot be enforced in court, while a specific lien can.
    II. A specific lien is held by only one person, while a general lien must be held by two or more.
    III. A specific lien is a lien against a certain parcel of real estate, while a general lien covers all of the debtor's property.
        a. I only
        b. II only
        c. III only
        d. I and II only

17. Someone seeking to be excused from the dictates of a zoning ordinance because of hardship should request a
    a. building permit.
    b. certificate of alternative usage.
    c. variance.
    d. certificate of nonconforming use.

18. Which of the following tax advantages are NOT associated with owner-occupied personal dwellings?
    a. Ability to depreciate the property
    b. Capital gains treatment of resale profits
    c. Installment sales treatment of owner-financed resales
    d. Deductibility of mortgage interest

19. Under the concept of riparian rights, the owners of property adjacent to navigable rivers or streams have the right to use the water and
    a. may erect a dam across the navigable river or stream.
    b. are considered to own the submerged land to the center point of the waterway.
    c. are considered owners of the water adjacent to the land.
    d. are considered to own the land to the edge of the water.

20. A leasehold estate that automatically renews itself at each expiration is the tenancy
    a. for years.
    b. from period to period.
    c. at will.
    d. at sufferance.

21. A homeowner may deduct which of the following items related to his personal residence on his federal income tax return?
    I. Interest on a mortgage loan
    II. Real estate taxes
    a. I only
    b. II only
    c. Both I and II
    d. Neither I nor II

REAL ESTATE BROKERAGE

22. In the typical real estate transaction in North Carolina, who is responsible for paying for title insurance?
    I. Buyer
    II. Seller
    III. Real estate agent
    a. I only
    b. II only
    c. III only
    d. I and II only

23. Steering is the practice of
    a. leading prospective homeowners to or away from certain areas.
    b. refusing to make loans to people residing in certain areas.
    c. requiring brokers to join a multiple-listing service.
    d. illegally setting commission rates.

24. All of the following terminate an offer EXCEPT
    a. revocation of the offer before its acceptance.
    b. the death of the offeror before acceptance.
    c. a counteroffer by the offeree.
    d. an offer from a third party.

25. Fred and Karen enter into a contract wherein Karen will purchase Fred's vacation lot for $10,000. Shortly thereafter, Karen changes her mind. Valerie would like to buy Fred's lot on the same terms as Karen. Fred agrees and enters into a new contract with Valerie. Fred and Karen tear up their original contract. This is known as
    a. assignment.   c. substitution.
    b. novation.   d. rescission.

26. An offer to purchase real estate is a binding contract after it has been signed, communicated and accepted by which of the following?
    I. Buyer
    II. Seller
    III. Broker
       a. I only
       b. II only
       c. I and II only
       d. I, II and III

27. A broker enters into a listing agreement with a seller wherein the seller will receive $120,000 from the sale of a vacant lot and the broker will receive any sales proceeds exceeding that amount. This type of agreement is called a(n)
    a. exclusive-agency listing.
    b. exclusive-right-to-sell listing.
    c. net listing.
    d. multiple listing.

28. The Civil Rights Act of 1866 prohibits in all cases discrimination based on a person's
    I. race.
    II. religion.
    III. familial status.
       a. I only
       b. II only
       c. III only
       d. I, II and III

29. With an option to purchase real estate, the optionee
    a. must purchase the property but may do so at any time within the option period.
    b. is limited to a refund of the option consideration if the option is exercised.
    c. cannot obtain third-party financing on the property until after the option has expired.
    d. has no obligation to purchase the property during the option period.

30. On Monday, Tom makes a written offer to buy Kyle's vacant lot for $12,000. On Tuesday, Kyle counteroffers, saying he will accept Tom's offer if Tom raises the price to $13,500. Tom does not reply, so on Friday, Kyle changes his mind and accepts Tom's original price of $12,000. Under these circumstances, there is
    a. a valid agreement because Kyle accepted Tom's offer exactly as it was made.
    b. a valid agreement because Kyle accepted before Tom withdrew his original offer.
    c. no valid agreement because Tom's offer was not accepted within 72 hours of its having been made.
    d. no valid agreement because Kyle's counteroffer was a rejection of Tom's offer; once rejected, an offer cannot be accepted.

31. A broker took a listing and later discovered that her client had previously been declared incompetent by the court. The listing is now
    I. unaffected because the broker was acting in good faith.
    II. of no value because the listing is void.
       a. I only
       b. II only
       c. Both I and II
       d. Neither I nor II

32. Agent Green calls several property owners in a neighborhood, stating that several minority homebuyers are moving into the area and that this will decrease property values. Then agent Green tries to solicit listings from these owners. Under the federal Fair Housing Act of 1986, this would be considered
    a. blockbusting.   c. steering.
    b. redlining.   d. lawful conduct.

33. Which of the following is(are) NOT usually prorated between the seller and buyer at closing?
    a. Recording charges
    b. Real estate taxes
    c. Prepaid rents
    d. Interest

34. In North Carolina, who is responsible for paying the excise tax on the sale of a property?
    I. Buyer
    II. Seller
    a. I only
    b. II only
    c. Both I and II
    d. Neither I nor II

35. Marie believes that she has been the victim of an unfair discriminatory practice committed by a local real estate broker. In accordance with federal regulations, how long does Marie have to file her complaint against the broker?
    a. 90 days
    b. 180 days
    c. 9 months
    d. 1 year

36. Broker Bob obtains an open listing on Fairfield's property. The house is sold by broker Nancy. Which of the following statements is true regarding the commission?
    I. Broker Bob and broker Nancy will share the commission.
    II. Broker Bob is not entitled to a commission.
    III. Broker Bob is entitled to 100 percent of the commission.
    a. I only
    b. II only
    c. III only
    d. I and II, depending on the terms of the purchase and sale agreement

37. An agency relationship is created between a broker and a property owner when the
    a. broker puts forth reasonable effort to sell the owner's property.
    b. parties enter into a listing agreement.
    c. broker finds a ready, willing and able buyer.
    d. broker finds a buyer who actually purchases the owner's property.

38. Broker Dickerson found a buyer for Presser's house. The buyer put down an earnest money deposit with the broker, and the parties signed a sales contract. Before the sale was closed, a title search revealed a defect in the seller's title, making it impossible for Presser to deliver good title. Which of the following statements is(are) true?
    I. The buyer was entitled to cancel the sale without penalty.
    II. The seller was entitled to keep the buyer's deposit if the buyer canceled the sale.
    III. Both seller and buyer had to contribute to Dickerson's commission because the sale could not go through as agreed.
    a. I only
    b. II only
    c. III only
    d. II or III only

39. Which of the following listings provides the strongest protection of the broker's interests?
    a. Net
    b. Exclusive agency
    c. Exclusive right to sell
    d. Open

40. Which of the following contracts does NOT have to be in writing?
    a. Contract to sell real estate
    b. Listing agreement
    c. One-year lease
    d. Agreement creating an easement

41. On the settlement statement, the earnest money deposit appears as a
    a. credit to the seller and a debit to the buyer.
    b. debit to the seller and a credit to the buyer.
    c. credit to the seller.
    d. credit to the buyer.

42. A seller's agent must disclose his or her agency status to a prospective buyer
    a. before closing the transaction.
    b. before presenting the buyer's offer to the seller.
    c. at first substantial contact.
    d. before the seller accepts the buyer's offer.

43. A property manager tries to
    I. maximize the property owner's net profit.
    II. maintain or increase the value of the property.
    a. I only
    b. II only
    c. Both I and II
    d. Neither I nor II

44. Property management agreements create an agency relationship between the
    I. manager and the tenant.
    II. owner and the manager.
    a. I only
    b. II only
    c. Both I and II
    d. Neither I nor II

45. The cost of preparing a deed is usually paid by the
    I. seller.
    II. buyer.
    a. I only
    b. II only
    c. Both I and II
    d. Neither I nor II

46. A broker had been trying to sell Mary's house for $75,000. Sam, an African American, saw the house and was interested in it. When Sam asked the broker how much the house was, the broker said $95,000. Under the Fair Housing Act of 1968, such a statement is
    a. legal because all that is important is that Sam be given the opportunity to buy the house.
    b. legal because the representation was made by the broker and not directly by the owner.
    c. illegal because the difference in the offering price and the quoted price was greater than 10 percent.
    d. illegal because the terms of the potential sale were changed for Sam.

47. A broker receives a deposit with a written offer that indicates that the offeror will leave the offer open for the seller's acceptance for ten days. On the fifth day, and prior to acceptance by the seller, the offeror notifies the broker that he is withdrawing his offer and demanding the return of the deposit. In this situation, which of the following statements is true?
    a. The offeror cannot withdraw the offer— it must be held open for the full ten-day period.
    b. The offeror has the right to withdraw the offer and have the deposit returned any time before he is notified of the seller's acceptance.
    c. The offeror can withdraw the offer, but the seller and the broker will each retain one-half of the forfeited deposit.
    d. The offeror can withdraw the offer, but the broker will declare the deposit forfeited and retain all of it in lieu of a commission.

48. The purchase price shows up on the closing statement as a
    a. debit to the buyer and a credit to the seller.
    b. credit to the buyer and a debit to the seller.
    c. debit to the buyer only.
    d. credit to the seller only.

NORTH CAROLINA REAL ESTATE LICENSE LAW

49. Which of the following statements is(are) true of the North Carolina Real Estate Commission?
    I. It issues broker and salesperson licenses and regulates the activities of licensees.
    II. It determines the maximum commission a broker may charge on any one transaction.
    a. I only
    b. II only
    c. Both I and II
    d. Neither I nor II

50. In North Carolina, a person must be licensed as a real estate broker to perform which of the following for others and for a fee?
    I. Rent apartments in several different complexes to tenants
    II. Negotiate an exchange of property
    a. I only
    b. II only
    c. Both I and II
    d. Neither I nor II

51. Which of the following statements is(are) true of license law regulations?
    I. They require that a broker have the owner's permission before placing a "For Sale" sign on any property.
    II. They permit a real estate salesperson to advertise another person's property under the salesperson's own name alone.
    a. I only
    b. II only
    c. Both I and II
    d. Neither I nor II

52. Which of the following statements is(are) true regarding a broker's trust account records?
    I. They must be kept for a period of three years.
    II. They are private and not subject to inspection by the North Carolina Real Estate Commission.
    a. I only
    b. II only
    c. Both I and II
    d. Either I or II

53. Rental payments received by a broker must be deposited into a trust or an escrow account
    a. no later than three banking days following receipt of the money.
    b. immediately.
    c. no later than two business days after receipt.
    d. as long as both the listing broker and the selling broker agree to do so.

54. Each broker-in-charge can head
    a. one or more offices.
    b. no more than one office.
    c. no more than 12 salespeople.
    d. no more than three branch offices.

55. In North Carolina the annual license pocket renewal card must be
    I. carried by the agent on his or her person at all times when doing business as a licensee.
    II. displayed at the business address where the licensee works.
    a. I only
    b. II only
    c. Both I and II
    d. Neither I nor II

56. A broker may establish one or more branch offices, provided that
    a. each office has a broker-in-charge.
    b. each office has at least five salespeople.
    c. the broker supervises the salespeople at each office.
    d. the broker uses a different trade name for each branch.

57. Before a real estate agent may act as a dual agent, the parties must
    a. be informed and must consent to the broker representing both parties'
    b. give their wrtitten consent after full disclosure.
    c. agree to split the commission payment.
    d. give the Real Estate Commission their written consent.

58. Which of the following activities may a person perform for compensation without holding a real estate license?
    a. Selling the house of his or her neighbor
    b. Selling lots in a new subdivision
    c. Leasing their own property
    d. Selling time-shares

59. If Brown is given a power of attorney to sell Smith's property, which of the following statements is true?
    a. Brown must get a real estate license.
    b. Brown does not have to be licensed.
    c. Brown does not have to be licensed, but she must have the North Carolina Real Estate Commission approve the sale before it closes.
    d. Brown must get a temporary real estate license.

60. The provisions of the license law do NOT apply to which of the following persons?
    a. Salesperson working only on a part-time basis
    b. Property manager renting units in several apartment buildings and receiving a fee for each unit rented
    c. Attorney at law who also operates a real estate business
    d. Executor of an estate

61. Which of the following activities by a broker does NOT violate the license law?
    a. Drafting deeds and wills
    b. Working on listings submitted to a multiple-listing service
    c. Advertising property for sale, indicating only a telephone number for prospective buyers to call
    d. Accepting a commission from both a buyer and a seller in a transaction without full disclosure to the buyer and seller

62. A time-share is considered
    a. real property.
    b. personal property.
    c. a fraudulent scheme that must be avoided by all licensees.
    d. to be the purchase of a unit for at least one week a year for at least three years.

63. A developer of a time-share must place all funds received by purchasers
    a. in a trust account within ten business days of receipt.
    b. in an escrow account for ten days after receipt.
    c. into stocks and bonds.
    d. back into the time-share project.

REAL ESTATE FINANCE

64. A mortgage requires monthly payments of $875.70 for 20 years and a final payment of $24,095. The final payment is known as what type of payment?
    a. Wraparound   c. Balloon
    b. Variable   d. Accelerated

65. A lender may sell a loan originated by a bank in which of the following markets?
    a. Primary   c. Mortgage
    b. Secondary   d. Investor

66. In North Carolina, a trustee is the conditional holder of title to mortgaged real estate. North Carolina is considered what type of state?
    a. Title theory   c. Statutory share
    b. Lien theory   d. Strict forfeiture

67. Wilma purchases a condominium unit and obtains financing from a local savings and loan association. In this situation, which of the following best describes Wilma?
    I. Vendor
    II. Grantor under a deed of trust
    III. Trustee
    a. I only
    b. II only
    c. III only
    d. I and II only

68. A building sold for $60,000, with the purchaser putting 10 percent down and obtaining a loan for the balance. The lending institution charged a 1 percent loan origination fee. What was the total of the down payment and the loan fee?
    a. $540   c. $6,540
    b. $6,000   d. $6,600

69. Which of the following statements is(are) true of a wraparound loan?
    I. It encompasses an existing loan plus a new loan.
    II. It typically involves only one lender.
    III. It is unlawful in North Carolina under any circumstances.
    a. I only
    b. II only
    c. I and II only
    d. I and III only

70. If a condominium sold for $40,000 and the buyer obtained an FHA-insured mortgage loan for $38,500, how much money would be paid in discount points if the lender charged four points?
    a. $1,600   c. $1,500
    b. $1,540   d. $385

71. Gerald is purchasing a home under a land contract. Until the contract is paid in full, Gerald has
    a. legal title to the premises.
    b. no interest in the property.
    c. a legal life estate in the premises.
    d. equitable title to the property.

72. Jim has just made the final payment on his mortgage loan to his bank. Regardless of this fact, the lender will hold a lien on Jim's mortgaged property until which of the following is recorded?
    I. Satisfaction of mortgage
    II. Mortgage novation
    III. Estoppel letter
    a. I only
    b. II only
    c. III only
    d. I and III only

73. Discount points on a real estate loan are a potential cost to both the seller and the buyer. The points are
    a. set by the FHA and VA for their loan programs.
    b. charged only on conventional loans.
    c. limited by government regulations.
    d. determined by the market.

74. *Acceleration* is a term associated with which of the following documents?
    a. Listings
    b. Mortgages
    c. Leases
    d. Purchase and sales contracts

75. Anne's real estate loan indicates that if she transfers title to the property, the lender must be paid in full immediately. This is known as which of the following clauses?
    a. Acceleration
    b. Alienation
    c. Subordination
    d. Habendum

76. Paul defaulted on his mortgage loan payments, and the lender foreclosed. At the foreclosure sale, Paul's property sold for $64,000; the unpaid loan balance at the time of foreclosure was $78,000. What must the lender do in an attempt to recover the $14,000 that Paul still owes?
    a. Sue for specific performance
    b. Sue for damages
    c. Seek a deficiency judgment
    d. Seek a judgment by default

77. Which of the following is true of a term mortgage loan?
    a. All of the interest is paid at the end of the term.
    b. The debt is partially amortized over the life of the loan.
    c. The length of the term is limited by state statutes.
    d. The entire principal amount is due at the end of the term.

78. A real estate loan that uses both real estate and personal property as collateral is known as which of the following types of loans?
    a. Blanket
    b. Package
    c. Growing equity
    d. Graduated payment

79. The total cost of a loan, including both the interest rate and all loan fees, is what type of rate?
    a. Annual percentage
    b. Adjustable mortgage
    c. Market mortgage
    d. Annual capitalization

REAL ESTATE VALUATION

80. A residence with leaky plumbing is suffering from
    a. functional obsolescence.
    b. curable physical deterioration.
    c. incurable physical deterioration.
    d. external obsolescence.

81. Which of the following statements is true of the market value of a parcel of land?
    a. It is an estimate of the present worth of future benefits.
    b. It represents a measure of past expenditures.
    c. It is the price the seller wants for the property.
    d. It is the same as the market price.

82. Each of the following should be similar in legitimate comparables EXCEPT
    a. location.
    b. sales price.
    c. date of sale.
    d. square footage.

83. If the annual net income from a commercial property is $22,000 and the capitalization rate is 8 percent, what is the value of the property, using the income approach?
    a. $275,000
    b. $200,000
    c. $183,000
    d. $176,000

84. If an appraiser used all three approaches to estimating value of one particular building, which approach would probably set the higher limits of value?
    a. Sales comparison approach
    b. Gross rent multiplier approach
    c. Income approach
    d. Cost approach

85. Paul has just been hired to appraise a property for loan purposes. The property is an elegant old mansion that has been converted into three apartments. Which approach to value may Paul use as an alternative to the income approach?
    a. Highest and best use approach
    b. Sales comparison approach
    c. Replacement cost approach
    d. Gross rent multiplier

86. Mary built a $125,000 home in a residential neighborhood. The block next to hers is going to be rezoned to allow a mix of residential and retail uses. Because of this future zoning change, the value of her home dropped to $100,000. This is due to the principle of
    a. substitution.
    b. competition.
    c. anticipation.
    d. supply and demand.

87. An appraiser is using the cost approach to value. After determining the replacement cost of the building, she will
    a. estimate depreciation.
    b. add back the land value.
    c. Both a and b
    d. Neither a nor b

88. Which of the following is(are) an element(s) of value?
    I. Scarcity
    II. Demand
    III. Utility
    a. I only
    b. II only
    c. I and II only
    d. I, II and III

89. Most appraisers try to estimate a property's
    a. market price.
    b. market value
    c. value in use.
    d. cost

90. The principle that states that the maximum value of a property tends to be set by the cost of purchasing an equally desirable and valuable replacement property is called the principle of
    a. replacement.
    b. competition.
    c. substitution.
    d. highest and best use.

91. Which of the following is NOT a principal factor in choosing a comparable sale for appraisal purposes?
    a. Location
    b. Date of sale
    c. Excise tax rate
    d. Amenities

92. Sharon is appraising an owner-occupied, single-family residence. The method that is the most reliable in estimating its value is the
    a. sales comparison approach.
    b. cost approach.
    c. income capitalization approach.
    d. gross rent multiplier method.

93. Steve's house is three blocks away from an international airport. This is an example of
    a. functional obsolescence.
    b. economic obsolescence.
    c. physical deterioration.
    d. deferred maintenance.

94. The art of analyzing and effectively weighing the findings from the different appraisal methods is called
    a. averaging.
    b. capitalization.
    c. final estimating.
    d. reconciliation.

95. When determining net income, which of the following are not deducted from gross income?
    a. Mortgage payments
    b. Management costs
    c. Utility costs
    d. Insurance expenses

REAL ESTATE MATHEMATICS

96. A borrower computed the interest he was charged for the previous month on his $60,000 loan balance as $412.50. What is his interest rate?
    a. 7.5 percent
    b. 7.75 percent
    c. 8.25 percent
    d. 8.5 percent

97. Assuming that the listing broker and the selling broker in a transaction split their commission equally, what was the sales price of the property if the commission rate was 6.5 percent and the listing broker received $2,593.50?
    a. $39,900
    b. $56,200
    c. $79,800
    d. $88,400

98. A seller wants to net $65,000 from the sale of her house after paying the broker's fee of 6 percent. Her gross sales price will be
    a. $69,149.
    b. $68,900.
    c. $61,321.
    d. $61,100.

99. The commission rate is 7 3/4 percent on a sale of $50,000. What is the dollar amount of the commission?
    a. $3,500
    b. $3,875
    c. $4,085
    d. $4,585

100. Margaret is purchasing a $107,000 home with an 80 percent loan. The lender is charging two and one-half discount points. Margaret's loan discount expense will total
    a. $2,675.
    b. $2,140.
    c. $2,575.
    d. $1,980.

101. If the quarterly interest at 7.5 percent is $562.50, what is the principal amount of the loan?
    a. $7,500
    b. $15,000
    c. $30,000
    d. $75,000

102. Assume a house is sold for $84,500 and the commission rate is 7 percent. If the commission is split 60/40 between the selling broker and the listing broker (60 percent going to the selling broker and 40 percent going to the listing broker), and each broker splits her share of the commission evenly with her salesperson, how much will the listing salesperson receive from this sale?
    a. $1,183
    b. $1,775
    c. $2,366
    d. $3,549

103. Glenn is purchasing Sylvia's home for $67,000. Sylvia will have to pay excise taxes in the amount of
    a. $268.
    b. $155.
    c. $134.
    d. $112.

104. Gretchen purchases a $37,000 property, depositing $3,000 as earnest money. If she can obtain a 75 percent loan-to-value loan on the property and no additional items are prorated, how much more cash will she need at the settlement?
    a. $3,250
    b. $3,500
    c. $5,250
    d. $6,250

105. Joseph wants to net $72,000 on the sale of his home. He has agreed to pay a brokerage commission of 6 percent. What is the minimum sales price that will ensure Joseph's getting his $72,000?
    a. $76,596
    b. $76,320
    c. $77,890
    d. $75,935

106. The Larches enter into a purchase contract with the Elvons to buy the Elvons' house for $84,500. The buyers deposit $2,000 as earnest money and obtain a new mortgage loan for $67,600. The purchase contract provides for a March 15 settlement. The buyers and sellers prorate the year's estimated real estate taxes (using the 360-day method) of $880.96, which are unpaid. The buyers have additional closing costs of $1,250, and the sellers have other closing costs of $850. How much cash must the buyers bring to the settlement?
    a. $16,638
    b. $15,966
    c. $16,238
    d. $16,338

107. Ben sold his house to Marsha for $105,000. He owned the house for five years and made a profit of 25 percent on the sale over his previous purchase price. What did Ben originally pay for the house?
    a. $84,000
    b. $80,000
    c. $78,750
    d. $95,000

108. Beth got a real estate loan to buy a small lot and had to pay a 1 percent loan fee, which was deducted directly from the proceeds of the loan. She received $4,455 in cash from her lender. How much did she borrow?
    a. $4,550
    b. $4,500
    c. $5,000
    d. $4,575

109. The comparable property has a physical feature that is superior to the subject property to the value of $8,000. Which of the following is true?
    a. The $8,000 adjustment will be subtracted from the subject's value.
    b. The $8,000 adjustment will be subtracted from the comparable's sales price.
    c. The $8,000 adjustment will be added to the subject's value.
    d. The $8,000 adjustment will be added to the comparable's sales price.

110. A real estate agent had an annual income of $30,000. With each transaction, she received one-fourth of the total commission paid by the seller. Her commission rate was always 7 percent. What is the total value of all the property she sold during the year?
    a. $857,143
    b. $3,428,571
    c. $1,714,286
    d. $2,000,000

Answer Key

Chapter 1
Basic Real Estate Concepts

1. c   2
2. b   3–4
3. b   4
4. a   5
5. d   5
6. a   4–5
7. d   9
8. c   12
9. c   8–9
10. a   13
11. d   12
12. c   6–7
13. b   10
14. a   10
15. d   12
16. d   10
17. d   10–11
18. b   9

Chapter 2
Property Ownership and Interests

1. b   18
2. a   22
3. c   18–19
4. d   23
5. b   21
6. a   21–22
7. a   23
8. c   18–19
9. c   26
10. c   29
11. b   38–39
12. a   26

13. b   26
14. a   25–26
15. c   26
16. d   39
17. c   29–30
18. a   29
19. c   34
20. b   29–30
21. b   33
22. b   34
23. c   45
24. c   42
25. b   43
26. a   25
27. d   25
28. c   19–20
29. a   20
30. a   43
31. c   43 $.80 + .50 = $1.30 city/county tax rate (.013); $1,600 annual taxes ÷ .013 = $123,076.92 assessed value
32. b   43 $133,000 assessed value × .01678 tax rate = $2,331.74 annual taxes ÷ 12 months = $185.97833 = $185.98 monthly tax liability
33. a   43 $2,000 annual taxes ÷ $184,000 assessed value = .0108695 × $100 = $1.08695 = $1.09 per $100.00 of assessed value
34. b   21
35. a   21–22
36. a   34
37. d   36–37
38. c   25, 215
39. c   29–30
40. b   31–32
41. c   29, 31

42. c 22
43. b 30
44. b 38
45. a 35
46. d 30–31
47. b 73
48. b 38–39

Chapter 3
Property Description

1. c 52
2. b 54
3. b 53–54
4. c 60
5. c 60
6. c 60
7. d 60

Chapter 4
Transfer of Title to Real Property

1. d 74
2. a 72 $75,000 sales price ÷ 500 =
     150 × $1.00 = $150
3. b 62
4. c 72–73
5. b 64
6. c 74
7. c 72
8. d 62
9. a 62
10. d 64
11. c 75
12. a 75
13. a 78
14. d 75
15. c 76–77
16. c 73
17. b 73
18. b 78–79
19. a 27
20. d 25
21. a 62

Chapter 5
Land-Use Controls

1. a 94
2. d 85
3. b 84–86
4. a 84–85
5. b 85
6. b 85
7. c 84–85, 92
8. c 86

9. a 87
10. b 94–95
11. a 86
12. d 84–85
13. b 94–95
14. a 95
15. c 86
16. b 87–88
17. a 87
18. c 88
19. c 92
20. d 95
21. b 86
22. b 86
23. b 84–85

Chapter 6
Real Estate Brokerage and the Law of Agency

1. a 108
2. b 111–112
3. b 115
4. b 103
5. a 106
6. b 106
7. b 101–102
8. a 163
9. d 126
10. a 108
11. c 124
12. c 124–125
13. b 101, 125
14. d 115–119
15. b 108
16. d 115
17. c 115
18. b 119
19. c 119
20. c 122
21. c 125
22. b 110
23. c 113–114
24. d 121–123

Chapter 7
Fair Housing and Ethical Practices

1. c 137
2. a 134
3. d 134
4. b 145
5. c 145
6. a 146
7. b 135
8. c 139

9. c 145
10. b 137
11. a 140
12. b 134
13. d 140
14. c 143
15. b 141
16. c 142
17. d 137
18. a 146
19. b 145–146
20. b 143–144
21. c 138
22. d 146

Chapter 8
Basic Contract Law/Agency Contracts

1. d 156
2. b 162
3. b 161
4. b 156
5. d 154
6. b 155
7. a 160
8. c 155
9. b 154
10. b 163
11. c 165–166
12. c 167
13. b 163
14. b 175
15. a 163
16. d 164–166
17. d 171
18. a 165
19. c 164
20. a Rule A.0104
21. a 172
22. a 164
23. d 166
24. c 164
25. d 161

Chapter 9
Sales Contracts and Practices

1. b 201
2. b 203
3. d 197–198
4. b 197
5. d 197

6. b 174 $85,000 seller desired net + $1,000 closing costs + $65,000 loan payoff = $151,000 ÷ .93 (100% – 7%) = $162,365.59 sales price (Rounded up to $162,366.00
7. c 197
8. b 198
9. a 197
10. b 202
11. d 202
12. b 197–198
13. b 203

Chapter 10
Landlord and Tenant

1. b 226
2. b 211
3. a 216
4. c 217–218
5. d 217
6. b 218
7. c 217–218
8. b 224
9. a 212
10. a 216
11. d 212
12. d 212
13. c 218
14. d 218
15. b 225
16. a 213
17. c 213
18. b 212
19. a 216
20. d 215–216
21. d 216
22. b 212
23. d 217
24. b 216
25. a 224
26. a 225
27. b 218

Chapter 11
Property Management

1. a 236
2. c 235
3. a 236
4. c 236
5. b 238
6. d 236
7. c 231
8. b 232

9. c   237
10. a   232
11. d   235   2-4BR × \$1,000/mo = \$2,000 × 12 mos. = \$24,000 rent received; 25-3BR × \$850/mo = \$21,250 × 12 mos. = \$255,000 × .95 (5% vacancy); 10-2BR × \$750/mo = \$7,500 × 12 mos. = \$90,000 × .95 (5% vacancy) = \$85,500 rent received; 11-1BR × \$650.00/mo = \$7,150 × 12 mos. = \$85,800 × .90 (10% vacancy) = \$77,220; Total rent received = \$428,970 × .12 mgmt fee = \$51,476
12. c   235–236
13. a   236
14. b   232

Chapter 12
Real Estate Financing: Principles

1. b   245
2. a   249
3. b   257
4. d   256   \$120,000 loan × .03 (3 discount points) = \$3,600
5. b   257
6. c   246
7. b   255
8. b   256   \$2,700 points ÷ \$90,000 loan = .03 = 3 points
9. a   261
10. d   247–248
11. b   260
12. a   245
13. b   256
14. c   249
15. d   261
16. b   261
17. d   262
18. b   262
19. a   251
20. c   253
21. b   249
22. b   262
23. b   254
24. a   246
25. b   259
26. b   262

Chapter 13
Real Estate Financing: Practices

1. a   277–278
2. a   276
3. b   282
4. b   277

5. b   288
6. d   274
7. c   279
8. b   276
9. a   283
10. b   276
11. c   269
12. b   288
13. a   269
14. d   280–281
15. c   283–284
16. a   285
17. a   286   Housing Expense = \$750 ÷ .28 = \$2,678.57, round up to \$2,679; Recurring Obligations \$750 + \$500 = \$1,250 ÷ .36 = \$3,472.222 rounded to \$3,472
18. a   284
19. c   270
20. d   281
21. d   281
22. c   277–278
23. a   288
24. c   272
25. c   202, 276
26. d   278
27. d   289
28. c   269   \$114,500 appraised value × .80 = \$91,600 loan amount
29. c   268
30. a   286   \$982 PITI + \$745 recurring obligations = \$1,727 ÷ .36 = \$4,797.22 × 12 months = \$57,566 annual income
31. c   285   \$60,000 annual income ÷ 12 months = \$5,000 monthly income × .36 = \$1,800 maximum PITI and Recurring obligations; \$1,800 – (\$160 taxes/Ins + \$700) = \$940 maximum PI ÷ 6.67 loan factor = \$140.92953 × \$1,000 = \$140,929.53
32. c   286   \$42,000 annual gross income ÷ 12 months = \$3,500 × .36 = \$1,260 – \$500 = \$760.00

Chapter 14
Closing the Real Estate Transaction

1. b   306
2. a   302
3. c   300–301
4. d   308   \$1,800 annual taxes ÷ 360 days = \$5.00 per day; Jan 1 - Sep 15 = 255 days × \$5.00 = \$1,275 sellers "liability"; Seller prepaid \$1,800 – \$1,275 = \$525 Credit seller/debit buyer

5. c 309 $400 rent ÷ 30 days = $13.333 × 15 days = $199.995 = $200 debit seller/ credit buyer

6. c 256, 269 $50,000 sales price × .90 = $45,000 (loan amount) × .02 = $900 (loan fees) + $5,000 (down payment) = $5.900

7. b 306
8. d 304
9. a 304
10. d 304
11. b 304
12. c 310
13. d 300
14. b 300
15. b 311
16. d 300
17. d 297
18. d 301
19. b 310
20. a 310

Chapter 15
Basic Residential Construction

1. a 332
2. b 327
3. d 327
4. c 324
5. c 332
6. a 324
7. c 333
8. c 324
9. c 327
10. c 331

Chapter 16
Real Property Valuation

1. b 337
2. c 354
3. b 349
4. d 351-352 Net operating income (NOI) of $24,000 ÷ $300,000 value = .08 = 8%
5. c 351
6. b 338
7. c 351
8. b 351
9. c 349
10. b 345–346
11. b 349
12. d 349
13. c 351
14. b 336
15. b 337
16. b 351

17. a 349
18. c 346
19. b 353
20. b 351
21. b 350
22. a 352
23. a 348
24. b 351
25. d 350
26. a 339
27. c 351, 353 Gross income of $6,000 – $1,000 mgt. ex. – $300 taxes – $1,100 repairs = $3,600 [Debt service is not an operating expense]
28. d 346
29. c 346

Subject	Comparable		Sold for $140,000
2100 SF	1900 SF (200 × $72)	=	+$14,400
4BR	3 BR (1× $2,000)	=	+ $2,000
2 CG	1 CG (1× $1,500)	=	+ $1,500
No patio	Patio (1× $2,000)	=	– $2,000
No Pool	Pool (1× $14,000)	=	– $14,000
2.5 baths	2 baths (½ = $800)	=	+ $ 800
1 acre	1.5 acre (½ = $15,000)	=	– $15,000
	Subject Property =		$127,700

30. d 346

CompA	Comp B	Comp C	Comp D
$73,000	$74,000	$62,000	$71,000
–$ 3,000	–$ 2,000	+$ 3,500	–$ 5,000
$70,000	$72,000	$65,500	$66,000

Range = $65,500 low to $72,000 high

Chapter 17
Property Insurance

1. d 361–362
2. b 363
3. a 364
4. a 363
5. d 364
6. c 365
7. a 363
8. b 364–365
9. c 362
10. b 363

Chapter 18
Federal Income Taxation of Real Property Ownership

1. c 371
2. a 373
3. c 369
4. b 372

5. d 370
6. d 371–372
7. b 372
8. a 372
9. c 371–372 $127,500 sales price less selling expenses of $750 = $126,750 amount realized – $75,000 original cost = $51,750
10. a 371–372 The entire gain would be subject to taxation if the property were an investment property.
11. b 371 $72,000 basis + $15,000 addition + $3,000 deck = $90,000. Roof repairs and fixing broken windows would be considered ordinary repairs or maintenance and would not increase the adjusted basis.

Chapter 19
Environmental Issues and the Real Estate Transaction

1. b 379
2. c 380
3. c 381
4. a 380–381
5. a 384
6. c 384
7. b 386
8. d 388
9. c 384
10. d 379
11. b 381–382
12. c 382

Chapter 20
Real Estate Mathematics

1. b $123,000 × 0.05 = $6,150

2. a $73,000 0.06 = $4,380 gross commission ÷ 2 = $2,190 × 0.30 = $657

3. b $356,000 ÷ $1,200,000 = 0.2966666 = 29.67% LTV

4. c $135,000 × 0.065 = $8,775 gross commission × 0.55 = $4,826.25 × 0.60 = $2,895.75

5. a 2% + 5%+ 3% = 10% commission; $2,000 ÷ 0.10 = $20,000 sales price

    Al: $20,000 × 0.02 = $400
    Broker: $20,000 × 0.05 = $1,000
    Betty: $20,000 × 0.03 = $600

6 d $75,000 + $250,000 = $325,000 new assessed value × 0.01678 = $5,453.50 ÷ 12 months = $454.46

7. a 350 acres × 43,560 (sq. ft./acre) = 15,246,000 sq. ft. ÷ 1,300' = 11,727.69' depth; 11,727.69 × 6,000' frontage = 70,366,140 sq. ft. ÷ divided by 43,560 = 1,615.4 acres

8. c 660' × 660' = 435,600 sq. ft. ÷ 43,560 = 10 acres ÷ 2 = 5 acres in each lot

9. b $5,000 profit ÷ $20,000 = 25%

10. c $20,000 × 5 lots = $100,000 original value; $17,000 × 9 = $153,000 present value – $100,000 = $53,000 profit ÷ $100,000 = 0.53 = 53%

11. d $135,000 net + $950 closing costs + $53,500 loan payoff = $189,450 ÷ 0.935 (100% – 6.5%) = $202,620.32

12. a $180,000 × 0.85 = $153,000 loan amount ÷ 1,000 = 153 × 6.65 = $1,017.45 PI. Taxes: $996 ÷ 12 months = $83. Insurance: $480 ÷ 12 months = $40. $1,017.45 PI + $83 T + $40 I = $1,140.45 PITI

13. c $1,017.45 PI × 360 payments = $366,282 PI – $153,000 P = $213,282

14. a $153,000 × .07 = $10,710 I ÷ 12 months = $892.50 I. $1,017.45 PI – $892.50 I = $124.95 P. $153,000 P – $124,95 P = $152,875.05

15. c $185,500 × 0.80 = $148,400 loan × 0.01 = $1,484 origination fee; $148,400 × 0.015 = $2,226 discount points; $1,484 + $2,226 = $3,710

16. d $37,100 down payment + $400 attorney fees + $3,710 loan fees + $371 revenue stamps = $41,581

17. c $105,000 × 0.90 = $94,500 original debt $105,000 – $94,500 = $10,500 original equity $105,000 × 1.20 = $126,000 new value $94,500 × 0.92 (100% – 8%) = $86,940 new debt $126,000 – $86,940 = $39,060 new equity $39,060 – $10,500 = $28,560 increase in equity $28,560 ÷ $10,500 = 2.72 = 272%

18. a $40,800 ÷ 12 months = $3,400 monthly gross income; Housing: $895 ÷ $3,400 = 0.26 = 26%: Yes; Recurring Obligations: $895 + $425 = $1,320 ÷ $3,400 = 0.39 = 39%: No

19. a $719.32 PI + $135 TI + $500 = $1,354.32 total debt ÷ 0.36 = $3,762 monthly income × 12 = $45,144

20. d $53,000 ÷ 12 = $4,416.67 monthly income; $4,416.67 × 0.36 = $1,590 maximum recurring obligations; $1,590 – $150 TI – $650 recurring obligations = $790 maximum PI; $790 ÷ 8.0462 = $98.182993 × 1,000 = $98,182.99

21. b $38,500 ÷ 12 months = $3,208.33 monthly income; $3,208.33 × .36 = $1,155 maximum recurring obligations; $1,155 – $700 = $455

22. d $575 × 3 = $1,725 ÷ 30 = $57.50/day Nov 1 to Nov 14 = 14 days × $57.50 = $805 to seller $1,725 – $805 = $920 debit seller/credit buyer

23. a 82,000 debit seller/credit buyer $82,000 × 0.07 = $5,740 divided by 360 days = $15.944/day; Aug 1 to Aug 11 = 11 days × $15.944 = $175.38 debit seller/credit buyer

24. b $1,260 ÷ 360 days = $3.50/day Jan 1 to Nov 15 = 315 days × $3.50 = $1,102.50 seller's share of taxes $1,260 – $1,102.50 = $157.50 credit seller/debit buyer

25. b $150,000 sales price – $11,250 commission – $50,000 loan payoff – $157.50 taxes – $150 deed preparation – $300 revenue stamps = $88,142.50 net to seller

26. d $150,000 sales price + $280 interim interest + $900 origination fee + $900 discount points + $185 title insurance + $380 insurance policy + $550 attorney fee – $90,000 loan – $3,000 earnest money deposit – $157.50 taxes = $60,037.50

Math for 25 and 26:
Commission: $150,000 × 0.075 = $11,250
Interim interest: $90,000 × 0.07 = $6,300 ÷ 360 days = $17.50/day. Feb 15 to end of month = 16 days × $17.50 = $280
Origination fee: $90,000 × 0.01 = $900
Discount points: $90,000 × 0.01 = $900
Tax proration: $1,260 ÷ 360 days = $3.50/day × 45 days (Jan 1 to Feb 15) = $157.50
Revenue stamps: $150,000 ÷ 500 = $300

27. d Comps #1 and #2 are the same except for square footage: $110,000 – $100,000 = $10,000 ÷ 200 sq. ft. (3,000 – 2,800) = $50 per sq. ft.

Comp #2 and Comp #3: $110,000 –
$86,000 = $ 24,000
3,000 sq. ft. - 2,600 sq. ft. =
400 sq. ft. × $50 = $–20,000
Value of garage: $ 4,000

	Comp # 1	Comp #2	Comp # 3
	$100,000	$110,000	$ 86,000
Square feet:	$+10,000	-0-	$+20,000
Garage:	$ 4,000	$ –4,000	-0-
	$106,000	$106,000	$106,000

28. a

29. b

30. c

31. d

Math for 28 through 31

$120,000 basis	$165,000
$ +1,600	$–11,550 commission
$+16,000	$ –1,300 closing cost
$137,600 adjusted basis	$152,150 amount realized

Gain: $152,150 amount realized – $137,600 adjusted basis = $14,550

Answer key to closing statement worksheet from Chapter 14

Closing Statement Worksheet				
	Buyer's Statement		Seller's Statement	
	Debit	Credit	Debit	Credit
Purchase price	$110,000.00			$110,000.00
Earnest money		$ 5,000.00		
Principal amount of new loan		88,000.00		
Interim interest	391.10			
Payoff of existing loan			$ 82,750.00	
Seller's accrued interest			344.79	
Loan origination fee	880.00			
Discount points	1,320.00			
Appraisal	150.00			
Credit report	50.00			
Property survey	200.00			
Pest inspection report	75.00			
Broker's commission			6,600.00	
Hazard insurance	345.00			
Property taxes	229.04		870.96	
Title insurance premium	250.00			
Revenue stamps			220.00	
Document (deed) preparation			50.00	
Recording fees	14.00		7.00	
Attorney's fees	500.00			
Escrow account deposit	500.00			
Subtotals	114,904.14	93,000.00	90,842.75	110,000.00
Balance due from buyer		21,904.14		
Balance due to seller			19,157.25	
Totals	$114,904.14	$114,904.14	$110,000.00	$110,000.00

Computation of figures on settlement statement:

Principal amount of new loan:	$110,000 sales price × 80% loan = $88,000 loan

Buyer's interim interest:

$88,000 loan amount × 10% = $8,800 annual interest
$8,800 annual interest ÷ 360 days = $24.444 daily interest
$24.444 daily interest × 16 days (Oct 15 to Oct 30) = $391.10
    interest

Seller's accrued interest:

$82,750 loan balance × 10% = $8,275 annual interest
$8,275 annual interest ÷ 360 days = $22.986 daily interest
$22.986 daily interest × 15 days (Oct 1 to Oct 15) = $344.79
    interest

Property taxes:

$1,100 ÷ 360 days = $3.056 daily taxes
January 1 to October 15 = 285 days
285 × $3.056 = $870.96 (seller's taxes)
$1,100.00 – $870.96 = $229.04 (buyer's taxes)

Revenue stamps:

$110,000 ÷ $500 = 220 × $1 = $220

Broker's commission:

$110,000 × 6% = $6,600

Loan origination fee:

$88,000 × 1% = $880

Discount points:

$88,000 × 1.5% = $1,320

Buyer's statement:

Buyer's debits	$114,904.14
– Buyer's credits	$ 93,000.00
	$ 21,904.14 balance (cash) due from buyer

Seller's statement:

Seller's credits	$110,000.00
– Seller's debits	$ 90,842.75
	$ 19,157.25

A. **Settlement Statement**

U.S. Department of Housing
and Urban Development

OMB Approval No. 2502-0265

B. Type of Loan

1. ☐ FHA	2. ☐ FmHA	3. ☐ Conv. Unins.	6. File Number:	7. Loan Number:	8. Mortgage Insurance Case Number:
4. ☐ VA	5. ☐ Conv. Ins.				

C. Note: This form is furnished to give you a statement of actual settlement costs. Amounts paid to and by the settlement agent are shown. Items marked "(p.o.c.)" were paid outside the closing; they are shown here for informational purposes and are not included in the totals.

D. Name & Address of Borrower:	E. Name & Address of Seller:	F. Name & Address of Lender:

G. Property Location:	H. Settlement Agent:	
	Place of Settlement:	I. Settlement Date:

J. Summary of Borrower's Transaction		K. Summary of Seller's Transaction	
100. Gross Amount Due From Borrower		**400. Gross Amount Due To Seller**	
101. Contract sales price	110,000	401. Contract sales price	110,000
102. Personal property		402. Personal property	
103. Settlement charges to borrower (line 1400)	4,904.14	403.	
104.		404.	
105.		405.	
Adjustments for items paid by seller in advance		Adjustments for items paid by seller in advance	
106. City/town taxes to		406. City/town taxes to	
107. County taxes to		407. County taxes to	
108. Assessments to		408. Assessments to	
109.		409.	
110.		410.	
111.		411.	
112.		412.	
120. Gross Amount Due From Borrower	114,904.14	**420. Gross Amount Due To Seller**	110,000
200. Amounts Paid By Or In Behalf Of Borrower		**500. Reductions In Amount Due To Seller**	
201. Deposit or earnest money	5,000	501. Excess deposit (see instructions)	
202. Principal amount of new loan(s)	88,000	502. Settlement charges to seller (line 1400)	7,747.96
203. Existing loan(s) taken subject to		503. Existing loan(s) taken subject to	
204.		504. Payoff of first mortgage loan	82,750.00
205.		505. Payoff of second mortgage loan	
206.		506. Accrued Interest- mortgage	344.79
207.		507.	
208.		508.	
209.		509.	
Adjustments for items unpaid by seller		Adjustments for items unpaid by seller	
210. City/town taxes to		510. City/town taxes to	
211. County taxes to		511. County taxes to	
212. Assessments to		512. Assessments to	
213.		513.	
214.		514.	
215.		515.	
216.		516.	
217.		517.	
218.		518.	
219.		519.	
220. Total Paid By/For Borrower	93,000	**520. Total Reduction Amount Due Seller**	90,842.75
300. Cash At Settlement From/To Borrower		**600. Cash At Settlement To/From Seller**	
301. Gross Amount due from borrower (line 120)	114,904.14	601. Gross amount due to seller (line 420)	110,000
302. Less amounts paid by/for borrower (line 220)	(93,000)	602. Less reductions in amt. due seller (line 520)	(90,842.75)
303. Cash ☐ From ☐ To Borrower	21,904.14	**603. Cash** ☐ To ☐ From Seller	19,157.25

Section 5 of the Real Estate Settlement Procedures Act (RESPA) requires the following: • HUD must develop a Special Information Booklet to help persons borrowing money to finance the purchase of residential real estate to better understand the nature and costs of real estate settlement services; • Each lender must provide the booklet to all applicants from whom it receives or for whom it prepares a written application to borrow money to finance the purchase of residential real estate; • Lenders must prepare and distribute with the Booklet a Good Faith Estimate of the settlement costs that the borrower is likely to incur in connection with the settlement. These disclosures are manadatory.

Section 4(a) of RESPA mandates that HUD develop and prescribe this standard form to be used at the time of loan settlement to provide full disclosure of all charges imposed upon the borrower and seller. These are third party disclosures that are designed to provide the borrower with pertinent information during the settlement process in order to be a better shopper.

The Public Reporting Burden for this collection of information is estimated to average one hour per response, including the time for reviewing instructions, searching existing data sources, gathering and maintaining the data needed, and completing and reviewing the collection of information.

This agency may not collect this information, and you are not required to complete this form, unless it displays a currently valid OMB control number.

The information requested does not lend itself to confidentiality.

L. Settlement Charges

	Paid From Borrowers Funds at Settlement	Paid From Seller's Funds at Settlement
700. Total Sales/Broker's Commission based on price $ 110,000 @ 6.00 % = $6,600		
Division of Commission (line 700) as follows:		
701. $ to		
702. $ to		
703. Commission paid at Settlement		6,600
704.		
800. Items Payable In Connection With Loan		
801. Loan Origination Fee 1.00 %	880.00	
802. Loan Discount 1.5 %	1,320.00	
803. Appraisal Fee to	150.00	
804. Credit Report to	50.00	
805. Lender's Inspection Fee		
806. Mortgage Insurance Application Fee to		
807. Assumption Fee		
808.		
809.		
810.		
811.		
900. Items Required By Lender To Be Paid In Advance		
901. Interest from 10/15 to 10/30 @$ 24.444 /day	391.10	
902. Mortgage Insurance Premium for months to		
903. Hazard Insurance Premium for 1.0 years to	345.00	
904. years to		
905.		
1000. Reserves Deposited With Lender		
1001. Hazard insurance months @ $ per month		
1002. Mortgage insurance months @ $ per month		
1003. City property taxes months @ $ per month		
1004. County property taxes months @ $ per month		
1005. Annual assessments months @ $ per month		
1006. Escrow account deposit months @ $ per month	500.00	
1007. months @ $ per month		
1008. months @ $ per month		
1100. Title Charges		
1101. Settlement or closing fee to		
1102. Abstract or title search to		
1103. Title examination to	250.00	
1104. Title insurance binder to		
1105. Document preparation to		50.00
1106. Notary fees to		
1107. Attorney's fees to	500.00	
(includes above items numbers:)		
1108. Title insurance to		
(includes above items numbers:)		
1109. Lender's coverage $		
1110. Owner's coverage $		
1111.		
1112.		
1113.		
1200. Government Recording and Transfer Charges		
1201. Recording fees: Deed $ 7.00 ; Mortgage $ 7.00 ; Releases $ 7.00	14.00	7.00
1202. City/county tax/stamps: Deed $; Mortgage $		
1203. State tax/stamps: Deed $ 220.00 ; Mortgage $		220.00
1204.		
1205.		
1300. Additional Settlement Charges		
1301. Survey to	200.00	
1302. Pest inspection to	75.00	
1303. buyer's property tax 10/16 to 12/30	229.04	
1304. seller's property tax 1/1 to 10/15		870.96
1305.		
1400. Total Settlement Charges (enter on lines 103, Section J and 502, Section K)	4904.14	7,747.96

License Law Appendix
Real Estate License Law

1. a *
2. c *
3. a *
4. a *
5. c *
6. a *
7. b *
8. b *
9. b *
10. d *
11. d *
12. c *
13. b *
14. d *
15. c *
16. b *
17. b *
18. d *
19. a *
20. c *
21. c *
22. c *
23. d *
24. b *

Sample Exam

1. b   53
2. c   44
3. c   53
4. a   63
5. d   74
6. b   69
7. a   72 $75,000 value ÷ 500 = 150 × $1.00 = $150.00
8. b   78
9. a   64
10. a   27
11. b   215
12. a   86
13. d   78, 226
14. b   84
15. a   69
16. c   36–37
17. c   86
18. a   370
19. d   19
20. b   216
21. c   370
22. a   311
23. a   145
24. d   160

25. b   161
26. c   197
27. c   171
28. a   134
29. d   203
30. d   197–198
31. b   156
32. a   145
33. a   310
34. b   72, 311
35. d   140–141
36. b   164–165
37. b   162
38. a   197–198
39. c   166
40. c   226
41. d   311
42. c   115
43. c   231
44. b   232
45. a   311
46. d   137
47. b   157
48. a   310
49. a *
50. c *
51. a *
52. a *
53. a *
54. b *
55. a *
56. a *
57. a *
58. c *
59. a *
60. d *
61. b *
62. a *
63. b *
64. c   253
65. b   282–283
66. a   244
67. b   246
68. c   255–256 $60,000 × .10 down = $6,000 Down Payment = $54,000 loan × .01 = $540 + $6,000 = $6,540
69. a   277
70. b   256 $38,500 loan × .04 = $1,540
71. d   202
72. a   257
73. d   255
74. b   247
75. b   249
76. c   262

77. d 251
78. b 276
79. a 288
80. b 349
81. a 336
82. b 345
83. a 352 $22,000 NOI ÷ .08 = $275,000
84. d 347–349
85. d 352
86. c 339
87. c 347–348
88. d 336
89. b 337
90. c 338
91. c 345
92. a 345
93. b 350
94. d 354
95. a 351–352
96. c 398–399 $412.50 monthly interest × 12 months = $4,950 annual interest ÷ $60,000 loan amount = .0825 = 8.25%
97. c 165 $2,593.50 × 2 = $5,187 gross commission ÷ .065 (6.5%) = $79,800
98. a 174 $65,000 seller net ÷ .94 (100% – 6%) = $69,148.936 rounded to $69,149
99. b 165 Sales price of $50,000 × .0775 (7¾%) = $3,875
100. b 256 $107,000 sales price × .80 (80%) = $85,600 loan × .025 = $2,140

101. c 251 $562.50 × 4 (Quarterly) = $2,250 annual interest × .075 = $30,000
102. a 165 $84,500 sales price × .07 (7%) = $5,915 gross commission × .40 (to listing broker = $2,366 ÷ .50 = $1,183 to listing salesperson
103. c 72 $67,000 ÷ 500 = 134 × $1.00 = $134
104. d 314 Purchase price of $37,000 × .75 = $27,750 loan amount. $37,000 – $27,750 = $9,250 down payment less $3,000 deposit = $6,250
105. a 404 Seller net of $72,000 ÷ .94 (100% – 6%) = $76,595.744 rounded to $76,596
106. b 314 $84,500 Purchase Price less $67,000 loan, less $2,000 deposit, less $183.53 prorated taxes, plus $1,250 closing costs = $15,966.47 rounded to $15,966; proration of taxes: $880.96 ÷ 360 days = $2.447 per day × 75 days (Jan 1-Mar 15) = $183.25 credit buyer/ debit seller
107. a 404 $105,000 sales price (present value) ÷ 1.25% (100% + 25%) = $84,000
108. b 256 $4,455 ÷ .99 (100% – 1%) = $4,500
109. b 346 Comparable is superior, value is subtracted from comparable sales price
110. c 165, 403 $30,000 annual income ÷ .25 (one-fourth split) = $120,000 ÷ .07 (commission rate) = $1,714,286 value

* Answers to these and all license law questions can be found in Appendix A: Real Estate License Law, Commission Rules, and Trust Account Guidelines.

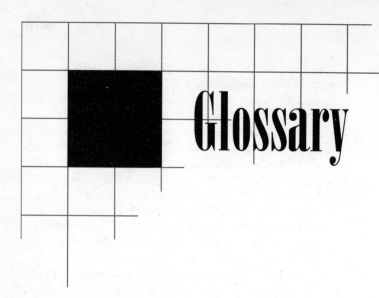

Glossary

abstract of title The condensed history of a title to a particular parcel of real estate, consisting of a summary of the original grant and all subsequent conveyances and encumbrances affecting the property and a certification by the abstractor that the history is complete and accurate.

acceleration clause The clause in a mortgage or deed of trust that can be enforced to make the entire debt due immediately if the borrower defaults on an installment payment or another covenant.

accession Acquiring title to additions or improvements to real property as a result of the annexation of fixtures or the accretion of alluvial deposits along the banks of streams.

accretion The increase or addition of land by the deposit of sand or soil washed up naturally from a river, lake or sea.

accrued items On a closing statement, items of expense that are incurred but not yet payable, such as interest on a mortgage loan or taxes on real property.

acknowledgment A formal declaration made before a duly authorized officer, usually a notary public, by a person who has signed a document.

acre A measure of land equal to 43,560 square feet, 4,840 square yards, 4,047 square meters, 160 square rods or .4047 hectare.

actual eviction The legal process that results in the tenant's being physically removed from the leased premises.

actual notice Express information or fact; that which is known; direct knowledge.

adjustable-rate mortgage (ARM) A loan characterized by a fluctuating interest rate, usually one tied to a bank or savings and loan association cost-of-funds index.

adjusted basis *See* basis.

ad valorem tax A tax levied according to value, generally used to refer to real estate tax. Also called the *general tax.*

adverse possession The actual, open, notorious, hostile and continuous possession of another's land under a claim of title. Possession for a statutory period may be a means of acquiring title.

affidavit of title A written statement, made under oath by a seller or grantor of real property and acknowledged by a notary public, in which the grantor (1) identifies himself or herself and indicates marital status, (2) certifies that since the examination of the title on the date of the contracts no defects have occurred in the title and (3) certifies that he or she is in possession of the property (if applicable).

agency The relationship between a principal and an agent wherein the agent is authorized to represent the principal in certain transactions.

agency coupled with an interest An agency relationship in which the agent is given an estate or interest in the subject of the agency (the property).

agent One who acts or has the power to act for another. A fiduciary relationship is created under the *law of agency* when a property owner, as the principal, executes a listing agreement or management contract authorizing a licensed real estate broker to be his or her agent.

agricultural fixture In North Carolina, a fixture used in farming operations that is considered real property rather than personal property.

air lot A designated airspace over a piece of land. An air lot, like surface property, may be transferred.

air rights The right to use the open space above a property, usually allowing the surface to be used for another purpose.

alienation The act of transferring property to another. Alienation may be voluntary, such as by gift or sale, or involuntary, as through eminent domain or adverse possession.

alienation clause The clause in a mortgage or deed of trust that states that the balance of the secured debt becomes immediately due and payable at the lender's option if the property is sold by the borrower. In effect, this clause prevents the borrower from assigning the debt without the lender's approval.

allodial system A system of land ownership in which land is held free and clear of any rent or service due to the government; commonly contrasted to the feudal system. Land is held under the allodial system in the United States.

American Land Title Association (ALTA) policy A title insurance policy that protects the interest in a collateral property of a mortgage lender that originates a new real estate loan.

amortized loan A loan in which the principal as well as the interest is payable in monthly or other periodic installments over the term of the loan.

annual percentage rate (APR) The relationship of the total finance charges associated with a loan. This must be disclosed to borrowers by lenders under the Truth-in-Lending Act.

anticipation The appraisal principle that holds that value can increase or decrease based on the expectation of some future benefit or detriment affecting the property.

antitrust laws Laws designed to preserve the free enterprise of the open marketplace by making illegal certain private conspiracies and combinations formed to minimize competition. Most violations of antitrust laws in the real estate business involve either *price fixing* (brokers conspiring to set fixed compensation rates) or *allocation of customers or markets* (brokers agreeing to limit their areas of trade or dealing to certain areas or properties).

appraisal An estimate of the quantity, quality or value of something. The process through which conclusions of property value are obtained; also refers to the report that sets forth the process of estimation and conclusion of value.

appreciation An increase in the worth or value of a property due to economic or related causes, which may prove to be either temporary or permanent; opposite of depreciation.

appurtenance A right, a privilege or an improvement belonging to, and passing with, the land.

appurtenant easement An easement that is annexed to the ownership of one parcel and allows the owner the use of the neighbor's land.

assemblage The combining of two or more adjoining lots into one larger tract to increase their total value.

assessment The imposition of a tax, charge or levy, usually according to established rates.

assignment The transfer in writing of interest in a bond, a mortgage, a lease or another instrument.

assumption of mortgage Acquiring title to property on which there is an existing mortgage and agreeing to be personally liable for the terms and conditions of the mortgage, including payments.

attachment The act of taking a person's property into legal custody by writ or another judicial order to hold it available for application to that person's debt to a creditor.

attorney's opinion of title An abstract of title that a lawyer has examined and has certified to be, in his or her opinion, an accurate statement of the facts concerning the property ownership.

automatic extension A clause in a listing agreement that states that the agreement will continue automatically for a certain period of time after its expiration date. In many states, use of this clause is discouraged or prohibited.

avulsion The sudden tearing away of land, as by earthquake, flood, volcanic action or the sudden change in the course of a stream.

balance The appraisal principle that states that the greatest value of a property will occur when the type and size of the improvements are proportional to each other as well as to the land.

balloon payment A final payment of a mortgage loan that is considerably larger than the required periodic payments because the loan amount was not fully amortized.

bargain and sale deed A deed that carries with it no warranties against liens or other encumbrances but that does imply that the grantor has the right to convey title. The grantor may add warranties to the deed at his or her discretion.

baseboard A board around the bottom of a wall perpendicular to the floor. Sometimes called *wains*, baseboards cover the gap between the floor and the wall, protecting the wall from scuffs and providing a decorative accent.

base line The main imaginary line running east and west and crossing a principal meridian at a definite point, used by surveyors for reference in locating and describing land under the rectangular (government) survey system of legal description.

basic form (HO-1) An insurance policy covering buildings and personal property against loss or damage from fire, lightning, removal, windstorm, hail, explosion, riot, smoke, vandalism and theft.

basis The financial interest that the Internal Revenue Service attributes to an owner of an investment property for the purpose of determining annual depreciation and gain or loss on the sale of the asset. If a property was acquired by purchase, the owner's basis is the cost of the property plus the value of any capital expenditures for improvements to the property, minus any depreciation allowable or actually taken. This new basis is called the *adjusted basis.*

bench mark A permanent reference mark or point established for use by surveyors in measuring differences in elevation.

beneficiary (1) The person for whom a trust operates or in whose behalf the income from a trust estate is drawn. (2) A lender in a deed of trust loan transaction.

bilateral contract *See* contract.

binder An agreement that may accompany an earnest money deposit for the purchase of real property as evidence of the purchaser's good faith and intent to complete the transaction.

blanket loan A mortgage covering more than one parcel of real estate, providing for each parcel's partial release from the mortgage lien upon repayment of a definite portion of the debt.

blockbusting The illegal practice of inducing homeowners to sell their properties by making representations regarding the entry or prospective entry of persons of a particular race or national origin into the neighborhood.

blue-sky laws A common name for those state and federal laws that regulate the registration and sale of investment securities.

boot Money or property given to make up any difference in value or equity between two properties in an *exchange.*

branch office A secondary place of business apart from the principal or main office from which real estate business is conducted. A branch office usually must be run by a licensed real estate broker working on behalf of the broker.

breach of contract The violation of any terms or conditions in a contract without legal excuse; for example, failure to make a payment when it is due.

broad form (HO-2) An insurance policy covering more perils than the *basic form.* This form also covers falling objects; weight of snow, ice or sleet; collapse of buildings; malfunctioning heating systems; accidental discharge of water or steam; and electrical currents that are artificially generated.

broker One who acts as an intermediary on behalf of others for a fee or commission.

brokerage The bringing together of parties interested in making a real estate transaction.

broker-in-charge Required for each brokerage firm and each branch office, the person responsible for displaying all licenses properly, notifying the Real Estate Commission of any change of business address or trade name, ensuring that all advertising is done properly, maintaining the trust account and trust account records properly, retaining and maintaining all real estate transaction records properly and supervising all salespeople associated with the firm or office.

buffer zone A strip of land, usually used as a park or designated for a similar use, separating land dedicated to one use from land dedicated to another use (e.g., residential from commercial).

building code An ordinance that specifies minimum standards of construction for buildings to protect public safety and health.

building permit Written governmental permission for the construction, alteration or demolition of an improvement, showing compliance with building codes and zoning ordinances.

bulk transfer *See* Uniform Commercial Code.

bundle of legal rights The concept of land ownership that includes *ownership of all legal rights to the land*—for example, possession, control within the law and enjoyment.

business cycle The upward and downward fluctuations in business activities generally characterized by four stages: expansion, recession, depression and revival.

buydown A financing technique used to reduce the monthly payments for the first few years of a loan. Funds in the form of discount points are given to the lender by the builder or seller to buy down or lower the effective interest rate paid by the buyer, thus reducing the monthly payments for a set time.

buyer-agency agreement A principal-agent relationship in which the broker is the agent for the buyer, with fiduciary responsibilities to the buyer. The broker represents the buyer under the law of agency.

capital gain The profit earned from the sale of an asset.

capitalization A mathematical process for estimating the value of a property using a proper rate of return on the investment and the annual net operating income expected to be produced by the property. The formula is expressed as

$$\frac{\text{Income}}{\text{Rate}} = \text{Value}$$

capitalization rate The rate of return a property will produce on the owner's investment.

cash flow The net spendable income from an investment, determined by deducting all operating and fixed expenses from the gross income. When expenses exceed income, a *negative cash flow* results.

cash rent In an agricultural lease, the amount of money given as rent to the landowner at the outset of the lease, as opposed to sharecropping.

caveat emptor A Latin phrase meaning "Let the buyer beware."

ceiling joist Attached to the top plate of a wall, these joists carry the weight of the roof.

certificate of reasonable value (CRV) A form indicating the appraised value of a property being financed with a VA loan.

certificate of sale The document generally given to the purchaser at a tax foreclosure sale. A certificate of sale does not convey title; normally, it is an instrument certifying that the holder received title to the property after the redemption period passed and that the holder paid the property taxes for that interim period.

certificate of title A statement of opinion on the status of the title to a parcel of real property based on an examination of specified public records.

chain of title The succession of conveyances, from some accepted starting point, whereby the present holder of real property derives title.

change The appraisal principle that holds that no physical or economic condition remains constant.

chattel *See* personal property.

Civil Rights Act of 1866 An act that prohibits racial discrimination in the sale and rental of housing.

closing statement A detailed cash accounting of a real estate transaction showing all cash received, all charges and credits made and all cash paid out in the transaction.

cloud on title Any document, claim, unreleased lien or encumbrance that may impair the title to real property or make the title doubtful; usually revealed by a title search and removed by either a quitclaim deed or suit to quiet title.

clustering The grouping of homesites within a subdivision on smaller lots than normal, with the remaining land used as common area.

COALD An acronym for the agent's specific duties in an agency relationship: care, obedience, accounting, loyalty and disclosure.

Code for Equal Opportunity Adopted by the National Association of REALTORS®, suggests conduct for REALTORS® belonging to member boards who have adopted it and wish to comply with both the letter and the spirit of the fair housing laws.

code of ethics A written system of standards for ethical conduct.

codicil A supplement or an addition to a will, executed with the same formalities as a will, that normally does not revoke the entire will.

coinsurance clause A clause in insurance policies covering real property that requires that the policyholder maintain fire insurance coverage generally equal to at least 80 percent of the property's actual replacement cost.

commingling The illegal act by a real estate broker of placing client or customer funds with personal funds. By law, brokers are required to maintain a separate *trust* or *escrow account* for other parties' funds held temporarily by the broker.

commission Payment to a broker for services rendered, as in the sale or purchase of real property; usually a percentage of the selling price of the property.

common elements Parts of a property that are necessary or convenient to the existence, maintenance and safety of a condominium or are normally in common use by all of the condominium residents. Each condominium owner has an undivided ownership interest in the common elements.

common law The body of law based on custom, usage and court decisions.

community property A system of property ownership based on the theory that each spouse has an equal interest in the property acquired by the efforts of either spouse during marriage. A holdover of Spanish law found predominantly in western states; the system was unknown under English common law.

comparable Property used in an appraisal report that is substantially equivalent to the subject property.

competition The appraisal principle that states that excess profits generate competition.

competitive market analysis (CMA) A comparison of the prices of recently sold homes that are similar to a listing seller's home in terms of location, style and amenities.

comprehensive plan *See* master plan.

condemnation A judicial or an administrative proceeding to exercise the power of eminent domain, through which a government agency takes private property for public use and compensates the owner.

conditional-use permit Written governmental permission allowing a use inconsistent with zoning but necessary for the common good, such as locating an emergency medical facility in a predominantly residential area.

condition subsequent May qualify a fee simple estate by dictating some action or activity that the new owner must not perform. The former owner retains a right of reentry, so if the condition is broken, the former owner can take repossession of the property.

condominium The absolute ownership of a unit in a multiunit building based on a legal description of the airspace the unit actually occupies, plus an undivided interest in the ownership of the common elements, which are owned jointly with the other condominium unit owners.

confession of judgment clause Permits judgment to be entered against a debtor without the creditor's having to institute legal proceedings.

conformity The appraisal principle that holds that the greater the similarity among properties in an area, the better they will hold their value.

Conner Act A North Carolina law that states that many types of real estate documents are not valid as to third parties unless the documents are recorded. These documents include deeds, mortgages, purchase contracts, installment land contracts, assignments, options, leases of three years or more, easements and restrictive covenants.

consideration (1) That received by the grantor in exchange for his or her deed. (2) Something of value that induces a person to enter into a contract.

construction loan *See* interim financing.

constructive eviction The actions of a landlord that so materially disturb or impair a tenant's enjoyment of the leased premises that the tenant is effectively forced to move out and terminate the lease without liability for any further rent.

constructive notice The notice given to the world by recorded documents. All people are charged with knowledge of such documents and their contents, whether or not they have actually examined them. Possession of property is also considered constructive notice that the person in possession has an interest in the property.

contingency A provision in a contract that requires a certain act to be done or a certain event to occur before the contract becomes binding.

contract A legally enforceable promise or set of promises that must be performed and for which, if a breach of the promise occurs, the law provides a remedy. A contract may be either *unilateral,* by which only one party is bound to act, or *bilateral,* by which all parties to the instrument are legally bound to act as prescribed.

contribution The appraisal principle that states that the value of any component of a property is what it gives to the value of the whole or what its absence detracts from that value.

conventional loan A loan that requires no insurance or guarantee.

conveyance A term used to refer to any document that transfers title to real property. The term is also used in describing the act of transferring.

cooperating broker *See* listing broker.

cooperative A residential multiunit building whose title is held by a trust or corporation that is owned by and operated for the benefit of persons living within the building, who are the beneficial owners of the trust or stockholders of the corporation, each possessing a proprietary lease.

co-ownership Title ownership held by two or more persons.

corporation An entity or organization, created by operation of law, whose rights of doing business are essentially the same as those of an individual. The entity has continuous existence until it is dissolved according to legal procedures.

correction lines Provisions in the rectangular survey (government survey) system made to compensate for the curvature of the earth's surface. Every fourth township line (at 24-mile intervals) is used as a correction line on which the intervals between the north and south range lines are remeasured and corrected to a full six miles.

cost approach The process of estimating the value of a property by adding to the estimated land value the appraiser's estimate of the reproduction or replacement cost of the building, less depreciation.

cost recovery An Internal Revenue Service term for *depreciation.*

counteroffer A new offer made in response to an offer received. It has the effect of rejecting the original offer, which cannot be accepted thereafter unless revived by the offeror.

covenant A written agreement between two or more parties in which a party or parties pledge to perform or not perform specified acts with regard to property; usually found in such real estate documents as deeds, mortgages, leases and contracts for deed.

covenant of quiet enjoyment The covenant implied by law by which a landlord guarantees that a tenant may take possession of leased premises and that the landlord will not interfere in the tenant's possession or use of the property.

credit On a closing statement, an amount entered in a person's favor—either an amount the party has paid or an amount for which the party must be reimbursed.

curtesy A life estate, usually a fractional interest, given by some states to the surviving husband in real estate owned by his deceased wife. Most states have abolished curtesy.

datum A horizontal plane from which heights and depths are measured.

debit On a closing statement, an amount charged; that is, an amount that the debited party must pay.

decedent A person who has died.

dedication The voluntary transfer of private property by its owner to the public for some public use, such as for streets or schools.

deed A written instrument that, when executed and delivered, conveys title to or an interest in real estate.

deed in lieu of foreclosure A deed given by the mortgagor to the mortgagee when the mortgagor is in default under the terms of the mortgage. This is a way for the mortgagor to avoid foreclosure.

deed in trust An instrument that grants a trustee under a land trust full power to sell, mortgage and subdivide a parcel of real estate. The beneficiary controls the trustee's use of these powers under the provisions of the trust agreement.

deed of trust *See* trust deed.

deed of trust lien *See* trust deed lien.

deed restriction Clause in a deed limiting the future uses of the property. Deed restrictions may impose a vast variety of limitations and conditions—for example, they may limit the density of buildings, dictate the types of structures that can be erected or prevent buildings from being used for specific purposes or even from being used at all.

default The nonperformance of a duty, whether arising under a contract or otherwise; failure to meet an obligation when due.

defeasance clause A clause used in leases and mortgages that cancels a specified right upon the occurrence of a certain condition, such as cancellation of a mortgage upon repayment of the mortgage loan.

defeasible fee estate An estate in which the holder has a fee simple title that may be divested upon the occurrence or nonoccurrence of a specified event. Two categories of defeasible fee estates exist: fee simple on condition precedent (fee simple determinable) and fee simple on condition subsequent.

deficiency judgment A personal judgment levied against the borrower when a foreclosure sale does not produce sufficient funds to pay the mortgage debt in full.

delivery and acceptance The actual delivery of a deed by a grantor and the actual or implied acceptance of the deed by the grantee.

demand The amount of goods people are willing and able to buy at a given price; often coupled with *supply.*

density zoning Zoning ordinances that restrict the maximum average number of houses per acre that may be built within a particular area, generally a subdivision.

Department of Housing and Urban Development (HUD) A federal cabinet department officially known as the U.S. Department of Housing and Urban Development; active in national housing programs. Among its many programs are urban renewal, public housing, model cities, rehabilitation loans, FHA subsidies and water and sewer grants.

depreciation (1) In appraisal, a loss of value in property due to any cause, including *physical deterioration, functional obsolescence* and *external obsolescence.* (2) In real estate investment, an expense deduction for tax purposes taken over the period of ownership of income property.

descent The acquisition of an estate by inheritance in which an heir succeeds to the property by operation of law.

developer A person or company that attempts to put land to its most profitable use through the construction of improvements.

devise A gift of real property by will. The donor is the devisor, and the recipient is the devisee.

discount point A unit of measurement used for various loan charges; one point equals 1 percent of the amount of the loan.

dominant tenement A property that includes in its ownership the appurtenant right to use an easement over another person's property for a specific purpose.

dormer A projection built out from the slope of a roof, used to house windows on the upper floor and to provide additional headroom. Common types of dormers are the gable dormer and the shed dormer.

dower The legal right or interest, recognized in some states, that a wife acquires in the property her husband held or acquired during their marriage. During the husband's lifetime, the right is only a possibility of an interest; upon his death, it can become an interest in land.

dual agency Representing both parties to a transaction. This is unethical unless both parties agree to it, and it is illegal in many states.

due-on-sale clause A provision in a mortgage that states that the entire balance of the note is immediately due and payable if the mortgagor transfers (sells) the property.

duress The unlawful constraint or action exercised on a person whereby the person is forced to perform an act against his or her will. A contract entered into under duress is voidable.

earnest money Money deposited by a buyer under the terms of a contract, to be forfeited if the buyer defaults but applied to the purchase price if the sale is closed.

easement A right to use the land of another for a specific purpose, such as for a right-of-way or utilities; an incorporeal interest in land.

easement by condemnation An easement created by the government or a government agency that has exercised its right under eminent domain.

easement by necessity An easement allowed by law as necessary for the full enjoyment of a parcel of real estate; for example, a right of ingress and egress over a grantor's land.

easement by prescription An easement acquired by continuous, open and hostile use of property for the period of time prescribed by state law.

easement in gross An easement that is not created for the benefit of any *land* owned by the owner of the easement but that attaches *personally to* the easement owner. For example, a right granted by Eleanor Franks to Joe Fish to use a portion of her property for the rest of his life would be an easement in gross.

economic life The number of years during which an improvement will add value to the land.

emblements Growing crops, such as grapes and corn, that are produced annually through labor and industry; also called *fructus industriales*.

eminent domain The right of a government or municipal quasi-public body to acquire property for public use through a court action called *condemnation*, in which the court decides that the use is a public use and determines the compensation to be paid to the owner.

employee Someone who works as a direct employee of an employer and has employee status. The employer is obligated to withhold income taxes and Social Security taxes from the compensation of the employee. *See also* independent contractor.

employment contract A document evidencing formal employment between employer and employee or between principal and agent. In the real estate business, this generally takes the form of a listing agreement or management agreement.

enabling acts State legislation that confers zoning powers on municipal governments.

encroachment A building or some portion of it—a wall or fence, for instance—that extends beyond the land of the owner and illegally intrudes on the land of an adjoining owner or on a street or an alley.

encumbrance Anything—such as a mortgage, tax or judgment lien; an easement; a restriction on the use of the land; or an outstanding dower right—that may diminish the value or use and enjoyment of a property.

environmental obsolescence *See* obsolescence.

Equal Credit Opportunity Act (ECOA) The federal law that prohibits discrimination in the extension of credit because of race, color, religion, national origin, sex, age or marital status.

equalization The raising or lowering of assessed values for tax purposes in a particular county or taxing district to make them equal to assessments in other counties or districts.

equalization factor A factor (number) by which the assessed value of a property is multiplied to arrive at a value for the property that is in line with statewide tax assessments. The *ad valorem tax* would be based on this adjusted value.

equitable lien *See* statutory lien.

equitable right of redemption The right of a defaulted property owner to recover the property prior to its sale by paying the appropriate fees and charges.

equitable title The interest held by a vendee under a contract for deed or an installment contract; the equitable right to obtain absolute ownership to property when legal title is held in another's name.

equity The interest or value that an owner has in property over and above any indebtedness.

erosion The gradual wearing away of land by water, wind and general weather conditions; the diminishing of property by the elements.

escheat The reversion of property to the state or county, as provided by state law, in cases where a decedent dies intestate without heirs capable of inheriting or when the property is abandoned.

escrow The closing of a transaction through a third party called an *escrow agent,* or *escrowee,* who receives certain funds and documents to be delivered upon the performance of certain conditions outlined in the escrow instructions.

escrow account The trust account established by a broker under the provisions of the license law for the purpose of holding funds on behalf of the broker's principal or some other person until the consummation or termination of a transaction.

escrow instructions A document that sets forth the duties of the escrow agent as well as the requirements and obligations of the parties when a transaction is closed through an escrow.

estate in land The degree, quantity, nature and extent of interest a person has in real property.

estate taxes Federal taxes on a decedent's real and personal property.

estate (tenancy) at sufferance The tenancy of a lessee who lawfully comes into possession of a landlord's real estate but who continues to occupy the premises improperly after his or her lease rights have expired.

estate (tenancy) at will An estate that gives the lessee the right to possession until the estate is terminated by either party; the term of this estate is indefinite.

estate (tenancy) for years An interest for a certain, exact period of time in property leased for a specified consideration.

estate (tenancy) from period to period An interest in leased property that continues from period to period—week to week, month to month or year to year.

estoppel A method of creating an agency relationship in which someone states incorrectly that another person is his or her agent and a third person relies on that representation.

estoppel certificate A document in which a borrower certifies the amount owed on a mortgage loan and the rate of interest.

estover Necessities that are allowed by the law; for example, the right of a life tenant to use some of the property's resources to pay for needed repairs.

ethics The system of moral principles and rules that becomes the standard for conduct.

eviction A legal process to oust a person from possession of real estate.

evidence of title Proof of ownership of property; commonly a certificate of title, an abstract of title with lawyer's opinion, or a Torrens registration certificate.

exchange A transaction in which all or part of the consideration is the transfer of *like-kind* property (such as real estate for real estate).

exclusive-agency listing A listing contract under which the owner appoints a real estate broker as his or her exclusive agent for a designated period of time to sell the property, on the owner's stated terms, for a commission. The owner reserves the right to sell without paying anyone a commission if he or she sells to a prospect who has not been introduced or claimed by the broker.

exclusive-right-to-sell listing A listing contract under which the owner appoints a real estate broker as his or her exclusive agent for a designated period of time to sell the property, on the owner's stated terms, and agrees to pay the broker a commission when the property is sold, whether by the broker, the owner or another broker.

executed contract A contract in which all parties have fulfilled their promises and thus performed the contract.

execution The signing and delivery of an instrument. Also, a legal order directing an official to enforce a judgment against the property of a debtor.

executory contract A contract under which something remains to be done by one or more of the parties.

express agreement An oral or a written contract in which the parties state the contract's terms and express their intentions in words.

express contract *See* express agreement.

external depreciation The reduction in a property's value caused by outside factors (those that are off the property).

external obsolescence *See* obsolescence.

Fair Housing Act The federal law that prohibits discrimination in housing based on race, color, religion, sex, handicap, familial status or national origin.

Fannie Mae A quasi-government agency established to purchase any kind of mortgage loans in the secondary mortgage market from the primary lenders.

Farmer's Home Administration (FmHA) An agency of the federal government that provides credit assistance to farmers and other individuals who live in rural areas.

Federal Deposit Insurance Corporation (FDIC) An independent federal agency that manages the insurance funds for deposits in commercial banks and savings and loan associations.

Federal Home Loan Mortgage Corporation (FHLMC) *See* Freddie Mac.

Federal National Mortgage Association (FNMA) *See* Fannie Mae.

Federal Reserve System The country's central banking system, which controls the nation's monetary policy by regulating the supply of money and interest rates.

fee simple absolute The maximum possible estate or right of ownership of real property, continuing forever.

fee simple defeasible *See* defeasible fee estate.

feudal system A system of ownership usually associated with precolonial England, in which the king or other sovereign is the source of all rights. The right to possess real property was granted by the sovereign to an individual as a life estate only. Upon the death of the individual, title passed back to the sovereign, not to the decedent's heirs.

FHA loan A loan insured by the Federal Housing Administration and made by an approved lender in accordance with the FHA's regulations.

fiduciary One in whom trust and confidence are placed; a reference to a broker employed under the terms of a listing contract or buyer agency agreement.

fiduciary relationship A relationship of trust and confidence, as between trustee and beneficiary, lawyer and client or principal and agent.

Financial Institutions Reform, Recovery and Enforcement Act (FIRREA) An act that restructured the savings and loan association regulatory system; enacted in response to the savings and loan crisis of the 1980s.

financing statement *See* Uniform Commercial Code.

fiscal policy The government's policy in regard to taxation and spending programs. The balance between these two areas determines the amount of money the government will withdraw from or feed into the economy, which can counter economic peaks and slumps.

fixture An item of personal property that has been converted to real property by being permanently affixed to the realty.

floor joist A horizontal board laid on edge, resting on the beams that provide the main support for the floor. The subflooring is nailed directly to the joists.

footing A concrete support under a foundation, chimney or column that usually rests on solid ground and is wider than the structure being supported. Footings are designed to distribute the weight of the structure over the ground.

foreclosure A legal procedure whereby property used as security for a debt is sold to satisfy the debt in the event of default in payment of the mortgage note or default of other terms in the mortgage document. The foreclosure procedure brings the rights of all parties to a conclusion and passes the title in the mortgaged property to either the holder of the mortgage or a third party who may purchase the realty at the foreclosure sale, free of all encumbrances affecting the property subsequent to the mortgage.

foundation wall The masonry or concrete wall below ground level that serves as the main support for the frame structure. Foundation walls form the side walls of the basement.

fractional section A parcel of land less than 160 acres, usually found at the edge of a rectangular survey.

fraud A deception intended to cause a person to give up property or a lawful right.

Freddie Mac A corporation established to purchase primarily conventional mortgage loans in the secondary mortgage market.

freehold estate An estate in land in which ownership is for an indeterminate length of time, in contrast to a *leasehold estate*.

front footage The measurement of a parcel of land by the number of feet of street or road frontage.

functional obsolescence A loss of value to an improvement to real estate arising from functional problems, often caused by age or poor design.

future interest A person's present right to an interest in real property that will not result in possession or enjoyment until some time in the future, such as a reversion or right of reentry.

gable The triangular portion of an end wall rising from the level top wall under the inverted *V* of a sloping roof that aids water drainage. A gable can be made of weatherboard, tile or masonry and can extend above the rafters.

gambrel A curb roof, having a steep slope and a flatter one above, as seen in Dutch colonial architecture.

gap A defect in the chain of title of a particular parcel of real estate; a missing document or conveyance that raises doubt as to the present ownership of the land.

general agent One who is authorized by a principal to represent the principal in a specific range of matters.

general lien The right of a creditor to have all of a debtor's property—both real and personal—sold to satisfy a debt.

general partnership *See* partnership.

general warranty deed A deed in which the grantor fully warrants good clear title to the premises. Used in most real estate deed transfers, a general warranty deed offers the greatest protection of any deed.

Ginnie Mae A government agency that plays an important role in the secondary mortgage market. It sells mortgage-backed securities that are backed by pools of FHA and VA loans.

girder A heavy wooden or steel beam supporting the floor joists and providing the main horizontal support for the floor.

government check The 24-mile-square parcels composed of 16 townships in the rectangular (government) survey system of legal description.

government lot A fractional section in the rectangular (government) survey system that is less than one quarter-section in area.

Government National Mortgage Association (GNMA) *See* Ginnie Mae.

government survey system *See* rectangular (government) survey system.

graduated-payment mortgage (GPM) A loan in which the monthly principal and interest payments increase by a certain percentage each year for a certain number of years and then level off for the remaining loan term.

grantee A person who receives a conveyance of real property from a grantor.

granting clause Words in a deed of conveyance that state the grantor's intention to convey the property at the present time. This clause is generally worded as "convey and warrant," "grant," "grant, bargain and sell" or the like.

grantor The person transferring title to or an interest in real property to a grantee.

gross income multiplier (GIM) A figure used as a multiplier of the gross annual income of a property to produce an estimate of the property's value.

gross lease A lease of property according to which a landlord pays all property charges regularly incurred through ownership, such as repairs, taxes, insurance and operating expenses. Most residential leases are gross leases.

gross rent multiplier (GRM) The figure used as a multiplier of the gross monthly income of a property to produce an estimate of the property's value.

ground lease A lease of land only, on which the tenant usually owns a building or is required to build as specified in the lease. Such leases are usually long-term net leases; the tenant's rights and obligations continue until the lease expires or is terminated through default.

growing-equity mortgage (GEM) A loan in which the monthly payments increase annually, with the increased amount being used to reduce directly the principal balance outstanding and thus shorten the overall term of the loan.

habendum clause That part of a deed beginning with the words "to have and to hold," following the granting clause and defining the extent of ownership the grantor is conveying.

heir One who might inherit or succeed to an interest in land under the state law of descent when the owner dies without leaving a valid will.

highest and best use The possible use of a property that would produce the greatest net income and thereby develop the highest value.

hip A pitched roof with sloping sides and ends.

holdover tenancy A tenancy whereby a lessee retains possession of leased property after the lease has expired and the landlord, by continuing to accept rent, agrees to the tenant's continued occupancy.

holographic will A will that is written, dated and signed in the testator's handwriting.

home equity loan A loan (sometimes called a *line of credit*) under which a property owner uses his or her residence as collateral and can then draw funds up to a prearranged amount against the property.

homeowner's insurance policy A standardized package insurance policy that covers a residential real estate owner against financial loss from fire, theft, public liability and other common risks.

homestead Land that is owned and occupied as the family home. In many states, a portion of the area or value of this land is protected or exempt from judgments for debts.

Housing and Community Development Act of 1974 An act that added gender as a protected class under the Fair Housing Act.

HVAC An acronym for heating, ventilation and air-conditioning.

hypothecate To pledge property as security for an obligation or a loan without giving up possession of it.

implied agreement A contract under which the agreement of the parties is demonstrated by their acts and conduct.

implied contract *See* implied agreement.

implied warranty of habitability A theory in landlord/tenant law in which the landlord renting residential property implies that the property is habitable and fit for its intended use.

improvement (1) Any structure, usually privately owned, erected on a site to enhance the value of the property—for example, a fence or a driveway. (2) A publicly owned structure added to or benefiting land, such as a curb, sidewalk, street or sewer.

income capitalization approach The process of estimating the value of an income-producing property through capitalization of the annual net income expected to be produced by the property during its remaining useful life.

incorporeal right A nonpossessory right in real estate; for example, an easement or a right-of-way.

independent contractor Someone who is retained to perform a certain act but who is subject to the control and direction of another only as to the end result and not as to the way in which the act is performed. Unlike an employee, an independent contractor pays all expenses and Social Security and income taxes and receives no employee benefits. Most real estate salespeople are independent contractors.

index method The appraisal method of estimating building costs by multiplying the original cost of the property by a percentage factor to adjust for current construction costs.

inflation The gradual reduction of the purchasing power of the dollar, usually related directly to the increases in the money supply by the federal government.

inheritance taxes State-imposed taxes on a decedent's real and personal property.

installment contract A contract for the sale of real estate whereby the purchase price is paid in periodic installments by the purchaser, who is in possession of the property even though title is retained by the seller until a future date, which may not be until final payment. Also called a *contract for deed* or *articles of agreement for warranty deed.*

installment sale A transaction in which the sales price is paid in two or more installments over two or more years. If the sale meets certain requirements, a taxpayer can postpone reporting such income until future years by paying tax each year only on the proceeds received that year.

insulation Pieces of plasterboard, asbestos sheeting, compressed wood-wool, fiberboard or other material placed between inner and outer surfaces, such as walls and ceilings, to protect the interior from heat loss. Insulation works by breaking up and dissipating air currents.

interest A charge made by a lender for the use of money.

interim financing A short-term loan usually made during the construction phase of a building project (in this case, often referred to as a *construction loan*).

Interstate Land Sales Full Disclosure Act A federal law that regulates the sale of certain real estate in interstate commerce.

intestate The condition of a property owner who dies without leaving a valid will. Title to the property will pass to the decedent's heirs as provided in the state law of descent.

intrinsic value An appraisal term referring to the value created by a person's personal preferences for a particular type of property.

investment Money directed toward the purchase, improvement and development of an asset in expectation of income or profits.

involuntary alienation *See* alienation.

involuntary lien A lien placed on property without the consent of the property owner.

joint tenancy Ownership of real estate between two or more parties who have been named in one conveyance as joint tenants. On the death of a joint tenant, the decedent's interest passes to the surviving joint tenant or tenants by the *right of survivorship.*

joint venture The joining of two or more people to conduct a specific business enterprise. A joint venture is similar to a partnership in that it must be created by agreement between the parties to share in the losses and profits of the venture. It is unlike a partnership in that the venture is for one specific project only, rather than for a continuing business relationship.

judgment The formal decision of a court upon the respective rights and claims of the parties to an action or a suit. After a judgment has been entered and recorded with the county recorder, it usually becomes a general lien on the property of the defendant.

judicial precedent In law, the requirements established by prior court decisions.

junior lien An obligation, such as a second mortgage, that is subordinate in right or lien priority to an existing lien on the same realty.

laches An equitable doctrine used by courts to bar a legal claim or prevent the assertion of a right because of undue delay or failure to assert the claim or right.

land The earth's surface, extending downward to the center of the earth and upward infinitely into space, including things permanently attached by nature, such as trees and water.

land contract *See* installment contract.

law of agency *See* agency.

lease A written or an oral contract between a landlord (the lessor) and a tenant (the lessee) that transfers the right to exclusive possession and use of the landlord's real property to the lessee for a specified period of time and for a stated consideration (rent). By state law, leases for longer than a certain period of time (generally one year) must be in writing to be enforceable.

leasehold estate A tenant's right to occupy real estate during the term of a lease, generally considered to be a personal property interest.

lease option A lease under which the tenant has the right to purchase the property either during the lease term or at its end.

lease purchase The purchase of real property, the consummation of which is preceded by a lease, usually long-term; typically done for tax or financing purposes.

legacy A disposition of money or personal property by will.

legal description A description of a specific parcel of real estate complete enough for an independent surveyor to locate and identify it.

legally competent parties People who are recognized by law as being able to contract with others; those of legal age and sound mind.

lessee *See* lease.

lessor *See* lease.

leverage The use of borrowed money to finance an investment.

levy To assess; to seize or collect. To levy a tax is to assess a property and set the rate of taxation. To levy an execution is to officially seize the property of a person to satisfy an obligation.

liability coverage Insurance providing protection of the property owner against financial claims of others.

license (1) A privilege or right granted to a person by a state to operate as a real estate broker or salesperson. (2) The revocable permission for a temporary use of land—a personal right that cannot be sold.

lien A right given by law to certain creditors to have their debts paid out of the property of a defaulting debtor, usually by means of a court sale.

lien theory Some states interpret a mortgage as being purely a lien on real property. The mortgagee thus has no right of possession but must foreclose the lien and sell the property if the mortgagor defaults.

life cycle costing In property management, comparing one type of equipment with another based on both purchase cost and operating cost over its expected useful lifetime.

life estate An interest in real or personal property that is limited in duration to the lifetime of its owner or some other designated person or persons.

life tenant A person in possession of a life estate.

limited partnership *See* partnership.

liquidated damages An amount predetermined by the parties to a contract as the total compensation to an injured party should the other party breach the contract.

liquidity The ability to sell an asset and convert it into cash, at a price close to its true value, in a short period of time.

lis pendens A recorded legal document giving constructive notice that an action affecting a particular property has been filed in either a state or a federal court.

listing agreement A contract between an owner (as principal) and a real estate broker (as agent) by which the broker is employed as agent to find a buyer for the owner's real estate on the owner's terms, for which service the owner agrees to pay a commission.

listing broker The broker in a multiple-listing situation from whose office a listing agreement is initiated, as opposed to the *cooperating broker*, from whose office negotiations leading up to a sale are initiated. The listing broker and the cooperating broker may be the same person.

littoral rights (1) A landowner's claim to use water in large navigable lakes and oceans adjacent to his or her property. (2) The ownership rights to land bordering these bodies of water up to the high-water mark.

loan origination fee A fee charged to the borrower by the lender for making a mortgage loan. The fee is usually computed as a percentage of the loan amount.

loan-to-value ratio The relationship between the amount of the mortgage loan and the value of the real estate being pledged as collateral.

lot-and-block (recorded plat) system A method of describing real property that identifies a parcel of land by reference to lot and block numbers within a subdivision, as specified on a recorded subdivision plat.

management agreement A contract between the owner of income property and a management firm or an individual property manager that outlines the scope of the manager's authority.

mansard An architectural style in which the top floor or floors of a structure are designed to appear to be the roof. Such a roof has two slopes on each of the four sides of the building, with the upper slope less steeply inclined.

market A place where goods can be bought and sold and a price established.

marketable title A good or clear title, reasonably free from the risk of litigation over possible defects.

Marketable Title Act Provides that if a chain of title can be traced back for 30 years without a problem, it becomes a marketable title. The act is designed to eliminate obsolete defects in a chain of title.

market value The most probable price property will bring in an arm's-length transaction under normal conditions on the open market.

master plan A comprehensive plan to guide the long-term physical development of a particular area.

mechanic's lien A statutory lien created in favor of contractors, laborers and materialmen who have performed work or furnished materials in the erection or repair of a building.

meridian One of a set of imaginary lines running north and south and crossing a base line at a definite point, used in the rectangular (government) survey system of property description.

metes-and-bounds description A legal description of a parcel of land that begins at a well-marked point and follows the boundaries, using directions and distances around the tract, back to the place of beginning.

mill One-tenth of one cent. Some states use a mill rate to compute real estate taxes; for example, a rate of 52 mills would be $.052 tax for each dollar of assessed valuation of a property.

minor Someone who has not reached the age of majority and therefore does not have legal capacity to transfer title to real property.

monetary policy Governmental regulation of the amount of money in circulation through such institutions as the Federal Reserve Board.

month-to-month tenancy A periodic tenancy under which the tenant rents for one month at a time. In the absence of a rental agreement (oral or written), a tenancy is generally considered to be month to month.

monument A fixed natural or artificial object used to establish real estate boundaries for a metes-and-bounds description.

mortgage A conditional transfer or pledge of real estate as security for the payment of a debt. Also, the document creating a mortgage lien.

mortgage banker A mortgage loan company that originates, services and sells loans to investors.

mortgage broker An agent of a lender who brings the lender and borrower together. The broker receives a fee for this service.

mortgagee A lender in a mortgage loan transaction.

mortgage lien A lien or charge on the property of a mortgagor that secures the underlying debt obligations.

mortgagor A borrower in a mortgage loan transaction.

multiperil policy An insurance policy that offers protection from a range of potential perils, such as those of fire, hazard, public liability and casualty.

multiple-listing clause A provision in an exclusive listing for the authority and obligation on the part of the listing broker to distribute the listing to other brokers in the multiple-listing organization.

multiple-listing service (MLS) A marketing organization composed of member brokers who agree to share their listing agreements with one another in the hope of procuring ready, willing and able buyers for their properties more quickly than they could on their own. Most MLSs accept exclusive-right-to-sell or exclusive-agency listings from their member brokers.

negotiable instrument A written promise or order to pay a specific sum of money that may be transferred by endorsement or delivery. The transferee then has the original payee's right to payment.

net lease A lease requiring that the tenant pay not only rent but also costs incurred in maintaining the property, including taxes, insurance, utilities and repairs.

net listing A listing based on the net price the seller will receive if the property is sold. Under a net listing, the broker can offer the property for sale at the highest price obtainable to increase the commission. This type of listing is illegal in many states.

net operating income (NOI) The income projected for an income-producing property after deducting losses for vacancy and collection and operating expenses.

nonconforming use A use of property that is permitted to continue after a zoning ordinance prohibiting it has been established for the area.

nonfreehold estate *See* leasehold estate.

nonhomogeneity A lack of uniformity; dissimilarity. Because no two parcels of land are exactly alike, real estate is said to be *nonhomogeneous.*

North Carolina Condominium Act of 1986 Specifies that a condominium is created and established when the developer of the property executes and records a declaration of its creation in the county where the property is located. The declaration must include any covenants, conditions or restrictions on the use of the property. Other requirements include disclosure and other consumer protection measures in connection with new residential condominium unit sales.

North Carolina Fair Housing Act of 1983 State fair housing law containing similar prohibitions to those of the federal fair housing law. Unlike the federal law, however, the North Carolina law does not exempt owners who are selling their own property, and it does exempt the rental of a unit in a one-unit to four-unit residential building if the owner or one of the owner's family members lives in one of the units.

North Carolina Human Relations Council The state agency responsible for enforcing the North Carolina Fair Housing Act of 1983.

North Carolina Residential Rental Agreements Act The state act that makes the obligations of the landlord and the tenant mutually dependent. If either the landlord or the tenant fails to fulfill a duty, the other party is no longer responsible for fulfilling his or her equivalent duty.

North Carolina Tenant Security Deposit Act The state act that regulates the amount of money that can be required as a security deposit and what the landlord can do with that deposit. The amount of the deposit depends on the term of the tenancy.

North Carolina Time Share Act The portion of North Carolina real estate law that defines time-shares and regulates their development and sales.

note *See* promissory note.

novation Substituting a new obligation for an old one or substituting new parties to an existing obligation.

nuncupative will An oral will declared by the testator in his or her final illness, made before witnesses and afterward reduced to writing.

obsolescence The loss of value due to factors that are outmoded or less useful. Obsolescence may be functional or economic.

occupancy permit A permit issued by the appropriate local governing body to establish that the property is suitable for habitation by meeting certain safety and health standards.

offer and acceptance Two essential components of a valid contract; a "meeting of the minds."

offeror/offeree The person who makes the offer is the offeror. The person to whom the offer is made is the offeree.

Office of Equal Opportunity (OEO) The federal agency under the direction of the secretary of the Department of Housing and Urban Development, which is in charge of administering the federal Fair Housing Act.

Office of Thrift Supervision (OTS) Monitors and regulates the savings and loan industry. OTS was created by the Financial Institutions Reform, Recovery and Enforcement Act (FIRREA).

open-end loan A mortgage loan that is expandable by increments up to a maximum dollar amount, the full loan being secured by the same original mortgage.

open listing A listing contract under which the broker's commission is contingent on the broker's producing a ready, willing and able buyer before the property is sold by the seller or another broker.

option An agreement to keep open for a set period an offer to sell or purchase property.

option listing A listing with a provision that gives the listing broker the right to purchase the listed property.

ostensible agency A form of implied agency relationship created by the actions of the parties involved rather than by written agreement or document.

package loan A real estate loan used to finance the purchase of both real property and personal property, such as in the purchase of a new home that includes carpeting, window coverings and major appliances.

parol evidence rule A rule of evidence providing that a written agreement is the final expression of the agreement of the parties, not to be varied or contradicted by prior or contemporaneous oral or written negotiations.

participation mortgage A mortgage loan wherein the lender has a partial equity interest in the property or receives a portion of the income from the property.

partition The division of cotenants' interests in real property when all parties do not voluntarily agree to terminate the co-ownership; takes place through court procedures.

partnership An association of two or more individuals who carry on a continuing business for profit as co-owners. Under the law, a partnership is regarded as a group of individuals rather than as a single entity. A *general partnership* is a typical form of joint venture in which each general partner shares in the administration, profits and losses of the operation. A *limited partnership* is a business arrangement whereby the operation is administered by one or more general partners and funded, by and large, by limited or silent partners, who are by law responsible for losses only to the extent of their investments.

party wall A wall that is located on or at a boundary line between two adjoining parcels of land and is used or is intended to be used by the owners of both properties.

patent A grant or franchise of land from the U.S. government.

payment cap The limit on the amount the monthly payment can be increased on an adjustable-rate mortgage when the interest rate is adjusted.

payoff statement *See* reduction certificate.

percentage lease A lease, commonly used for commercial property, whose rental is based on the tenant's gross sales at the premises. It usually stipulates a base monthly rental plus a percentage of any gross sales above a certain amount.

percolation test A test of the soil to determine whether it will absorb and drain water adequately to use a septic system for sewage disposal.

periodic estate (tenancy) *See* estate (tenancy) from period to period.

personal property Items, called *chattels*, that do not fit into the definition of real property; movable objects.

physical deterioration A reduction in a property's value resulting from a decline in physical condition; can be caused by action of the elements or by ordinary wear and tear.

pier A column, usually of steel-reinforced concrete. Piers are evenly spaced under a structure to support the weight. May also refer to the part of the wall between the windows or other openings that bears the wall weight.

planned unit development (PUD) A planned combination of diverse land uses, such as housing, recreation and shopping, in one contained development or subdivision.

plat map A map of a town, section or subdivision indicating the location and boundaries of individual properties.

plottage The increase in value or utility resulting from the consolidation (assemblage) of two or more adjacent lots into one larger lot.

point of beginning (POB) In a metes-and-bounds legal description, the starting point of the survey, situated at one corner of the parcel. All metes-and-bounds descriptions must follow the boundaries of the parcel back to the point of beginning.

police power The government's right to impose laws, statutes and ordinances, including zoning ordinances and building codes, to protect the public health, safety and welfare.

power of attorney A written instrument authorizing a person, the attorney-in-fact, to act as agent for another person to the extent indicated in the instrument.

prepaid item On a closing statement, an item that has been paid in advance by the seller, such as an insurance premium and some real estate taxes, for which he or she must be reimbursed by the buyer.

prepayment penalty A charge imposed on a borrower who pays off the loan principal early. This penalty compensates the lender for interest and other charges that would otherwise be lost.

price fixing *See* antitrust laws.

primary mortgage insurance (PMI) Insurance coverage used for obtaining conventional loans with higher than normal loan-to-value ratios.

primary mortgage market The mortgage market in which loans are originated, consisting of lenders such as commercial banks, savings and loan associations and mutual savings banks.

principal (1) A sum loaned or employed as a fund or an investment, as distinguished from its income or profits. (2) The original amount (as in a loan) of the total due and payable at a certain date. (3) A main party to a transaction—the person for whom the agent works.

principal meridian The main imaginary line running north and south and crossing a base line at a definite point, used by surveyors for reference in locating and describing land under the rectangular (government) survey system of legal description.

prior appropriation A concept of water ownership in which the landowner's right to use available water is based on a government-administered permit system.

priority The order of position or time. The priority of liens is generally determined by the chronological order in which the lien documents are recorded. Tax liens, however, have priority even over previously recorded liens.

private mortgage insurance (PMI) Insurance provided by a private carrier that protects a lender against a loss in the event of a foreclosure and deficiency.

probate A legal process by which a court determines who will inherit a decedent's property and what the estate's assets are.

procuring cause The effort that brings about the desired result. Under an open listing, the broker who is the procuring cause of the sale receives the commission.

progression An appraisal principle that states that between dissimilar properties, the value of the lesser-quality property is favorably affected by the presence of the better quality property.

promissory note A financing instrument that states the terms of the underlying obligation, is signed by its maker and is negotiable (transferable to a third party).

property insurance A policy that provides property owner coverage for the basic structure on that property.

property manager Someone who manages real estate for another person for compensation. Duties include collecting rents, maintaining the property and keeping up all accounting.

property reports The mandatory federal and state documents compiled by subdividers and developers to provide potential purchasers with facts about a property prior to its purchase.

proprietary lease A lease given by the corporation that owns a cooperative apartment building to the shareholder for the shareholder's right as a tenant to an individual apartment.

prorations Expenses, either prepaid or paid in arrears, that are divided or distributed between buyer and seller at the closing.

protected class Any group of people designated as such by the Department of Housing and Urban Development (HUD) in consideration of federal and state civil rights legislation; currently includes ethnic minorities, women, religious groups, the handicapped and others.

public offering statement The document all prospective time-share purchasers must receive before signing a sales contract. The statement must disclose all material facts about the property, as required by the state.

puffing Exaggerated or superlative comments or opinions.

pur autre vie "For the life of another." A life estate pur autre vie is a life estate that is measured by the life of a person other than the grantee.

purchase-money mortgage (PMM) A note secured by a mortgage or deed of trust given by a buyer, as borrower, to a seller, as lender, as part of the purchase price of the real estate.

pyramiding The process of acquiring additional properties by refinancing properties already owned and investing the loan proceeds in additional properties.

quantity-survey method The appraisal method of estimating building costs by calculating the cost of all of the physical components in the improvements, adding the cost to assemble them and then including the indirect costs associated with such construction.

quiet title A court action to remove a cloud on the title.

quitclaim deed A conveyance by which the grantor transfers whatever interest he or she has in the real estate, without warranties or obligations.

rafter One of a series of sloping beams that extends from the exterior wall to a center ridgeboard and provides the main support for the roof.

range A strip of land six miles wide, extending north and south and numbered east and west according to its distance from the principal meridian in the rectangular (government) survey system of legal description.

rate cap The limit on the amount the interest rate can be increased at each adjustment period in an adjustable-rate loan. The cap may also set the maximum interest rate that can be charged during the life of the loan.

ratification A method of creating an agency relationship in which the principal accepts the conduct of someone who acted without prior authorization as the principal's agent.

ready, willing and able buyer One who is prepared to buy property on the seller's terms and is ready to take positive steps to consummate the transaction.

real estate Land; a portion of the earth's surface extending downward to the center of the earth and upward infinitely into space, including all things permanently attached to it, whether naturally or artificially.

Real Estate Commission The state governmental agency whose primary duties include making rules and regulations to protect the general public involved in real estate transactions, granting licenses to real estate brokers and salespeople and suspending or revoking licenses for cause.

real estate investment syndicate *See* syndicate.

real estate investment trust (REIT) Trust ownership of real estate by a group of individuals who purchase certificates of ownership in the trust, which in turn invests the money in real property and distributes the profits back to the investors free of corporate income tax.

real estate license law The state law enacted to protect the public from fraud, dishonesty and incompetence in the purchase and sale of real estate.

real estate mortgage investment conduit (REMIC) A tax entity that issues multiple classes of investor interests (securities) backed by a pool of mortgages.

real estate recovery fund A fund established in some states from real estate license revenues to cover claims of aggrieved parties who have suffered monetary damage through the actions of a real estate licensee.

Real Estate Settlement Procedures Act (RESPA) The federal law that requires certain disclosures to consumers about mortgage loan settlements.

The law also prohibits the payment or receipt of kickbacks and certain kinds of referral fees.

real property The interests, benefits and rights inherent in real estate ownership.

REALTOR® A registered trademark term reserved for the sole use of active members of local REALTORS® boards affiliated with the National Association of REALTORS®.

reconciliation The final step in the appraisal process, in which the appraiser combines the estimates of value received from the sales comparison, cost and income capitalization approaches to arrive at a final estimate of market value for the subject property.

reconveyance deed A deed used by a trustee under a deed of trust to return title to the trustor.

recording The act of entering or recording documents affecting or conveying interests in real estate in the recorder's office established in each county. Until it is recorded, a deed or mortgage ordinarily is not effective against subsequent purchasers or mortgagees.

rectangular (government) survey system A system established in 1785 by the federal government, providing for surveying and describing land by reference to principal meridians and base lines.

redemption The right of a defaulted property owner to recover his or her property by curing the default.

redemption period A period of time established by state law during which a property owner has the right to redeem his or her real estate from a foreclosure or tax sale by paying the sales price, interest and costs. Many states do not have mortgage redemption laws.

redlining The illegal practice of a lending institution denying loans or restricting their number for certain areas of a community.

reduction certificate (payoff statement) The document signed by a lender indicating the amount required to pay a loan balance in full and satisfy the debt; used in the settlement process to protect both the seller's and the buyer's interests.

reference to recorded plat *See* lot-and-block (recorded plat) system.

registration certificate The document that developers of time-shares in North Carolina must obtain from the Real Estate Commission before they can offer a project's time-shares for sale to the public.

regression An appraisal principle that states that between dissimilar properties, the value of the better quality property is affected adversely by the presence of the lesser quality property.

Regulation Z Implements the Truth-in-Lending Act requiring credit institutions to inform borrowers of the true cost of obtaining credit.

release deed A document, also known as a *deed of reconveyance*, that transfers all rights given a trustee under a deed of trust loan back to the grantor after the loan has been fully repaid.

remainder interest The remnant of an estate that has been conveyed, to take effect and be enjoyed after the termination of a prior estate, such as when an owner conveys a life estate to one party and the remainder to another.

rent A fixed, periodic payment made by a tenant of a property to the owner for possession and use, usually by prior agreement of the parties.

rent schedule A statement of proposed rental rates, determined by the owner or the property manager or both, based on a building's estimated expenses, market supply and demand and the owner's long-range goals for the property.

replacement cost The construction cost at current prices of a property that is not necessarily an exact duplicate of the subject property but serves the same purpose or function as the original.

reproduction cost The construction cost at current prices of an exact duplicate of the subject property.

rescission The legal remedy of canceling, terminating or annulling a contract and restoring the parties to their original positions. Contracts may be rescinded due to mistake, fraud or misrepresentation. There is no need to show any money damage.

Resolution Trust Corporation The organization created by the Financial Institutions Reform, Recovery and Enforcement Act (FIRREA) to liquidate the assets of failed savings and loan associations.

restrictive covenant A clause in a deed that limits the way the real estate ownership may be used.

revenue stamps *See* transfer tax.

reverse-annuity mortgage (RAM) A loan under which the homeowner receives monthly payments based on his or her accumulated equity rather than a lump sum. The loan must be repaid at a prearranged date or upon the death of the owner or the sale of the property.

reversionary interest The remnant of an estate that the grantor holds after granting a life estate to another person.

reversionary right The return of the rights of possession and quiet enjoyment to the lessor at the expiration of a lease.

ridgeboard A heavy horizontal board, set on edge at the apex of the roof, to which the rafters are attached.

right of first refusal The right of a person to have the first opportunity to either purchase or lease real property. In a lease situation, a right of first refusal might give the tenant the right either to purchase the property, if offered for sale, or to renew the lease or lease adjoining space. In some condominiums, the association of apartment owners retains the right of first refusal on any sale of a unit.

right of survivorship *See* joint tenancy.

right-of-way The right given by one landowner to another to pass over the land, construct a roadway or use the land as a pathway, without actually transferring ownership.

riparian rights An owner's rights in land that borders on or includes a stream, river or lake. These rights include access to and use of the water.

risk management The evaluation and selection of appropriate property and other insurance.

roofing felt Sheets of flat or other close-woven, heavy material placed on top of the roof boards to insulate and waterproof the roof.

roofing shingle Thin, small sheet of wood, asbestos, fiberglass, slate, metal, clay or other material used as the outer covering for a roof. Shingles are laid in overlapping rows to completely cover the roof surface. Shingles are sometimes used as an outer covering for exterior walls.

rules and regulations Real estate licensing authority orders that govern licensees' activities. They usually have the same force and effect as statutory law.

R-value The insulation value of materials. The higher the *R-value*, the more resistant the material is to the transfer of heat.

sale and leaseback A transaction in which an owner sells his or her improved property and, as part of the same transaction, signs a long-term lease to remain in possession of the premises.

sales comparison approach The process of estimating the value of a property by examining and comparing actual sales of comparable properties.

salesperson A person who performs real estate activities while employed by or associated with a licensed real estate broker.

satisfaction of mortgage A document acknowledging the payment of a mortgage debt.

secondary mortgage market A market for the purchase and sale of existing mortgages, designed to provide greater liquidity for mortgages; also called the *secondary money market*. Mortgages are first originated in the *primary mortgage market*.

section A portion of township under the rectangular (government) survey system. A township is divided into 36 sections, numbered 1 through 36. A section is a square with mile-long sides and an area of one square mile, or 640 acres.

security agreement *See* Uniform Commercial Code.

security deposit A payment by a tenant, held by the landlord during the lease term and kept (wholly or partially) on default or destruction of the premises by the tenant.

separate property Under community property law, property owned solely by either spouse before the marriage, acquired by gift or inheritance after the marriage or purchased with separate funds after the marriage.

servient tenement Land on which an easement exists in favor of an adjacent property (called a *dominant estate*); also called a *servient estate*.

setback The amount of space local zoning regulations require between a lot line and a building line.

severalty The ownership of real property by one person only; also called *sole ownership*.

severance Changing an item of real estate to personal property by detaching it from the land; for example, cutting down a tree.

sharecropping In an agricultural lease, the agreement between the landowner and the tenant farmer to split the crop or the profit from its sale, actually sharing the crop.

shared-appreciation mortgage (SAM) A mortgage loan in which the lender, in exchange for a loan with a favorable interest rate, participates in the profits (if any) the borrower receives when the property is eventually sold.

siding Boards nailed horizontally to the vertical studs, with or without intervening sheathing, to form the exposed surface of the outside walls of the building. Siding may be made of wood, metal or masonry sheets.

sill The lowest horizontal member of the house frame, which rests atop the foundation wall and forms a base for the studs. The term can also refer to the lowest horizontal member in the frame for a window or door.

situs The personal preference of people for one area over another, not necessarily based on objective facts and knowledge.

slab A flat, horizontal reinforced concrete area, usually the interior floor of a building but also an exterior or a roof area.

sole plate That which connects the studs to the flooring.

special agent One who is authorized by a principal to perform a single act or transaction. A real estate broker is usually a special agent authorized to find a ready, willing and able buyer for a particular property.

special assessment A tax or levy customarily imposed against only those specific parcels of real estate that will benefit from a proposed public improvement like a street or sewer.

special warranty deed A deed in which the grantor warrants, or guarantees, the title only against defects arising during the period of his or her tenure and ownership of the property and not against defects existing before that time, generally using the language "by, through or under the grantor but not otherwise."

specific lien A lien affecting or attaching only to a certain, specific parcel of land or piece of property.

specific performance A legal action to compel a party to carry out the terms of a contract.

split-level Usually a house in which two or more floors are located directly above one another, and one or more additional floors, adjacent to them, are placed at a different level.

square-foot method The appraisal method of estimating building costs by multiplying the number of square feet in the improvements being appraised by the cost per square foot for recently constructed similar improvements.

statute of frauds That part of a state law that requires that certain instruments, such as deeds, real estate sales contracts and certain leases, be in writing to be legally enforceable.

statute of limitations That law pertaining to the period of time within which certain actions must be brought to court.

statutory lien A lien imposed on property by statute—a tax lien, for example—in contrast to an *equitable lien*, which arises out of common law.

statutory redemption The right of a defaulted property owner to recover the property after its sale by paying the appropriate fees and charges.

steering The illegal practice of channeling home seekers to particular areas, either to maintain the homogeneity of an area or to change the character of an area, which limits their choices of where they can live.

stigmatized property Property regarded as undesirable because of events that occurred there; also called *psychologically impacted property*. Some conditions that typically stigmatize a property are murder, gang-related activity, proximity to a nuclear plant and even the alleged presence of ghosts.

straight-line method A method of calculating depreciation for tax purposes, computed by dividing the adjusted basis of a property by the estimated number of years of remaining useful life.

straight (term) loan A loan in which only interest is paid during the term of the loan, with the entire principal amount due with the final interest payment.

subagent One who is employed by a person already acting as an agent; typically a reference to a salesperson licensed under a broker (agent) who is employed under the terms of a listing agreement.

subdivider One who buys undeveloped land; divides it into smaller, usable lots; and sells the lots to potential users.

subdivision A tract of land divided by the owner, known as the subdivider, into blocks, building lots and streets according to a recorded subdivision plat, which must comply with local ordinances and regulations.

subdivision and development ordinances Municipal ordinances that establish requirements for subdivisions and development.

subdivision plat *See* plat map.

subflooring Boards or plywood sheets nailed directly to the floor joists, serving as a base for the finish flooring. Subflooring is usually made of rough boards, although some houses have concrete subflooring.

sublease *See* subletting.

subletting The leasing of premises by a lessee to a third party for part of the lessee's remaining term. *See also* assignment.

subordination Relegation to a lesser position, usually in respect to a right or security.

subordination agreement A written agreement between holders of liens on a property that changes the priority of mortgage, judgment and other liens under certain circumstances.

subrogation The substitution of one creditor for another, with the substituted party succeeding to the legal rights and claims of the original claimant. Subrogation is used by title insurers to acquire from the injured party rights to sue to recover any claims they have paid.

substitution An appraisal principle that states that the maximum value of a property tends to be set by the cost of purchasing an equally desirable and valuable substitute property, assuming that no costly delay is encountered in making the substitution.

subsurface rights Ownership rights in a parcel of real estate to the water, minerals, gas, oil and so forth that lie beneath the surface of the property.

suit for possession A court suit initiated by a landlord to evict a tenant from leased premises after the tenant has breached one of the terms of the lease or has held possession of the property after the lease's expiration.

suit to quiet title A court action intended to establish or settle the title to a particular property, especially when a cloud on the title exists.

supply The amount of goods available in the market to be sold at a given price. The term is often coupled with *demand.*

supply and demand The appraisal principle that follows the interrelationship of the supply of and demand for real estate. As appraising is based on economic concepts, this principle recognizes that real property is subject to the influences of the marketplace, as is any other commodity.

surety bond An agreement by an insurance or a bonding company to be responsible for certain possible defaults, debts or obligations contracted for by an insured party; in essence, a policy insuring one's personal or financial integrity. In the real estate business, a surety bond is generally used to ensure that a particular project will be completed at a certain date or that a contract will be performed as stated.

surface rights Ownership rights in a parcel of real estate that are limited to the surface of the property and do not include the air above it (*air rights*) or the minerals below the surface (*subsurface rights*).

survey The process by which boundaries are measured and land areas are determined; the on-site measurement of lot lines, dimensions and position of a house on a lot, including the determination of any existing encroachments or easements.

syndicate A combination of people or firms formed to accomplish a business venture of mutual interest by pooling resources. In a *real estate investment syndicate,* the parties own or develop property, with the main profit generally arising from the sale of the property.

tacking Adding or combining successive periods of continuous occupation of real property by adverse possessors. This concept enables someone who has not been in possession for the entire statutory period to establish a claim of adverse possession.

taxation The process by which a government or municipal quasi-public body raises monies to fund its operation.

tax credit An amount by which tax owed is reduced directly.

tax deed An instrument, similar to a certificate of sale, given to a purchaser at a tax sale. *See also* certificate of sale.

tax lien A charge against property, created by operation of law. Tax liens and assessments take priority over all other liens.

tax sale A court-ordered sale of real property to raise money to cover delinquent taxes.

tenancy by the entirety The joint ownership, recognized in some states, of property acquired by husband and wife during marriage. Upon the death of one spouse, the survivor becomes the owner of the property.

tenancy in common A form of co-ownership by which each owner holds an undivided interest in real property as if he or she were sole owner. Each individual owner has the right to partition. Unlike joint tenants, tenants in common have the right of inheritance.

tenant One who holds or possesses lands or tenements by any kind of right or title.

tenant improvement Alteration to the interior of a building to meet the functional demands of the tenant.

testate Having made and left a valid will.

testator A person who has made a valid will. A woman often is referred to as a *testatrix*, although testator can be used for either gender.

tier (township strip) A strip of land six miles wide, extending east and west and numbered north and south according to its distance from the base line in the rectangular (government) survey system of legal description.

time is of the essence A phrase in a contract that requires the performance of a certain act within a stated period of time.

time-share A form of ownership interest that may include an estate interest in property and that allows use of the property for a fixed or variable time period.

title (1) The right to or ownership of land. (2) The evidence of ownership of land.

title insurance A policy insuring the owner or mortgagee against loss by reason of defects in the title to a parcel of real estate, other than encumbrances, defects and matters specifically excluded by the policy.

title search The examination of public records relating to real estate to determine the current state of ownership.

title theory Describing those states that interpret a mortgage to mean that the lender is the owner of mortgaged land. Upon full payment of the mortgage debt, the borrower becomes the landowner.

top plate That which connects the stud to the ceiling framing.

Torrens system A method of evidencing title by registration with the proper public authority, generally called the *registrar*, named for its founder, Sir Robert Torrens.

township The principal unit of the rectangular (government) survey system. A township is a square with six-mile sides and an area of 36 square miles.

township strip *See* tier.

trade fixture An article installed by a tenant under the terms of a lease and removable by the tenant before the lease expires.

transfer tax Tax stamps required to be affixed to a deed by state or local law.

trust A fiduciary arrangement whereby property is conveyed to a person or an institution, called a *trustee*, to be held and administered on behalf of another person, called a *beneficiary*. The one who conveys the trust is called the *trustor*.

trust deed An instrument used to create a mortgage lien by which the borrower conveys title to a trustee, who holds it as security for the benefit of the note holder (the lender); also called a *deed of trust*.

trust deed lien A lien on the property of a trustor that secures a deed of trust loan.

trustee The holder of bare legal title in a deed of trust loan transaction.

trustee's deed A deed executed by a trustee conveying land held in a trust.

trust funds Those monies received by a real estate licensee while acting as an agent in a real estate transaction. Generally, trust funds include earnest money deposits, down payments, tenant security deposits, rents and monies received from final settlements.

trustor A borrower in a deed of trust loan transaction.

Truth-in-Lending Act *See* Regulation Z.

undivided interest *See* tenancy in common.

unenforceable contract A contract that has all the elements of a valid contract, yet neither party can sue the other to force performance of it. For example, an unsigned contract is generally unenforceable.

Uniform Commercial Code A codification of commercial law, adopted in most states, that attempts to make uniform all laws relating to commercial transactions, including chattel mortgages and bulk transfers. Security interests in chattels are created by an instrument known as a *security agreement.* To give notice of the security interest, a *financing statement* must be recorded. Article 6 of the code regulates *bulk transfers*—the sale of a business as a whole, including all fixtures, chattels and merchandise.

Uniform Settlement Statement The standard HUD Form 1 required to be given to the borrower, lender and seller at or before settlement by the settlement agent in a transaction covered under the Real Estate Settlement Procedures Act. The lender must retain its copy for at least two years.

unilateral contract A one-sided contract wherein one party makes a promise to induce a second party to do something. The second party is not legally bound to perform; however, if the second party does comply, the first party is obligated to keep the promise.

unit-in-place method The appraisal method of estimating building costs by calculating the costs of all of the physical components in the structure, with the cost of each item including its proper installation, connection, etc.; also called the segregated cost method.

unit of ownership The four unities traditionally needed to create a joint tenancy—unity of title, time, interest and possession.

usury Charging interest at a higher rate than the maximum rate established by state law.

valid contract A contract that complies with all the essentials of a contract and is binding and enforceable on all parties to it.

VA loan A mortgage loan on approved property made to a qualified veteran by an authorized lender and guaranteed by the Department of Veterans Affairs to limit the lender's possible loss.

value The power of a good or service to command other goods in exchange for the present worth of future rights to its income or amenities.

variance Permission obtained from zoning authorities to build a structure or conduct a use that is expressly prohibited by the current zoning laws; an exception from the zoning ordinances.

vendee A buyer, usually under the terms of a land contract.

vendor A seller, usually under the terms of a land contract.

voidable contract A contract that seems to be valid on the surface but may be rejected or disaffirmed by one or both of the parties.

void contract A contract that has no legal force or effect because it does not meet the essential elements of a contract.

voluntary alienation *See* alienation.

voluntary lien A lien placed on property with the knowledge and consent of the property owner.

wall stud The vertical member to which horizontal pieces are attached. Studs are placed 16 to 24 inches apart and serve as the main support for the roof and the second floor.

waste An improper use or an abuse of a property by a possessor who holds less than fee ownership, such as a tenant, life tenant, mortgagor or vendee. Such waste ordinarily impairs the value of the land or the interest of the person holding the title or the reversionary rights.

will A written document, properly witnessed, providing for the transfer of title to property owned by the deceased, called the *testator.*

workers' compensation acts Laws that require that an employer obtain insurance coverage to protect employees who are injured in the course of their employment.

wraparound loan A method of refinancing in which the new mortgage is placed in a secondary, or subordinate, position. The new mortgage includes both the unpaid principal balance of the first mortgage and whatever additional sums are advanced by the lender. In essence, it is an additional mortgage in which another lender refinances a borrower by lending an amount exceeding the existing first mortgage amount without disturbing the existence of the first mortgage.

zoning ordinance An exercise of police power by a municipality to regulate and control the character and use of property.

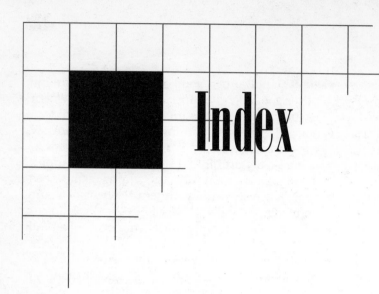

Index

A

Abstract of title, 76
Accelerated cost recovery system, 375
Acceleration clause, 247, 249
Acceptance, 63, 197
According to value, 36
Accord and satisfaction, 160–61
Accounting, 118–19
Accretion, 20
Accrued items, 306, 307–8
Active income, 375
Actual notice, 78
Actual-days-in-the-month method, 307
Addenda, 200, 201
Adjustable-rate mortgage, 252–53
Adjusted basis, 371, 373
Adjustment period, 252
Administrator, 74
Ad valorem taxes, 42–43
Adverse possession, 74
Advertising, 146, 288
Aesthetic zoning, 87
Affidavit
    of lien waiver, 298
    of title, 298
Age-life method, 350
Agency, 101, 102
    agreements, 114
    creation of, 106–7
    definitions, 102–3
    disclosure, 114–15, 128–29, 172–73
    law of, 101–2
    relationships, 106–14
    rentals and, 114
    scope of authority, 107–8
    termination of, 108
types of agreements, 176, 179
Agent, 102
    duties, liabilities of, 115, 118–24
    duty to disclose zoning, 87
    responsibilities to third parties, 120–21
Agricultural fixtures, 24
Agricultural property, 10
Agriculture, Department of, 275
Air rights, 19
Alienation, 62–64
Alienation clause, 249
Allocating markets/customers, 128

Allocation of costs, 232
All-risk form (HO-3), 363
ALTA policy, 76–77, 305
American Institute of Real Estate
    Appraisers, 354
American Land Title Association, 76–77,
    305
American Society of Appraisers, 354, 355
American Society of Farm Managers and
    Rural Appraisers, 354
Americans with Disabilities Act (ADA),
    94, 144–45, 215, 239–40
Amortization, 406, 408
Amortized loans, 250
Annexation, 22
Annexation method, 22
Annual percentage rate, 288
Anticipation, 339
Antitrust laws, 127–28
Appraisal, 7, 43, 146, 335–36, 355
    calculations, 410
    fees, 306
    process, 339–42
Appraisal Institute, 355
Appraisal methods
    cost approach, 347–51
    income capitalization approach, 351–
        54
    reconciliation, 354
    sales comparison approach, 345–47
Appraisal Qualifications Board, 336
Appraisal Standards Board, 336
Appraiser, 269
Appraising, profession of, 354–55
Appurtenance, 18–20
Appurtenant, 20
Architectural types, styles, 324, 325–26
Area
    measurements, 400–401
    preferences, 5
Asbestos, 379–81
Assessment, 43–45
Assessment office, 8
Assignment, 160, 224
Assumption
    fee, 408
    loan interest, 310
    rules, 270, 274
Attorney-in-fact, 106

Attorney's fee, 305
Attorney's opinion on title, 77
Auction, 159
Avulsion, 20

B

Backup offer, 201
Balloon framing, 327, 329
Balloon payment loan, 253–54
Banker's month method, 307
Banker's year, 307
Bank Insurance Fund, 280
Bare legal title, 246
Baseboards, 332
Basic form (HO-1), 361–62
Basis, 371
Beneficiary, 74, 246
Bilateral contract, 154–55
Biweekly loans, 254
Blanket mortgage, 276
Blockbusting, 145
Boards of REALTORS®, 127
Bonding, 88
Boot, 374
Borrower, rights, duties of, 257
Breach
    of contract, 161–62
    of duty, 124
Broad form (HO-2), 363
Broker, 7
    authority to prepare documents, 162
    commission, 304, 398
    fair housing and, 142–44
    listing agreement duties, 171
    protection clause, 172
Brokerage, 7, 101, 128
    business, nature of, 125–28
    commission, 403
    defined, 103, 106
    fee, 171
Broker-in-charge, 102, 113
Broker-salesperson relationship, 125
BTU, 333
Budgeting expenses, 235–36
Buffer zone, 85
Building code, 90, 92–93, 96, 333
Building permit, 92–93
Built-up roof, 332
Bundle of legal rights, 18, 61

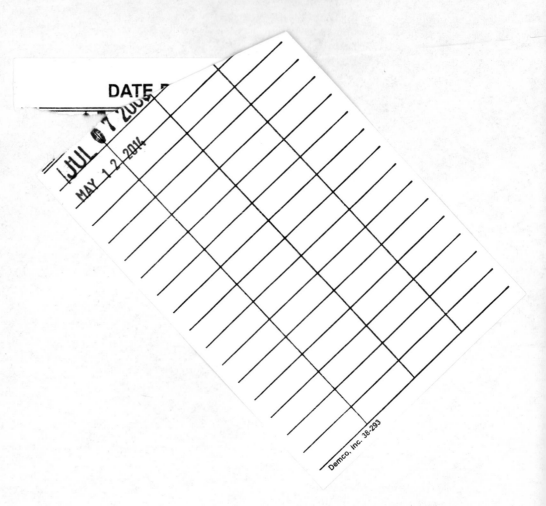

DATE

JUL 07 2005

MAY 1 2 2014

Demco, Inc. 38-293